Beginning
ASP.NET 2.0 with C#

Beginning ASP.NET 2.0 with C#

Chris Hart, John Kauffman, David Sussman, and Chris Ullman

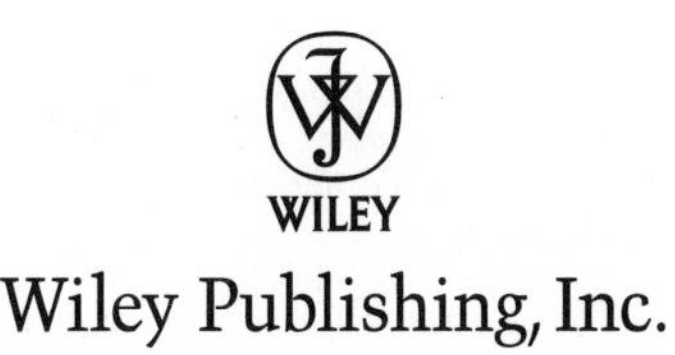

Wiley Publishing, Inc.

Beginning ASP.NET 2.0 with C#

Published by
Wiley Publishing, Inc.
10475 Crosspoint Boulevard
Indianapolis, IN 46256
www.wiley.com

Published simultaneously in Canada

ISBN-13: 978-0-470-04258-8
ISBN-10: 0-470-04258-3

Manufactured in the United States of America

10 9 8 7 6 5 4 3 2 1

1B/SQ/QU/QW/IN

For general information on our other products and services please contact our Customer Care Department within the United States at (800) 762-2974, outside the United States at (317) 572-3993 or fax (317) 572-4002.

Library of Congress Cataloging-in-Publication Data:

Beginning ASP.net 2.0 with C# / Chris Hart ... [et al.].
p. cm.
Includes index.
ISBN-13: 978-0-470-04258-8 (paper/website)
ISBN-10: 0-470-04258-3 (paper/website)
1. Active server pages. 2. Web sites—Design. 3. Microsoft .NET. 4. C# (Computer program language) I. Hart, Chris, 1976-
TK5105.8885.A26B4535 2006
005.2'76—dc22
2006007661

Wiley also publishes its books in a variety of electronic formats. Some content that appears in print may not be available in electronic books.

About the Authors

Chris Hart

Chris normally works at Trinity Expert Systems Plc, based in Coventry (UK), but is currently on maternity leave. She's worked on several major .NET, SharePoint, and CMS applications. She enjoys having a job where she gets to learn and play with new technologies on a regular basis, often working on-site with customers. She's been using .NET since the pre-Alpha days, and yet still enjoys the fun of working with beta software.

Chris lives in Birmingham (UK, not Alabama) with her extremely understanding husband James and baby Nathan, and is discovering that motherhood is more challenging than developing a CMS system for a major client. She's currently trying to work out how to make the home network toddlerproof.

I'd like to thank James for being so understanding — this was the hardest one yet, and you were great. Thanks also to my brother Rob for your inspiring creativity — best of luck in your final year at Uni. Thanks to Lou for designing the Wrox United site, and for being such a fantastic friend. Finally, thanks to Nathan for waiting eight more days after I finished my final drafts before arriving into the world.

Chris Hart contributed Chapters 3–5 and 11 and Appendix C to this book.

John Kauffman

John Kauffman was born in Philadelphia, the son of a chemist and a nurse. He received his degrees from The Pennsylvania State University, the colleges of Science and Agriculture. His early research was for Hershey foods in the genetics of the chocolate tree and the molecular biology of chocolate production. Since 1993 John has focused on explaining technology in the classroom and in books.

In his spare time, John is an avid sailor and youth sailing coach. He also enjoys jazz music and drumming. In addition to technical material, he manages to read the New Yorker magazine from cover-to-cover each week.

John Kauffman contributed Chapters 1, 2, 7, and 8 and Appendix D to this book.

Dave Sussman

Dave Sussman is an independent trainer, consultant, and writer, who inhabits that strange place called beta land. It's full of various computers, multiple boot partitions, VPC images, and very occasionally, stable software. When not writing books or testing alpha and beta software, Dave can be found working with a variety of clients helping to bring ASP.NET projects into fruition. He is a Microsoft MVP, and a member of the ASP Insiders and INETA Speakers Bureau. You can find more details about Dave and his books at his official website (`www.ipona.com`) or the site he shares with Alex Homer (`http://daveandal.net`).

Dave Sussman contributed Chapters 6, 9, 14, and 15 and Appendix E to this book.

Chris Ullman

Chris Ullman is a freelance web developer and technical author who has spent many years stewing in ASP/ASP.NET, like a teabag left too long in the pot. Coming from a Computer Science background, he started initially as a UNIX/Linux guru, who gravitated towards MS technologies during the summer of ASP (1997). He cut his teeth on Wrox Press ASP guides, and since then, he has written on over 20 books, most notably as lead author for Wrox's bestselling Beginning ASP/ASP.NET 1.x series, and has contributed chapters to books on PHP, ColdFusion, JavaScript, Web Services, C#, XML, and other Internet-related technologies too esoteric to mention, now swallowed up in the quicksands of the dot.com boom.

Quitting Wrox as a full-time employee in August 2001, he branched out into VB.NET/C# programming and ASP.NET development and started his own business, CUASP Consulting Ltd, in April 2003. He maintains a variety of sites from `www.cuasp.co.uk`, his "work" site, to `www.atomicwise.com`, a selection of his writings on music and art. The birth of his twins Jay and Luca in February 2005 took chaos to a new level. He now divides his time between protecting the twins from their over-affectionate three-year-old brother Nye, composing electronic sounds on bits of dilapidated old keyboards for his music project Open E, and tutoring his cats in the art of peaceful co-existence and not violently mugging each other on the stairs.

Chris Ullman contributed Chapters 10, 12, 13, and 16 and Appendix B to this book.

Credits

Senior Acquisitions Editor
Jim Minatel

Development Editor
Brian Herrmann

Technical Editor
Dan Maharry

Production Editor
Felicia Robinson

Copy Editor
Kim Cofer

Editorial Manager
Mary Beth Wakefield

Production Manager
Tim Tate

Vice President and Executive Group Publisher
Richard Swadley

Vice President and Executive Publisher
Joseph B. Wikert

Graphics and Production Specialists
Jennifer Click
Alicia B. South
Julie Trippetti

Quality Control Technicians
John Greenough
Brian Walls

Project Coordinator
Bill Ramsey

Proofreading and Indexing
Techbooks

Chris Ullman: All my love to my wife Kate and the boys.

Acknowledgments

Chris Hart

I'd like to thank James for sharing me with a laptop while I wrote this book—this was the hardest one yet, and you were great. Thanks also to my brother Rob for your inspiring creativity—best of luck in your final year at Uni. Finally, big thanks to Lou for designing the Wrox United site, and for being such a fantastic friend.

John Kauffman

I gratefully acknowledge the help of the Microsoft ASP.NET 2.0 development team, particularly Bradley Millington. It was Brad who first demonstrated the enormous capability of the ASP.NET 2.0 data controls to me and has continued to tutor me in the best use of the code his team developed. I also deeply appreciate the ongoing advice and friendship of my co-author Dave Sussman.

Dave Sussman

I would like to thank everyone on the ASP.NET team for supplying interim builds and answering many questions; Dan Maharry for his invaluable reviewing; and Brian Herrmann for coping admirably with not only my writing, but also my occasional stroppy fits.

Chris Ullman

Thanks to everyone on the author team (Dave, Chris, and John) for being available for my Messenger and email queries, thanks to Dan for being an honest reviewer and always ready with good advice, and thanks to Jim and Brian for being patient on the chapters—I got there eventually!

Contents

Introduction

There are many different technologies available today for developing complex web sites and web applications, and with so many to choose from, it's great that there's one technology in particular that stands out from the crowd and is such a joy to use. ASP.NET 2.0 is a fantastic technology that enables you to develop web sites and applications with very little hassle. Developing web applications was never this easy, yet even though it may appear simple, there is real power and depth to this technology that enables it to host even the most complex applications available today.

With every new release from Microsoft comes a new way of thinking, new technologies designed to make your life easier, and the best-ever programming experience; ASP.NET 2.0 is no exception to this rule. Whether you have developed web applications before, or if you are completely new to the world of web development, there's a lot to learn about this particular version of the technology.

Built on top of version 2.0 of the .NET Framework, ASP.NET 2.0 extends the functionality first seen in ASP.NET 1.0 and 1.1. At its core, you have a *control-based, event driven* architecture, which means that you have the ability to add small blocks of code to a page, see dynamic results with minimal effort, and react to user input to provide a smooth and intuitive user experience.

The biggest change since the previous edition of ASP.NET is in the amount of code you have to write—the ASP.NET team aimed for a 70% reduction in the amount of code you write, and having spent time myself working with ASP.NET 2.0 in the field, even if this claim does sound somewhat large, the reduction in time spent with fingers on keys is very noticeable. The mundane and repetitive tasks that you would have previously had to complete have been simplified. For example, providing user login functionality to a site is now a very swift process—adding a few controls to a page and setting up some user accounts is pretty much all you need to do to get basic user login functionality implemented on a site, and personalizing the user experience is just a step away from there.

Now add the new development environment designed for building ASP.NET 2.0 applications, Visual Web Developer (available on its own, or as part of Visual Studio 2005), and you will find building dynamic, feature-rich applications to be a fast, smooth process.

Visual Web Developer is a new innovation from Microsoft, and was developed mostly in response to developer demand. Previous editions of Visual Studio .NET were not great when it came to web programming, and you'd often find your code had been "fixed" for you behind the scenes, as your HTML came out looking very different from the way it went in originally. Visual Web Developer has a fantastic HTML editing environment, and a really smooth and intuitive interface for developing complex ASP.NET applications. Best of all, it's a low-cost product, which makes it accessible to a wide audience who may not be able to afford the complete Visual Studio package.

Who This Book Is For

This book will teach you how to program web applications in ASP.NET 2.0 that can display data stored in a database, provide a personalized user experience to your users, and even offer shopping functionality. All of these sorts of web applications can be developed using ASP.NET 2.0, so if these are the sorts of applications that you are interested in developing, then this is a great place to start.

This book is for anyone new to web programming, or who has a small amount of knowledge of web programming concepts. Maybe you want to start a career as a web developer? Or perhaps you just want to learn how to use some cool server-side technology to put together some sites in your spare time? In either case, this book will teach you what you need to know, and give you a good feel for how the technology works, how to use the Visual Web Developer environment to speed up your development, and to give you total control over the development process.

The earlier chapters in this book will ease you in to the world of ASP.NET development, and if you already have some knowledge of programming, then you will find these early chapters a swift and pleasant read. Note, though, that ASP.NET 2.0 has a lot of neat tricks and tools at its disposal, and we'll be introducing these throughout the book. As with other Wrox *Beginning* books, you'll find that the concepts discussed in one chapter are then used and extended in other chapters.

What This Book Covers

This book teaches you ASP.NET 2.0, with the help of the Visual Web Developer IDE (Integrated Development Environment). Working through this book, you will learn how to develop powerful data-driven web applications, and even to expose functionality using web services. Here's how the book shapes up over the next 16 chapters.

Chapter 1: An Introduction to ASP.NET 2.0 and the Wrox United Application

This chapter provides an overview of ASP.NET 2.0 and the Visual Web Developer environment, and will give you a chance to create and run a simple page. You'll also learn about the Wrox United sample website, which we'll use in examples throughout the book to demonstrate different aspects of ASP.NET 2.0.

Chapter 2: Site Design

Now that you've gained some familiarity with creating simple pages, this chapter will discuss the concept of site design, and introduce the concept of a master page, which can be used to provide a consistent look for all pages on a site. We'll also introduce Web.config and global.asax—two important ASP.NET files that control the behavior of a site, and the concept of a site map, for defining a site page hierarchy.

Chapter 3: Page Design

This chapter starts by providing a quick crash-course (or a refresher course as the case may be) in HTML and XHTML development, and introduces the crucial concept of server controls. The chapter continues by demonstrating several of the built-in server controls in action to provide navigation functionality on a site.

Chapter 4: Membership and Identity

One of the big new features of ASP.NET 2.0 is the addition of the Login server controls, so this chapter introduces these controls, alongside discussions of how to create user accounts, how to configure roles, and how to enable login functionality on a site.

Chapter 5: Styling with Themes

After the functionality of a site has been developed, it's important to make a site look and feel the right way. This chapter introduces CSS style sheets, and integrates them into the discussion of ASP.NET's Theme functionality, making it simple to keep your functionality and your site styling cleanly separated—great for future maintainability!

Chapter 6: Events and Code

Reacting to events involves writing code, so this chapter talks about server-side coding concepts and how web servers work. We walk you through the basics of HTTP so that you will gain an understanding of the *postback*, and how you can write code to handle postback events.

Chapter 7: Reading Data

Developing a site will almost always involve reading data stored in a database, and displaying that data on the screen, so this chapter talks about how you can use ASP.NET controls (such as the `GridView`, `DataLists`, and `DetailsView` controls) to connect to a database and display data. This chapter also discusses reading data stored in an XML file.

Chapter 8: Writing Data

The storing and updating of data is the next topic to be covered in this book, and in this chapter, you learn some useful techniques for safely updating the data stored in the database using parameters and referring to data using keys that uniquely identify items in a database.

Chapter 9: Code

This chapter teaches you the fundamental programming concepts that you need to understand if you are to become a fully-fledged .NET developer. We start by taking you thorough basic variables and data types, before looking at collections, statements, operators, branches, and loops. Then we introduce some object orientation and talk about classes, properties, methods, and simple class design principles.

Chapter 10: Componentization

Having learned all about the principles of code in the previous chapter, this chapter takes those building blocks and talks about creating pages with separate code files, and about how to design applications with logic stored in different classes or files. This chapter also introduces the concept of user controls, which are great for storing pieces of code that can be reused across pages on a site.

Chapter 11: Roles and Profiles

Following on from simple user accounts and roles as introduced in Chapter 4, this chapter builds on the concept of site design, and changing the appearance of a site depending on which user is accessing the site. This chapter also looks at storing user profiles and populating profiles in code, as well as switching the theme used on a site according to user preferences.

Chapter 12: Web Services

At this stage in the book, you'll have gained sufficient experience with ASP.NET 2.0 and coding that you should now be ready to enter the world of Web Services. First, we show you how to consume a third party Web Service, and use that functionality on a page. Next, you get the chance to build your own Web Services, and learn about proxies and WSDL.

Chapter 13: E-Commerce

Adding e-commerce functionality to a site can be a bit tricky, so this chapter walks you through the e-commerce facilities built in to the Wrox United sample application, looking at how to implement a product catalog, and build a shopping cart system that links in to user's profiles.

Chapter 14: Performance

You may find your rather lovely web applications may crawl to a halt if you haven't quite tweaked them the right way to make them perform well under heavy loading, so this chapter talks about many of the different ways you can enhance the performance of an application. This includes concepts such as disposing of objects, using stored procedures, and making efficient use of caching.

Chapter 15: Dealing with Errors

Errors happen whenever you develop any application, so in this chapter, we talk you through some of the most common ways to handle errors, how to trap exceptions, and how to present custom error pages to users of your site. After all, users don't need to know that your database server collapsed, but they would like to know that if the site is down, the faults will be rectified shortly. You can then use some of the excellent debugging and tracing functionality available in ASP.NET.

Chapter 16: Deployment, Builds, and Finishing Up

In the final chapter of the book, we talk you through the ideal way to deploy a finished web application to a live server. The application used as an example is the Wrox United application, which you can publish using both the Visual Web Developer tools, and what's known as XCOPY deployment. We also look at testing the deployment and looking out for common deployment problems. The final part of the chapter reviews the different parts of the Wrox United application, and recaps where each part of the application was discussed in the book. Finally, we give you some pointers as to where you can head next to further your ASP.NET development career.

How This Book Is Structured

This book explains concepts step-by-step, using worked examples and detailed explanations, to tell the story of how to develop ASP.NET applications. Each chapter assumes knowledge developed in previous chapters, so you will likely find a front-to-back study approach works best to understand the concepts explained. There are four authors who worked on this book as a team, and we all worked quite closely together (with some great editorial support), to give you a steady and complete tutorial of the basics of developing ASP.NET applications.

What You Need to Use This Book

To gain the most from this book, you should have the following software installed on your system:

- A minimum of Windows XP Home Edition as your operating system
- Microsoft Visual Web Developer
- Microsoft SQL Server 2005 Express Edition

Because Visual Web Developer includes the .NET Framework and ASP.NET 2.0, these three pieces of software are all you will need to develop ASP.NET applications.

Conventions

To help you get the most from the text and keep track of what's happening, we've used a number of conventions throughout the book.

Try It Out

The *Try It Out* is an exercise you should work through, following the text in the book:

1. They usually consist of a set of steps.
2. Each step has a number.
3. Follow the steps through with your copy of the code.

How It Works

After each *Try It Out*, the code you've typed will be explained in detail.

> **Boxes like this one hold important, not-to-be forgotten, information that is directly relevant to the surrounding text.**

Tips, hints, tricks, and asides to the current discussion are offset and placed in italics like this.

As for styles in the text:

- We *italicize* new terms and important words when we introduce them.
- We show keyboard strokes like this: Ctrl+A.
- We show file names, URLs, and code within the text like so: `persistence.properties`.
- We present code in two different ways:

```
In code examples, we highlight new and important code with a gray background.
```

```
The gray highlighting is not used for code that's less important in the present
context, or has been shown before.
```

Source Code

As you work through the examples in this book, you may choose either to type in all the code manually or to use the source code files that accompany the book. All of the source code used in this book is available for download at `www.wrox.com`. When you are at the site, simply locate the book's title (either by using the Search box or by using one of the title lists) and click the Download Code link on the book's detail page to obtain all the source code for the book.

Because many books have similar titles, you may find it easiest to search by ISBN. For this book, the ISBN is 0-470-04258-3 (changing to 978-0-470-04258-8 as the new industry-wide 13-digit ISBN numbering system is phased in by January 2007).

After you download the code, just decompress it with your favorite compression tool. Alternately, you can go to the main Wrox code download page at `www.wrox.com/dynamic/books/download.aspx` to see the code available for this book and all other Wrox books.

Errata

We make every effort to ensure that there are no errors in the text or in the code. However, no one is perfect, and mistakes do occur. If you find an error in one of our books, like a spelling mistake or faulty piece of code, we would be very grateful for your feedback. By sending in errata, you may save another reader hours of frustration, and at the same time, you will be helping us provide even higher quality information.

To find the errata page for this book, go to `www.wrox.com` and locate the title using the Search box or one of the title lists. Then, on the book details page, click the Book Errata link. On this page, you can view all errata that has been submitted for this book and posted by Wrox editors. A complete book list, including links to each's book's errata, is also available at `www.wrox.com/misc-pages/booklist.shtml`.

If you don't spot "your" error on the Book Errata page, go to `www.wrox.com/contact/techsupport.shtml` and complete the form there to send us the error you have found. We'll check the information and, if appropriate, post a message to the book's errata page and fix the problem in subsequent editions of the book.

p2p.wrox.com

For author and peer discussion, join the P2P forums at `p2p.wrox.com`. The forums are a web-based system for you to post messages relating to Wrox books and related technologies and interact with other readers and technology users. The forums offer a subscription feature to e-mail you topics of interest of your choosing when new posts are made to the forums. Wrox authors, editors, other industry experts, and your fellow readers are present on these forums.

At `http://p2p.wrox.com`, you will find a number of different forums that will help you not only as you read this book, but also as you develop your own applications. To join the forums, just follow these steps:

1. Go to `p2p.wrox.com` and click the Register link.
2. Read the terms of use and click Agree.
3. Complete the required information to join as well as any optional information you wish to provide and click Submit.
4. You will receive an e-mail with information describing how to verify your account and complete the joining process.

You can read messages in the forums without joining P2P, but in order to post your own messages, you must join.

After you join, you can post new messages and respond to messages other users post. You can read messages at any time on the web. If you would like to have new messages from a particular forum e-mailed to you, click the Subscribe to This Forum icon by the forum name in the forum listing.

For more information about how to use the Wrox P2P, be sure to read the P2P FAQs for answers to questions about how the forum software works as well as many common questions specific to P2P and Wrox books. To read the FAQs, click the FAQ link on any P2P page.

An Introduction to ASP.NET 2.0 and the Wrox United Application

At the end of the twentieth century something unprecedented happened to personal computers. Previously relegated to the realm of the business office and teenagers who never saw the light of day, the explosion of the Internet lead to computers acquiring a glamour, an aura of excitement that had never been associated with them before. Prior to the 1990s, it was almost embarrassing to admit you worked with computers, and then suddenly everyone wanted one. Every business had to be attached to the Internet, and many families wanted their own web site. If you had to name one piece of technology that became synonymous with the explosion, it was undoubtedly the web browser. However, without anything to view on a web browser, it becomes virtually useless. You need information, and like mushrooms sprouting up in a forest, hundreds of web sites on every imaginable subject were born.

The late '90s were a time of vast upheaval. Business empires were founded on the simplest ideas — a search engine (Google) or an online store for buying books (Amazon). Everyone wanted to know how to build a web site for themselves. HTML (HyperText Markup Language) enabled them to do that, but it was soon obvious that it only went so far. You could display pictures and text, but what happened if you wanted more than that? What happened if you wanted a site that was reactive, that received information from your users and was automatically updated without someone having to beaver away writing new web pages every time? What if you wanted to attach a database to the Internet, or you wanted to display a stock catalogue, or you wanted to personalize your site to everyone who visited it, or you just wanted it to look good for your family and friends who visited it?

The race was on and several competing technologies were created for doing this from CGI and PHP to Java. Microsoft's own entry into the race was ASP and what made it particularly attractive was that it was simpler to pick up and learn than most of its rivals, but it also had some exciting features — the ability to store details of users as they moved through pages on a web site, and controls such as calendars and ad rotators that you could just stick into your pages like HTML tags. ASP was a huge success. Microsoft went one step further — it created the .NET Framework, and ASP.NET became a "grown up" version of its ASP technology, using its mature programming languages VB.NET and C#. The leap forward in power was amazing, but Microsoft lost partial site of one critical aim — simplicity. Web sites suddenly became things you needed expensive consultants to build and cutting-edge designers to visualize. It was out of the hands of those who so empowered the boom.

ASP.NET 2.0 is the big step back in the right direction. Microsoft recognized that one thing people who build web sites don't want to do is have to code. Code is dull; code is geeky. However, Microsoft also recognized that some people still have to code for a living. And more than that, these coders have to build the same things, over and over again: a login mechanism, a menu system, a shopping cart, a funky theme for your site's backdrop applied to every page — something every web site requires. Two guiding principles seem to be at work here: make it easier for the novice to use and reduce the amount of repetitive work the developer has to do. Claims for ASP.NET 2.0 boast "70 percent less code" is needed; ASP.NET 2.0 also comes with a multitude of controls to enable the developer to create login systems and menus in minutes.

Late in 2003 we saw the previews of the new version of Active Server Pages named ASP.NET 2.0. Everyone knew that these claims weren't just hyperbole and that the way developers create web applications was going to change fundamentally. Microsoft expanded the powerful features of earlier ASP versions while greatly reducing the effort to implement those features. The ease of implementation meant a reduction in the cost of developing complex sites. Or, put another way, there would now be a large expansion of the number of people that have the capability to build a complex site.

In addition to ASP.NET 2.0 comes a new, affordable tool for creating these web sites: Visual Web Developer Express. Microsoft's previous attempts at providing tools for helping create dynamic web sites have been clunky (Front Page) or have never really taken off (Visual Interdev), but this time they've got it right. Visual Web Developer is part of the Visual Studio.NET suite, but a scaled-down version of Visual Web Developer Express will be free in the foreseeable future. It allows you to drag and drop a site together within minutes, is instantly recognizable to developers, and allows easy creation and management of your web pages.

This book leads you step-by-step through creating dynamic, data-driven, complex web sites using ASP.NET 2.0. To those ends, this chapter explains the basic ideas and examines the completed sample site. You then learn how to use Visual Web Developer Express (VWD) to build ASP.NET 2.0 sites.

Specifically, this chapter covers five topics:

- An introduction to ASP.NET 2.0
- A review of the Internet programming problems that ASP.NET 2.0 solves
- An explanation of how ASP.NET 2.0 fits in with other technologies
- A tour of the dynamic features of a site built with ASP.NET 2.0
- Understanding the tool you will use to build ASP.NET 2.0 (ASPX) pages — Visual Web Developer Express (VWD)

In previous books, we've been pleased if our readers can create a single page by the end of the chapter, but ASP.NET 2.0 inspires much greater ambitions, and you will have the structure and outline of a working web site up by the end of the second chapter. Your web site will be focused around a hapless soccer (football) team named Wrox United and will be able to display their news and results, sell their merchandise, screen their footage, and offer different views of the site depending on whether you are a customer or an administrator. And, as always, a list of gotchas and some exercises are included to help you review the concepts covered in this chapter.

The Site You Will Build

Go to www.wroxunited.net and have a good look at the site (the main page is shown in Figure 1-1). This site is built entirely in ASP.NET 2.0 and is the site you will build in the book. Likewise, it is the site that you will learn how to create a working miniature of in just two chapters.

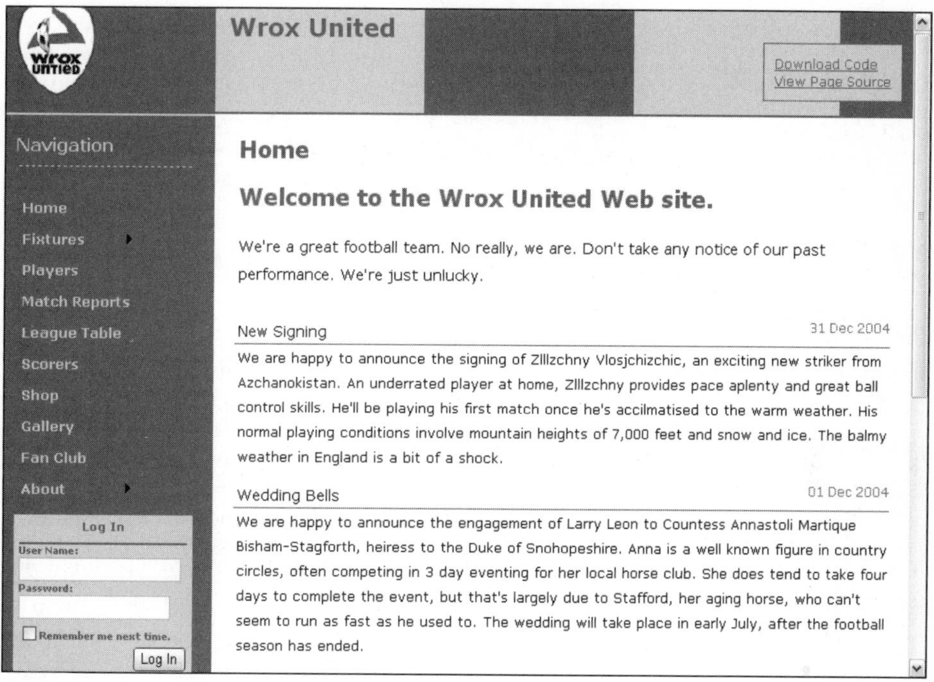

Figure 1-1

On the home page alone you can see a menu system, a login control, and some news items — these are all things that would have taken considerable time and code to create in any previous version of ASP or ASP.NET. If you take the example of a login mechanism, you'd have to think of accepting a user ID and password, checking that against an existing set of users and passwords, making sure the password wasn't corrupted in any way, and making sure that password was transmitted securely. So just to do something relatively trivial, you'd be talking at least an hour or two of your time, with not much to show for it. Now this could take seconds.

Click the View Page Source link — it doesn't matter if you don't understand what you see yet — there are fewer than 10 lines of ASP.NET 2.0 code. All the coding in this book is done in C#. You can download the complete site in C# from www.wrox.com. A working copy of the site is also hosted at www.WroxUnited.net, although under the covers that public site is written in VB.

```
<%@ Page Language="VB" Trace="false" MasterPageFile="~/site.master"
AutoEventWireup="false" codefile="Default.aspx.cs" Inherits="_Default" %>
<%@ Register TagPrefix="wu" TagName="News" Src="News.ascx" %>

<asp:Content ID="Content1" ContentPlaceHolderID="mainContent" Runat="server">

    <h2>Welcome to the Wrox United Web site.</h2>
```

```
        <p>We're a great football team. No really, we are. Don't take any notice
        of our past performance. We're just unlucky.</p>

        <wu:news id="News1" runat="server" ItemsToShow="5"></wu:news>

    </asp:Content>
```

Step through the different links in the menu and see how league tables and fixture lists work, and see how few lines of code there are. Notice how the theme and style of the site remains consistent throughout, yet there is no evidence of how this is done. Welcome to ASP.NET 2.0. This is about to revolutionize how you build web sites from now on. You're going to look at some of the features behind the Wrox United site in more detail shortly, but first let's talk about what ASP.NET 2.0 offers.

ASP.NET 2.0 — A Powerful Tool to Build Dynamic Web Sites

The World Wide Web (WWW) on the Internet provides a wide expanse of connectivity. Virtually everyone that uses computers has access to the Internet. But this pervasive reach was achieved by establishing very minimal standards. Information is transmitted in ASCII characters, without a built-in capability for machine-level code. The client requirements are very minimal — in fact the Internet itself does not have any standards for how a browser works, and thus multiple browsers for multiple operating systems (OS) and platforms exist. It is easy for us, in 2005, to forget that the Internet was designed to send simple static pages of text with images and links.

The story of the past 15 years of Internet programming is an effort to provide sophistication and complexity to the user experience without violating the WWW rules that demand extreme simplicity in page design. Users expect an experience that comes close to desktop applications such as word processing and database access. But such a level of complexity has not been easy to implement in the web given its minimal configuration.

ASP.NET 2.0 fundamentally reduces the barriers for development of complex web sites. The ASP.NET development team at Microsoft looked at thousands of pages, sites, and scenarios to create a list of common objectives of site owners. The list included about 20 goals, including reading data, a unified login and authentication procedure, consistency in site appearance, and customization of pages for different browser platforms. The team then set to work to create bundles of code that would achieve each objective in the right way, with a minimum of developer effort and with Microsoft performing extensive tests of that code. This set of capabilities is available as *classes* (encapsulated and ready-to-use batches of code) in ASP.NET 2.0. The end result is simple — developers can very quickly put together (and easily maintain) a complex site by merely assembling the building blocks Microsoft has developed in ASP.NET 2.0. Instead of writing 50 or so lines of code (as in earlier versions of ASP), the designer can now simply drag and drop a control to the page and answer some questions in a wizard. This control generates a small amount of code for your page and the server uses that code to build pages in HTML that are then sent to the browser. Because HTML is sent to the browser, there is no requirement for special capabilities on the browser beyond the display of HTML and the execution of a single simple JavaScript script. Any browser that can display HTML can display ASP.NET 2.0 pages. This includes not only desktop browsers, but also PDAs, cell phones, and other devices.

Because all the code for these controls is run on the server before a web browser ever gets a hold of a page, these controls are known as *server-side controls*. The next section looks at what some of these server-side controls can do.

Simple Solutions for Common Web Site Tasks

Microsoft's survey of sites in earlier versions of ASP created a list of common objectives that site programmers were implementing. Some objectives were easy to achieve but time-consuming, whereas others were too complex for all but the most sophisticated developers. Overall, the programmers' solutions varied from brilliant to dysfunctional. Not only were the observed solutions sometimes poor, but they also represented a tremendous waste of time, because thousands of programmers spent time planning, writing, and testing code that had the same purpose. This section goes through 11 of the objectives for which ASP.NET 2.0 offers built-in solutions. As you will see in Chapter 3 and beyond, these solutions are in the form of ASP.NET 2.0 server-side controls that contain code to execute settings and behaviors. By simply placing one of these controls on a page, the designer gets all of the behavior that would have been hand-coded in the past.

Consistency and Personalization

Web designers tend to desire two conflicting design features. On the one hand, they want a consistent look to the entire site. But conversely, they want users to be able to customize the site to the user's taste in colors, font size, and other features. ASP.NET 2.0 offers a `MasterPage` control that allows a site to be consistent in the layout of its headers, menus, and links. Within that consistent layout, a designer can add a control that allows users to pick one of several themes to apply to all pages.

Navigation

Every site requires tools for navigation, generally in three forms. Users need a menu. They also need to be able to see where they are currently located in a site. And last, they want to be able to easily navigate up or down a level. ASP.NET 2.0 supports an XML file called a SiteMap. ASP.NET 2.0 controls can then render menus and other navigation aids based on the site map and the name of the current page.

Login, Security, and Roles

Many sites need a login system that can check a potential user's ID and password against a list and then authorize or deny entry. Although basic implementations are not difficult, only a small percentage of programmers are successful in creating a system that conforms to best security practices. ASP.NET 2.0 offers a few controls that create and implement a logon better than most of us can program by hand. Beyond simple site entry, the system offers password reminders and a system to create new users. A user can also be assigned a *role* that determines what pages and features will be available for that user to view. For example, all users can view the employee phonebook, but only users with the role of Manager can view pages to change information about employees.

Connection to Data

Although most dynamic web sites are connected to data, few designers are successful in implementing the full suite of features that users desire. In sites built with older ASP versions, Microsoft observed many problems in efficiency and security. Furthermore, even modest objectives required scores of lines of code. ASP.NET 2.0 provides a rich suite of data features through two groups of controls for working with data. *Data source* controls offer the behavior of connecting to sources of data. *Data-bound* controls take that information and render it into HTML. The several data source controls can connect to almost any source of data, and the data-bound controls offer the user tables, lists, trees, and other presentations. Working together, these controls offer the user the capability to page through data, as well as to sort and edit data.

Code

Almost every web site requires customized code because it is impossible for ASP or any other web site technology to anticipate the needs of all businesses. ASP.NET 2.0 supports more than 20 different languages. Regardless of the language the programmer uses, the code is translated into a single intermediate language prior to execution. ASP.NET 2.0 controls are executed on the server, but the programmer also has the option of writing code (for example Java or other client-side script) in a block to go out for execution on the client.

Componentization

Web sites are easier to develop and maintain if various parts can be created independently of each other. Traditional ASP relied on large pages containing content, HTML, ASP controls, and scripts of code. ASP.NET 2.0 provides more efficient models and structures to divide the site into logical parts. For example, code is normally kept in separate files from the presentation layer (the text and HTML tags). Furthermore, Visual Web Developer offers wizards to easily create objects to provide data resources.

Web Services

Enterprises offer information and services on their own sites. For example, from its worldwide headquarters, `www.Ford.com` can give you a list of colors and price quotes. But the past few years have seen a demand for those services to be available to other sites. For example, a local Ford dealer may want to offer the list of colors and prices at `www.YourLocalFordDealer.com`. Web Services allow a *consumer* site (the local dealer) to obtain information from a *provider* site (Ford headquarters). The local Ford dealer can display real-time data using web services provided by the Ford corporate site, but keep the user on the page of the local site. ASP.NET 2.0 offers a complete web-services solution that conforms to the specifications of SOAP (Simple Object Access Protocol, a way to ask for data from a web service) and XML (Extensible Markup Language, a format for data).

Performance and Caching

After the designer writes a page on the development machine, it is compiled into the single uniform language of .NET 2.0 called the Microsoft Intermediate Language (MSIL). Then it is copied to the deployment machine. The first time it is requested, the page undergoes a further compilation into the Common Language Runtime (CLR), which optimizes the page for the hardware that will serve it. This two-step process achieves the dual aims of consistency for software and optimization for hardware. Both steps have undergone intensive performance analysis from the .NET 2.0 team. The great aspect for beginners is that all of this compilation occurs automatically.

ASP.NET 2.0 easily enables *caching* of pages so that subsequent requests are served faster. When cached, the final version of a page is stored in the server's RAM so that it can be immediately sent on the next request rather than having the server rebuild the page. Furthermore, the designer can specify that only parts of pages can be cached, a process known as *fragment caching*. Fragment caching accelerates the service of non-changing portions of a page while still allowing the dynamic fragments to be custom generated. If you are using Microsoft SQL Server 7 or higher, you also have the option of *data invalidation caching* for portions of the page that are data-dependent but less variable (perhaps a list of employees or your retail outlets). Data invalidation caching keeps a page in cache until it gets a message from SQL Server that the underlying data has changed. You cache a set of data with a designation to receive a SQL data changed notice. SQL Server notifies .NET when the data has changed, which triggers ASP.NET 2.0 to perform a reread.

Errors and Exception Handling

Any web site, indeed any system, needs to respond to errors. ASP.NET 2.0 provides a system to respond to errors. The response can be in code or it can be a redirect to an error page. The error page can be unique to the error or it can be a single error page for the entire site. The .NET 2.0 Framework also allows for multiple levels of error handling. If an error occurs in a data read, it can be handled at the level of the data source. If it is not handled, the error bubbles up to the next level and can be handled there. Unhandled errors continue to bubble up through layers with the designer having the option to resolve the problem at the most effective level.

Deployment

In the past, sites deployed to Windows or Linux required a series of setup steps that registered and configured the site on the host machine. The ASP.NET 2.0 team set a goal of XCOPY deployment, naming it after an old DOS command that performed a simple copy of a folder and all of its subfolders. A simple XCOPY deploys your site from the development machine to the deployment host. All registrations and machine-level customizations occur automatically when the first request hits the site.

Development Tools

Microsoft has spent considerable effort improving tools for building ASP pages, namely the Visual Studio, Visual Web Developer, and Visual Web Developer Express products. Although they are not part of ASP.NET 2.0, these IDEs (Integrated Development Environments) allow drag-and-drop building of pages. Most common actions are either automatic or guided with wizards. In cases where typing is required, the IDE provides intelligent completion of most phrases. This book uses the freely downloadable VWD Express.

Where Does ASP.NET 2.0 Fit with Other Technology?

Many people have questions about how ASP.NET 2.0 fits in with all of the other web-related terms (most of them acronyms). We will clarify this now — where does ASP.NET 2.0 fit with other software that is running on the server? What is its role, and what are the roles of the other pieces of technology?

ASP.NET 2.0 is part of the .NET 2.0 Framework. The .NET Framework is a brand of Microsoft that sets software standards for Internet connectivity using web services and XML. Many Microsoft products conform to the .NET standard, including various server software, data-management systems, and desktop applications. ASP.NET 2.0 is the subset of .NET 2.0 that offers software for generating dynamic web sites. The software is published in a set of classes holding various controls that execute their behavior on the web server. In our day-to-day designing of pages, we work with these server-side controls. Because ASP.NET 2.0 is a subset of the .NET 2.0 Framework, this book sometimes uses features of ASP.NET 2.0 and sometimes uses features of the .NET 2.0 Framework. Use of these various features will be essentially seamless.

As a Microsoft product, ASP.NET 2.0 runs on Windows. For development, it works on the desktop with Windows 2000 or later (including both XP Home and XP Pro). At deployment, the normal OS is Windows Server 2003 or another Windows OS version designed for higher loads. Within Windows, ASP.NET 2.0 works with the Internet Information Server to read pages from disk and send them to requestors. Alternatively, on the development desktop, ASP.NET 2.0 can be tested with a lightweight web server named the ASP.NET Development Server that is distributed with development tools such as VWD.

When a designer uses the ASP.NET 2.0 controls to connect with data, two more levels of interaction are introduced. The data controls use a technology named ActiveX Data Objects (ADO.NET), but fortunately the use of ADO.NET is behind the scenes for us. Those ADO.NET objects, in turn, interact with the source of data. The source of data can be Microsoft SQL Server (as used in this book) or almost any other source of data including relational databases such as Oracle or MySQL, and non-relational sources such as XML or text files.

Microsoft offers tools for several levels of developers to build ASP.NET 2.0 web sites. The most comprehensive product is Visual Studio, which contains tools for building applications for Windows and applications for the web. The web construction part is named Visual Web Developer. A free (but less capable) alternative is the Visual Web Developer Express. Front Page can work, but it focuses more on static HTML pages and thus lacks the set of tools that makes designing the dynamic, data-intensive ASP.NET 2.0 pages such a pleasure. Creating pages in Notepad was long the preferred method of ASP developers and is still theoretically possible; however, the necessary management of web sites and web pages make this impractical, laborious, and far more prone to errors.

Enough of the theory — let's see ASP.NET 2.0 in action. During the course of this book you will build a complete web site for a hapless football (soccer) team named Wrox United. A completed example is hosted at `www.wroxunited.net`, which you explore in the next section to observe the range of features ASP.NET 2.0 supports. Then in the remainder of the book, you will build the same site on your desktop. For this exercise, you do not have to install software on your machine. The remainder of the book, however, relies on your completion of the setup outlined in Appendix B.

Exploring the Wrox United Application

This section explores the site as built by the authors, which you will build as well. It is hosted at `www.wroxunited.net`. Open your browser and direct it to that address.

- **Master pages and site map (discussed in Chapter 2):** Click through several pages to observe the uniform layout across the top and left side of the page. This design consistency derives from an easy-to-implement feature called Master Pages. Second, note the maroon box in the lower-right of each page that indicates your current page and its relationship to parent pages back to the home page. This feature was created with the ASP.NET 2.0 Site Map and Navigation controls.

- **Server-side controls (discussed in Chapter 3):** Go to the Players page. All of the data comes from two server-side controls — a data source control to connect to the database and a data-bound control to display the information. Most of the behavior of ASP.NET 2.0 pages is encapsulated in server-side controls. These include links like the shopping cart at the bottom-left, images such as the logo at the top-left, and text boxes such as the logon section at the lower-left.
- **Login and security system (discussed in Chapter 4):** On the home page, log in as User Name `Lou` and Password `lou@123`. Then log out. Authentication systems can require a tremendous amount of work to create and even then frequently contain security holes. ASP.NET 2.0 offers a very simple system based on several server-side controls including the login and password verification schemes, and a system to e-mail a clue for forgotten passwords.
- **Events (discussed in Chapter 6):** Browse to the Shop page, click an item, and add the item to your cart (of course, this is not a real shopping site, just a demo). An event occurred as you clicked the Add to Cart button and that event was handled by custom code that created an order and added the item to the order.
- **Data reads (discussed in Chapter 7):** Browse to the Players page where the names and joining dates are read from a SQL Server Express database. Many kinds of information on the site are held in data stores that are read by ASP.NET 2.0 server-side controls on the page. Browse back to the home page and observe the menu. Even these menu choices are read from an XML file that holds a map of the site.
- **Data writes (discussed in Chapter 8):** Browse to Shop, click the car sticker, and click Add to Cart. You have just written a value to a database. The behavior of writing your order to the database was implemented by two ASP.NET 2.0 server-side controls. The designer of the site did not have to do any custom code.
- **Code behind the controls (discussed in Chapter 9):** From the home page, click Shopping Cart at the lower-left of the page. We have written custom code that executes when the page is loaded, checks if there are currently any items in the shopping cart, and renders a page appropriate for the cart contents: either empty or a list of contents. Although the capabilities of the ASP.NET 2.0 server-side controls are impressive, they cannot cover every possible case. An ASP.NET 2.0 site offers numerous places that a designer can add custom code.
- **Components (discussed in Chapter 10):** Browse to the Fixtures page. Although the data is stored in a SQL Server database, the ASP.NET 2.0 page does not read it directly. There is a component that reads that data and then sends it on to the ASP.NET 2.0 page. That component can be reused by other web sites or by Windows applications that run on a local network without the Internet.
- **Roles (discussed in Chapter 11):** If you had administrative rights, you could log in and see different screens. After you have installed the site on your local machine, you will experiment with this feature in Chapter 4. ASP.NET 2.0 goes beyond just logging in visitors. They can be authorized to have sets of privileges called *roles*. The public site does not allow non-authors to log in as administrators, so there is no need to take action at this point.
- **E-commerce (discussed in Chapter 13):** From the menu, go to Shop, and click a few items to add to your cart. Now on the bottom of the menu, click Shopping Cart and view its contents. The most complex part of the site is the shopping cart. ASP.NET 2.0 does not have a pre-built e-commerce solution, but because so much behavior is built into the ASP.NET 2.0 controls, designers can develop features such as e-commerce much more quickly than in the past.
- **Performance (discussed in Chapter 14):** Under the covers, the data is being cached where appropriate and objects are being disposed as early as feasible. The site also uses Generics to improve the performance of lists.

- **Errors and exception handling (discussed in Chapter 15):** As you navigate the site, you can try entering data of the wrong type or clicking to save data without entering any information. In these cases, the mistake is handled gracefully.
- **Deployment (discussed in Chapter 16):** At this point, you will not walk through a deployment. However, keep in mind that for ASP.NET 2.0, the transfer for a site from a development machine to a deployment machine generally entails only a few steps that copy the databases to the data server and then perform a simple file copy of the site folder and its subfolders to the new server.

This walkthrough gave you a taste of what you will learn to create in this book. Most of the features explored were implemented with very little code that we wrote. The behavior was performed by code that Microsoft baked into a set of server-side controls that are the components of ASP.NET 2.0. We merely placed these controls on pages and set various properties.

Getting Started with Your Wrox United Site

Now that you have observed the finished site as publicly hosted, you can begin creating the same site on your desktop. If you have not installed Visual Web Developer Express, SQL Express, the sample database, and the sample site (outlined in Appendix B) then do so now. Start by reading the overview at the beginning of the appendix and then work your way through each step. You can be sure of your installation by performing the check at the end of each section.

This chapter and the next chapter set up the basic framework of the site as you learn how to use VWD and establish some design parameters for the site. Because VWD offers drag-and-drop solutions to most tasks, you will be able to create the entire site with a minimum of typing. In the cases where some typing is necessary, you can cut and paste from text files in this book's download at `www.wrox.com`. All pages are in the download in their final form, but creating ASPX pages yourself is a better way to learn ASP than merely copying completed pages from our reference set.

VWD Express — A Development Environment

A fundamental difference between most animals and humans is the ability to use tools. In the early days of programming, the tools to write programs were very primitive. Today we enjoy the benefits of very sophisticated tools for software development. Engineers have taken almost every area of human weakness (primarily related to the capacity of memory and the brain's interface to the world) and created compensating tools. These tools are pulled together into a type of software called an Integrated Development Environment (IDE). The IDE used in this text is Visual Web Developer Express (VWD).

VWD contains a number of development tools. First is an editor in which you can build a web page. This editor is enhanced with IntelliSense, a tool that finishes typing commands and offers appropriate choices for the developer. In addition, a toolbar contains icons that can be dragged to the editor and automatically type a block of code into the editor. Another way to automatically get code into a page is with the many wizards that pop up when you attempt a more complex task. VWD also contains a mini File Manager to organize ASPX and associated files and folders. Similarly, there is a Data Explorer that offers navigation through the data sources of the web site. A suite of troubleshooting tools is also included. Finally, VWD ships from Microsoft with a web server for testing named ASP.NET

Development Server, which is covered in the next section. If you go beyond the scope of this book, you can discover tools for more complex scenarios, including the management of code versions among a team of developers.

Introducing the ASP.NET Development Server

ASP.NET Development Server was mentioned earlier as the lightweight web server that comes with VWD. This is the lightweight server that was known as Cassini during the Beta releases of VWD. Both ASP.NET Development Server and IIS (included with the .NET Framework) can serve all ASPX and associated pages, so at deployment there is no need to make changes to your site. But a number of differences exist between the servers.

The two servers use different security models. IIS is a service, and every service in Windows requires a user. The special user for IIS is named ASPNET. ASP.NET Development Server runs as an application that uses the currently logged-in Windows user. That makes ASP.NET Development Server easier to install because there is no need to create a specific ASPNET account in Windows. In fact, the installation of ASP.NET Development Server is transparent when VWD is installed.

ASP.NET Development Server has three downsides. First, it is a tool for designers to test pages on their development machine and thus it does not scale to more than one user. Second, because of the simplifications to the user model, ASP.NET Development Server cannot support a robust security scheme. ASP.NET Development Server should run only in a closed environment or behind a robust firewall. Third, when you run a page in ASP.NET Development Server, it locks the page back in VWD. In order to unlock the page, you must close the browser, which can be inconvenient when you're making and testing many changes to a site. Therefore, many developers use IIS even on their development machines so they do not have to close a page in the browser before working on it in VWD. The downside is that you have to configure your development machine to provide IIS, set up the appropriate authorizations, establish security controls, and create a virtual root. You learn how to set this up in Appendix B. If you don't want to go through the IIS setup, you can still use ASP.NET Development Server and just close the browser between modifications.

VWD's Solution Explorer

An ASP.NET 2.0 web site is stored as a family of files. You need to be able to organize these files, including the tasks of viewing their names and relationships, copying, creating, and deleting. You can view and manipulate them in Windows Explorer, but it is inconvenient to switch between VWD and Windows Explorer. VWD includes an explorer-like tool called the Solution Explorer, shown in Figure 1-2. The Solution Explorer is displayed by default on the right of the screen, or you can redisplay it by pressing Ctrl+Alt+L. Think of it as a Windows Explorer that considers your web root to be the highest level and does not require you to switch out of VWD. Note that the Toolbox may be placed behind the Solution Explorer, as illustrated in Figure 1-2.

The layout of Solution Explorer is instantly familiar to anyone who uses Windows Explorer. Click the plus and minus icons to expand or contract folders. The icons in the toolbar start from the left with a tool that switches from the Solution Explorer to a view of properties (more on that later in this chapter). The double horizontal arrows perform a refresh. The double file icon automatically hides or expands nested subfiles. The next two icons open the selected files to display either their user interface (design) or their code. The double browser icon is used to copy the entire site to the deployment machine. The right-most icon, with the hammer, opens a Web Administrator tool to manage features of the site.

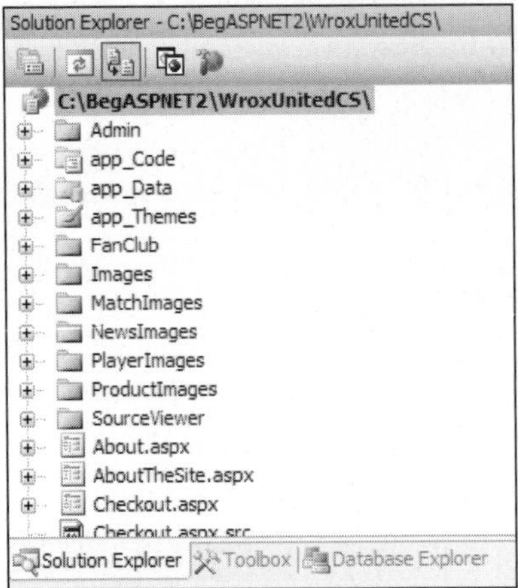

Figure 1-2

At the bottom of the Solution Explorer may be a small task bar that shows tabs for the Solution Explorer, Toolbox, Data Explorer, and/or Properties windows. To conserve monitor real estate these four tools are frequently stacked and the tabs offer quick switching. For example, in Figure 1-2, the Toolbox is also open (albeit hidden behind the Solution Explorer) and clicking the Toolbox tab would hide the Solution Explorer behind it. They are not strictly part of the Solution Explorer, but rather the pane that holds the four stacked tools.

In the main pane of the Solution Explorer is the list of files that make up your site. At the top is the root, generally in `C:\websites\MyWebSiteName`. In the case of WroxUnitedCS, `C:\BegASPNET2\WroxUnitedCS` is used. The files are displayed in their subfolders. Using the same techniques as Windows Explorer, you can expand, collapse, cut, copy, and paste files among folders. Solution Explorer recognizes the implied link between an .aspx file and its .aspx.cs file (more on these in Chapters 6 and 9). If you copy the .aspx file, the code file moves with it.

You can also right-click a folder and select Add Existing Item. The resulting dialog box enables you to navigate anywhere on your computer and network (including FTP sites) to bring in files. For example, when you begin to build your project, there are times you are asked to use an image or text file from this book's download at `www.wrox.com`. You can use Solution Explorer to add the item to your web site from your download folder.

During development, ASP.NET 2.0 sites do not contain a special system of file registration. The files, including ASPX pages, code files, data files, and images are all contained in a normal Windows folder and subfolder structure. If you do not have VWD open, you can cut, copy, and paste your site files directly from Windows Explorer.

The Solution Explorer, like the Toolbar, Data Explorer, and Properties window discussed in the next section, can be placed on the page in one of two modes: *floating* or *dockable*. Floating allows the window to be placed anywhere on the screen, similar to a normal window of a base size (not maximized). The dockable mode automatically places the window in one of five locations: top, bottom, left, right, or stacked on another window. Change the mode by selecting one of the windows, and click through Window⇨Floating or dockable in the menu. In dockable mode you will see some translucent positioners when you drag the window's title bar, (see Figure 1-3). Drag the title bar onto one of these positioners, and the window automatically sizes and places itself in the correct dock.

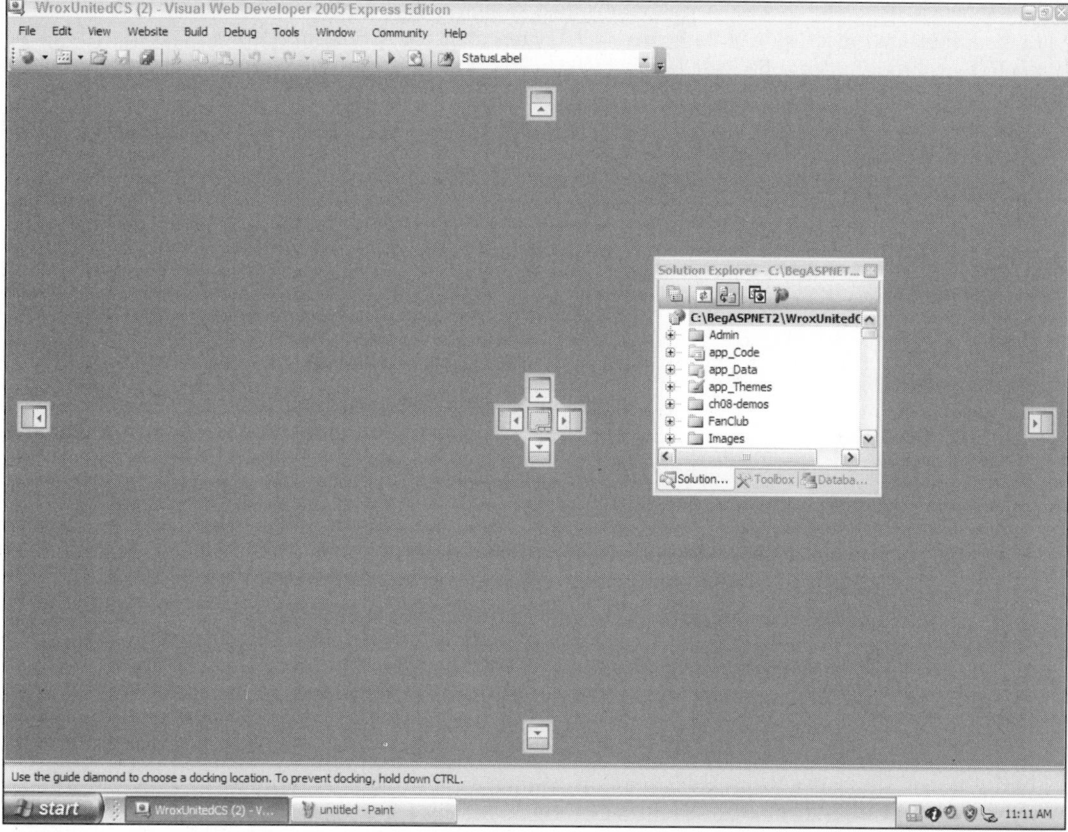

Figure 1-3

Now that you have learned to modify the VWD Express IDE, you can move on to the techniques of creating web sites and pages within those sites.

Creating, Opening, and Using Web Sites and Pages with VWD

To create a new site, you only have to open VWD and click Menu⇨File⇨New Site. From the wizard, select an ASP.NET web site. Assuming you will create a local copy for development, set the location to File System and browse to the path. Normally this would be `C:\BegASPNET2\MyWebsiteName` (our practice site allows backward compatibility with earlier books by using `C:\BegASPNET2\WroxUnited`). This book uses the C# choice in the Language list. VWD automatically creates a folder, a default page, and a subfolder for data.

ASP.NET 2.0 introduces a very simple model for file organization and code registration for a web site. All files for the site are stored in a folder and its subfolder. At the time of deployment, that entire group is copied from the development machine to the host. Therefore, you are not required to create a virtual root as in former versions of ASP. Deployment is further simplified by VWD: if you select Menu⇨Website⇨Copy Website, VWD opens an FTP screen that you can use to send new or updated files to your host.

To edit an existing site, choose Menu⇨File⇨Open Web Site. If you are working locally, you can browse to the folder. On the left side of the screen, VWD presents a menu with options to work directly on pages via FTP or through a local IIS installation.

After you create the web site, you can add pages. We usually start by adding some folders to organize the pages. Right-click an existing folder and click the option to add a folder. The options are a regular folder or one of the folder names that are reserved in ASP.NET, including ones for Code, Themes, and Web References.

To add a page, right-click a folder and click Add New Item. A wizard presents many choices. For now, you simply need to create a Web Form, but take a look at the other options to get a feel for the capability of VWD and ASP.NET 2.0. Give your new page a name and set its language. Later chapters discuss the two checkboxes. Having introduced you to creating web sites and pages, the following Try It Out puts that knowledge to use, asking you to create the Wrox United site and a couple of practice pages.

The Sample Code (Download) Directories

To make things easy, each chapter has its own code, and there are two directories for each chapter, held under one of two higher-level directories. There is a Begin directory, which contains the samples ready for you to work through — it's the samples without any changes. The End directory contains the samples with the Try It Outs completed, so you can use these as a reference as you are working through the examples, or to cut and paste code if the example directs you to do this.

The Begin and End directories appear under a Chapters directory, with each chapter having its own directory. So the starting set of samples for this chapter is under `Chapters\Begin\Chapter01`, and the finished code for this chapter is under `Chapters\End\Chapter01`. Some chapters work on the main WroxUnitedCS application, and will therefore contain a copy of the WroxUnitedCS directory, whereas others have non-WroxUnitedCS samples. The reason for this is that some techniques are easier to digest in smaller samples, rather than in a fully working application. All of the techniques, however, are used in the main application.

Because each chapter has a separate directory, some with complete copies of WroxUnitedCS, the samples are quite large. However, the advantage is that each chapter is kept separate from the others, which allows you to work through chapters without mixing up which code came from which chapter.

In addition to the code for the chapters, there is a WroxUnitedCS application that contains the final application. This may differ slightly from the samples, but only in that the data may be more complete, and some of the pages look a little nicer.

Try It Out — Creating the Wrox United Site and Two Practice Pages

1. Open VWD. Choose Menu⇨File⇨New Web Site. Select the template for an ASP.NET web site and locate it in the File System at `C:\Websites\WroxUnitedCS` (you can use the Browse button to navigate to this directory). Make sure the Language choice is set to Visual C#. Click OK. You should see your folder on the right side of the screen in the Solution Explorer. If not, choose View⇨Solution Explorer. Note that VWD automatically builds three items: a folder named `App_Data`, a page named `Default.aspx`, and (if you expand `Default.aspx`) a file named `Default.aspx.cs`, which will hold code for the default page.

2. In the center of VWD, you will see a space for editing pages with the `Default.aspx` page opened. Note in the bottom-left a choice of Design and Source. Click each in turn to observe the code and the results of the code. In Design View, click the page and type the simple text **Home Page**. Press Ctrl+S to save.
3. Create a folder for images by going to your Solution Explorer and right-clicking the root of your site (this will probably show as `C:\...\Chapter01`, as the Solution Explorer hides part of the path) and then clicking Add Folder of the regular type. Name the nascent folder **Images**.
4. You can manipulate your site's files and folders outside of VWD. Open Windows Explorer and navigate to `C:\BegASPNET2\Chapters\Begin\Chapter01` to see the same set of folders and files as you see in VWD's Solution Explorer.
5. Returning to VWD, right-click the nascent Images folder and click Add an Existing Item. Browse to the folder where you stored the download for this book, probably named `C:\BegASPNET2\WroxUnitedCS`. Open the Images folder and select all the images. Click Add to actually copy those images from the download folder to your site's image folder.
6. Staying in VWD, now create your next page, the history of Wrox United. Right-click the site's root (`C...\Chapter01` at the top of the Solution Explorer) and select Add New Item from the menu. Select the Web Form template and give it the name **History**. Accept the other default settings. Click Add and switch to Design View. Rather than typing text on the page, you can copy a short history of the team from a file included in the download. Switch to Windows Explorer and navigate to your downloaded `Chapter01\Begin\Chapter01` folder. Look for the file named `History.txt`, open it, and select the paragraphs. Switch back to VWD and paste the text into the page. Click the diskette icon on the toolbar to save.
7. Repeat step 6 for a Mishaps page, whose contents come from `Mishaps.txt`.

How It Works

In this exercise, you created your site and the first few pages. By using the menu choices in VWD to create a site, you automatically get some standard folders and files. You followed the Microsoft recommendation of storing the site in the `C:\Websites` directory. As you saw with the Images folder, it is easy to add subfolders to the root to organize your files.

When you created a page in VWD, you were offered a few dozen templates. You selected Web Form as the standard plain ASP.NET 2.0 web page. By using cut and paste, you have no problems bringing in text from other files.

You also learned that there is no requirement for a special file indexing or storage mechanism in VWD. The files sit in the folders organized by Windows on the hard drive. However, it is better to create and add files in VWD when possible to keep the Solution Explorer view and other VWD features immediately up-to-date with your changes.

Running a Page

After a page is created, it can be served to a user. Because the server actually executes code in the server-side controls to create the final HTML page, this serving of the page is also called *running* the page, as if you were running a program. VWD has a green triangle tool icon to initiate a run or you can press F5 or choose Menu⇨Debug⇨Run. VWD then performs several steps:

1. All pages in the site are compiled to the Microsoft Intermediate Language (MSIL) that is then stored with supporting files in an assembly. At this point, development language differences (for example VB and C#) disappear because the result is in MSIL. However, there is no optimization for the hardware that will serve the page.
2. The assembly is Just In Time (JIT)—compiled from MSIL to Native Code that is optimized for the serving machine.
3. A lock is placed on the page that prevents changes in VWD Design View while the page is opened by ASP.NET Development Server.
4. VWD starts ASP.NET Development Server and your browser is opened with a request to ASP.NET Development Server for the page.

> **A common mistake for beginners is to attempt to change a page in VWD's Design View while it is still open in a browser served by ASP.NET Development Server.**

As your site gets larger, you'll find that the compilations take longer. You can press Ctrl+F5 to run a page with a compilation of only that page. In the following Try It Out, you practice running the History and Mishaps pages created in the previous Try It Out.

Try It Out Running a Page

1. In VWD's Solution Explorer, double-click the `History.aspx` file to open it (if it is not already open).
2. Click the Run icon (green arrow) on the toolbar. If there is a message to add a Web.config with a Debug, accept the suggestion. Note that your browser opens and displays the History page.
3. In the Windows tray, the icon of a yellow page with a gear indicates that ASP.NET Development Server is running. Double-click it and you will see that it is pointing to your web site. Close your browser so ASP.NET Development Server unlocks the page.
4. Return to VWD and open the Mishaps page. This time, watch the lower-left corner of VWD as you start to run the page. You will see a message that the build has started and a brief display of an error list box. After seeing the Mishaps page in your browser, switch back to VWD. Note that the page (in Design View) is locked while it is served.

How It Works

This Try It Out focused on running pages from VWD. You can start the run by clicking the green arrow. This action starts ASP.NET Development Server. It also opens your browser and sends a request to ASP.NET Development Server for the page. When ASP.NET Development Server is running, you can see the icon for the server in the Windows system tray.

Design Surface

The center of the VWD interface is occupied by the large Design Surface. This is the area where you will do most of your work of adding content to ASP.NET 2.0 pages. You can switch between Design View, which displays a simile of the final page in a browser-like display, or you can switch to Source View, which displays code in a text screen (see Figure 1-4). In general, the Design View is easier and faster for most work because it supports more drag-and-drop features. You can switch to Source View when you need to make those minor changes that are beyond the capability of the VWD drag-and-drop interface.

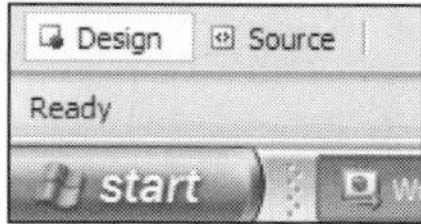

Figure 1-4

When you add a control to a page in Design View, a Common Tasks Menu may pop up. This mini menu contains the most frequently used setup features for the control. Not all controls have smart task panels, but if it is available, it can be opened and closed using the small black triangle at the top corner (shown in Figure 1-5) of a control that is selected.

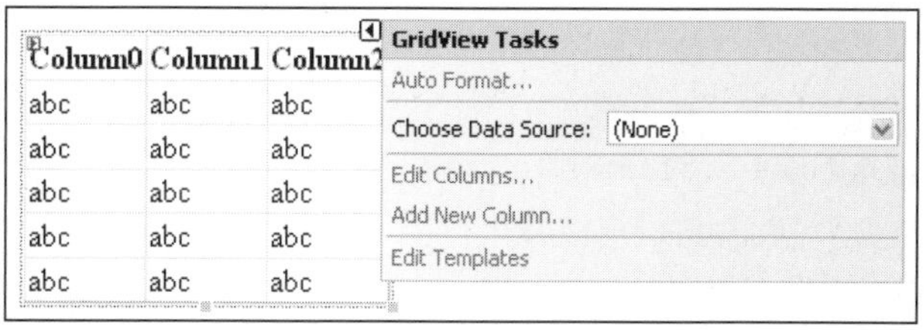

Figure 1-5

You can change several default settings in the Design Surface by opening the Tools menu and selecting Options. These options change the way the pages appear to you, as the programmer, when they are opened for editing in VWD. These are not the settings for the appearance of the page to the web site visitor. You can select to start pages in Design View or Source View, as well as the automatic opening of the smart task panel. Being able to revise the number of spaces for tabs and indents helps your projects conform to your company's specifications for web page code.

At the bottom edge of the Design Surface is a navigation tool that is useful in large and complex documents. You can read the navigation tags to find out where the insertion bar (cursor) is currently setting. The current setting is highlighted, as depicted in Figure 1-6. You can also click a tag and the entire tag will be selected in the Design Surface.

Figure 1-6

The designer is, in many ways, like a word processor. But VWD also offers the two alternatives to viewing a page (Design and Source) as well as enhancements for navigating through the page. The next section discusses how VWD helps you to add features to the page.

Toolbox

VWD offers the set of ASP.NET server-side controls in a Toolbox for easy drag-and-drop onto the page. Chapter 3 discusses in detail the various server-side controls and how they are used; here you will just get a feel for how to use the Toolbox in general. The Toolbox can be displayed by choosing Menu⇨View⇨Toolbox or by pressing Ctrl+Alt+X. When the Toolbox is displayed, you can move it to a new location on the screen by dragging its title bar. As you drag the Toolbox to different areas, it will render a compass icon that enables you to drop the toolbar toward the top, bottom, left, or right, as well as on top of other windows. If you are trying to maximize the size of your design surface, you can stack your Solution Explorer and Toolbox on top of each other at one location on the screen.

The Toolbox is organized into several panels that group similar controls. The panels can be expanded to show their tools or collapsed to save space. There is some variation among installations, but a typical set of panels includes the following:

- **Standard** for the majority of ASP.NET 2.0 server-side controls
- **Data** for data source and data-bound controls
- **Validation** for controls that reject user input that does not meet your range of acceptable values
- **Navigation** for menus and breadcrumbs
- **Login** for the authentication controls
- **WebParts** for larger components in sites that the user can rearrange or hide
- **HTML** for generic (non-ASP) tags
- **General** for customization

Figure 1-7 depicts the Toolbox as it appears on your screen.

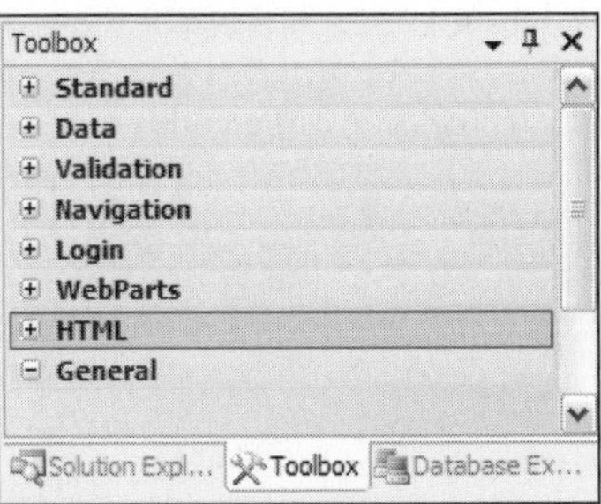

Figure 1-7

Clicking the plus icon expands a panel to show its list of available controls. Figure 1-8 shows the Data and Login panels expanded.

The General panel starts out empty. After you have created part of a page, you can select that page and drag it into the General panel to create your own reusable tool. This is useful if you want to duplicate a set of a couple controls with formatting onto several pages.

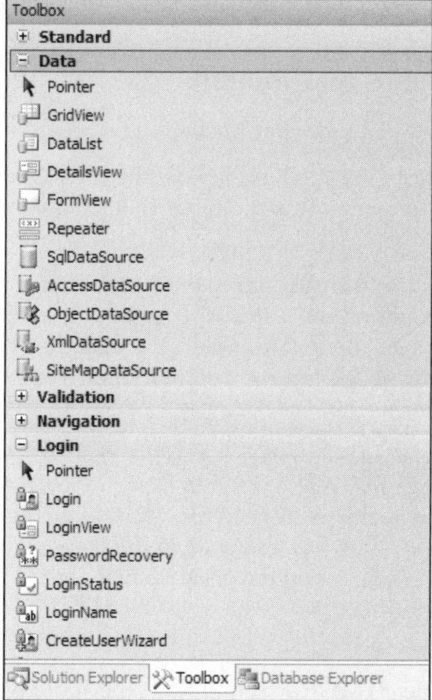

Figure 1-8

On the right side of the Toolbox title bar there is a pushpin icon, shown in Figure 1-9. When clicked, the pushpin turns horizontal, meaning that the Toolbox will automatically hide when not in use, leaving only its title bar exposed.

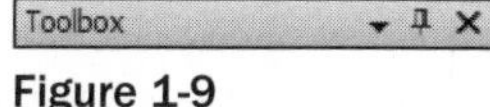

Figure 1-9

The appearance of the Toolbox changes as it is used. For example, the titles of each panel will change as they are selected.

When your mouse moves over the Toolbox title bar, the Toolbox expands for your employment, as shown in Figure 1-10.

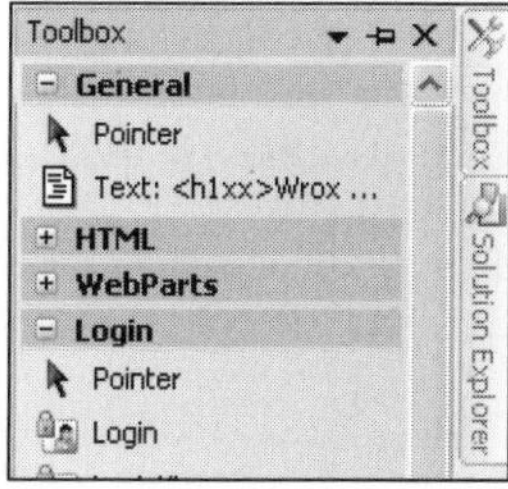

Figure 1-10

In this Try It Out, you practice using the Design and Source Views and Toolbox features of VWD.

Try It Out Using the Views and Toolbox

1. Continue working in VWD with your Mishaps page.
2. Switch to Design View. In the Toolbox, expand the HTML panel and scroll down to the bottom of the panel. Drag a Horizontal Rule from the Toolbox onto the page (anywhere between paragraphs).
3. Your next objective is to add a calendar to the bottom of the History page. Open the Standard panel of the Toolbox and find the ASP.NET calendar control. Drag it to the page. (Double-clicking performs the same operation.) Select the calendar with a single click and notice the small right-facing arrow in the top-right corner. Click it to expose the smart task panel. Click Autoformat, select a format, and click Apply. Observe how easy it is to modify many rendering criteria simultaneously using VWD's dialog interface.
4. Open your History page in VWD. View it in Design View. Move your insertion bar up to the first line to the tag that begins with `<%@ Page...>`. Note that the navigation guide (at the bottom of the design panel) shows that you are in the `<Page>` tag. Click the `<Page>` tag. You will see that the entire tag is selected in the design panel.

How It Works

As you saw, by adding a simple HTML Horizontal Rule, the Toolbox offers the ability to drag and drop elements to the page rather than typing out their tags. Even complex constructs like a calendar are added with just a drag-and-drop. When you are on the page, you can modify an element by using the smart task panel.

Properties Window

An object, such as a web page, a ListBox server-side control, or a connection to a data source, has *properties*. Properties are settings that determine how the object appears and behaves. In earlier versions of ASP, many goals were achieved by writing lengthy and complex code. In ASP.NET 2.0, however, most of that code has been pre-written by Microsoft and encapsulated within the server-side controls. Properties determine how that behavior will be exercised. Properties can be very simple, such as BackgroundColor, or very complex, such as EnablePaging. Likewise, the values assigned to a property can be as simple as BLUE or as complex as a multiple-line SQL statement. Property values can be set by typing them directly into the Code View or by using the Properties window, which is shown in Figure 1-11.

Display the Properties window by pressing F4 or by choosing Menu⇨View⇨Properties. The properties are organized into panels that can be collapsed or expanded (similar to the Toolbox). For example, in Figure 1-11 the top three panels are collapsed. At the top of the Properties window is a drop-down list containing the names of all controls on the page currently open. Below that are icons to arrange the list of properties categorically or alphabetically. The lightning icon changes the Properties window so that it displays events (a topic covered in Chapter 6) rather than properties. The body of the window displays property names on the left and their current values on the right. At the bottom sits a box that gives some help on the currently selected property.

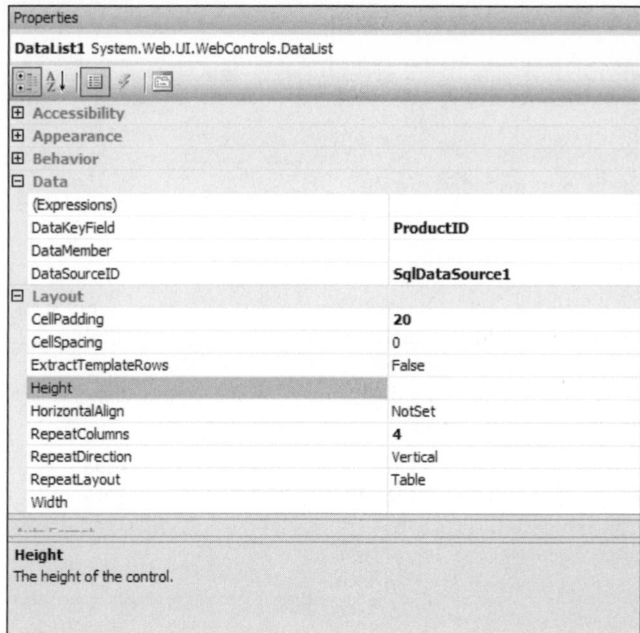

Figure 1-11

The fundamental technique used to change properties is to select an object, usually a control, and then find the property of interest and set it. You can select the object with a single click on the object in Design View or by locating the insertion bar in the object in Source View. Alternatively, you can select an object from a drop-down list at the top of the Properties window. One common mistake arises when you attempt to change the properties but have not first actually selected the object you want to change. You end up changing an object that was still selected from earlier work.

You have several options for setting the value of a property. If the property has a limited number of allowed values (such as true and false), you can double-click the property name to toggle through the values. If there are more than a few options, but still a finite amount, the values will be in a drop-down list. Some properties have many options, and their value box offers an ellipses button that takes you to a dialog box. Some properties can accept strings, so their values are set in text boxes. It is always better to select or to toggle a value rather than type it. After a value has been changed, you must press Enter or Tab or click another property in order to set the value. At that time, the Design View will render the change.

You can also set property values by typing into the Source View. Locate the insertion bar within a tag and press the space bar to display an IntelliSense list of all the properties that can be inserted at the location of the insertion bar. Type the first letter or two and then type an equals sign. IntelliSense displays all of the legal values (if the list is finite), and again type the first letter or two of the value you desire. Finish by typing a space. Note that there will be no value list if the range of possible property values is not finite. For example, if the value is a SQL statement, you will have to type the statement without IntelliSense.

Error List Window

When problems arise you have two major paths for obtaining clues about the problem. First is an error report on the page delivered to the browser, and second is the Error List window within VWD.

ASP.NET 2.0 displays an error report (shown in Figure 1-12) on the page sent to the browser if the following shaded line is in your `Web.config` file:

```
<system.web>
        <compilation debug="true">
         </compilation>
```

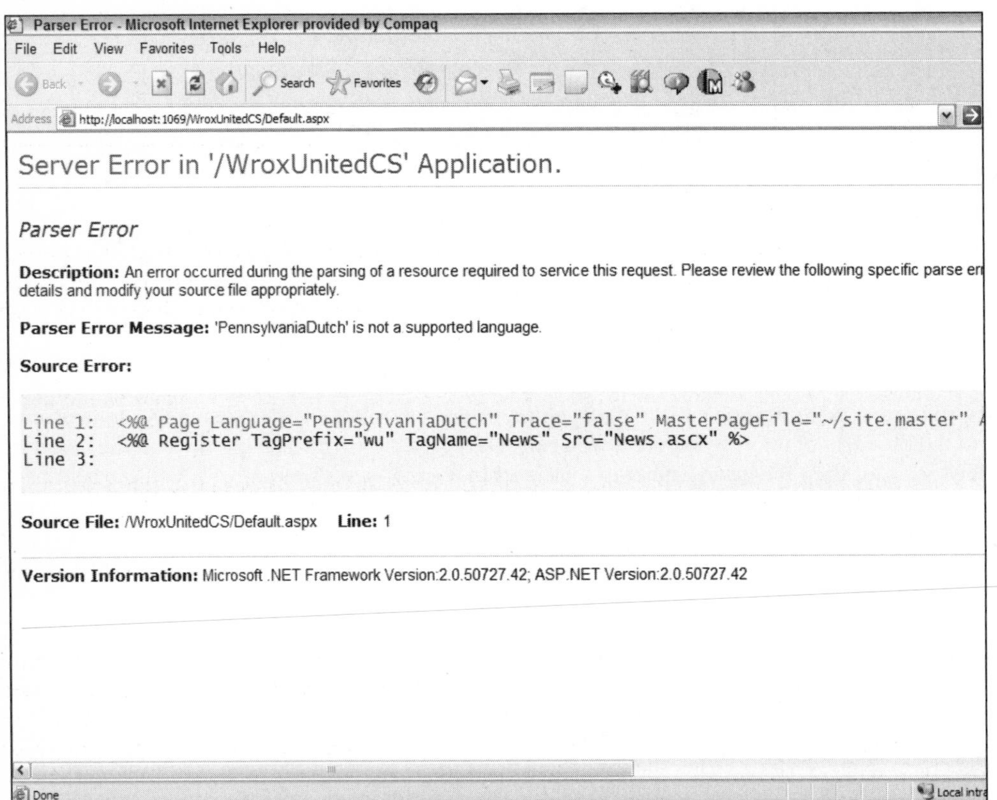

Figure 1-12

Note that the first time you run (F5) a page, you get a default of `<compilation debug="true" strict="false" explicit="true"/>`.

Because the default is `true`, you will have debug turned on if there is no specific attribute. So `debug=true` for the following case as well where there are no changes to the default. Of course, having the default literally set to `true` helps other programmers on your team that may be looking through your settings:

```
<system.web>
        <compilation></compilation>
```

A fatal error on the page produces a characteristic white-and-yellow page on your browser with an error message. Just below the yellow block is the name of the offending file and the line containing the failure. As with all errors, the error may actually be related to the line number displayed, but this should give you a good clue. Note that when you deploy a site, the `debug` command in `Web.config` should be set to `false` to improve performance and to reduce information given to hackers. Error handling is covered in greater depth in Chapter 15.

The second way to identify errors comes from within VWD itself via the Error List window, depicted in Figure 1-13. By default, the window is hidden until you run a page. You can force it to be displayed by choosing Menu⇨View⇨Error List. The window displays all of the errors encountered during the conversion of the page into the MSIL.

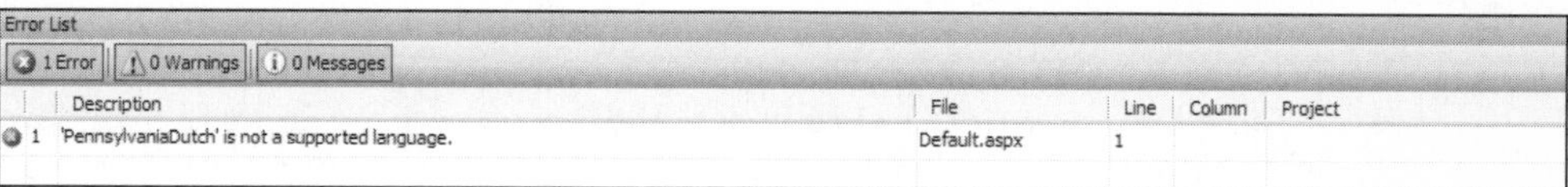

Figure 1-13

Note that the top of the Error List window has three clickable icons: Errors, Warnings, and Messages, which display different lists of items created when the page was built. Hiding a type of item does not remove it from the list; rather, doing so only hides the item so the list is shorter. The second column from the left identifies the order in which the errors occurred.

Errors cause the page as a whole, or some portion of it, to fail. This includes, for example, references to objects that do not exist.

Warnings are problems that could be solved by VWD while building the page (for example, the lack of a closing tag).

Messages are sets of texts that the programmer can include in the code to appear when IIS is building the page.

When viewing the list of items, you can sort by clicking a column heading. If you hold Shift you can click a second column for tiebreakers (to determine the order for records with the same value in the primary column). You can also resize the columns by dragging their dividers, or re-order them by dragging the column name left or right. Double-clicking an item allows you to open the offending file and jump the cursor to the offending line.

In this Try It Out, you practice changing properties of an image control on the History page. Then you create some errors and observe the results.

Try It Out — Using the Properties and Error Lists Windows

1. Open the History page in Design View. In the Solutions window, open the Images folder and drag the JPEG named "logo-yellow" to the top of the History page. VWD automatically creates an image with its source set to the JPEG.

2. Click the image once to select it, and then switch to the Properties window (or open it with F4). Change the height from 447 to 100 and press Enter to set the value. As you can see, changes are immediately visible in the design panel.

3. Now modify properties from Source View. Find the `<img>` control and within it the property (attribute) for height. Change it from 100 to 300. Click the green arrow (or press F5) to run the page and see the result.

4. Close your browser and return to Source View. Locate your insertion bar in the `<img>` tag immediately after the closing quote of `height="300"` and press the space bar. This opens the IntelliSense list with all of the properties that are suitable at this point in your page. Press the t key and then the i key to move down the list to the Title property. Press the equal (=) key to close the IntelliSense and type in **"Wrox Logo In Yellow"** including the start and end quotes. Run the page, and in your browser note that when you mouse over the image you see the title you created. Close the browser.

5. Next, introduce a non-fatal error. Open the History page in Source View and find the `<h1>` tag near the top of the page. Change the `<h1>` tag to `<H1xx>` and run the page. The browser opens and you can see that the text "Wrox United — a potted history" fails to render in the heading-one style. Close the browser and switch back to VWD to observe the Errors List window. If not the Errors List window is not already visible, choose Menu➪View➪Error List to view it. Note that two errors were entered in the list. First was a note that "h1xx" on line 3 is not supported. Second, the closing tag of `</h1>` on line 4 no longer matches an opening tag.

6. Your last experiment is to introduce a fatal error. In Source View, go to the top of the page and change the first line from `Language="C#"` to `Language="Esperanto"` and run the page.

7. You will deal with solving many kinds of errors in each chapter of this book. For now, return your page to its original form by deleting the `<img>` tag, restoring the goofy `<h1xx>` to the proper `<h1>`, and changing the language back to C#.

8. Save the page.

How It Works

You experimented with three ways to change a property. First you worked in Design View and changed a property by typing its new value into the Properties window. Next you made a change by typing a new value into the source code. Last, you used IntelliSense to guide you through adding a property to an existing control.

You observed the results of two types of errors: fatal and non-fatal. In the first case, ASP.NET 2.0 could still render the page even though the faulty tag of `<h1xx>` left your text as default, not heading one. Although the page rendered, back in VWD an error message was logged on to the Error List window. You introduced a more serious error when you changed the language value to a non-supported language. ASP.NET 2.0 could not overcome this error and so you see two results. In the browser you got the error page with troubleshooting information, and back in VWD you got entries to the error list.

VWD's Database Explorer

When you begin to work with data (in Chapter 7) you can use tools in VWD to gain knowledge about your data sources. This information includes the exact names of tables and columns. In fact, as you will see later in this book, you can drag columns to the designer and VWD does all the work of setting up the proper controls to display data from those columns. For now, understand that in the Solution Explorer you can double-click the name of an Access MDB to open that file in Access (assuming Access is installed). For SQL Server databases (as used in this book), you can use a tool named the Database Explorer to do even more exploration of a database and change its data and properties. These features are discussed in detail in Appendix D.

Summary

Microsoft has revised large parts of ASP.NET in version 2.0. The overall biggest benefit is that tasks, which formerly required custom coding, can now be implemented by dragging pre-built controls to the page. These pre-built controls include tools for logging on users, navigation, connecting to stores of data, displaying data, creating a consistent look to the site, and offering customization options to the user. The result is both faster and more robust development of dynamic web pages. On top of this, Microsoft has made version 2.0 easier to deploy and faster in performance. As with earlier versions of ASP, the execution of code (that is, the building of dynamic pages) occurs on the server and only standard HTML is sent to the browser. Thus, ASP.NET 2.0 is compatible with all browsers.

Three tools are available from Microsoft for creating ASP.NET 2.0 pages. The one used in this book, Visual Web Developer Express (VWD), is a free download as of 2005. VWD displays the organization of pages on your site, and helps you build new pages or modify existing pages. VWD also comes with a lightweight web server named ASP.NET Development Server for testing your pages. After building a page, you can click Run to have VWD start ASP.NET Development Server, start your browser, build the page, and serve it to the browser. This chapter also covered the following topics:

- VWD offers many options for the way that you view and work with pages during their development. Tabs enable switching between Design View (which displays a good facsimile of how the browser will render the page) and Source View (which shows the tags and code that generate the page).
- When you create a new site or add pages, VWD offers wizards and templates that walk you through the most common setups. In this chapter, you looked at how to create a new page based on one of several dozen templates, followed by working with the Toolbox. This source of pre-built objects is a focus of building pages in all the exercises of this book. To organize the large Toolbox, the tools are divided into groups.
- Another window displays properties of whichever object is currently selected. You can, for example, select a text box and see its size, background color, and dozens of other properties. The remainder of this book goes into the details of many properties of objects that ASP.NET 2.0 supports on a page.
- When a page is built as a result of the VWD Run command, you get some feedback on how the process fared. Fatal errors are listed, as well as warnings about potential problems with the page. Double-clicking any of those errors leads you to the offending line in the site.

This first chapter focused on an introduction to ASP.NET 2.0 and how to build your first pages using VWD. Chapter 2 moves on to some of the ASP.NET 2.0 features that govern the look and feel of all the pages on a site.

Exercises

1. Explain the differences among the .NET 2.0 Framework, ASP.NET 2.0, VWD, and IIS.
2. List some differences between ASP.NET Development Server and IIS.
3. When you drag the title bar of the toolbar it will only go to certain locations and certain sizes. How can you put the title bar where you want it?

4. How can you copy a .jpg file in `C:\MyPhotos` into your site for display on a page?
5. You want to add a subfolder to your site, but Folder is not one of the items listed in Add Items. Why?
6. Microsoft has written extensive code to make it easier for programmers to create web pages. How does a programmer actually use that code?
7. Why are there no tools in the General panel of the Toolbox?

Site Design

When you start to develop a web site, you'll often have a good idea of what the site needs to be able to do. For example, a blog site needs the ability to store blog entries by categories, for adding comments to blog entries, and an administration section, at the very least. Alternatively, consider a simple retail store that wants to enter the realm of e-business by having a web site that enables customers to browse and buy their products. Each and every site needs to be carefully thought about and designed before you can start work, and only then can you start putting code together to implement a site.

Before jumping into the discussion and implementation of specific techniques, you should understand the development of good site design with an eye toward the features supported by the ASP.NET 2.0 server-side controls. After all, a well-designed site is easier to create, easier to use, and easier (and cheaper) to maintain.

In this chapter, you'll learn about the following concepts:

- How to start the design process for a site, and consider all the requirements for the site before you start coding
- Using Master and Content pages to implement a consistent look and feel to a site using this great new ASP.NET 2.0 feature
- Constructing a site map that defines which pages exist on a site, and how these pages relate to each other hierarchically
- Storing central configuration data and code that is used by all pages on a site using the `Web.config` and `Global.asax` files

At the end of the chapter are some exercises to help you gain a bit more familiarity with the concepts learned.

General Design Objectives

Designing a fully functional web application is a big task. If you're developing your own site, you may have thought long and hard about what you want your site to be about, so you know what it is you're trying to do before you start. However, if you are developing a site for a customer, you must make sure you are careful and thorough about how you agree on a design for a site. In a professional development environment, this process normally includes the following steps:

1. Develop a functional model that describes exactly how the site should function. What happens when the user clicks the Log In button? What features are available when a user wants to view a product? These questions, and many others, need to be answered before you start work, so you don't end up developing something that the customer doesn't want.
2. Identify which technologies you have available to use in the implementation of the site. Many hosting packages have different levels of support for databases, and limitations on the overall size of a site, so make sure you talk about this early on and make sure you can use all the technologies you would like to use.
3. Develop a technical specification that describes how you will implement the required functionality. For example, on a blog site, how will you make sure that when the user clicks the button to post a new blog entry, the text that has been entered is saved in the database? Be as thorough as you can, because you may not be the one who has to maintain the site later.

This may sound like quite a lot of work, but even for smaller businesses or sole trading contractors, following this process will help you to maintain a happy relationship with your customer, and potentially secure future work with either that customer or any of their friends or business contacts.

When you move from the business side of things into the implementation phase, you start to think about how to create the application, and how to actually design the site in line with what the customer wants. Creating a web application requires more than just correct use of the ASP.NET 2.0 server-side controls, because the process of actually designing and laying out the pages of the site is just as important.

Note that the term *design* can have two meanings. The first is the selection of colors and layout, which are typically created by a design artist for the site. The second definition includes the intellectual construction and coordination of the parts of the site. This includes the plans for the architecture of the information. In your case, you want to store as much information as possible in a relational database. This chapter concentrates on the second definition. The next chapter considers how to design each page in a site, using a healthy mix of HTML and ASP.NET controls.

The Wrox United sample site has the following site-wide design objectives that are implemented in this chapter:

- Facilitate troubleshooting as much as possible during the development, so that it's a simple process to track down errors.
- Set site-wide standards for coping with errors after deployment.
- Create a consistent look for all pages.

Additional general design objectives are covered later in the book, including an interface for a login system to identify members (Chapter 4), applying consistent styling and themes to a site (Chapter 5), and sourcing as much information as possible on databases or XML data files (Chapters 7 and 8).

Master and Content Pages

A site benefits from a consistent look and feel, and you'll rarely find sites on the Internet that deviate from having a generic site layout, which generally includes the following:

- A common header and menu system for the entire site
- A bar on the left side of the page offering some page navigation options
- A footer providing copyright information and a secondary menu for contacting the webmaster

These elements will be present on every page and they not only provide essential features, but the consistent layout of these elements signal to users that they are still in the same site. Although this appearance can be built with include files in HTML, ASP.NET 2.0 provides more robust tools with the Master page and Content page system.

A Master page defines the layout to be used by all pages based on the Master. It's the overall parent that controls your layout, specifying how big your header will be on every page, where your navigation features will be placed, and the text to display in the footer on every page — a bit like a cookie cutter for each page. The Master page contains some of the content available to each page on the site, so standard copyright footer text can be defined here, along with positioning the main site logo at the top of the page. After the standard features of the Master are defined, you then add some *placeholders* — named regions on a page that define where content that varies from page to page will be positioned.

A Content page is a page based on a Master, and is where you add the content for each page on a site that varies from page to page. The Content page contains text, HTML, and controls within `<asp:content>` tags. When the Content page is requested, its content is combined with a copy of the Master page, with the specific content defined in the Content page placed within the specified placeholder on the Master page. Then the whole package is delivered to the browser, as shown in Figure 2-1.

Fortunately, the heavy lifting for this architecture is performed by ASP.NET 2.0. You only have to create the Master and Content pages as laid out in the next two sections.

Creating a Master Page

You create a Master page in VWD's Solution Explorer by right-clicking the root of the site, selecting Add Item, and designating the type as a Master Page. By default, the name for a new Master page is `MasterPage.master` and is located in the root of the site. The Master page has three parts.

First are some basic page tags and designations (such as the designation of a Master, `DOCTYPE`, `xmlns`, `html`, and `head` tags) that are required by any rendered page. This content is entered only once in the Master page, to reduce repetition. `DOCTYPE` and `xmlns` refer to the place the server can look up the definitions of tags used by the page. Note that these tags will not appear in the Content pages:

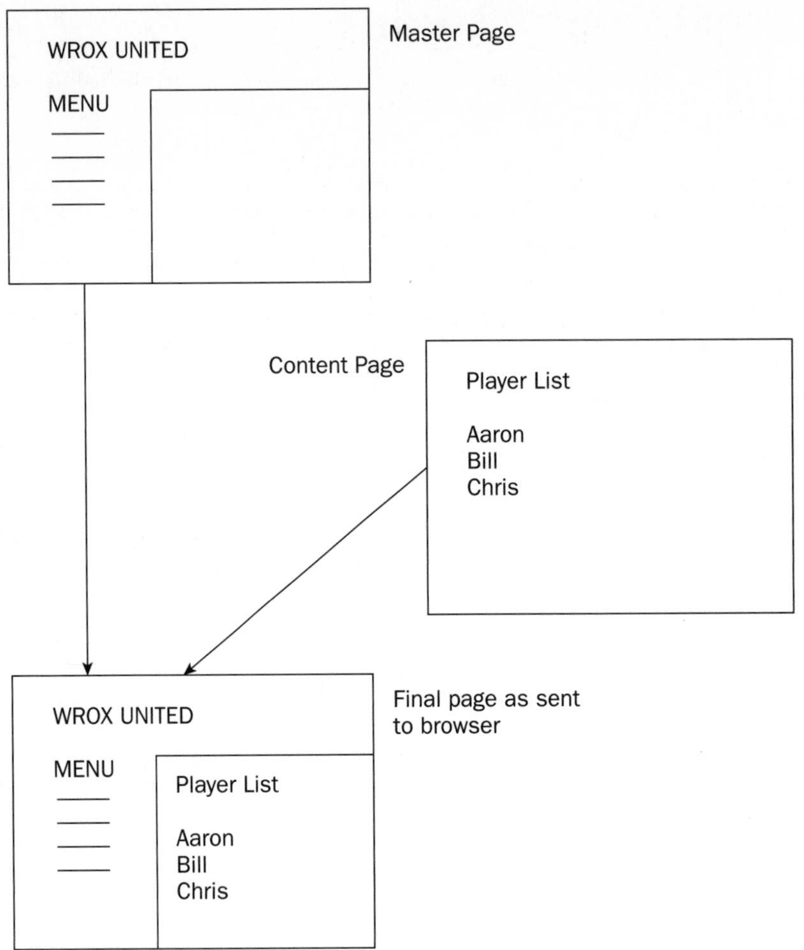

Figure 2-1

```
<%@ master language="C#" %>

<!DOCTYPE HTML PUBLIC "-//W3C//DTD XHTML 1.0 Transitional//EN"
"http://www.w3.org/TR/xhtml1/DTD/xhtml1-transitional.dtd">

<html xmlns="http://www.w3.org/1999/xhtml">

<head id="PageHead" runat="server">
  <meta http-equiv="Content-Type" content="text/html; charset=utf-8" />
  <meta http-equiv="Content-Language" content="en-uk" />
  <title>Wrox United</title>
  <link rel="stylesheet" type="text/css" href="site.css" runat="server" />
</head>
```

The second part of the Master page is a place for scripts that will be run on all pages (such as `Page_Load` code, which runs each time a page is loaded). For example:

```
<script runat="server">
  Sub Page_Load(ByVal sender As Object, ByVal e As System.EventArgs)
    ' ...
  End Sub
</script>
```

Third, the Master page includes some HTML for layout, and the start/end tags `<asp:content ... ContentPlaceHolderID="xxx>` and `</asp:content>` tags. The material from the Content page will be placed between these tags. For example:

```
<body>
  <form id="mainForm" runat="server">
    <div id="header">...</div>
    <div id="sidebar">...</div>
    <div id="content">
      <asp:contentplaceholder id="mainContent" runat="server" />
    </div>
    <div id="footer">
      <p class="left">
         All content copyright &copy; Wrox Press and its subsidiaries 2006.</p>
    </div>
  </form>
</body>
</html>
```

In summary, each Master page must include the following elements:

- Basic HTML and XML typing tags
- `<%@ master ... %>` on the first line
- An `<asp:ContentPlaceHolder>` tag with an ID

The Master page is now available as a container to hold other pages. You create those Content pages in the next section.

Creating Content Pages

As with most of ASP.NET 2.0, VWD saves you typing. Starting in the Solution Explorer, right-click the root and select Add New Item. Generally, you will pick a Web Form (there is no special template for a Content page). At the bottom of the dialog box is the option to Select master page (see Figure 2-2). When this box is checked and you click Add, you will be led to an additional dialog box that asks which Master page to use for the new Content page.

The second dialog box (shown in Figure 2-3) allows you to pick which Master page to use. Select the Master page. Change the name from the default of `MasterPage.master to site.master` and click OK.

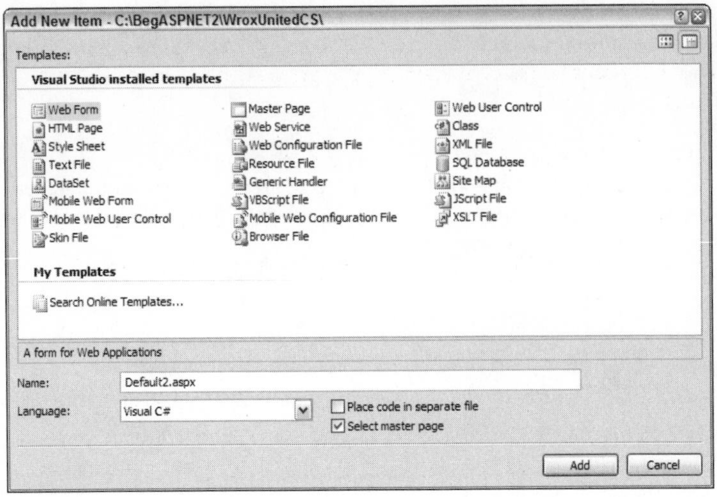

Figure 2-2

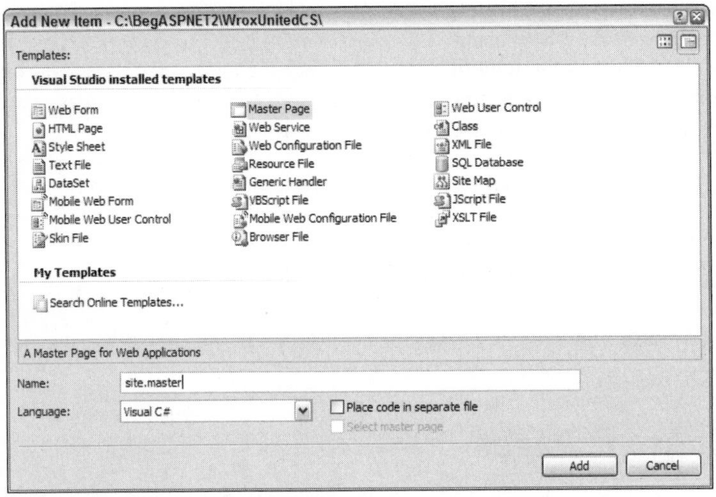

Figure 2-3

VWD sets two values in the Content page. They are not shown in Design View, but switching to Source View reveals them, as displayed in the following code:

```
<%@ Page Language="C#" MasterPageFile="MyMasterPage.master" %>
<asp:Content ID="Content1"
ContentPlaceHolderID="Content Place Holder ID in Master Page"
Runat="Server">

... content goes here

</asp:Content>
```

The Master page to use is stated in the first directive. Second, VWD includes an `<asp:content>` control with a property that designates the ID of the placeholder in the Master page. A Master page may have many places where Content pages can be inserted. This designator identifies which placeholder to fill with this particular page.

To summarize, the Content page exhibits the following three features:

- Lack of the HTML `<!DOCTYPE HTML ... >` and XML `<html xmlns=...>` typing tags
- `<%@ page MasterPageFile= ... %>` on the first line to instruct ASP.NET 2.0 which Master page to use
- An `<asp:content>` tag

The theory is not difficult and the typing is done automatically by VWD. In the following sample, you see Master and Content pages working together.

A Sample of Master and Content Pages

Almost all of the exercises in this book can be carried out in Design View (without working directly in code). But it is interesting to take a look at how VWD builds pages by switching to Source View. The following code shows an example of a Master page (named "research.master") for a corporation and a Content page called "mission statement." The first shaded line designates the Master page, and the second shaded area is a control that defines a content placeholder, where the content developed on a Content page will be inserted:

```
<%@ Master Language="C#" %>
<!DOCTYPE html PUBLIC "-//W3C//DTD XHTML 1.1//EN"
"http://www.w3.org/TR/xhtml11/DTD/xhtml11.dtd">
<html xmlns="http://www.w3.org/1999/xhtml" >
<head runat="server"> <title>CorporateMaster</title></head>
<body>
Corporation Name
    <form id="form1" runat="server">
    <div>
        <asp:contentplaceholder
               id="ContentPlaceMissionStatement"
                 runat="server">
        </asp:contentplaceholder>
    </div>
    </form>
</body>
</html>
```

Following is the Content page for this example. The highlighted section designates the Master page and the control that delineates the material to be put in the Master page. The ID of the `ContentPlaceHolder` must match the ID of the `ContentPlaceHolder` in the Master page. The following listing is complete; there are no additional tags or attributes at the top of the page:

```
<%@ Page Language="C#" MasterPageFile="~/research.master" Title="Untitled Page" %>

<asp:Content ID="Content1"
  ContentPlaceHolderID="ContentPlaceHolderMissionStatement"
```

```
    Runat="Server">

Our Mission Statement is to provide value to the customer.

</asp:Content>
```

Note that a Content page must have a very minimal set of tags. The Content page does not have tags such as `<!DOCTYPE>` or `<html xmlns="http://www.w3.org/1999/xhtml">`. Nor does the Content page contain `<head>` information. This data will be provided by the Master page.

Using Cascading Style Sheets in a Master Page

A Master page is a good location to declare a link to a Cascading Style Sheet (CSS). CSS is a feature of HTML, not ASP.NET 2.0, so the topic isn't covered in depth in this book. However, CSS is discussed as it relates to themes in Chapter 5. There is also a brief reference for HTML and CSS in Appendix E. In short, a CSS contains formatting for various styles to be applied to pages and controls, so that when a page is rendered, the elements on a page, the style of the text, buttons, links, and so on, appear formatted according to the style definition in the CSS. This saves the designer from having to include (and maintain) many individual style format tags for frequently used designs. A CSS also speeds page loading because the CSS is loaded just once by the browser, and then reused directly from the client-side cache for each subsequent page that uses that style sheet. On a Master page, you should include the following kind of link (highlighted with a gray background) in the `<head>` section to link a page with a CSS:

```
<head id="PageHead" runat="server">
    <title>Wrox United</title>
    <link rel="stylesheet" type="text/css" href="MySite.css" runat="server" />
</head>
```

In the following Try It Out, you get the chance to create the Master page for the Wrox United site. You will be adding content and features in the exercises of each chapter of this book. At this point, you will simply create the shell of the Master page. You will add many parts to the Master page later in the book, so if it seems a bit incomplete now, hang in there.

Try It Out — Creating a Master Page and Importing a CSS

1. Open the sample site for this chapter, located at `C:\BegASPNET2\Chapters\Begin\Chapter02`. You will start by importing a CSS file the authors have created for you. Right-click the root of the site and select Add Existing Item, as shown in Figure 2-4.

2. Navigate to the folder where you downloaded the files for this book (`C:\BegASPNET2\WroxUnitedCS`), select `site.css`, and click Add. CSS is an HTML topic (not ASP.NET), but if you want to open the file, you can observe styles set for the HTML of the body, such as `<h1>`, `<h2>`, and so forth. There is no need for you to modify this file. Observe that you now have a `site.css` file in the list of files displayed in the Solution Explorer. If you opened the CSS file, close it now.

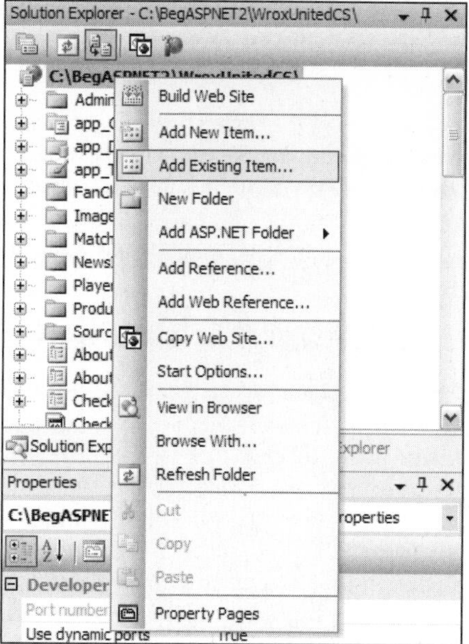

Figure 2-4

3. Again, right-click the root, but this time select Add New Item and use the Master Page template. Name the page **site.master**. Ensure that the check box for Select Master Page is not checked (that option is only for Content pages). After VWD creates the page, you can observe it in Design View, although it is empty at this point. Notice in Source View that VWD has added several tags and controls for you (see the following code). The first tag is a designation that this will be a Master page and the second tag is the normal document-type designation. Following that is a place to insert scripts and then an XMLNS value. Observe that in the <body>, VWD created a contentplaceholder:

```
<%@ master language="C#" %>
<!DOCTYPE HTML PUBLIC "-//W3C//DTD XHTML 1.0 Transitional//EN"
"http://www.w3.org/TR/xhtml1/DTD/xhtml1-transitional.dtd">

<script runat="server">
</script>

<html xmlns="http://www.w3.org/1999/xhtml">

<head id="PageHead" runat="server"> ... </head>

<body>
  <form id="Form1" runat="server">
    <div>
      <asp:contentplaceholder id="mainContent" runat="server" />
    <div>
  </form>
</body>
</html>
```

4. You want to change the name of the form from the generic VWD names to something more applicable to your situation. Switch to Source View and change the `<form id="form1" runat="server">` to `<form id="MainForm" runat="server">`.

5. Switch back to Design View to set the style sheet. At the top of the Properties box, drop down the list of controls and select Document. Set the `Debug` property to `True`. At the bottom of the properties list, find Style Sheet (see Figure 2-5), click its ellipses, and browse to `site.css`. Click OK.

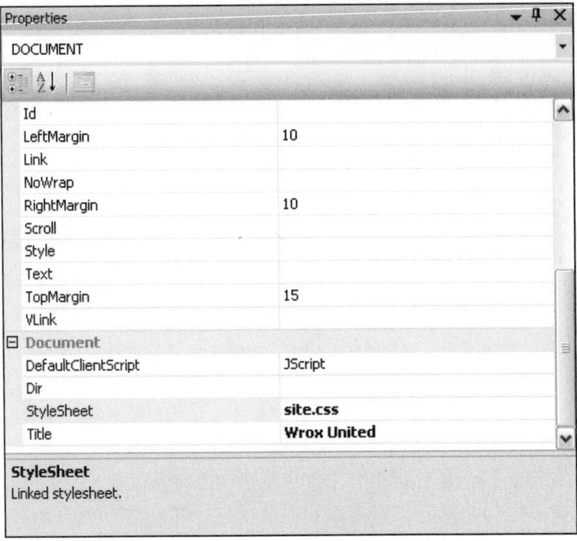

Figure 2-5

Adding `<div>` tags divides the page for easier formatting. Your Master page will use four `<div>` sections within the `<form>`. Some of these will then contain additional `<div>` tags within them (lower-level `<div>`). The first `<div>` is automatically created by VWD; the others you will add. A `<div>` can be dragged onto a page from the HTML section of the toolbar, but it is difficult to get it located properly in Design View. You will use Source View to get exact placement.

6. Switch to Source View and find the default `<div>` within the form. Select from the beginning of the `<div>` tag to the end of the `</div>` tag, and note that the Properties window now shows properties for the `<div>`, including a `style` attribute that sets the width and height. Set the `id` property to `content`.

7. Staying in Source View, add another `<div>` by dragging the control from the HTML section of the toolbar to a position above the `<div id="content">`, but still within the `<form>`. Set its `id` property to `header`.

8. Add two more `<div>` tag sets within the form. Place one just below the header with the ID of `sidebar` and one at the bottom of the page, just above the form closing tag with an `id` of `footer`.

9. Staying in Source View, now create lower-level `<div>` tags, which will reside inside of the `<div>` you created earlier. In the `header <div>`, drag in a `<div>` and give it an `id` of **logo**. Follow the `logo <div>` with some simple text for display, shown here:

```
<form id="mainForm" runat="server">

  <div id="header">
    <div id="logo"></div>
    <h1>Wrox United</h1>
  </div>
```

10. In the `sidebar` `<div>` add the text **Navigation**, as shown in the following code:

```
<div id="sidebar">
  <h3>Navigation</h3>
</div>
```

11. You will add controls to the `content` `<div>` in the next few chapters, but for now, add a lower-level **<div id=>** with an `id` of **itemcontent**:

```
<div id="content">
  <div class="itemContent">
    <asp:contentplaceholder id="mainContent" runat="server" />
  </div>
</div>
```

12. In the `footer` `<div>` add two notices of copyright:

```
  <div id="footer">
    <p class="left">
      All images and content copyright &copy; Wrox Press and its subsidiaries 2006.
    </p>
    <p class="right">
      Website designed by
        <a href="http://www.frogboxdesign.co.uk" title="croak">Frog Box Design</a>
    </p>
  </div>
</form>
```

How It Works

You started by simply importing to your site a CSS that the authors created for you and included in the download for this book. (Actually, the authors are lame at design. We originally thought red, pink, and orange went well together, so we asked a designer at `www.frogboxdesign.co.uk` to make the design palatable.) Because CSS is an HTML topic, the structure of the style sheet is not discussed here (see Appendix E for some details).

The more important objective, however, is to use VWD to help you create a Master page with the three basic components. By using the Master page template, you got the basic HTML and XML typing tags. VWD also added for you the `<%@ master ... %>` on the first line. Finally, VWD provided a single `<div>` with an `<asp:ContentPlaceHolder>` tag. Every placeholder tag must have an ID, so you changed the ID so that it made sense in your context.

You then did some basic modifying of the Master page to support features you will add later in the book. All of these are actually HTML features, not ASP.NET 2.0. First, you used VWD IntelliSense to add a link to the CSS sheet you imported. Then you created several more `<div>` tags to organize the page into header, sidebar, content, and footer sections.

The following Try It Out complements the previous exercise in that you will now create a Content page to fill the placeholder of the `site.master`. Because of its simplicity, the "about the site" page is a good starting point.

Try It Out Create Content Pages

1. In VWD and with Wrox United open, right-click the root of the site. Select Add New Item and select the template type of Web Form. Name it **About.aspx** and make sure that both Select Master Page and Place Code in Separate File are checked as in Figure 2-6, even though there will be no code. (If you don't set code in a separate file, the framework tags for code will be in the .aspx file. It's better to stay consistent with the rest of the site and keep the container tags and the code in a separate file.)

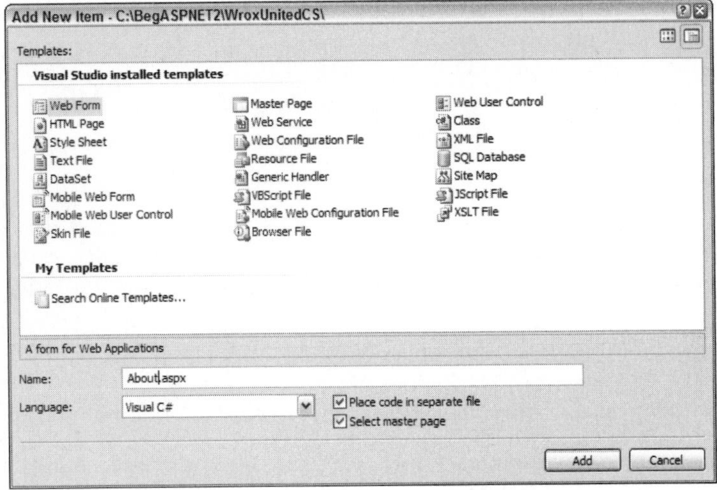

Figure 2-6

2. In the second dialog, select `site.master` for the Master page and click OK, as in Figure 2-7.

3. In Design View, type in a few lines, such as the following:

```
The site was initially written by Dave, while design & graphics were done by Lou.
Conformance is XHTML 1.0 Transitional and CSS 2.1.
```

4. As an aside, you can experience that VWD helps you with non-ASP tags, such as a hyperlink. Staying in Design View, look on the Toolbox's Standard panel for the `Hyperlink` control and drag one to the end of the first sentence in the preceding code. In the properties box set the text to `Frog Box Design` and the `NavigationURL` property to `www.frogboxdesign.co.uk`. VWD will automatically take care of all the typing to create the link.

5. Look at the page in Design View and note that the Master page contributes the framework, and the Content page only has the text you typed. Switch to Source View and note that the About page designates its Master page and that its content will go into the `MainContent` placeholder.

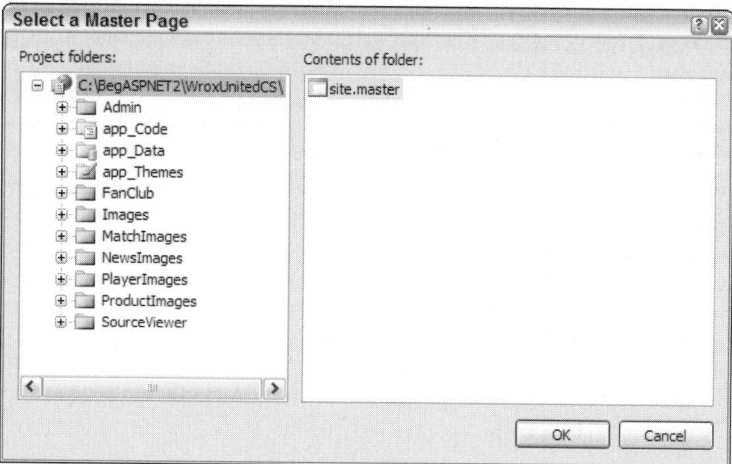

Figure 2-7

How It Works

The general steps to create a page start with selecting the parent folder in the Solution Explorer. In many cases this is the root of the web site `C:\BegASPNET2\WroxUnitedCS`, but in some cases it can be a lower folder such as the location of `FanClub.aspx` in the folder `C:\BegASPNET2\WroxUnitedCS\FanClub`.

Observe how a Content page has the three features work with the `site.master` page. The initial tag `<%@ Page... >` must contain the `MasterPageFile` attribute. Because you might move the files into a different folder structure, you refer to the Master page's location with an initial tilde (~) that indicates that it will be in the root of the site. Second, the material of the Content page is held within an ASP.NET server-side control named `asp:Content` with a `ContentPlaceHolderID` attribute that points to one of the locations for content in the Master page. Third, because the HTML and XMLNS tags will be brought in with the Master page, you omit them from all the Content pages.

Additional Capabilities of Master Pages

Although not implemented in Wrox United, several additional features are available that you can use with Master and Content pages. Multiple levels of Master pages can contribute to a final page. One of several Master pages can be served depending on the requesting browser. And a Master page can support several content placeholders.

Multiple Levels of Master Pages

Although the technique is not used on Wrox United, your pages can inherit multiple levels of Master pages. This feature provides a way to display standard content from several levels of hierarchy. For example, a Content page named `Publication.aspx` can establish its Master as `Research.master`, which can in turn declare its Master as `Corporate.master`. The final rendering will be of `Research.aspx` surrounded by `Research.master`, and all of that surrounded by `Corporate.master`. One problem is that the space remaining for content is reduced at each level. VWD does not contain automatic tools to create multiple levels of Masters. In fact, if you have multiple levels, you can only open those pages in Source View.

To create pages with multiple levels of Masters you must include in the middle-level page tags that both indicate its Master page (up a level) and its content placeholders (for the lower level). Recall that a Master page must have `<%@ Master ... %>` on the first line, and that a lower-level or Content page must have `<%@ Page MasterPageFile= %>` on its first line. In the case of a middle page that is both a Content and Master page, the tag must start with `<%@ Master ...` and also contain `... MasterPageFile= %>`.

Also recall that a Master page contains an `<asp:ContentPlaceHolder>` tag whereas the Content page has an `<asp:content>` tag. In the case of a middle layer, there must be an `<asp:content>` holding the ID of the Master's `<ContentPlaceHolder>` tag. Then within that tag there is an `<asp:ContentPlaceHolder>` tag that will be used by the next level down.

The following example illustrates a Corporate Master page, then a Research department Master page, and finally a `Publication.aspx` page that holds the content. The Corporate page is shown in the following code. Note that its content placeholder is defined in the shaded lines:

```
<%@ Master Language="C#" %>
<!DOCTYPE html PUBLIC "-//W3C//DTD XHTML 1.1//EN"
"http://www.w3.org/TR/xhtml11/DTD/xhtml11.dtd">
<html xmlns="http://www.w3.org/1999/xhtml" >
<head runat="server">
  <title>CorporateMaster</title>
</head>
<body>
Corporation Name
  <form id="form1" runat="server">
    <div>
      <asp:contentplaceholder
                  id="ContentPlaceHolderCorporate"
                  runat="server">
      </asp:contentplaceholder>
    </div>
  </form>
</body>
</html>
```

The Research department Master page is illustrated by the following code. This page is the most complex, because it is a Content page for the Corporate page, and a Master page for the Publication page. Notice the use of `Master` and `MasterPageFile=` on the first line that establishes this as content for the Corporate Master page. Then observe that the `<asp:ContentPlaceHolder>` will house other pages as content (in this case the Publication page). The content placeholder must sit wholly within the `<asp:content>` tags:

```
<%@ Master MasterPageFile="~/Corporate.master"  Language="C#" %>

<asp:Content runat="server"
  ContentPlaceHolderID="ContentPlaceHolderCorporate">

Research Department

    <asp:contentplaceholder
        id="ContentPlaceHolderResearch"
        runat="server">
```

```
        </asp:contentplaceholder>

    </asp:Content>
```

Code for the `Publication.aspx` page (designed with content only) is shown in the following code. Here you only need to designate a Master page. This page, which sits at the lowest level, is not a Master page:

```
<%@ Page Language="C#" MasterPageFile="~/Research.master" Title="Untitled Page" %>

<asp:Content ID="Content1"
  ContentPlaceHolderID="ContentPlaceHolderResearch"
  Runat="Server">

Publication text

</asp:Content>
```

Master Pages Support Multiple Content Placeholders

The examples so far have used a single `<asp:ContentPlaceHolder>` in the Master page and a single `<asp:content>` tag in the Content page. ASP.NET 2.0 supports multiple content placeholders. However, each must have its own ID, as in the following example:

```
<%@ Master Language="C#" %>

<form id="form1" runat="server">
  <asp:contentplaceholder runat="server" id="TopContent" />
  <asp:contentplaceholder runat="server" id="MiddleContent" />
  <asp:contentplaceholder runat="server" id="BottomContent" />
</form>
</body>
</html>
```

The content can then have `<asp:content>` tags that have `ContentPlaceHolderID` values equal to the ID values in the Master page:

```
<%@ Page Language="C#" MasterPageFile="~/research.master" Title="Untitled Page" %>

<asp:Content ID="Content1" ContentPlaceHolderID="TopContent" Runat="Server">
  Text to go in Top section
</asp:Content>

<asp:Content ID="Content1" ContentPlaceHolderID="MiddleContent" Runat="Server">
  Text to go in Middle section
</asp:Content>

<asp:Content ID="Content1" ContentPlaceHolderID="BottomContent" Runat="Server">
  Text to go in Bottom section
</asp:Content>
```

Dividing content into several `<asp:ContentPlaceHolder>` tags helps with the layout of the Master page.

Creating a Site Map

To enable navigation features of ASP.NET 2.0, you need to have a standard way to describe each of the pages of the site. This standard should not only include the names of all of the site's pages, but also a sense of their hierarchy. For example, the page of a player's statistics would be a subpage of the general players list, and that would be a subpage of the home page:

```
Home
- Players
-- Player Statistics
```

Defining this sort of hierarchy is an important part of site design, because you want to know (before you start coding) what pages need to be developed, which links will be relevant to users on different pages, and where the user is likely to want to go after viewing a specific page. Drawing up a site tree, like the simple one shown here, is the first step you need to take. Then you can move to the next stage and define this hierarchy in code.

ASP.NET 2.0 holds this information in an XML file named `web.sitemap`. You can use this file as the source of data for menu and navigation controls, which are discussed in Chapter 3.

> **What Microsoft offers in ASP.NET 2.0 is a way to *use* site data in menus and navigation controls if that data is stored according to the `web.sitemap` standards. VWD includes a template with the tags for a `web.sitemap` file. But as of this writing there is no tool to scan the site and generate the actual data that goes into those tags. Third parties will surely fill this gap, but for now you must type the information into the `web.sitemap` file.**

The site map must be an XML file with the exact name `web.sitemap` and must be located in the root of the web application. XML is a standard for holding data, somewhat like a database, but in a human-readable text form. Each item of data is held in a *node*, and in this case a node would represent one page of the site with data for the page URL, title, and description. An XML file holds the nodes in a tree-like structure so ASP.NET 2.0 will know which pages are to be considered children of a parent page. For example, a page of *Corporate Departments* would be a parent to children pages with details on *Sales*, *Research*, and *Accounting*. The first tags in the file are standard for XML files to identify the version and the XMLNS, as shown in the following code:

```
<?xml version="1.0" encoding="utf-8" ?>
<siteMap xmlns="http://schemas.microsoft.com/AspNet/SiteMap-File-1.0" >
```

These first two lines are automatically typed for you when you use VWD to add an item to the root from the template site map. The node names are simple: `<siteMap>` containing `<siteMapNode>` tags. Each tag represents a web page and can include the following attributes (all attributes of the `<SiteMapNode>` tag are strings):

- **Title:** Describes the page (this is not linked to the `<Title>` tag in the header of the page, although it could have the same value).
- **URL:** The location of the page described in this node.
- **Description:** A description of the page.

Note that a URL can contain *querystring* data, which is additional information defined at the end of the URL string of a page, which is sent as part of a request to display a page. For example, a general reference to a page would be similar to the first line in the following code, whereas a reference to a page with some data (for example, the month to display on the calendar) would be similar to the third line:

```
url="Calendar.aspx"

url="Calendar.aspx?Month=May"
```

The hierarchy (parent/child relationships) of pages listed in the site map is established by including a child node within its parent's open and close tags. Notice in the following code how the two subpages (Members and Calendar) occur within the open and close tags for the Home page (shown with a gray background). The indentation is only for the human eye; it does not affect the hierarchy. Note that the tags for the child pages (Members and Calendar) can use the single tag format of `<Tag... />`. But because the parent page (Home) has children (it contains other nodes), it must use the two-tag format of `<Tag>...</ Tag>`:

```
<siteMap>
  <siteMapNode title="Home" url="Default.aspx" description="Home page for MySite">
    <siteMapNode title="Members" url="Members.aspx" description="All Members" />
    <siteMapNode title="Calendar" url="Calendar.aspx" description="Club Events" />
  </siteMapNode>
</siteMap>
```

To create two child pages within Calendar (grandchildren to the Home page) you take two steps. First convert the Calendar `<SiteMapNode>` to the two-tag format and then add the two child tags as shown in the following highlighted code. Remember, as stated in the preceding note box, you must do all of this by typing in the Source View of the `web.sitemap` file. VWD offers neither a tool to perform an automatic scan and build, nor a way to drag and drop from the Solution Explorer into the `web.sitemap` file.

```
<siteMap>
  <siteMapNode title="Home" url="Default.aspx" description="Home page for MySite">
    <siteMapNode title="Members" url="Members.aspx" description="All Members" />
    <siteMapNode title="Calendar" url="Calendar.aspx" description="Club Events">
        <siteMapNode title="Calendar of Racing Events"
                 url="Calendar\Racing.aspx" description="Racing Events" />
        <siteMapNode title="Calendar of Social Events"
                 url="Calendar\Social.aspx" description="Social Events" />
    </siteMapNode>
  </siteMapNode>
</siteMap>
```

Note that there is another attribute that you can specify on a `<SiteMapNode>` element: the `roles` attribute. As you learn in Chapter 11, this attribute is used in the Wrox United site map file. There may be some situations where you will want to allow a user to know of the existence of a page, even if the user is denied access to the page. In this way, you can offer a link to a user, but when they click that link, they are prompted to log in as a user with sufficient privileges before they can view the page.

In the next Try It Out you create a `web.sitemap` for Wrox United. You won't be able to see the results of your hard work until you reach the next chapter, where you learn the concept of navigation controls, but this stage is a way of putting your paper-based design for the structure of a site into code, so it's important to get it right.

Try It Out Create a Site Map

1. Right-click the root of the site in Solution Explorer and select Add New Item. Choose the template named Site Map and name it **web.sitemap**. Note that VWD added the first two tags automatically and gave you the framework for three nodes. The first is the highest level (Home) and the next two are children.

2. Modify the first `<siteMapNode>` to represent your Home page with the following code:

```
<siteMapNode title="Home" url="Default.aspx" description="Wrox United Home Page">
```

3. Modify the next `<siteMapNode>` (the first child) as follows:

```
<siteMapNode title="Fixtures" url="Fixtures.aspx" description="Match Fixtures">
```

4. Copy an entire blank `<siteMapNode>` to the clipboard so you can paste it without having to retype the tag.

5. Create two children to Fixtures, as highlighted here:

```
<siteMapNode title="Fixtures" url="Fixtures.aspx" description="Match Fixtures">
  <siteMapNode title="Future Fixtures"
               url="Fixtures.aspx?type=future"
               description="Who we're going to be playing" />
  <siteMapNode title="Past Fixtures"
               url="Fixtures.aspx?type=past"
               description="Who we've already played" />
</siteMapNode>
```

   As you can see, there are two subnodes within the Fixtures section of the site that enable you to view details of both future and past fixtures.

6. There are quite a few more nodes to specify to complete this example, so to save you some time, we've included the rest of the nodes in a file called `web.sitemap.remainder` in the chapter directory (`C:\BegASPNet2\Chapters\begin\Chapter02`). All you have to do is open this file in Notepad, copy the entire contents of the file, and paste the contents into your version of the file right at the bottom. Alternatively, feel free to just import our `web.sitemap` file into your site.

7. At this point there is no good test for your `web.sitemap` file because the controls that display the data aren't discussed until Chapter 3, but having an understanding of this foundation is very important because you can use it to add navigation features to a site.

How It Works

In this exercise, you undertook the tasks to create a site map file. Recall that VWD does not include a tool to automatically create this file, but does include a simple template to pre-type some tags to get started. ASP.NET 2.0 will only use this file when it is named `web.sitemap`, so try to avoid any temptation to change the name.

You added a new item of the site map template and switched to Source View. VWD adds the initial tags and the tags for the first node. But you then have to manually type all of the data and begin copying and pasting tags for all of the rest of the pages and their data. (Obviously, the third party that writes a program to automate this task will enjoy good sales.)

General Guidelines for Site Design

Prior to designing any web site, you benefit from reviewing the principles of a good site design. In this book, you should keep in mind three general concepts:

- Endeavor to separate the presentation from the information. For example, design the title, layout, and format of a page (the presentation). On that page, put a control that is configured to get and display information (such as the list of players for the team). By dividing these goals, you are able to make updates to each without impacting the other. For example, when a new player is added to the team, you enter the information about the player into the site's database, and the page automatically displays the new list of players on the team without you having to modify the presentation layer.
- Strive for a consistent look and feel throughout the site. By keeping the same colors, logo, and arrangement on the screen, you develop a sense of presence. The loyal followers immediately feel at home with the team colors. Return visitors will be able to use the same set of learned behaviors for using the site.
- Make the site as easy to navigate as possible. First, a menu bar on all pages provides easy jumps form one part of the site to another. Use ASP.NET 2.0 tools to indicate where the currently viewed page is located in the site.

Standard Files for ASP.NET 2.0 Applications

ASP.NET 2.0 uses two files, common to every ASP.NET site, to hold configuration information and code that applies to the entire site. These are the `Web.config` and `Global.asax` files, respectively.

- `Web.config` contains configuration settings for a site; for example, for specifying a standard customized error page to display to end users if anything on the site breaks.
- `Global.asax` contains code that handles events raised by any page on the entire site; for example, code that is run each time a user first accesses the site (the start of a session).

Web.config Holds Settings for the Entire Site

`Web.config` stores values that apply to the entire site. Structured as an XML file and located in the root, nodes hold information in three major areas:

- Application settings for feature availability used in development versus deployment
- Connection strings that hold values used when reading or writing from a data source
- System.Web and System.Net settings that hold everything else

System.Web settings are then broken into several subcatagories, including the following (not all are used in WroxUnitedCS):

- HTTP Modules that point the page to other pages for execution of code
- Debugging routines that should be turned on at the time of compilation
- Authentication Technique

- Role Manager settings (on or off?)
- Anonymous Identification settings (permitted or not)
- Error handling settings
- Web.SiteMap file data used for navigation and menus
- Profile data that is used for identifying users
- E-mail settings for the Simplified Mail Transfer Protocol (SMTP) (not used in WroxUnitedCS)
- Definition of Namespaces that identify the location of objects within larger objects (not used in WroxUnitedCS)

System.Net holds just one setting for your purposes: a series of values for sending e-mail.

You can amend the contents of this file in two ways; the first is to edit it by hand in VWD, which, thankfully, is not too tricky to do. The alternative is to use the ASP.NET Web Site Administration Tool, which you can launch from within VWD. Go to the main VWD menu and select Website➪ASP.NET Configuration. A series of dialog boxes enable you to set values that VWD will change in Web.config without directly opening the file. You can have a look at this tool later on in the last Try It Out in this chapter.

The following explanation of the structure of a `Web.config` file takes a look at parts of the Wrox United `Web.config` file, looking at sections from the top of the file and working down. If you open the file, you can see that the structure (with opening and closing tags, each with attributes, and sometimes with child nodes) is the same as for any other XML file. Application-wide configuration settings are made by adding appropriate nodes and attributes. Text within the special `<!-- -->` characters is treated as a comment, which you can add to the file to help other users understand what each part of the file is used for.

When VWD creates a `Web.config` *file it includes many comments that provide advice for the settings of each section. A list of all of the values is contained in a text file located at* `C:\Windows\Microsoft.NET\Framework\v2.xxx\CONFIG\Web.config.Comments`.

The following is the start of the Wrox United `Web.config` file that you can view in the download. Feel free to import it into your site instead of typing a new web.config yourself.

```
<?xml version="1.0"?>
<!-- Note: As an alternative to hand editing this file you can use the web admin
     tool to configure settings for your application. Use the Website->Asp.Net
     Configuration option in Visual Studio.
     A full list of settings and comments can be found in machine.config.comments
     usually located in \Windows\Microsoft.Net\Frameworks\v2.x\Config -->

<configuration>
```

Three lines of code here are added by default to all new Web.config files. The first line contains the XML declaration, specifying that the `Web.config` file follows the XML standard. The next section is a large comment that reminds you that you can use the administration tool, instead of editing the code. The last item to note is the root node for the file; the `<configuration>` node contains all child nodes with settings relating to the content stored on the site.

The next section contains a custom application setting that can be useful to change the way the sample application runs for different environments. The large section between <!-- and --> is a note to programmers from VWD and is not part of the actual settings:

```
<!--
  Mode defines certain feature availability:
    Full: No restrictions
    Real: Runs as if a real site, without the view code and download links
-->
<appSettings>
  <add key="mode" value="Full" />
</appSettings>
```

The next section, the connection string section, holds sets of information about data sources. This string generally includes authentication information that you can use to connect your code to the data stored in your database. Connection strings are discussed in detail in Chapter 7. For now, simply notice that within the connection strings section you have one or more tags that add strings:

```
<!--
       define the connection string to the database
 -->
 <connectionStrings>
    <add name="WroxUnited"
         connectionString="     Data Source=.\SQLEXPRESS;
                                AttachDbFilename=|DataDirectory|WroxUnited.mdf;
                                Integrated Security=True;
                                User Instance=True"
         providerName="System.Data.SqlClient"/>
 </connectionStrings>
```

Note that the connectionString attribute wraps here because of page width limitations. This line of code should remain on one line in your code.

After the connection strings, the remainder of the settings are within the <system.web> tag. They can be in any order — here the httpModules setting is covered first. This value allows the site to handle user-selected themes centrally, without requiring code in pages. Themes are covered in Chapter 5, and although the httpModule isn't covered in detail in this text, the code is well commented:

```
<system.web>
  <httpModules>
    <add name="Page" type="Wrox.Web.GlobalEvents.ThemeModule" />
  </httpModules>
```

Next within System.Web is the compilation value. When set to true (as illustrated in the following code), ASP.NET 2.0 will provide output to the page describing any problems that were found during the build of the page. This feature is useful when you're developing the site, but it should be set to false prior to deployment:

```
<system.web>
  <compilation debug="true">
  </compilation>
```

Wrox United declares site-wide values for three security settings: authentication, roles, and profiles. Chapters 4 and 11 discuss these functions in detail. The section of `Web.config` in the following code gives you a preview of what you will learn to write. Notice how the settings establish the page to use for log-on (`Default.aspx`) and then turn on the Role Manager. You then have a set of tags that create the Member type of role. Again, these are explained in detail in Chapters 4 and 11. The following code listing saves space by not listing the VWD programmers help comments. Also, there is a break in the WroxUnited `Web.config` between the second and third settings. where there are other settings.

```
<authentication mode="Forms">
  <forms loginUrl="Default.aspx"></forms>
</authentication>

<roleManager enabled="true"/>
<anonymousIdentification enabled="true"/>
```

```
...
```

```
<profile enabled="true">
  <properties>
    <add name="MemberName"/>
    <add name="Name"/>
    ...
    <add name="Cart" serializeAs="Binary" type="Wrox.Commerce.ShoppingCart"
         allowAnonymous="true"/>
  </properties>
</profile>
```

The next section concerns handling errors that can (and will) affect the day-to-day running of your site. Chapter 15 discusses error handling in detail, but as an introduction, ASP.NET can be set to redirect the user to a custom error page if there is a problem. The file to display in the case of an error is declared in the `Web.config` `defaultRedirect` setting as follows:

```
<!-- The <customErrors> section enables configuration of what to do if/when an
unhandled error occurs during the execution of a request.  Specifically, it enables
developers to configure html error pages to be displayed in place of a error stack
trace. -->
```

```
      <customErrors mode="RemoteOnly">
   <error statusCode="404" redirect="missingPage.aspx"/>
      </customErrors>
```

So, for example, if your database server was the victim of a power cut, your users don't need to know the details, but they'd like to be reassured, along the lines of "Sorry, there is a fault—we're working hard to fix the problem. Normal service will resume shortly." Local administrators, on the other hand, would like to know what the problem is so that they can get it back up and running as quickly as possible. The `RemoteOnly` attribute in this example means that remote users see the friendly message, whereas the administrator will see all the details of any error.

The last setting of System.Web identifies the file that will hold the site map, an index to all of the pages, and their relationships to each other (as covered in Chapter 2). ASP.NET 2.0 also requires the identification of what Provider, or reading tool, to use for the site map.

```
<!-- Redefine the Site Map Provider, to add the security trimming attribute, which
is off by default -->
    <siteMap defaultProvider="AspXmlSiteMapProvider" enabled="true">
      <providers>
        <clear/>
        <add name="AspXmlSiteMapProvider"
                type="System.Web.XmlSiteMapProvider,
                System.Web,
                Version=2.0.3600.0,
                Culture=neutral,
                PublicKeyToken=b03f5f7f11d50a3a"
                siteMapFile="web.sitemap"
                securityTrimmingEnabled="true"/>
      </providers>
    </siteMap>
```

The last group of settings is in System.Net. Although not explicitly used in the WroxUnitedCS application, it could be used so that automated e-mails can be sent to a user when they forget their password, and request that the password be sent in an e-mail. Regardless of how the e-mail is created, you must declare the SMTP (Simplified Mail Transfer Protocol) in `Web.config` as follows:

```
  <system.net>
    <mailSettings>
      <!-- these settings define the mail server settings from: the user name from
which the email is sent - this is the application that is sending the message host:
the name of your mail server userName: the name the application will use to log
into the mail server password: the password for the above user name
      -->
      <smtp from="admin@your-domain.com">
        <network host="your-mail-server-name"
                 userName="your-user-name"
                 password="your-password" />
      </smtp>
    </mailSettings>
  </system.net>
```

Finally, as with all XML files, each opening tag must have a closing tag, so you finish up the file with the following:

```
  </system.web>
</configuration>
```

`Web.config`, as you have seen, holds site-wide settings to which all other pages can refer. This saves you from having to repeatedly specify the same pieces of information in every page that needs it, and you have one place to go to change settings.

Later in the book, you'll be adding more capabilities to all your site pages, including adding code to deal with various events that happen on each page. But, in the same way that you don't want to specify the same settings in every page, if you need to have the same behavior repeated on multiple pages, you'll need a way to share that code. There was no executable code in `Web.config` — for that you need another site-wide file — the `Global.asax` file.

Global.asax Holds Code for the Entire Site

Whereas `Web.config` holds values, `Global.asax` holds code. `Global.asax`, like `Web.config`, resides in the root of the site. Writing code is discussed in detail in Chapter 9, but for now you can get an overview of `Global.asax`.

The code in `Global.asax` executes in one of three cases. First is the case of the application as a whole starting or stopping. Second is when each user starts or stops using the site. Third is in response to special events taking place that could happen on any page, such as a user logging in or an error occurring. Each of these is known as an event. When each of these events occurs, ASP.NET lets `Global.asax` know, and by editing `Global.asax`, you can put code into it that will be executed in response to the events.

You'll be using `Global.asax` to share code across all the pages of the Wrox United web site later in the book.

Editing Site Configuration Through a Web Browser

Now, it's perhaps a little daunting looking at the complex XML syntax of `Web.config` and the code in `Global.asax`. Editing these files to make changes to the overall configuration and behavior of your application requires a good understanding of the files' syntax rules, and accurate typing to avoid introducing little errors. Conveniently, though, ASP.NET 2.0 provides a graphical tool that lets you modify many of the settings you could manually enter in `Web.config`, through the Web Site Properties dialog box.

Bring up the Web Site Administration Tool by clicking the ASP.NET Configuration button at the top of the Solution Explorer, as shown in Figure 2-8.

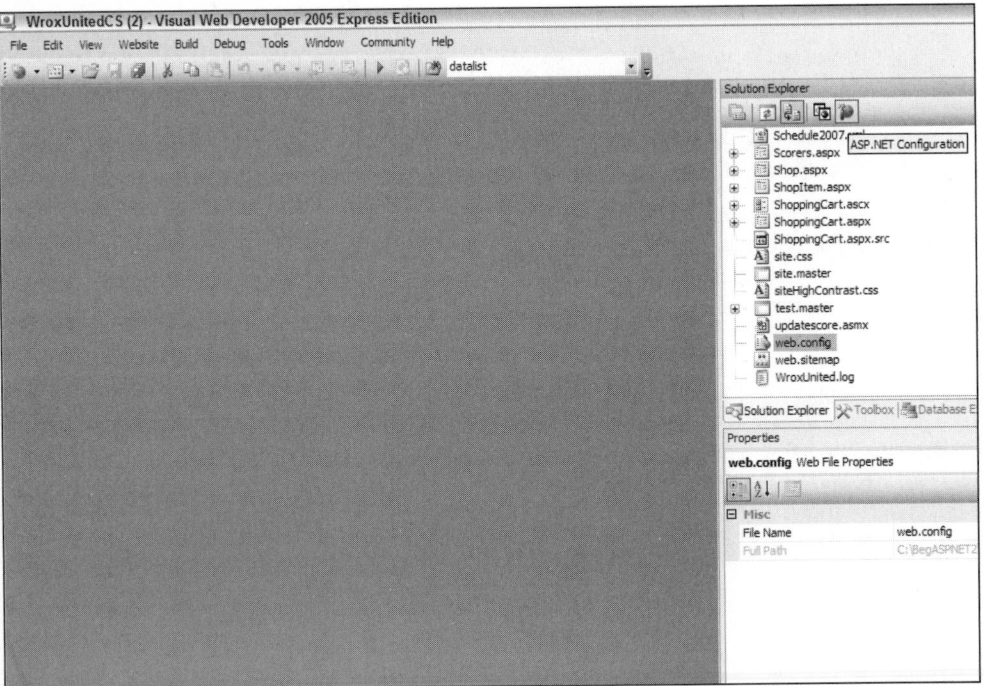

Figure 2-8

The Properties window opens, as shown in Figure 2-9.

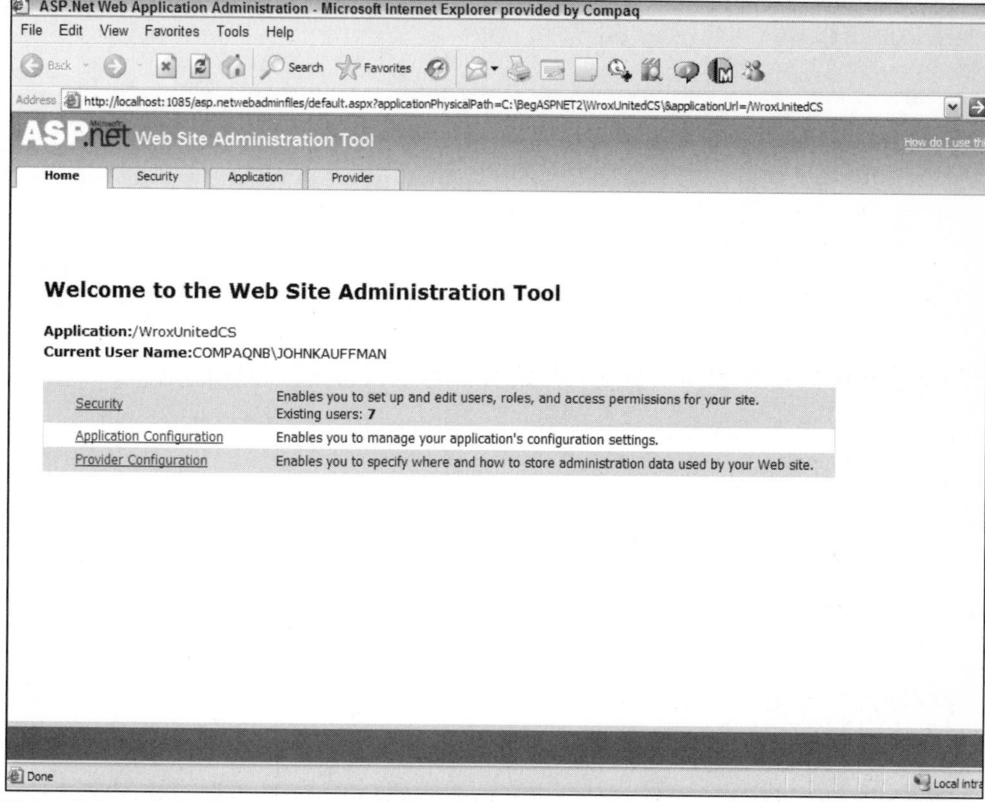

Figure 2-9

As you can see, VWD has actually opened up a web browser showing a web site that is built into ASP.NET, called the ASP.NET Administration Tool, through which you can edit the settings of your web application. You'll be using this administration tool in depth later in the book, but for now, you can explore the Application Configuration section of the tool. Figure 2-10 shows what options are presented to you by this page.

Although you can't administer everything that you looked at earlier, some of the key sections from `Web.config` are represented here. You have the ability to edit application settings (the contents of the `<appSettings>` element you looked at earlier), e-mail settings (the `<smtpMail>` section you saw in the `Web.config` file), and debugging and error handling (the `<compilation>` and `<customErrors>` sections you examined before).

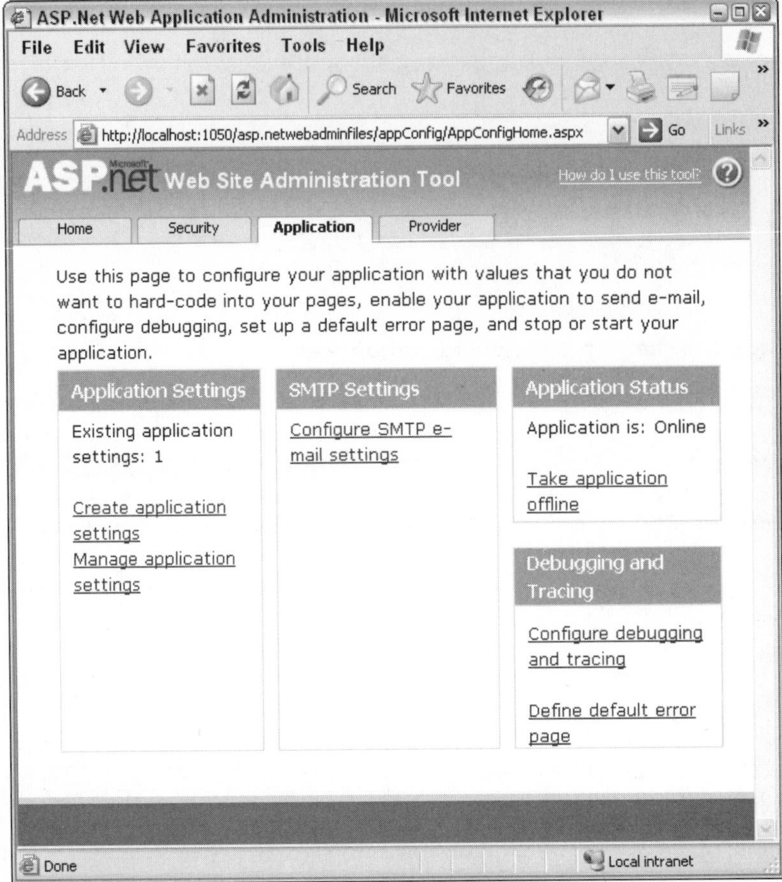

Figure 2-10

In this Try It Out, you see how the ASP.NET Administration Tool edits the `Web.config` file for you.

Try It Out — Changing Settings with the Administration Tool

1. Working in VWD's Solution Explorer, import into your site `missingPage.aspx` from the download files (`C:\BegASPNET2\WroxUnitedCS`).
2. Open the Web Site Administration Tool by clicking the icon on the Solution Explorer.

> **If you have imported the WroxUnitedCS web.config from the download at `www.wrox.com`, you will find that it uses a namespace called Wrox, which has not yet been created in this book. Ignore the warning to this effect.**

3. Navigate to the Application Configuration page, and click Define Default Error Page.

4. Select the Specify a URL to Use as the Default Error Page option, and select `MissingPage.aspx` as the page to redirect users to when an error occurs.
5. Click the Save button.
6. Return to VWD, and open the `Web.config` file.
7. Scroll down until you find the `<customErrors>` section of the configuration, and notice that the value of the `defaultRedirect` attribute has been changed to the path of the page you chose in the Administration Tool:

```
<customErrors mode="RemoteOnly" defaultRedirect="MissingPage.aspx">
</customErrors>
```

How It Works

The Administration Tool is just a friendlier way to edit some of the settings present in `Web.config`, including the default error page. When you change the application's error handling setting through the Administration Tool, it edits `Web.config` for you—without your having to get your hands dirty editing XML data.

Troubleshooting Site Design Errors

Now that you have a good idea of what goes into site design, here are the most common errors you might run into when using Master pages, and the other facilities you've looked at in this chapter:

- The reference to the Master page is misspelled in a Content page. This will prevent ASP.NET from being able to find the Master page template for a page. To avoid this, whenever possible, use the VWD check box in the template dialog box to create the master reference.
- A mismatch between the ID of the content placeholder in the Master page and the `ContentPlaceHolder` ID property of the `content` tag in the Content page will prevent your page from displaying. Double-check that they match.
- The `Web.config` or `Global.asax` files are very strict about their syntax, and errors in them (such as typos) can be hard to track down. You can get around having to edit `Web.config` by using the ASP.NET Administration Tool, so you can be sure you haven't introduced typographical errors into the file.

Summary

Web sites are easy to create, use, and maintain if they are well designed. ASP.NET 2.0 offers several tools to organize the design of the site.

In this chapter, you learned that Master and Content pages create a consistent look and feel to the site. Master pages provide the consistent sections of the pages along with a position for the material contained in the Content page. Whenever possible, create the Master and Content pages using the Add New Item choice after right-clicking the root of the site in the Solution Explorer. A Master page must have the normal HTML and XML typing tags, `<%@ master ... %>` on the first line, and an `<asp:Content PlaceHolder>` tag with an ID. Content pages must not have the basic HTML and XML typing tags, must have <%@ page masterPageFile= %> on the first line, and must at some point use an <asp:content> tag to contain the material to be displayed. A Master page <head> can contain the link to a CSS if you are using one. Additionally, this chapter covered the following topics:

- Your site can implement multiple levels of Master pages. You can also create several Master pages to be served depending on the requesting browser. Furthermore, a Master page can support several <ContentPlaceHolder> tags provided that each has its own ID.
- Site maps contain a description of each file and its relationship to surrounding files. This XML file can then be read by ASP.NET 2.0 server-side controls to create navigation aids. VWD does not have a way to automatically create a site map, but the XML structure is not hard to understand because each page is a SiteMapNode.
- Two files hold information for an entire application. Web.config holds settings such as connection strings used with a data source, debugging routines for compilation, security settings, and values for handling errors, among other settings. Global.asax holds code for the entire site, including code to run when the application as a whole starts or stops. Additional code blocks can run when each user starts or stops using the site. Global.asax also houses code that can run on any page.

In the next chapter, you learn about the various server-side controls and how to use them to build proper pages. You will construct the Wrox United home page and fill in some of the Master page you created in this chapter.

Exercises

1. Describe the functional difference between the Web.config file and Global.asax.
2. What files discussed in this chapter are in XML format?
3. Take a look at the code for a Content page. Why does it lack directives and tags?

```
<!DOCTYPE HTML PUBLIC "-//W3C//DTD XHTML 1.0 Transitional//EN"
"http://www.w3.org/TR/xhtml1/DTD/xhtml1-transitional.dtd">
<html xmlns="http://www.w3.org/1999/xhtml">
<head ></head>
```

4. What values must match between a set of Master and Content pages?

Page Design

Successful web sites are generally easy to use, intuitive, and clearly presented. It's your job (possibly with the help of a friendly designer) to ensure that the sites you develop are not just functional, but can be presented in a meaningful manner. After you have a basic site outline structure in place, you need to make decisions about how to present the information and user interface elements.

ASP.NET, in conjunction with VWD, has some great tools for designing and laying out pages. Recall that you've already created a few pages with simple content simply by dragging and dropping from the Toolbox in VWD. Designing an entire site is obviously going to involve a whole lot more dragging and dropping, but there are ways of making this process less painful.

This chapter looks at the following topics:

- Creating and laying out static pages
- HTML and the HTML viewer in VWD
- Server controls and dynamic content
- Configuring controls in Design View
- The controls available in the web control library
- Adding dynamic navigation controls to a page, and getting them to work without writing a single line of code

If you have experience programming in HTML, some of this chapter may cover familiar territory, but the toolset available for working with HTML in VWD is quite advanced, so it's worth sticking around and enjoying a light refresher.

Static Page Design

The term *static* refers purely to the fact that the page shown in Figure 3-1, like many others on the Internet, is view-only (imagine an HTML page with nothing but text, or just a series of images) — you don't always want to have every page in a site include a form for submitting information, or react to user input. Static pages contain, by definition, content that doesn't change (or that rarely needs to be updated). Imagine you had a personal web site that contained an "About Me" page—you might want to change the content from time to time (if you move, change jobs, or get married), but on the whole, you're not likely to want to change that page more than a couple of times a year.

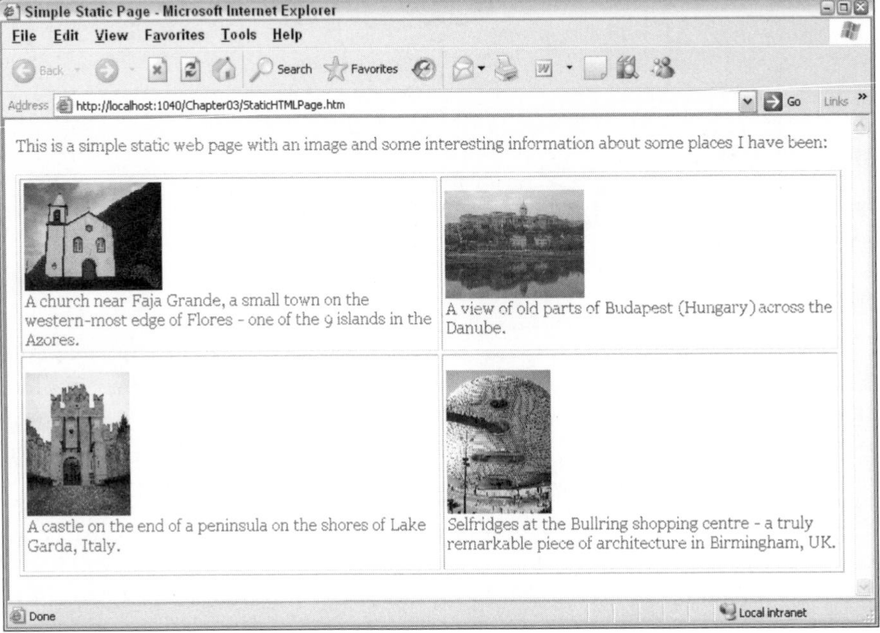

Figure 3-1

Static pages remind me of the Web circa 1995—most of the sites I'd view at the time would be simple, plain sites, and the joy of just playing with HTML tables for layout was enough to keep me occupied for a few afternoons. Time for a quick Try It Out—you're going to create a really simple page and see what this page looks like in HTML view, looking at how HTML elements are structured.

Try It Out — Creating a Static Page

Fire up VWD and get started. This is a light run-through—you don't have to do much at this stage, just follow the steps and feel comfortable with the techniques.

1. First, it will help if you download the base code for this chapter from `www.wrox.com`. Make sure you place the base code folder in the following location: `C:\BegASPNET2\Chapters\Begin\Chapter03`.
2. Open VWD and select Open Web Site from the main menu. In the dialog box that appears, select the Chapter03 folder and click Open (see Figure 3-2).
3. In the Solution Explorer on the right (shown in Figure 3-3), right-click the Chapter03 site and select Add New Item.
4. The Add New Item dialog box appears, where you need to select a new HTML page called `StaticHTMLPage.htm`, and click Add (see Figure 3-4).

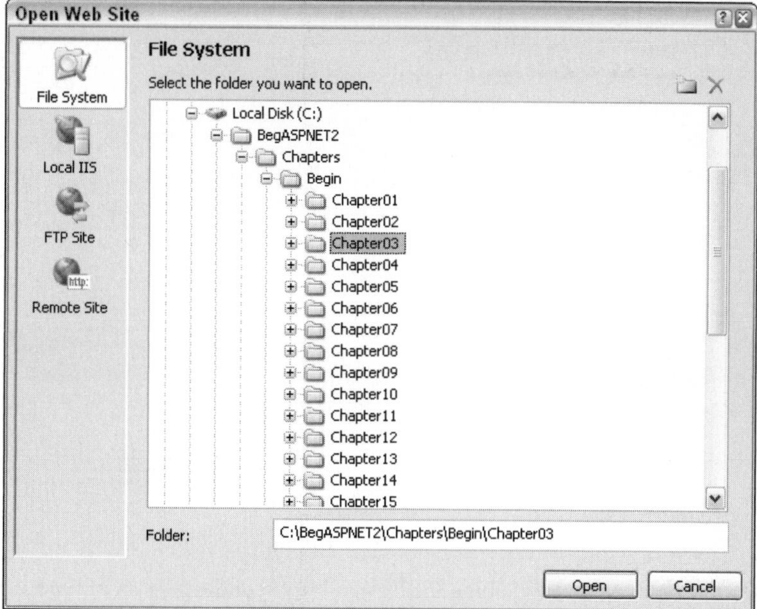

Figure 3-2

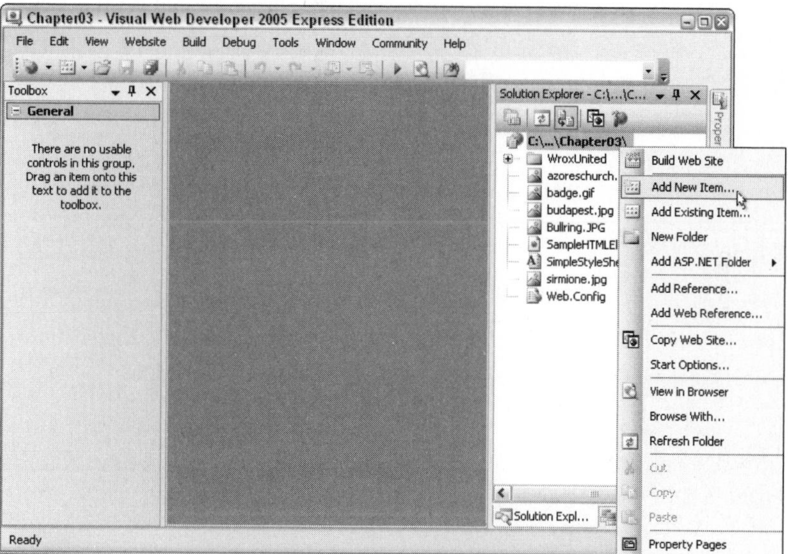

Figure 3-3

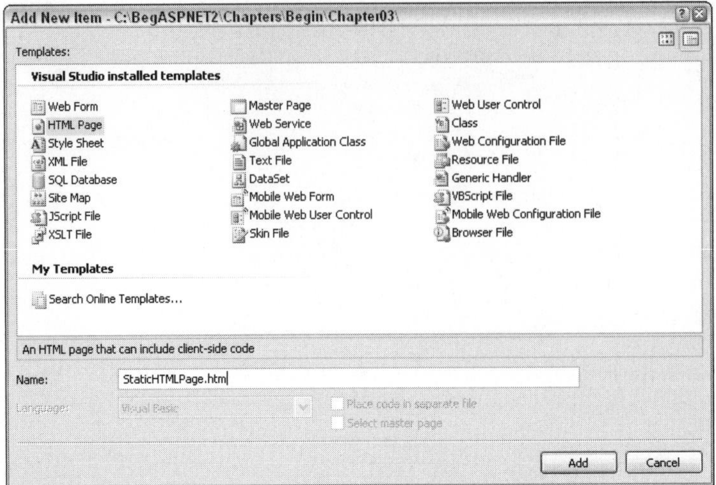

Figure 3-4

5. Switch to Design View by clicking the Design button at the bottom of the page, and then type in some text, as depicted in Figure 3-5.

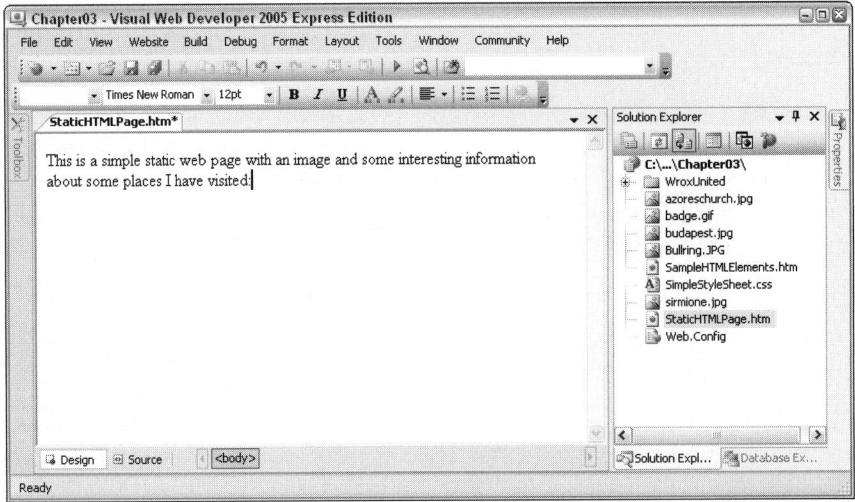

Figure 3-5

Don't worry about the actual text — this is a simple example, and you don't have to publish this on the web.

6. Next, from the toolbar select Layout➪Insert Table to add a table to the page. Give it two rows, two columns, and borders and padding if you like, all of which appear in Figure 3-6.

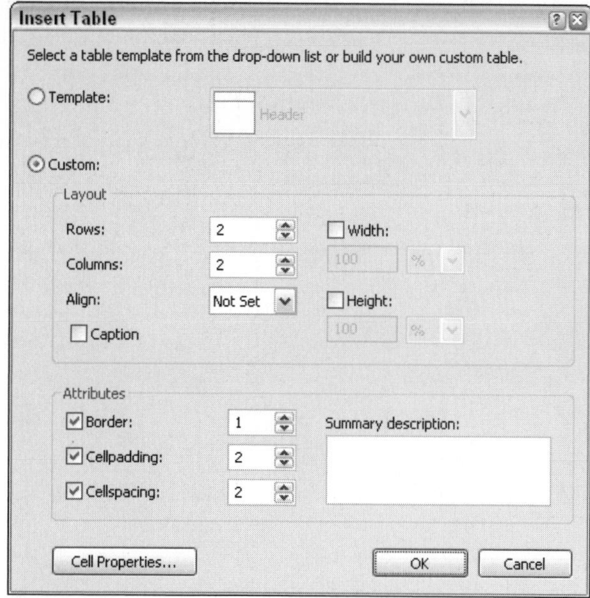

Figure 3-6

7. After you have a table, you can add content within each cell. Try adding some text to a cell, and then drag an image tag from the HTML section of the Toolbox on the left of VWD onto the page, as shown in Figure 3-7.

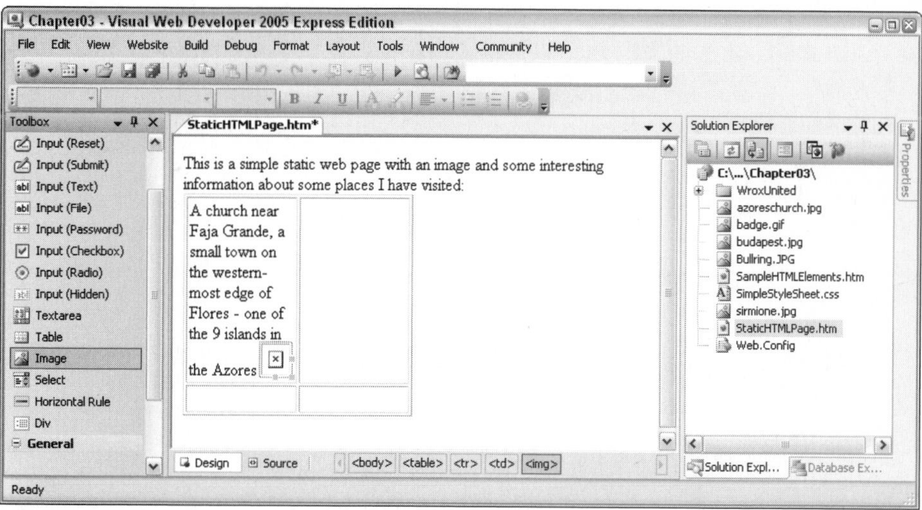

Figure 3-7

When you have a table in the designer, you can click the `<table>` button at the bottom of the screen to select only that element on the page (see Figure 3-8) — you can then modify the padding and border attributes on the table by changing the values in the Properties box on the right.

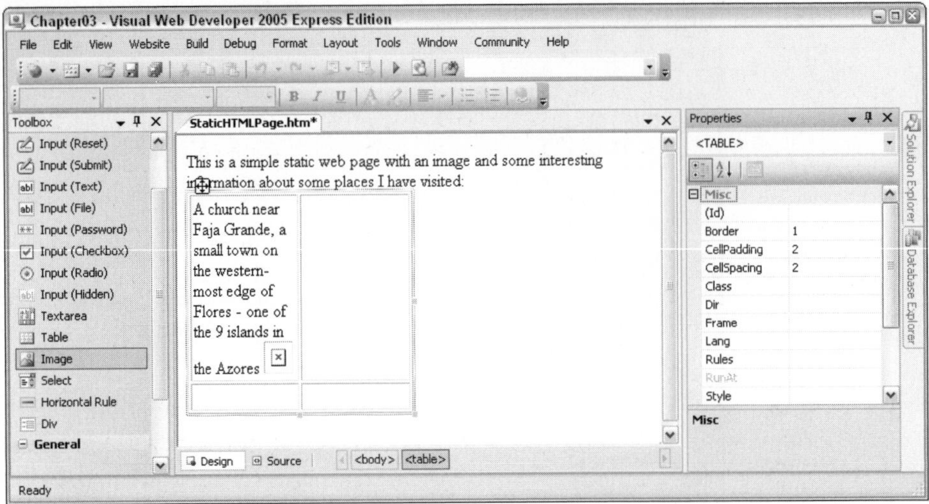

Figure 3-8

8. Click the Source button at the bottom of the screen and you can see the HTML that's generated for you (see Figure 3-9). With some small tweaks, you can add a small amount of styling and some links to your images.

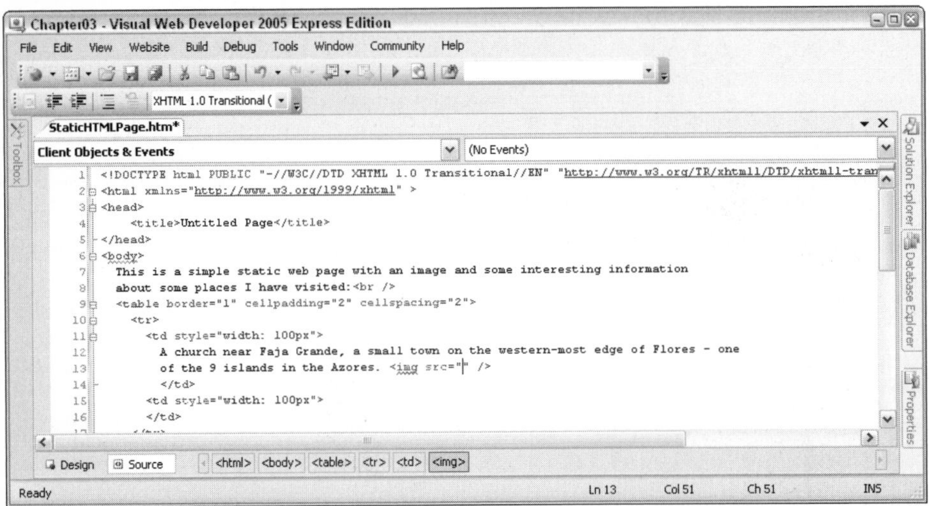

Figure 3-9

9. To turn the nascent page into the finished example, I added some more text and images to my version. Here's the code for the version of the finished page that you can download from `www.wrox.com`—notice the `<style>` attribute on the `<body>` tag:

```
<body style="color: darkolivegreen; font-family: georgia">
  This is a simple static web page with an image and some interesting information
  about some places I have been:<br />
  <br />
```

```
    <table cellspacing="3" cellpadding="3" border="1">
      <tr>
        <td>
          <img src="azoreschurch.jpg" height="100" /><br />
          A church near Faja Grande, a small town on the western-most edge
          of Flores - one of the 9 islands in the Azores.</td>
        <td>
          <img src="budapest.jpg" height="100" /><br />
          A view of old parts of Budapest (Hungary) across the Danube.</td>
      </tr>
      <tr>
        <td style="height: 192px">
          <img src="sirmione.jpg" width="100" /><br />
          A castle on the end of a peninsula on the shores of Lake Garda, Italy.</td>
        <td style="height: 192px">
          <img src="bullring.jpg" width="100" /><br />
          Selfridges at the Bullring shopping centre - a truly remarkable piece of
          architecture in Birmingham, UK.<br /></td>
      </tr>
    </table>
  </body>
```

When you finish adding content to the page, you can view the page by pressing Ctrl+F5. The result is a page that looks like Figure 3-10 (which is the same as Figure 3-1).

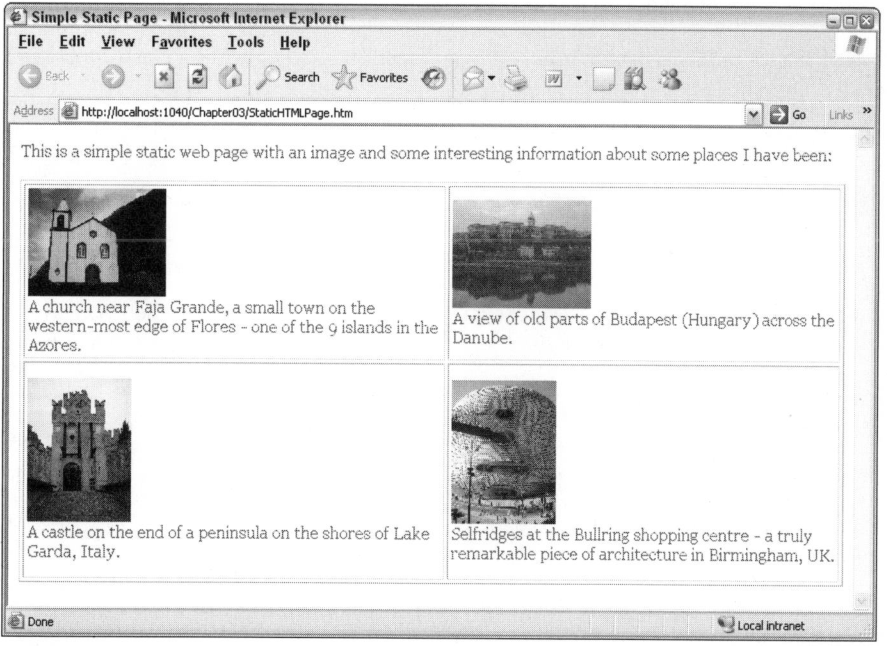

Figure 3-10

How It Works

As you proceed through this chapter, you'll become increasingly familiar with the technique of adding layout elements in the design window, and making some changes either in the Properties pane on the right, or by modifying the code manually. Static elements such as the ones used in this example (simple text within a body tag, tables, and images) are used throughout both static and dynamic pages, and understanding how to add and integrate these elements is all part of building dynamic web applications.

In this example, you gained a bit of practice in working with a simple HTML layout of a page. For example, the elements on the page were laid out in a simple HTML table, and within each of the cells in the table were some text and some images:

```
<td>
  <img src="azoreschurch.jpg" height="100" /><br />
   A church near Faja Grande, a small town on the western-most edge of Flores - one
   of the 9 islands in the Azores.
</td>
```

The body tag in the rendered page has some simple styling attached to it that defines the color and font used for the text on the page:

```
<body style="color: darkolivegreen; font-family: georgia">
```

This attribute will apply to all of the elements within the opening and closing `<body>` tags, hence all of the content of the visible page.

Don't worry if a lot of this is new to you — the next section is designed as a crash course in HTML to help you get up to speed.

The World of HTML

If you are unfamiliar with HTML, here are some of the basic concepts you need to understand:

- An HTML file is human-readable text with a few extra brackets — when you browse a web page, your web browser will understand how to convert the bracketed bits into something that looks interesting.
- The bracketed bits are called *elements*, though strictly speaking, the element normally consists of two *tags* that open and close the element, and sometimes have textual or other HTML content between them. Some elements have only a single tag.
- Elements have *attributes* that give the browser extra information about how the element should appear on the page.

  Here's a simple HTML element:

```
<div id="divUserDetails"
style="width:300px;height:100px;float:left;background:darkred;color:white">
  These are my details, my favorite color, and my hobbies
</div>
```

In this example, the `<div ...>` and `</div>` parts are *tags* describing the `div` *element*, the `id=""` and `style=""` bits are *attributes*, and the text between the two tags is the content of the element.

- *Rendering* is the process of turning HTML code into visual elements, so the preceding code will render as shown in Figure 3-11.

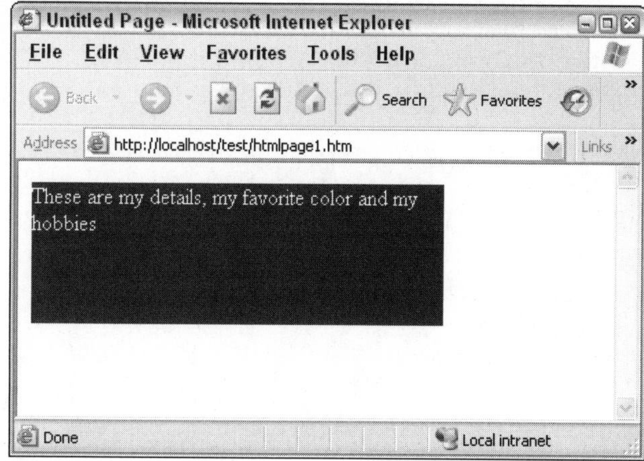

Figure 3-11

The following table contains some of the HTML elements you're likely to run into.

Element	Description	Example Usage
`<img>`	An image tag. This tag places an image on a page.	`<img src="myimage.gif" />`

`<div>`	A paragraph-style block of text. Text contained in a `<div>` element can be positioned on a page using various attributes. For example, to place two `div` elements side-by-side, you could have one with a `float:left` style, and one with a `float:right` style.	`<div style="float:left" >Left-hand content here</div>`
		`<div style="float:right">`
		`Right-hand content here</div>`

`<span>`	A tag used to format characters of text, so you could surround a word in a sentence with a `<span>` tag and make the span have bold styling to highlight that word.	`<div>`
		`Some standard text with a <span style="font-weight: bold">`
		`bold</span> word in the middle`
		`</div>`

`<table>`
`<tr>`
`<td>`
	A table element that contains rows (`<tr>`) and cells (`<td>`). Commonly used to position elements on a page, should ideally be used only for tabular data. According to accessibility guidelines, `<div>` elements should be used for layout and positioning, but a lot of sites still use tables because they are simpler to develop.	`<table border="1">`
		`<tr>`
		` <td>The contents of a cell</td>`
		` </tr>`
		`</table>`

Table continued on following page

Element	Description	Example Usage
<a>	An anchor element. Defines a hyperlink on a page, enabling the developer to specify both the target content (in the href attribute) and the text to display to the user.	Some text with a <a href="page.htm"> hyperlink </a> in it
<head> <body>	The two main parts of an HTML page are the <head> and the <body>. The <head> is where the <title> element and <link> elements (along with a variety of metadata) are placed. The <body> contains the display elements.	<html> <head> <title>Page Title</title> </head> <body> Contents of page </body> </html>
<form> <input>	A form element. When creating a site that has a data entry form, the elements that are used to transmit data to the server must be contained within a <form> element. The HTML <input> element is quite versatile. With a type attribute of text, it appears as a text box on the screen. With a type of submit, it appears as a button that, when clicked, submits the form to the server.	<form id="form1" runat="server"> <input id="Text1" type="text" /> <input id="Submit1" type="submit" value="submit" /> </form>
<title> <link>	Within the <head> of the page, the <title> element controls the text in the title bar of the page. The <link> is most often used to link a page with a CSS style sheet.	<head> <title>Page Title</title> <link rel="Stylesheet" type="text/css" href="MyCss.css" /> </head>

<script>	Can contain either client-side script (script run on the browser, normally written in JavaScript, or possibly VBScript), or server-side .NET code.	<script language=
		"JavaScript">
		alert('Hello World!');
		</script>
		<script runat="server">
		protected void Page_Load(
		object sender,
		EventArgs e)
		{
		...
		}
		</script>

Element	Description	Example Usage
  <hr /> 	Used to help to lay out a page, the tag adds a line break to a string of text, and the forcibly enters a non-breaking space character; hence two words (or elements) separated only by a character cannot be split apart over two lines. The <hr /> element displays a horizontal line across the page.	This is a string of text with a line break and a space. <hr /> Two images separated by a space: <img src="1.gif"> ;<img src="2.gif">

A sample HTML page called SampleHTMLElements.htm that includes these simple examples is available in the code download for this chapter, and it appears as shown in Figure 3-12.

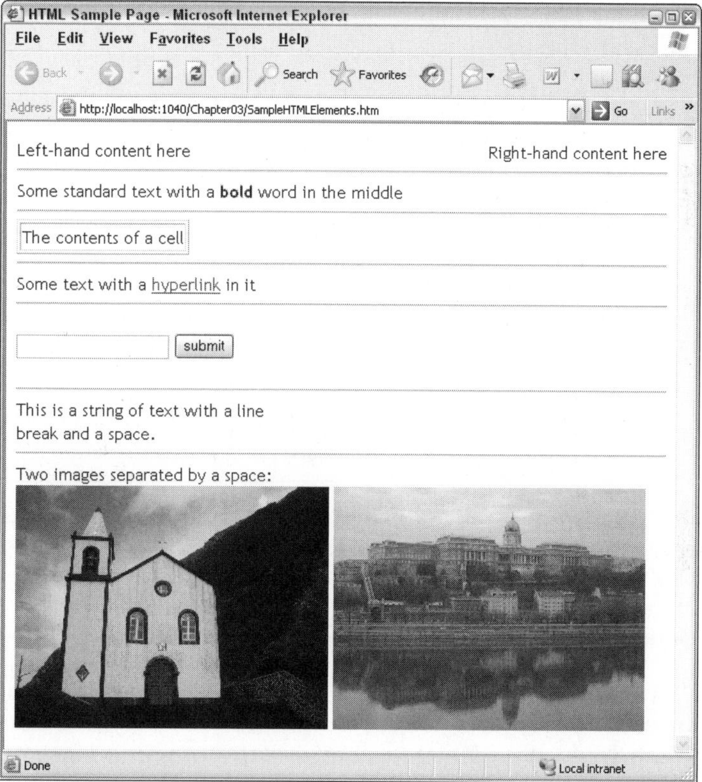

Figure 3-12

Gaining familiarity with the common elements in HTML is a necessity for any ASP.NET developer, and not only do you have to understand how to use these elements, you have to learn how to use them correctly, in adhering to the standards and making sure that sites you develop are accessible by as many users as possible.

It's very easy to end up with HTML that's almost impossible to maintain, with tags and styling all over the place. Many older tools for constructing HTML pages would take pride in destroying your carefully crafted HTML code, and supposedly correct your code to follow the guidelines within the tool. Anyone who used older versions of FrontPage would have cursed many a time at the fact that simply opening an HTML page and closing it in FrontPage would permanently mangle your HTML code. Thankfully, VWD has one of the best HTML editors I've ever used.

Perhaps the best way to make your code clean and easy to maintain is to adhere to a common standard. The introduction of XHTML brought many more guidelines to web development, and following these guidelines is a great way to improve your technique.

From HTML to XHTML Code

Although most people speak of HTML code, the fact is that if you write good HTML code, you're actually writing XHTML. XHTML is a set of rules that, if you follow them when you write HTML code, result in code that is more standards-compliant, and hence more likely to render as you want it to on a variety of different client browsers.

The core rules of XHTML are as follows:

- Always close your tags (so you always have both a `<p>` and a `</p>` for a paragraph) or use self-closing tags (such as `<br />` instead of `<br>`).
- Tag and attribute names must be lowercase (so `<div id="myDiv">` is acceptable, but `<Div ID="myDiv">` is not) because XHTML is case-sensitive (so `<div>`, `<Div>` and `<DIV>` are all different entities to XHTML).
- Attribute values must be enclosed within double quotes.

This is only a brief summary of XHTML. If you want to know more about the rules, refer to the W3 site `www.w3.org/TR/xhtml1/` where you can learn all about the XHTML standard. Section 4 of that page deals specifically with the way XHTML differs from standard HTML.

In essence, the aim of XHTML is to provide a common set of guidelines for web developers and browser developers to to follow. With newer web browsers such as Firefox starting to gain ground on the Microsoft Internet Explorer–dominated landscape, it's important that all parties agree to support XHTML in all future iterations of their products to move away from the old problem of developing a site that worked just fine on Internet Explorer, but looked awful on Netscape.

The move toward XHTML as the standard language of the web is gradual, and will likely never happen fully (with browsers likely to support older tags and markup for many years yet for backward compatibility), but you'll find that future maintenance of web sites that you write today will be much simpler if you follow the XHTML guidelines. You should be less likely to see your sites break when the next version of Internet Explorer or Firefox arrives.

Visual Web Developer has a great feature for helping you to develop standards-compliant web sites. If you open up `SampleHTMLElements.htm` in VWD, you'll notice that there is a toolbar at the top of the page (see Figure 3-13) that lists Internet Explorer 6.0 as the target for the web page.

Now if you change the selection so that your page is supposed to target the XHTML 1.1 standard, you'll see plenty of red squiggly underlining, as shown in Figure 3-14.

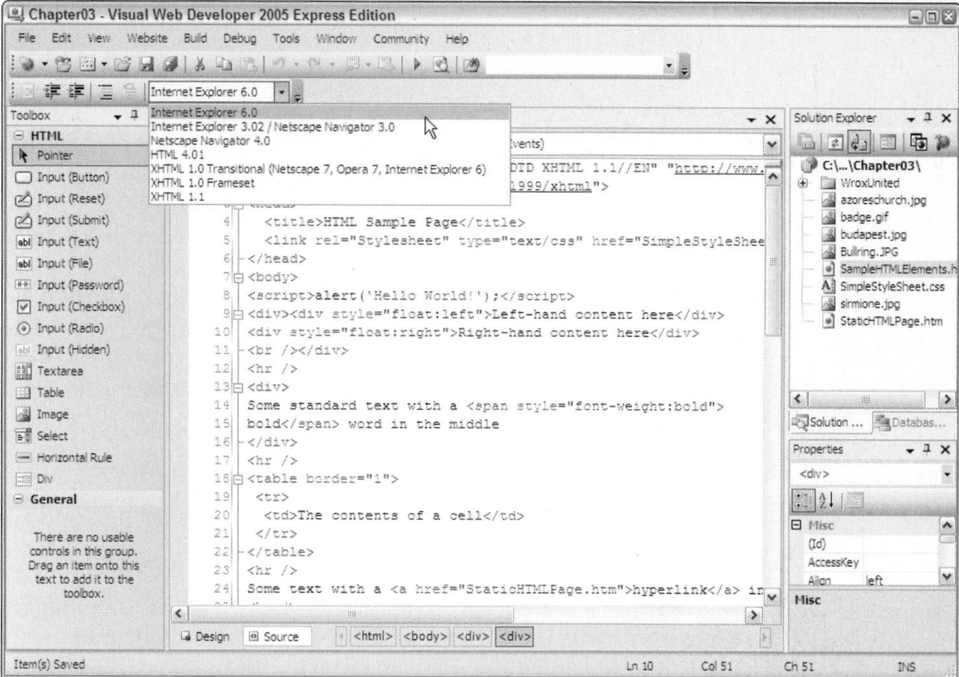

Figure 3-13

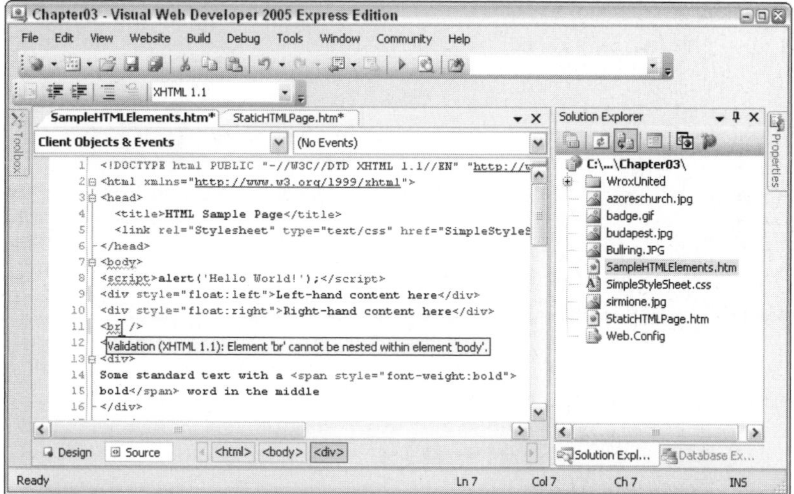

Figure 3-14

The highlighted error shown in Figure 3-14 refers to the fact that `<br />` tags are supposed to only appear within a block element, such as a `<div>`. If you changed the first part of the page to be enclosed within a `<div>` element, this error would be fixed, without any discernable change to the appearance of the page:

```
<div>
  <div style="float:left">Left-hand content here</div>
  <div style="float:right">Right-hand content here</div>
  <br />
</div>
```

Switch the validation target back to Internet Explorer 6.0 and you will see that the highlighted errors will all disappear. Building a site for a specific browser, like IE 6.0, gives you more flexibility with the code you write, but you cannot guarantee that your site will appear as designed on other browsers.

The rules of XHTML are also followed in any code that ASP.NET generates dynamically. You haven't created much in the way of dynamic content so far, so let's move on to looking at how you can make pages a bit more exciting.

Dynamic Content

In order to move from the static world of HTML to the dynamic world of ASP.NET, it's important to know what is meant by dynamic content.

When you click a button on a form on a web page, you expect something to happen — and most of the time (if the page has been coded correctly), something does happen. You might submit an order form for a stack of CDs by clicking a button. You might also select an item on a menu on a page — take, for example, a menu from the Wrox United web site. Clicking the menu causes the menu contents to pop out (see Figure 3-15) and become selectable in a similar way to clicking your Start button.

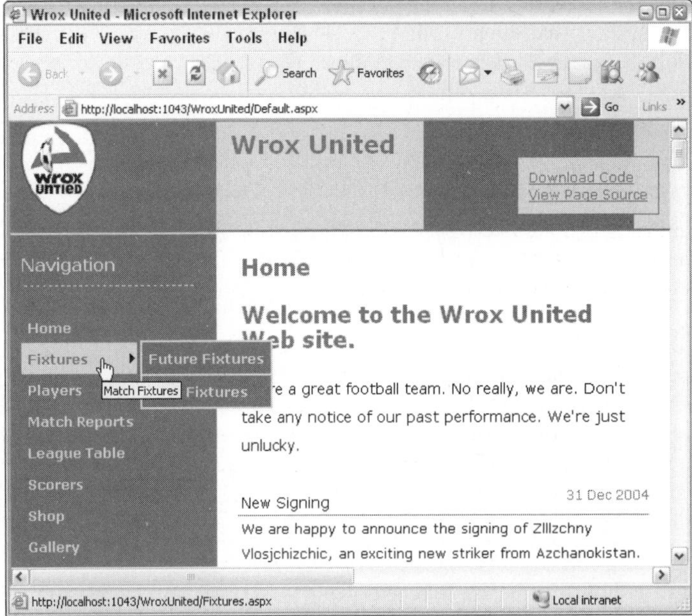

Figure 3-15

Now notice that there's no lag between clicking the menu and clicking a different menu — the page responds just like your own system. Your browser's actually executing some local code in order to display these items. Click a button or a hyperlink on a form and the page will likely take longer to respond. Clicking buttons, hyperlinks, or other similar elements on a page causes your browser to start talking to the server, asking for something, or sending some data.

Dynamic Client Code and Dynamic Server Code

Hovering over the menu on the Wrox United web site will run some code on the page that is likely written in JavaScript, a programming language that most browsers can understand and run, and is used to provide quick responses to user input. The page won't flicker and refresh (unlike clicking a hyperlink) because the browser already knows what to display when you hover over the menu. This is an example of dynamic *client* code.

When a more complicated response is required (for example, when you submit an order on a shopping site or when you want to search for a specific item on a shopping site), the page submits information back to the web server for processing. The processing on the server is dynamic *server* code, and this is the code that you will learn to write over the course of this book.

Server-side code can be written in many different languages, not just ASP.NET with VB.NET, C#, or other .NET languages. You probably have heard of PHP and perhaps JSP (Java Server Pages) — these are just two examples of other languages used by developers to write server-side code. Each language has its strengths and weaknesses, but you'll be hard-pressed to find a server-side technology that's as easy to use and as powerful as ASP.NET.

When it comes to creating dynamic pages in ASP.NET, the fastest way to build a dynamic page is to drag server controls onto the page, set properties on those controls, and eventually write code to customize their functionality. This *drag-and-drop* architecture has improved greatly in the latest edition of ASP.NET, making it possible to create the structural framework for an entire site without having to write any code.

Introduction to Server Controls

When you look at the Visual Web Developer Toolbox, you'll notice several different sections, each containing a different set of tools. Many of these tools are *server controls*, and you'll be using these controls regularly when you develop ASP.NET applications.

> **A server control appears on the source code for an ASP.NET page as a tag; for example, `<asp:textbox ... />`. These tags are not standard HTML elements, so a browser will not be able to understand them if they appear on a page. However, when you request an ASP.NET page from a web server, these tags are converted into HTML elements dynamically, so the browser only receives HTML content that it can understand.**

This section starts by taking a look at some of the categories of controls available to you, and then discussing how they work.

The Server Control Toolbox

At first glance, the array of server controls in the Toolbox can be quite overwhelming. Not only do you have standard web page elements to choose from (such as radio buttons, hyperlinks, and drop-down lists), but other categories of controls are also available (shown minimized in Figure 3-16) that contain even more controls. The Toolbox changes appearance depending on which type of page is being edited, so Figure 3-16 is the standard appearance when you're working on ASP.NET pages.

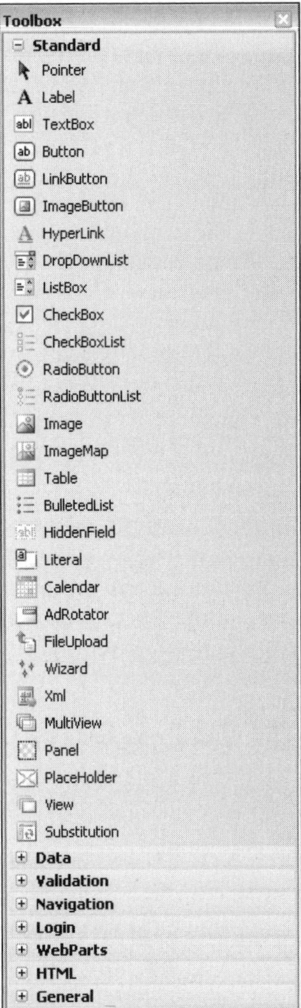

Figure 3-16

The categories of controls available are as follows:

- **Standard:** Common controls that make up 90 percent of all pages.
- **Data:** Controls used to connect to data sources (databases or XML files).

- **Validation:** Controls that can be added to a page to validate user input (for example, to ensure that certain text boxes contain data or that data has been entered in the correct format).
- **Navigation:** Controls used to provide a simple and quick solution to making a site navigable (for example, dynamic menus and breadcrumbs of hyperlinks).
- **Login:** A set of controls that make it simple to move from a completely open site to one that has personalized areas.
- **WebParts:** Controls that make it possible to create Sharepoint-style sites with drag-and-droppable sections, known as Web Parts, which enable the user to rearrange their view of a site.
- **HTML:** Simple HTML elements.

Throughout the rest of this book, you'll be introduced to many of the controls in each category. Later in this chapter, you can play with some of the navigation controls when you build some menus for the Wrox United site.

What Are Server Controls?

Let's start from first principles. When you create a simple HTML page and save it to your local file system, you can view that page in your browser by double-clicking the file. This is fine if you're putting together a static HTML site and want to test the output, but there's no point in developing a web site that users would have to download to view. That's why, when a web site is deployed, it is uploaded to a *web server*, which everyone can access via its URL (Uniform Resource Locator).

When the site is hosted on a web server, people can access the site from other machines and browse through the HTML pages. However, if the server has the right software installed, you can then do much more than offer static HTML pages. When you request an HTML page, the server looks up the file and sends it to you. When you request an ASP.NET page (a page with the file extension `.aspx`), the server looks up the file on its file system and reads the file, and then it performs some processing before sending the resulting page back to you. The "performs some processing" bit is the magic that makes ASP.NET work.

The extra processing that the server performs includes the capability to read an ASP.NET page and convert the server controls in that page into HTML that the browser can understand. Remember, your browser doesn't speak ASP.NET. A web browser is a simple thing that only speaks HTML and possibly JavaScript—it cannot process ASP.NET code. The *server* reads the ASP.NET code and processes it, *converting* anything that is ASP.NET-specific to HTML and (as long as the browser supports it) a bit of JavaScript, and sends the freshly generated HTML back to the browser.

The process of converting ASP.NET code to HTML is how server controls work—you can happily create pages that contain server controls when you are developing the source .aspx page, yet the browser that requests that page from the web server will only receive HTML and JavaScript (see Figure 3-17). This is a key concept to understand, and the process is discussed in more detail in Chapter 6.

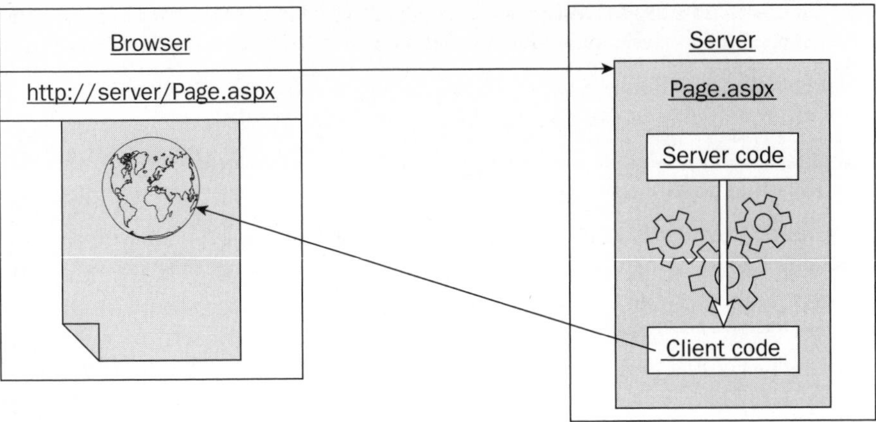

Figure 3-17

You can see how this works with the aid of a simple example. The following Try It Out is a really simple example to demonstrate the differences between the ASP.NET code and HTML code.

Try It Out Adding Server Controls in Design View

1. Reopen the Chapter03 web site.
2. Right-click the root of the web site and select Add New Item.
3. In the dialog box that appears (shown in Figure 3-18), select Web Form, call the page **ServerControls.aspx**, select your preferred language from the drop-down list, and leave both of the check boxes unchecked.

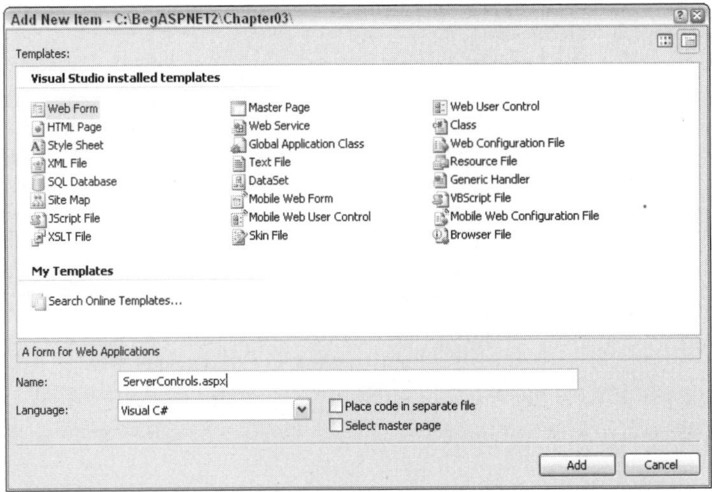

Figure 3-18

4. If you are not already in Design View, switch into that mode and double-click a TextBox control from the Standard section of the control toolbox on the left (see Figure 3-19) to add it to the main body of the page.

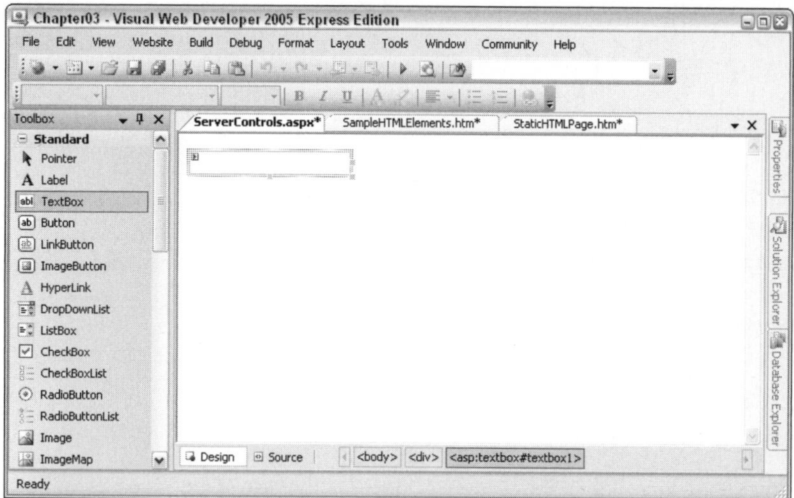

Figure 3-19

5. You're actually ready to view the page now, so right-click on the page and select View in Browser. Your browser should start and display the page shown in Figure 3-20.

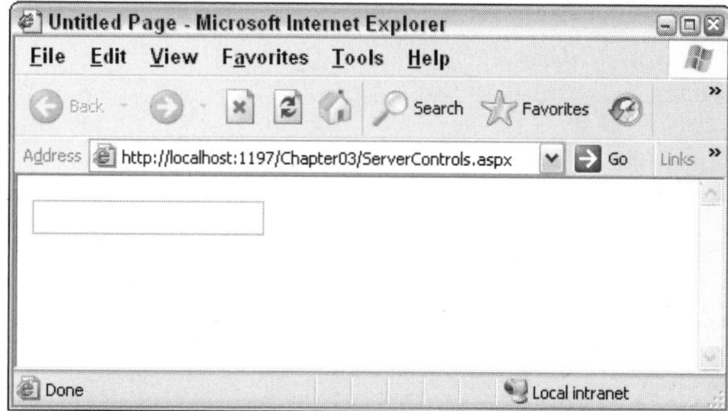

Figure 3-20

Note that the number displayed in the address bar (after the word "localhost") is a fairly random number that is generated whenever you first request a server-side page from a project.

How It Works

In this example, you only added a single server control to an ASP.NET page and viewed the page in the browser. It's not exactly the most exciting example in the world, but the point is to see how server-side code is changed into client-side code.

Click the View menu in the browser and select View Source. You should see the code shown in Figure 3-21 appear within Notepad.

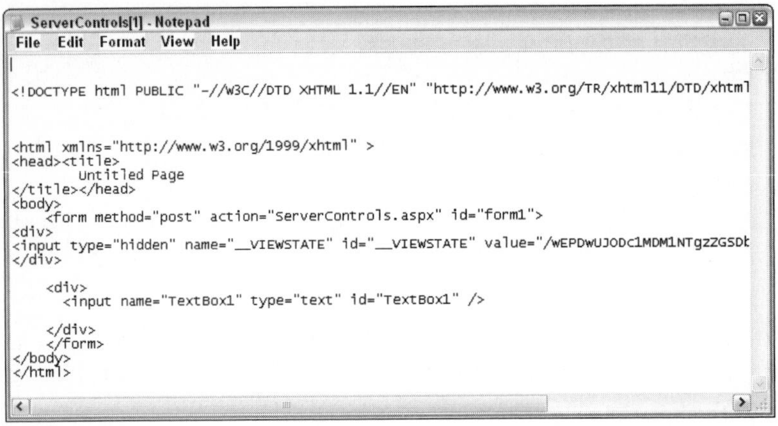

```
ServerControls[1] - Notepad
File  Edit  Format  View  Help

<!DOCTYPE html PUBLIC "-//W3C//DTD XHTML 1.1//EN" "http://www.w3.org/TR/xhtml11/DTD/xhtml


<html xmlns="http://www.w3.org/1999/xhtml" >
<head><title>
	Untitled Page
</title></head>
<body>
    <form method="post" action="ServerControls.aspx" id="form1">
<div>
<input type="hidden" name="__VIEWSTATE" id="__VIEWSTATE" value="/wEPDwUJODc1MDM1NTgzZGSDk
</div>

    <div>
      <input name="TextBox1" type="text" id="TextBox1" />

    </div>
    </form>
</body>
</html>
```

Figure 3-21

This code is the client-side code — the rendered output of the page. Compare this with the original code — return to VWD and click the Source View of the page (see Figure 3-22).

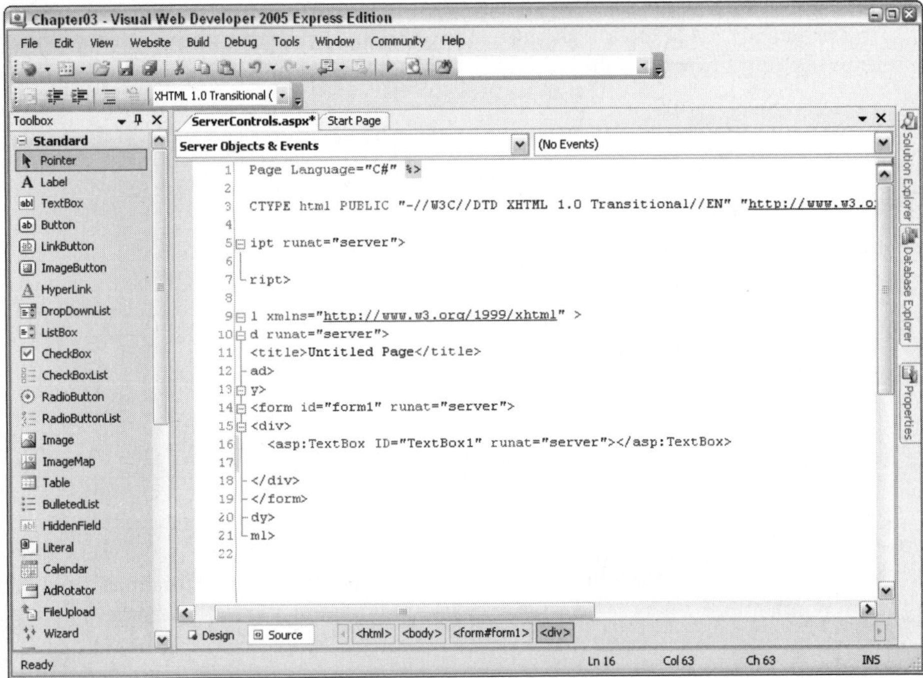

Figure 3-22

Note the lines that describe the control with the ID of `TextBox1`. Here are those lines, as they appear in the original source code for the page:

```
<div>
  <asp:TextBox ID="TextBox1" runat="server"></asp:TextBox>

</div>
```

And here is the equivalent line in the rendered source code:

```
<div>
  <input name="TextBox1" type="text" id="TextBox1" />

</div>
```

Notice that the original `TextBox1` control has been converted from an ASP.NET control to an HTML element. The server received the request for the page and was able to glean, from the original request, that the browser could understand HTML, so the server produced an HTML version of the control along with the rest of the page back to the browser. The browser then does the legwork in converting that HTML code to a viewable web page.

Source View in VWD

Visual Web Developer has two main modes when it comes to building and editing pages. The Design View is one that you've spent a little while working in now, and it's the Design View that you'll concentrate on using (where you can) in this book to avoid having to type too much code. However, Source View is really useful for editing a page and fixing nagging problems, so it's worthwhile taking a look at this now and gaining some familiarity. Add another control to the page you were just working on, this time in Source View.

Try It Out Adding Server Controls in Source View

1. Head back into VWD and ensure that you are in Source View for the `ServerControls.aspx` page (click the link at the bottom of the window to switch between Design View and Source View). In the code that appears, click the line immediately below the code representing the `TextBox` control that you added in the previous example.

```
<div>
  <asp:TextBox ID="TextBox1" runat="server"></asp:TextBox>

</div>
```

2. You have two options available to you when you add server controls in Source View: you can either type the code, or drag and drop the control from the Toolbox, much like the technique used in Design View. Do it the hard way first — start typing the following code:

```
<asp:Image
```

   Before you even finish the word "Image," you'll notice some handy tooltips popping up, as shown in Figure 3-23, trying to guess what you're typing.

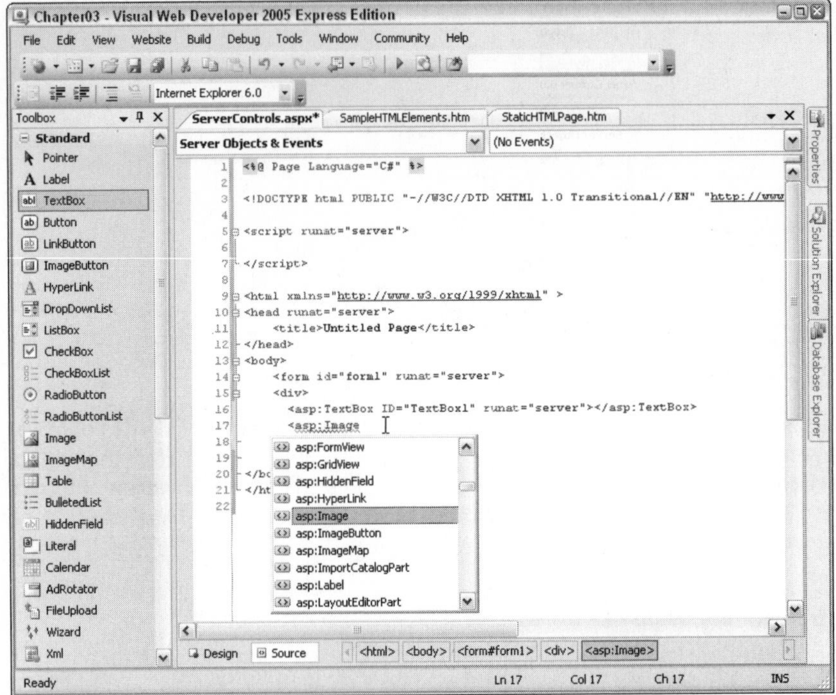

Figure 3-23

> **This is a feature available to VWD and Visual Studio known as IntelliSense, and it's designed to make your life as a developer a little easier. To accept a suggestion, you can scroll through the list with the arrow keys and then press the Tab or Enter key or the spacebar, or click the suggestion with your mouse. To forcibly show any relevant IntelliSense, press Ctrl+Space and the popup will appear.**

3. Continue to enter the code as follows:

```
<div>
  <asp:TextBox ID="TextBox1" runat="server"></asp:TextBox>
  <asp:Image ID="MyImage" runat="server" ImageUrl="~/azoreschurch.jpg" />
</div>
```

   Notice that VWD presents you with a list of local images when you enter the `ImageUrl` property (see Figure 3-24).

4. Add one more control to the page; this time, add it using the double-click technique. Add a blank line before the `</div>`, position your cursor in this line, and double-click the `Hyperlink` control (see Figure 3-25) in the Toolbox to add it to the page.

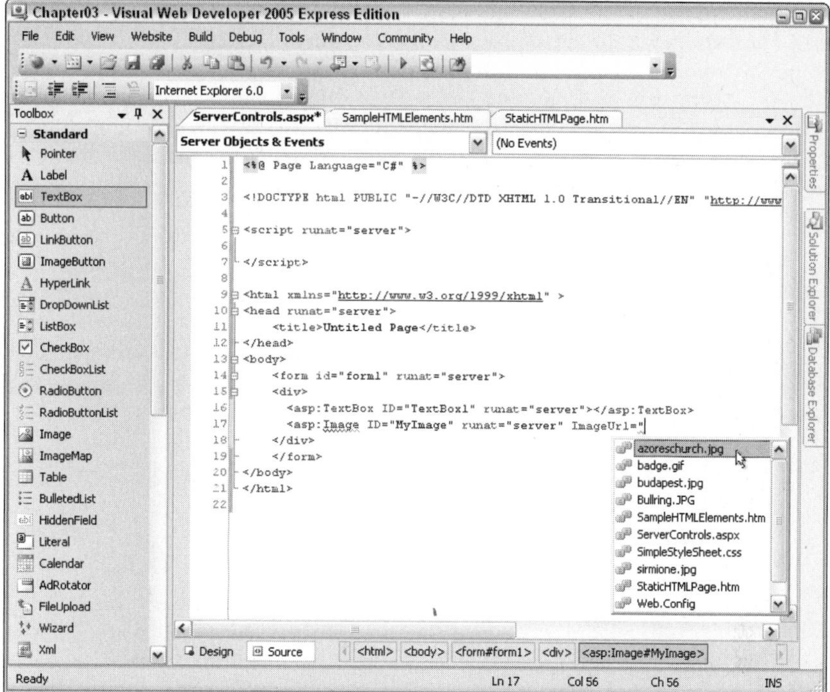

Figure 3-24

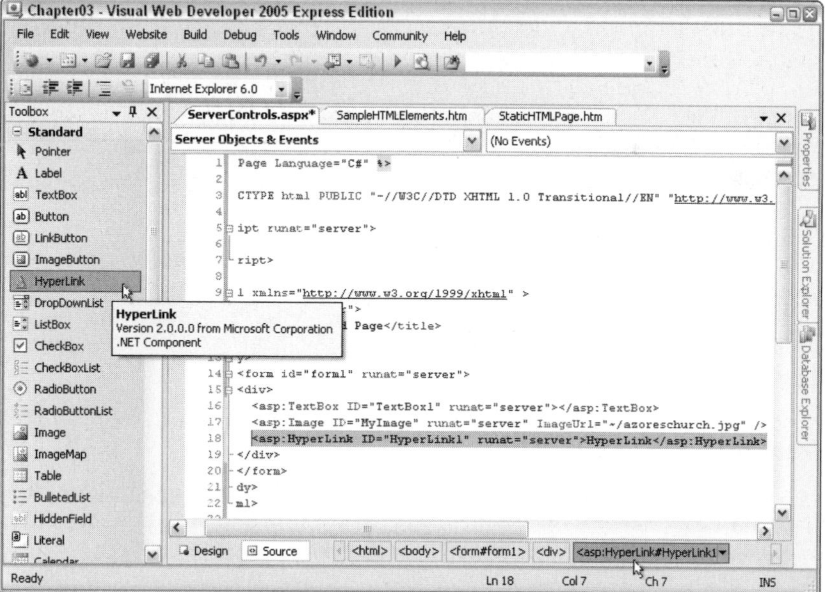

Figure 3-25

5. You'll still have to edit this control before you can run the page successfully, so position your cursor anywhere within the `Hyperlink`'s definition and then cast your eye over to the Properties pane on the right. (If it is hidden, as in Figure 3-25, you will need to pop it out from the side by hovering your mouse over the Properties tab at the right-hand edge of your screen, or select View⇨Properties Window.) Notice a property called `NavigateUrl` near the bottom of the list of properties. Enter **http://www.wroxunited.net** as the value for this property and press Enter. Take a look at Figure 3-26 and you'll notice a new attribute of the hyperlink tag called `NavigateUrl` appear on the page with the value you entered.

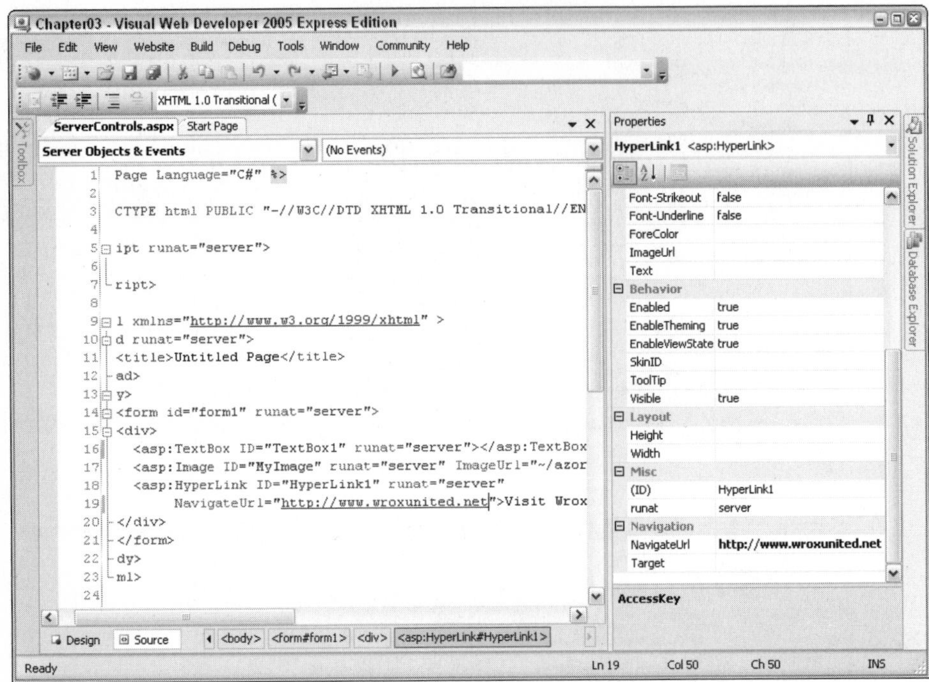

Figure 3-26

6. Switch over to Design View and see how it looks — you'll notice all three controls on the page in one line. If you'd prefer them to appear one below the other, simply type **
** after each control to add an HTML line break character in Source View. You might also want to change the display text of the hyperlink control (the text immediately before the `</asp:HyperLink>` closing tag) to some text of your choosing.

```
<body>
  <form id="form1" runat="server">
    <div>
      <asp:TextBox ID="TextBox1" runat="server"></asp:TextBox><br />
      <asp:Image ID="MyImage" runat="server" ImageUrl="~/azoreschurch.jpg" /><br />
      <asp:HyperLink ID="HyperLink1" runat="server"
           NavigateUrl="http://www.wroxunited.net">Visit Wrox United Online!
      </asp:HyperLink>
    </div>
  </form>
</body>
```

Notice the bar at the bottom of the screen next to the Design and Source buttons. There's an orange highlight on the element that is underneath the current cursor position (see Figure 3-26). This element hierarchy changes whenever you select different elements in either Design View or Source View.

7. Run the page again and view the results, which are depicted in Figure 3-27.

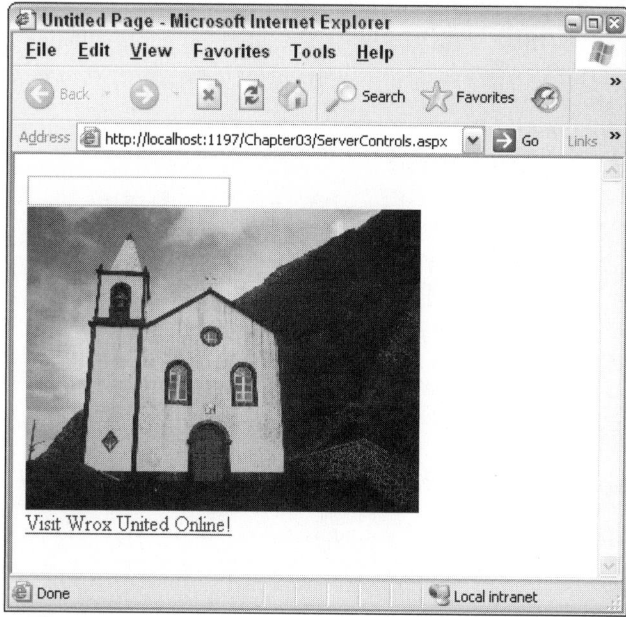

Figure 3-27

How It Works

In this example, you gained a bit more familiarity with the drag-and-drop method of page design, and with using Source View to manually craft pages. You also saw that VWD has lots of features that spring into action at different times to help you with this process.

Here's a walkthrough of the code that was generated in VWD. The main content region of the page was surrounded by a `<div>` control, and within this are the three controls added to the page:

```
<div>
  <asp:TextBox ID="TextBox1" runat="server"></asp:TextBox><br />
  <asp:Image ID="MyImage" runat="server" ImageUrl="~/azoreschurch.jpg" /><br />
  <asp:HyperLink ID="HyperLink1" runat="server"
       NavigateUrl="http://www.wroxunited.net">Visit Wrox United Online!
  </asp:HyperLink>
</div>
```

Now take a look at the rendered source. While the page is running in the browser, select View⇨Source from the main menu in your browser, and see how the contents of the `<div>` have been changed:

```
<div>
  <input name="TextBox1" type="text" id="TextBox1" /><br />
  <img id="MyImage" src="azoreschurch.jpg" style="border-width:0px;" /><br />
  <a id="HyperLink1" href="http://www.wroxunited.net">Visit Wrox United Online!</a>
</div>
```

Web browsers don't know anything about ASP.NET server controls, so when the page is requested, the ASP.NET processor on the web server kicks in and starts converting the server-side elements into simple HTML that the browser is more happy to receive. The `TextBox` control maps straight onto an HTML `<input>` element. The `Image` control is converted into an `<img>` element, but notice how the `ImageUrl` attribute is converted into the `src` attribute:

```
ImageUrl="~/azoreschurch.jpg"
```

The name of the file (or URL to the image) in the `ImageUrl` is converted to the `src` attribute:

```
src="azoreschurch.jpg"
```

If the file is local to the project, the file is prefixed with `~/` on the server side.

The `HyperLink` control also mapped fairly directly to its rendered equivalent, where the `NavigateUrl` is easily converted to the `href` attribute of the `a` tag.

In this simple example, you didn't really gain a lot from using server controls instead of coding the HTML, but bear in mind that this page is completely static. If you wanted to respond to user input, react to events, or obtain data from a database, you would need to use server-side code. Server controls make the process of working with visual elements on the server possible.

Types of Server Controls

Many of the ASP.NET server controls that exist are ASP.NET equivalents of HTML elements, so there is a text box, a button, a hyperlink, a drop-down list, and so on. These controls look like the elements that they will eventually be turned into, but there is more to them than that. Each control has a common set of properties (for example, they all have an ID, and controls such as the text box, label, and so on all have a Text property), which makes it easier to work with these controls in code. Having learned the different categories of controls earlier in this chapter, you can concentrate on some of the most commonly used controls as you tour the server controls you can add to a site.

Standard Controls

These controls are the Web equivalents of the tools that you encounter when using Windows applications. Web pages that include these controls have that standard application feel that we're all familiar with, so the process of adding them to pages is quick and simple. Here are some of the most commonly used controls:

- **TextBox control:** Used for entering text on a page, commonly seen on order forms on shopping sites, or for logging in to a site.
- **Button control:** From submitting an order to changing preferences on a web site, clicking a button on a page normally causes information to be sent to the server, which reacts to that information and displays a result.

- **Label control:** Used for displaying simple text in a specified position on a page. The `Label` control is an easy way to change the text on part of a page in response to user interaction.
- **Hyperlink control:** Used for providing hyperlink functionality on a page that enables navigation to other parts of a site, or to other resources on the Internet.
- **Image control:** Used for displaying images on a page. The server can change the image that is displayed in the control programmatically in response to user input.
- **DropDown List control:** Used for offering the user a list of options to choose from; collapses when not in use to save space.
- **Listbox control:** Used for offering a fixed-size list of items to choose from.
- **CheckBox and Radio Button controls:** Used for selecting optional extras with either a yes/no or "this one out of many" style, respectively.

Figure 3-28 shows the ASP.NET Web Site Administration Tool screen that you will learn to use in the next chapter for administering user accounts. On this screen, you'll see many of these controls in one place.

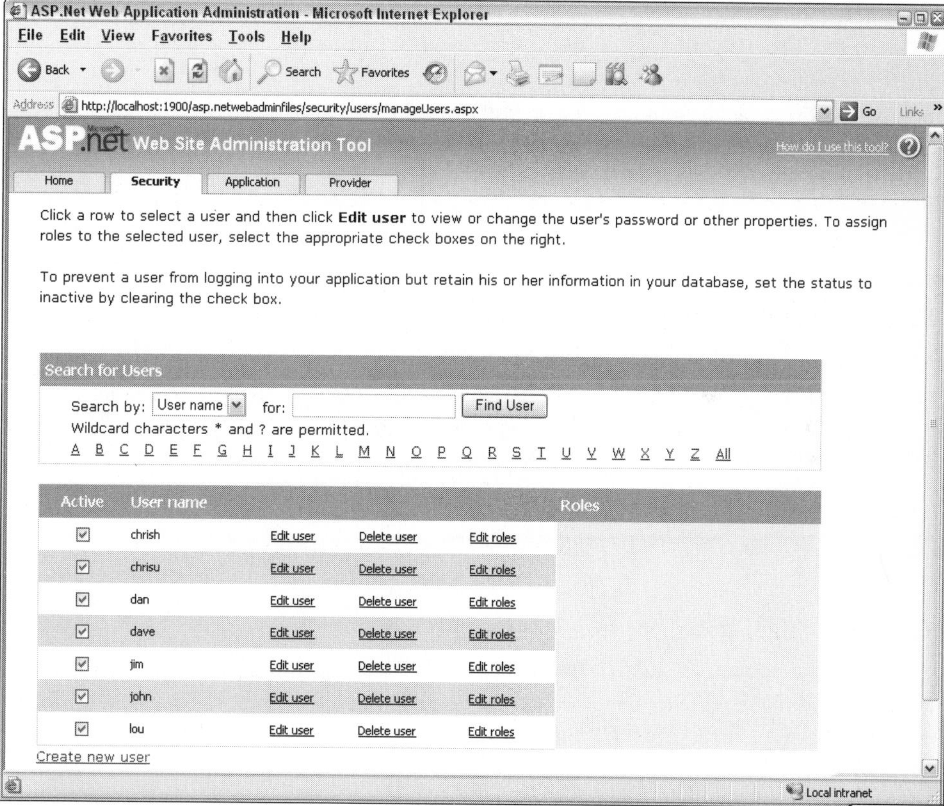

Figure 3-28

The `Search by:` label on the page is likely to be a `Label` control, and it's next to a `DropDownList` control. The `for:` label is next to a `TextBox`, which is next to a `Button` control. Next to each user name is a `CheckBox` control for selecting the user, and some `HyperLink` controls for managing the user account. In the next chapter, you'll become very familiar with this configuration application, and it's a great example of many types of controls all on one page.

HTML Controls

Often when you're creating a site, you don't need to do anything with a control on the server. In these situations, you might just want to add simple static HTML to part of a page; for example, just to position elements on a page or to provide a container for groups of elements. The HTML Control Toolbox contains drag-and-drop versions of the most commonly used HTML elements for this purpose. If you browse through this section of the Toolbox (see Figure 3-29), you'll notice HTML controls for client-side elements such as the Input (Text) box, the `Table` control, and the `Div` control.

Figure 3-29

The controls on the toolbar are just a handy way to add the most common HTML elements to a page, and you are not restricted to using only those HTML elements. In Source View, you can add any valid HTML element you like; for example, an anchor tag `<a>` for hyperlinks, or a `<span>` for highlighting text within a section of a page.

Elements such as the `Table` control and the `Div` control are containers and hence can contain other controls within their definitions. For example, in a `Table` control, you can have different controls nested within each table cell. Within a `Div` control, you can also place a wide variety of elements and controls. You can nest server-side controls within static, non-server HTML elements such as these for laying out a page.

HTML Controls as Server Controls

You can turn any HTML element into a server control by adding a `runat="server"` attribute to the element. As you'll see in Chapter 6, you can work with *any* server controls (HTML or ASP.NET) on a page dynamically using code when a page is submitted to the server. For example, after you add an ASP.NET `TextBox` control to a page, you can set the value to be displayed in the text area using code running on the server. However, after you add a `runat="server"` attribute (and give the element a unique ID) to, for example, a `div` element, you can then specify what the `div` should display and where it should be positioned on the page dynamically, using code running on the server.

Additionally, because you can add a `runat="server"` to *any* HTML element, you could use an `Input type="text"` control instead of the ASP.NET `TextBox` control if you like. The same goes for the other types of HTML elements that have direct equivalents in the ASP.NET Toolbox.

Should I Use HTML Controls or ASP.NET Server Controls?

This question only really relates to simple elements on a page, such as the text box, the button, tables, and so on. Complicated server controls such as the `Calendar` control exist to speed up development time for sites, so there's no real question of which to use in cases like these. The approach taken by most developers, when making the choice about which type of control to add to a page, is to use ASP.NET's standard-server controls for the majority of server-side controls on a page and static HTML elements for layout.

Although this works in most situations (and indeed you'll find that many situations require server controls where HTML controls simply can't offer the correct functionality), you may find exceptions to the rule. For example, adding `runat="server"` to HTML elements is a technique I often use with HTML `div`s or tables. If I know that I want to show or hide parts of a page depending on user input, I can convert those elements I need to work with on the server into server controls, and then dynamically toggle their visibility. Though it's also easy to create sites that offer the same functionality using standard server controls, the design team I work with only produces page layouts using simple HTML, so it's sometimes easier to convert some of those HTML elements to run on the server than it is to recode the site to use the built-in ASP.NET server controls. There is no real right or wrong approach here, so use your own judgment, but be aware that you may encounter code written by others that takes a different, but equally viable, approach.

Navigation Controls

The three out-of-the-box controls available for navigating a site provide a wealth of functionality for very little effort. Compare this to the situation that was in place previously for ASP.NET developers and you'll see that this is a big improvement — what would have previously been a couple of work items on a task list that might take a couple of hours each for a developer to code now takes a few seconds. The `Menu`, `TreeView`, and the `SiteMapPath` controls are new in ASP.NET 2.0, and are quick and simple to set up. Following is an overview of these controls. You'll add both of these controls to the Wrox United site later.

The SiteMapPath Control

This control is used to add breadcrumb functionality to a site, giving you a visual aid to remind you where you are in the site hierarchy. This is demonstrated in the Wrox United site, as shown in Figure 3-30.

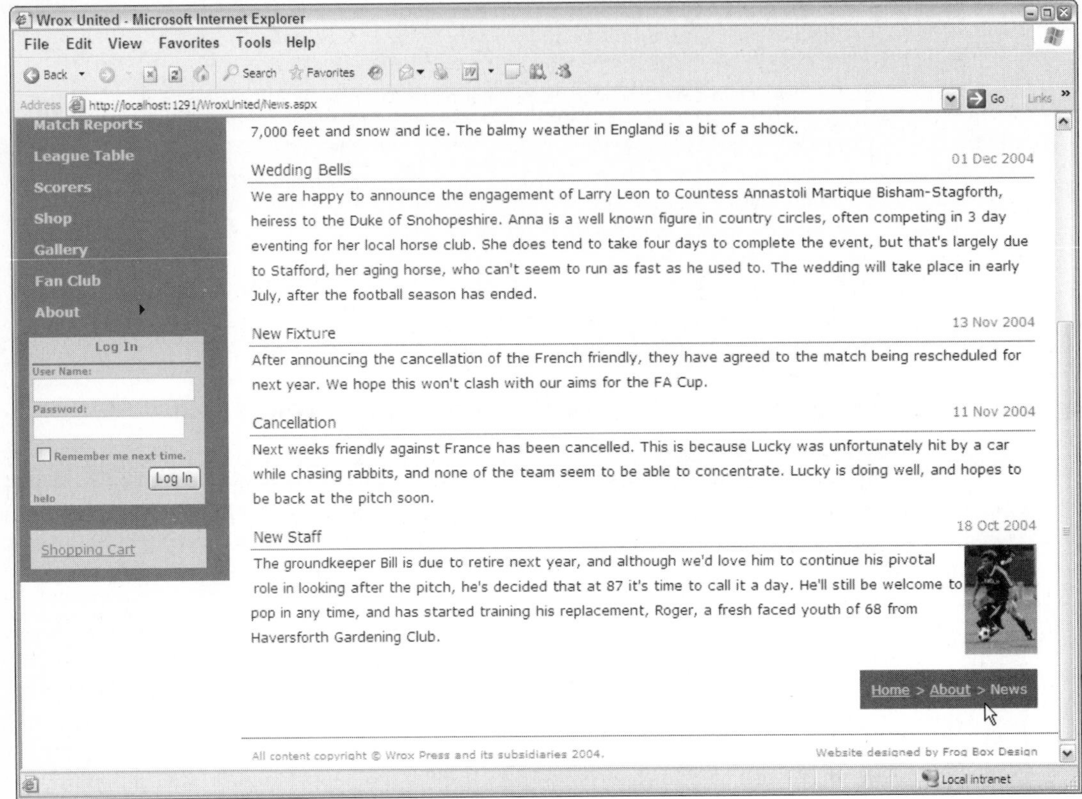

Figure 3-30

The term *breadcrumb* most likely comes from the old fairy tale of Hansel and Gretel — two children who went for an adventure in the woods, leaving a trail of breadcrumbs behind them to help them to find their way home. As you click through pages on a site, you may pass through to different sections and subsections of the site, until you are several links deep into an application. A breadcrumb helps you to go back to a specific point in your navigation path without having to rely on the back button on the browser. You may have encountered situations where you can't hit the back button to head back a link — a bit like a crow eating your breadcrumbs. Some pages submit information to the server in such a way that you can't go back without resending the information.

You'll find breadcrumb functionality available on many different sites across the Internet. One such site is the Wrox United site, as shown previously in Figure 3-30. However, in order to add one of these controls to the site, you need to have a `Web.SiteMap` file at hand. (Got one? Excellent! If not, you need to go back to Chapter 2 and learn how to create one.)

When you have a `Web.SiteMap` available to your application, adding a `SiteMapPath` control and seeing some results is easy — all you need to do is add it to a page. To add it to Wrox United, the best thing to do would be to add the control to the Master page so that all of the content pages will suddenly have breadcrumbs at their feet.

For this next Try It Out, you need to work with the Chapter03 version of the Wrox United application (stored within the `Chapter 03` folder in the code download as `WroxUnited`). This version of the site has been modified to enable you to try out these examples.

If you open the Chapter 3 version of the `WroxUnited` application as it stands, you'll see what's shown in Figure 3-31. If it doesn't look quite like the figure, don't worry — VWD has some problems displaying pages that use CSS, so you may see most of the site without having to scroll down.

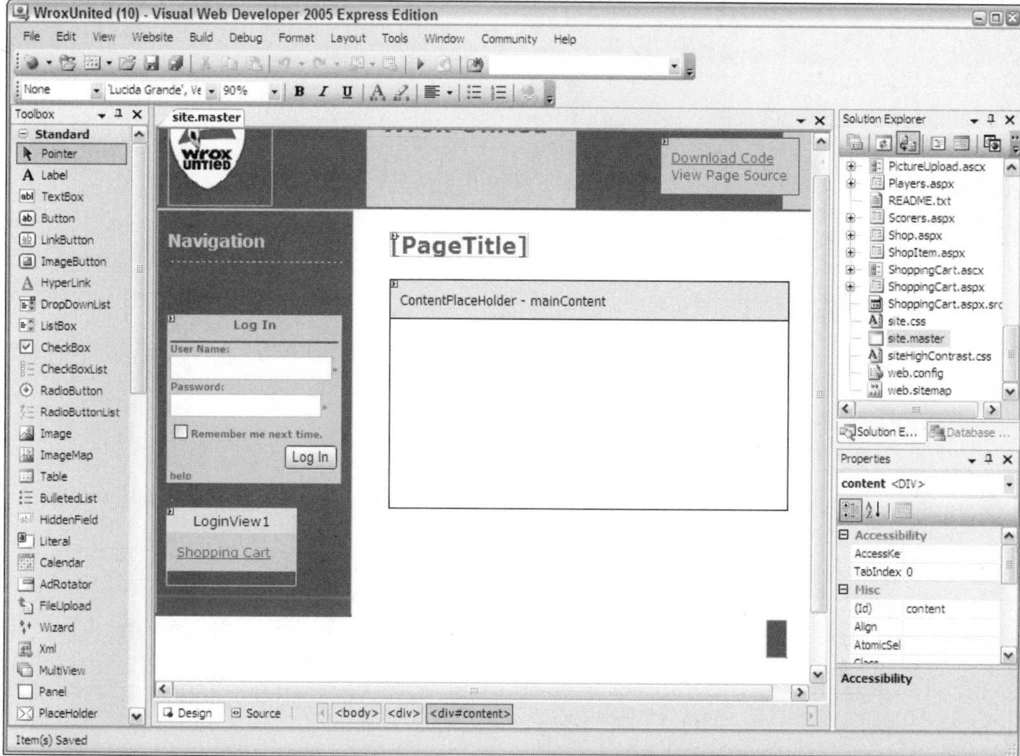

Figure 3-31

Although the site looks fairly normal, two things are missing: the links on the left of the page and the breadcrumbs at the bottom of the page. In the following Try It Out example, you'll add these to the site and see how simple it is to add navigation. Before running this example, close down the `Chapter03` project from Visual Web Developer.

Try It Out — Adding the SiteMapPath Control

1. Open the Chapter 3 version of the Wrox United application (`C:\BegASPNET2\Chapters\Begin\Chapter03\WroxUnited`) and open the `site.master` file. Make sure you're in Design View.

2. Place your cursor inside the Breadcrumbs `div` at the bottom of the page—it's the red blob in the bottom right of the page. You'll know when you've found the right spot when you see `<div#breadcrumbs>` highlighted at the bottom of the window, as shown in Figure 3-32.

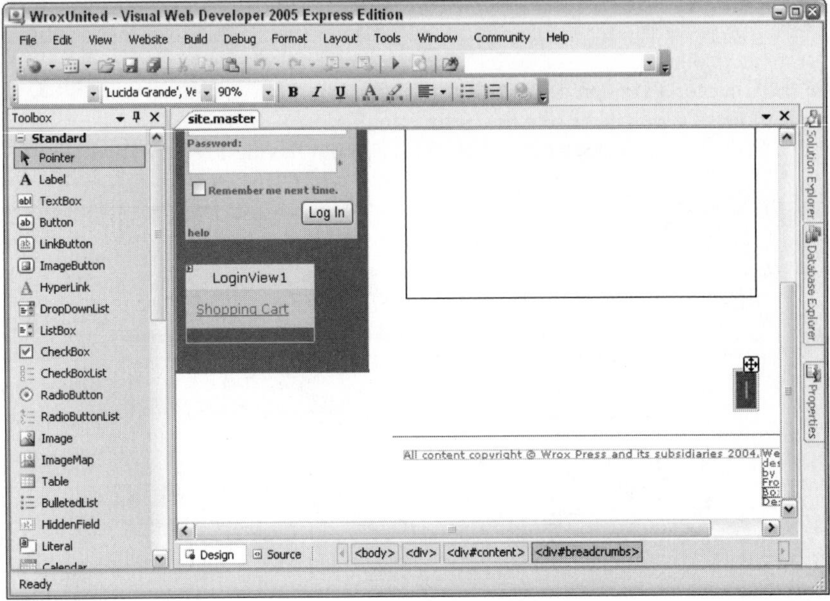

Figure 3-32

3. Now drag a `SiteMapPath` control into the Breadcrumbs `div` from the Navigation section of the Toolbox (see Figure 3-33).

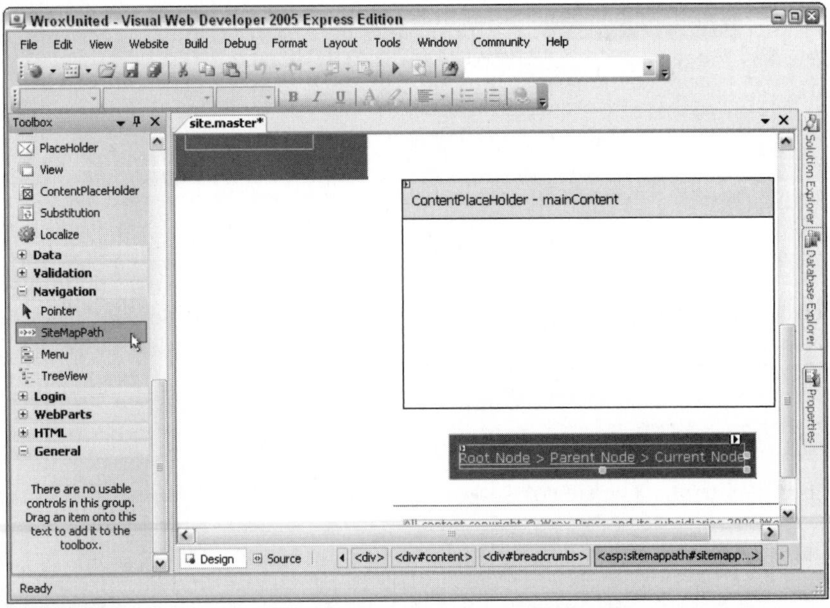

Figure 3-33

4. Ignore the Common Task menu on this one — the only modification to make here is to change the name of the control. Ensure that the `SiteMapPath` control is selected and change its ID to crumbs in the Properties panel. Notice the mouse cursor in Figure 3-34 highlights the ID property for the control.

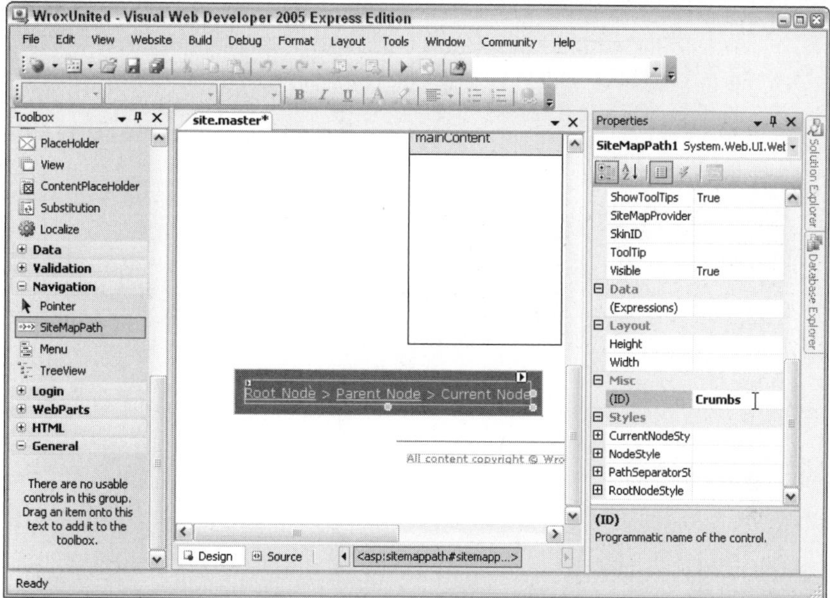

Figure 3-34

5. Run the site again by launching `Default.aspx` and see the results of your hard work down at the bottom of the page, as shown in Figure 3-35. Notice that the URL my browser is using is `http://localhost:1100/WroxUnited/`. Your port number (the bit after the colon) will be different.

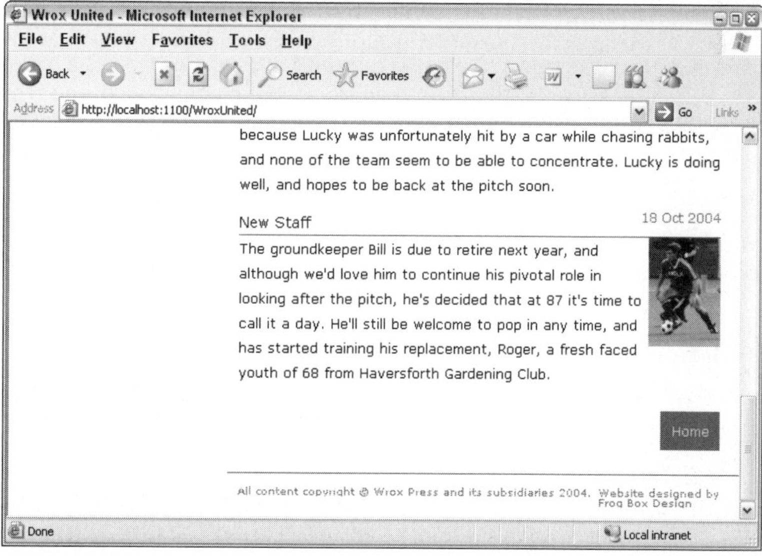

Figure 3-35

6. Browse to the History page by changing the `Default.aspx` part of the URL to `History.aspx`. Figure 3-36 shows how the rendered `SiteMapPath` control changes at the bottom of the page.

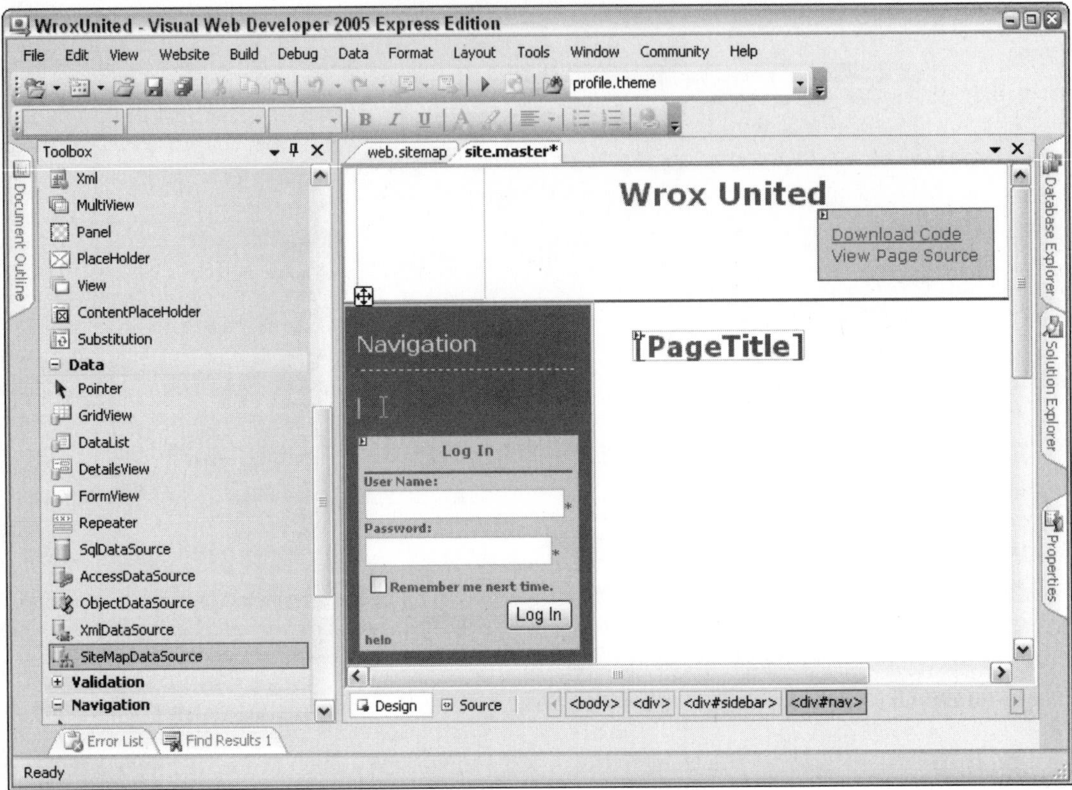

Figure 3-36

How It Works

In this example, you added a simple `SiteMapPath` control to a modified version of the Wrox United web site to give users some visual feedback as to which page is being viewed, and where in the site hierarchy that page resides. Adding the control to the page is enough to achieve this, because there is a `Web.SiteMap` file included in the application files.

The `SiteMapPath` control hooks in to the `Web.SiteMap` (if it exists) and renders content dynamically by figuring out which page the user is currently viewing, and where that page is situated in relation to the order of nodes in the site map. Here's the `Web.SiteMap` code that relates to the nodes you looked at:

```
<siteMap>
  <siteMapNode title="Home" url="Default.aspx"
               description="Wrox United Home Page">
...
    <siteMapNode title="About" description="About the club" url="about.aspx">
      <siteMapNode title="History" url="History.aspx"
                   description="The history of the club" />
```

Notice that the `History` node resides within the `About` node, which in turn resides within the `Home` node, so when you look at the `History` page, you know that the page below must be the `About` page, and the root node is the `Home` node — which is exactly what you saw on the `SiteMapPath` control:

```
Home > About > History
```

If you navigated to a different part of the hierarchy (to the Match Fixtures, Future Fixtures, or Past Fixtures page), the display would have changed appropriately. So, navigating to `Fixtures.aspx?type=future` would present the following:

```
Home > Fixtures > Future Fixtures
```

This is how the `SiteMapPath` control that was added to the page appears in code:

```
<div id="breadcrumbs">
  <asp:SiteMapPath ID="crumbs" runat="server">
   </asp:SiteMapPath>
</div>
```

Without customizing the control (no specific attributes have been set), the nodes are rendered. The style used for the control is controlled in the style sheet for the page. (Chapter 5 looks at styling pages.)

SiteMapPath Control Properties

In the previous Try It Out, you added a `SiteMapPath` control without modifying it and the list of nodes was displayed. If you'd modified it to change the number of levels displayed, it could have been used in quite a different way; perhaps to display the name of the current page in a header. For example:

```
<asp:SiteMapPath ID="PageTitle" Runat="server" ParentLevelsDisplayed="0">
</asp:SiteMapPath>
```

With this modification, the site map node would display only the name of the current page. In the case of `History.aspx`, the `SiteMapNode` would simply say `History`.

Another modification that could be made would be to change the path separator character. For example:

```
<asp:SiteMapPath ID="crumbs" runat="server" PathSeparator=" : ">
</asp:SiteMapPath>
```

Again, if you were then to navigate to the `History.aspx` page, you'd see the following:

```
Home : About : History
```

In addition to these two properties, you can set many other attributes to customize this control. The following table describes some of these properties in a bit more detail.

Attribute	Description	Options (default in bold)
RenderCurrentNodeAsLink	Specifies whether the active node is clickable, or whether the current node appears as plain text.	True / **False**
PathDirection	Sets whether the breadcrumbs appear in order from the root link to the current link (from left to right) or vice versa.	**RootToCurrent** / Current ToRoot
PathSeparator	Sets the character to use as the separator marker between nodes.	>, any ASCII character

Having looked at how the SiteMapPath control works, it's time to move on to look at the remaining two navigation controls: the Menu control and the TreeView control. To use these controls on a page, you need to add a different type of control to provide the data to these controls: the SiteMapDataSource control.

The SiteMapDataSource Control

This control is a non-visual control, and is used to expose the nodes defined in the Web.SiteMap file in a way that the Menu and TreeView controls can understand, and to make it possible to amend the content that these controls will display.

To add this control to a site, you only have to drag a copy onto a page. That's all there is to it. The code that's generated for you will appear as follows in Source View:

```
<asp:SiteMapDataSource ID="SiteMapDataSource1" runat="server" />
```

In the next Try It Out, you will do this for yourself so that you will be able to use the Menu control. The Menu control is used in the full Wrox United site to provide the means to navigate the Wrox United site, so you won't have to keep typing in links. Let's see how this works in connection with the SiteMapDataSource control.

The Menu Control

The Menu control provides a mixture of static and dynamic menu functionality. When you add this control to a page, you have the option of making the menu completely dynamic, so an entire navigational structure can be displayed in the menu, a bit like a Start menu. Alternatively, you can adopt a more traditional approach and opt for a fixed menu, or one mixing this functionality. The dynamic bits use client-side JavaScript that ASP.NET generates for you (again, without you having to lift a finger).

To add a menu control to the site, you first need to add the SiteMapDataSource control, which specifies what links your menu will have access to and the order in which they appear. You'll do both of these now in a Try It Out based on the WroxUnited application.

Try It Out — Adding a Menu Control to Wrox United

1. Open `site.Master` and switch to Design View. Position your cursor in the `nav` div on the left of the page, as shown in Figure 3-37.

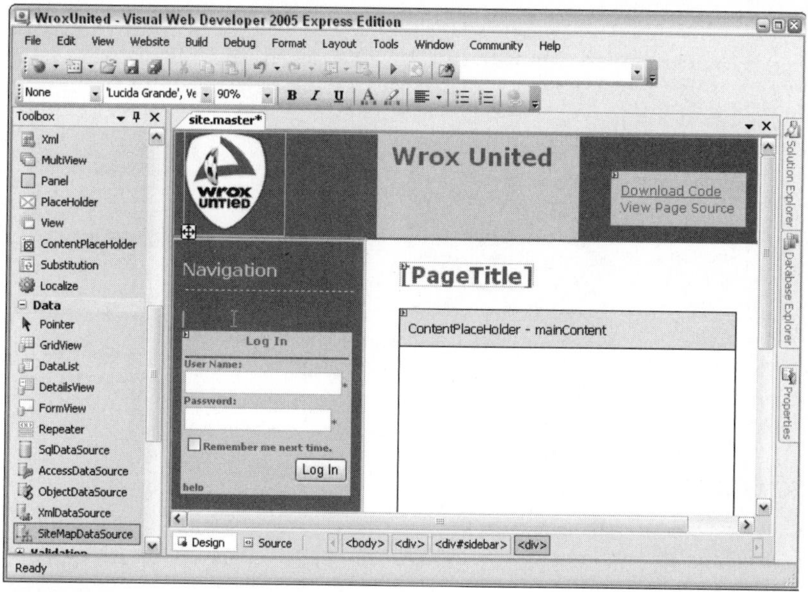

Figure 3-37

2. Drag a `SiteMapDataSource` control (highlighted on the left in Figures 3-38 and 3-39) onto the page inside the `nav` div (you'll find it hiding in the Data tool group on the Toolbox), and, in the Properties pane, rename the control **siteData**.

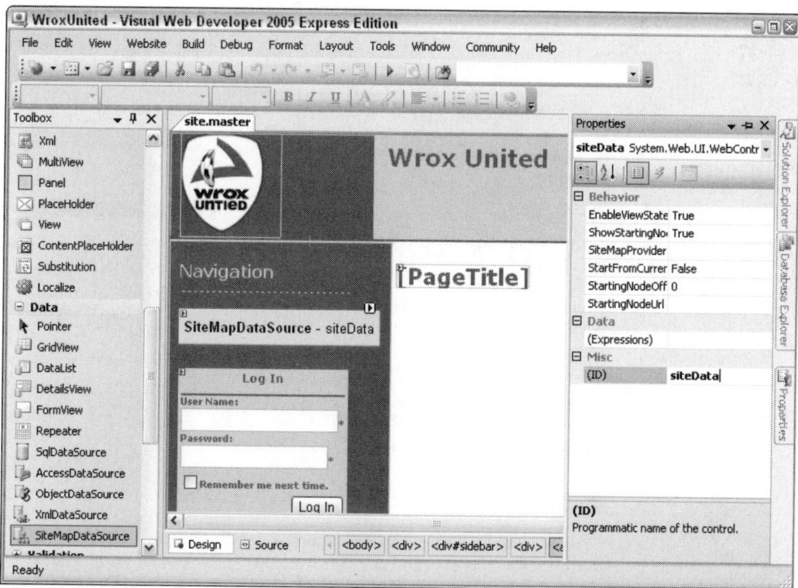

Figure 3-38

That's all the groundwork you need to do. Next, you'll add the `Menu` control itself.

3. Drag a `Menu` control onto the page next to the right edge of the `SiteMapDataSource` control. You will see a fly-out dialog box appear as shown in detail in Figure 3-39 — this is the Smart Tasks window.

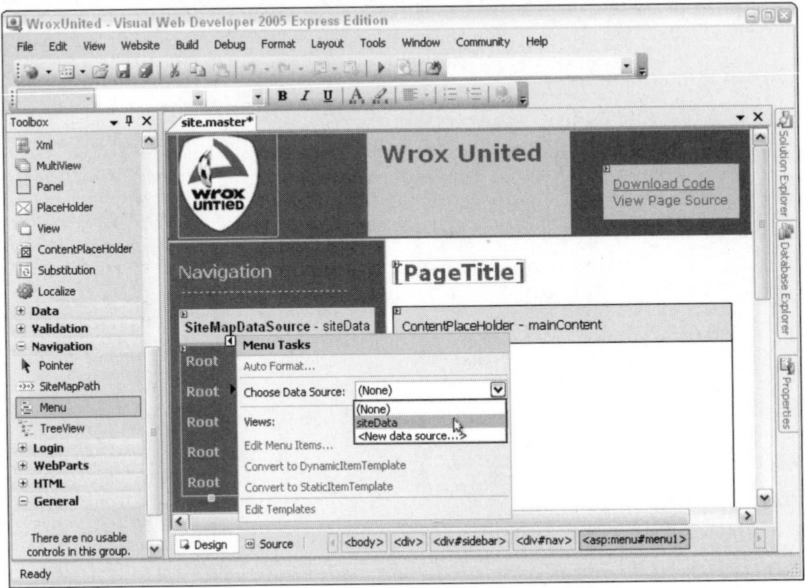

Figure 3-39

In the dialog box, choose the `siteData` data source that you generated in step 3. After this has been set, the menu will change as shown in Figure 3-40.

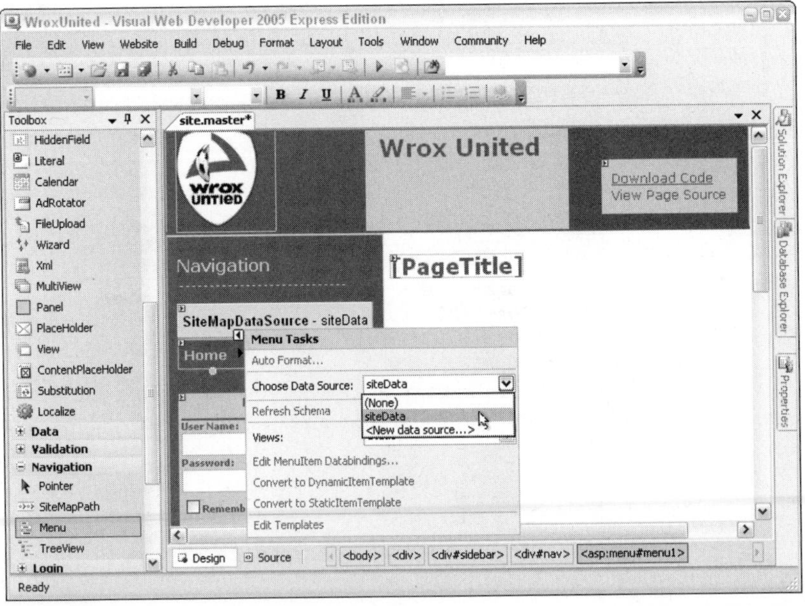

Figure 3-40

4. Click the small arrow at the top-right corner of the `Menu` control to close the pop-out menu. Now, with the menu selected, change the menu's `StaticDisplayLevels` to **2** using the Properties pane. You'll immediately notice a difference — have a look at Figure 3-41.

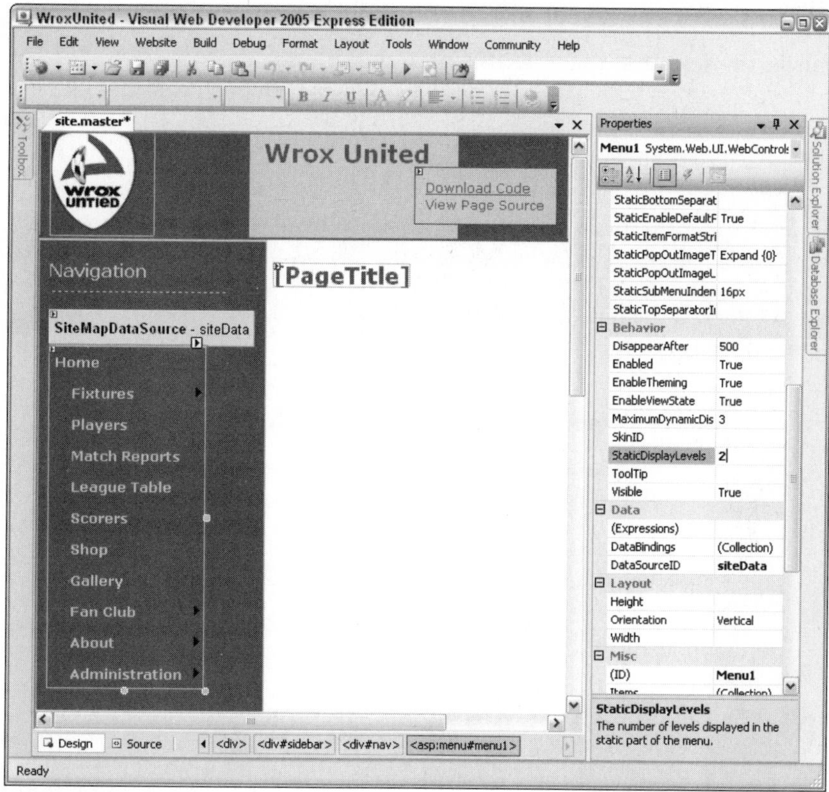

Figure 3-41

Note that if your links appear in red, rather than yellow, then you should switch to Source View and ensure that your `menu` control is within a div with an ID of `"nav"`:

```
<div id="sidebar">
  <h3>Navigation</h3>
    <div id="nav">
      <asp:SiteMapDataSource ID="siteData" runat="server" />
      <asp:Menu ID="Menu1" runat="server" DataSourceID="siteData"
                StaticDisplayLevels="2">
      </asp:Menu>
```

5. Some properties need to have values set before this control will work and behave as it does on the full version of Wrox United. Switch to Source View, and add the following properties in the code:

```
<asp:Menu ID="Menu1" runat="server" DataSourceID="siteData" StaticDisplayLevels="2"
      orientation="Vertical"
      StaticSubMenuIndent="0"
      disappearafter="200"
```

```
        AccessKey="m"
        EnableViewState="false">
        <DynamicMenuStyle CssClass="dynamicMenu" />
        <DynamicMenuItemStyle CssClass="dynamicMenuItem" />
</asp:Menu>
```

6. Run the site again and you'll see the screen shown in Figure 3-42.

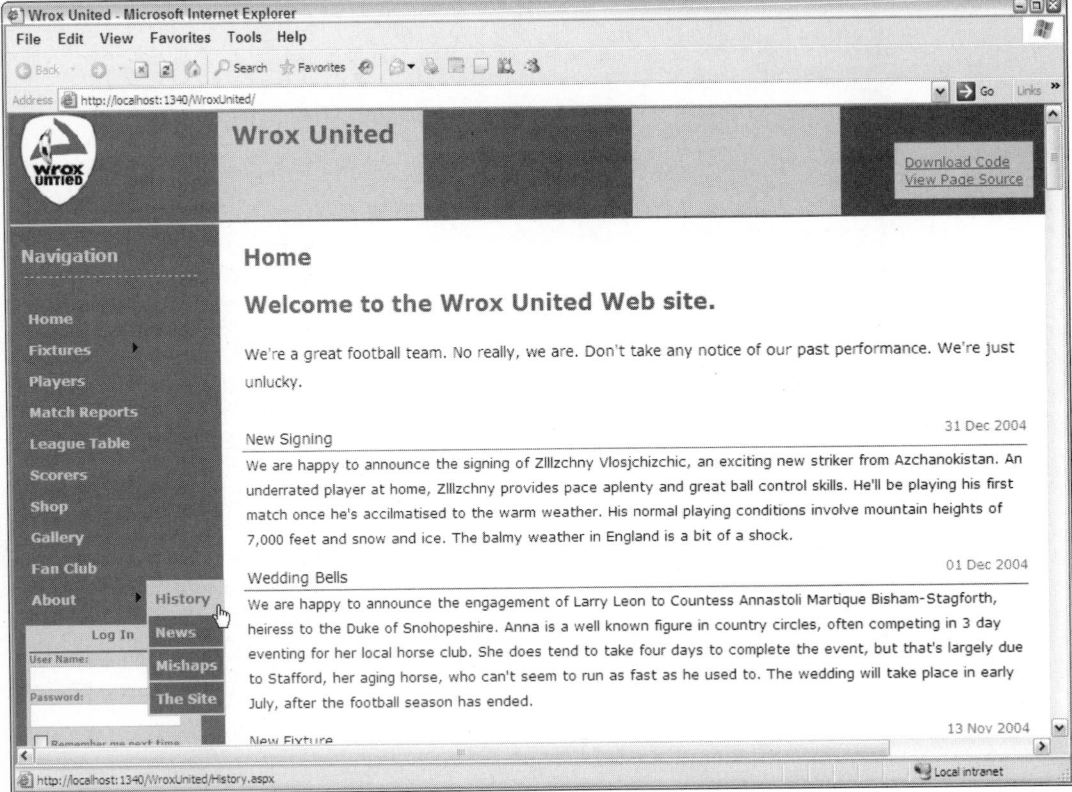

Figure 3-42

Notice that you can hover over the About link and a flyout appears with submenu items, including the History page, displayed. This is out-of-the-box dynamic functionality at its finest.

How It Works

The `Menu` control that was added to the Master page read the contents of the `SiteMapDataSource` control (`siteData`) and rendered a set of links corresponding to the data stored in that data source. The `SiteMapDataSource` itself required no customization (other than a quick renaming). By default, the `SiteMapDataSource` will read the `Web.SiteMap` file and act as a middle-man for the `menu` control so that it can display links corresponding to the contents of the `Web.SiteMap` file.

The `SiteMapDataSource` can be customized if required using the parameters described in the following table.

Property	Values	Result
EnableViewState	True/False	Specifies whether the SiteMapDataSource control retains its data on postbacks.
ShowStartingNode	True/False	Specifies whether the root node should be displayed on any control dependent on this data source.
SiteMapProvider	Any valid provider	Can be used to specify a custom provider (necessary if, for example, site map data is stored in a completely different structure such as a .csv file or a database instead of the Web.SiteMap file).
StartFromCurrentNode	True/False	If set to true, then only sublinks from the current node (active page) are shown, instead of the entire hierarchy.
StartingNodeOffset	Integer values	Used to shift the starting point of the hierarchy inward. This could be useful if you only want a Menu control to show submenu links, and not the full site structure. If the menu in Wrox United had this value set to 1, the menu would ignore all the first-level menu items, and only show the next level in the hierarchy. In the case of the Wrox United hierarchy, this would show the Future and Past Fixtures, History, News, and similar links.
StartingNodeUrl	String representing a URL of a page defined within the Web.SiteMap file	Used to specify a different point at which to start the hierarchy.

Binding a menu to a SiteMapDataSource control is a simple way to generate a hierarchy of links from the Web.SiteMap data file, but it is possible to do much more via this data source control, including binding to a completely different data source, and combining different controls (other than a menu) to the data. If you're the sort of person who has to work with site map information stored in a completely different format (other than Web.SiteMap), then in order to get a working SiteMapDataSource control, you'll need to have a custom SiteMapProvider class available. Creating custom providers is an involved process, which is beyond the scope of this chapter. For more information on this process, refer to *Professional ASP.NET 2.0*, by Bill Evjen, Wrox Press.

The Menu control itself was changed slightly in this example to include some additional property values. Here's a look at these values:

```
<asp:Menu ID="Menu1" runat="server" DataSourceID="siteData" StaticDisplayLevels="2"
       orientation="Vertical"
       StaticSubMenuIndent="0"
       disappearafter="200"
       AccessKey="m"
       EnableViewState="false">
       <DynamicMenuStyle CssClass="dynamicMenu" />
       <DynamicMenuItemStyle CssClass="dynamicMenuItem" />
</asp:Menu>
```

The additional attributes on the `Menu` control itself are fairly simple. The two on the first line in the listing (`DataSourceID` and `StaticDisplayLevels`) were set in the Properties pane in the example. The remaining attributes control the following:

- `Orientation`: Used to have a horizontal menu bar on a page.
- `StaticSubMenuIndent`: Controls the depth of indentation used to render submenu items, if the levels are set to appear in static mode.
- `DisappearAfter`: Dictates how long a flyout will remain visible before disappearing.
- `AccessKey`: Enables keyboard shortcuts for enhanced usability.
- `EnableViewState`: An ASP.NET feature that, if set to `true`, is used to maintain control state when a page is posted back to the server. This is used, for example, on text boxes, when submitting data to the server, for keeping the values in the text box when the page refreshes. This is unnecessary in this control, and will slightly improve page performance if disabled.

In addition to these attributes are two properties that help to define the visible style of the rendered control. `DynamicMenuStyle` controls the appearance of the flyout itself, and `DynamicMenuItemStyle` controls the appearance of the links. CSS controls the styling for these items. You'll learn more about this in Chapter 5.

There is just one last navigation control to consider in this chapter: the `TreeView` control. This control is very similar to the `Menu` control.

The TreeView Control

The `TreeView` and the `Menu` controls are very similar to implement, though the rendered experience is quite different. With a `TreeView` control, you end up with a user experience more akin to using Windows Explorer to work through the files stored on your file system, with expandable nodes that contain sublevels.

Deploying the control is similar to deploying a `Menu` control—you just drag it onto the page and select the `SiteMapDataSource` control to use to provide its data. If this control were used on the Wrox United site, it would appear as shown in Figure 3-43.

Notice that the Home node and the Fixtures nodes are expanded in the preceding view, though the About link is collapsed. If you replaced this control yourself, aside from some minor styling quirks, this could easily be used to navigate the site instead of the `Menu` control.

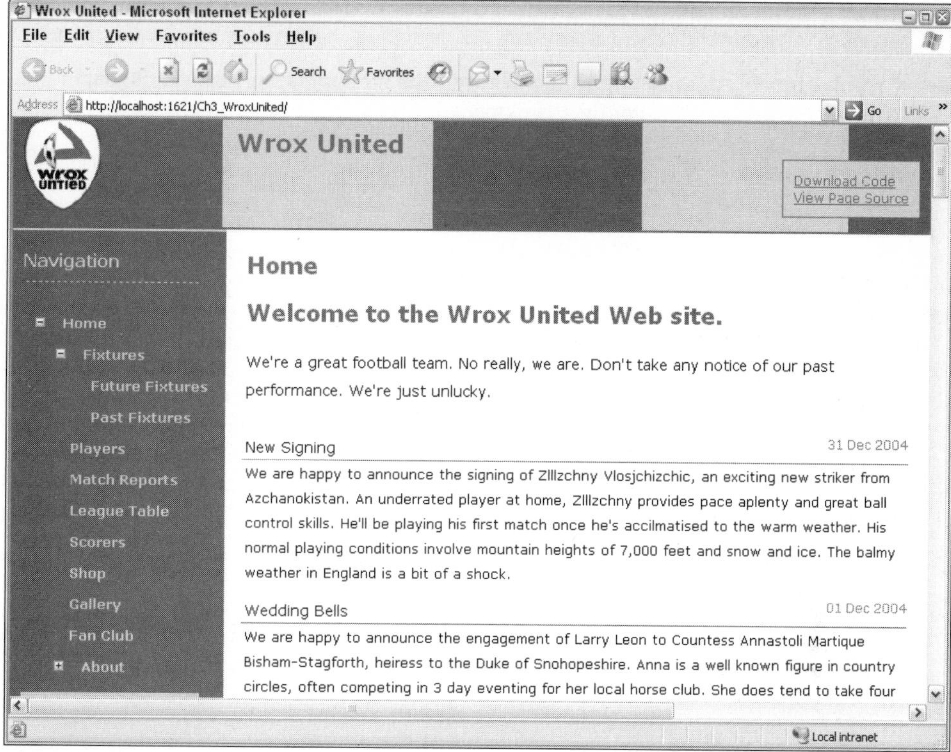

Figure 3-43

Summary

This chapter looked at the differences between code that the browser can understand and server controls, which the server can convert into a format that is displayable on the browser. In particular, you should now feel comfortable with the following facts:

- HTML is the language that the browser can understand, and is used throughout web programming to form the web pages we view on any site.
- XHTML is a version of HTML that follows a strict set of guidelines, with the aim that both current and future browsers will be able to speak the same language, thus removing some of the uncertainty when you're developing a web site.
- Client-side code and server-side code are two different entities. Server-side code is processed on the server, and is processed and turned into client-side code that the browser can understand.
- ASP.NET's server controls can be used to construct complex sites in a short time via the VWD environment, and can be added to a page either in Design View or in Source View.

- ❑ Server controls are converted (by the server) into HTML that the browser can understand, and JavaScript for dynamic client-side elements, provided the browser has JavaScript support.
- ❑ Complex functionality can be added to a web site for navigating around the pages in a site with minimal effort on the part of the developer.

The next chapter starts to look at how you can personalize a site by using server controls and some neat ASP.NET functionality to log in to the web site.

Exercises

These exercises are designed to help you get more comfortable with the VWD interface. The sample code (available from `www.wrox.com`) is an end solution, but you'll obviously gain more knowledge and understanding by trying out these exercises for yourself. Answers to these exercises are in Appendix A.

1. Practice using the drag-and-drop functionality of VWD to put together a simple web page that displays the following information:
    - ❑ The WroxUnited Logo (available for free download from `www.wrox.com`), or just use any small image of your choice.
    - ❑ The names of the players and some information about each of them, arranged in a table, as shown in Figure 3-44.

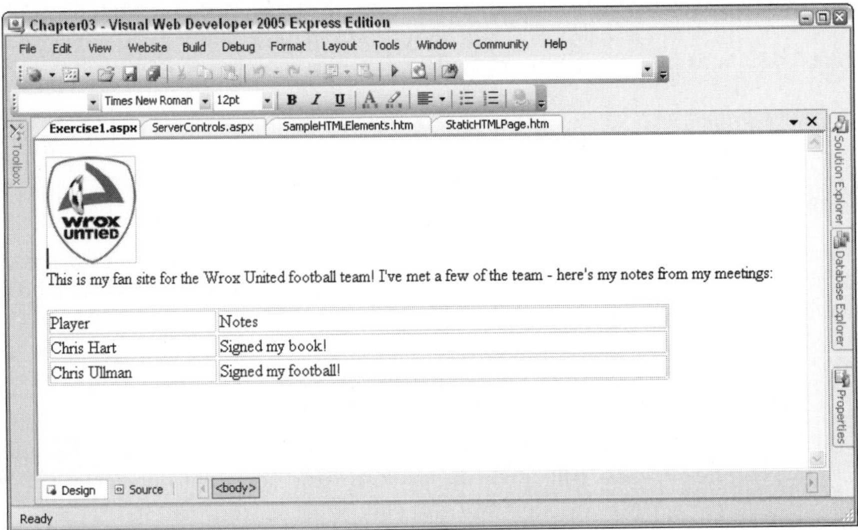

Figure 3-44

2. Return to Wrox United and go to the Master page. Try deleting the `Menu` control and replacing it with a `TreeView` control. Bind that control to the `siteData` data source, and you should see a fully populated tree of items, both in Design View (shown in Figure 3-45) and when you run the page (shown previously in Figure 3-43).

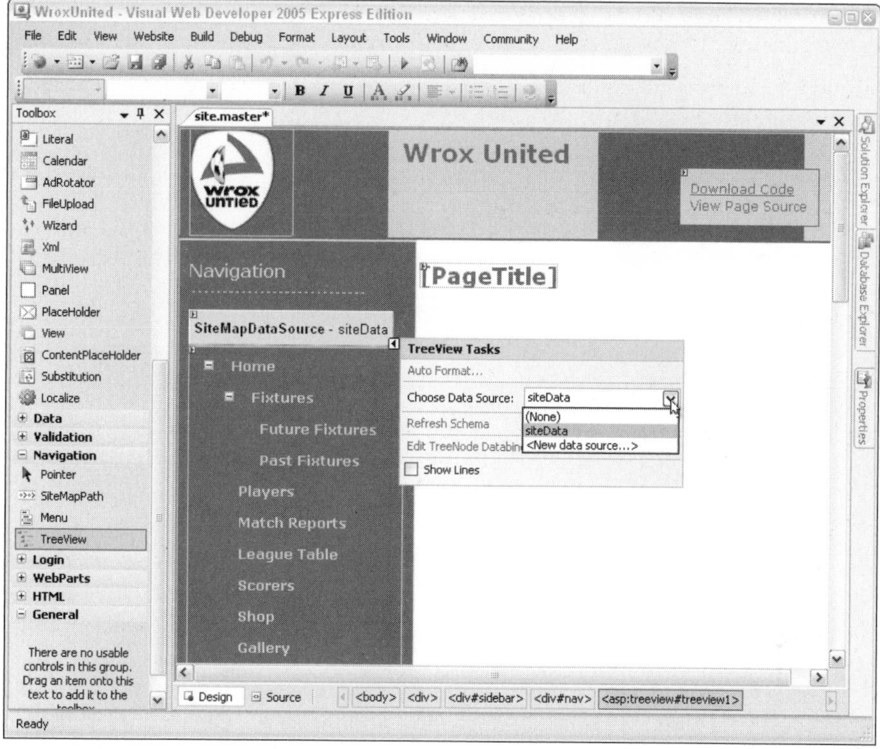
WroxUnited - Visual Web Developer 2005 Express Edition
File Edit View Website Build Debug Format Layout Tools Window Community Help
Toolbox
Literal
Calendar
AdRotator
FileUpload
Wizard
Xml
MultiView
Panel
PlaceHolder
View
ContentPlaceHolder
Substitution
Localize
Data
Validation
Navigation
Pointer
SiteMapPath
Menu
TreeView
Login
WebParts
HTML
General
There are no usable controls in this group. Drag an item onto this text to add it to the toolbox.
site.master*
Wrox United
Download Code
View Page Source
Navigation
[PageTitle]
SiteMapDataSource - siteData
Home
Fixtures
Future Fixtures
Past Fixtures
Players
Match Reports
League Table
Scorers
Shop
Gallery
TreeView Tasks
Auto Format...
Choose Data Source: siteData
Refresh Schema
Edit TreeNode Databin
(None)
siteData
<New data source...>
Show Lines
Solution Explorer
Database Explorer
Properties
Design
Source
<body> <div> <div#sidebar> <div#nav> <asp:treeview#treeview1>
Ready

Figure 3-45

Membership and Identity

The concept of membership appeals to human beings on a low level, and stems from the sense of wanting to belong to a group. We want to feel part of the team, and for others to know who we are, so it was only a matter of time before the Web jumped on the bandwagon and adopted this concept as a way of life. If you sit down and consider how many web sites you have logged in to and stored a simple user profile, you may find that you're a member of many more groups than you first imagined. From sites that sell books and gadgets to community sites that discuss the merits of owning a Ford Puma, or that enthuse about a BBC TV comedy show called *Look Around You*, I know I'm a member of far too many sites to name. And then there is the familiar dilemma of "which username and password do I use to log in to this site?"

One of the most successful sites on the Web, Amazon.com, started life as a bookstore, but has evolved into something much larger. When you log in to Amazon now, you find entire pages on the site that offer only those items related to your spending habits.

In this chapter, you learn how to personalize sites using some of the membership features available to ASP.NET 2.0. This chapter discusses the following:

- The concepts of identity, authentication, and authorization
- The membership server controls, including the `Login` control
- Storing member profiles so that they can be retrieved
- Restricting access to certain areas of a site to allow only specified members
- Personalizing a site based on the active user profile

You'll also extend the Wrox United sample application so that you can log in to the site and personalize the site according to a set of stored preferences based on the membership profile.

Security Basics

You need to feel comfortable with some key important concepts before you start to put together web applications involving membership, and those are the concepts of identity, authentication, and authorization.

Identity — Who Am I?

When you think of your identity, you can use several unique features to describe yourself. For example, you may be a woman with blonde hair who enjoys watching sci-fi shows and building PCs, but that's not necessarily of interest to someone who is interested in my skills on the badminton court. Identity information stored on a web site will likely be tailored to only relevant aspects of a person. For example, a shopping web site can store your name, telephone number, e-mail address, and home address, which are all facts that are relevant to the sale of goods. They may not care about your interests (unless they are as big as Amazon), so they won't need to store that sort of information about you, but that doesn't stop you from having those aspects of your identity.

So your identity, the concept of who you are, is a collection of a wide range of facts. You may even have a résumé (or CV as we Brits call it) that puts many of these facts down on paper, but these facts again are only those relevant to potential employers. It's up to you to decide which facts to store on your résumé, and which facts to leave off. The same is true when you store membership information about members on a web site in that you should choose which facts you need to know about the members of a site early in the development process.

Authentication — This Is Who I Am

When you attempt to log in to a web site, you pass in certain credentials; for example, an e-mail address and password combination. The web site then has to determine that you are who you claim to be, so the e-mail address and password combination that you enter must match the combination stored on file on the server for the specified e-mail address.

The process of *authentication* is all about proving you are who you say you are. The e-mail and password combination is a tried and tested method adopted by many of the web sites out there offering retail or community services, and although it's not bulletproof, as long as you choose a strong enough password and don't tell it to anyone, and as long as the site is coded well, your profile will be kept unique for your use only.

Authorization — This Is What I Can Do

After you pass in your username and password to a web site, the web server then not only verifies that the password matches the username, but it also checks to see what permissions you have been granted by the webmaster of that site. The next step from authentication is *authorization*, and this is the process of retrieving more information about the type of user account you have with a site.

Take, for example, a banking web site. After your login credentials are verified, the server looks to see what level of access you have to the site. Like most users of a bank site, you'll be authorized to check your balances and perhaps transfer money between accounts or pay bills. If, however, the bank was the victim of a security scare (like many *phishing* e-mails circulating around the Internet), you may find that you suddenly lack permission to add third-party standing orders to your account via the online application until the security issues have been resolved. This switching off of functionality may well be controlled by the administrators of the server by setting a special flag against either a subset of users or all users, stating that they no longer have authority to amend their account details.

Logging In to a Site

The process of logging in to a site, from a user's perspective, is a case of entering a set of credentials, and then being shown a different user interface corresponding to your profile. Commonly, this will happen by username and password combination; however, more secure sites, such as banking web sites, can use other methods of logging in, including PINs and security certificates. The general principle of authentication remains the same, though, regardless of the method used to pass those authentication credentials to the server. And after you're authenticated, it's a simple matter to inquire about whether you have the required level of access for the resource you're looking for via the authentication mechanism.

ASP.NET Security

ASP.NET 2.0 has some great tools available to help with implementing a login-authentication-authorization framework with minimal effort. In previous editions of ASP.NET, you would have to write code to implement a login framework, to authenticate against a database, and to react to the currently logged-in user. Though you will still eventually find yourself having to write code for working with users (as you'll discover in later chapters), a lot of the pain of the initial process has been taken away with the inclusion of some great controls and wizards. In this section, you learn more about the server controls available for working with logins, and the ASP.NET Web Application Configuration utility.

Login Controls

In this section, you start the process of building up a simple mock web site with just two pages; a `Default.aspx` as the front page and a `login.aspx` page for logging in to the site. You'll work through a series of steps using Try It Out examples, and then pause along the way to look at what's going on behind the scenes. Later in this chapter, you'll take some of these principles and apply them to the Wrox United web site to integrate the login framework into that application.

This section introduces the following controls:

- The `Login` control, which provides text boxes, buttons, and built-in validation to enable you to add login functionality to a page with a single drag-and-drop operation.
- The `LoginView` control, which provides a way of altering the appearance of the page dependent on whether a user is logged in or not, or showing different content to different groups of users.
- The `LoginStatus` control, which gives a simple bit of feedback to users so that they know whether they have remembered to log in to the site.

In the following Try It Out, you put some of these controls to use. This example builds up the skeleton site by creating the pages and adding the login controls.

Try It Out — Personalized Site: Web Page Design

1. Open VWD and create a new blank web site in your `C:\BegASPNET2\Chapters\Begin` directory called **Chapter04**. By default, you should have a page called `Default.aspx` already added to the project, as shown in Figure 4-1.

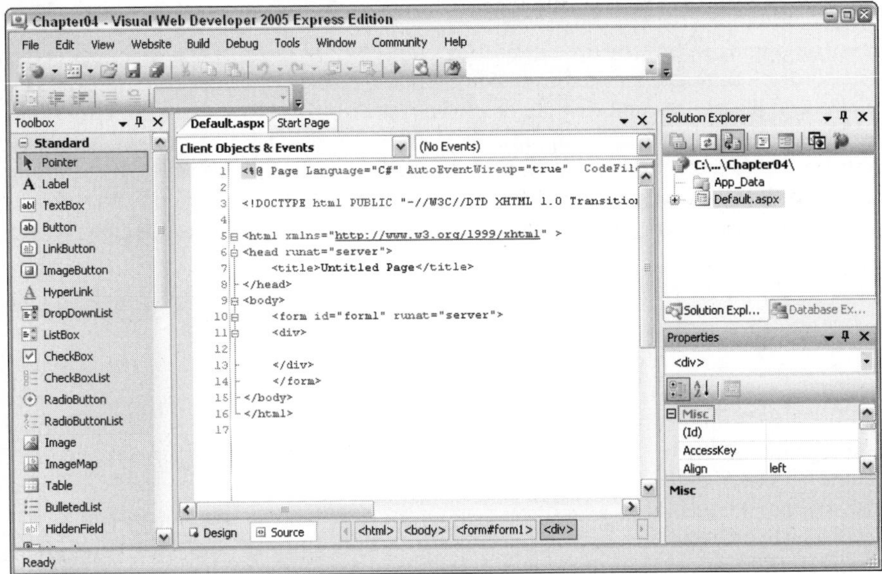

Figure 4-1

2. Time to add some controls. Switch to Design View, drag on a `LoginView` control from the Login controls section of the Toolbox (see Figure 4-2). In the Common Tasks menu that appears, ensure that Anonymous Template is selected and type **You are not logged in** in the main box.

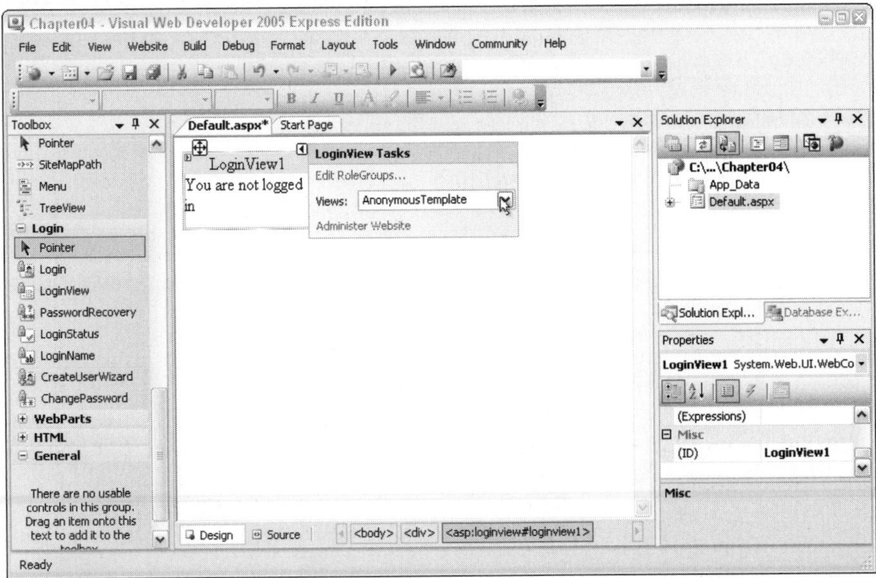

Figure 4-2

3. Pop out the Common Tasks menu again by clicking the small arrow in the top right and select LoggedInTemplate from the drop-down list, then type **You are logged in** in the box. This will ensure that the page will tell you when you're logged in or not.

4. Drag a `LoginStatus` control onto the page underneath the `LoginView` control, as shown in Figure 4-3. This control will give you a hyperlink to either log in or log out, depending on whether or not you're currently logged in.

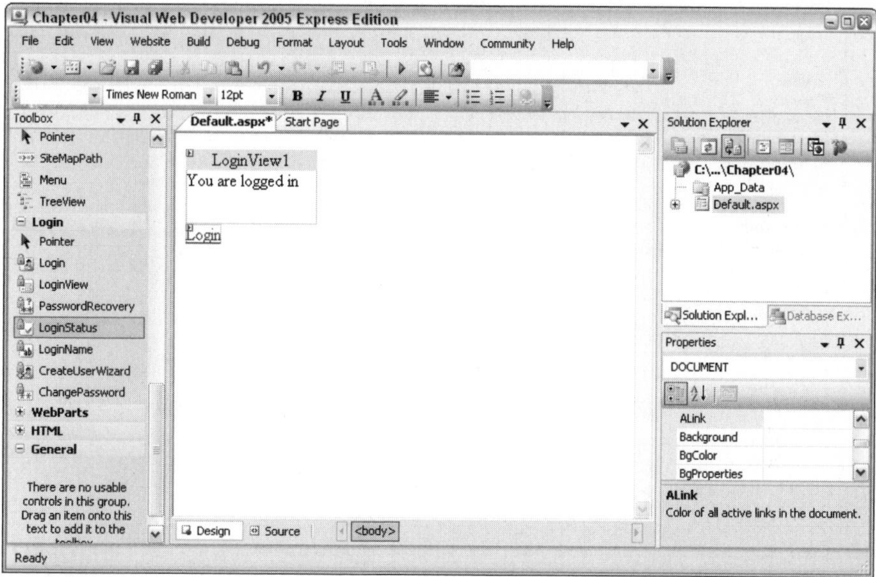

Figure 4-3

5. The next step is to create a login page, so right-click the root of the web site in the Solution Explorer and select Add New Item. In the dialog box that appears, depicted in Figure 4-4, select Web Form and call it **Login.aspx**.

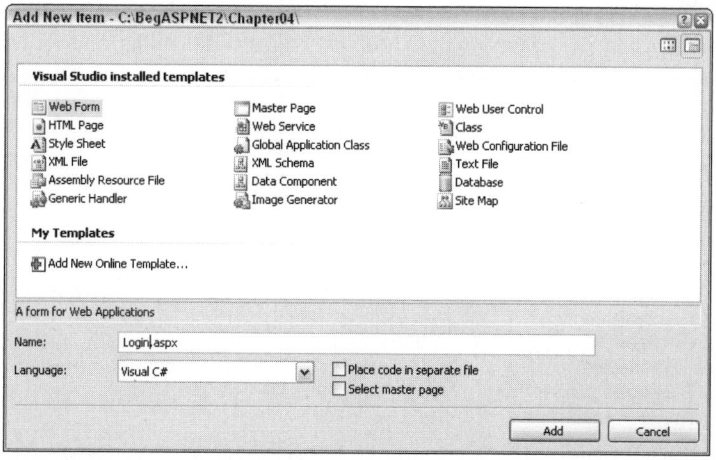

Figure 4-4

6. In the newly created page, switch to Design View and drag a `Login` control onto the page from the Login section of the Toolbox, as shown in Figure 4-5.

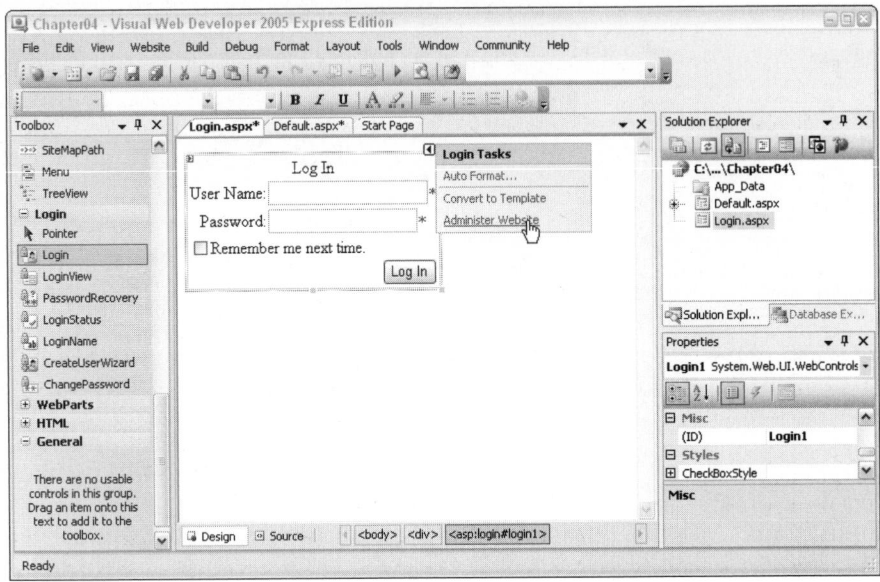

Figure 4-5

7. In the flyout that appears, you have the option of administering the web site. At this stage, you have the framework ready to roll, but you'll need to configure the site by adding some user accounts before the site will work, so click the Administer Website link in the flyout to launch the ASP.NET Web Application Configuration Tool, which is covered in the next Try It Out example.

How It Works

These controls are quite powerful, and although you're not quite at the stage of running the example, you can feel confident that you're only a few steps away from having a fully functional (if a little simplistic) application for trying out login functionality. These controls are a new addition to this edition of ASP.NET. Previously, you would have had to add text boxes and buttons, and write lines of VB.NET or C# code to handle the login process, to display messages relating to whether or not you are logged on, and to change the view of the page depending on the current user. At this stage, all you've had to do is drag and drop a couple of controls onto a page, and you'll be pleased to know that this is all you need to do to get the framework of an application together.

First take a look at the controls that were added to the pages, starting with the `Default.aspx` page.

Viewing the source on `Default.aspx` displays the following code:

```
<asp:LoginView ID="LoginView1" Runat="server">
  <LoggedInTemplate>
    You are logged in
  </LoggedInTemplate>
  <AnonymousTemplate>
```

```
    You are not logged in.
  </AnonymousTemplate>
</asp:LoginView>
<asp:LoginStatus ID="LoginStatus1" Runat="server" />
```

You can see that two controls are defined in the code: a `LoginView` control for displaying login information and a `LoginStatus` control that can be used to control the login and logout processes. Note that if you configured your site as in this example, you will not see the anonymous template message because anonymous users are denied access to the site (and are redirected straight to the login page).

In the `Login.aspx` page, you will see the following code has been added:

```
<asp:Login ID="Login1" Runat="server">
</asp:Login>
```

Everything has been pre-written, so you don't see any text boxes, and you don't see any validation code—you just see a single line of code. ASP.NET 2.0 has tools available so that you can actually create complex controls like this yourself, but that's a bit beyond this chapter.

Try It Out Personalized Site: User Account Configuration

When you click the administration link in step 7 of the previous Try It Out, the web page shown in Figure 4-6 is displayed (note that the port number used will be different whenever you launch this for the first time).

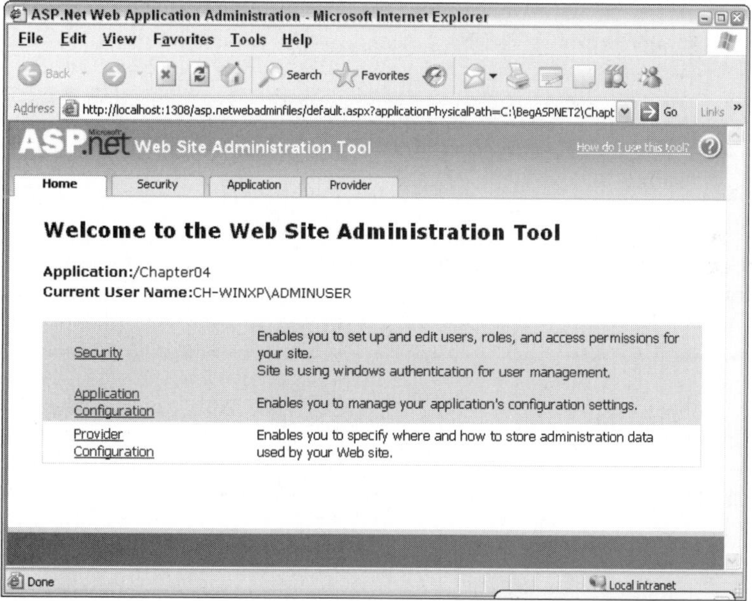

Figure 4-6

Now follow these steps:

1. Click the Security link to take you to the Security settings administration tab, shown in Figure 4-7.

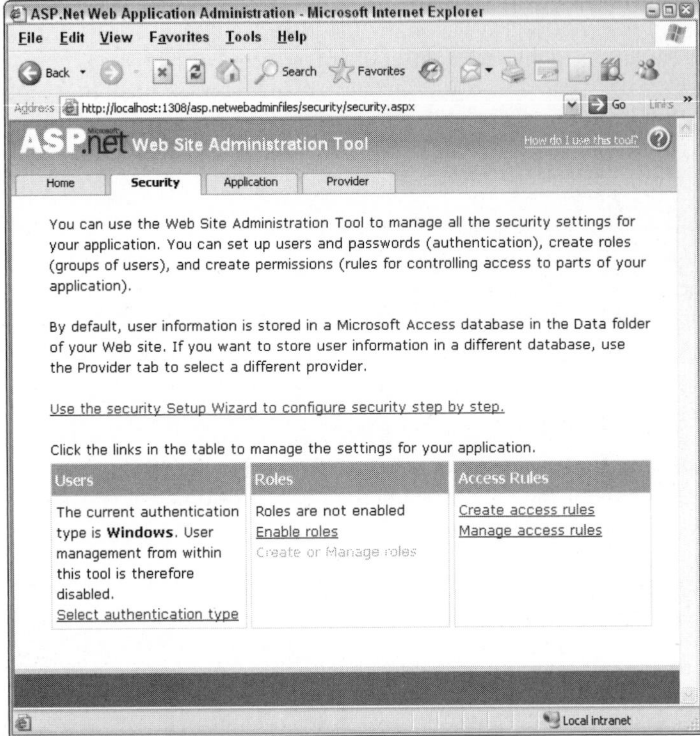

Figure 4-7

2. In this page you will see a hyperlink that enables you to launch the Security Setup Wizard. Click this link to proceed to the first stage in the wizard, as depicted in Figure 4-8.

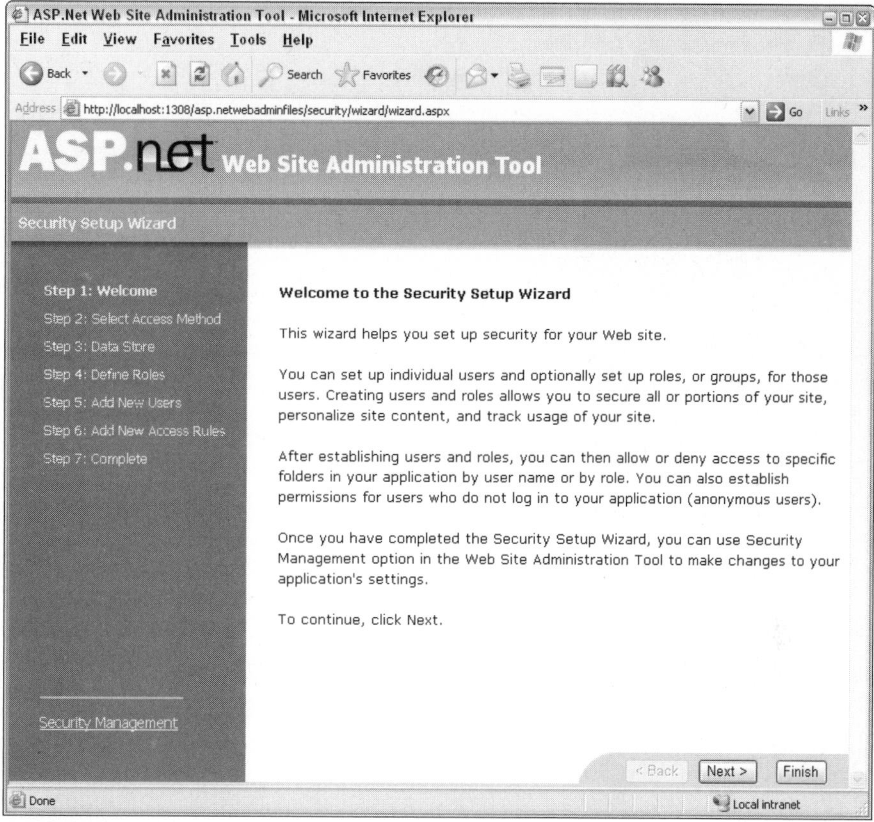

Figure 4-8

3. Click Next to skip past the first page, and you'll arrive at the screen shown in Figure 4-9. Select the From the Internet radio button to enable both anonymous users and users who have to log in via the web.

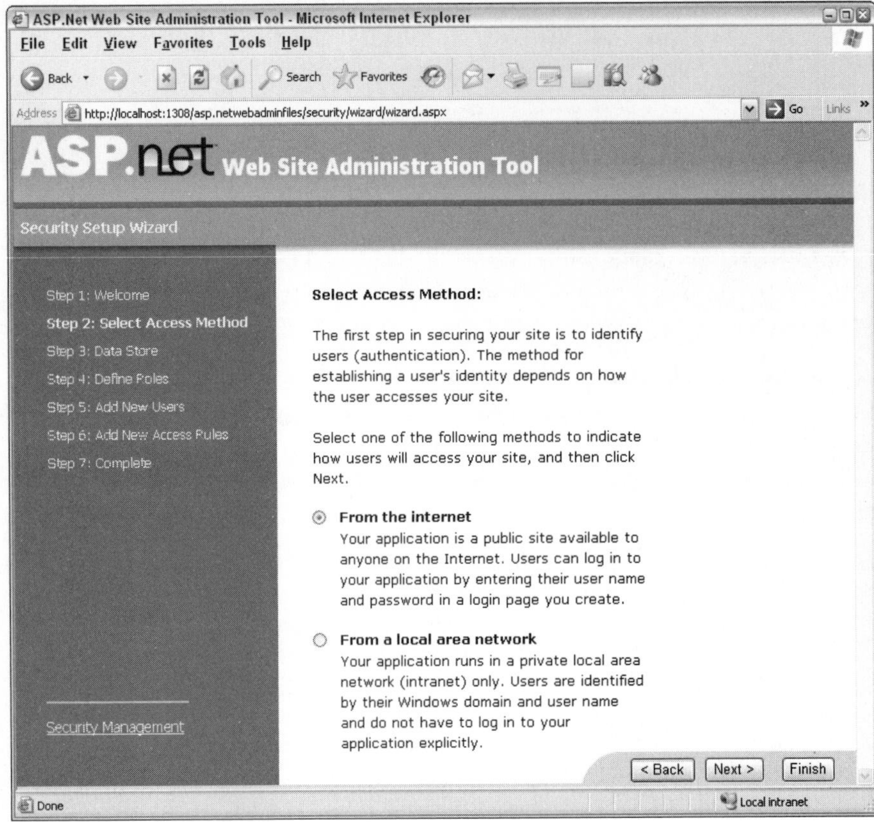

Figure 4-9

Click Next to continue to the next screen, displayed in Figure 4-10.

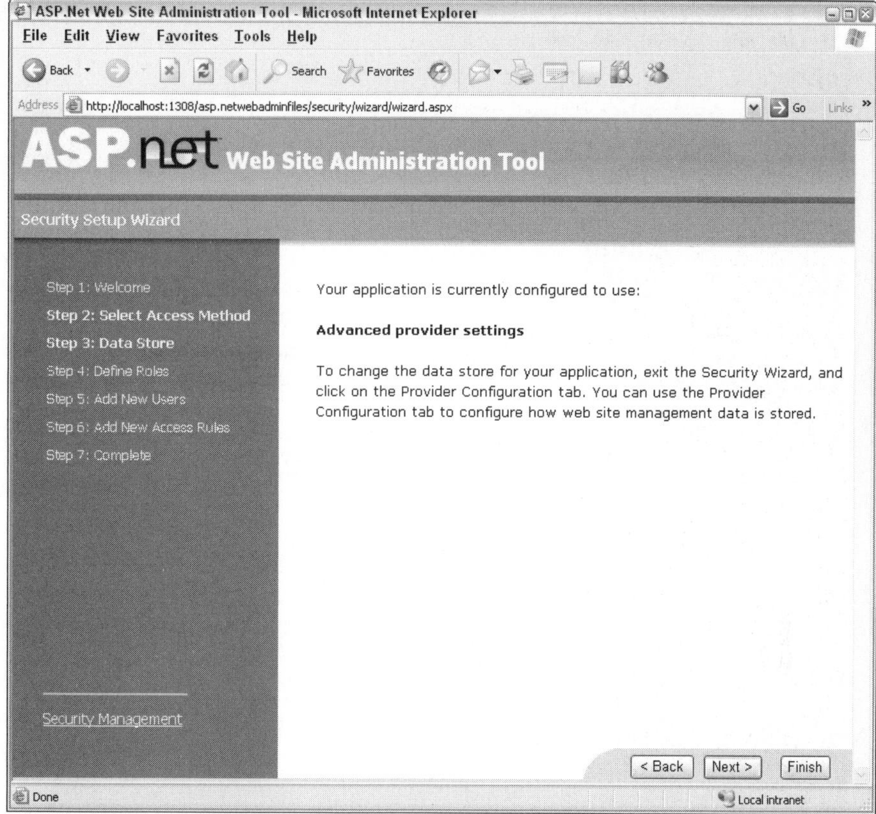

Figure 4-10

You can skip straight past this step and click Next to continue — the default provider will enable all of the required functionality without additional work. In the next screen, you are asked if you want to define any roles for the web site. In this example, you can skip this step — you will be defining roles later in this chapter. Keep the check box unchecked and click Next.

4. When you reach the screen shown in Figure 4-11, you will be prompted to enter some details for a user.

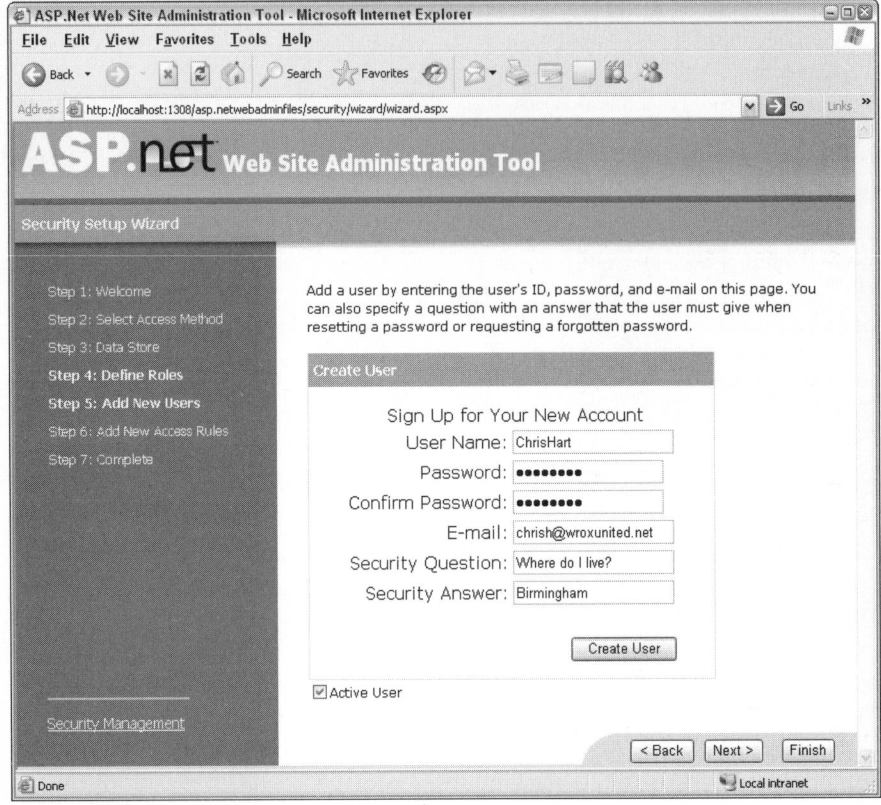

Figure 4-11

5. As shown in Figure 4-12, enter some details for a user of the site — these could be your name, my name, anyone's name. Just make sure you don't forget the password you enter — you'll need this later. Clicking the Create User button shows a confirmation prompt, at which point you can click Continue to create another user. At this stage, you should create two users — one standard user and one that you'll use later as the administrator of the site.

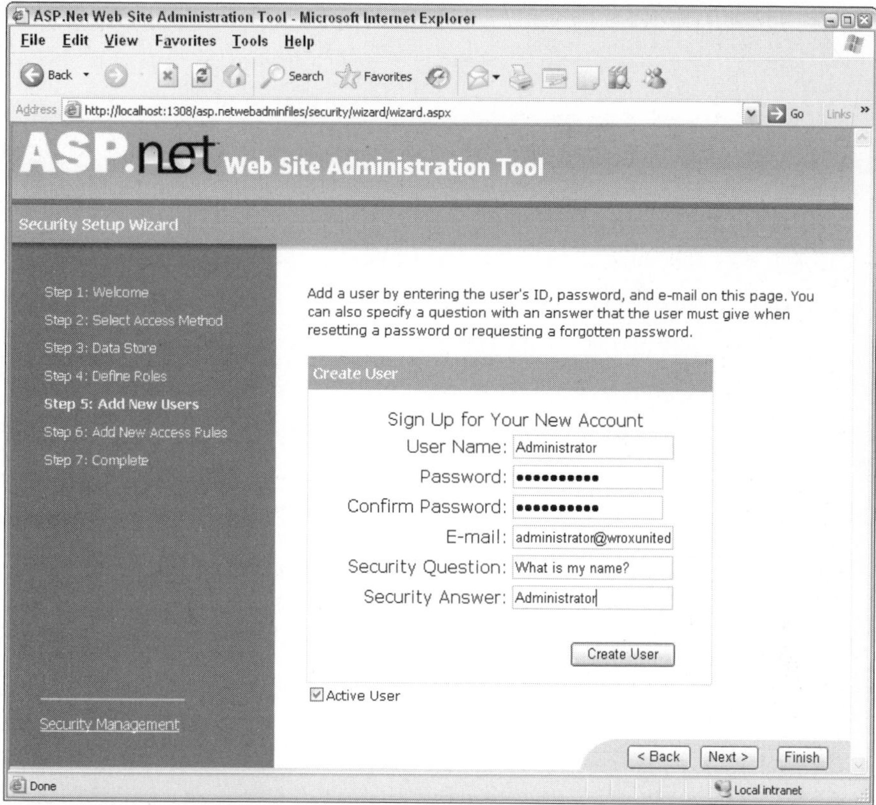

Figure 4-12

Later, you'll be able to give these users appropriate access permissions for the site. Note that you don't get the option to make these users members of any roles at this stage — this is done later in the setup process. Click Next to continue.

6. The next step is to define the accessibility levels for the site, defining who is able to see the content of the site, and who is denied access. At this stage, you can add permissions to users directly. Later, you will add those users to groups and assign rights and permissions to entire groups of people. As illustrated in Figure 4-13, you need to grant the Allow permission to each user individually, and deny access to all anonymous users. To set permissions for a user, select the User radio button, enter the username in the box next to the radio button, select Allow, and click Add This Rule. To deny access to anonymous users, select the Anonymous Users radio button, click Deny in the Permission section, and click Add This Rule.

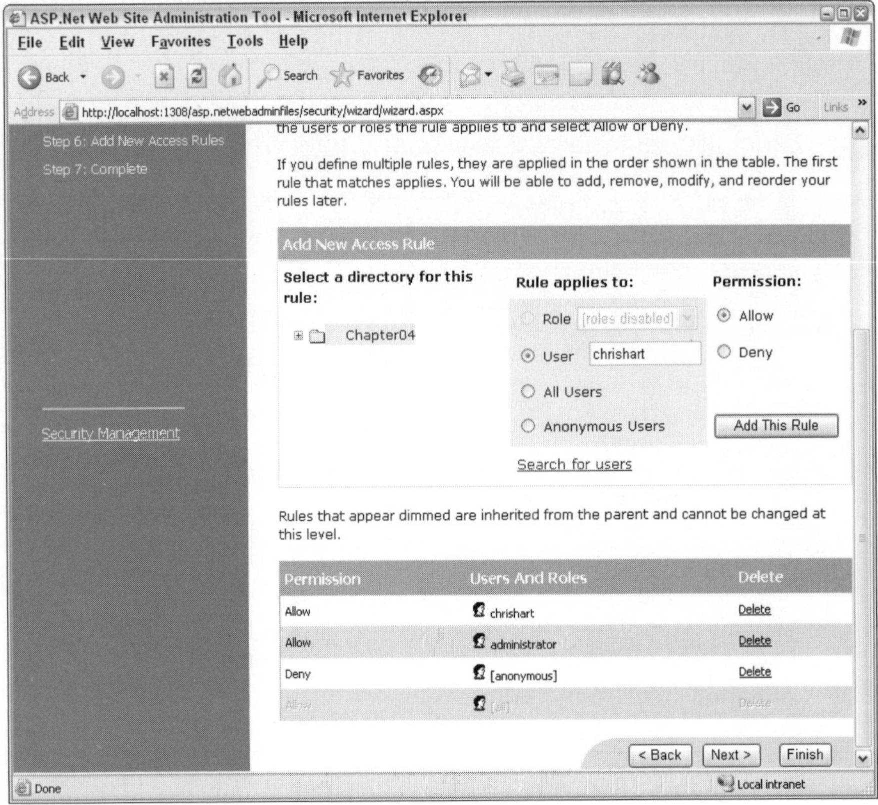

Figure 4-13

After you click Next, you should see that you have completed the wizard, which means that you should now have a web site with some user profiles and some access rights restrictions. All that remains is to try out the pages.

7. Back in VWD, select the `Default.aspx` page from the solution explorer and press Ctrl+F5 to run the page — you should see the screen shown in Figure 4-14.

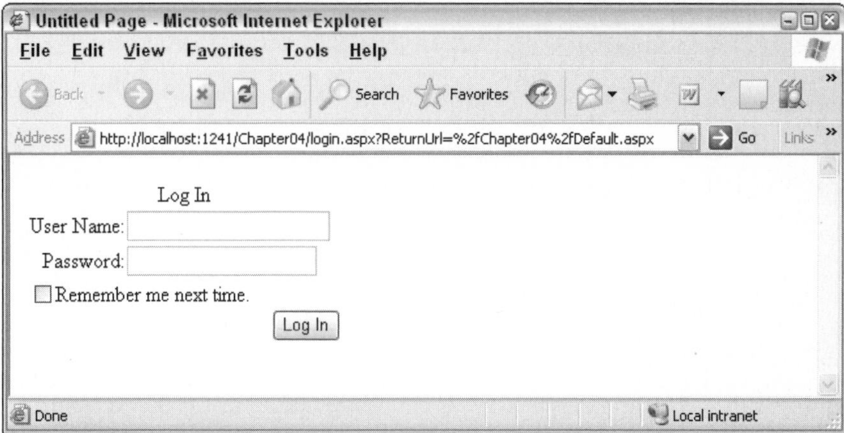

Figure 4-14

Because anonymous access is denied for the site, you are immediately taken to the login page. Notice that the address of the page indicates that your intention was to view the `Default.aspx` page.

8. Before you log in, try entering some invalid credentials (a username and password that don't exist, but not a blank password). You should see the message shown in Figure 4-15.

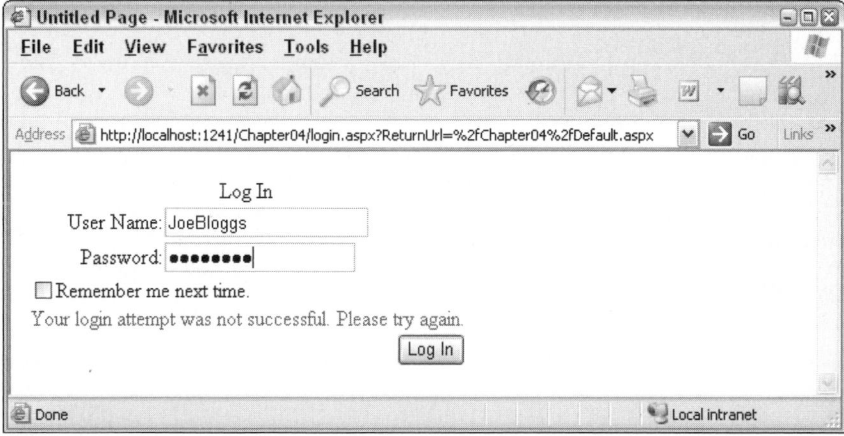

Figure 4-15

9. Try to log in as one of the user accounts available to the site. You are automatically taken back to the `Default.aspx` page, as illustrated in Figure 4-16.

Figure 4-16

Clicking the Logout link takes you back to the `Login.aspx` page — the site will not let anyone view pages without being logged in first.

How It Works

The `Login` controls available to ASP.NET pages are a real gift from the Microsoft teams. I've lost count of the number of sites I've worked on that had custom login functionality, all coded by hand, and now all I have to do is drag a few controls onto a page. On top of that, the wizards available for configuring user accounts and permissions make it even easier to get results up and running quickly. You may prefer to use your own user account data store, or even to link in to Active Directory user accounts, but this can be changed later in your development process.

This Try It Out simply walked you through the process of configuring user accounts. Though that is a necessary process, the Website Administration Tool is more interesting in what it creates behind the scenes. First, the user account profiles that were created have to be stored in some central repository, so the tool creates a new profile database for you for this purpose. Take a look at the `Chapter04` folder in your `C:\BegASPNET2\Chapters\Begin\Chapter04` directory and you should see a folder called `App_Data`. Right-click and select Refresh Folder, and you should see a file called `AspNetDB.mdf`. This is a Microsoft SQL database file, and you can view the structure and contents of the database tables within the VWD environment, as shown in Figure 4-17. (You'll learn more about this process when you get to the database chapters.)

The other part of the configuration was to assign some permissions to user accounts for accessing the site. By running the wizard, you're able to run through this process quite easily. After the wizard is finished, you have a new file in your solution called `Web.config` (the configuration file that stores preferences related to the way the application runs on your server — see Chapter 2 for more details). If you look in the `Web.config` file stored in your `Chapter04` folder, you will see the statements shown in Figure 4-18.

Notice that the `<allow ... />` and `<deny ... />` parts of the configuration file reflect the permissions that were set as part of the example. You can add and modify these statements yourself directly in the `Web.config` file by typing them in, or you can use the Administration Tool to streamline the process, whichever you prefer.

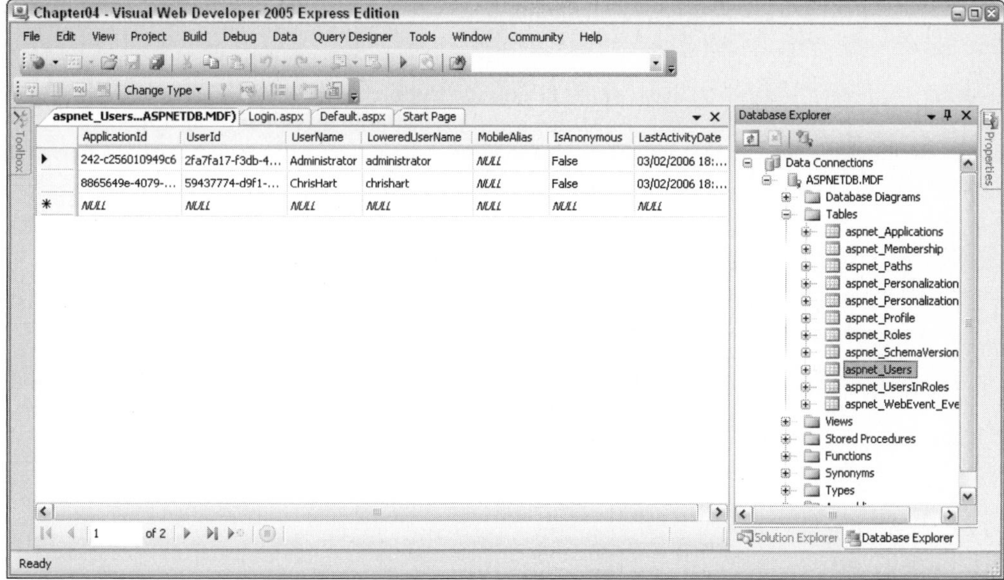

Figure 4-17

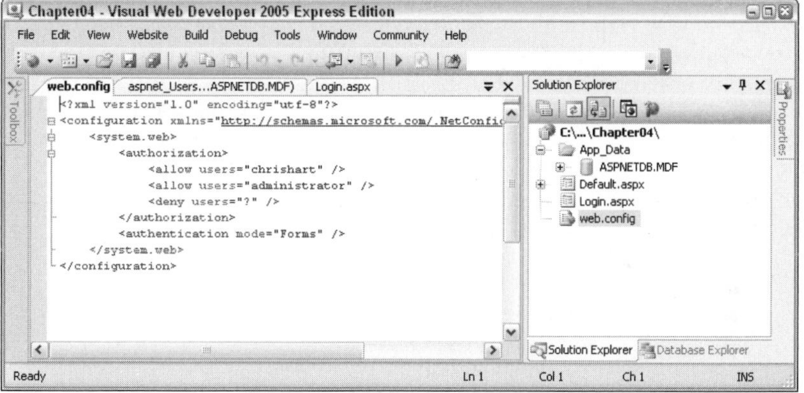

Figure 4-18

The `LoginView` control can do much more than display specific text to users depending on whether or not they're logged in. In Chapter 11, you'll see that this control can be used to change the appearance of a page entirely based on not just user identity, but also on roles. This control can contain text, HTML, or even other controls. The next Try It Out shows an example of this.

Personalization

The capability to personalize a site to reflect the preferences of the currently logged-in user is a great way to give a site a sense of community. Although you won't be doing too much personalization in this site, the next chapter explores some of the features available to ASP.NET developers to give users a more personalized user interface and browsing experience.

A useful addition to any personalized site is to provide feedback to logged-in users to confirm that they have been correctly identified. The LoginName control is a simple way to add this functionality. In this Try It Out, you learn how this control is used. For this example, you will need to enable anonymous access.

Try It Out Displaying User-Specific Information

1. You can choose which way you want to enable anonymous access — you can either edit the Web.config file (refer to the previous "How It Works") or you can launch the Web Site Administration Tool. To relaunch the tool, right-click the administration site icon in your system tray and select Open in Web Browser. Alternatively, to modify the Web.config file, simply open it up in VWD and change the following highlighted line of code:

```
<authorization>
  <allow users="?" />
  <allow users="administrator" />
  <allow users="chrishart" />
</authorization>
```

   The question mark represents all unknown (anonymous) users, so by changing deny to allow, you can enable anonymous access.

2. Next you need to make a slight change to the web page code to add the LoginName control. Open Default.aspx and pop up the Common Task menu next to the LoginView control (click the small right-hand arrow next to the control and select the LoggedInTemplate, as shown in Figure 4-19). Change the text to **You are logged in as**, and then drag a LoginName control to the end of the text.

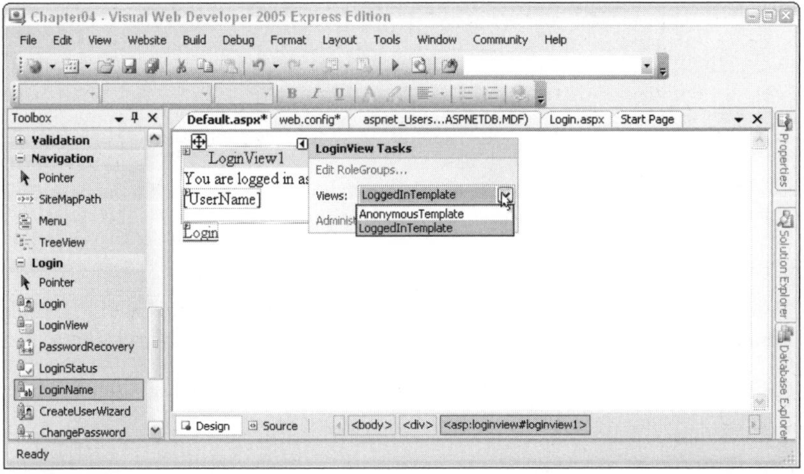

Figure 4-19

3. There is no need to make any amendments to the LoginName control after it's been added to the page, so all that remains is to save your changes and run the page. The first thing you should see is the anonymous user's perspective on the site, shown in Figure 4-20.

Figure 4-20

4. Click the Login link and log in to the site. When you are logged in, you should see something similar to Figure 4-21, depending on which user account you used.

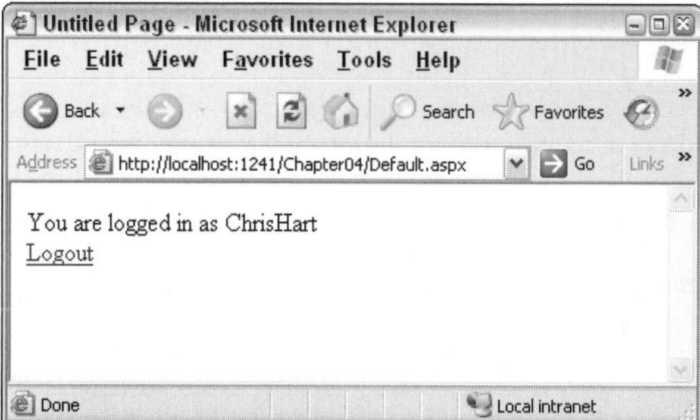

Figure 4-21

How It Works

The LoginName control is a quick and easy way to display a user's currently logged-in identity on a site. If you switch to Source View for the page, you can see the LoginName control, shown here with a gray background:

```
<LoggedInTemplate>
  You are logged in as
  <asp:LoginName ID="LoginName1" runat="server" />
  <br />
</LoggedInTemplate>
```

Some HTML code has been added to my code. Because I pressed Return after the `LoginName` control (so that the `LoginStatus` control would appear on the next line), there's a `<br />` HTML tag in the code. This is the HTML code for a simple line break. You'll often find tags like this, added to your code after you switch from Design View to Source View. The two most common tags are the ` ` character, which is a non-breaking space (a space character that keeps the items immediately before and after it on the same line), and `<br />`, which is a simple line break. The bit of code that is most relevant in this case is not the HTML, but the `LoginName`'s source. Again, there's hardly anything exciting to see in the generated source, because ASP.NET does all the hard work of finding out what the currently logged-in user's name is behind the scenes, and inserts it when the page is rendered.

Note that the `LoginName` control was not added to the Anonymous template, but then there's no reason to do so—if you view the site as an anonymous user, the control will not display anything when it is rendered.

Earlier in the chapter, the concept of roles was discussed. The following section takes a look at what roles are and how they are used to refine the membership characteristics of a site.

Membership

Defining which users can access a site is a perfectly viable way to build a small site, but it would have to be very small and remain small to be a manageable solution. A far better solution would be to define a set of user roles, and add user accounts to the appropriate roles. When users are members of a role, you can assign permissions based on a role.

For example, consider a typical site configuration scenario: all the members of an Administrators role can access the site, and can access all areas of the site. All members of a Users role can access the site, but cannot access certain restricted areas. All anonymous users will see a cut-down version of the site, but without any personalization, and certainly without any permissions for visiting restricted areas of a site.

Chapter 11 examines roles in more detail, including refining the Wrox United site to make good use of roles. In the meantime, you can experience roles for yourself in the next Try It Out, because the `Chapter04` example site is extended to include roles. In this example, you will be defining two roles: Users and Administrators. These roles have to be created before you can add users to the roles.

Try It Out — Adding Users to Roles

1. Start by launching the Web Site Administration Tool. If you've been running the tool recently, you can right-click the icon in your system tray for the administration site and select Open in Web Browser. Or, as an alternative, you can click Website⇨ASP.NET Configuration from the main VWD menu bar. When the tool is up and running, select the Security tab and click the Enable Roles link, as shown in Figure 4-22.
2. The Create or Manage Roles link should be enabled, so click it to enter the Create New Role screen. Create the two roles, Users and Administrators, by entering a role name in the text box and clicking Add Role (see Figure 4-23).

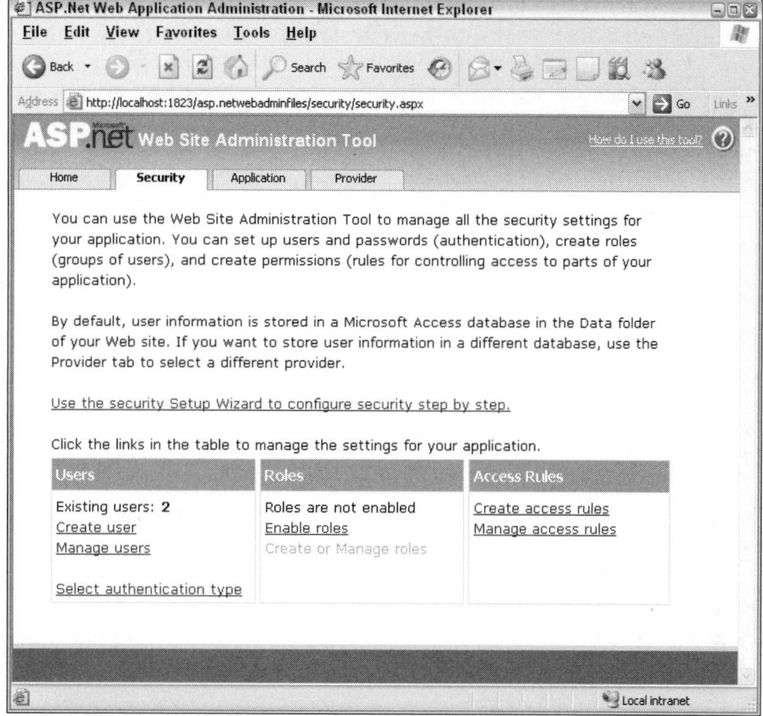

Figure 4-22

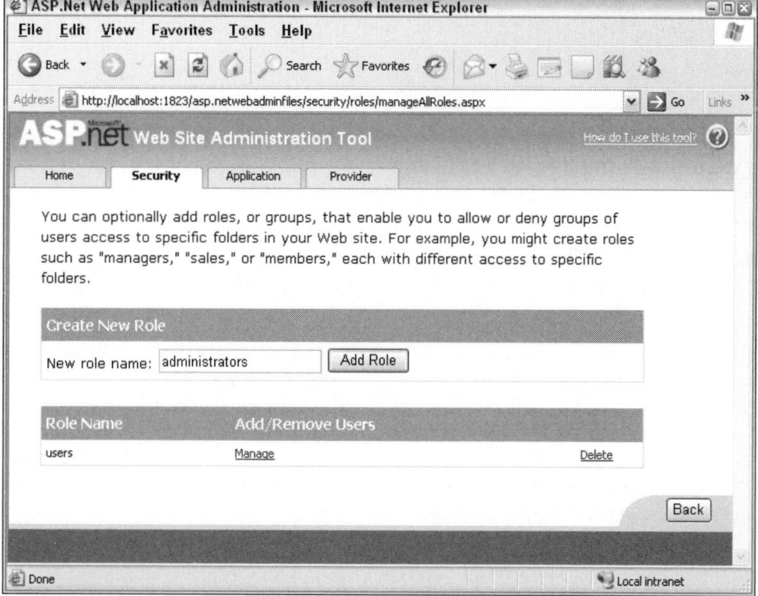

Figure 4-23

3. Click the Manage link for the Administrators group, and then search for the Administrator user account, using the search tools shown in Figure 4-24. The easiest way to find the Administrator account is to search for all accounts beginning with the letter *A*, so type `a*` in the text box and click Find User. Add the Administrator account to the Administrators role by checking the User Is In Role check box.

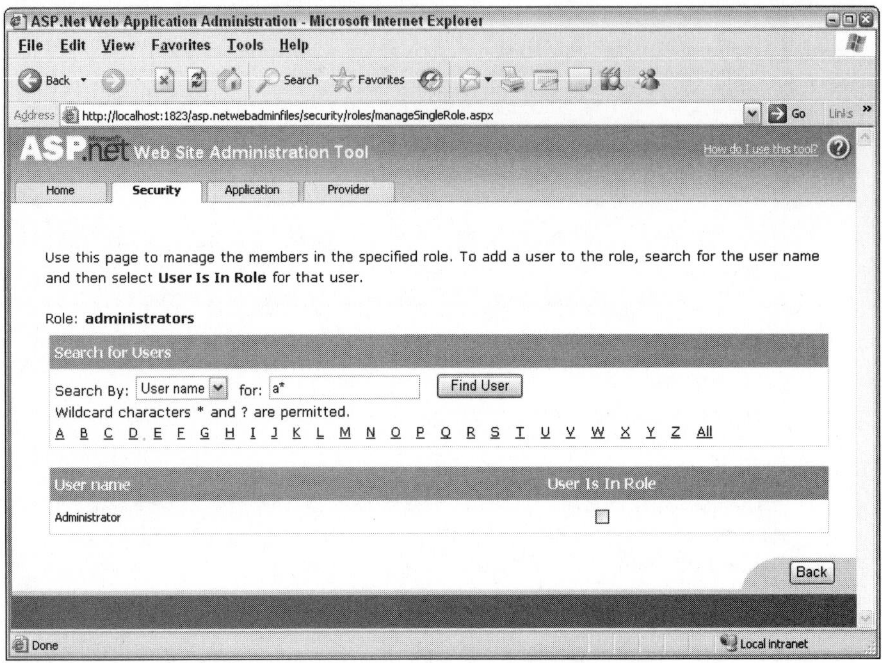

Figure 4-24

4. Add the remaining user accounts to the Users role in the same way.

5. Click the Security tab to return to the main Security section of the Administration Tool. Then click the Manage access rules link to return to managing the access rules for the site. In the same interface as you used in the earlier example for managing access rules (see Figure 4-13), remove the access rules for the individual user accounts, and instead grant access to the site to both the Administrators and Users groups. As you delete rules, you'll be prompted as shown in Figure 4-25.

6. Add the new permissions on a role-by-role basis with the interface shown in Figure 4-26.

   After you have added the rules, you should see the list of rules shown in Figure 4-27.

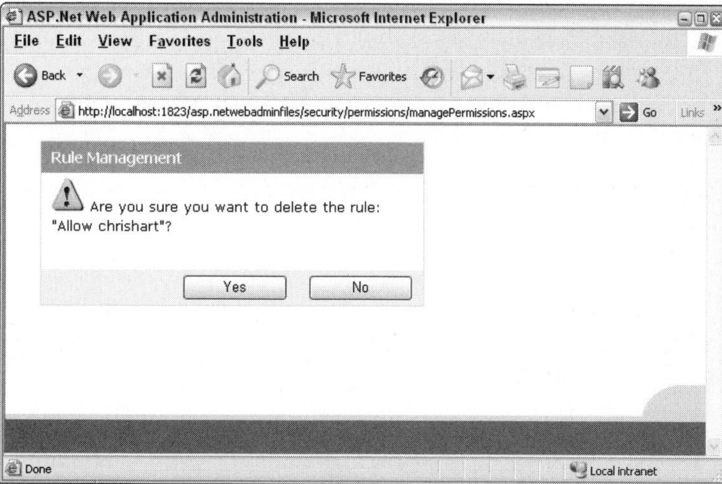

Figure 4-25

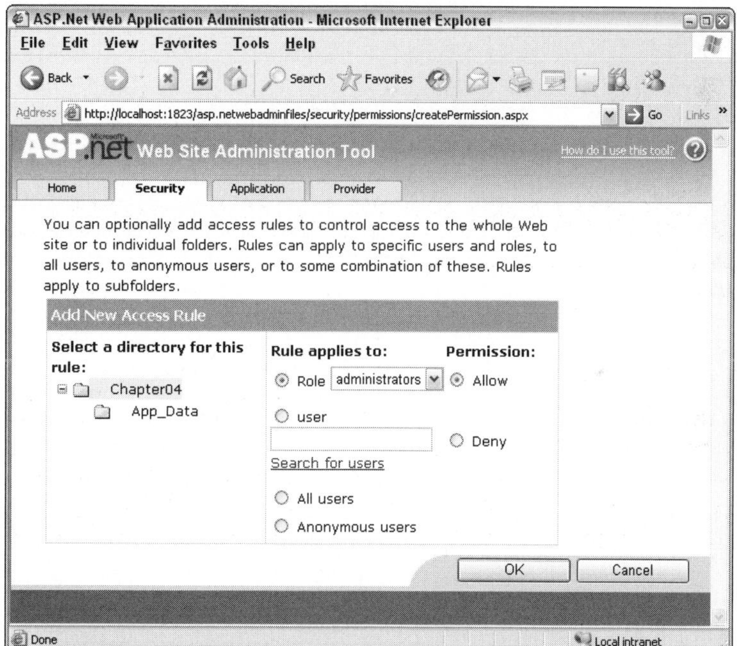

Figure 4-26

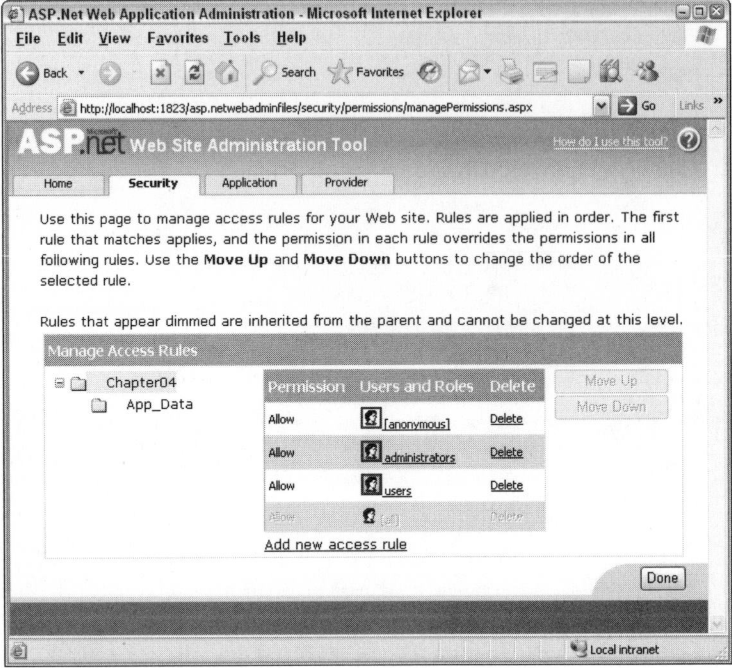

Figure 4-27

7. If you run the application again now, you should be able to log in as any of the user accounts and access the site as before. If you change the permissions for one of the roles, all members of that role will be affected, hence you could block access to all non-administrative users if you wanted.

How It Works

All of the changes in this example were made via the magic Web Site Administration interface, which simplifies the process of adding role definitions and access rules. If you were to do this by hand, as you will see in just a moment, you would have to manipulate the contents of the Roles table in the `AspNetDB.mdf` database that was shown earlier to include two role definitions, and then add users to those roles by changing the UsersInRoles table by hand. Then you would have to manipulate the `Web.config` file to change the access permissions to the site.

This configuration process was all handled for you automatically by the tool, so it's made configuration and administration quite a lot simpler. However, this is a Visual Web Developer and Visual Studio 2005 feature, not an ASP.NET feature, so you would have to do this by hand if you didn't have access to the VWD environment.

If you return to the Source View of your `Web.config` file, you'll see the following changes have been made (shown with a gray background):

```
        <roleManager enabled="true" />
        <authorization>
```

```
        <allow users="?" />
        <allow roles="administrators" />
        <allow roles="users" />
    </authorization>
```

In addition, the process of enabling roles has modified the user profile database slightly, by adding two new tables: one to store roles and one that tells you which users are members of which roles (see Figure 4-28).

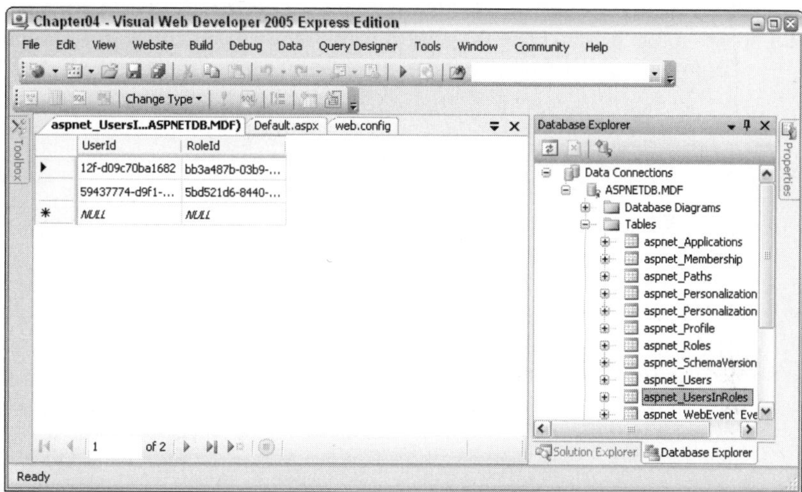

Figure 4-28

Authentication

One area not yet discussed is that of how the authentication works for this application, and what options are available in ASP.NET for authentication. The examples so far have relied on what's known as Forms authentication. So, what is Forms authentication, and what are the other options available?

- **Forms authentication:** Login requests are made by filling in a form on a web page and submitting that form to the server. When the server receives the request, a cookie is written to the user's local machine, and this cookie is passed back to the server by the browser along with each request that is sent so that the user remains authenticated for as long as is required.
- **Windows authentication:** Login pages pass user credentials to a web server (IIS only, not the web server built into VWD). The web server then handles the authentication using whichever method is configured on the virtual directory that the application is running within. IIS hooks in to the Windows operating system and Active Directory domain structures, which means that it can rely on user profiles that are stored externally, and use standard Windows credentials to log in to the site. Depending on the configuration of your site, and depending on which user account you used to log in to your machine, you may not even have to log in to the site directly, because your current Windows credentials can be passed to the web server automatically for authentication. This is really handy when it comes to developing intranet applications.

- **Passport authentication:** Login credentials are passed to a Microsoft Passport server where user profiles are stored centrally. You may be familiar with this from logging in to a Hotmail account. And because you can configure Windows to log on to a Passport account on startup, you can access your Hotmail inbox without even having to type a password.

Forms Authentication Model

This section looks at how Forms authentication works. Consider the following scenario:

- The user — let's call him Bob — wants to view Page A, which can't be accessed by anonymous users, so when Bob tries to view Page A, the browser instead displays a login page, as shown in Figure 4-29.

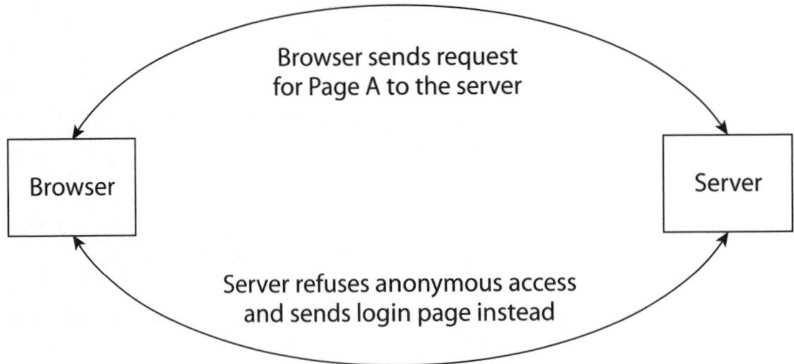

Figure 4-29

- Bob is now looking at a login page. Because Bob registered with this site previously, he logs in to the site using his username and password combination. Figure 4-30 shows the interaction between Bob's browser and the server.

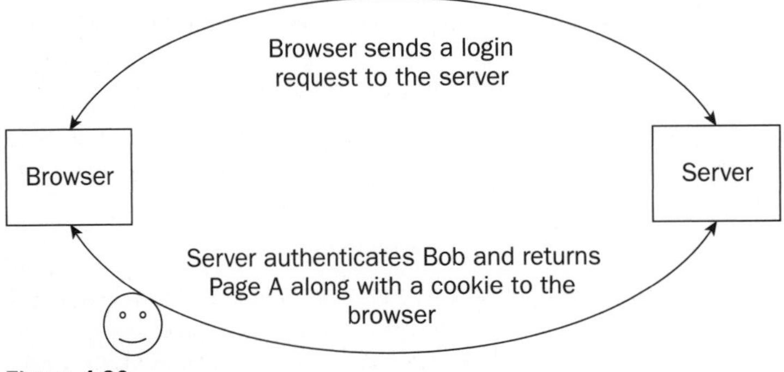

Figure 4-30

- Bob can now view Page A and is a happy user. Next, Bob wants to view Page B by following a link from Page A. Along with the request for the page, Bob's browser sends a copy of the cookie to the server to let the server know that it's Bob who's trying to view the page. The server knows who Bob is, and likes Bob, so it sends Bob Page B as requested, as shown in Figure 4-31.

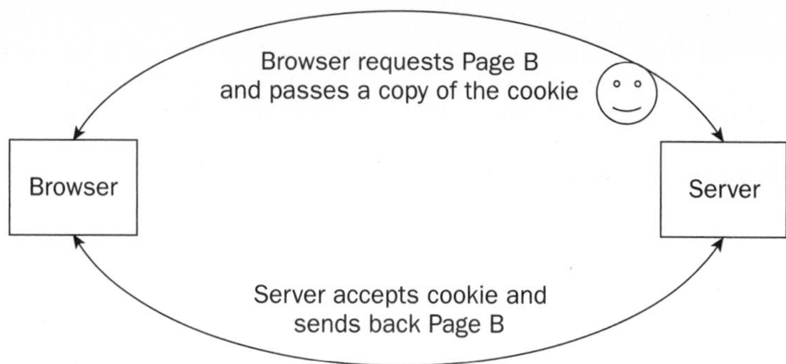

Figure 4-31

- If Bob now requests the site's home page, the browser will tack on the cookie to the request, so even though the home page is not restricted content, the cookie is still sent to the server. Because the page isn't restricted, the server doesn't worry about the cookie, ignores it, and sends back the home page.
- Bob then heads back to Page A. Because the cookie is fresh on Bob's machine, the cookie is sent to the server. The server is still happy with Bob, so it lets Bob view the page.
- Bob goes off and makes himself a coffee. He then makes some lunch. By the time he gets back to his computer, 25 minutes have elapsed. Bob now wants to view Page B again, but the cookie on his machine has expired. The server doesn't receive a cookie along with the page request, so Bob has to log back in again.

Cookies on a user's machine are normally set to expire after a specific amount of time has elapsed. In this scenario, the server gives out cookies with a 20-minute expiry, which means that as long as the user keeps making requests within 20 minutes of each other, the cookie will remain active. However, more than 20 minutes away from the site and the user will have to log back in to the site to view restricted content.

The login page built in the earlier examples included a box that offered you the "remember my details for next time" option. This writes a more permanent cookie to your browser's cookie collection so that your account name is pre-populated when you revisit the site. Because you should never store password information in a cookie, you should always have to enter your password, but at least your username field is filled in for you on each visit.

Other methods of authentication — Windows and Passport — provide the end user with a similar experience. For example, the Windows authentication model relies on the web server (which will likely be IIS) to control access to the site, but it can also incorporate the timeout mechanism to block users that have been idle for too long. To configure Windows authentication, you need to specify which users or roles from the corporate Active Directory (AD) domain can access a site. These users can then access the site whenever they are logged on using their login details to a PC on the corporate network.

It's also possible to view a Windows authenticated site from outside of the corporate environment, though you are asked to enter your standard Windows logon credentials when you attempt to access a page protected by Windows authentication.

Passport authentication isn't as widely adopted as Microsoft perhaps would have liked, but some sites on the Internet do link to the Passport network to handle web site authentication (for example, Expedia.com). Passport authentication relies on the entire repository of user accounts being accessible from anywhere in the wired world, a bit like a central active directory for web accounts.

This book uses Forms authentication to handle all authentication with the Wrox United application.

Wrox United Security

The Wrox United site that you've been working on so far needs to have some security applied to it if you want to be able to include some personalization in the site. In the finished site (`www.wroxunited.net`), you'll see that there is shopping cart functionality built in to the site. Additionally, the finished site will also have an administration area, where you can edit fixtures, team members, and much more. This all means that you're going to have to add some users and roles at some stage. Because you have gained plenty of experience of using the configuration tool, you can now perform the first stage in this process. The next Try It Out walks you through the user accounts and roles configuration for the Wrox United site. At this stage, you don't have to worry about locking down parts of the site — that's a task for later in the book.

Try It Out — Configuring Security in the Wrox United Site

1. Open the final version of the Wrox United site in VWD. Then click the Website menu and select ASP.NET Configuration. This launches the configuration tool for the site. Figure 4-32 shows the configuration screen that is displayed for the finished version of the site.

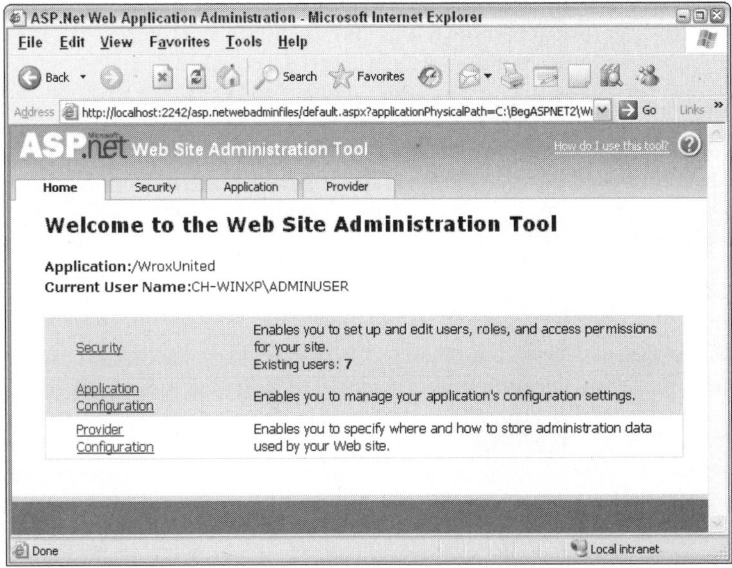

Figure 4-32

2. Click the Security link to go to the section where you can configure users and roles. As you did previously in this chapter, launch the security setup wizard. As you walk through the wizard, select the following:

    - The application will be used over the Internet.
    - Roles are enabled.
    - Roles should be defined for Administrator, FanClubMember, Manager, Owner, and Reporter (see Figure 4-33).

3. Look at the user accounts. The user accounts predefined with the Wrox United application are shown in Figure 4-34.

4. Take a look at the configuration for the finished application. You'll see that the preconfigured user accounts are each members of different roles, so while the ChrisH account is a member of the Reporter role, Jim is a member of the Owners role, and Lou is a member of the Fan Club.

5. After you finish the wizard, look at a couple of subfolders within the WroxUnited directory that contain specific areas of the site — the Admin and the FanClub sections. These areas have some access restrictions on them.

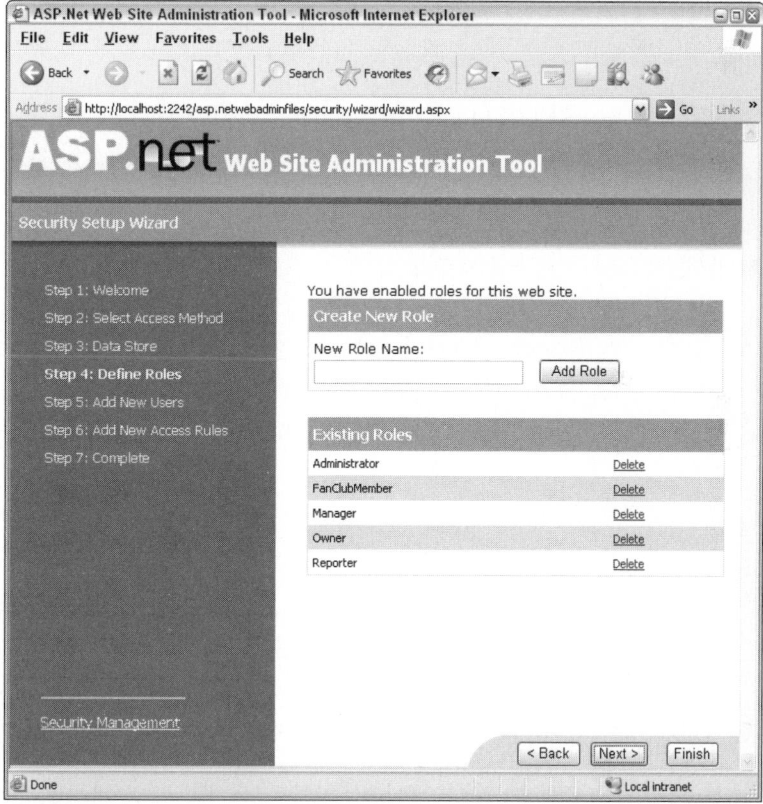

Figure 4-33

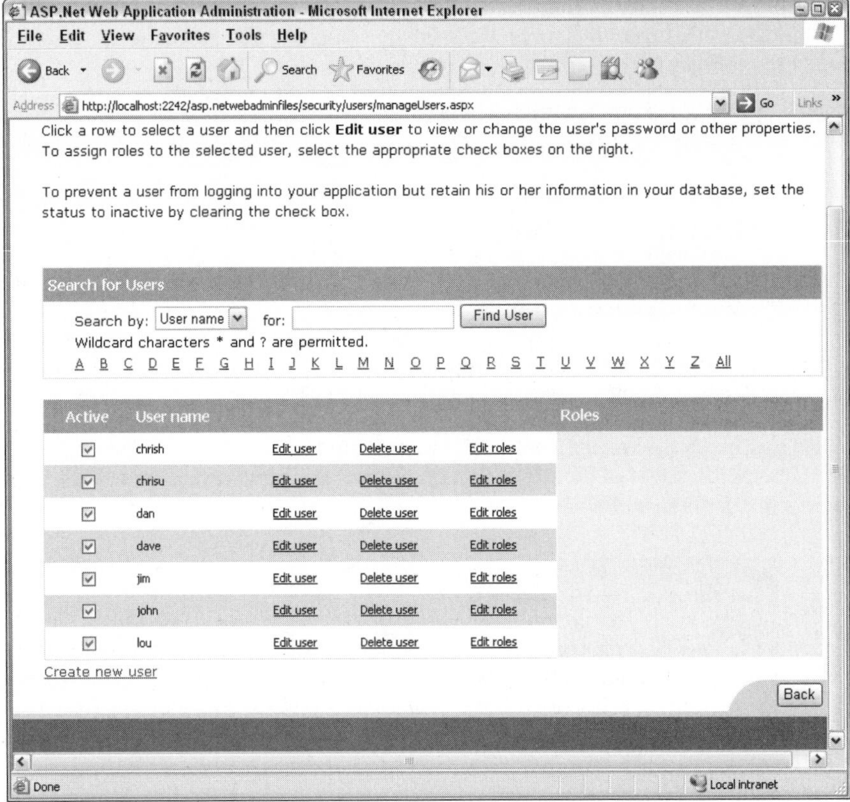

Figure 4-34

6. Go to the section for managing Access Rules and you'll see the following rules:
   - For the main WroxUnited folder, anonymous access is allowed.
   - For the FanClub folder, only members of the FanClub role can access the folder — all other users are denied access.
   - For the Admin folder, access is denied to all users.

How It Works

With the Wrox United application, you have access to the configuration of a fully functional web application. Feel free to have a look through this configuration using both the Administration Tool and the `Web.config` file to see how the basic permissions are enabled. This example is only a taste of what will come later in the book, because Chapter 11 covers the details of role-based access to a site and shows you different techniques for enabling and disabling content by role.

The code generated for filtering access to the FanClub folder has been added to the `Web.config` file that lives within the `FanClub` folder. This code is as follows:

```
<?xml version="1.0" encoding="utf-8"?>
<configuration>
  <system.web>
    <authorization>
      <allow roles="FanClubMember" />
      <deny users="*" />
    </authorization>
  </system.web>
</configuration>
```

Notice that the FanClubMember role has been defined as the only role that has permission to access the content in this folder.

The directory-level permission created in this example has created a restricted zone in the site. Chapter 11 walks through some examples using the Administration section and the Fan Club sections, demonstrating different parts of ASP.NET 2.0 technology. These examples will rely on an understanding of the foundations built in this section.

Summary

This chapter discussed the basics of security, the concept of identity, and the process involved in logging on to a site. These are familiar concepts to anyone who spends time on the Internet, surfing fan sites, community portals, or online shops. Because these concepts are so universal, you've seen how ASP.NET 2.0 is designed to make the process of creating sites that use this functionality.

The core concepts to understand are as follows:

- **Identity:** The concept of an individual as described by a set of attributes that make that individual unique.
- **Authentication:** The concept of identifying a user to a server by passing a set of credentials to the server. If the server can identify the user attempting to connect, he or she will be authenticated.
- **Authorization:** The process of taking authenticated user credentials and comparing them against a set of access control list information, providing the answer to the question "can this user access the requested resource?"
- **Personalization:** The capability to provide information that is specific to the currently logged-in user.
- **Membership:** The concept of belonging. This chapter considered the concept of users being members of specific roles.

The next chapter expands on the concept of personalization and looks at how ASP.NET sites can be personalized.

Exercises

1. Change the configuration of your Chapter 4 web site to allow anonymous access, but to deny access to one specific user account.

2. Add a subfolder to the Chapter 4 web site called **Admin**. Within this folder, add a page called **MainAdmin.aspx** with a `LoginName` control on it and any other controls you might want. Change the access permissions for that specific folder so that only members of the Administrators group can view the page.

Styling with Themes

The process of developing any web application usually revolves around two main areas: functionality and appearance. The functionality aspect of a web application includes the structure of the site, the behavior of the controls, the user experience, code for securing the application, what happens when the user clicks a button, and so on. The appearance of a site is somewhat more aesthetic, and involves the use of color, images, the layout of pages, and to some extent, the style of code that is rendered to the browser. A successful application will strike a good balance between the two sides, providing a visually pleasant site that is easy to use and to work with for all users, and it's the balancing act between the two sides where many sites fail.

This chapter starts by introducing the fundamental tools available for styling web applications, before introducing the styling capabilities of Visual Web Developer. It goes through the basics of styling individual controls before moving style information into a separate CSS file, and then introduces themes — a new technique for styling pages and sites.

In this chapter, the following topics are discussed:

- Styling a web site, from styling individual elements to the use of CSS style sheets
- Developing style sheets for an application in VWD
- Using ASP.NET 2.0's themes and skins to rapidly develop styled web content that conforms to a standard look and feel
- Adding style to the Wrox United site using themes and skins

Additionally, this chapter also discusses the concepts of usability and accessibility, which are two important areas of web design that should be considered when developing any web site.

Styling a Site

It may sound obvious, but the front page appearance of a site is the first thing your visitors will see, and although we are told never to judge a book by its cover (particularly in the case of Wrox author mug shots!), most of us will still have an initial impression of a site based on its appearance, whether it's a fairly neutral response (it's okay, it does the job, where's the search box?), a positive response (neat, slick, pretty, show me more!), or a negative response (yuk, messy, I'm going somewhere else!). Initial impressions count, so it's important that you get them right.

In any site design there are common elements; for example, some kind of header that gives you a company name, an idea of what the site is about, or a reflection of why you are looking at the site. You will also find areas such as menus, search boxes, groups of links, footers, and so on. A page without these sorts of elements will only be relevant to a specific audience; for example, a developer proving a concept, or the reader of a book who's trying out some new technology. Positioning these elements precisely is important, as is structuring the content to fit the style of site you're trying to develop.

Styling and laying out a site is an integral part of web development. Although laying out a site is one aspect, the styling of a site can be a bit trickier. This chapter focuses on styling pages and the rules and hierarchy involved in this process — laying out elements and positioning items on a page is part of web design that is discussed throughout this book.

Style Attributes

The easiest and quickest way to change the way an element appears on a page is to add a `style` attribute. The `style` attribute can be applied to any visible element on a page. For example:

```
<div style="font-weight:bold;color:red;border-bottom:solid 2pt navy">This is a
styled "div" tag</div>
```

Figure 5-1 shows how this `style` attribute will look in Internet Explorer.

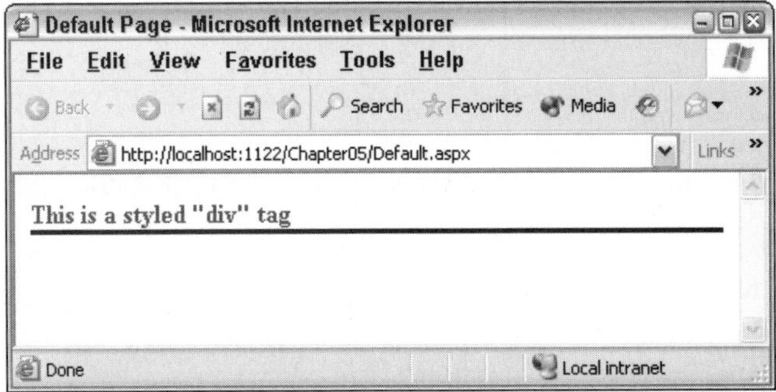

Figure 5-1

In the following Try It Out, you start by creating a web site that you can use to host all of the examples in this chapter.

Try It Out Styling a Simple Page, Part 1 — Element by Element

1. In VWD, open the starter web site called Chapter05 (`C:\BegASPNET2\Chapters\Begin\Chapter05`). This starter site contains just a few files to give you a head start on the examples within this chapter.

2. Add a new blank .aspx page and call it `Default.aspx`. Switch straight to Source View and type the following highlighted lines of code between the `Form` tags:

```
<form id="form1" runat="server">
    <div style="font-weight:bold; color:red; border-bottom:solid 2pt navy;">
    This is a styled "div" tag
    </div>
</form>
```

Notice how Visual Web Developer helps you as you type in the style information (see Figure 5-2).

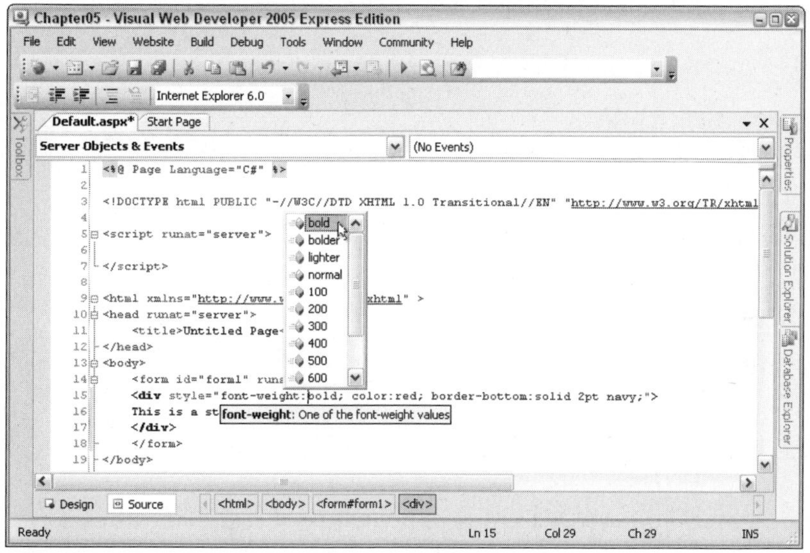

Figure 5-2

3. Switch over to Design View and see how your formatting has been applied to the page, as shown in Figure 5-3.

4. Notice how the `style` tag has the style attribute information visible in the properties pane. If you click somewhere within the value for the `Style` attribute, you'll notice the ellipsis button (. . .) next to the style information. Click this button and you will see the Style Builder dialog box, shown in Figure 5-4.

   This dialog box comes in very handy when you are styling elements, because you won't have to remember the individual syntax for each style. All you need to do is select the attributes you want to apply to the element and click OK to apply the style. Go ahead and do that with another page.

5. Create another .aspx page and call it **StyledPage1.aspx**. In this page, add a simple `<div>` element with the text **This is highlighted text** and a Heading 1 (`h1`) element with the text **This is also highlighted text**.

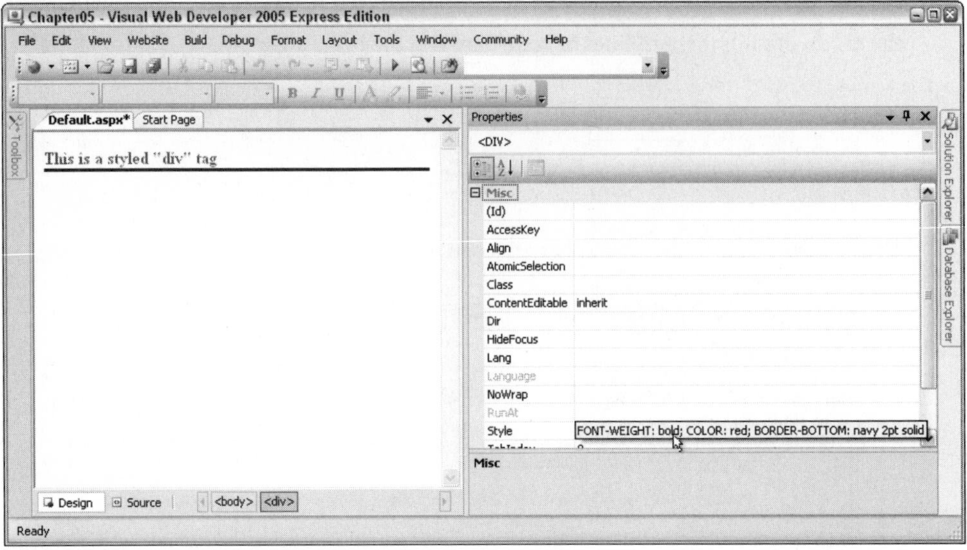

Figure 5-3

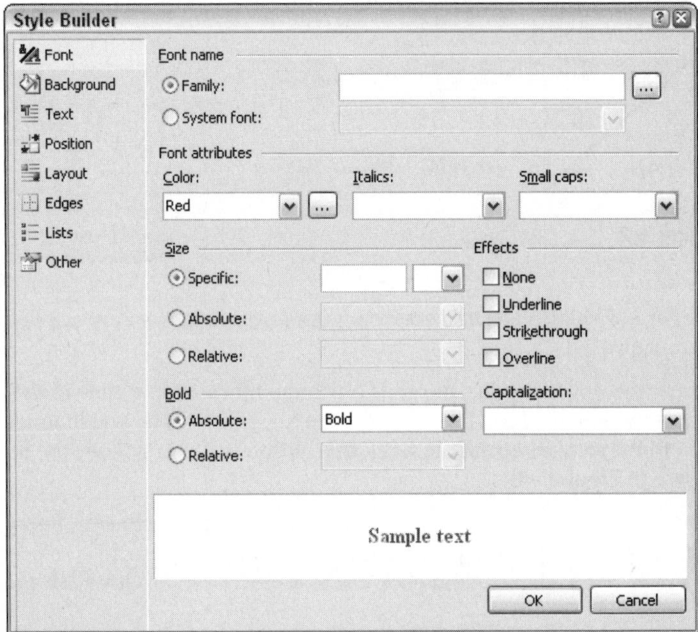

Figure 5-4

6. Using the Style Builder dialog box (see Figure 5-5), set the style for both elements to use the Trebuchet MS font family, and set them to appear in Navy. This will add the following code to Source View for you automatically:

```
<div style="font-family: 'Trebuchet MS';Color: Navy;">
  This is highlighted text.</div>
<h1 style="font-family: 'Trebuchet MS';Color: Navy;">
  This is also highlighted text.</h1>
```

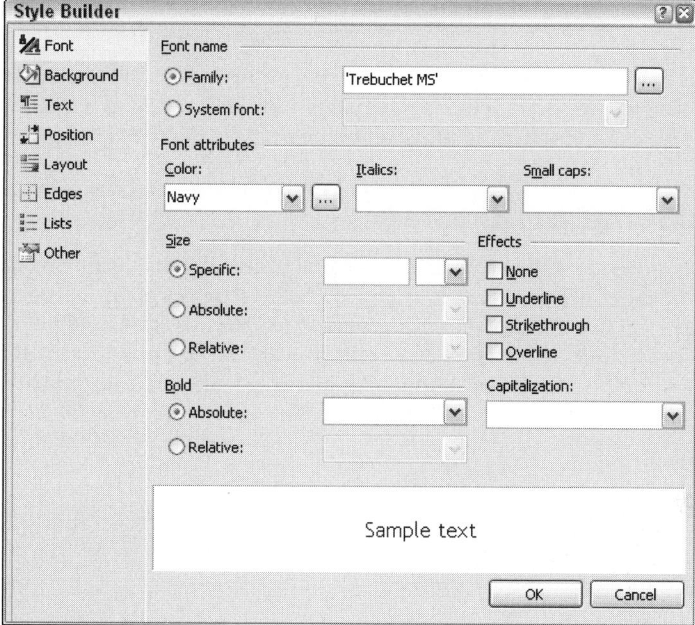

Figure 5-5

7. View the page in your browser to see the finished article. It should look similar to Figure 5-6.

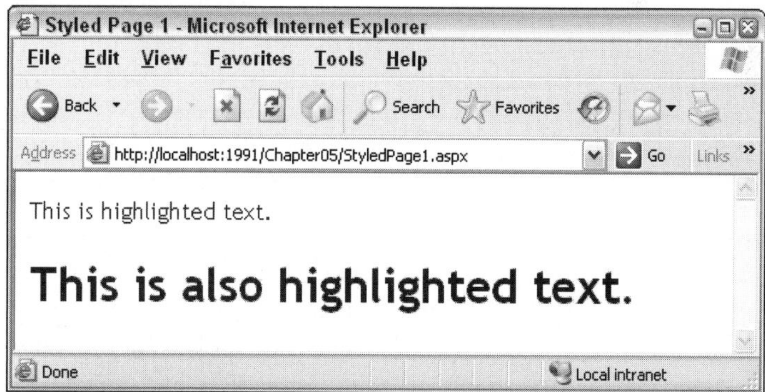

Figure 5-6

How It Works

Now it might not look fantastic, but it didn't take long to change how this element appeared on the page. This technique can then be applied to each element on the site. You can apply many different style attributes to a site, and so Appendix E includes some of the most common elements to help you to pick out your favorite styles for a site.

The good news is that having learned to style elements on a page, it's just a short step to reorganizing your code into using a style sheet. The style attributes on HTML elements use exactly the same syntax as the style syntax used in style sheets, so move on to the next section and tidy up all this style code.

CSS — Cascading Style Sheets

The concept of style sheets has been around for several years now (it was first made a recommendation by the W3C in December 1996), and every well-designed web application will be backed by a well-defined CSS style sheet that defines a specific look and feel for the site. Using a style sheet, you are able to define how every type of element on a page will appear, and you can also create definitions for specific styles that you can pick and choose from to apply to specific elements on a page. For example, you can specify that every instance of a `<div>` tag should contain navy text, or you can define a style *class* called `HighlightedText` that you can apply to any `<div>`, or other similar element, on a page. Here's a section from a style sheet that defines these styles:

```
div
{
  font-family: 'Trebuchet MS';
  Color: Navy;
}

.HighlightedText
{
  font-family: 'Trebuchet MS';
  Color: Navy;
}
```

Notice that the only difference between these two is that the `HighlightedText` class has a period before the name of the custom class. This identifies the section as a class that can be applied to any element you want, instead of defining default styling for a particular type of element.

To apply a style to an element, you don't need to do anything to the element itself. As long as your page knows where the style information for the page can be found, the style will be applied automatically (locating style information is discussed in just a moment). However, to specify a custom class to be used to style an element, you use the `Class` attribute. For example:

```
<div class="HighlightedText">This is highlighted text.</div>
<h1 class="HighlightedText">This is also highlighted text.</h1>
```

Although you can't see the color of the text in this printed book, you can see that the font style that was defined in the preceding style class has been applied to these two elements in Figure 5-7.

Figure 5-7

Of course, if you try this out for yourself, you'll see that the font has also been rendered in navy blue.

Style Syntax

Style definitions are surrounded by curly brackets (braces). The position of the opening brace is usually either next to the name of the element or class, or on the following line. For example, the `div` style can be rewritten as follows:

```
div{
  font-family: 'Trebuchet MS';
  Color: Navy;
}
```

You can choose whichever presentation style you prefer — personally, I like my braces to all line up in a vertical line.

Style information can also be applied to elements like anchor tags (<a>) with some specific modifiers to provide some dynamic hover-style appearance as follows:

```
a:link, a:visited
{
  color: #cc3300;
  text-decoration: underline;
}
a:hover
{
  text-decoration: none;
}
a:active
{
  color: #ff9900;
  text-decoration: underline;
}
```

This code will render red links with underline on a page that, when you hover your mouse over them, lose their underline, and when you click them, they momentarily appear slightly orange. This is to provide you with some feedback that you are hovering over a link, and that you have just clicked a link.

The comma-separated items mean that the following style information will be applied to both style definition items (in this case, the `a:link` and `a:visited` items).

The first step in moving to a fully CSS-based layout is to decide what styles you want to use for each element and construct a set of style definitions.

> **You can put style definitions in two places so that they can be used in a web page. The first option is to embed style information at the top of the web page within a `<style>` tag, placed within the `<head>` element. The other option is to create a separate external style sheet to store the style definitions, and to link that external style sheet to each web page that it should be applied to.**

In the next sections, you look first at placing style definitions within the `<style>` tags on a page, and then see how to attach an external CSS style sheet.

Moving from Style Attributes to a Style Section

If you are only interested in styling a single page, you can embed style information in the `<head>` section of the HTML for the page as follows:

```
<html xmlns="http://www.w3.org/1999/xhtml" >
<head runat="server">
  <title>Styled Page 1</title>
  <style>
    .HighlightedText
    {
      font-family: 'Trebuchet MS';
      Color: Navy;
    }
  </style>
</head>
<body>
  <form id="form1" runat="server">
    <div class="HighlightedText">This is highlighted text.</div>
    <h1 class="HighlightedText">This is also highlighted text.</h1>
  </form>
</body>
</html>
```

This code is the same code used to display the previous example. Notice how you can embed the style information quite easily within the `<head>` of the page using the `<style>` tag. This technique is fine for single pages — in fact, if you ever save a Word document as HTML, you'll see that this technique is used to define the document styles in use so that the document can be rendered as HTML. I just saved this document from within Word 2003 as a Web Page (Filtered), which produces HTML code that's a lot cleaner than the standard auto-generated code when you just save as a Web Page from Word. After I saved it, I viewed the source code that was generated, and found the following style definition that describes how some of the highlighted sections of code used in this chapter are defined:

```
p.code, li.code, div.code
  {margin-top:0cm;
  margin-right:0cm;
  margin-bottom:0cm;
  margin-left:30.0pt;
  margin-bottom:.0001pt;
  line-height:112%;
  font-size:8.5pt;
  font-family:Courier;}:
```

This technique isn't really ideal for constructing a web site with style information applied to many different pages, because you would have to copy the <style> tags and style definitions across to all of the pages in the site individually. The solution for that scenario is to move to a separate CSS.

Moving to a Separate CSS

This step is perhaps the simplest to achieve. When you have style definitions encapsulated within <style> tags, it's a really simple matter to extract that information into a separate style sheet. All you need to do is create a file with the file extension of .css, copy across all the style information from your web page, and then add a link to that style sheet as follows:

```
<head runat="server">
  <title>Styled Page 2</title>
  <link href="StyleSheet.css" rel="stylesheet" type="text/css" />
</head>
```

The style sheet file contains only style information, so say you had a style sheet with all of your style code in it:

```
.HighlightedText
{
    font-family: 'Trebuchet MS';
    color: Navy;
}
a:link, a:visited
{
    color: #cc3300;
    text-decoration: underline;
}
a:hover
{
    text-decoration: none;
}
a:active
{
    color: #ff9900;
    text-decoration: underline;
}
```

You can then link that style sheet to your web page, and make a minor addition to the page code:

```
<form id="form1" runat="server">
  <div class="HighlightedText">This is highlighted text.</div>
  <h1 class="HighlightedText">This is also highlighted text.</h1>
  <div><a href="default.aspx">This is a sample link</a></div>
</form>
```

When you view this page you'll see the result shown in Figure 5-8.

Figure 5-8

Go ahead and try these concepts. In the next Try It Out, you create a simple styled page that is based on the `StyledPage1.aspx` that you created earlier.

Try It Out Styling a Simple Page, Part 2 — Using CSS

1. Create another new page in your Chapter05 web site and call it `StyledPage2.aspx`.

2. Copy the `<div>` and heading from `StyledPage1.aspx` and remove the `style` attributes from each element. In their place, add a `class` attribute, and give it a value of `"HighlightedText"`:

```
<form id="form1" runat="server">
  <div class="HighlightedText">
    This is highlighted text.</div>
  <h1 class="HighlightedText">
    This is also highlighted text.</h1>
</form>
```

3. Add a hyperlink to the page below the heading with the text **This is a sample link**. Enter `"default.aspx"` as the value for the `href`:

```
<form id="form1" runat="server">
  <div class="HighlightedText">
    This is highlighted text.</div>
  <h1 class="HighlightedText">
    This is also highlighted text.</h1>
  <div><a href="default.aspx">This is a sample link</a></div>
</form>
```

4. After the hyperlink, add a line break, followed by an ASP.NET `Label` control. Remember that server controls have a different set of properties than standard controls, so set the label's `CssClass` property to `"HighlightedText"`, and the `Font-Italic` property to `"true"`:

```
    This is also highlighted text.</h1>
  <div><a href="default.aspx">This is a sample link</a></div><br />
  <asp:Label CssClass="HighlightedText" Font-Italic="true" ID="Label1"
    runat="server" Text="This is an ASP.NET label"></asp:Label>
</form>
```

5. Right-click the Chapter05 site in the Solution Explorer and select Add New Item. Select StyleSheet from the list of icons and accept the default name: `StyleSheet.css`. In this file, add the following code:

```
.HighlightedText
{
  font-family: 'Trebuchet MS';
  color: Navy;
}
a:link, a:visited
{
  color: #cc3300;
  text-decoration: underline;
}
a:hover
{
  text-decoration: none;
}
a:active
{
  color: #ff9900;
  text-decoration: underline;
}
```

Notice how you get the same syntax help when you work with a CSS style sheet as when you work with `<style>` attributes on a HTML control in Source View, as displayed in Figure 5-9.

Also notice the Build Style icon on the toolbar. If you click this button, it launches the Style Builder dialog box. You can try this out for yourself — add another element definition (a `<div>`, perhaps), and add the opening and closing curly braces. Place your cursor between those braces and click the button to launch the style builder. After you have selected the styles you want, just click OK and your styles appear as CSS items in the `StyleSheet.css` file.

6. There is just one final thing to do, which is to tell your page to refer to the styles defined in the .css file. Switch back to `StyledPage2.aspx` and flip to Design View. You should see the screen shown in Figure 5-10.

7. Now drag and drop the `StyleSheet.css` file icon from the Solution Explorer onto the design surface. As soon as you do that, your page will change appearance (see Figure 5-11).

If you run the page now, you'll see pretty much the same thing in your browser window.

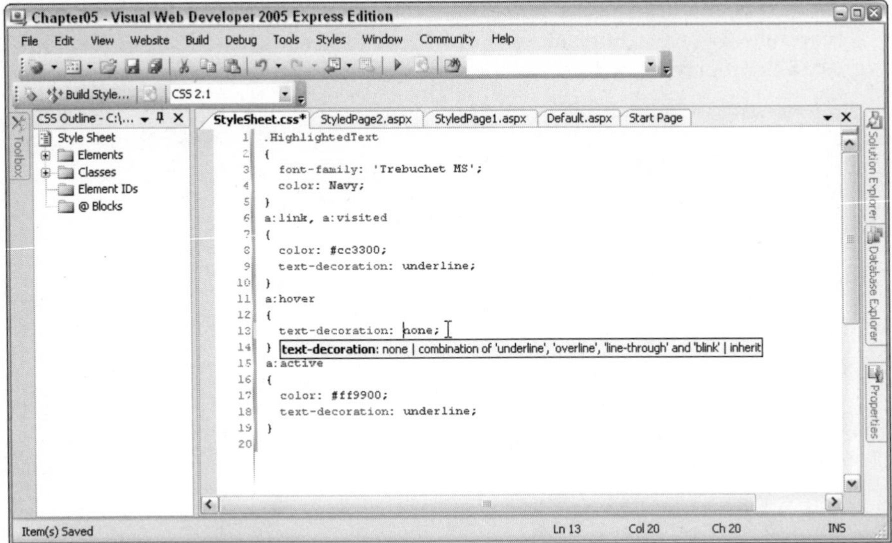

Figure 5-9

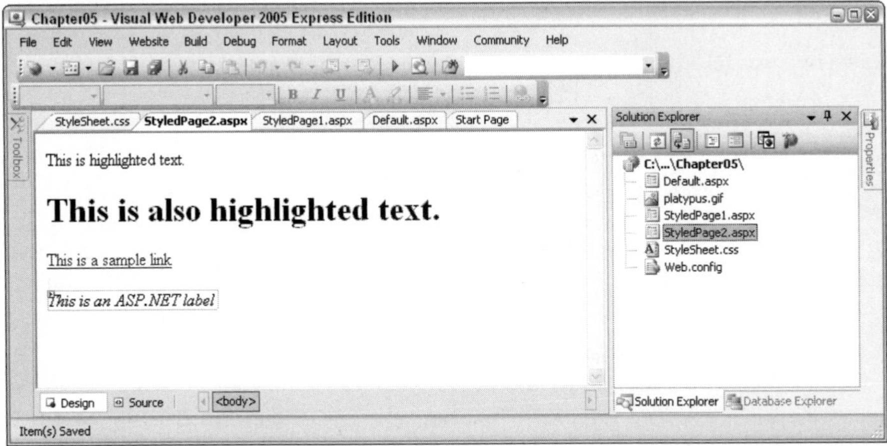

Figure 5-10

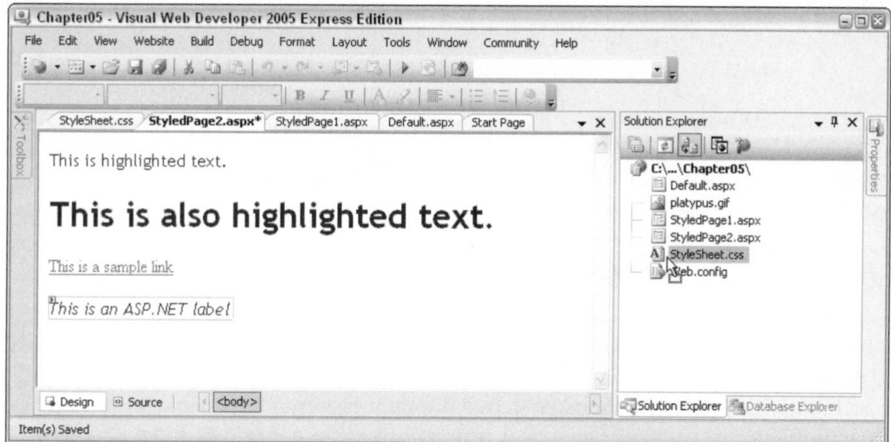

Figure 5-11

How It Works

Only two things are required to style an HTML element on a page using a separate CSS file. One is the class to be used by the element, and the other is a link that the page will use to locate the CSS file. When you dragged the CSS file onto the design surface of the page, the following code was added for you at the top of the page:

```
<html xmlns="http://www.w3.org/1999/xhtml">
<head runat="server">
  <title>Styled Page 2</title>
  <link href="StyleSheet.css" rel="stylesheet" type="text/css" />
</head>
```

That link at the top of your page tells your page where to find its style information. From that moment on, any `class` attributes in the page will attempt to refer to the CSS style sheet for the styling information for those elements. If the class cannot be found, no styles are applied, unless they are specified manually in the `Style` attribute of the element.

HTML elements with `class` attributes specified can also have additional style information specified in the `Style` attribute. Any styles defined in the `Style` attribute will override those specified in the CSS file, giving you the chance to fine-tune the appearance of selected elements on your page.

Server controls are somewhat different. Because a server control will be converted to appropriate HTML when it is rendered, the available properties will be different. In this example, you used a `Label` control. The `Label` control is a relatively simple control, so there's not a huge amount of styling you can add to it. In this case, you added a link to the CSS style, and defined one additional style. The `CssClass` attribute used by server controls relates directly to the `class` attribute found on HTML elements. The individual style attributes are similar to the individual parts found in the HTML style attributes:

```
<asp:Label CssClass="HighlightedText" Font-Italic="true" ID="Label1"

  runat="server" Text="This is an ASP.NET label"></asp:Label>
```

When the label is rendered, the following code is generated:

```
<span id="Label1" class="HighlightedText" style="font-style:italic;">This is an
ASP.NET label</span>
```

Notice that the custom style attributes are converted to a standard `style` tag on the browser. Because CSS styling is applied on the client side, once the page is rendered the `class` and `style` attributes on the HTML elements will have styles and CSS styling applied just like static HTML elements.

Limitations of CSS and Server-Side Code Styles

When you style a site using CSS, you can specify how specific elements will appear on a page. This works just fine in a static HTML web site, but when it comes to server-side elements, you will start to run into problems. Take, for example, a simple ASP.NET `Panel` control. If you drag a `Panel` control onto a page, add some text, and view the page in two different browsers (for example, Internet Explorer and an older or more limited browser like Links), you will see different results when you view the source of the page. Here's some example source code:

```
    <form id="form1" runat="server">
      <asp:Panel ID="Panel1" runat="server" Height="50px" Width="125px">This text
is contained within an ASP.NET Panel control
      </asp:Panel>
    </form>
```

Now, viewed in Internet Explorer 6 and Firefox 1.5, the following source code has been generated:

```
<form method="post" action="StyledPanels.aspx" id="form1">
  <div>
    <input type="hidden" name="__VIEWSTATE" id="__VIEWSTATE"
      value="/wEPDwULLTEwODU4OTkxMzRkZHehxD/SHmjEeZzCKx7+bB752B3R" />
  </div>

  <div id="Panel1" style="height:50px;width:125px;">
    This text is contained within an ASP.NET Panel control
  </div>
</form>
```

Now if you view that same page in an older browser (for example, Mozilla 5.0), you'll see the following:

```
<form name="form1" method="post" action="StyledPanels.aspx" id="form1">
  <input type="hidden" name="__VIEWSTATE" id="__VIEWSTATE"
    value="/wEPDwULLTEwODU4OTkxMzRkZHBovyeleyCJNtOpi+uco+l/zE5a" />

  <div id="Panel1">
    This text is contained within an ASP.NET Panel control
  </div>
</form>
```

Notice how the `Panel` has been rendered to a `<div>` control in both cases, but in the second case, it has lost its height and width information. It's a small change in this case, but it's a great improvement over ASP.NET 1.1, which renders ASP.NET `Panel` controls as HTML tables on Mozilla, Firefox, and other non-Internet Explorer browsers. For example:

```
<table id="Panel1" cellpadding="0" cellspacing="0" border="0" height="50"
width="125">
    <tr><td>
      This text is contained within an ASP.NET Panel control
    </td></tr>
  </table>
```

Although ASP.NET 2.0 has removed a lot of issues like this from our day-to-day programming lives, the problem still remains that what you see on the server side isn't the same as you will see on the client side, and you can't guarantee that an element will always be rendered in the same way on every browser. What ASP.NET 2.0 attempts to do is to provide a mechanism for specifying the appearance of an element based on its server-side control type, not on its client-side control type, so that when a control is rendered on different browsers, consistency is maintained where possible. This is achieved using themes and skins.

Themes

Themes are used to define the look and feel of a web site, similarly to how pages are styled using CSS. However, unlike CSS, themes can specify how server-side elements, such as a `TreeView` control, will appear when they are rendered on the browser. Remember that server controls have to be converted to standard HTML and possibly JavaScript if a browser is to understand how to render them on a page. A themed server control will have `style` attributes applied to each of the relevant client-side elements that are generated when the page is requested.

A theme can be used in one of two ways. It can be used as a Stylesheet theme, which acts in a similar way to a regular CSS style sheet. The alternative is to use your theme as a Customization theme, which changes the order of preference for style rules that you may be used to, so that the Customization theme will specify the style to use for each element, overriding any style preferences specified in a separate style sheet, or even in the `style` attributes of an element.

The basic method for creating a theme is the same, whichever way you use it. Additionally, you can choose to use one theme throughout an entire site, or a different theme on each page.

Creating a Theme

The process of creating a theme involves creating a `.skin` file, which defines the appearance of each element on the page, and placing this skin file within a folder, the name of which specifies the name of the theme. All themes are stored within a folder in an application directory called `App_Themes`. Here's a look at a sample skin file:

```
<asp:Calendar runat="server" Font-Names="Century Gothic" Font-Size="Small">
    <OtherMonthDayStyle BackColor="Lavender" />
    <DayStyle ForeColor="MidnightBlue" />
    <TitleStyle BackColor="LightSteelBlue" />
</asp:Calendar>

<asp:TreeView runat="server" ExpandDepth="1" Font-Names="Century Gothic"
  BorderColor="LightSteelBlue" BorderStyle="Solid" >
    <SelectedNodeStyle Font-Bold="True" ForeColor="SteelBlue" />
    <RootNodeStyle Font-Bold="True" />
    <NodeStyle ForeColor="MidnightBlue" />
    <LeafNodeStyle Font-Size="Smaller" />
```

```
    <HoverNodeStyle ForeColor="SteelBlue" />
</asp:TreeView>

<asp:Label SkinId="textLabel" runat="server" Font-Names="Century Gothic" Font-
Size="10pt" ForeColor="MidnightBlue"></asp:Label>

<asp:ImageButton SkinId="homeImage" runat="server" ImageUrl="~/platypus.gif" />
```

This file contains definitions for four types of elements. The ASP.NET `TreeView` control and the ASP.NET `Calendar` control in this file define how each of the calendars and tree view controls on a site will appear. Notice that these controls have no `ID` tag — this is a feature of all skin files. Each element within a skin file appears without an ID. At run time, if you have a page that has this theme specified as the default theme, and contains a `Calendar` control, the calendar on the page will automatically inherit the styles defined in this file.

The other two controls in this skin file, the `Label` and the `Image Button` controls, have associated `SkinIds`. These attributes enable you to create sites with many different types of `Label` controls or `Image Button` controls on them, and style selected instances of those controls using the skin data provided — the link to the skin file is controlled by the `SkinId` property. If you want to include two `Label` controls on a web page and style one of them using a theme, you can use the following syntax:

```
<asp:Label ID="Label1" SkinID="textLabel" runat="server" Text="Label">
  Styled label</asp:Label>
<asp:Label ID="Label2" runat="server" Text="Label">Unstyled label</asp:Label>
```

The `SkinID` property in this example specifies the style to apply to this control, as long as it has been defined in the theme used on that page.

In the following Try It Out, you create a simple theme in VWD and see how to define style formatting. You'll use this theme, and one other, in the examples later in this chapter.

Try It Out — Creating Themes

1. In VWD, open up the Chapter05 web site. Right-click the `C:\...\Chapter05\` folder at the top of the Solution Explorer and select Add ASP.NET Folder⇨Theme. You will see the screen shown in Figure 5-12.
2. This creates a new folder within the application called `App_Themes`, and a new empty folder within `App_Themes` that you will have to name. Name the new folder **Blue**.
3. Right-click the `App_Themes` folder and add a new Theme folder named **Red**. You now have two themes available to your site, although you don't yet have any skin files containing style definitions. This is the next part.
4. Right-click the Blue folder and select Add New Item. Select Skin File and call it **BlueBits.skin**, as shown in Figure 5-13.
5. Click Add. Take a look at the resulting file (see Figure 5-14) and you'll see some default comments that overview some of the basics of skin files.

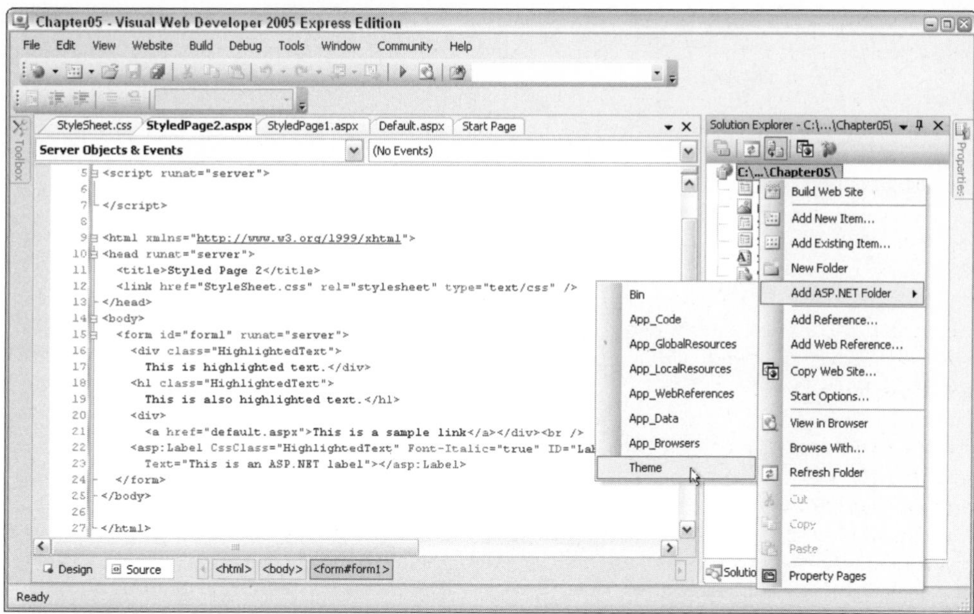

Figure 5-12

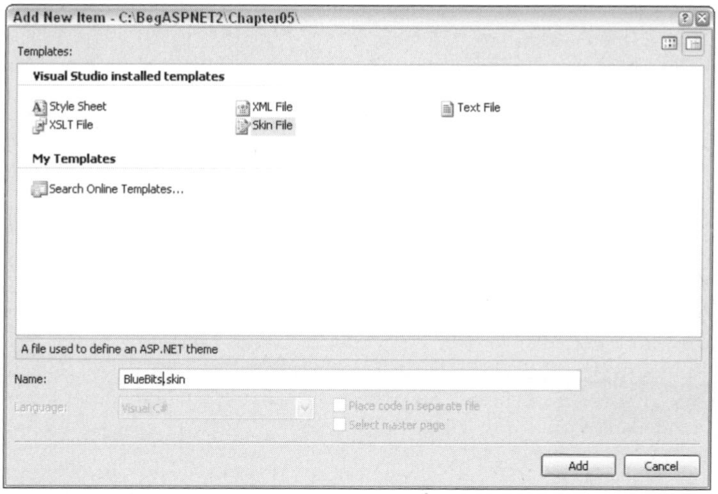

Figure 5-13

6. Repeat this step to add a skin file for the Red theme, called **RedBits.skin**.

7. For these examples, you'll find it really handy to create a simple ASP.NET page for trying out new styles before you add controls to a skin file. Create a new web page by right-clicking the `C:\...\Chapter05` root in the Solution Explorer and selecting Add New Item, selecting a Web Form, calling it **SkinSource.aspx**, and clicking OK.

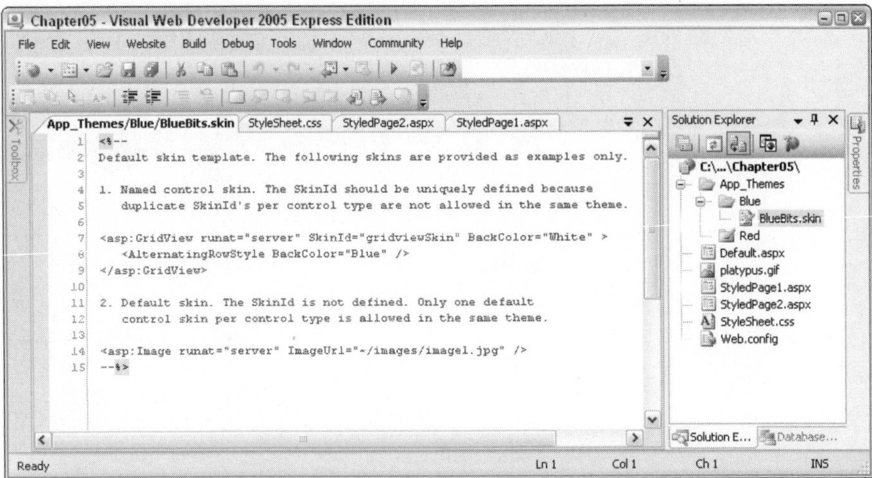

Figure 5-14

8. Drag two `Calendar` controls onto the page. These controls need some styling, and the first step is to manually add some styles to each of these controls so that the first one can be used in a blue theme, and the second can be used in a red theme. In just a moment, you'll see the styles to use for these controls — first, Figure 5-15 shows how they will look when they are styled.

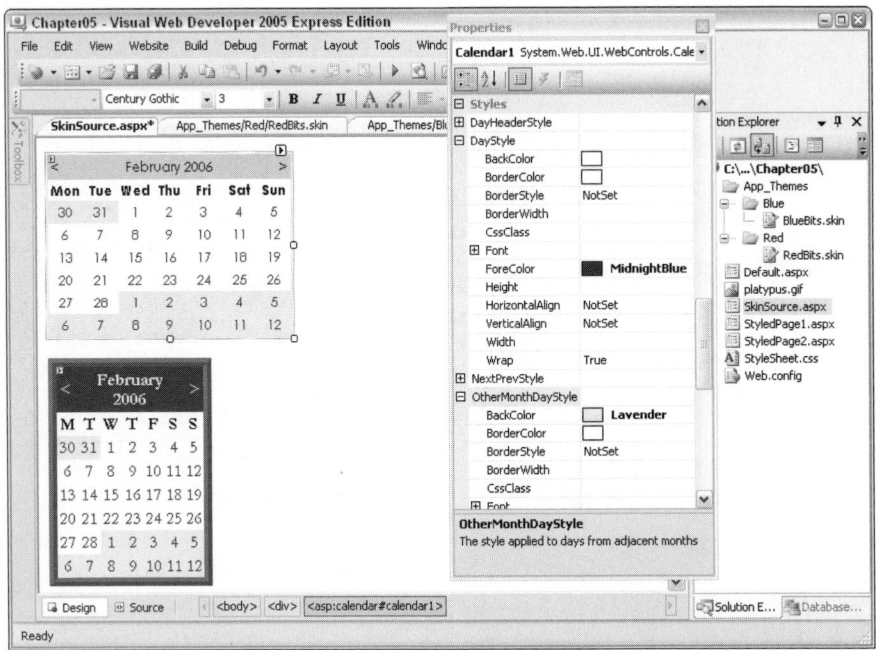

Figure 5-15

Notice that the Properties pane contains many different style options for the `Calendar` control. Set the properties as shown in the following tables.

Blue Skin

Attribute	Style
Font-Names	Century Gothic
Font-Size	Small
OtherMonthDayStyle - BackColor	Lavender
DayStyle - ForeColor	MidnightBlue
TitleStyle - BackColor	LightSteelBlue

Code

```
<asp:Calendar ID="Calendar1"
  runat="server"
  Font-Names="Century Gothic"
  Font-Size="Small">
    <OtherMonthDayStyle
      BackColor="Lavender" />
    <DayStyle
      ForeColor="MidnightBlue" />
    <TitleStyle
      BackColor="LightSteelBlue" />
</asp:Calendar>
```

Red Skin

Attribute	Style
Font-Names	Garamond
Font-Size	Medium
BorderColor	Chocolate
BorderStyle	Ridge
BorderWidth	8px
DayNameFormat	FirstLetter
OtherMonthDayStyle - BackColor	BlanchedAlmond
DayStyle - ForeColor	Maroon
TitleStyle - BackColor	Maroon
TitleStyle - Font-Bold	True
TitleStyle - ForeColor	# FFFFC0

Code

```
<asp:Calendar ID="Calendar2"
  runat="server"
  Font-Names="Garamond"
  Font-Size="Medium"
  BorderColor="Chocolate"
  BorderStyle="Ridge"
  BorderWidth="8px"
  DayNameFormat="FirstLetter">
    <OtherMonthDayStyle
      BackColor="BlanchedAlmond" />
    <DayStyle ForeColor="Maroon" />
    <TitleStyle BackColor="Maroon"
      Font-Bold="True"
      ForeColor="#FFFFC0" />
</asp:Calendar>
```

9. Now drag a `Label` control onto the page and style it with a bit of color and font styling. The following code creates two labels and defines styles that should match with your blue and red themes:

```
<asp:Label ID="Label1" runat="server" Text="Blue Styled Label" Font-Names="century
gothic" Font-Size="10pt" ForeColor="MidnightBlue"></asp:Label>

<asp:Label ID="Label2" runat="server" Font-Names="garamond" Font-Size="11pt"
ForeColor="DarkRed" Text="Red Styled Label"></asp:Label>
```

After you finish defining styles, you are ready for the next phase.

10. Open the `BlueBits.skin` file in VWD and copy and paste the HTML for your blue `Calendar` and `Label` controls in the `SkinSource.aspx` page into the skin file. Remove the `ID` tags for each of them.

11. Remove the `Text` attribute and add a `SkinID` attribute to the `Label` control to give it a unique style reference that you can use later (see the bold text in the following listing):

```
<asp:Calendar runat="server" Font-Names="Century Gothic" Font-Size="Small">
    <OtherMonthDayStyle BackColor="Lavender" />
    <DayStyle ForeColor="MidnightBlue" />
    <TitleStyle BackColor="LightSteelBlue" />
</asp:Calendar>

<asp:Label SkinId="textLabel" runat="server" Font-Names="Century Gothic"
  Font-Size="10pt" ForeColor="MidnightBlue"></asp:Label>
```

12. Repeat steps 8 and 9 for the red controls, placing them in the `RedBits.skin` definition file:

```
<asp:Calendar runat="server" Font-Names="Garamond" Font-Size="Medium"
BorderColor="Chocolate" BorderStyle="Ridge" BorderWidth="8px"
DayNameFormat="FirstLetter">
    <OtherMonthDayStyle BackColor="BlanchedAlmond" />
    <DayStyle ForeColor="Maroon" />
    <TitleStyle BackColor="Maroon" Font-Bold="True" ForeColor="#FFFFC0" />
</asp:Calendar>

<asp:Label SkinId="textLabel" runat="server" Font-Names="Garamond" Font-Size="11pt"
ForeColor="DarkRed" />
```

It's simply a case of repeating the process for any other controls you might want to add to your skin file. In the next Try It Out, you'll be adding a `Calendar` control and a `Label` control to pages and seeing how these themes change their appearance. You'll also add a `TreeView` control and an `ImageButton` control, so you will need to have some more information in your skin file to render these.

13. Add the following code to the blue skin (`BlueBits.skin`) file to specify styling for the `TreeView` and `ImageButton` controls:

```
<asp:TreeView runat="server" ExpandDepth="1" Font-Names="Century Gothic"
BorderColor="LightSteelBlue" BorderStyle="Solid" >
    <SelectedNodeStyle Font-Bold="True" ForeColor="SteelBlue" />
    <RootNodeStyle Font-Bold="True" />
    <NodeStyle ForeColor="MidnightBlue" />
    <LeafNodeStyle Font-Size="Smaller" />
    <HoverNodeStyle ForeColor="SteelBlue" />
</asp:TreeView>

<asp:ImageButton SkinId="homeImage" runat="server" ImageUrl="~/platypus.gif" />
```

14. Add similar code to the red skin (`RedBits.skin`) file to specify how to style a `TreeView` control:

```
<asp:TreeView runat="server" ExpandDepth="1" Font-Names="Garamond"
BorderColor="Chocolate" BorderStyle="Ridge">
    <SelectedNodeStyle Font-Bold="True" ForeColor="Chocolate" />
    <RootNodeStyle Font-Bold="True" />
    <NodeStyle ForeColor="DarkRed" />
    <LeafNodeStyle Font-Size="Smaller" />
    <HoverNodeStyle ForeColor="Chocolate" />
</asp:TreeView>

<asp:ImageButton SkinId="homeImage" runat="server" ImageUrl="~/platypus.gif" />
```

That's all there is to it as far as creating a theme is concerned. You should now have two themes available to your Chapter05 pages: blue and red.

How It Works

The presence of a .skin file within an App_Themes in your web application is all that's needed to make the themes within the folder available to your application. If you are hosting your web sites on a web server running IIS, you can alternatively place your themes within your <drive>:\Inetpub\wwwroot\aspnet_client\<version> folder, which makes them available to all of the applications hosted on your server.

You can create more than one .skin file for each theme you work on. All you need to do is create another .skin file within the theme's directory and create more control definitions within this file. This may help you to split up your .skin file definitions into smaller pieces. For example, if you created a site that had two different fonts in use on it (for example, one for text and one for code snippets), you could have styles defined in two .skin files: one containing the body text styles and one containing code snippet styles.

You can also include CSS style sheets in themes and use styles generated by your friendly designer on your web site. You'll see how this works later on. First, you need to have a go at putting these red and blue themes into action!

The .skin files that formed the themes in the previous example define some standard control styles that can be applied to any instance of a Calendar control on a page, or any instance of a Label control with the appropriate SkinID on a page. In this Try It Out, you apply these themes to some simple pages in a site. Note that the entire code for this chapter is available to download from www.wrox.com.

Try It Out Applying Themes to Pages

1. Start by creating a Master page for the site. This is going to be a very small and simple site, but having a Master page will help you to navigate consistently around the site. Call the Master page **ThemedMaster.master**. Into the Master page, add a TreeView control on the left-hand side of the page, and place the ContentPlaceholder to the right by using the following HTML. Notice the style attributes on the two bold <div> elements that will help to lay out the contents of the page in two columns:

```
<body>
  <form id="form1" runat="server">
    <div style="float:left;padding-right:15px">
     <asp:TreeView ID="TreeView1" runat="server">
      </asp:TreeView>
    </div>
    <div style="float:left">
      <asp:contentplaceholder id="ContentPlaceHolder1" runat="server">
      </asp:contentplaceholder>
    </div>
  </form>
</body>
```

2. You'll need to create a simple web.sitemap for this example to act as the data source for the `TreeView` control. Right-click the Chapter05 folder and select Add New Item. Add a web.sitemap with the following code:

```
<?xml version="1.0" encoding="utf-8" ?>
<siteMap xmlns="http://schemas.microsoft.com/AspNet/SiteMap-File-1.0" >
  <siteMapNode url="ThemeDefault.aspx" title="Default" description="Default Page">
    <siteMapNode url="ThemePage1.aspx" title="Page1" description="Themed Page 1" />
    <siteMapNode url="ThemePage2.aspx" title="Page2" description="Themed Page 2" />
    <siteMapNode url="Default.aspx" title="SubPage" description="Sub Page">
      <siteMapNode url="StyledPage1.aspx" title="Page1" description="Page 1" />
      <siteMapNode url="StyledPage2.aspx" title="Page2" description="Page 2" />
    </siteMapNode>
  </siteMapNode>
</siteMap>
```

3. Add a `SitemapDataSource` to the Master page and set the `DataSource` for the `TreeView` control — just like you did in Chapter 3. You should now have the following code:

```
<body>
  <form id="form1" runat="server">
    <div style="float:left;padding-right:15px">
      <asp:TreeView ID="TreeView1" runat="server" DataSourceID="SiteMapDataSource1">
      </asp:TreeView>
      <asp:SiteMapDataSource ID="SiteMapDataSource1" runat="server" />
    </div>
    <div style="float:left">
      <asp:contentplaceholder id="ContentPlaceHolder1" runat="server">
      </asp:contentplaceholder>
    </div>
  </form>
</body>
```

Figure 5-16 shows what you should see in Design View.

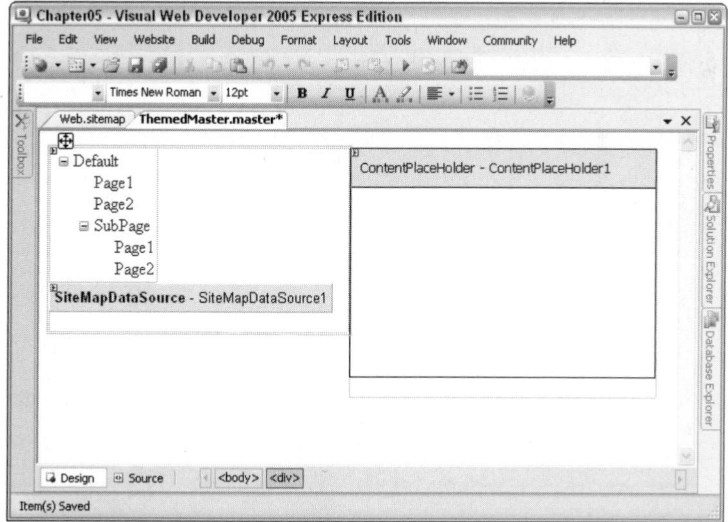

Figure 5-16

4. Time to build some content pages. In this example, you create three very simple pages. The first one is called `ThemeDefault.aspx`. Start by right-clicking the Chapter05 folder and select Add New Item. Make sure you check the box to specify a Master page for the new page and select the Master page you just created when prompted (see Figure 5-17).

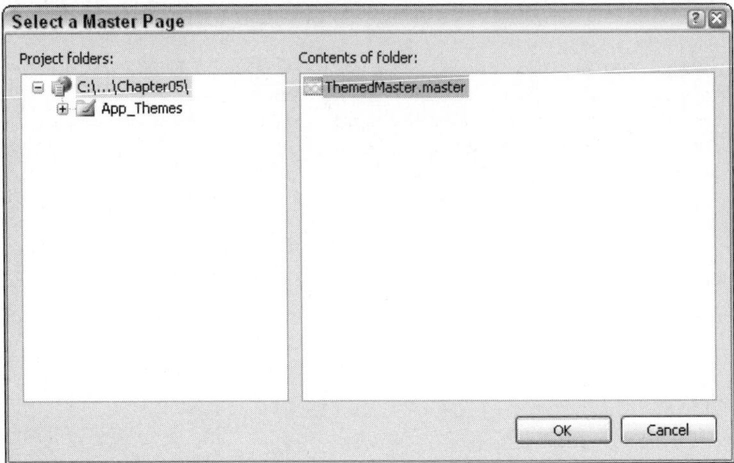

Figure 5-17

5. In the `Content` placeholder on this new page, type in some plain text: **"Default page!"**, and then drag two `Label` controls onto the page. Set the first `Label` control's `text` property to `"Styled label"`and the second `Label` control's `text` property to `"Unstyled label"`. Finally, set the first `Label` control's `SkinID` property to `textLabel`. This will link up the `Label` control to use the skinned label's styling. Your page should look like Figure 5-18.

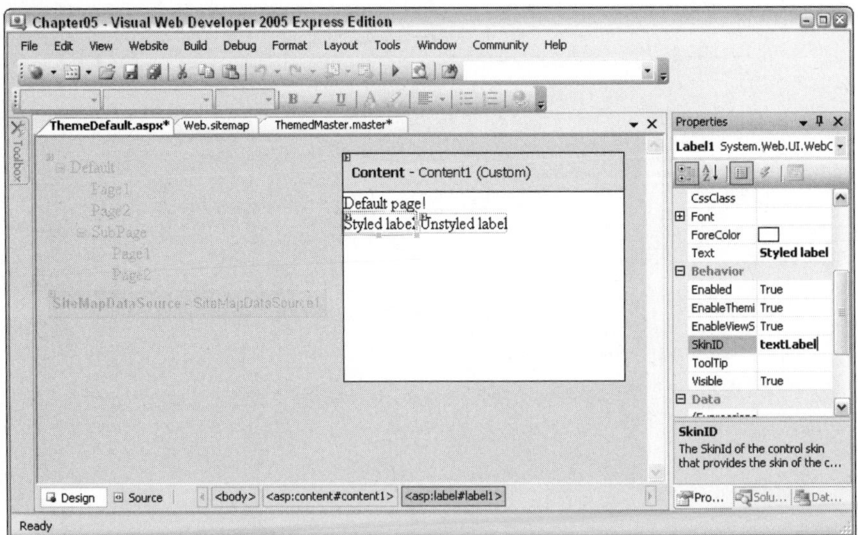

Figure 5-18

6. Specify which theme to use for this page. Let's use the blue theme. If you are in Design View, click the gray area and view the properties for the Document. In this properties list, you should set the `Theme` property to `Blue`. Save the page and that's the first one out of the way.

   If you prefer to use Source View and work with HTML directly, your code should be similar to the following — notice the `MasterPageFile` and `Theme` attributes (in bold) on the `@Page` directive at the top of the page that control the layout and style for this page:

```
<%@ Page Language="C#" MasterPageFile="~/ThemedMaster.master" Title="Untitled Page"
Theme="Blue" %>
<asp:Content ID="Content1" ContentPlaceHolderID="ContentPlaceHolder1"
  Runat="Server">
    Default page!<br />
    <asp:Label ID="Label1" SkinID="textLabel" runat="server" Text="Label">
      Styled label</asp:Label>
    <asp:Label ID="Label2" runat="server" Text="Label">
      Unstyled label</asp:Label>
</asp:Content>
```

7. Add two more pages in the same way. Call them **ThemePage1.aspx** and **ThemePage2.aspx**. Make sure that you specify the same Master page for these content pages.

8. In `ThemePage1.aspx`, enter the text **Page 1** and add a `Calendar` control onto the Content area of the page. Set the page's `Theme` property to `Blue`. The source code for this page should look like this:

```
<%@ Page Language="C#" MasterPageFile="~/ThemedMaster.master" Title="Untitled Page"
Theme="Blue" %>
<asp:Content ID="Content1" ContentPlaceHolderID="ContentPlaceHolder1"
  Runat="Server">
    Page 1<br />
    <asp:Calendar ID="Calendar1" runat="server"></asp:Calendar>
</asp:Content>
```

9. In `ThemePage2.aspx`, enter the text **Page 2** and add an `ImageButton` control to the page. Set its `SkinID` property to `homeImage` and the `PostBackUrl` property to `ThemeDefault.aspx`. This means that if a user clicks the image, they will be taken back to the `ThemeDefault.aspx` page. Finally, set the page's `Theme` property to `Red`. The source code for this page should look like this:

```
<%@ Page Language="C#" MasterPageFile="~/ThemedMaster.master" Title="Untitled Page"
Theme="Red" %>
<asp:Content ID="Content1" ContentPlaceHolderID="ContentPlaceHolder1"
   Runat="Server">
    Page 2<br />
    <asp:ImageButton ID="ImageButton1" SkinID="homeImage" runat="server"
      PostBackUrl="ThemeDefault.aspx" />
</asp:Content>
```

10. You've finished the groundwork, so it's time to see the results of your hard work. Click the `ThemeDefault.aspx` in the Solution Explorer and press Ctrl+F5 to run the page (see Figure 5-19).

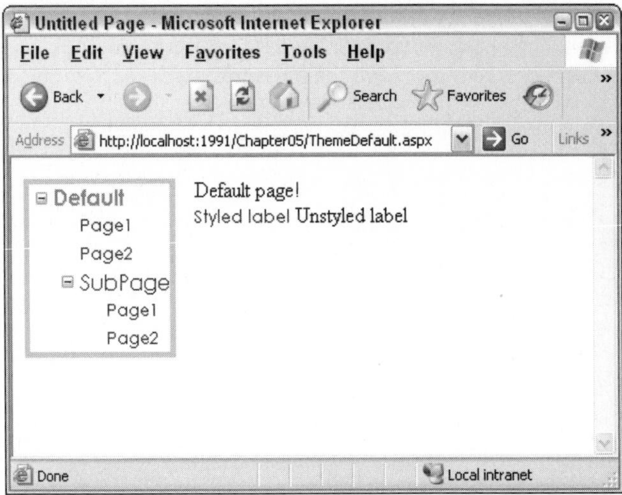

Figure 5-19

11. Click through to Page 1 to see the `Calendar` control, shown in Figure 5-20.

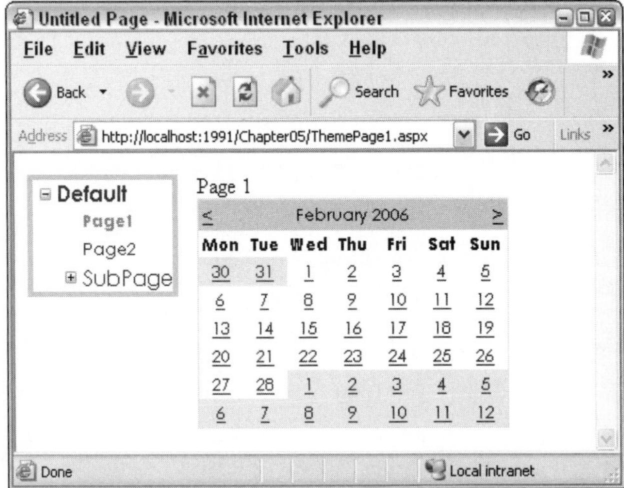

Figure 5-20

Page 2 (see Figure 5-21) includes the `ImageButton` control, and will use the red theme.

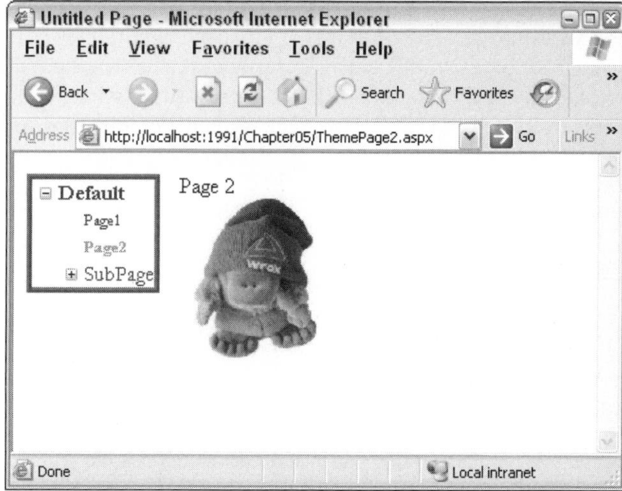

Figure 5-21

12. Change the `Theme` attribute on Page 1 to use the red theme. Save the page and view it again. It should look like Figure 5-22.

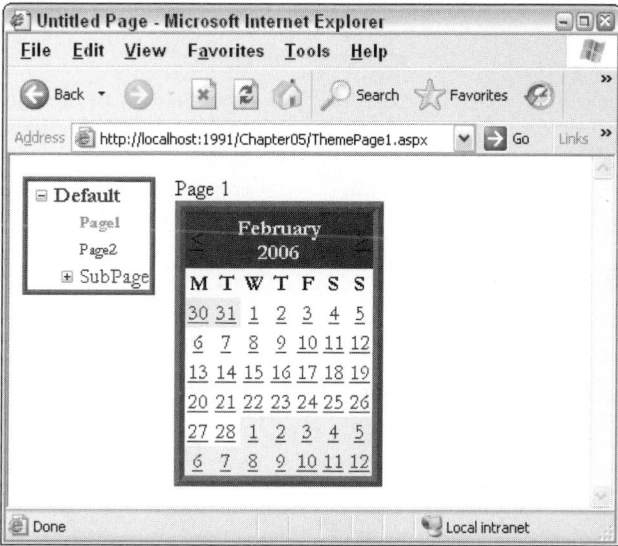

Figure 5-22

How It Works

In this example, the themes built in the previous Try It Out example have been applied to a simple collection of pages. Master pages were first discussed in Chapter 2, and in this chapter you've seen that when you have a page that uses a Master page, the entire rendered page is treated as a single entity.

Remember how you set the ThemeDefault.aspx page to use the blue theme, but you didn't specify any Theme property on the Master page? The truth is that you can't actually specify a theme directly on a Master page in any case. Your pages in this example showed how changing the Theme property on each page styled the entire page (including the TreeView control added to the Master page) with the same consistent look and feel. That style can easily be switched on different pages, as you saw with Page 1 in this Try It Out.

The main pieces of code that you need to be aware of are the Theme property in the Page directive and the SkinID attribute on server controls. Adding just these two pieces of information to a page resulted in the finished pages. Take ThemePage2.aspx as an example:

```
<%@ Page Language="C#" MasterPageFile="~/ThemedMaster.master" Title="Untitled Page"
Theme="Red" %>
<asp:Content ID="Content1" ContentPlaceHolderID="ContentPlaceHolder1"
   Runat="Server">
    Page 2<br />
    <asp:ImageButton ID="ImageButton1" SkinID="homeImage" runat="server"
      PostBackUrl="ThemeDefault.aspx" />
</asp:Content>
```

The Theme attribute at the top of the page specifies which theme should be applied to the entire page, including the contents of the Master page that it's connected to. The SkinID property specifies which skin of an ImageButton control to apply to the ImageButton on the page, so if you had many different ImageButton control styles defined in your skin file, this attribute would specify which one to use on your page.

In the preceding example, you used the Theme attribute specified at the top of each page to indicate which theme to use to style a page. There is another attribute that you can use to style the elements on a page: the StyleSheetTheme attribute. Both the Theme attribute and the StyleSheetTheme attribute take the name of the theme to apply as the value, and both are used to style pages using themes, but the attribute you choose to use can result in slightly differently rendered pages. Here's why.

Customization Themes — You Have Control!

The pages in the previous example used the Theme attribute, which means that you have just used *Customization* themes to style each of the pages in the example. A Customization theme has total control over the styling of elements on a page. If you manually style elements on a page controlled by a Customization theme, those styles will only be applied if the elements to which they are added are not already styled by the theme.

Stylesheet Themes — CSS for Server Controls

If you'd prefer to use your themes like a style sheet, you can easily choose to do so by using the StyleSheetTheme attribute at the top of a page. This change in attribute means that you can still give developers the freedom to add some small amounts of styling to controls using style attributes on each tag, while providing a common look and feel for a site in the theme itself.

The best way to see the differences between Stylesheet themes and Customization themes is to have a play, so in this Try It Out you modify the previous example to see the differences.

Try It Out — Customization and Stylesheet Themes

1. Open `ThemeDefault.aspx` and add **Font-Bold="true"** to the code for the `Styled label`. Alternatively, switch to Design View, select the `Styled label`, select the Font node from the Properties tab, and specify that the font should be bold:

```
<asp:Label ID="Label1" SkinID="textLabel" runat="server"
  Text="Styled label" Font-Bold="True"></asp:Label>
```

2. Run the page and you'll see a bold label, as depicted in Figure 5-23.

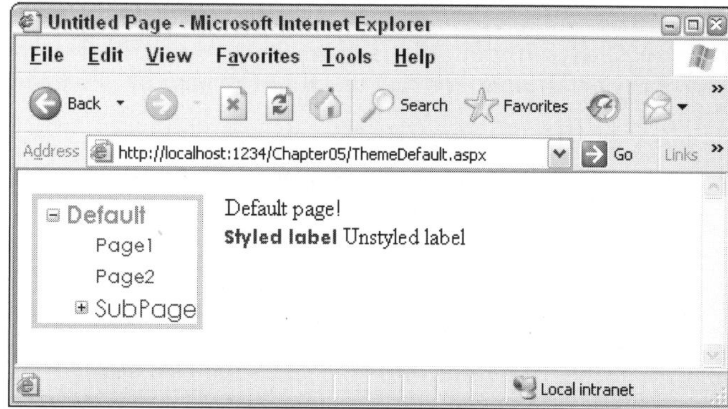

Figure 5-23

3. Edit the label declared with the `SkinId="textLabel"` in the `BlueBits.skin` file and add the following bolded declaration:

```
<asp:Label SkinId="textLabel" runat="server" Font-Names="Century Gothic"
  Font-Size="10pt" ForeColor="MidnightBlue" Font-Bold="False"></asp:Label>
```

4. Run the page again and the label will no longer be bold, as shown in Figure 5-24.

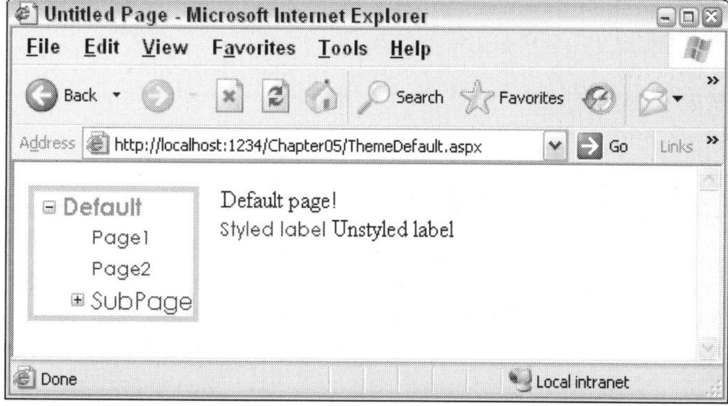

Figure 5-24

5. Change the `Theme` attribute at the top of the `ThemeDefault.aspx` page to read **StyleSheetTheme** instead of `Theme`. Alternatively, in Design View, edit the properties for the page and specify that the page's `StyleSheetTheme` should be `Blue`, and delete the `Theme` property. Run the page again and you'll see that the label is now bold once more.

How It Works

The first step in this exercise was to add a `Font-Bold="True"` attribute to the label. Because the bold attribute hadn't been specified in the Customization theme, the style in the page was applied successfully and the control was rendered with bold blue text.

However, adding a `Font-Bold="False"` to the skin's `textLabel` control overrides the style in the page because the page is still using the Customization theme (the `Theme` attribute at the top of the page). As a result, the second time you ran the page, you saw that the page now has a non-bold blue label.

The last step was to change to using a `StyleSheetTheme` instead of a `Theme` attribute at the top of the page. This enabled the page's styles to once more take priority, and so the bold blue label returned the third time the page was run.

Using a Stylesheet theme or a Customization theme is completely up to you. Choosing a Customization theme gives your designer a bit more control over the look and feel of a site, whereas the Stylesheet theme lets you play with control rendering yourself. Bear in mind, though, that if you start adding your own style attributes to controls, you may find that your site appears somewhat strange if you ever decide to change the contents of the theme, or switch to a completely different theme.

Using Both Stylesheet Themes and Customization Themes

No rules in ASP.NET specify that you can only use a Stylesheet theme or a Customization theme in your pages. If you want to have two levels of styling available to your pages, some mandatory and some optional, you can use both types of theme on your site.

For example, you may specify that major page elements must stay consistent from page to page. The `<body>` tag of a page must always be in a certain font, and the `Menu` control must always contain a certain style of node, but you may want to only use styling on `Label` controls as a guideline or default style. You can therefore create one theme that defines rules for main page elements and `Menu` controls and specify that theme to be used as the Customization theme. You can then create a different theme with some other style information in it that you can apply to a site as you create it and override certain element styles, and then apply the second theme as a Stylesheet theme. The following is the order of application when it comes to styling:

1. Stylesheet theme
2. CSS styles
3. Element styles
4. Customization theme

Styles specified in a Customization theme will always override all other settings.

Themes and CSS Together

CSS is a great way to style a site, so it's great that there's a really simple way to integrate style sheets in your themes. All you need to do is add a style sheet file to the theme's directory and slot it in right next to your skin files. Your non-ASP.NET designer will certainly be pleased that you can easily integrate his designs in your server-side pages.

Because this isn't a tough concept, you can jump straight in with a quick example that shows how this works.

Try It Out Integrating CSS and Themes

1. Return to VWD, right-click the Blue theme folder, and select Add New Item. In the dialog box that pops up, add a new style sheet and call it **BlueStyleSheet.css**.
2. In the newly created style sheet, add the following code:

```
body
{
   font-family:Arial;
}
.bigtext
{
    font-size:xx-large;
}
```

3. Return to `ThemeDefault.aspx` and add a `CssClass` attribute to the unstyled label, with a value of **"bigtext"**:

```
<asp:Label ID="Label2" CssClass="bigtext" runat="server" Text="Unstyled label">
</asp:Label>
```

4. Run the page and you'll see that the label has xx-large text style applied (see the CSS style sheet definition), and the default font for the page (everything within the `<body>` tag) is formatted using Arial as the font face, as shown in Figure 5-25.

Figure 5-25

5. Go to the `BlueBits.skin` file and add another `Label` control definition. Set its `SkinID` to **"bigLabel"**, give it a `CssClass` attribute of **"bigtext"**, and save the file:

```
<asp:Label SkinId="bigLabel" runat="server" CssClass="bigtext"></asp:Label>
```

6. In `ThemeDefault.aspx`, remove the `CssClass` attribute from the label and set its `SkinID` attribute to **"bigLabel"**:

```
<asp:Label ID="Label2" SkinID="bigLabel" runat="server" Text="Unstyled label">
</asp:Label>
```

Notice that the IntelliSense in VWD kicks in here and helps out by giving you the option of specifying which label style to use (see Figure 5-26), because you now have more than one available in your selected theme.

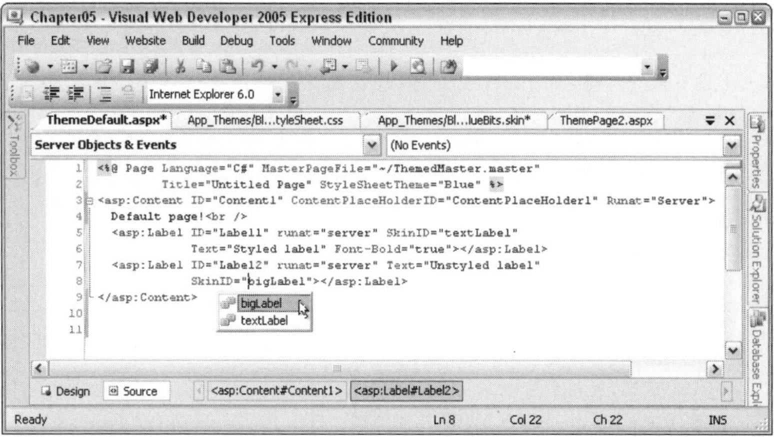

Figure 5-26

Note that you will get the IntelliSense support here only if you have saved the skin file before going back into the `ThemeDefault.aspx` page.

Running the page again will render the same result. The only differences are whether the skin file or the page contains the styling information.

How It Works

By adding a CSS style sheet to a theme folder, that style sheet is now available to all pages that use that theme. After the theme has been applied, whether it's a Customization theme or a Stylesheet theme, the styles in the style sheet are available both to the skin files within the theme's folder, and within the page itself.

The same rules apply to CSS-styled server controls from a Customization versus Stylesheet theme perspective — if you apply a CSS style to an element in a theme and apply a different style to an element on a page, the result will vary according to which type of theme you have applied. If you apply a Customization theme, the theme defined in the skin file will overrule any styles or CSS classes specified in the .aspx page, whereas the opposite is true if you specify that your theme be used as a Stylesheet theme.

Applying Styling to a Site

In most situations, you will likely want to apply a consistent look and feel to all pages within a site. Although you could just specify that all of your pages in the site use the same theme, it's quicker and easier to specify the default theme for the site in a central location. In ASP.NET 2.0, you can add a value to the `Web.config` file for your site to specify the default theme for your pages. You used the `Web.config` file in Chapter 4 when you specified site access permissions for different user accounts. Because a `Web.config` file is the central location for all site-wide settings, this is where you can store default theme settings for your site. The basic syntax for this is as follows:

```
<?xml version="1.0"?>
<configuration>
  <appSettings/>
  <connectionStrings/>
  <system.web>
    <pages theme="myTheme" styleSheetTheme="myOtherTheme" />
```

You can specify both a Stylesheet theme and a Customization theme in the `Web.config` file. If a theme is specified in the `Web.config` file and no theme is specified in a page, the theme in the `Web.config` will be applied. Additionally, if your `Web.config` specifies a Customization theme for a site and you specify a Stylesheet theme for your page, the Customization theme from the `Web.config` will be applied. Here's a slightly amended order of application for themes, including the `Web.config` themes:

1. `Web.config` Stylesheet theme
2. Page Stylesheet theme
3. CSS styles
4. Element styles
5. `Web.config` Customization theme
6. Page Customization theme

> **If you want to completely control the appearance of an entire site, use a Customization theme in the `Web.config` file.**

In the next Try It Out, you quickly specify a site-wide theme for the pages in the small application you've been building in this chapter so far.

Try It Out — Applying Themes to a Site

1. If you don't have a `Web.config` file in your project, right-click the Chapter05 folder and select Add New Item. In the dialog box, create a new Web configuration file (`Web.config`) and click OK.

2. Add the following line of code (highlighted in bold) to the `Web.config` file and save the file:

```
<?xml version="1.0"?>
<!--
    Note: As an alternative to hand editing this file you can use the
```

```
        web admin tool to configure settings for your application. Use
        the Website->Asp.Net Configuration option in Visual Studio.
        A full list of settings and comments can be found in
        machine.config.comments usually located in
        \Windows\Microsoft.Net\Framework\v2.x\Config
    -->
    <configuration>
        <appSettings/>
        <connectionStrings/>
        <system.web>
          <pages theme="red" styleSheetTheme="blue" />
```

3. Remove all `Theme` and `StyleSheetTheme` attributes from all of the pages used in this chapter and run the application. All of the pages in the site will now be rendered in the red theme, but note in Figure 5-27 the result in the `ThemeDefault` page.

Figure 5-27

How It Works

The resulting output in the `ThemeDefault.aspx` page seems to be a bit of a mixture of two different themes, yet you specified that all pages in a site should use the red Customization theme. However, in the previous example, you added a CSS file and some additional style information to the blue theme. Because the blue theme is set as a Stylesheet theme for the site, and because there are no equivalents for these styles in the red theme, these styles are picked up from the blue theme and applied to the body text and the `"Unstyled label"` label control.

The first line of HTML code is part of the body of the page:

```
Default page!<br />
```

This is styled using the blue theme's `body` style from the `BlueStyleSheet.css` file:

```
body
{
   font-family:Arial;
}
```

The next item in the code for this page is the `"Styled label"` control, which has a `SkinID` of `textLabel`:

```
        <asp:Label ID="Label1" SkinID="textLabel" runat="server" Text="Styled label"
    Font-Bold="True"></asp:Label>
```

Because this `SkinID` exists in both themes, the red theme is applied, because this theme is set to be the Customization theme in the `Web.config` file:

```
<asp:Label SkinId="textLabel" runat="server" Font-Names="Garamond" Font-Size="11pt"
ForeColor="DarkRed" />
```

Here's the line of code in the `Web.config` again:

```
        <pages theme="red" styleSheetTheme="blue" />
```

Remember that the theme attribute represents the Customization theme. However, the specified Customization theme in this case, the red theme, has no `SkinID` for a `"bigLabel"`, so the blue theme is used instead:

```
        <asp:Label ID="Label2" SkinID="bigLabel" runat="server" Text="Unstyled
    label"></asp:Label>
```

The last item on the page is styled according to the blue theme:

```
<asp:Label SkinId="bigLabel" runat="server" CssClass="bigtext"></asp:Label>
```

The `Label` control is still part of the body of the page, and because no additional font information has been specified for the control, it also inherits the CSS style for the body of the page from the blue theme.

The final example in this chapter concerns themes used in the Wrox United application. The following section takes a quick look at the themes and styling in the application.

Themes in Wrox United

The themes defined for the Wrox United site control the appearance of the team's site. Two themes are available for the site: a red theme and a blue theme. The normal, everyday theme is the red theme, and it reflects the team's home outfit in blocks of bold red and yellow. The other theme available to contrast with the red theme is the blue theme, which is designed mainly to show up the differences between two different themes being applied to a site. Figure 5-28 shows the site in its traditional Wrox Red colors.

The way that themes are applied in Wrox United is slightly different from the techniques that you've looked at in this chapter, because it relates to user preferences. As you saw in Chapter 4, you can add user accounts to a web site to enable users to log in to a site. When a user is logged on to the Wrox United site, there is some code that enables that user to store personal information (the user's name, address, and so on), and to store personal preferences, such as the theme to apply to the site when the user logs on.

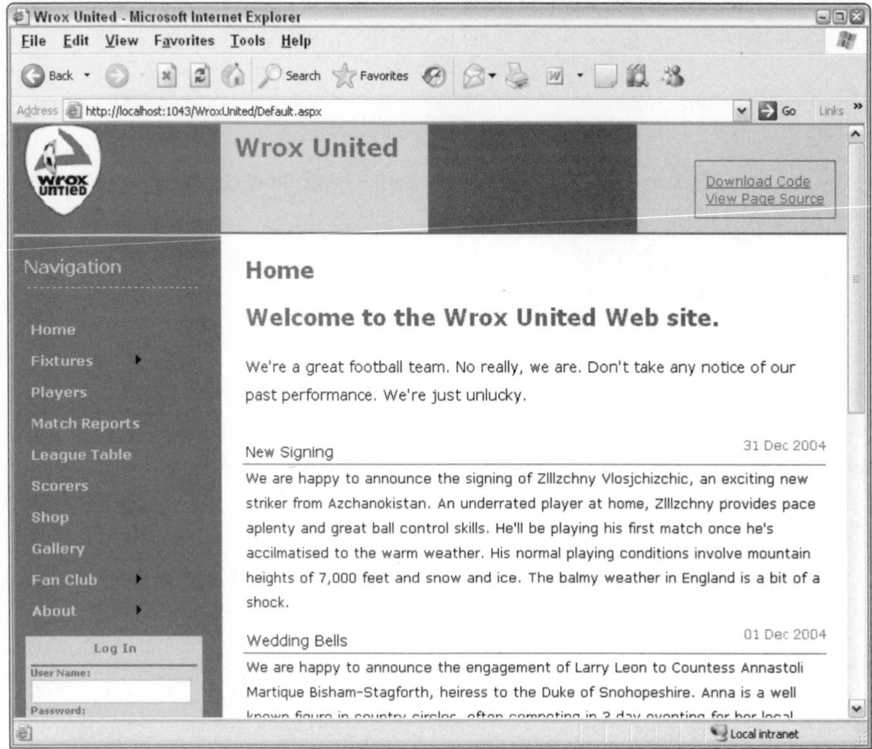

Figure 5-28

The code that handles the theme switching is explained in detail in Chapter 11, because it involves an understanding of several techniques that have not yet been covered in the book. However, in the following Try It Out, you can see how the themes are applied to the Wrox United site, and it steps through the most interesting bits in the theme definitions for the Wrox United site.

Try It Out Using Themes in Wrox United

1. Open your local copy of the Wrox United application — this should be stored within your `C:\BegASPNET2\WroxUnited` folder.

2. Press Ctrl+F5 to run the site and you'll be taken to the main front page in its default color scheme. In the login box near the bottom of the left-hand column, log in as the user **Lou**, password **lou@123**. In the box that appears below the login box, click the Modify Account link, as highlighted by the hand-style cursor in Figure 5-29.

3. In the screen that appears (see Figure 5-30), select the Wrox Blue theme from the Theme drop-down list and click Save Changes.

4. Click the Home link at the top of the menu at the side of the page to go back to the front page of the site and you'll now see the site rendered with the blue theme, as shown in Figure 5-31.

   You might not be able to see the difference that clearly in a printed book, but because it's quite easy to try out for yourself, give it a go and see the changes for yourself.

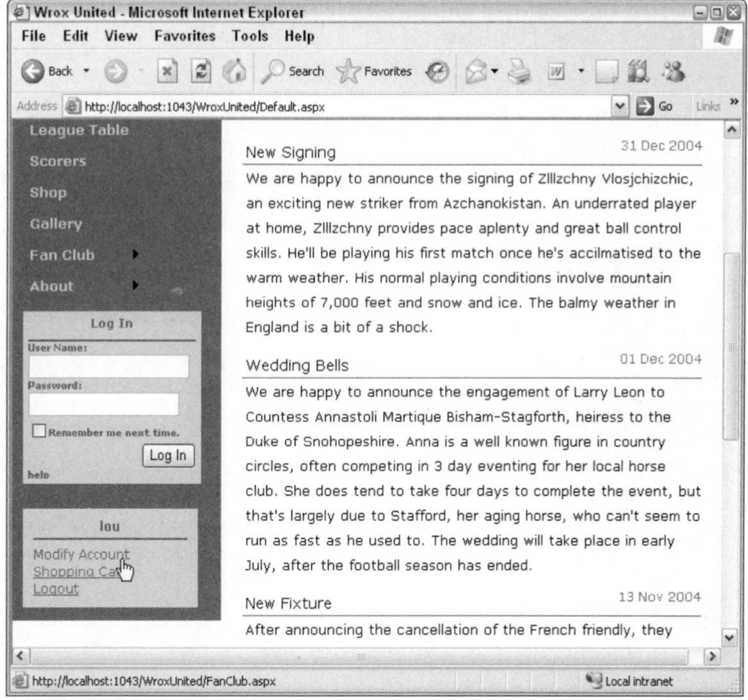

Figure 5-29

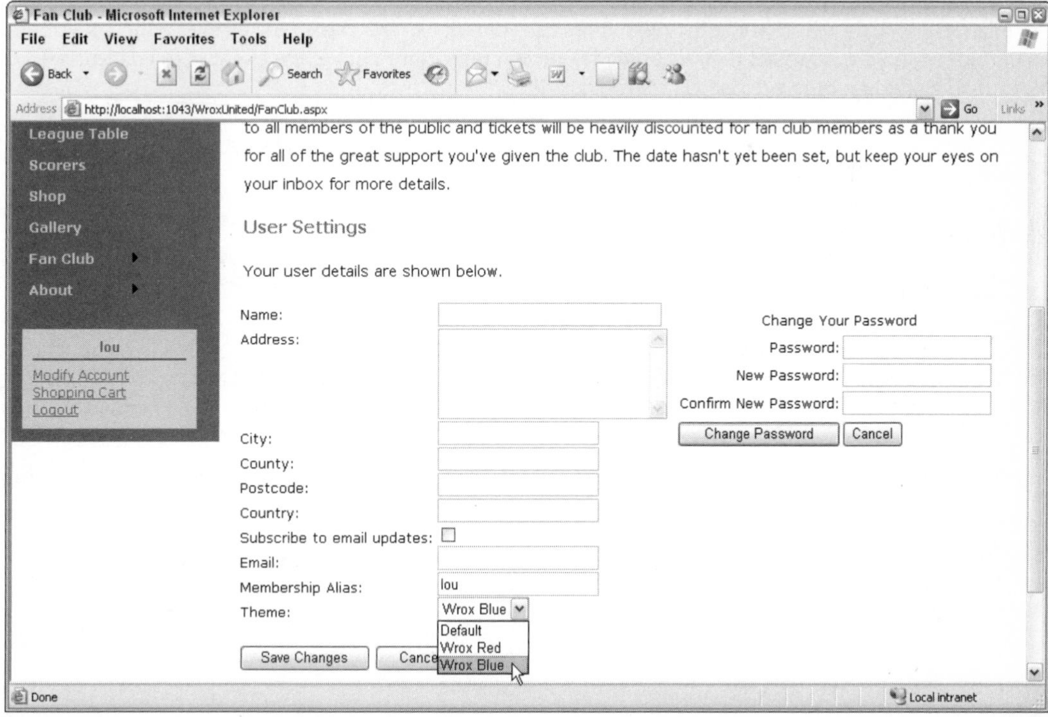

Figure 5-30

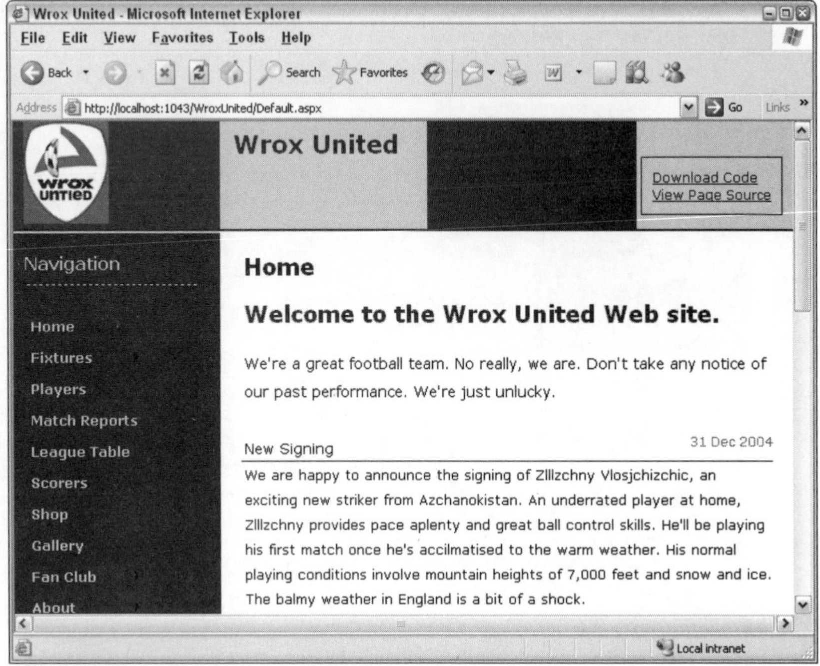

Figure 5-31

How It Works

This example demonstrated the theme-switching capability of the Wrox United site, which is something you look at in a lot more detail in Chapter 11, but the important part of the exercise to concentrate on here is the styling of the site itself.

Many styles are in use on this site, so look at the Wrox Red theme first and see how the styling is applied to the elements on the page using this theme.

The Wrox United red skin (the `WroxRed.skin` file within the WroxRed Theme folder) is included with the rest of the code for the site (available at `www.wrox.com`). The following listing shows some of the styles defined in this skin file:

```
<asp:Label runat="server" ForeColor="#000000" BackColor="transparent"></asp:Label>

<asp:TextBox runat="server" ForeColor="#000000" BorderWidth="1px"
  BorderStyle="Solid" BorderColor="#ff0000" BackColor="Transparent"></asp:TextBox>

<asp:Button runat="server" BorderStyle="Solid" BorderColor="#ff0000"
  BorderWidth="1pt" ForeColor="#000000" BackColor="#ffe5e5"></asp:Button>

<asp:HyperLink runat="server" Font-Underline="True" BorderStyle="None">
```

```
</asp:HyperLink>
```

Notice that there are specific style definitions for `Label`, `TextBox`, `Button`, `HyperLink`, and `Calendar` controls, which means that every instance of a control of each of those types will be styled as defined in this skin file.

Here's the `TextBox` definition:

```
<asp:TextBox runat="server" ForeColor="#000000" BorderWidth="1px"

  BorderStyle="Solid" BorderColor="#ff0000" BackColor="Transparent"></asp:TextBox>
```

The `TextBox` has been styled so that it has a thin solid red border around it. Note that the value specified for the `BorderColor` attribute doesn't actually say "red," but instead it uses the hexadecimal representation of a pure, bright red color.

The hash symbol (#) indicates that the color to be applied is provided as a hexadecimal value. The next two characters control how much red to add to the control, from 00 to FF. The next two characters control the level of green to apply, and the last two control the level of blue. The hexadecimal value 000000 represents a pure black (none of each color), whereas the value FFFFFF renders as white (all of every color).

The hexadecimal counting system (sometimes known as Base 16) means that the hex value FF corresponds to the decimal value of 256. With 256 different values for each component, that enables you to choose from one of 16 million possible color values!

The Wrox Red theme also has an associated CSS style sheet, `WroxRed.css`, which is also available in the code for download. The following is an extract from this file:

```
html, body {
  margin: 0;
  padding:0 5px 0 5px;
  background-color: #f00;
  color: #000;
}

title {
  color: #f66;
}

#nav {
  background-color: #f00;
  width: 20px;
  float: left;
  margin-left: -1px;
  padding: 10px;
}

#content {
  padding: 10px;
  margin-left: 230px;
  width: 100%;
}
```

The styles in use in this theme define some simple color and positioning for some of the elements used on the site. The `#nav` definition and the `#content` definition are used to match all elements on a page with an ID set to `nav` or `content`, respectively, rather than specifying the `class` attribute, or specifying a specific element type to style.

Styling and Layout Best Practices

The concepts discussed in this chapter can be used for both good and evil. You can have as many style definitions in your site as you like, but if you have little or no sense of style, you could make a big mess of things. And style is nothing without layout— the two go hand in hand. Pages need to be structured sensibly so that any user can view and understand what you're trying to tell them. Now that you've grasped the basics of styling and presenting a site, the two concepts you need to learn about now are usability and accessibility.

Usability

Usability is all about keeping users on your site, and giving them the best possible user experience while they browse. Users want to see prompt responses to their requests, they want to be able to find what they want, and they want to be able to understand what the site is all about. A site that has fifteen fonts on it will appear cluttered, hard to read, and most likely look like it was put together by someone who'd never spent time reading content on a web site.

The goal of every web development team is to make a site as usable as possible, which requires developers working together with designers to provide an attractive and intuitive user interface. This is where you can start to employ the techniques discussed in this chapter. The core principles of usability are as follows:

- **Learnability:** Design the user interface so that it takes a minimum of time for a first-time visitor to understand the design and use the site.
- **Efficiency:** Make the site efficient so that experienced users can accomplish tasks swiftly.
- **Memorability:** A user should be able to remember how to use the system next time they come to visit.
- **Bugability:** Squash those errors where possible, and if errors occur, make them user-friendly and recoverable.
- **Satisfaction:** Users should like and enjoy using your site.

Usability is an art that has been written about by many people, but the main site you should refer to when it comes to usability guidelines is `www.useit.com/`, which is the web site owned by Jakob Nielsen. All developers should spend some time looking in to this area and gain some key insights into making your sites really effective.

Accessibility

Accessibility is all about making sites *accessible* by all users. For example, web users who are partially sighted access the web with the assistance of a screen reader, which reads the contents of a web site aloud. Alternatively, these users could have their screens set to a much lower resolution, where most sites would be unable to fit on the screen. At another end of the spectrum, you could also find mobile users connecting to the web using a Pocket PC device that's only capable of displaying 320 × 240 pixels of information at one time. The browsers used on different devices like Pocket PCs employ some great techniques for scaling images to make a site fit on a screen. You could also find yourself having to cater to users who have very limited-functionality browsers — perhaps browsers that don't allow the use of JavaScript for client-side code, or that don't display images on a page to save on bandwidth. If an image were missing from a page, it would be nice to know what the image was supposed to represent to give it some context in the absence of the image itself.

At the core of accessibility are some facts that will help you to make your sites as accessible as possible. For example, if you have a screen reader reading out your source code, you should always include an HTML `alt` attribute on your images, so that the screen reader can describe what the image represents. You should always provide code that can render your site on browsers that don't support HTML frames using the `<noframes>` element, and you should avoid, where possible, using many levels of nested HTML tables to lay out a site, because a screen reader will read out the contents of every cell and row.

Many different guidelines are available for making a site accessible, and the best place to start reading is the `www.w3.org/WAI/` site. This site is the home page for the Web Accessibility Initiative and is packed full of useful and important advice.

Despite the existence of myriad resources, the vast majority of developers in the world have never given a second thought to making a site truly accessible. Many more have thought about it and made some changes to their site in an attempt to make it more accessible, but building truly accessible sites is actually quite difficult.

Take for example the Wrox United web site. This book concentrates on teaching you how to build ASP.NET web sites. The main focus is teaching what is possible, the techniques you can use, and how you can get results quickly. To make this site truly accessible would take a fair bit more time, and perhaps that would be the topic for another book.

Learn as much as possible about building accessible web sites for any public site you develop, because it's actually illegal (though not often enforced) to only provide an inaccessible web site, as described in Section 508 (see `www.section508.gov`) in the U.S., and the Disability Rights Commission's (DRC) Disability Discrimination Act (DDA) Code of Practice (`www.opsi.gov.uk/acts/acts1995/95050--c.htm`) in the UK. Prosecution for inaccessibility is quite rare, but because it's entirely possible to design accessible web sites, it's worth adding accessible web design to your skill set for both those with disabilities, and for your own professional reputation.

Summary

This chapter discussed all of the different ways of styling a page and its elements, and demonstrated numerous methods for controlling look and feel. The new skinning and themeing capabilities of ASP.NET 2.0 provide you with a great way to combine all available techniques into one easily applied package.

This chapter discussed the following:

- How to apply style attributes to elements

- How to move style attribute information into <style> sections in a page, then into a separate CSS file
- Creating ASP.NET themes and applying them to pages
- The differences between Customization themes and Stylesheet themes
- Integrating themes and CSS
- Applying a consistent style to all pages in a site
- The issues of usability and accessibility and why they are so important in today's Internet world

The next chapter moves on to discuss the issues of raising and handling events in code, as you are introduced to the concept of a postback-driven architecture.

Exercises

1. You have an ASP.NET `Label` control on a page. The label has a `font-italic="true"` attribute, and a `CssClass="maintext"` attribute:

```
<asp:label id="myLabel" CssClass="maintext" font-italic="true"
```

```
  text="This is a label"></asp:label>
```

The page has an associated CSS style sheet (not associated with a theme) that defines a `.maintext` style class. This style class has the following attributes:

```
.maintext
{
  color: Navy;
  font-family: Verdana;
  font-weight: Bold;
  font-style: normal;
}
```

How will the label appear when it is rendered?

2. You add a `Theme="ExerciseTheme"` to the preceding page. You place the CSS style sheet from the previous exercise within the ExerciseTheme theme folder. How will the label control appear now?

3. You define a skin for all labels within the ExerciseTheme theme folder and specify the following attributes:

```
<asp:Label CssClass="maintext" runat="server" font-italic="false"></asp:Label>
```

How will the label appear now?

Events and Code

We've managed to avoid lots of code so far, but you can't get away from it completely, so now it's time to get your hands dirty. You're not only going to look at code, but also the event architecture of ASP.NET and how web servers work. The reason for this is simply because knowing how web servers process pages enables you to understand how the architecture of ASP.NET works. In turn this leads to understanding how and why the ASP.NET events work.

In particular, this chapter looks at the following:

- A high-level overview of the Internet HTTP protocol
- The problems brought by web servers and how the ASP.NET event architecture solves those problems
- How server-side code works, and how it is created and used
- How events relate to the controls placed on a page, and the various types of events that you can use

The chapter starts by looking at web servers and the HTTP protocol.

Web Server Architecture

HTTP stands for *HyperText Transfer Protocol*, and it's the method of communicating with web servers. The protocol defines the commands that web servers can accept, and how browsers interact with them. The key point is that a web browser requests a page from the server. The server processes that page and sends the results back to the browser. The browser only understands HTML or JavaScript. HTML is the language that describes the layout of text and images on the page, and JavaScript enables programming on the client, within the browser. It's the web server's job to ensure that only the required content is sent back to the client browser.

Chapter 3 briefly discussed the difference between static and active content, and went on to look at the HTML and server controls, so you've seen that server controls need to be processed on the server, and that they emit HTML for the browser. What you need to do now is look at how this process actually works: what happens when you fire up your browser and type a URL into the address box, what happens when you press a button on a page, how the web server keeps track of the pages, and so on.

HTTP works by having a set of commands that browsers send to a web server. The two most common of these commands are `GET` and `POST`. The `GET` command is what a browser sends when a web page is to be fetched — it's what happens when you type a URL into the browser's address bar and press Return; it simply means "get me this web page." The `POST` command is for when something is to be sent back to the web server — for example, when you fill in a form and press a button. In reality the `POST` command actually fetches a page, but it also sends the form data back to the web server.

You don't need to know the rest of the HTTP commands or how any of them work in detail, but it's useful to know the terms and to understand that HTTP is very simple.

HTTP Is Stateless

One of the things you have to understand about HTTP is that it is *stateless*, meaning that it retains no knowledge from one request to the next. So when you request a page from a web server, the page is sent to you, and the server immediately forgets everything about you; each request stands alone. HTML doesn't help much either, because it's simple a language for the representation of the contents of the page; like HTTP, HTML doesn't retain content. For example, consider a simple web page that has a text box and a button. In your browser you enter some text and press the button. The data you entered is sent back to the web server, the web server process the page (making changes as necessary), and the page is sent back to the browser to be redisplayed. However, because there is no retention of data, the text box comes back empty — it's as though the web server has forgotten your text.

Why is this a problem? Well, it poses some real issues when writing applications, because very often you want some form of data retention. For example, consider the checkout page at an online store, such as the one at the Wrox United online shop, as shown in Figure 6-1.

Figure 6-1

The checkout involves several steps, each of which requires users to supply some form of information: making sure they are logged in, checking their address, and authorizing payment. As far as HTTP is concerned, each step is a separate request from the user; the page loading is one request, pressing the Next button is another request, and so on.

When you fill in some details on a page and press a button, that information is posted back to the web server (the term *posted* derives from the actual HTTP `POST` command used). When you reach the last of the checkout steps, you need all of the information entered by the user, not just the data supplied with the last step. Because HTTP and HTML don't retain this information for you, you have to store it yourself. In non-ASP.NET environments this can be quite complex and time consuming, but luckily for us the server controls are clever; they retain their state across *postbacks*. This means you don't have to do anything special; if you press a button to post the information back to the server, when the page is refreshed the text boxes still have their data. This is one of the big differences between standard HTML and server controls, and is one of the reasons why we use server controls.

The server controls remove even more of a burden from us. Consider the checkout page shown earlier, which has several text boxes, and that's only one step; there's also the login details, plus the credit card details, plus the management of the steps themselves. Server controls are used for all of the text entry, but there is also a Wizard control, designed specially for use in situations like this. It manages the steps, creates the menu of steps on the left, and provides the Previous and Next buttons. All you have to do is define what you want within those steps. When you get to the last step everything the user has typed in is available, and the order can be processed.

Server-Side Events

So far you've seen a very simple view of what happens when you interact with a web server — you press a button and something happens. So what is it that actually happens on the server, in your ASP.NET page? Well, simply put, there are a number of events that run; some that always run, some that only run depending on what the user has done (which button they've pressed), and some that run due to other actions, such as data being changed. These events are ASP.NET's way of letting you know something has happened, and they allow you to take some action. For example, all ASP.NET pages have an event that runs when the page loads, and you can place code within this event to perform some action. Buttons have an event that runs when you click them, lists have an event that runs when you select a list item, and so on, and these events are what give you the power to control how the web page reacts to the user.

Before digging into the code, some terms need explaining. When an event happens it is called *firing* or *raising*. That is, the event is raised or the event is fired. Both terms are valid, and which you use is a matter of preference (I prefer raised, because fired always makes me think of a poor little event being stuffed into a cannon at a circus before being launched into a tiny net to amuse the crowd). Both terms are used regularly in the .NET documentation and on various online sites and articles.

The code that is run when the event is raised is called the *event procedure* or *event handler*. Any code you put in here becomes part of the event procedure and runs when the event is raised. For example, consider a page with two buttons. Each of these buttons could have its own event procedure, while there is a separate event procedure for when the page loads, as illustrated by Figure 6-2.

Figure 6-2 shows three event procedures. This first is the `Page_Load` event, which is raised by ASP.NET when the page loads, and allows you to prepare the page for the user, perhaps fetching data from a database.

The other two events are generated by the user when a button is clicked; each button has its own event handler. For example, the first button might save some user-entered details, whereas the second button cancels user-entered details.

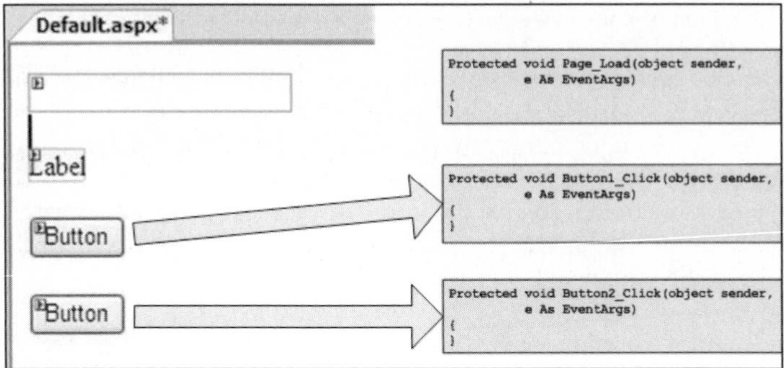

Figure 6-2

Adding Events to the Page

Adding events to ASP.NET pages is simple because Visual Web Developer (VWD) provides a way to do this for you. It allows you to select the page or a control and for the allowable events to be listed. You can then instruct VWD to create the event procedure for you. The first thing that needs to be discussed is where the events are created, because there are two places where events can be created. The first is in the same file as the ASP.NET controls, and this is called *code inline*. The second place to create events and code is in a separate file and this is called *code-behind*. Where the code is created depends upon a simple checkbox on the Add New Item dialog, as shown in Figure 6-3.

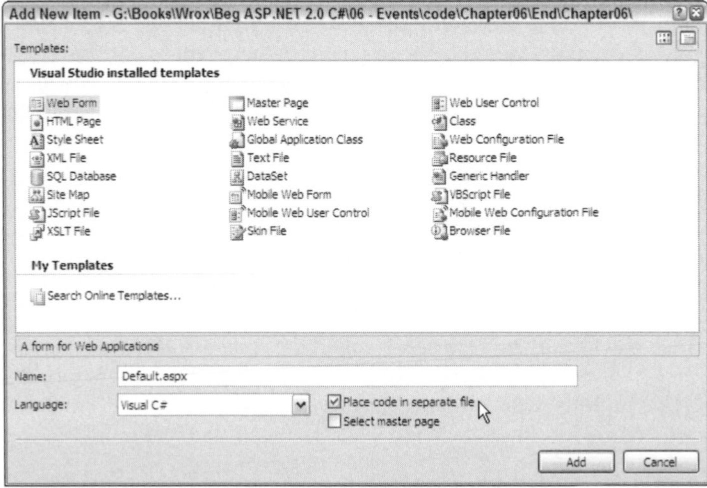

Figure 6-3

You can use either code inline or code-behind, because it doesn't make any difference to ASP.NET, but code-behind is the accepted standard, and all of the pages in the Wrox United application use code-behind, as do all of the examples in this chapter.

In the following Try It Out, you give events a go and add some events to a page.

Try It Out Adding Page and Control Events

1. Start Visual Web Developer, and open the web site at `C:\BegASPNET2\Begin\Chapter06`. You should see a screen similar to Figure 6-4.

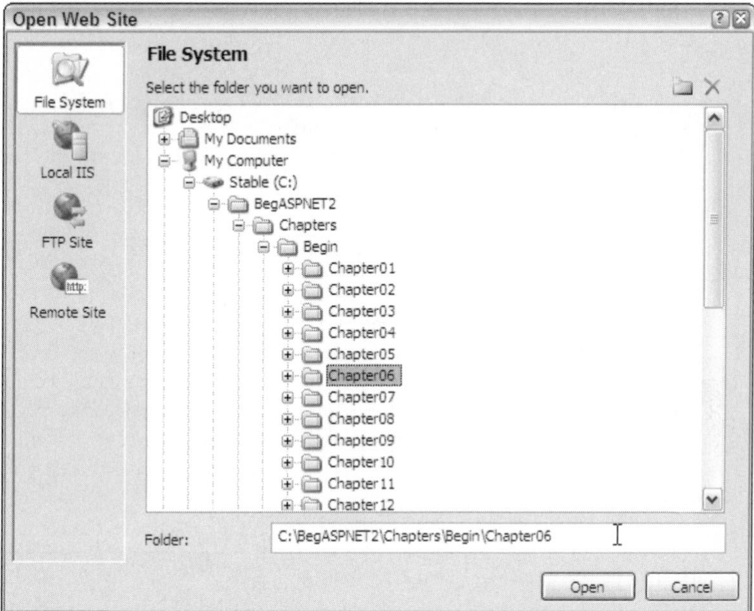

Figure 6-4

2. Open the `Default.aspx` file and switch from Source View to Design View.
3. Drag a `Label`, a `TextBox`, and two `Button` controls onto the page, so that it looks like Figure 6-5.

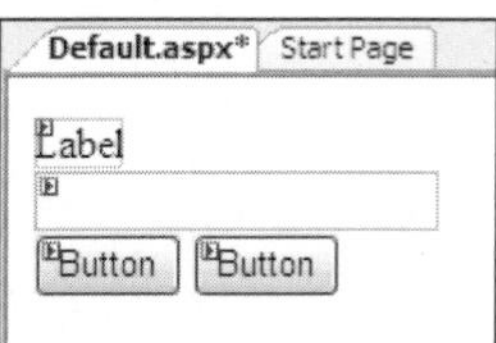

Figure 6-5

4. In an empty area of the page, double-click the left mouse button to load the code file associated with the page and create an empty event procedure for you, called Page_Load, as shown in Figure 6-6.

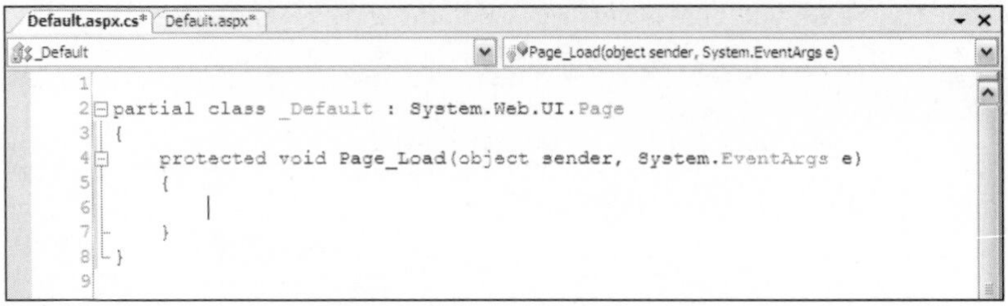

Default.aspx.cs* Default.aspx*

_Default | Page_Load(object sender, System.EventArgs e)

```
partial class _Default : System.Web.UI.Page
{
    protected void Page_Load(object sender, System.EventArgs e)
    {

    }
}
```

Figure 6-6

5. Switch back to the page design and double-click the first button, `Button1`. The event procedure `Button1_Click` for this button is created (see Figure 6-7), underneath the event procedure for the page.

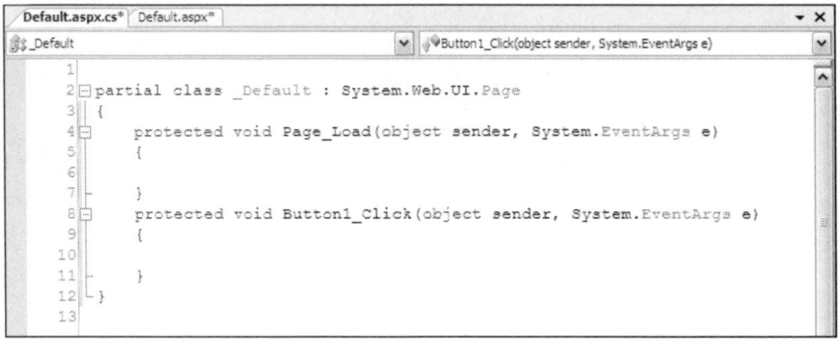

Default.aspx.cs* Default.aspx*

_Default | Button1_Click(object sender, System.EventArgs e)

```
partial class _Default : System.Web.UI.Page
{
    protected void Page_Load(object sender, System.EventArgs e)
    {

    }
    protected void Button1_Click(object sender, System.EventArgs e)
    {

    }
}
```

Figure 6-7

6. Repeat step 5, but for the second button, `Button2`, which will create the event procedure `Button2_Click`, as shown in Figure 6-8.

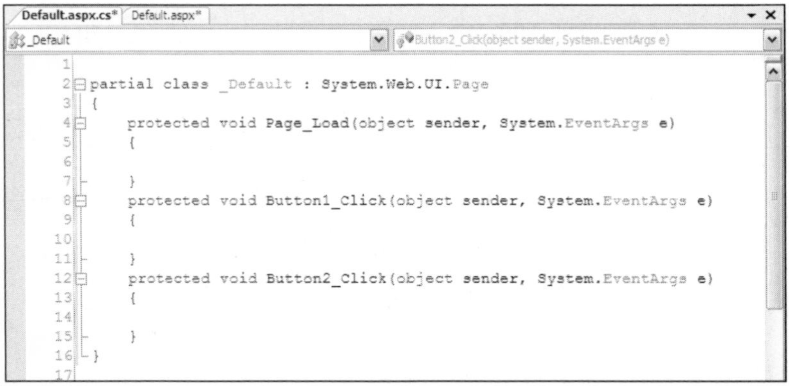

Default.aspx.cs* Default.aspx*

_Default | Button2_Click(object sender, System.EventArgs e)

```
partial class _Default : System.Web.UI.Page
{
    protected void Page_Load(object sender, System.EventArgs e)
    {

    }
    protected void Button1_Click(object sender, System.EventArgs e)
    {

    }
    protected void Button2_Click(object sender, System.EventArgs e)
    {

    }
}
```

Figure 6-8

7. In the `Page_Load` event procedure, add the following line of code:

```
Label1.Text = "You entered " + TextBox1.Text;
```

- The event procedure will now look like this:

```
protected void Page_Load(object sender, System.EventArgs e)
{
  Label1.Text = "You entered " + TextBox1.Text;
}
```

8. In the `Button1_Click` event, add the following line of code:

```
TextBox1.Text = "You clicked button 1";
```

9. In the `Button2_Click` event, add the following line of code:

```
TextBox1.Text = "You clicked button 2";
```

10. Press F5 to run the example. Click OK if the Debugging Not Enabled dialog appears, accepting the default selection for adding a new `Web.config` file with debugging enabled. This is shown in Figure 6-9 and will only appear if debugging is not enabled, so clicking the OK button enables debugging and stops the dialog from appearing again. You may also receive another dialog or pop-up from a firewall if you have one running; this might be to warn you that a program is trying to access the Internet and if you have an option you should allow the access.

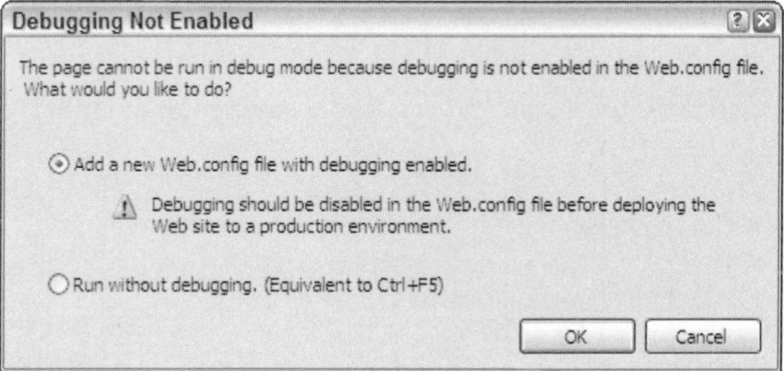

Figure 6-9

11. When the browser window appears you'll see a screen similar to Figure 6-10. Don't worry if the numbers after `localhost` are different, because VWD picks this number.

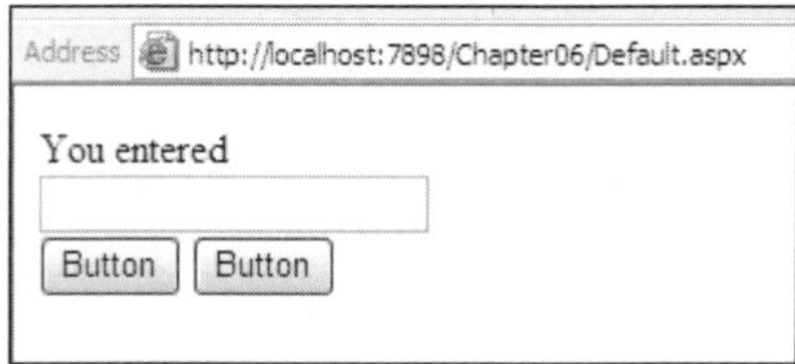

Figure 6-10

- Notice that the label has the text you set in the `Page_Load` event, but nothing else.

12. Enter your name into the text box and click the first button. For example, I entered Dave because that's my name, so the figures show Dave. Now the label has the text you entered (as shown in Figure 6-11), but the text box has the text set from the `Button1_Click` event.

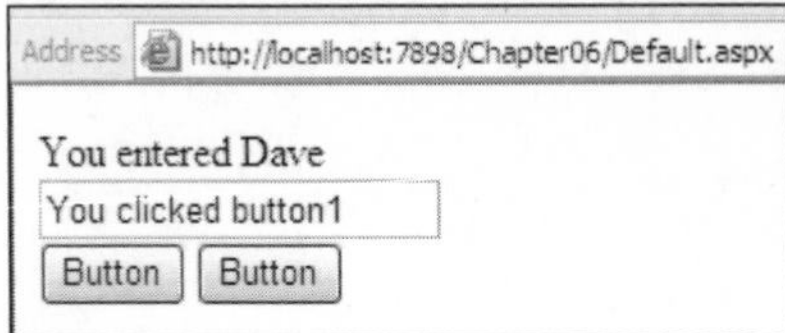

Figure 6-11

13. Now click the second button. Figure 6-12 shows that the label text has changed to what the text box contained in the previous step, and the text box contains the text from the `Button2_Click` event.

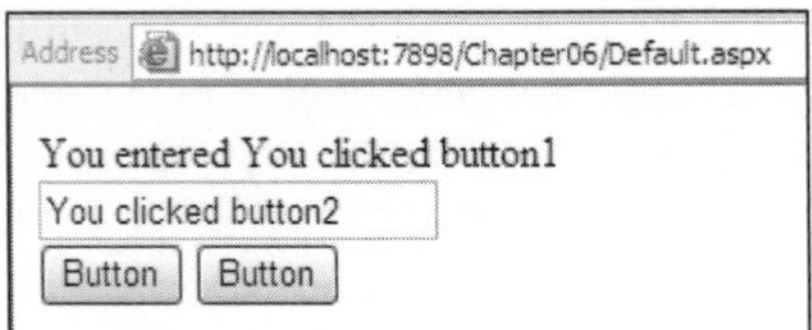

Figure 6-12

14. Now click the first button again, and you'll see something similar to Figure 6-13.

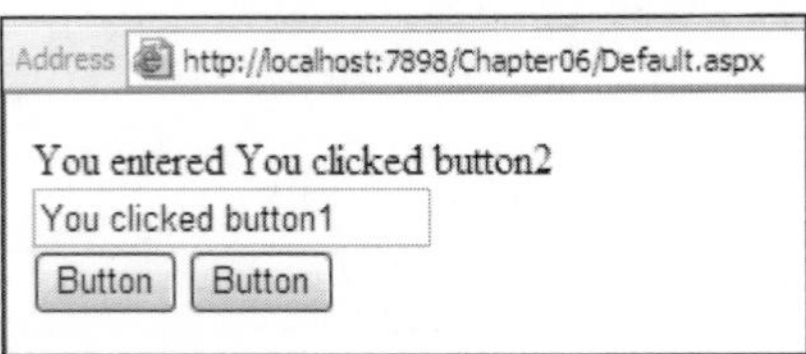

Figure 6-13

How It Works

Take a look at how this works, starting with the `Page_Load` event.

```
protected void Page_Load(object sender, System.EventArgs e)
```

This is known as the *declaration*, and tells you lots about the procedure. It has two main areas: the bits before the parentheses, and the bits within the parentheses. So at the beginning of the line you have the following:

```
protected void Page_Load
```

- `protected` tells you about who can use the procedure. In this case it means that only other programs within the same class can use this procedure. You don't need to worry about this for now; Chapter 9 looks at this in more detail.
- `void` tells you that this is an event procedure, and that it doesn't return a value. That means ASP.NET can simply call this and not expect anything back.
- `Page_Load` is the name of the event procedure. The name of event procedures can be anything, but you'll find certain standard usages appearing that are descriptive of the actual event. The `Page_Load` event is very descriptive because this event procedure will be used whenever the page is loaded into ASP.NET for processing.

Next you have the middle section; these are the parameters. There are two parameters, separated from each other by a comma:

```
object sender, System.EventArgs e
```

The parameters are simply variables that get passed into the event procedure by ASP.NET. Chapter 9 covers variables in more detail, so the actual syntax isn't explained here, but some details are worth knowing. By and large all events in ASP.NET have two parameters. The first, typically called `sender`, is the object that raised the event. In this case it is the actual page, because the page is saying "Hey, I've loaded and you can do your stuff now." For other events, such as those that buttons raise, the sender would be the button. The second parameter, `e`, is any additional information that the event procedure might need. For the `Page_Load` event there is no additional information, but later in the chapter you'll look at events where you do need some extra detail. Neither of these arguments is needed for your event procedure, but they are provided by ASP.NET in case they are required.

The way that these event procedures are run depends upon the event procedure. For the `Page_Load` event, this is automatic — ASP.NET automatically looks for a procedure called `Page_Load` and will run it when the page loads. For other controls, such as the buttons you placed on the form, the event procedure is linked to the control by way of an attribute — this is explained after you've looked at the code for the button event procedure.

Now that you've actually hooked your procedure into the event handling system of ASP.NET, you can run your own code:

```
  Label1.Text = "You entered " + TextBox1.Text;
```

This line of code simply sets the text for the label to some static text plus whatever text was entered into the text box. Don't worry too much about what the plus (+) means — Chapter 9 looks at that sort of thing in more detail.

Here are the event procedures for the buttons:

```
protected void Button1_Click(object sender, System.EventArgs e)
{
  TextBox1.Text = "You clicked button 1";
}
```

The declaration is very similar to the Page_Load one, apart from the name of the procedure. The big difference is that this event procedure isn't automatically linked to the button — this is done in the source of the page, and was added for you when you doubled-clicked the button. The source of the button is:

```
<asp:Button ID="Button1" runat="server"
  OnClick="Button1_Click" Text="Button" />
```

Here the event you are handling is the Click event, which is raised whenever the button is clicked. For each event there is an associated attribute, with the same name as the event but with On in front of it. So for the Click event you have an attribute called OnClick, and the contents of that attribute is the name of the event procedure. In the above code example, the OnClick attribute contains Button1_Click, which is the name of the event procedure. You could name the procedure anything you like, but having sensible names means it's easy to see what the event procedure does. The event procedure for the second button is similar, but with the obvious changes of the names and text.

Now look at what happens when the examples are run. When the page is first loaded, the Page_Load event procedure runs and the text for the label is set. However, because there is no text in the text box, the label only has "You entered" as its text. When you enter some text into the text box and click the first button, the page is loaded again, so the Page_Load event procedure is run, followed by the Button1_Click event procedure. So the text you entered into the text box is displayed in the label, and then the text box has new text set from within the Button1_Click event procedure. The important thing to note is that both event procedures run; the Page_Load event procedure will always be before event procedures for controls on the page.

This process is repeated as you continue to click the buttons.

The Postback Architecture

One of the problems you might have spotted is that the Page_Load event always runs, even when a button is clicked. There may be times when you want code to run when the page is first loaded, but not when buttons are clicked. For example, consider the previous example, where you displayed the contents of a text box in a label. When the page first loaded there was nothing in the text box so your label text was incomplete. The next Try It Out corrects this.

Try It Out Checking for Postback

1. If you are still running the browser from the previous example, close it.
2. In Visual Web Developer, change the Page_Load event procedure so that it looks like this:

```
protected void Page_Load(object sender, System.EventArgs e)
{
  if (Page.IsPostBack)
  {     Label1.Text = "You entered " + TextBox1.Text;
  }}
```

3. Save the page and press F5 to run it. Notice that the label text is Label — this is the default text for a Label control and you didn't change it when you placed the Label on the page. Enter some text and click a button, and you'll see that the label now has text. Close the browser.
4. Now change the Page_Load event to this:

```
protected void Page_Load(object sender, System.EventArgs e)
{
  if (Page.IsPostBack)
  {
    Label1.Text = "You entered " + TextBox1.Text;
  }
  else
  {
    Label1.Text = "Enter some text and press a button";
  }
}
```

5. Save the page and press F5 to run it. Now you have this more useful, new text when the page first loads, and different text when a button is pressed.

How It Works

Having different text at the first page load from subsequent page loads works because the ASP.NET page has a property called `IsPostBack`, which identifies whether or not the page has been posted back to — that is, whether a button has been pressed. If so, `IsPostBack` will be `true`. If it's the first time the page has loaded — that is, a button has not been pressed — `IsPostBack` will be `false`.

In the first code change you only displayed text if `IsPostBack` was true — if a button had been pressed. The second code change, in step 4, had different text for the two different situations.

It is important to know that this postback design only works when you are dealing with a single page, because `IsPostBack` gets reset when you move to another page. Consider two pages, Page1 and Page2, each with a `Page_Load` event procedure and a `Button1_Click` event procedure for a button. They also have a hyperlink to each other, allowing you to jump between the pages. You start with Page1, the `Page_Load` event procedure runs, and `IsPostBack` is `false`. You press the button and the `Page_Load` event is run again, followed by the `Button1_Click` event; in both event procedures `IsPostBack` would be `true`. You click the link to jump to Page2 and the `Page_Load` event procedure on that page runs, and `IsPostBack` in the `Page_Load` event on Page2 is `false`. Now you click the link to jump directly back to Page1, where the `Page_Load` event runs once more, but this time `IsPostBack` is `false` as well. The use of `IsPostBack` only works when you remain on the same page, so don't think that "the first time the page is loaded" means the very first time. The following table might help to make this clear.

Action	Page	Control	Events	IsPostBack
Page loads	Page1		`Page_Load`	`false`
Button clicked	Page1	`Button1`	`Page_Load` `Button1_Click`	`true`
Navigate to Page 2	Page2		`Page_Load`	`false`
Navigate to Page 1	Page1		`Page_Load`	`false`

What Events Are Available?

In the first example in this chapter you created event procedures by double-clicking the page and control. The questions that might be poised on your lips are what events are there, how can I find the events, and which events should I use? Well, the first two questions can be answered in the same way, and there is one main place to look — the Properties area on the page designer. Above the list of properties is an icon that looks like a lightning bolt, which only shows when the page is in Design View; clicking this icon shows a list of events for the control, as shown in Figure 6-14. If you double-click in the space to the right of an event, the code window will be displayed and the event procedure created for you, or like the code window selection, you'll be shown the event procedure if it already exists. By and large the events you'll be interested in will be grouped under Action or Data.

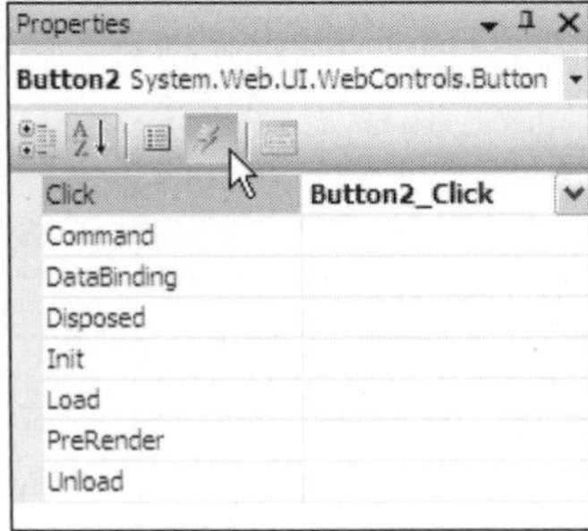

Figure 6-14

The other place to find a list of events is in the Help files, where details of each event and what they are used for is listed.

Which Events Should I Use?

If you start looking into the events that are available you'll soon realize that there are quite a few, and it's not always obvious which ones should be used. The following table details some of the most common controls and events; this isn't all of them, just the ones you'll find most useful.

Control	Event	Is raised when...

`Button`
`LinkButton`
`ImageButton`
	`Click`	The button is clicked.

`DropDownList` `ListBox`	`SelectedIndexChanged`	The selection on the list changes. This is useful for performing some action based on the new selection.
`CheckBox` `RadioButton`	`CheckChanged`	The status of the `CheckBox` or `RadioButton` changes. That is, when they either become checked or unchecked.

Control	Event	Is raised when...
CheckBoxList RadioButtonList	SelectedIndexChanged	The selection on the list changes.
Calendar	SelectionChanged	The selected date is changed.
	VisibleMonthChanged	The month is changed.
Login	Authenticate	The user is authenticated.
	LoggedIn	The user has logged in.
	LoginError	There is an error during the login process.
DataList	DataBound	An item is taken from a database and bound to the list.
GridView	RowDeleting	The current row is being deleted.
	RowUpdating	The current row is being updated.
	SelectedIndexChanged	The selected row has changed.
SqlDataSource	Deleted	A row has been deleted from the set of data.
	Inserted	A row has been inserted into the set of data.
	Updated	A row has been updated in the set of data.
Menu	MenuItemDataBound	An item is being bound to the menu.

Some of these are fairly obvious in their usage. For example, you've already seen the `Click` event of the button, and you can see that all of the button type controls have that same event. So if you don't want to have a standard button, but want to maybe have an image instead, you still use the `Click` event. Give this a try in the following Try It Out, but this time you'll use a different method for hooking into the event.

Try It Out — Manually Creating Events

1. If you have a running browser window, close it, and open `Default.aspx` in Visual Web Developer.
2. Create a Regular Folder called Images under the web site. You can use the right-click Add Folder menu on the web site for this, as shown in Figure 6-15.
3. Copy `AddToCart.gif` from the Images folder of the Wrox United site and place it in the Images folder you have just created.
4. In Design View place an `ImageButton` on the form, and set the `ImageUrl` property to `~/images/AddToCart.gif`.
5. Select the `TextBox` and change the `Columns` property from `0` to `50`.

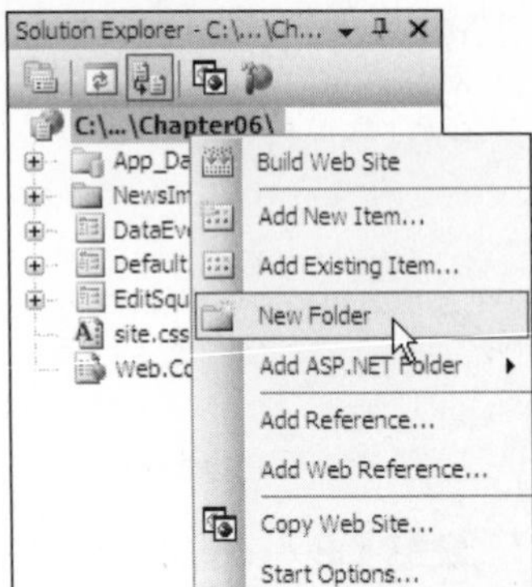

Figure 6-15

6. Switch to Source View and locate the `ImageButton` control. Change the declaration so that it looks like this:

```
<asp:ImageButton ID="ImageButton1" runat="server"
  OnClick="ImageButton_Click" ImageUrl="~/images/AddToCart.gif" />
```

7. Open the code file, `Default.aspx.cs`, and add the following code, just before the `End Class` statement:

```
protected void ImageButton_Click(object sender,
                    System.Web.UI.ImageClickEventArgs e)
{
  TextBox1.Text = "You clicked the ImageButton at position "+
                    e.X.ToString() + "," + e.Y.ToString();
}
```

8. Press F5 to run the page. Click several times in the `ImageButton`, moving the cursor so that you click in a different position. Notice how the coordinates of where you click are shown in the text box.

How It Works

The important bit of how this works is in the Source View, where the `ImageButton` control is defined. Here you added the following to it:

```
OnClick="ImageButton_Click"
```

This tells the control that for the `Click` event you want to run the procedure called `ImageButton_Click`—this is the same as for the standard button you used earlier. Within the code file, the event procedure declaration is similar, but the second parameter is different from the type you've seen before:

```
protected void ImageButton_Click(object sender,
                    System.Web.UI.ImageClickEventArgs e)
```

For the `Button`, the second parameter was `System.EventArgs`, but for the `ImageButton` it is `System.Web.UI.ImageClickEventArgs`. Remember that the second parameter can be used by ASP.NET to pass extra information into the event procedure, but for `Button` controls there was no extra information. For an `ImageButton` there is extra information, so the parameter is different—in this case it contains the `X` and `Y` coordinates of where on the image the mouse was clicked. You simply display these coordinates in the text box. You don't actually need these coordinates, but this is a great example of parameters having extra information.

A parameter name other than `System.EventArgs` *is actually a good indication that additional information may be available to you in the event procedure. You can find out what that information is by simply typing* `e.` *in the code window and looking at the IntelliSense that pops up.*

Events Aren't Triggered by Users Only

So far in this chapter the events you've seen have been explicitly generated by the user, by way of clicking a button. Some events, however, are generated in other ways. Some are indirectly generated by the user, perhaps by way of updating some data, and others are generated directly by ASP.NET. You can use the events regardless of how they are generated, and in this section you see how you can do this.

You're going to create some events from data in a database, and although data has not been covered yet, it's the events that are important. First, have a look at the news items on the Wrox United site (see Figure 6-16), found under the About⇨News menu item.

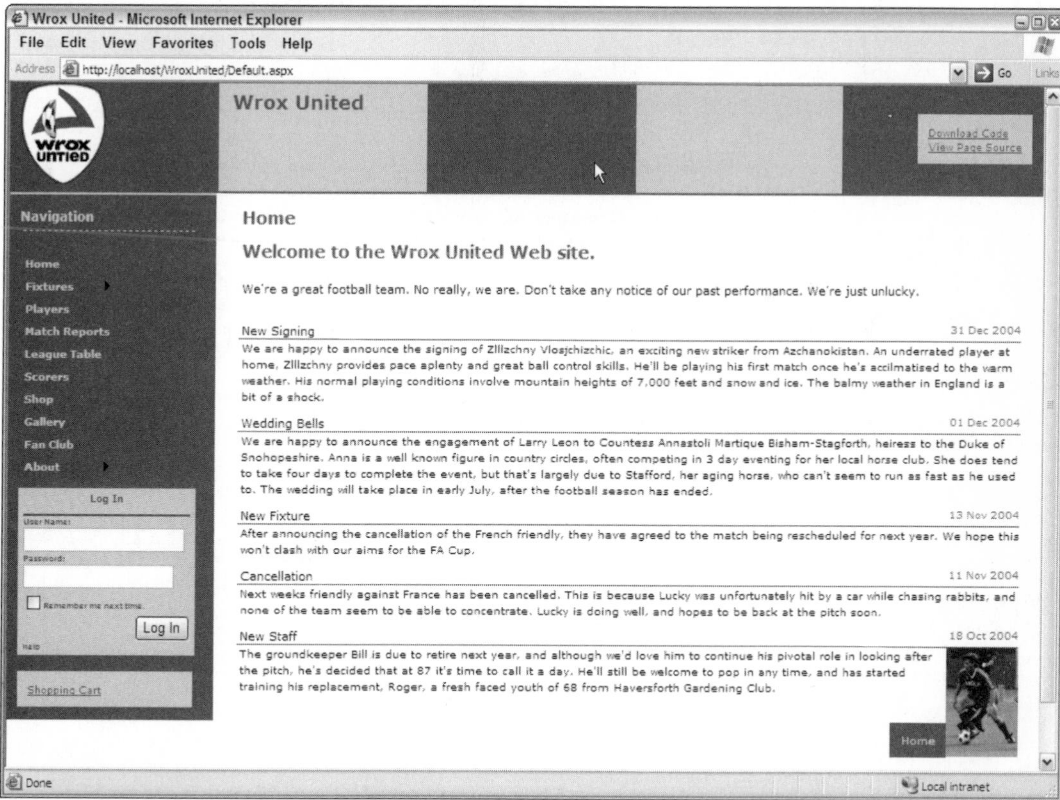

Figure 6-16

Here you can see that not all of the news items have a picture. In the following Try It Out, you see how the news items can be customized, by responding to events generated by controls that fetch data. You'll make sure that an image is only visible when there is a picture associated with the news item.

Try It Out Data Events

1. Close any open browser windows.
2. In Visual Web Developer open the DataEvents.aspx file from the Chapter06 web site.
3. Right-click the mouse button anywhere on the page, and select View in Browser from the menu that appears. You'll see a screen similar to Figure 6-17.
    - ❑ Notice that not all of the news items have images. For those that don't there is a small image with a red cross in it, indicating that the image is missing; this is the default. You need to modify the page to use events, so that if there is no image for the news item, that red cross isn't shown.
4. Close the browser and switch to Design View in Visual Web Developer.
5. Select the `DataList` control. There are only two controls on the page: `SqlDataSource` and `DataList`. The `DataList` control is bound to a database, so it shows Databound items—simply click anywhere on this control to select it.

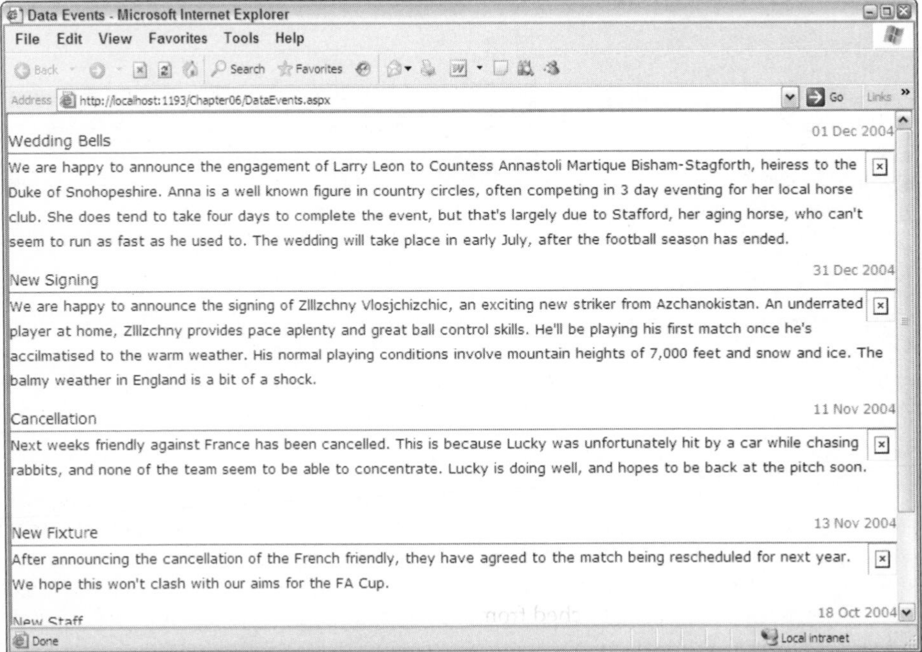

Figure 6-17

6. From the Properties box, select the events and double-click into the `ItemDataBound` event. Don't enter any text, just double-click, and this will open the code editor and create the empty event procedure for you.

7. Add the following code in the empty event procedure:

```
DataRowView row;
Image img;

if (e.Item.ItemType == ListItemType.Item ||
   e.Item.ItemType == ListItemType.AlternatingItem)
{
    row = (DataRowView)e.Item.DataItem;

    if (row["PictureURL"].ToString().Trim() == "")
    {
        img = (Image)e.Item.FindControl("NewsImage");
        img.Visible = false;
    }
}
```

8. Save the pages and switch back to the Design View of the page. Right-click the page and select the View in Browser menu item to view the page in the browser. Notice how the red cross images have disappeared.

How It Works

Before looking at the code you need to understand how HTML handles images. The image is created with an `img` tag, like so:

```
<img src="ImageName.gif"></img>
```

When the browser receives this HTML it displays the image, or that red cross if the image isn't found. When you use server controls for images, you use an `Image` control:

```
<asp:Image ImageUrl="ImageName.gif" runat="server" id="Image1"></Image>
```

This renders the same HTML as the first example. So if there's no physical file you get that red cross, which is exactly what's happening on this page; you need some way to not show the red cross image if there's no picture associated with the news story.

In the `DataEvents.aspx` page you use an `Image` server control, but the value for the `ImageUrl` property is fetched from a database. Databases are covered in the next two chapters, so it's not important to know how this works just yet. The important point is to realize that as each row of data (a news item) is fetched from the database it is bound to the `DataList`, which means that there will be an item in the `DataList` for each row in the table fetched from the database. Each row of data contains different bits of the news: the title, the description, and what you're really interested in for this example, the picture name. But not every news item has a picture, so you have to check to see if the database has a picture and if it doesn't, you make the `Image` control invisible. Take a look at the code that makes this possible.

First, you have the ItemDataBound event itself:

```
protected void DataList1_ItemDataBound(object sender,
        System.Web.UI.WebControls.DataListItemEventArgs e)
```

This event is raised when a row from the database is bound to a server control. Like the Click event of the ImageButton, the ItemDataBound event of the DataList supplies extra information to the event procedure in the form of the second parameter. This contains information about the row being bound, and contains a property called DataItem, which itself contains three properties:

- DataItem: The actual data item from the database.
- ItemIndex: The index number of the item being bound. This starts at 0 and increments by one for each row.
- ItemType: The type of the item in the DataList. This will be one of the following: AlternatingItem, EditItem, Footer, Header, Item, Pager, SelectedItem, or Separator.

The ItemType is used to determine what type of row item you are on. For example, if data is being bound into the header row, the ItemType would be Header. For the actual rows in this example, the ItemType will be Item or AlternatingItem (for each row and every other row). So your code, shown here, simply checks the ItemType, so you only work with the rows you are interested in:

```
If (e.Item.ItemType == ListItemType.Item ||
    e.Item.ItemType == ListItemType.AlternatingItem)
```

Next you can use the ItemType to access the actual data being bound to the Image control, so you can check to see if there is any data for the image. First, you extract the actual row of data—don't worry about the exact details of this code; data and data conversion are covered in the next few chapters. What's important to remember is that e.Item.DataItem is the actual data from the database for this row, and you check to see whether the PictureUrl column is empty:

```
row = (DataRowView)e.Item.DataItem;

if (row["PictureUrl"].ToString().Trim() == "")
```

If the PictureUrl column is empty, you want to access the Image control and make it invisible. Here you again use e.Item, but this time to find the Image control (NewsImage), and set its Visible property to false:

```
img = (Image)e.Item.FindControl("NewsImage");
img.Visible = false;
```

Several things in this example have not been explained fully because they are covered in more detail later in the book. Data binding and databases are covered in Chapter 7, and data conversion and casting, and the use of FindControl are covered in Chapter 9. You don't need to understand how these work at the moment, because the important thing is to know what is possible. In this case, you are seeing that an event is raised when an item from the database is bound to a server control. This event provides information about the underlying data and the row on the server control, thus giving you a lot of information.

This technique is also used on the menu. Chapter 3 looked at the navigation controls such as the Menu and SiteMapPath controls. One of the issues we have with the Wrox United web site is that we wanted the

SiteMapPath on every page, which means that every page has to be in the SiteMap file as XML nodes. However, we don't want all of the pages to appear in the Menu. For example, we don't want users to navigate directly to the Checkout page, because we only want them to access it from the Shopping Cart page. The problem we have is that we can have an item that appears in the SiteMap and SiteMapPath, but that doesn't appear in the Menu — the navigation framework doesn't cater for that situation. So we have to cheat.

What you do is use the MenuItemDataBound event in the master page (site.Master), as shown here:

```
protected void MyMenu_MenuItemDataBound(object sender,
                     System.Web.UI.WebControls.MenuEventArgs e)
{
    string text = e.Item.Text;

    if (text == "Checkout" || text == "Shop Item" ||
        text == "Shopping Cart")
        e.Item.Parent.ChildItems.Remove(e.Item);
}
```

As each menu item is taken from the SiteMap file and bound to the menu the MenuItemDataBound event is raised. Within this event procedure we check to see if the menu text is one of the pages we don't want to show, and if it is we remove the item from the menu. This means that the item still retains its place in the navigation structure, but that it won't show on the menu.

So you can see that events raised by ASP.NET are extremely useful. Despite the fact ASP.NET takes care of the data binding and display of data for us, we still have access to what's happening. The next section looks at another example, where events are raised indirectly by the user.

Indirect Events

Indirect events are raised by ASP.NET, but because of some action that the user took. For example, have a look at one of the administration pages, where the team owner can change the players in the squad, as shown in Figure 6-18.

Here there are two visible controls: the GridView at the top, showing all players, and the DetailsView at the bottom where the player details are edited. One of the things you have to do is make sure that the GridView is updated when the player details are changed. The following Try It Out shows how you can do this.

Try It Out Indirect Events

1. In the Chapter06 web site in Visual Web Developer, open the EditSquad.aspx page.
2. Click the right mouse button and select View in Browser from the menu.

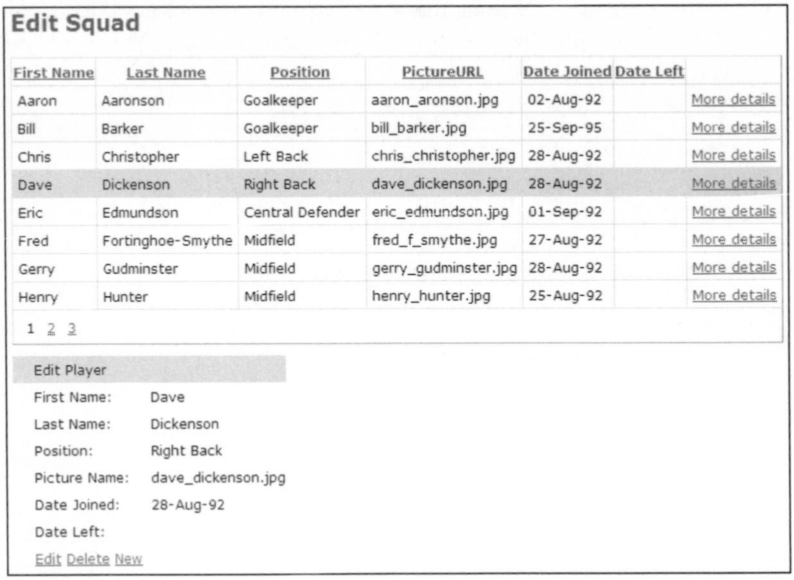

Edit Squad

First Name	Last Name	Position	PictureURL	Date Joined	Date Left	
Aaron	Aaronson	Goalkeeper	aaron_aronson.jpg	02-Aug-92		More details
Bill	Barker	Goalkeeper	bill_barker.jpg	25-Sep-95		More details
Chris	Christopher	Left Back	chris_christopher.jpg	28-Aug-92		More details
Dave	Dickenson	Right Back	dave_dickenson.jpg	28-Aug-92		More details
Eric	Edmundson	Central Defender	eric_edmundson.jpg	01-Sep-92		More details
Fred	Fortinghoe-Smythe	Midfield	fred_f_smythe.jpg	27-Aug-92		More details
Gerry	Gudminster	Midfield	gerry_gudminster.jpg	28-Aug-92		More details
Henry	Hunter	Midfield	henry_hunter.jpg	25-Aug-92		More details

1 2 3

Edit Player	
First Name:	Dave
Last Name:	Dickenson
Position:	Right Back
Picture Name:	dave_dickenson.jpg
Date Joined:	28-Aug-92
Date Left:	

Edit Delete New

Figure 6-18

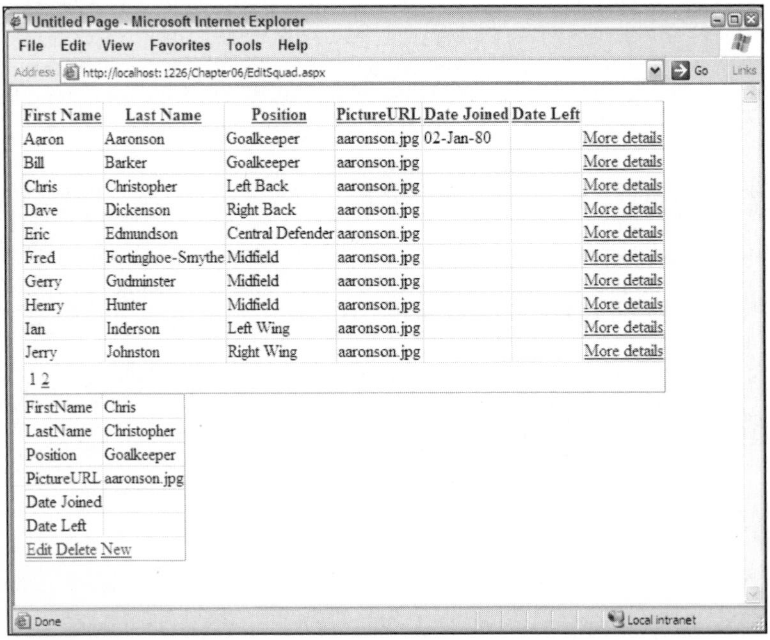

Untitled Page - Microsoft Internet Explorer

File Edit View Favorites Tools Help

Address http://localhost:1226/Chapter06/EditSquad.aspx Go Links

First Name	Last Name	Position	PictureURL	Date Joined	Date Left	
Aaron	Aaronson	Goalkeeper	aaronson.jpg	02-Jan-80		More details
Bill	Barker	Goalkeeper	aaronson.jpg			More details
Chris	Christopher	Left Back	aaronson.jpg			More details
Dave	Dickenson	Right Back	aaronson.jpg			More details
Eric	Edmundson	Central Defender	aaronson.jpg			More details
Fred	Fortinghoe-Smythe	Midfield	aaronson.jpg			More details
Gerry	Gudminster	Midfield	aaronson.jpg			More details
Henry	Hunter	Midfield	aaronson.jpg			More details
Ian	Inderson	Left Wing	aaronson.jpg			More details
Jerry	Johnston	Right Wing	aaronson.jpg			More details

1 2

FirstName	Chris
LastName	Christopher
Position	Goalkeeper
PictureURL	aaronson.jpg
Date Joined	
Date Left	

Edit Delete New

Done Local intranet

Figure 6-19

3. View the player details by clicking the More details link — pick Chris Christopher the Left Back.
4. Click the Edit link to allow the player details to be changed. Change his position from Left Back to Goalkeeper and click Update. Notice how the details show him as Goalkeeper, but the grid still shows him as Left Back, as in Figure 6-19.
   - You need to change this to make sure that the grid is updated with the new details.
5. Close the browser window and return to Visual Web Developer.
6. Create an event procedure for the `Updated` event of the `Details` data source, by selecting the `DetailsDataSource` control and double-clicking into the `Updated` event when viewing the events list in the properties window.
7. Add the following line of code into the empty event procedure:

```
GridView1.DataBind();
```

8. Save and close the code file.
9. From the web page, view the page in the browser and repeat the update process, changing the Position of Chris Christopher to Striker. Notice that when you click Update to save the changes the grid also changes.

How It Works

This code is extremely simple, and even though it relies on data binding, it is easy to understand. The key is that the page uses a `SqlDataSource` object, which is responsible for fetching the data from the database and making it available to the grid to display. The `SqlDataSource` control is just like other ASP.NET server controls, except that it doesn't actually display anything. So although it's on the page, nothing is shown to the user.

As well as providing data for the grid to show, the `SqlDataSource` also deals with data edits — inserting new rows, and updating and deleting existing rows, and for each of these actions there are events. One of these events is the `Updated` event, which is raised when the data is updated. So when you click the Update link, the `SqlDataSource` updates the database, and then raises the `Updated` event. The code in the `Updated` event simply tells the grid to rebind its data — to fetch it again and redisplay it. So what you're doing is using multiple controls, with a chain of actions that result in an event, as seen in Figure 6-20.

You can see that although you can easily construct pages by just dropping controls onto a page and configuring properties, knowing how these controls work is important. Without knowing that the update of the `DetailsView` generated a similar event for the data source, you might spend time trying to work out which event on the `DetailsView` could be used to refresh the grid.

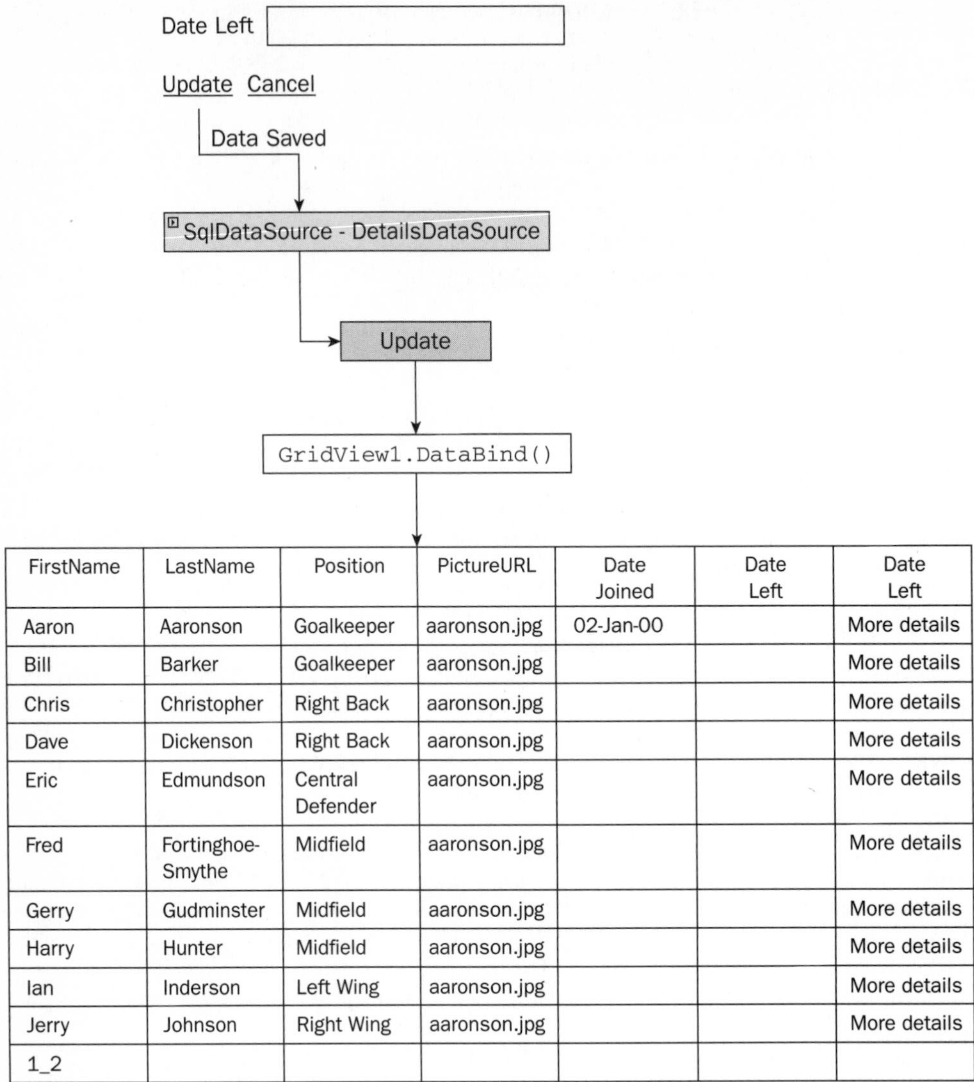

FirstName	LastName	Position	PictureURL	Date Joined	Date Left	Date Left
Aaron	Aaronson	Goalkeeper	aaronson.jpg	02-Jan-00		More details
Bill	Barker	Goalkeeper	aaronson.jpg			More details
Chris	Christopher	Right Back	aaronson.jpg			More details
Dave	Dickenson	Right Back	aaronson.jpg			More details
Eric	Edmundson	Central Defender	aaronson.jpg			More details
Fred	Fortinghoe-Smythe	Midfield	aaronson.jpg			More details
Gerry	Gudminster	Midfield	aaronson.jpg			More details
Harry	Hunter	Midfield	aaronson.jpg			More details
Ian	Inderson	Left Wing	aaronson.jpg			More details
Jerry	Johnson	Right Wing	aaronson.jpg			More details
1_2						

Figure 6-20

Canceling Events

So far in this chapter you've seen controls raise single events. Both the `Button` control and the `ImageButton` control raise a `Click` event, whereas other controls raise other events. One thing you have probably noticed is that the controls have quite a lot of events that could be raised, and you may not have realized that a single action can raise multiple events. For example, when updating data there is both an `Updating` and an `Updated` event. Likewise, there are pairs of events for adding new data

(`Inserting/Inserted`) and for data being deleted (`Deleting/Deleted`). The present tense event (`Inserting`, for example) is raised as the action is occurring, whereas the past tense event (such as `Deleted`) is raised after the event. For example, when deleting a row, the `Deleting` event is raised just before the row is deleted, and the `Deleted` event is raised after the event is raised.

For some events, the fact that they are raised before the actual action takes place gives you the opportunity to cancel the event. For example, consider the `EditSquad.aspx` file, where the team owner can change the squad. One of the things the owner wants is to make sure that any players that left during the playing season remain in the database — so you can't delete players between August 20 and May 31. To enable this, you need to allow deletion of players, but not within those dates. Give this a go in the next Try It Out.

Try It Out Canceling Events

1. Open the `EditSquad.aspx` file in the Visual Web Developer designer, and add a `Label` control at the very end of the page.
2. Set the `ID` of the `Label` control to `Message`, and clear the `Text` property.
3. Select the `DetailsDataSource` control, and on the events list double-click into the box next to the `Deleting` event to have the event procedure created for you.
4. In the empty event procedure, add the following code:

```
DateTime today = DateTime.Now;
int startYear;
int endYear;
DateTime seasonStart;
DateTime seasonEnd;

if (today.Month > 5)
{
    startYear = today.Year;
    endYear = today.Year + 1;
}
else
{
    startYear = today.Year - 1;
    endYear = today.Year;
}

seasonStart = new DateTime(startYear, 8, 20);      // 20th August
seasonEnd = new DateTime(endYear, 5, 31);          // 31st May

if (today >= seasonStart && today <= seasonEnd)
{
    e.Cancel = true;
    Message.Text = "Cannot delete players during the season";
}
else
{
    GridView1.DataBind();
    Message.Text = "";
}
```

5. Save the file and from the right mouse menu select View in Browser.
6. Make sure your system date is set between August 20 and May 31.
7. Select a player and try to delete him. You'll see a message telling you that players cannot be deleted during the season, and the player is not deleted.
8. Change the system clock so that the date is out of season—that is, between June 1 and August 19.
9. Select a player and try to delete him. You may want to add a new test player just so that you can delete him, to save you deleting real squad members.

How It Works

This example relies on the fact that the `Deleting` event is raised before the actual action takes place, which gives you the opportunity to cancel the event. One of the keys to how this works are the parameters of the event procedure, the declaration of which is shown here:

```
protected void DetailsDataSource_Deleting(object sender,
  System.Web.UI.WebControls.SqlDataSourceCommandEventArgs e)
```

You can see that the second parameter provides extra information, but not only that it allows you to send information back to ASP.NET. One of the properties of the parameter `e` is called `Cancel`, and if you set this to `true`, the event will be cancelled and the action (the deletion) will not take place. Take a look at the code used to determine whether or not the player should be deleted.

You start with some declarations, which will be used to store date information:

```
DateTime today = DateTime.Now;
int startYear;
int endYear;
DateTime seasonStart;
DateTime seasonEnd;
```

The first line sets the variable `today` to the current date. The variables `startYear` and `endYear` indicate the year in which the season starts and ends, and `seasonStart` and `seasonEnd` are the actual dates for the start and end of the season.

To determine the start and end year you see if the current date is after May. If it is, you know that the season has ended, or is already under way, so the start year is the current year and the end year is next year. If the current date is before May, you are in the second half of the season, so the start year was last year and the end year is the current year:

```
if (today.Month > 5)
{
    startYear = today.Year;
    endYear = today.Year + 1;
}
```

```
else
{
    startYear = today.Year - 1;
    endYear = today.Year;
}
```

Next you create the actual start and end dates of the season, using the start and end year already set:

```
seasonStart = new DateTime(startYear, 8, 20);      // 20th August
seasonEnd = new DateTime(endYear, 5, 31);          // 31st May
```

Now you check to see if the current date falls within the season start and end dates. If it does, you set the `Cancel` property of the parameter `e` to `true`, so when the event procedure ends the event action (the delete) will be cancelled. You also display a message to tell the user that players cannot be deleted during the season:

```
if (today >= seasonStart && today <= seasonEnd)
{
    e.Cancel = true;
    Message.Text = "Cannot delete players during the season";
}
```

If you are outside of the season, players can be deleted, so you simply clear any message and rebind the grid (so that the deleted player doesn't still show in the grid). Because you haven't set the `Cancel` property of parameter `e` to `true` (it is `false` by default), the action will take place, and the player will be deleted:

```
{
    GridView1.DataBind();
    Message.Text = "";
}
```

So what you've seen here is that some events can be cancelled, which allows you to build logic into your applications, enabling you to control the actions that are run. This also means that events that you think will run might not. For example, it was mentioned earlier that some of these events are paired. So, as well as the `Deleting` event, there is a `Deleted` event, and if you cancel the `Deleting` event the `Deleted` event isn't run. The logic of this is shown in Figure 6-21.

This process is also the same for inserted and updated items, where the `Inserting` and `Updating` event procedures are used. In all three cases you can set the `Cancel` property of the parameter to `true` to cancel the event.

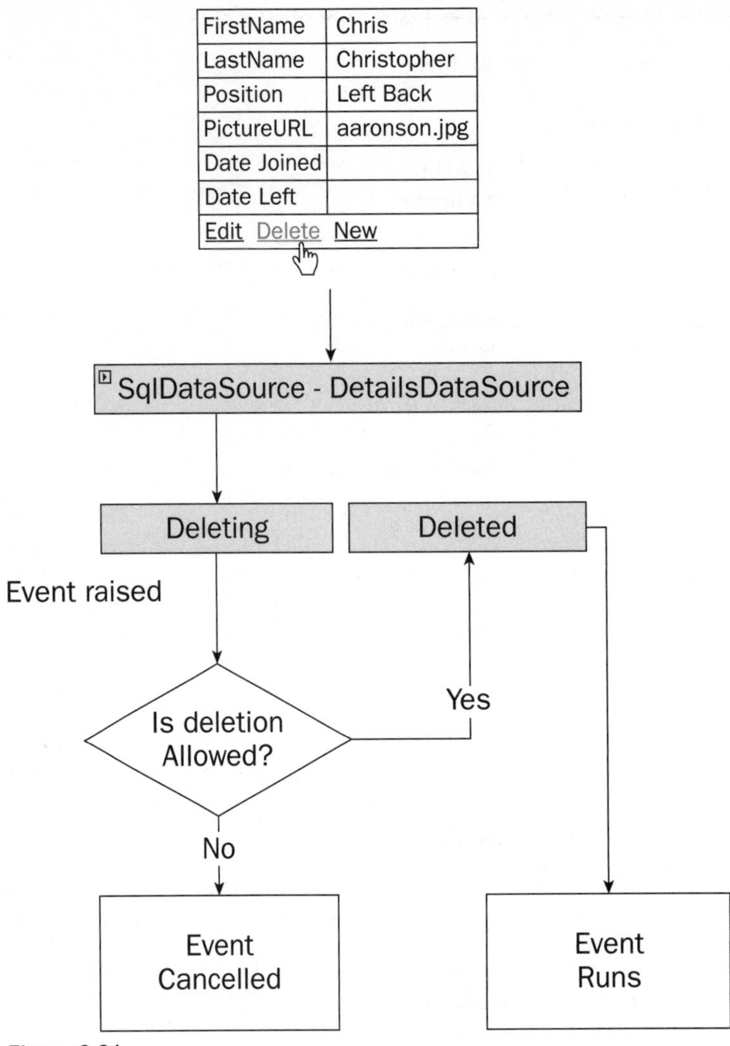

Figure 6-21

Global Events

So far in this chapter you've seen that events are raised by controls or by pages, but there is a third type of event — an *application* event. Application events are raised by ASP.NET in response to certain conditions, and these are stored in the Global Application Class, `global.asax`, a code-only file.

The `global.asax` page has several events:

- `Application_Start`, which is raised when the application first starts. This is when the first user accesses the site and should be used to set any initial start conditions.

- `Application_End`, which is raised when the application stops.
- `Session_Start`, which is raised when a user starts a session. This is when the user starts accessing the site for the first time, and includes the time when a user closes the browser window and opens it again.
- `Session_End`, which is raised when a user session ends. This isn't when the browser window is closed, because sessions have a timeout—if there is no user activity within that time, the session ends.
- `Application_Error`, which is raised when an unhandled error occurs.
- `Profile_OnMigrateAnonymous`, which is raised when an anonymous user logs in, and allows migration of any Profile properties.

You can create a Global Application Class in the same way as adding normal Web Forms, and when created, the first four events in the preceding list will be created for you. They'll have no code, but will be ready for you to add code if you need it.

In the Wrox United application, none of the first four events are used, but the latter two are. The `Application_Error` event is covered in Chapter 15, which looks at error handling, and the `Profile_OnMigrateAnonymous` event is covered in Chapter 11, which looks at the Profile.

Summary

This chapter covered a lot about events, and you've seen that they can be raised under a number of different circumstances. First you looked at the ASP.NET page itself, where an event is raised when the page is loaded, which allows you to take some action before anything is shown to the user. Additionally, this chapter examined the following topics:

- The ASP.NET page has the `IsPostback` property that allows you to identify whether this is the first time the page has been displayed, or whether the user has clicked a button.
- Button controls, where an event is raised when the user clicks the button. You saw that similar types of controls (the `Button` and `ImageButton` controls) have similar events (the `Click` event).
- Events that are raised by ASP.NET itself, both directly (such as the binding of data from a database) and indirectly (such as updating database records). These events give you an opportunity to interact with the process of displaying or updating data, and allow you to fine tune the interface and provide user feedback.
- How some events can be cancelled, thus canceling any action they trigger, such as another event. In the example you saw that you can stop the deletion of data by using an event procedure.

Now that you've had a look at events, and especially some related to data, it's time to look at databases in more depth. The next chapter looks at some of the data controls and shows you how data can be fetched from the database and displayed for easy use by the user.

Exercises

1. In the Chapter06 project create a new Web Form called Lists.aspx and add a `ListBox` control to the page, and add three list items with values of One, Two, and Three. Add a `Label` control and a `Button` control to the page. In the `Click` event of the `Button`, display the selected value of the `ListBox` in the `Label`.

2. Modify Exercise 1 so that just selecting an item in the list posts back to the server (meaning you don't need to click the button). You'll need to add an event procedure to the `ListBox`, and in that event procedure you can use the same code from the `Click` event of the `Button` to display the selected value in the `Label`. Hint: The terms *postback* and *automatic* might be useful in your hunt for correct properties.

3. Modify the `EditSquad.aspx` example so that the `GridView` is refreshed when a new player is added to the squad. The technique is similar to the code you already have, but you'll need to use a different event. Remember that you can use the drop-down lists in the code view to find the events.

Reading Data

The hallmark of dynamic web application pages is the capability to use information from a database. No other capability so widely expands the horizons of functionality for the visitor. The majority of information in an enterprise is held in databases, so it is imperative that a web application representing a business interact with that data. A tremendous effort by the ASP.NET 2.0 development team has reduced the knowledge and lines of code needed to work with data. This chapter and Chapter 8 explain how to implement the data-based features.

This chapter covers several major ideas:

- The theory of using data in ASP.NET 2.0, including a brief overview of the theory and terminology of databases, an introduction to ASP.NET 2.0 data source controls and data-bound controls, and the role of VWD in creating data-based pages
- Data source controls
- Data-bound selection lists
- Various data-bound controls, including `GridView`, `DataList`, `Repeater`, `DetailsView`, and `FormView`
- Data source controls with parameters
- Implementing multiple data controls that work together
- Working with XML data

By the end of the chapter, you will have the tools and experience to use ASP.NET 2.0 server-side controls to present on your pages information that comes from a database.

Introducing Databases

Before starting on the ASP.NET 2.0 data controls, take a moment to consider sources of data. Data can be broadly divided into one of three categories. *Relational* data is organized into sets of tables according to rules of normalization. This category includes the data held in Microsoft Access,

Microsoft SQL Server, Oracle, SAP, DB2, and MySQL. A second category of data resides in tree structures, such as XML files, the Windows registry, and the Windows file system. Last, data can be held in a wide range of miscellaneous types, such as Excel files, text files, or proprietary formats. This book (as per the vast majority of web site data interaction) discusses relational data and XML files.

Relational databases divide information into *tables*, and the tables contain *records* (also called rows). A record represents one instance of the topic of the table. A table contains multiple *fields*, or columns, that organize values by their type. For example, a table of employees could contain a record for each employee. The table's columns may be NameFirst, NameLast, DateOfHire, and so forth. For each column there would be a value for each record. A group of tables makes a database in most management systems. In Microsoft SQL Server, which is used in this book, one or more databases together make an instance of the server. Typically, tables contain only the data. The description of how the data is organized, the names of fields, and restrictions all reside in a separate structure of the database called metadata.

XML files are different from relational databases. First, instead of tables, the data is organized into a tree with branches of the tree holding finer and finer points of data. Each set of data and each individual datum are contained in a node. For example, an Employees XML file would have an Employees node that would represent the main trunk. Then there would be a limb for each employee. From that limb would be branches for FirstName, LastName, and so on. Second, an XML file is self-describing in that the metadata is included with the data. Each piece of information has an HTML tag that acts like a container that states the description of that data. For example, a datum like "John" would actually be stored as `<NameFirst>John</NameFirst>`. Although the self-descriptors can make an XML file huge, they make it easy to understand the data without having the metadata information.

Almost all sources of data have a system that controls who is allowed to use the data. The first step in security is authentication, wherein the system determines who is asking to use it. The topic of authentication was covered in detail in Chapter 4, so we won't spend much time on it here. Basically, there are two types of authentication: Windows Authentication (also known as Trusted Security) and SQL Authentication. The decision of which authentication to use is made when the database is installed. With SQL Server Express, you have the option of Windows Authentication or Mixed. Mixed means you can use either Windows Authentication or SQL Authentication. SQL Server Express installs, by default, with Mixed Authentication. This book uses Windows Authentication.

> *This book mainly uses Microsoft's SQL Server. The product is sold with different sets of features, but for our use the simplest version (SQL Server Express) is adequate. Fortunately, Microsoft provides SQL Server Express free of charge, and automatically installs with the instructions given in this book for the setup. The beauty of SQL Server Express is that when you deploy your site to the public, all of your code fits without modification into the full-featured SQL Server.*

After you are authenticated (you prove that you actually are who you say you are), there will probably be a set of rights and limitations for your use of the data. First are restrictions in how you can look at data. Database administrators (DBAs) generally restrict direct access to tables. Instead, data may only be available to you through a view or query that contains limited fields or records. Second, you may have limits on how (or if) you can change data. Last, even if you have the right to change data, there may be restrictions (called constraints) on how data can be changed. To use Wrox United as an example, you generally cannot delete a team that is listed in the schedule (thus leaving the schedule with the logical fault of a game without an existing team).

Using ASP.NET 2.0's Data Controls

Chapter 3 presented the idea that ASP.NET offers server-side controls. These controls contain code written by Microsoft that offers various behaviors, such as a drop-down list or a button. ASP.NET 2.0 has two sets of controls that are specific to working with data. The first set is *data source* controls that enable a page to connect to a source of data and to read from and write to that source. However, a data source control has no means to display data on an ASP.NET 2.0 page, which is where *data-bound* controls come into play. Data-bound controls display data to the user by rendering data onto a page. This chapter discusses data source controls and the reading behaviors of data-bound controls.

Almost all data source controls can work with almost all data-bound controls. This gives designers a mix-and-match solution. Pick the data source control that is optimized for the data and then pick a data-bound control that displays the information as desired.

Introducing Data Source Controls

ASP.NET 2.0 ships with several types of data source controls that are tailored to work with different types of data sources. These controls are as follows:

- The `SqlDataSource` control allows connections to most relational databases. The `Sql` in its name refers to databases that understand the SQL language. That includes almost every kind of database that holds its data in a relational format. Note that the `Sql` does not refer only to the Microsoft SQL Server database management system. `SqlDataSource` controls utilize one of several *providers* that are specific to different kinds of databases. The default provider is for Microsoft SQL Server. Another provider is for Oracle. Both of these are written in managed code, the most robust option in the .NET Framework. ASP.NET 2.0 contains an additional provider that can communicate with any database that is OLEDB-enabled (OLEDB is an acronym for Object Linking and Embedding for Databases). Because OLEDB is an old standard, it comprises almost every other database management system including IBM DB2, MySQL, and SAP. However, the provider for OLEDB connections is not written in managed code. That means it does not meet all the requirements of being .NET technology, but it still can work with .NET. We can expect third parties to publish more data source controls and providers and can hope that they are in proper managed code.

If you begin writing more advanced scenarios, you will discover that OLEDB data source controls are not part of the `System.Data` hierarchy. These controls actually reside in the `System.Web.UI.Controls` namespace. But this point does not arise for most scenarios where you can just drag data controls from the toolbar.

- The `AccessDataSource` control is a special case of the `SqlDataSource` control that contains a provider optimized for Microsoft Access.
- The `XMLDataSource` control allows connection to XML sources.

- The `SiteMapDataSource` control, a specialized form of the `XMLDataSource` control, is optimized for the specific architecture of the ASP.NET 2.0 web application site map (as you built in Chapter 2).
- The `ObjectDataSource` control connects to business objects you build yourself (discussed in Chapter 10).

Regardless of which data source control (and in the case of the `SqlDataSource`, which provider) you use, the data source control will enable a set of behaviors for your ASP.NET 2.0 page. These include a connection to the database and enablement of behaviors such as reading and writing data, which are available to data-bound controls that display data and receive input from the user.

> **If you are familiar with older versions of ASP, the ASP.NET 2.0 data source controls instantiate ADO.NET objects. Therefore, ADO.NET provides the underlying technology for data access. The creation and manipulation of ADO.NET objects for most scenarios is now handled automatically (and correctly and efficiently) by the higher-level data source control objects.**

In summary, the data source controls create the background infrastructure needed to use data. However, they do not create any rendering on the web page (see the next section for those capabilities). Rather, they make the data behaviors like reading and writing to data stores available to data-bound controls.

Introducing Data-Bound Controls

Data-bound controls provide the link between the data source controls and the user. They take the data and behaviors of the data source control and render it to the visitor. This division of labor works very well. You can select any data source control and link that to any of the data-bound controls. With just a few exceptions, it is a mix-and-match scenario.

Data-bound controls encapsulate remarkable amounts of behavior. For example, the `GridView` control can not only display data in a table, but it offers sorting, selecting, paging through subsets, and one-click transition to data editing. If your needs extend beyond these capabilities, you can write custom code hooked into events exposed by the `GridView` control.

There is one constraint on the compatibility of data source controls and data-bound controls. Each control is optimized for tabular data, tree data, or custom class data. For example, XML data is organized as a tree and thus best accessed with the `XMLDataSource` control and displayed in `Menu` or `SiteMapPath` data-bound controls. SQL Server data is organized into tables and thus accessed with the `SqlDataSource` control and displayed in `GridView` (tables) or `DetailsView`. List-type data-bound controls can display either source of data. You can twist the controls to cross-utilize types of data, but in general it is best to stick to their intended purpose.

Four general groups of data-bound controls ship with ASP.NET 2.0. Because there is overlap in their functionality, this chapter spends some time differentiating them. First you will look at their renderings, then a comparison chart, and finally a guide to selecting the correct data-bound control for your purposes.

Note that other controls, such as text boxes, can be data-bound. However, these independent controls are best connected to data in the context of a template within one of the controls just mentioned. This topic is discussed in detail in *Beginning ASP.NET 2.0 Databases* from Wrox, ISBN 0-4717-8134-7.

The trick with data-bound controls arises in the selection. It can be confusing in the first attempts to get the correct control for your purpose. To help, the following sections organize the data-bound controls into four groups. Later in the chapter, you will practice using each of them in a series of exercises.

Tabular Controls

Tabular controls produce the classic HTML table listing the data of records, albeit with opportunity for significant enhancements. These controls show multiple records in rows and one or more fields from each record as columns. The `GridView` control shows one value (datum) in each cell in a table layout. The `DataList` and `Repeater` controls behave in the same way, and render each cell with all of the fields for one record. Figure 7-1 shows how these controls look in a browser.

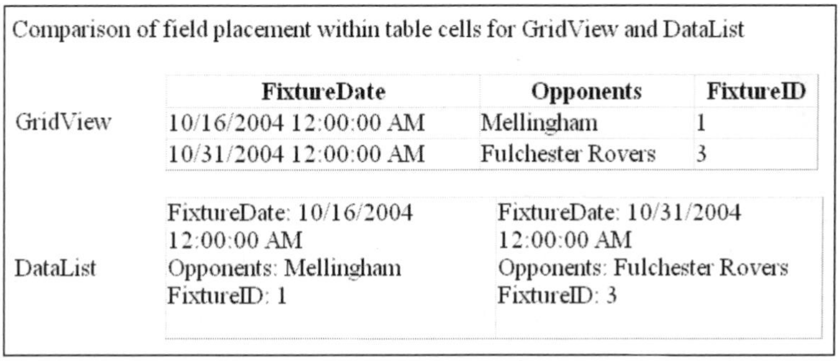

Comparison of field placement within table cells for GridView and DataList

	FixtureDate	Opponents	FixtureID
GridView	10/16/2004 12:00:00 AM	Mellingham	1
	10/31/2004 12:00:00 AM	Fulchester Rovers	3

DataList	FixtureDate: 10/16/2004 12:00:00 AM Opponents: Mellingham FixtureID: 1	FixtureDate: 10/31/2004 12:00:00 AM Opponents: Fulchester Rovers FixtureID: 3

Figure 7-1

The `GridView` control offers the most behaviors, as it can read, edit, and select records. The `DataList` control allows reading and editing, whereas the `Repeater` is a read-only control. The name of `DataList` is a bit confusing because you have a separate set of `List` controls that are optimized for selecting a record. The `DataList` is a display control in a tabular format.

Single Record Display Controls

Single record controls (`DetailsView` and `FormView`) display one record at a time. You can think of them as a deck of playing cards in a pile face up. At any moment all of the cards are there, but you can only see the top one. You have to navigate down through the deck to see other cards (see Figure 7-2 for an example of the `DetailsView` control). Single record controls have navigation features to permit the visitor to go to the next record, jump to a specific record, or fly to the first or last record. The `DetailsView` control provides some default layout when you create the control, whereas the `FormView` control creates a blank slate upon which you create the entire layout. Both of these data-bound controls support the reading, editing, and creation of new records.

Selection List Controls

Selection list controls are optimized to accept a user selection. These two controls display just one field from each record and stand by for a mouse-click. As shown in Figure 7-3, `ListBox` controls (right side of figure) are by default expanded, whereas `DropDownList` controls (left side of figure) display a single row until the user expands. As you would expect, these controls are display-only with no capability to change data.

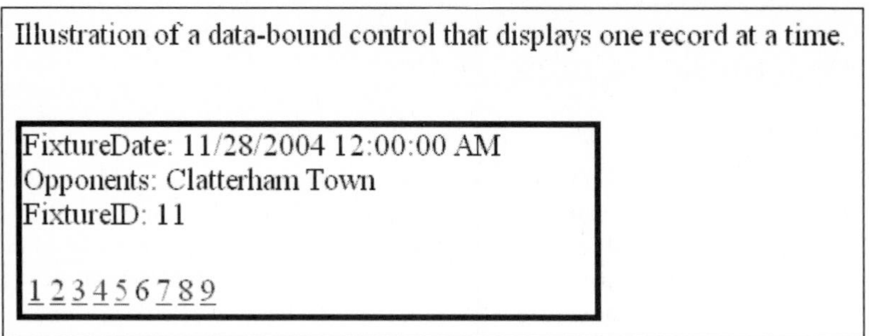

Illustration of a data-bound control that displays one record at a time.
FixtureDate: 11/28/2004 12:00:00 AM
Opponents: Clatterham Town
FixtureID: 11
1 2 3 4 5 6 7 8 9

Figure 7-2

Illustration of data-bound controls of the Selection Lists type.

DropDownList ListBox

Mellingham - 16 Oct 04

Mellingham - 16 Oct 04
Fulchester Rovers - 31 Oct 04
Wilstone Wanderers - 06 Nov 04
Wilstone Wanderers - 14 Nov 04

Figure 7-3

Tree Controls

Tree controls are optimized to handle data that are stored in nodes rather than tables. The `Menu` control provides a slide-out dynamic so that when you pass your mouse over a menu choice the submenu slides out. The `TreeView` control gives the user the option to expand or collapse nodes (see Figure 7-4). The `Menu` control is on the left of Figure 7-4, and the `TreeView` control is on the right. The `SiteMapPath` control offers a navigation trail that automatically updates based on the current page.

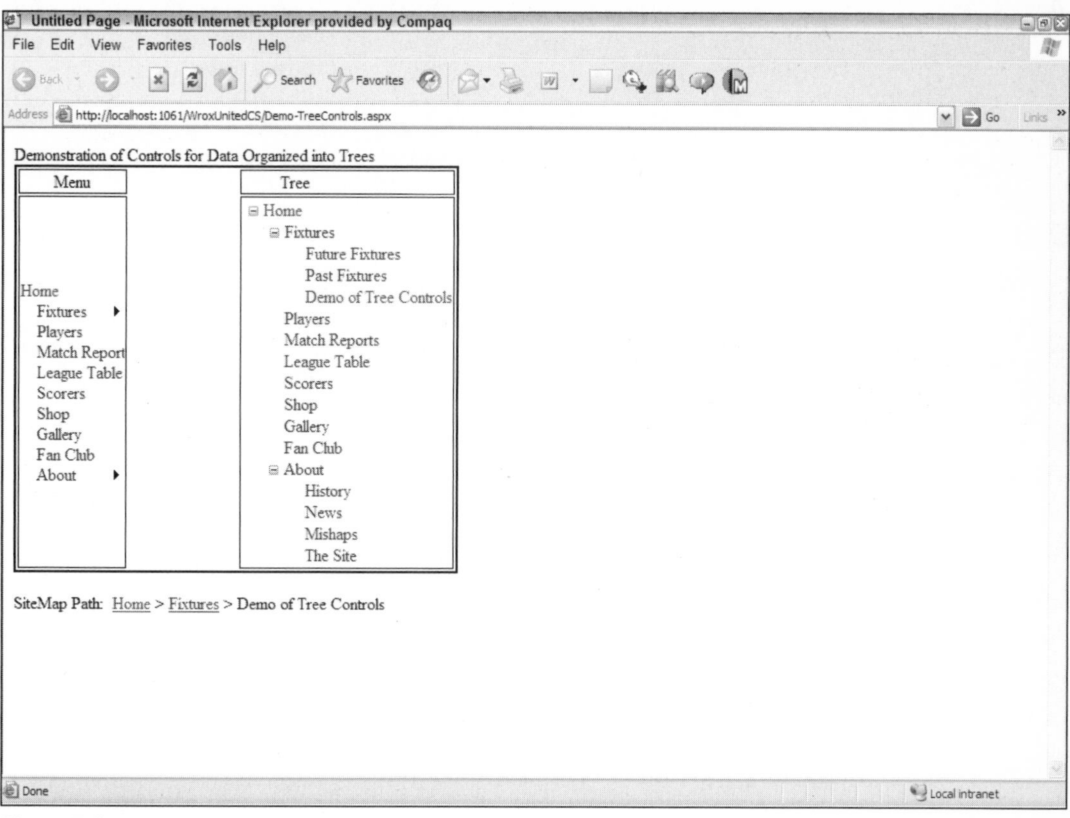

Figure 7-4

The following table summarizes the differences among the data-bound controls.

Control	Primary Data Structure	Capabilities	Description and Primary Uses
`GridView`	Table	Read and edit	Separate column for each field.
			Each field value in its own cell.
			Display multiple records in a grid.
			Edit existing records.
`DataList`	Table or Tree	Read and edit	All fields in one cell.
			One cell equals one record.
			Display multiple records in a grid.
			Create new record for `GridView`.

Table continued on following page

Control	Primary Data Structure	Capabilities	Description and Primary Uses
`Repeater`	Table or Tree	Read only	All fields in one cell.
			One cell equals one record.
			Display multiple records in a grid.Create new record for `GridView`.
`DetailsView`	Table or Tree	Read, edit, create	Display single records.
			Default structure provided.
			Edit existing records.
			Create new records.
`FormView`	Table or Tree	Read, edit, create	Display single records.
			No default structure.
			Edit existing records.
			Create new records.
`DropDownList` and `ListBox`	Table or Tree	Read only	List of a few fields.
			Invites a user selection.
			Display data for user selection.
`SiteMapPath`	Tree	Read only	List page names between home and current page.
			Used to identify current position in site.
`Menu`	Tree	Read only	Displays top-level nodes with the option to expand one sub-node at a time.
			Used to display a menu where there will be one selection.
`TreeView`	Tree	Read only	Displays top-level nodes with option to expand one or many subnodes.
			Used to display multiple subnodes simultaneously.

Data Source Controls and Data-Bound Controls Work Together

As discussed in the previous two sections, ASP.NET 2.0 offers two families of controls for working with data: data source controls and data-bound controls. This section takes a moment to look at how they work together. The data source control handles the behind-the-scenes connections to the data as well as a set of behaviors such as editing, sorting, and paging. The data-bound control presents the data and behavior to the user in actual renderings to the page.

The two controls you use on your page should match in type. Tabular-type data-bound controls such as `GridView` and `FormView` should be sourced by table-type data source controls such as the `SqlDataSource`. Tree-type data-bound controls should be sourced by an XML data source. Lists can be sourced by either type. Having said that, there are some exceptions. Some tree sources can be used with tabular data-bound controls. This combination generally requires an InfoPath statement that narrows the scope of information that is harvested from the tree source of data.

A data-bound control must have a property that sets its source to the data source control. In addition, for many behaviors there must be some coordination of properties between the pair of controls. For example, if editing is to be enabled, the data source control must have that option turned on and the data-bound control must also have its editing features enabled. As the controls are demonstrated later in the chapter, you will see more details of how data source and data-bound controls work together.

Configuring Data Controls with VWD

When you place a data source control on your page (in Design View) VWD leads you through a wizard to configure the various properties of the control. This procedure is remarkably cognizant of all the details required to work with data on a page.

You can add data interactions using VWD at several levels. If you like to create controls one at a time, you can drag a data source control and walk through its wizard, and then drag a data-bound control and connect it to the data source control. Alternatively, you can start with a data-bound control, and its wizard steps you through creating a data source control. You can even work at a higher level by opening the Database Explorer, selecting several fields, and dragging them to the page. VWD then creates both the data source controls and data-bound controls for you.

VWD also offers tools for editing data controls that already exist on the page. The Properties window offers a graphical user interface for changing settings. If you are working with code in Source View, you can move the insertion bar within a data control tag and press the space bar to get a list of the appropriate attributes in IntelliSense.

Last, VWD offers a very useful tool within wizards for building the SQL statements needed to display or modify data. Instead of you typing (and commonly mistyping) the names of fields and the SQL keywords, the wizard offers a drag-and-drop interface with check box options. When you click Finish, VWD builds the SQL statement for you.

The tools of VWD greatly speed the development of data pages. However, you may find that some of the default settings and tags created by VWD are not to your liking.The number of tags created by VWD can be overwhelming (like long lists of parameters), particularly for beginners. Advanced designers may want to substitute validation controls for the basic text boxes created by VWD. So although VWD does a large amount of the page construction for you, most designers follow on with tweaks or partial rewrites. You will see an example in a Try It Out later in this chapter.

Data Source Controls

This section moves from the theory to the practice by adding data source controls to a page. As mentioned in the previous section on VWD and data controls, a data source control is most easily created by adding a data-bound control to a page and letting the VWD wizard set up the data source control. However, at times you will have to create the data source control yourself, so you will walk through that process here. The first step, of course, is to decide which data source control to use based on your type of data. Take a look at a SQL Server Express data source (as used in this book).

The Basic Properties of Data Source Controls

Data source controls require several attributes. The obvious are an ID and the `runat="server"`. You must also specify which database on which server to use and your log on name and password for authentication. These data are held in a connection string. Next you must specify which records and fields to read from the data source. The data source control also requires a provider that describes how to interact with the database. (The default provider for the `SqlDataSource` control is the provider for Microsoft SQL Server.) In this case, VWD walks you through these specifications in a wizard.

In this chapter, you mostly work on a `Fixtures.aspx` page that will list Wrox United's schedule. In this Try It Out, you add the data source control using the VWD wizard and then examine the source code that the IDE created for you.

Try It Out Data Source Control

1. If you have not done so already, create a folder in the root of your site named App_Data. Right-click the new folder and select Add Existing Item. Navigate to your downloads for this book. Look in the `App_Data` folder and select the file named `WroxUnited.mdf`. Click OK to import the data file to your site.
2. Open the web site for the chapter (`C:\BegASPNET2\WroxUnitedCS`) and create a Web Form called `Fixtures.aspx` in the site's root using the web form template with the `site.master` page and with code in a separate page. Switch to Design View and type **Fixtures** in the content panel.
3. From the Data section of the toolbar (see Figure 7-5), drag a `SqlDataSource` control to the middle of the content pane. You may have to scroll down to see the new control.

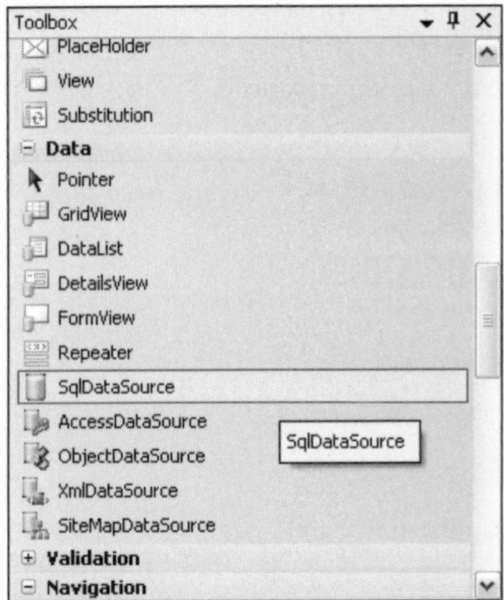

Figure 7-5

3. Click the small arrow at the top right of the control to open the smart task panel (as shown in Figure 7-6) and click Configure Data Source. A wizard starts. In the first dialog box, drop down the list of connections and select `WroxUnited.mdf`. Click Next. Do not save to the application configuration file.

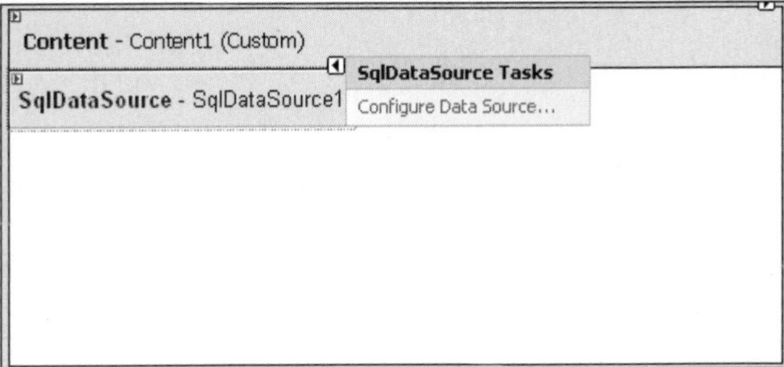

Figure 7-6

4. Click Next and in the dialog box, accept the choice to specify columns from a table. From the drop-down list, select the Fixtures table. Then select all of its fields by checking the asterisk (*) choice in the columns panel. See Figure 7-7 for an example.
5. Click Next. In the last step of the wizard, you have an opportunity to test your query. You should see several records and fields appear in the panel as in Figure 7-8. Click Finish.

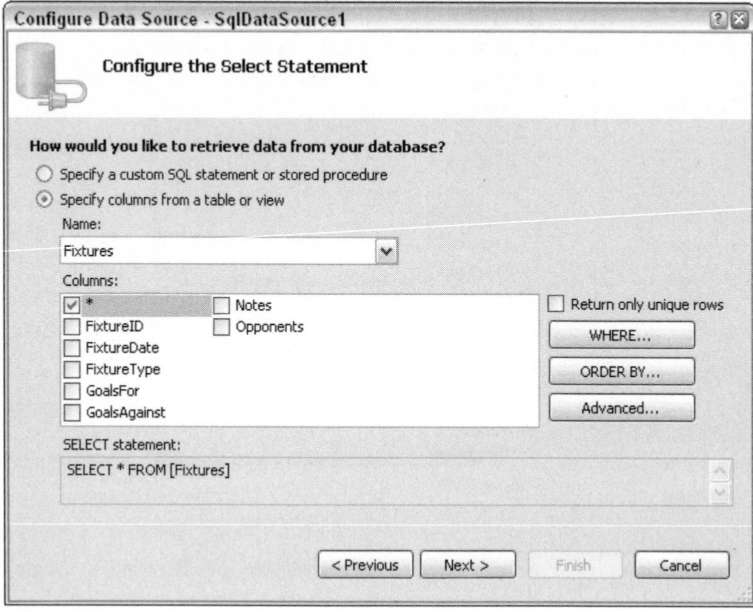

Figure 7-7

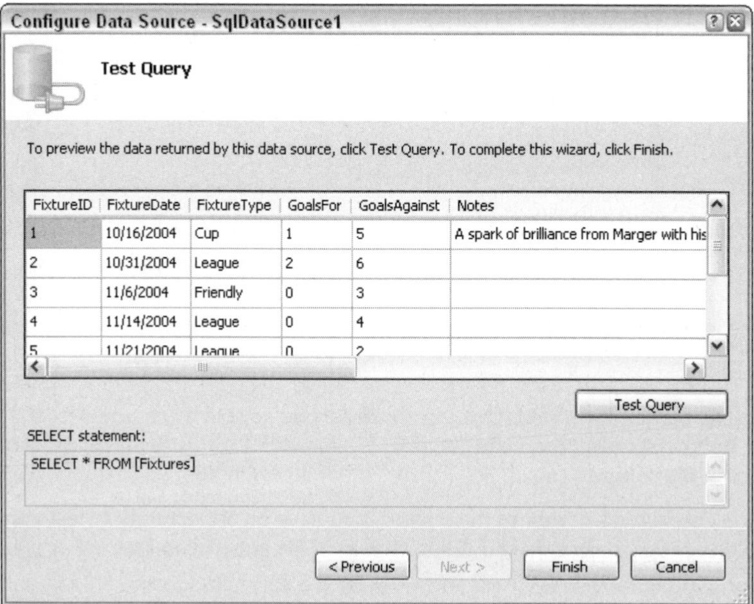

Figure 7-8

6. Run the page and observe that although you have created a data source control, there is no rendering. That will come when you add a data-bound control.

7. Close the browser and click Source View in VWD. Take a look at what VWD built for you in the `SqlDataSource` control. The `Fixtures.aspx` page appears as follows in Source View. Instead of `(local)\SQLExpress`, your server may be identified with a period (full stop) as `.\SQLExpress`:

```
<%@ Page Language="C#" MasterPageFile="~/site.master" AutoEventWireup="false"
CodeFile="Fixture.aspx.cs" Inherits="Fixture" title="Untitled Page" %>

<asp:Content ID="Content1" ContentPlaceHolderID="mainContent" Runat="Server">

<asp:SqlDataSource ID="SqlDataSource1" runat="server"

ConnectionString="Data Source=.\SQLEXPRESS;  AttachDbFilename=C:\BegAspNet2\
WroxUnitedCS\app_Data\WroxUnited.mdf; Integrated Security=True;
User Instance=True"

        providerName="System.Data.SqlClient"

        SelectCommand="SELECT * FROM [Fixtures]">

</asp:SqlDataSource>

</asp:Content>
```

How It Works

In this Try It Out, you used VWD to create a `SqlDataSource` control for you. Note how easy it was to drag the control and then answer the series of questions in the wizard. VWD typed each of the properties listed earlier in the section. The basic `ID` and `Runat` are there. Then you see a connection string holding the name of your server and database identified in connection string syntax as the initial catalog. In the wizard, you requested Windows Authentication and so VWD wrote the connection string with Integrated Security. That means you will allow Windows to certify who you are by using the name and password with which you logged in to Windows. Last, when you picked your data source to be a Microsoft SQL Server data file, VWD added a property to the data source control that sets the provider to use the `System.Data.SqlClient`.

Hiding the Connection String

In the preceding Try It Out, you placed the data of your connection string in the page. This leads to two problems. First, if the name of your server or database changes, you have to change the connection string in every page. Second, if you are using SQL Authentication, you have to present credentials (name and password). Although the connection string is never sent to the browser, it should still make any developer nervous to ever have that confidential authentication information on an ASP page.

Both of these problems can be solved by moving the connection string from the pages into a single entry of the `Web.config` file, and then referring to the entry rather than writing out the entire connection string in the page. This change can be made by simply accepting the offer to "save the connection string in the application configuration file" in the second page of the Data Source Configuration wizard.

In this Try It Out, you replace the data source control of `Fixtures.aspx` with a new data source control configured to use a connection string stored in the `Web.config` file.

Try It Out Hiding Connection Strings

1. Open your `Fixtures.aspx` page in Design View and delete the `SqlDataSource1` control.
2. Drag a new `SqlDataSource` control to the content panel of the page. Click Configure Data Source.
3. Make a new connection to the `WroxUnited.mdb` in the `App_Data` folder. Click test and OK. Click Next to move to the Save the Connection String panel.
4. This time leave the check on (as default) to save the connection string to the application configuration file and give it the name **WroxUnited** (see Figure 7-9). Click Next.

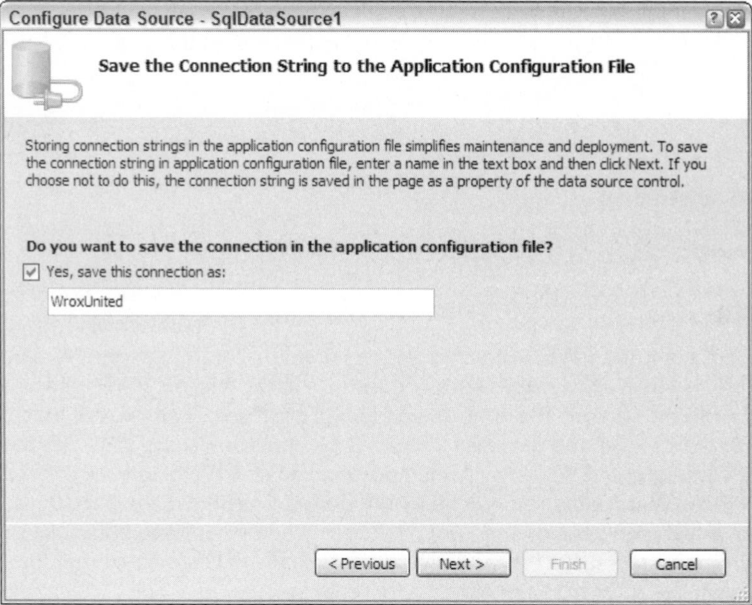

Figure 7-9

5. Continue with the rest of the wizard as before, using the fixtures table and selecting all of the columns. Click Next, test the query, and click Finish. Save the page.
6. In the end, your data source control will appear as follows in the `Fixtures.aspx` page:

```
<asp:sqldatasource id="SqlDataSource1" runat="server"
    connectionstring="<%$ ConnectionStrings:WroxUnited %>">
    SelectCommand="SELECT * FROM [Fixtures]"
</asp:sqldatasource>
```

7. Meanwhile, an addition has been created in `<connectionstrings>` section of the `Web.config` code. In the actual `Web.config` file, the connection string runs on across one long line. To make it easier to consider here, the line is broken into its sections:

```
<connectionStrings>
     <add name="WroxUnited"
         connectionString="Data Source=.\SQLEXPRESS;
         AttachDbFilename=|DataDirectory|WroxUnited.mdf;
         Integrated Security=True;
         Connect Timeout=30;
         User Instance=True"/>
         providerName="System.Data.SqlClient" />
</connectionStrings>
```

How It Works

Take a look at the `Fixtures.aspx` page in Source View and focus on the data source control. Notice that it now lacks the actual values for the connection string. Instead, you get a pointer to `connectionString` (which is understood to mean in the `Web.config` file) and within the connection strings to Wrox United.

Open the `Web.config` file. Go to the section on `connectionStrings`. The `<add>` tag indicates another connection string within the section. Following the name, you see the same information that you provided on the page in the previous Try It Out.

Details of the Connection String and Provider

The most complex parts of the data source control are the `connectionString` and the `provider`. The previous examples present the simplest case. The connection string has three parts when connecting to a SQL Server data source:

- First is the data source that means the name of the SQL server. A period (full stop) means the local server:

```
<connectionStrings>
     <add name=
      "WroxUnited" connectionString="Data Source=.\SQLEXPRESS;
```

- Second is the name of the database file to attach:

```
      AttachDbFilename=|DataDirectory|WroxUnited.mdf;
```

  Or alternatively:

```
AttachDbFilename= C:\BegAspNet2\ WroxUnitedCS\app_Data\WroxUnited.mdf;
```

- Last is the type of security to use:

```
Integrated Security=True;User Instance=True"/>
 </connectionStrings>
```

If you use another relational database manager (such as Oracle or MySql), you must specify a `provider` as follows. The `provider` for SQL Server is the default, so you did not have to use a provider in the Try It Out exercises of this book. But for other sources, you must use the following syntax. The `Sql` in `SqlDataSource` means that the control can be used with any SQL-compliant data source (not only Microsoft SQL Server). But if you use a data source other than Microsoft SQL Server, you must specify a provider for that source so that the named provider can override the default provider:

```
<asp:SqlDataSource ID="SqlDataSource1" Runat="server"
 providerName="System.Data.OracleClient"
```

ASP.NET 2.0 can use virtually any source of data, including OLEDB- or ODBC-enabled systems. Access files can be used for lightly loaded local sites, but complexities emerge when the MDB file has a security scheme. Extensive discussion of the permutations, advantages, and syntax are presented in several chapters of our sister book, *Beginning ASP.NET 2.0 Databases*.

Data-Bound Controls

Keep in mind the basic model of ASP.NET 2.0 for using data. Two controls must be on the page: a data source control and the data-bound control. The remainder of this chapter focuses on the various data-bound controls. It starts with selection lists; moves on to the `GridView`, `DataList`, and `Repeater`; the two single-record-display controls (`DetailsView` and `FormView`); and finally the tree view for hierarchical data. Along the way, we will pause to look at how multiple data-bound controls can be used to set parameters for each other.

You can add data-bound controls to a page (in Design View) using VWD in three ways:

- Add the data-bound control *after* adding a data source control and point to the existing data source control.
- Add the data-bound control directly *without* an existing data source control, and let the VWD wizard guide you through setting up a data source control.
- Add the field names directly from the Database Explorer to the page, and let VWD set up both an appropriate data-bound control and a data source control.

This list increases in terms of ease as you move down the list, but decreases some of your options. For example, a direct drag-and-drop of field names automatically creates a `GridView`, whereas in the second option you could create a `DropDownList`.

Data-Bound Selection Lists

Data-bound lists present the user with a set of data from the database and imply a request that the user select from the list. ASP.NET provides four types of lists for user selection: `DropDownList`, `ListBox`, `RadioButtonList`, and `CheckBoxList`. You can add the items in the selection list either by hard coding (static) or from a data source control (dynamic). After the user makes a selection, the value is available to your code or to other controls on the same page, or even controls on different pages.

> **It is easy to confuse the topic of this section (lists that request a user selection) with the control named `ASP.NET DataList`, which presents data without expectation of user selection. `ASP.NET DataList` is covered later in the chapter.**

All four of these selection controls support a pair of properties that are easily confused. The first is the DataTextField property, which determines the text that the user will see. Related, but different, is the DataValueField property that will hold the value that is used internally in your site to process the user's selection. For example, the DataTextField control may show a combination of a customer's full name and city. But that long and mixed value is not useful to select the single customer from your Customers table. So you set the selection list control's DataValueField property to be the customer ID number, and that neatly fits into your code to narrow the orders you receive to those for that one customer ID. When you use different fields as sources for the list control's DataText and DataValue, both fields must be included in the list of fields obtained by the appropriate data source control.

One additional property is of importance for all of the selection lists. AutoPostBack will rebuild and re-present the page after a selection is made. This is critical if there is code in the Page_Load event that you want to execute to reflect the user's selection, such as re-rendering a GridView to show a limited set of records based on the user's selection from a list box.

Items can be added to a list in three ways. The first way adds items using individual ASP.NET 2.0 tags. The second way binds the list to an array of values. Finally, the items can be read from a data source.

Adding List Items with Individual ASP.NET 2.0 Tags

When the items remain relatively static (for example, a list of states or provinces), you use hard coding to add items. Although the code can be long, it will execute faster than opening up a connection to a data source. Note that in some cases, although the original list of items may be static (the list of states), the items to appear in the selection list may be dynamic (only those states with customers). Items can be added with simple <asp:ListItem> tags as shown in the following code. In this example, you create a drop-down list for users to pick a player position. You want the user to see the full name of the position (such as Left Back), so that is the Text property. After the user makes a selection you, as a programmer, will want to actually work with your code for the position, so that is the Value property. Also note that you can set a default selection on the Central Defender position. For example, in the following code listing, the first item in the list will be for the Goalkeeper. The word Goalkeeper will appear in the list box as text and the value of GK will be the value you can work with if the user selects Goalkeeper. (The concepts of DataTextField and DataValueField are covered a bit later.)

```
<asp:DropDownList id="DropDownList1" runat="server">
    <asp:ListItem Value="GK">Goalkeeper</asp:ListItem>
    <asp:ListItem Value="LB">Left Back</asp:ListItem>
    <asp:ListItem Value="RB">Right Back</asp:ListItem>
    <asp:ListItem Value="CD" Selected="True">Central Defender</asp:ListItem>
</asp:DropDownList>
```

Binding List Items to an Array

A more sophisticated method for adding static items employs an array. You create an array in the Page_Load event, and then set the array as the data source for the list. Finally, you perform a *binding*. Binding, in ASP.NET 2.0, refers to the act of bringing data into a control. For example, when you bind a ListBox to a data source control the information from the data source is actually brought into the ListBox control. This is one of the few places in ASP.NET 2.0 where you use the version 1.x technique of performing binding as a distinct line of code. In most cases in version 2.0, the data controls automatically perform binding as needed. You carry out the steps in C# as follows:

```
<%@ Page Language="C#" %>
<!DOCTYPE html PUBLIC "-//W3C//DTD XHTML 1.0 Transitional//EN"
"http://www.w3.org/TR/xhtml1/DTD/xhtml1-transitional.dtd">
<script runat="server">
    protected String[] MyStates ={ "AK", "AL", "AR" };

    protected void Page_Load(object sender, EventArgs e)
        {
            DropDownList1.DataBind();
        }
</script>

<html xmlns="http://www.w3.org/1999/xhtml" >
<head runat="server"> <title>Demo-ListBind</title> </head>
<body>
    <form id="form1" runat="server">
    <div>
    <asp:DropDownList ID="DropDownList1" runat="server"
     DataSource="<%# MyStates %>" >
    </asp:DropDownList>
    </div>
    </form>
</body>
</html>
```

The first shaded line creates a variable named MyStates and fills it with three values. The third shaded line identifies that array (MyStates) as the one to be bound to DropDownList1. The second shaded line instructs the ASP.NET 2.0 page to, at the time of page load, actually perform the binding; that is, bring the values in MyStates into DropDownList1.

When you support variation in the items to be displayed, the population of the selection list should be based on a data source control. The selection list will have a property of DataSourceID with the value of the ID of the data source control. Then there are values for the DataTextField and DataValueField, which are set to fields included in the SelectCommand of the data source control.

Adding List Items from a Data Source

In many cases, the items of a list will be stored in a database, so it makes sense to populate the list from the database rather than creating an array or individual tags as shown in the previous sections. Because of ASP.NET 2.0's mix-and-match design of data source and data-bound controls, you can populate the list from a data source control. You just have to follow the VWD wizard to identify what data source to use to supply the information to the ListBox.

On the page, you want visitors to be able to limit the view of games to just one month. In this Try It Out, you start with a page that hard-codes the months, and then move to a dynamic binding. Note that the teams play games from October to December. You start with static binding for September to December. Then you improve the page to dynamically bind to the actual dates in the database of games.

Try It Out — Selection List Bound to a Data Source Control

1. Early in this chapter, you created a Fixtures.aspx page. Open it in VWD. Delete the existing SqlDataSource control and GridView.

2. Add some text similar to **Please pick a month**, and then drag a `ListBox` control from the Toolbox onto the content area. You will probably have to scroll down to see it, as in Figure 7-10.

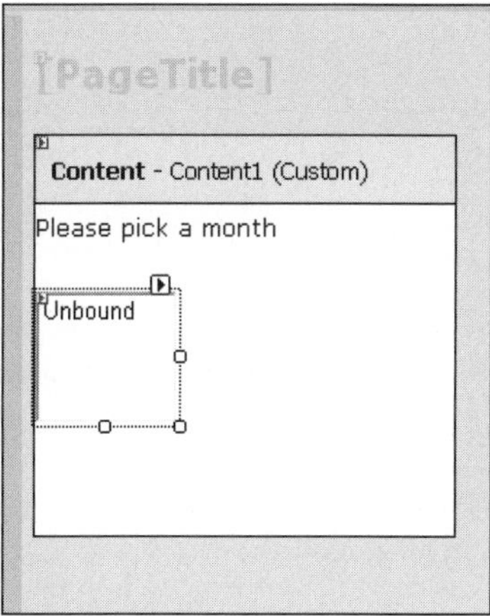

Figure 7-10

3. Because code-behind is used in this book, you have to write your code in a separate file. At the top of the Solution Explorer, click the View Code icon (the right-most icon in Figure 7-11) to open the editor panel.

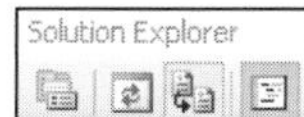

Figure 7-11

Notice that VWD automatically sets up the opening and closing lines of a `Page_Load` event for you (as shown in Figure 7-12). If it was not there (or for other events) you could have created it as follows: at the top left of the editor panel, expand the drop-down list and click the Fixtures object, and at the top-right, expand the drop-down list and select `Page_Load`.

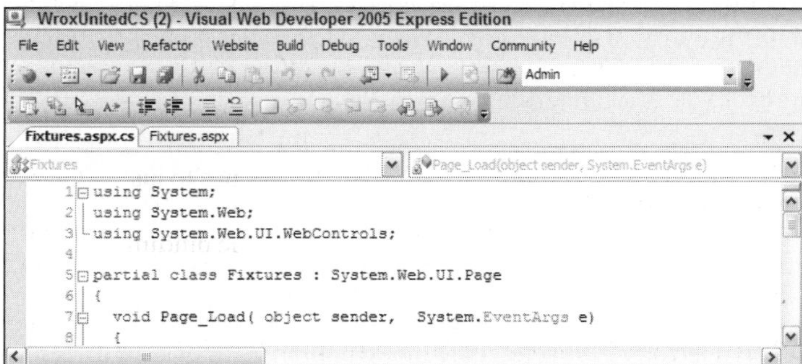

Figure 7-12

4. Add the following shaded lines to the `Page_Load` event. Note that around the list of numbers are braces ({}), not parentheses. Also note that the declaration of the array occurs *before* `Page_Load`:

```
public partial class Fixtures : System.Web.UI.Page
{
    protected Int32[] ListOfMonths = { 9, 10, 11, 12 };
    protected void Page_Load(object sender, EventArgs e)
    {
        ListBox1.DataBind();
    }
}
```

5. Direct the `ListBox` control to use your array for its source of data. Switch from the `Fixtures.aspx.cs` code page back to the `Fixtures.aspx` page and switch to Source View. Select the `ListBox` and modify its properties so that it will get its list of items from the data source control, as shown in the following shaded lines:

```
<%@ Page Language="C#" MasterPageFile="~/site.master" AutoEventWireup="true"
CodeFile="Fixtures.aspx.cs" Inherits="Fixtures" Title="Untitled Page" %>
<asp:Content ID="Content1" ContentPlaceHolderID="mainContent" Runat="Server">
    <h2>Fixtures</h2>
    (end of TIO-Selection List Bound to Data Source Control)<br />
    Please Pick a Month: <br />
    <asp:ListBox ID="ListBox1" runat="server"
      DataSource=<%# ListOfMonths %>  >
    </asp:ListBox></p>
</asp:Content>
```

6. Save and test the page in your browser by pressing F5. At this point, the list does not do anything beyond show the months (see Figure 7-13).

   But what if the team plays in January or February or you observe that there are no September games even though you have the ninth month in your list box? You want the pages to offer new choices in the list box automatically (dynamically). Now you will improve the `ListBox` control by binding it to the list of fixtures.

7. Drag a `SqlDataSource` control from the toolbar onto the fixtures page (the .aspx page, not the code page) to a point just after the `ListBox`, as shown in Figure 7-14 (you will probably have to scroll down to see it). Then open its smart task panel and configure its data source. Select the WroxUnited connection (not `WroxUnited.mdf`) and click Next.

8. Specify a custom SQL statement and click Next. Type the following statement:

```
SELECT DISTINCT MONTH(FixtureDate) AS FixtureMonth FROM Fixtures
```

9. Click Next, Test Query, and Finish.

10. Select your `ListBox` control and make some changes in the Properties window. Eliminate the `DataSource` value; add a `DataSourceID` value of `SqlDataSource1`; and set both the `DataTextField` and `DataValueField` to `FixtureMonth` (see Figure 7-15). If the Properties window is not already visible (usually in the bottom right of your screen) you can bring it back by pressing F4.

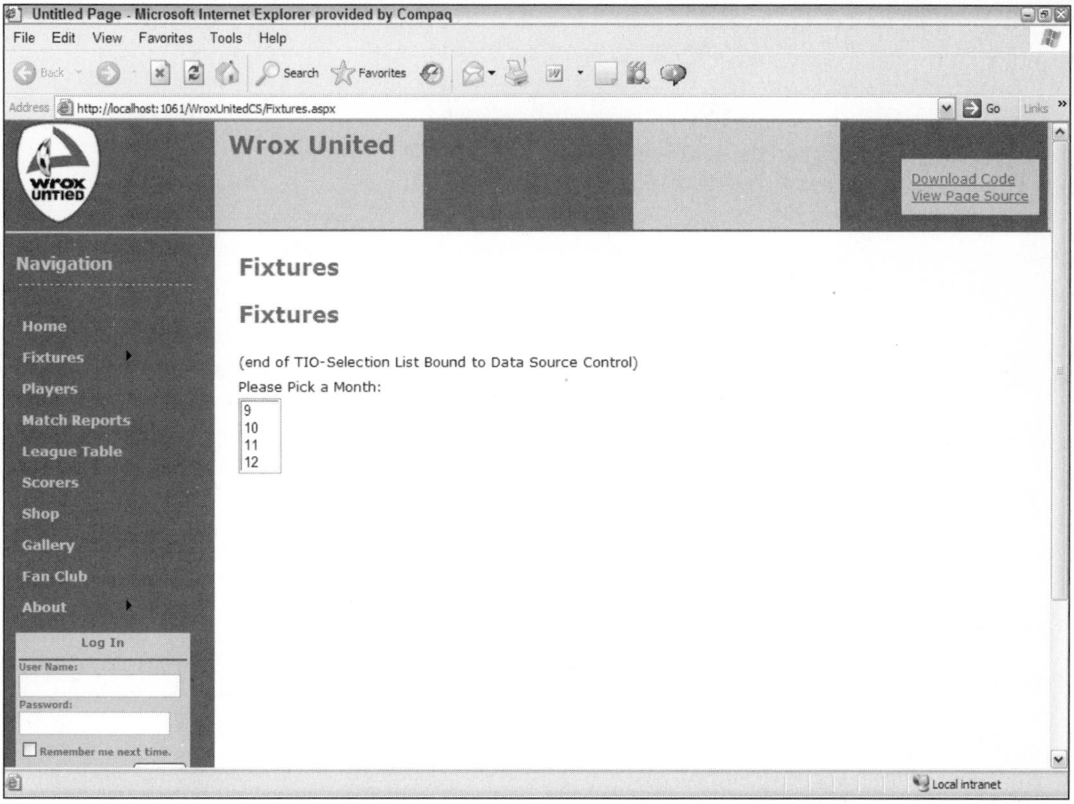

Figure 7-13

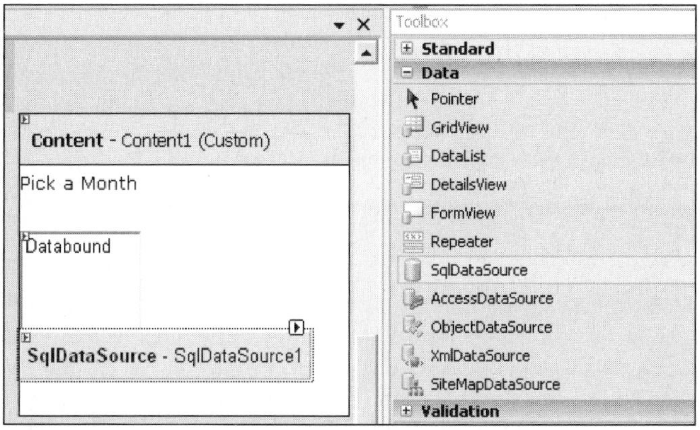

Figure 7-14

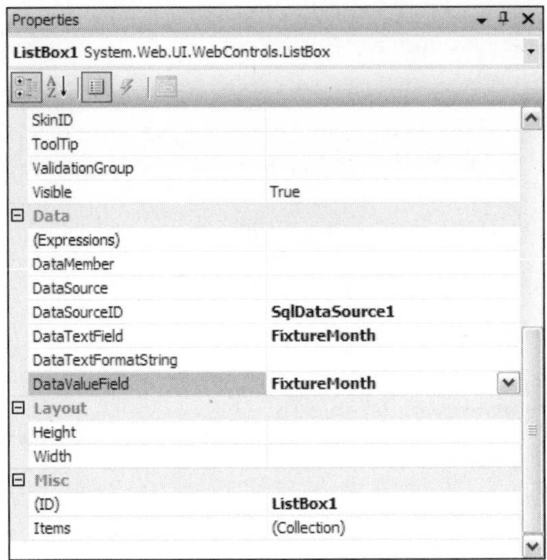

Figure 7-15

11. In Source View, remove the lines in the code page that are no longer needed — the lines shaded here. You could also remove the Page_Load event entirely; because they are devoid of internal lines, the beginning and ending lines of the procedure are not needed here. But as you develop the page in later chapters, you will need them again.

```
public partial class Fixtures : System.Web.UI.Page
{
    protected Int32[] ListOfMonths = { 9, 10, 11, 12 };
    protected void Page_Load(object sender, EventArgs e)
    {
        ListBox1.DataBind();
    }
}
```

12. Run the page. Now the ListBox control only shows the months with games — 9 is left out. Months will also automatically change if the Wrox United schedule adds games in another month.

How It Works

Adding a ListBox control is easy with VWD's drag-and-drop functionality. In the hard-coded technique, you created an array of integers and filled it with what you expected would be useful values. Then in the ListBox properties, you specified that the items of the list (its DataSource) should come from the values returned by a read of the array ListOfMonths. In the following shaded code, focus on the right side of the equals (=) sign. Everything within the <% %> is code that should be executed. An additional symbol, the #, indicates that you will be getting back a set of data. Then you state the name of the array you created. When this page is built by IIS, this line will read the contents of the ListOfMonths array and establish that set of values (9,10,11, and 12) as the source of data for the ListBox control. The closing bracket at the end of the line closes the <asp:Listbox> control and is not directly part of the data binding.

```
<asp:ListBox ID="ListBox1" runat="server"
  DataSource=<%# ListOfMonths %>  >
</asp:ListBox></p>
```

Last, back up in the code, you added a line to the `Page_Load` event that instructs ASP.NET 2.0 to actually bind the data of the array to the data-bound control.

Two problems exist with this technique. First, it uses the ASP.NET version 1.1 technique of binding by explicit command. Although that works (and is the only technique for hard-coded arrays) it does not utilize the automatic binding features of version 2.0. Second, if Wrox United changes the months in which it plays, then your list box choices are out of synch.

In the second technique, you created a new data source control that will read the actual months that are currently in the games list. However, those months are stored as full dates (such as 12/21/04), so you use a SQL function called `MONTH` to extract the number of the month from the date. And because more than one game is played in a month, you add the `DISTINCT` term to give you just one of each value. (These kinds of SQL tricks are discussed in Wrox's *Beginning SQL*.) Now you do not need the lines to create or fill the array and you can also get rid of the binding line (which ASP.NET 2.0 will do for you when you use an ASP.NET 2.0 data source control).

Notice the subtle but important difference between two properties of the `ListBox` control. `DataSource` is used when you are binding by explicit command to an ASP.NET version 1.1 source of data. `DataSourceID` is employed when you use ASP.NET 2.0 automatic binding to a data source control.

The GridView Control

The `GridView` data-bound control provides the classic display of tabular data. Each row represents one instance or record, and each column holds one field of data. A cell within the table displays a value that is appropriate for its intersection of record and column. By default, `GridView` displays all of the columns that are provided by the data source control, but you'll see how to show the user only a subset. The biggest advance in tabular data display comes when you activate two simple features of the `GridView` control: sorting and paging. *Sorting* allows the user to re-order the records according to taste. *Paging* allows you, as the designer, to specify the number of records to show at one time and then provide the user navigation tools to jump to different sets of records. Both of these features took hundreds of lines of codes to get right in earlier versions of ASP.NET, so they are huge timesavers that you get for free with ASP.NET 2.0.

Like all data-bound controls, the `GridView` control must have a data source control to provide the values. `GridView` was optimized to work with the data source controls for tabular data (such as `SQL`, `Access`, and `Data` controls), as opposed to the tree data of an `XML` source control.

Adding a GridView Control

VWD reduces control implementation to simple drag-and-drop. You can add a `GridView` control in VWD one of three ways. The techniques in the following list increase in the number of steps required as you go down the list: dragging and dropping a field is quickest, and adding the controls independently requires the most steps. However, in every case, you can go back and edit a `GridView` control's properties in Design View, or even modify the source code directly:

- From the Data Explorer window, select and drag field names to create a `GridView` control and automatically create a data source control — with no questions asked.
- From the toolbar, drag a `GridView` control to the page and let VWD walk you through the setup of a new data source control.
- From the toolbar, first add a data source control, and then drag on a `GridView` control and use the nascent data source control.

Regardless of which technique you use, when the `GridView` control is on the page, its smart task panel is open, as shown in Figure 7-16. Click the Auto Format option to quickly apply a set of colors, borders, and cell sizes. Note the first choice, the ability to remove a prior auto-formatting.

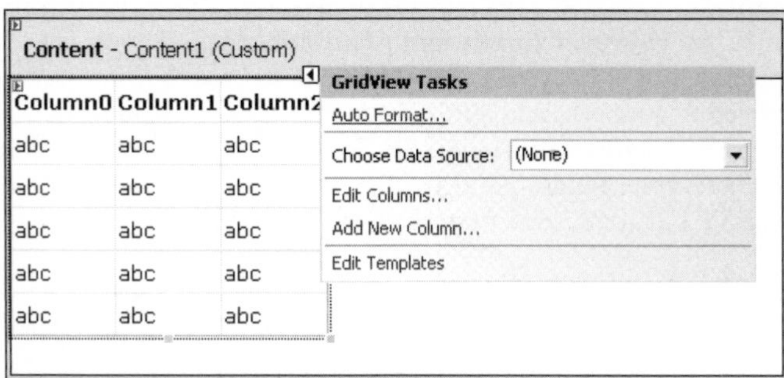

Figure 7-16

You can add or remove columns with three techniques. The easiest way is to use the smart task panel and click Edit Columns. Expand the entry for BoundField, select a field, and click Add. From the box below, you can select a field and click the X tool to delete (see Figure 7-17).

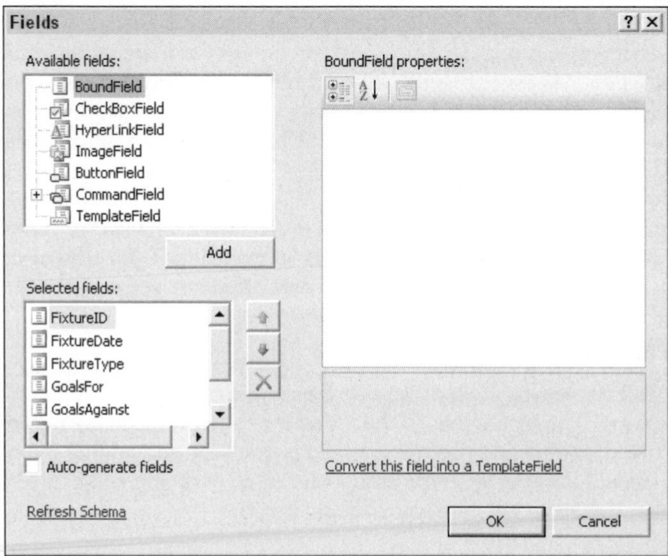

Figure 7-17

A second technique, while you have the Fields dialog box open, is to click the option in the bottom-left corner to Auto-Generate fields. This option displays all fields.

And last, you can switch to Source View and edit the list of fields.

Before moving on, take a look at the code that VWD builds for a `GridView` control. A data-bound control such as `GridView` will always have a `DataSourceID` property that points to the data source control providing the data. Note that the `DataSourceID` property points to a data source control and is used here. A similarly named property, the `DataSource`, is used in more advanced scenarios. First, display of all fields by including setting the `autogeneratecolumns` property to `true`, as follows:

```
<asp:gridview id="EmployeesTable" runat="server"
    datasourceid="EmployeesDataSource"
    autogeneratecolumns="True"
</asp:gridview>
```

The following syntax would only display three of the fields because you set the `autogeneratecolumns` to `false` and instead, will have a set of tags called `<Columns>`. Within those tags, you add an `<asp:BoundFIeld>` tag for each field. Note that ASP.NET 2.0 uses the terms *columns* and *fields* interchangeably here.

```
<asp:gridview id="EmployeesTable" runat="server"
    datasourceid="EmployeesDataSource"
    autogeneratecolumns="False"
</asp:gridview>
    <Columns>
        <asp:BoundField HeaderText="Hired Date" DataField="DateHire"
        </asp:BoundField>

        <asp:BoundField HeaderText="First Name" DataField="NameFirst"
        </asp:BoundField>

        <asp:BoundField HeaderText="Last Name" DataField="NameLast"
        </asp:BoundField>
    </Columns>
</asp:gridview>
```

Adding Paging and Sorting to a GridView Control

Designers faced an onerous task prior to ASP.NET 2.0 when they had to implement paging and sorting. The ASP.NET 2.0 design team took it upon itself to offer these features fully coded and ready to use. Select a `GridView` control and open its smart task panel by clicking the small triangle at the top right of the control to see check boxes to turn on paging and sorting as shown Figure 7-18.

Turning on paging and sorting requires three prerequisites. First, the `GridView` control must have its `DataSourceID` set to a valid data source control on the page. Second, for sorting only, that data source control must have its `DataMode` set to `Dataset` (which is the default), not `DataReader`. Third, sorting requires that fields have a header value so there is a target for users to click. The logic is that when a user requests a sort by clicking a `GridView` control, the `GridView` passes the request down to its data source control. The data source control revises the data and sends the new information back to the `GridView` control, which re-renders.

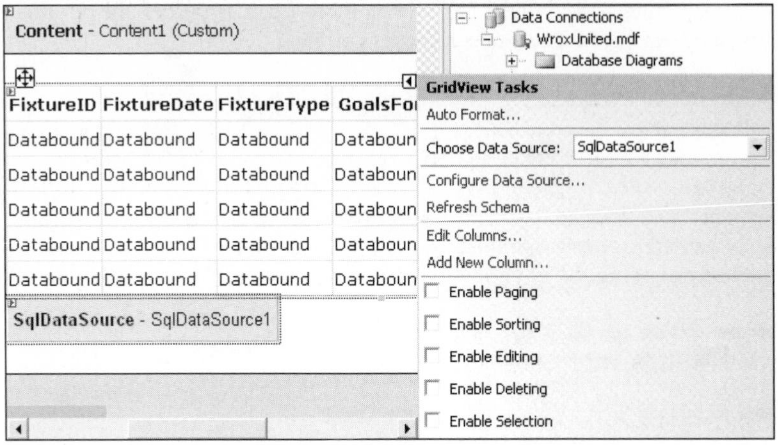

Figure 7-18

Checking sorting enables sorts on all columns. When the page is running, a user can click a second time on a column's header to change the direction of the sort. Individual columns can be sortable or not by going to Source View and removing the `SortExpression` property. In the following snippet built by VWD, the `Date` field is not sortable but the `Name` field will sort because after the sort option was checked, VWD added a `SortExpression` property to the `Name` field (the shaded line):

```
<asp:GridView ID="GridViewSemiSortable" runat="server"
    AllowSorting="True"
    AutoGenerateColumns="False"
    DataSourceID="SqlDataSource1">
    <Columns>
        <asp:BoundField DataField="Date"
            HeaderText="FixtureDate" />
        <asp:BoundField DataField="Name"
            HeaderText="FixtureType"
            SortExpression="FixtureType" />
    </Columns>
</asp:GridView>
```

Paging requires additional design elements to offer navigation tools to the user. As soon as the paging option is checked, the `GridView` control has an additional panel for `PagerSettings` in the Properties window, as shown in Figure 7-19.

The last entry is a setting for the number of records to show simultaneously (`PageSize`). For navigation, the highest-level property is `Mode`, where you can select one of four custom sets of tools. Selecting one of these sets of tools automatically sets the remainder of the properties for `PagerSettings`:

- `NextPrevious`: Displays only the Next and Previous options.
- `Numeric`: Displays a list of page numbers, with the number of pages to display set by `PageButtonCount`.
- `NextPreviousFirstLast`: Displays only the Next, Previous, First, and Last options.
- `NumericFirstLast`: Displays the numbers of pages and also the two terminal buttons.

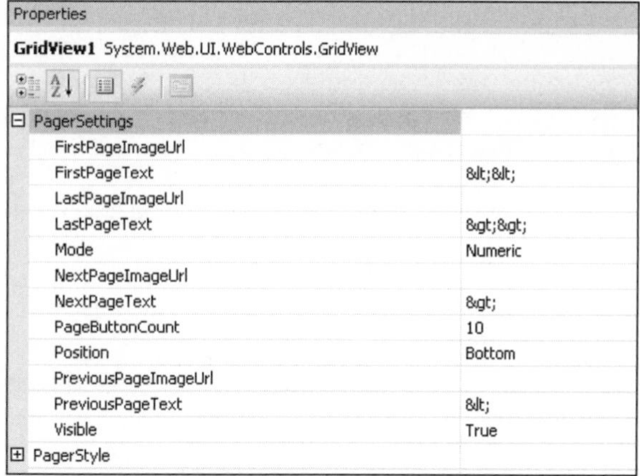

Figure 7-19

Of course, you can go beyond the option packages and set any property as desired. A common modification is to substitute site-specific images for the tools. Look carefully at the text properties. Sometimes the default words do not clearly relay the intention. For example, the term "last" when working with dates could mean the last record added in time, the last event to occur, or the last page that you viewed.

In the following Try It Out, you add a `GridView` of games. Each row will be a record from the Fixtures table; that is, one game. Columns will hold information such as the date and opponent of the game.

Try It Out Adding a GridView Control to Fixtures.aspx

1. Open your `Fixtures.aspx` page and use Design View.
2. Switch to (or open with Ctrl+Alt+S) the Database Explorer. Expand `WroxUnited.mdf`, expand Tables, and expand Fixtures, as shown in Figure 7-20. Select all of the fields and drag them to the bottom of the content section of the `Fixtures.aspx` page. VWD does all of the heavy lifting. Wait for it to finish and then run the page. Admire your work (although at this point there is no connection between the `ListBox` and the `GridView`) and close the browser.

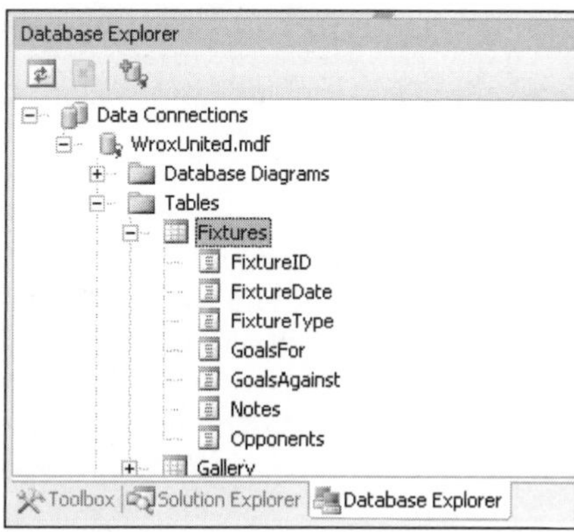

Figure 7-20

3. Continue in Design View and modify which fields are displayed. Looking at the scores, it might be just as good to delete those. Be sure the browser is not displaying the page, because that will lock it in VWD. Select the `GridView` and open its smart task panel. Click Edit Columns and in the bottom left, select the GoalsFor, and click the X icon to delete as shown in Figure 7-21. Repeat for the GoalsAgainst column. Click OK when you are finished.

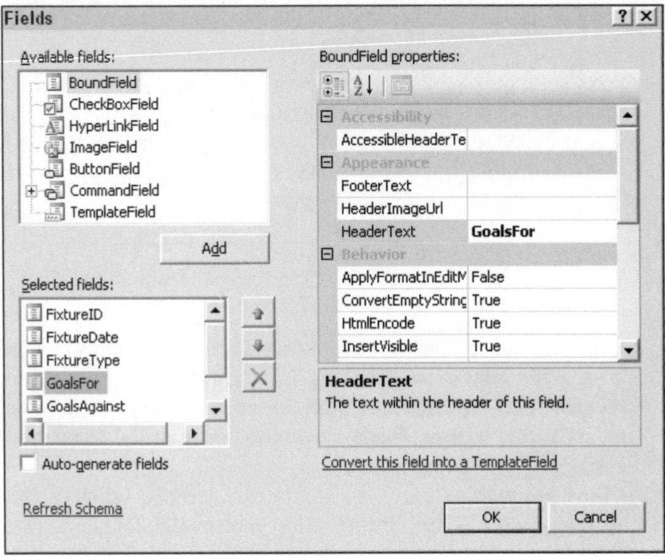

Figure 7-21

4. Turn on the check box for Enable Paging and then close the smart tasks panel. Look in the Properties window to find the `PageSize` property that you will set to two (Wrox United doesn't get invited to many games). Also note the section of `PagerSettings`. Set the mode to NumericFirstLast. Again, run in the browser, play with paging, and then close the browser.

5. Open the smart task panel and check Enable Sorting.

   - Because the Notes field is not logical for sorts, turn off sorting for that one field. Switch to Source View, and within the `GridView` control find the `BoundField` for Notes. Delete the entire property of `SortExpression="Notes"`. Save the file and check it in your browser.

How It Works

Adding a `GridView` control is simplicity itself with the help of VWD. This example demonstrated removing columns with the Edit Columns feature and it is just as easy to add columns. Turning on paging is as simple is checking the option, followed by setting properties for the control in the Properties window. The `PageSize` property is obvious, but other settings are under the `PagerSettings` group. Turning on sorting was easy. Removing the sort option from one column was similarly easy. All you had to do was go to Source View and delete that field's `SortExpression` property.

The DataList and Repeater Controls

The GridView control displayed data with each cell holding one piece of information (for example, the first name of employee 6). ASP.NET 2.0 offers the alternative of a table where all of the fields for one record are in one cell (one cell holds the first name, last name, ID, and date of hire, all for employee 6). Two data-bound controls render one record per cell: DataList and Repeater. The only difference is that the DataList control has default formatting and templates, but the Repeater control requires more setup by the designer.

Creating a DataList control is similar to creating a GridView control. You can drag and drop the data-bound control from the toolbar and a let VWD walk you through creation of a new data source control, or you can add the data source control by hand and then add the data-bound control. The DataList control's properties support the capability to set the Layout Repeat Direction so that records are ordered to increase horizontally across the page or vertically down the page, as well as the number of columns.

Templates offer the capability to lay out the space within a cell. For example, if you want a different set of fields in each DataList cell, want to change the cell's background to pink, and want to add a logo to each cell, you can modify the template. The exercise that follows walks you through changing a template.

Templates are invaluable, but there are several confusing points. First, templates by themselves do not display data. Rather, templates contain data-bound controls, such as labels, that do the actual display of data. Second, there are multiple templates for a given space. A DataList cell can have an Item Template (the normal display for data), an Alternating Item Template (to create every other record with a different color), a Selected Template (to change the appearance when selected), and an Edit Item template (to change the appearance during editing). Each of these templates is designed independently, as you will see. The third point of confusion is that you must enter into a specific template editing mode in order to make the changes — you cannot change a template by just selecting and modifying fields in Design View. After editing a template, you must explicitly end the template editing mode. Last, ASP.NET 2.0 uses the term *style* in context of templates. Styles primarily provide the properties for appearance (color, borders, and so forth), and the template primarily provides the layout of fields (but can also specify appearance). If a color or border is set in both the style and the template, the template will take precedence. It may seem that this is a minefield, but after you have worked with templates (as in the next exercise) you will find the template feature is well-designed.

Templates are also available in the GridView control and work the same way. The difference between a DataList control and a Repeater control is that the DataList control has a set of default templates, and the Repeater control is a blank space in which you must build all of the templates.

In this Try It Out, you practice using a DataList to display pictures from Wrox United matches. You will create a simple page that shows all of the pages and name it Gallery-All. Later in the chapter, you will create a more complex version as your final Gallery.aspx.

Try It Out DataList

1. Create a simple ASP.NET 2.0 Web Form page named **Gallery-all.aspx** in your site's root using the site.master and with the code placed in a separate page. Also, for this exercise, you will need some images that are supplied in the download. Check if you have already imported the

MatchImages folder from the download (`C:\BegASPNET2\WroxUnited`). If not, import it by right-clicking the root of the site in Solution Explorer and using Add Existing Item. In the end, you should have below the root a folder named `MatchImages`, and within there a JPEG of a player in action. Note that in other parts of the book, you will also use an Images folder that holds files such as `AddToCart.gif`, `ArrowFirst.gif`, and `logo_white.jpg`.

2. Start in Gallery-All by dragging a `DataList` control from the Data section of the Toolbox to the content area. Open its smart task panel, as shown in Figure 7-22, and click Choose Data Source. Click New Data Source for the wizard to create a data source control.

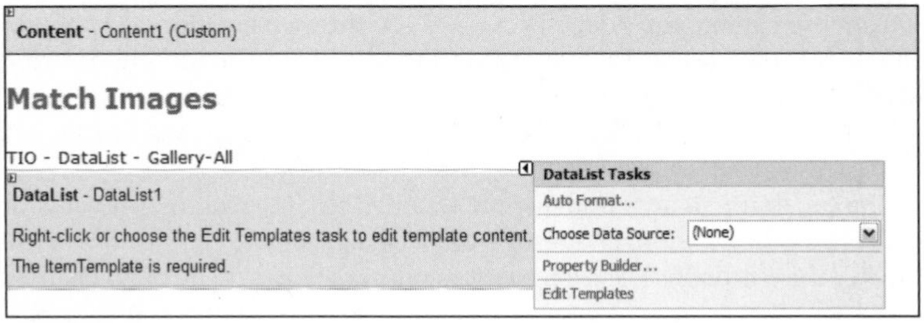

Figure 7-22

3. Select Database as the source and leave the name as SqlDataSource1. Click OK. Use the WroxUnited connection string (not `WroxUnited.mdf` because that choice will create a new connection).

4. From the Gallery table, check the five fields: `PictureURL`, `FixtureID`, `UploadedByMemberName`, `Notes`, and `PictureURL`. Then click Next, test the query, and finish. You can also use the wildcard (*) to select all fields, but having them listed in the SQL statement on the page makes it a little easier for understanding and troubleshooting when you look at the source code. At this point, VWD automatically creates the data source control and sets it as the source for the `DataList` control.

5. Run the page in your browser to test it (see Figure 7-23), noticing that you don't have the pictures yet. Close the browser.

6. Now you need to actually get the pictures displayed. Be sure your browser is closed and then in Design View select the `DataList` control, open its smart task panel, and click Edit Templates to see a screen similar to Figure 7-24. Select and then delete the line that has the text `PictureURL` and a `Label` control.

7. From the Toolbox, drag an `Image` control into the template just below the Picture ID field. Feel free to add a carriage return (by pressing Enter) to get the image control on its own line. On the `Image` control's smart task panel, click Edit Data Bindings, and select the property `ImageURL` to bind to the field `PictureURL`, as shown in Figure 7-25.

   The resulting source code follows. If you test the page in your browser, you'll notice that you are still not there. The `Image` control still does not have a URL that actually points to an image:

```
<asp:image id="Image1" runat="server"
  ImageUrl='<%# Eval("PictureURL")%>'  />
```

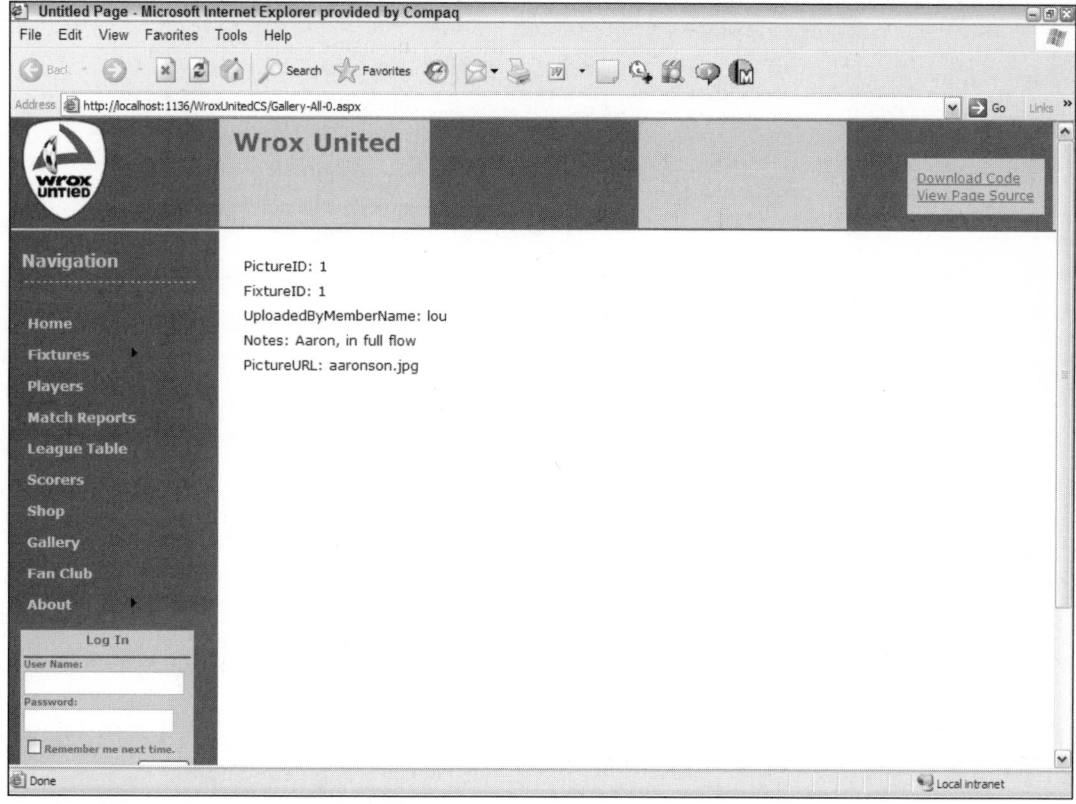

Figure 7-23

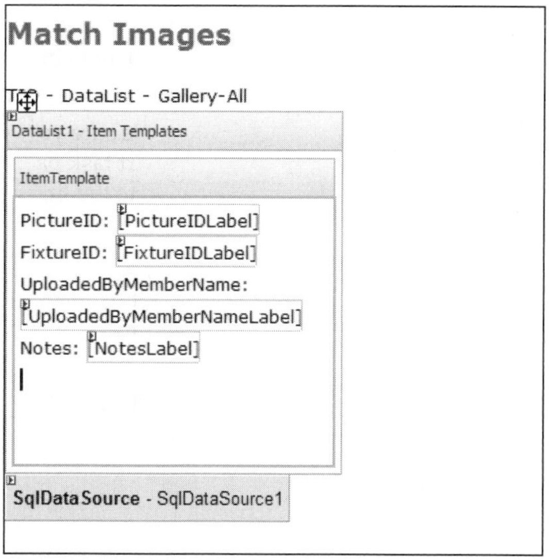

Match Images

TIO - DataList - Gallery-All

DataList1 - Item Templates

ItemTemplate

PictureID: [PictureIDLabel]

FixtureID: [FixtureIDLabel]

UploadedByMemberName: [UploadedByMemberNameLabel]

Notes: [NotesLabel]

SqlDataSource - SqlDataSource1

Figure 7-24

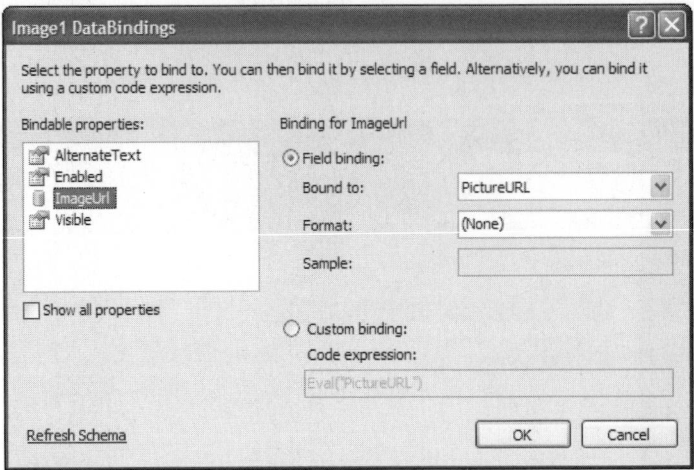

Figure 7-25

8. To get this to work, you must identify not only the name of the image file but also its path (folder). Staying in Source view, add the following argument to the `imageURL` property:

```
<asp:image id="Image1" runat="server"
 ImageUrl='<%# Eval("PictureURL", "~/MatchImages/{0}") %>'  />
```

9. Check your page in the browser (see Figure 7-26), shout "Eureka!" and then close the browser.

10. Now make some modifications to the `DataList`. Back in Design View, change the layout of the `DataList` control. Select the `DataList` control (see Figure 7-27), and in the Properties window change `RepeatColumns` to 3 and the `RepeatDirection` to Horizontal.

11. You'll finish with a little practice on templates. In Design View, select the `DataList` control and open its smart task panel. Click Edit Templates and, by default, you will be editing the Item template, shown in Figure 7-28.

12. Delete the "Notes:" text, but keep the label that shows the notes.

13. In the layout, move the `FixtureID` up higher in the template and the Member Name lower in the template. Edit the text `UploadedByMemberName` by adding some spaces between the words so it is easier to read. These finished actions are shown in Figure 7-29.

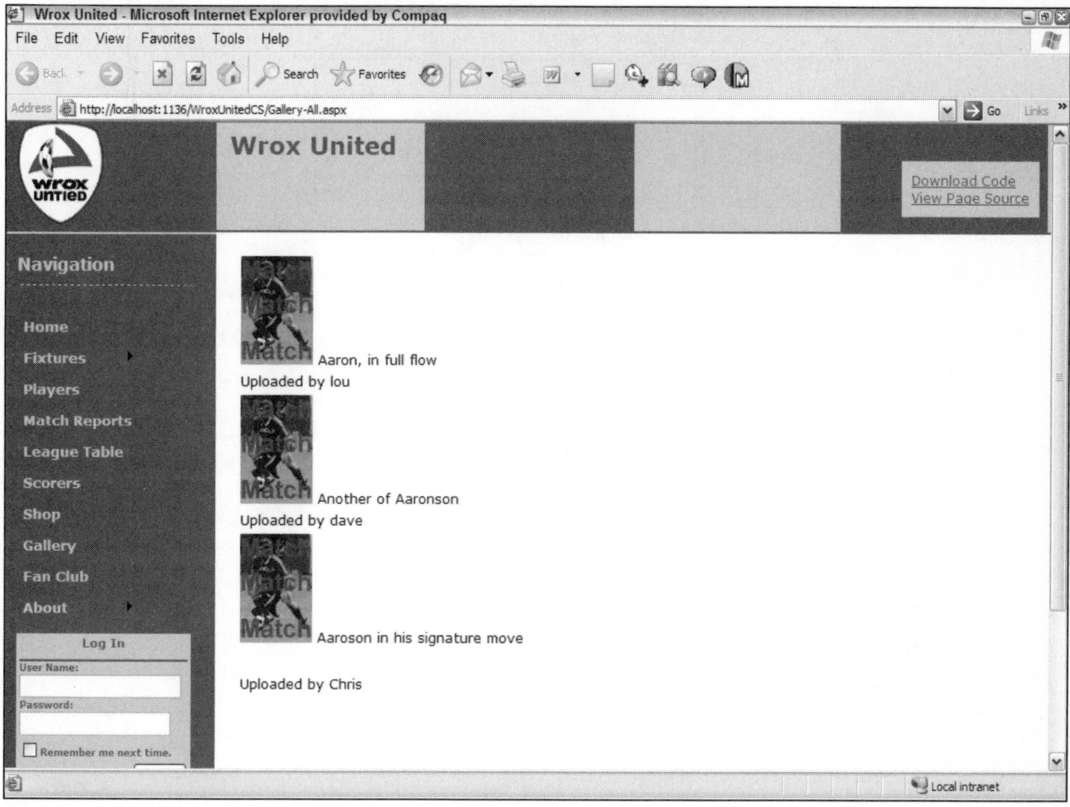

Figure 7-26

Properties

DataList1 System.Web.UI.WebControls.DataList

⊞ Accessibility	
⊞ Appearance	
⊞ Behavior	
⊞ Data	
⊟ Layout	
CellPadding	-1
CellSpacing	0
ExtractTemplateRows	False
Height	
HorizontalAlign	NotSet
RepeatColumns	**3**
RepeatDirection	**Horizontal**
RepeatLayout	Table
Width	
⊟ Misc	

Figure 7-27

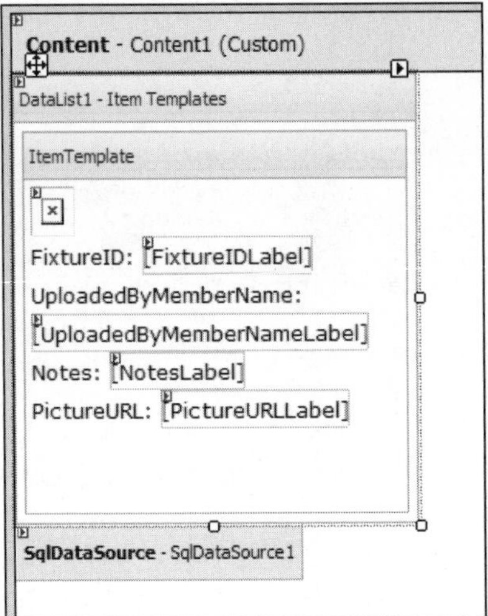

Figure 7-28

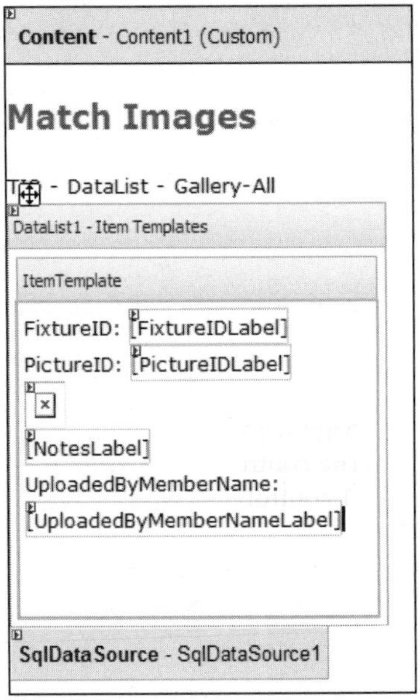

Figure 7-29

14. In the `DataList` control's smart task panel (which is probably still open), click End Template Editing. The page should look like the following in Source View:

```
<%@ Page Language="C#" MasterPageFile="~/site.master" AutoEventWireup="true"
CodeFile="Gallery-All.aspx.cs" Inherits="Gallery_All" Title="Untitled Page" %>
<asp:Content ID="Content1" ContentPlaceHolderID="mainContent" Runat="Server">
    <h2>
```

```
        Match Images</h2>
    TIO - DataList - Gallery-All<br />
    <asp:DataList ID="DataList1" runat="server"
    DataKeyField="PictureID"
    DataSourceID="SqlDataSource1">
        <ItemTemplate>
            PictureID:
            <asp:Label ID="PictureIDLabel" runat="server"
                Text='<%# Eval("PictureID") %>'></asp:Label><br />
            FixtureID:
            <asp:Label ID="FixtureIDLabel" runat="server"
                Text='<%# Eval("FixtureID") %>'></asp:Label><br />
            UploadedByMemberName:
            <asp:Label ID="UploadedByMemberNameLabel" runat="server"
                Text='<%# Eval("UploadedByMemberName") %>'></asp:Label><br />
            Notes:
            <asp:Label ID="NotesLabel" runat="server"
                Text='<%# Eval("Notes") %>'></asp:Label><br />
            <asp:Image ID="Image1" runat="server"
                ImageUrl='<%# Eval("PictureURL", "~/MatchImages/{0}") %>' />
            <br /><br />
        </ItemTemplate>
    </asp:DataList><asp:SqlDataSource ID="SqlDataSource1" runat="server"
        ConnectionString="<%$ ConnectionStrings:WroxUnited %>"
        SelectCommand="
            SELECT [PictureID], [FixtureID], [UploadedByMemberName],
                [Notes], [PictureURL]
            FROM [Gallery]">
    </asp:SqlDataSource>
</asp:Content>
```

15. Run the page to see the results of your work in your browser (see Figure 7-30).

How It Works

After the step 5, you had produced a page with names of picture files, not the actual images. This was because when VWD made the `DataList` control's default template, it saw there was text in the `PictureURL` field so it created a `Label` control, as follows:

```
...
<asp:DataList ID="DataList1" runat="server" DataSourceID="SqlDataSource1"
RepeatColumns="3" RepeatDirection="Horizontal">
        <ItemTemplate>
            <asp:label ID="label1" runat="server"
                Text='<%# Eval("PictureURL") %>'>
            </asp:Label>
```

In the next step, you changed the control from a `Label` to an `Image` control, as shown in the following code. This gave you an image but left the image rendered as a red x, meaning that the image could not be found.

```
<asp:Image ID="Image1" runat="server" ImageUrl='<%# Eval("PictureURL") %>' />
```

The problem is that an ASP.NET 2.0 page will, by default, look for an image file in the same folder as itself. The images are kept in a different folder named `MatchImages`. So, you can use a feature of the `ImageURL` property to add the relative path to the name of the picture file. You add a second argument that embellishes some text onto whatever value is provided by the database. In this case, you added the path. There are two new tricks in this syntax. First, in the formatting argument, you use a tilde (~) that means the root of the site. When you deploy the site to another server, you will not have to change all of the paths. Second, the syntax `{0}` indicates the place to plug in the value that comes from the database. So syntax such as the following will be translated into `C:\BegAspNet2\WroxUnitedCS\MatchImages\aaronson.jpg` for the first record before it is used as the `ImageURL`:

```
<asp:Image ID="Image1" runat="server"
 ImageUrl='<%# Eval("PictureURL", "~/MatchImages/{0}") %>' />
```

You finished the exercise by getting some practice with editing templates. Remember that you must shift into Edit Templates mode prior to making changes to the controls in a template that actually present the data. If you become perplexed by the unresponsiveness of VWD when you attempt to select or modify the `Label` and `Image` controls, you have forgotten to enter Edit Templates mode. You saw how fields could be selected and then deleted or moved.

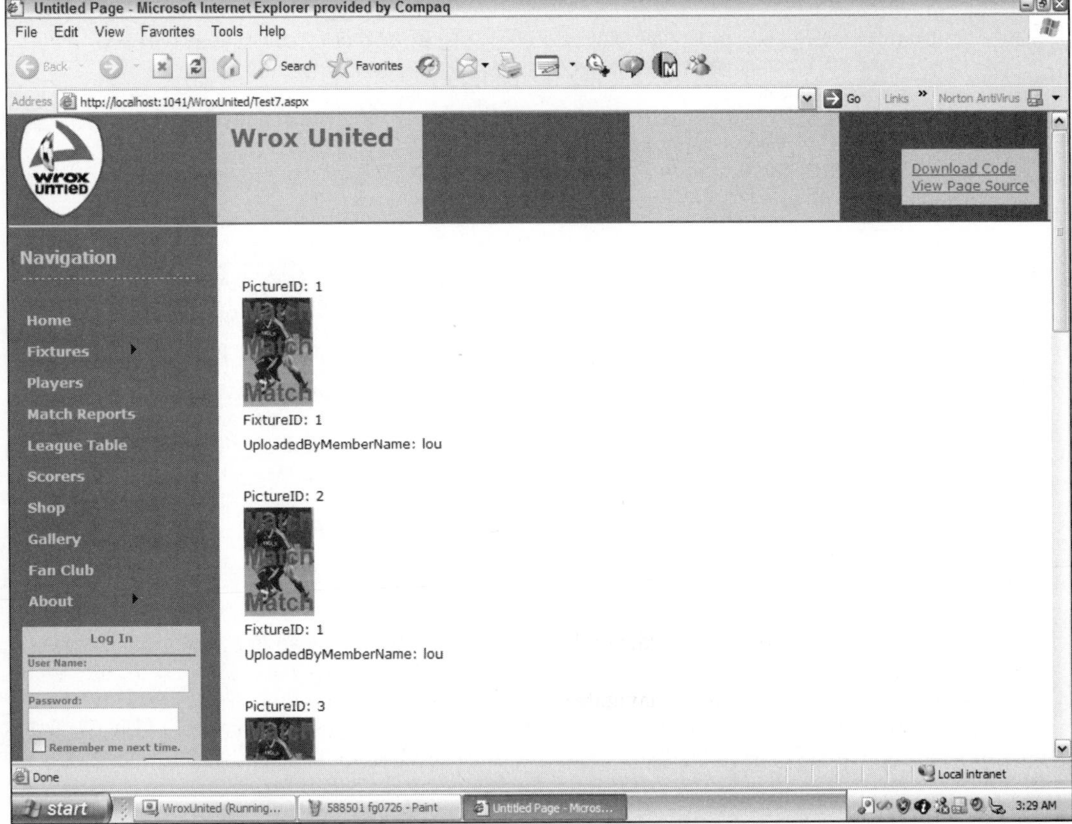

Figure 7-30

The DetailsView and FormView Controls

The three data-bound controls you have studied so far (`GridView`, `DataList`, and `Repeater`) display more than one record at a time. An alternative pair of data-bound controls display just one record at a time: `DetailsView` automatically creates a set of templates, and `FormView` is a blank slate upon which you build templates as desired. These are useful controls when you want to focus the user's attention on one record or need more screen real estate to display many fields for one record. They are also the preferred controls for adding or editing a record.

Like many other data-bound controls, `DetailsView` and `FormView` can be added to the page either directly, in which case VWD kicks off the wizard to create a data source control, or they can be added after a data source control is already on the page.

> **As you will study in Chapter 8, only `DetailsView` and `FormView` can accept the addition of new records. `GridView`, `DataList`, and `Repeater` can change, display, and modify existing records, but not create new records.**

Both the `DetailsView` and `FormView` controls rely on templates as described in the previous section. After creating the control, open the smart task panel and click Edit Templates. The appearance will change as you enter Template Edit Mode. Figure 7-31 shows the default mode.

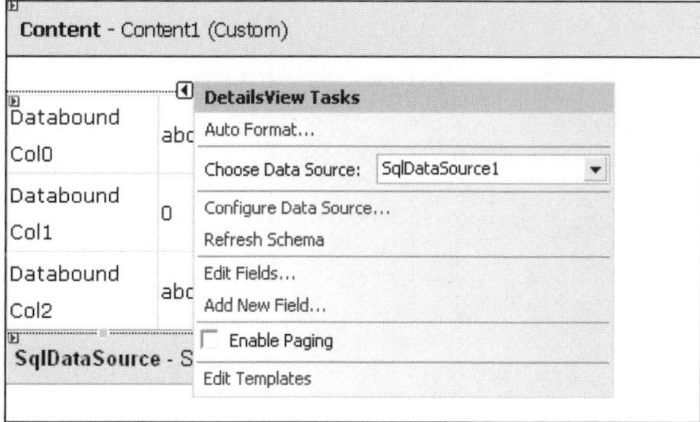

Figure 7-31

Figure 7-32 depicts the Template Edit mode where fields can be added, removed, or rearranged.

When you're displaying only one record, you have to make a decision whether or not to allow navigation from record to record. If you are showing details of a record selected in a `GridView` control, you would not want the user to be able to navigate off to other records because that would cause a loss of synchronization with the `GridView`. But if the `DetailsView` is standing alone, you can turn on paging with the check box in the smart task panel. The same Navigation Mode options are available as discussed for the `GridView`, such as `Numeric`, `FirstLast`, and `PreviousNext`.

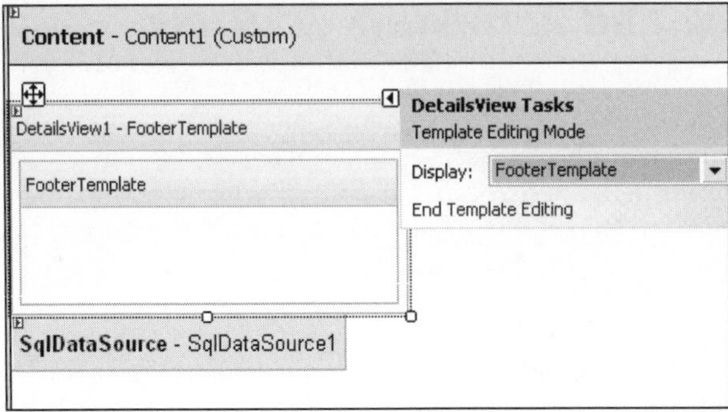

Figure 7-32

In this Try It Out, you practice looking at the information of one Wrox United match at a time using `DetailsView`.

Try It Out — Using DetailsView and FormView

1. Create a new page in the root of your site named **Fixtures-Stacked** using the Master page and putting the C# code in a separate file.
2. Working in Design View, drag a `DetailsView` control from the Toolbox onto the page, as shown in Figure 7-33.

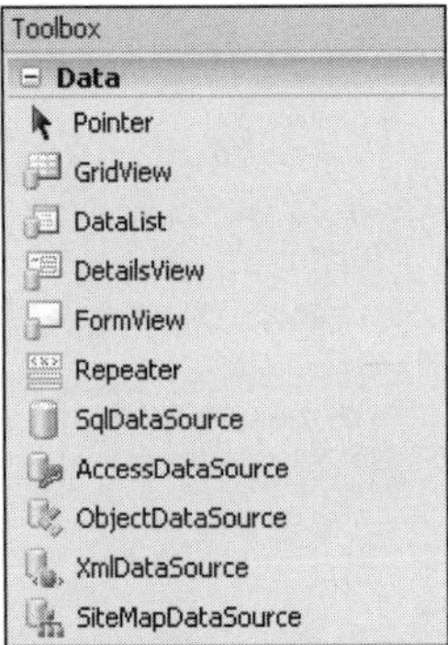

Figure 7-33

3. In the `DetailsView` control's smart task panel, choose its data source to be a new data source from Database with an ID of **SqlDataSource2** and using the existing Wrox United connection string. Be sure to name it **SqlDataSource2** because you will add a 1 later, and when the page is complete it will be logical to have the DetailsView as the second control. Include all of the fields from the Fixtures table. Test the query and finish the wizard.
4. Before testing the page in your browser, enable paging from the `DetailsView` control's smart task panel. In addition, in the Properties window, configure the Pager Settings / Mode to use `NumericFirstLast`.

5. Staying with the `DetailsView` control selected, in the Properties window change the `LastPageText` property to "Last Game of the Season" and `FirstPageText` property to "First Game of the Season." Finally, go to the Layout section, and set the Width to about 500px. (Alternatively, you can drag the right edge of the control in the Design View.

   The results are as follows:

```
<%@ Page Language="C#" MasterPageFile="~/site.master" AutoEventWireup="false"
CodeFile="Fixtures-Stacked.aspx.cs" Inherits="Fixtures_Stacked" title="Untitled
Page" %>

<asp:Content ID="Content1" ContentPlaceHolderID="mainContent" Runat="Server">

<asp:DetailsView ID="DetailsView1" runat="server"
    AllowPaging="True"
    AutoGenerateRows="False"
    DataKeyNames="FixtureID"
    DataSourceID="SqlDataSource2"
    Height="50px" Width="450px">
        <PagerSettings
            Mode="NumericFirstLast"
            FirstPageText="First Game of the Season"
            LastPageText="Last Game of the Season"
            />
        <Fields>
            <asp:BoundField DataField="FixtureID" HeaderText="FixtureID"
InsertVisible="False"
                ReadOnly="True" SortExpression="FixtureID" />
            <asp:BoundField DataField="FixtureDate" HeaderText="FixtureDate"
SortExpression="FixtureDate" />
            <asp:BoundField DataField="FixtureType" HeaderText="FixtureType"
SortExpression="FixtureType" />
            <asp:BoundField DataField="GoalsFor" HeaderText="GoalsFor"
SortExpression="GoalsFor" />
            <asp:BoundField DataField="GoalsAgainst" HeaderText="GoalsAgainst"
SortExpression="GoalsAgainst" />
            <asp:BoundField DataField="Notes" HeaderText="Notes"
SortExpression="Notes" />
            <asp:BoundField DataField="Opponents" HeaderText="Opponents"
SortExpression="Opponents" />
        </Fields>
    </asp:DetailsView>

    <asp:SqlDataSource ID="SqlDataSource2" runat="server"
        ConnectionString="<%$ ConnectionStrings:WroxUnited %>"
        SelectCommand="SELECT * FROM [Fixtures]">
    </asp:SqlDataSource>
</asp:Content>
```

6. Run the page in your browser to observe that only one match is shown at a time (see Figure 7-34).

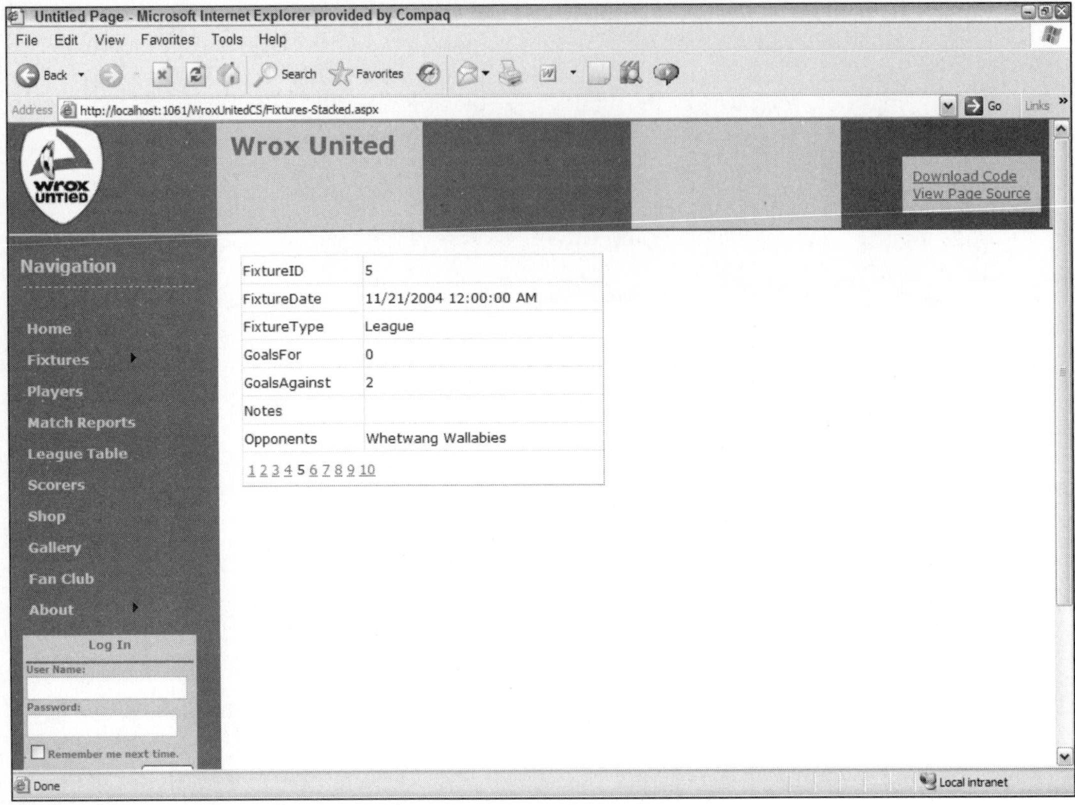

Figure 7-34

How It Works

The key point of this exercise is to create and view a presentation where one record is shown at a time, like the top playing card in a deck. You can use either `DetailsView` or `FormView`. In this case, you chose `DetailsView` because it does an automatic default layout for you.

The modifications you made to the `DetailsView` control were almost the same as those for other data-bound controls in earlier exercises. To move through the records of games, you enabled paging by checking the appropriate box in the control's smart task panel. To enhance the user experience, you specified a set of navigation tools in the Properties window of the control and modified their text to present a more logical user interface.

Data Source Controls with Parameters

So far in this chapter, you have created pages with fixed sets of data. With parameters, you can dynamically determine what data to display in a data-bound control. In ASP.NET 2.0, a *parameter* is a tag that holds a piece of data that can be used when a control carries out its task. For example, a parameter could hold a date, and that date is used to determine which game to show in a data-bound control. This section starts with a simpler case where you will look at how you can pass a parameter between pages. In the next section, you use parameters to enable two controls to work together. As with all of ASP.NET 2.0, the implementation is made even easier with tools in VWD. You will start with a simple page that picks up a value from a querystring and uses it to find one record of a table.

> **A querystring is a field name and value added to a HTTP request, as shown in the italicized part of the following URL (the text following the question mark):** `www.WroxUnited.com\PlayerInformation.aspx?PlayerLastName=Smith`.

When you created data source controls earlier in the chapter, you saw how to add only certain columns from a table in the "Configure the Select Statement" dialog step, but the wizard button captioned WHERE was not discussed (see Figure 7-35).

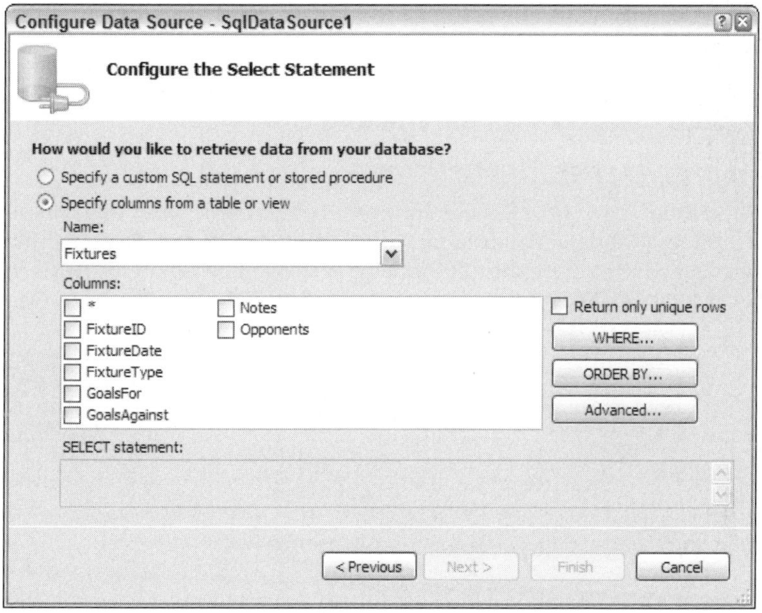

Figure 7-35

If you click the WHERE button of the wizard you get a dialog box that leads you through the options to limit the data set to only certain records. This step selects which column to use in the process of limiting records. Then the "source" drop-down list offers the choice of getting the data from a querystring. That opens a section for parameter properties. In the following code, you would enter **PlayerLastName** in the shaded box. These steps add a section to the data source control called `SelectParameters`, as shown in the following shaded code. `SelectParameters` is one type of parameter; you will encounter others later in the book.

```
<asp:SqlDataSource ID="SqlDataSource1" runat="server"
ConnectionString="<%$ ConnectionStrings:WroxUnited %>"
```

```
    SelectCommand=
     "SELECT * FROM [Players] WHERE ([PlayerLastName] = @PlayerLastName)">
       <SelectParameters>
          <asp:QueryStringParameter Name="PlayerLastName"
             DefaultValue="XXX" QueryStringField="PlayerLastName" Type="String" />
          </SelectParameters>
    </asp:SqlDataSource>
```

In this code, first notice that a `<SelectParameters>` is added in the shaded section. This is similar to a variable that will be filled by ASP.NET 2.0 with the value of `Smith` that comes in when you specify a querystring, as you did earlier. Then notice in the `SELECT` command that VWD has made the `WHERE` clause equal to a name starting with an at (@) sign. The @ symbol means a parameter — in this case, the parameter that holds the player's last name. Each time the page is opened or refreshed, it will search the querystring for a PlayerLastName value. Typing all of these would be a waste of time, so you will instruct VWD to do it for you in the next exercise.

In this Try It Out, you modify the previous Try It Out. Instead of presenting a `DetailsView` control with all of the games stacked up, you will present just one game. That one game will be determined by a game identifier (`FixtureID`) in the querystring.

Try It Out — Data Controls with Parameters

1. Make a new page named **Fixtures-One.aspx**.
2. Drag and drop a `DetailsView` control, open its smart task panel, and choose a new data source. Select a source of database and accept the default name. Select the WroxUnited connection and go to the configuration of the Select Statement. Select all the fields from the Fixtures table. Click the WHERE button to detour to the Add WHERE Clause box (see Figure 7-36).

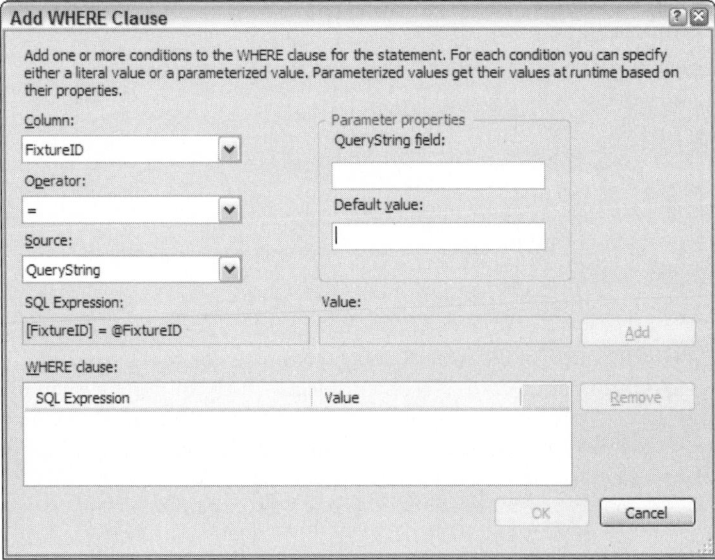

Figure 7-36

3. Select `FixtureID` from the drop-down list of columns.
4. Accept an operator of = and set the source to querystring. In the parameters properties panel, set the `QueryString` field to **FixID** (type in the name) and a default of `1`. Click Add and then click OK. Click Next and test. Notice that before the test runs, VWD gives you a chance to input the value that will be in the querystring. Try the default of `1`, and then also test various numbers between. (See Figure 7-37.)

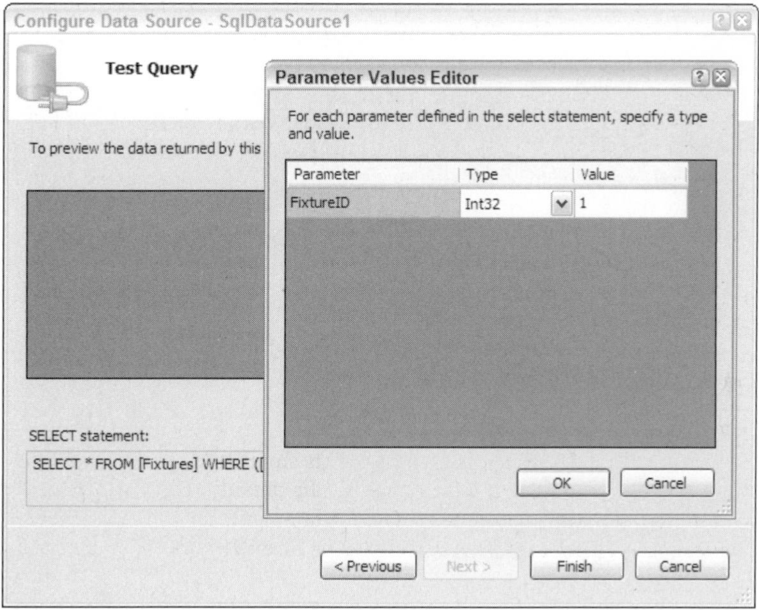

Figure 7-37

5. Click Finish. While the `DetailsView` is selected, change its width to about 450px. Your source code will end up as follows:

```
<%@ Page Language="C#" MasterPageFile="~/site.master" AutoEventWireup="true"
CodeFile="Fixtures-One.aspx.cs" Inherits="Fixtures_One" Title="Untitled Page" %>
<asp:Content ID="Content1" ContentPlaceHolderID="mainContent" Runat="Server">
    TIO - DataList - Gallery-All<br />
    <asp:DetailsView ID="DetailsView1" runat="server"
        AutoGenerateRows="False"
        DataKeyNames="FixtureID"
        DataSourceID="SqlDataSource1"
        Height="50px" Width="450px">
        <Fields>
            <asp:BoundField DataField="FixtureID"
                HeaderText="FixtureID"
                InsertVisible="False"
                ReadOnly="True"
                SortExpression="FixtureID" />
            <asp:BoundField DataField="FixtureDate"
                HeaderText="FixtureDate"
                SortExpression="FixtureDate" />
```

```
            <asp:BoundField DataField="FixtureType"
                HeaderText="FixtureType"
                SortExpression="FixtureType" />
            <asp:BoundField DataField="GoalsFor"
                HeaderText="GoalsFor"
                SortExpression="GoalsFor" />
            <asp:BoundField DataField="GoalsAgainst"
                HeaderText="GoalsAgainst"
                SortExpression="GoalsAgainst" />
            <asp:BoundField DataField="Notes"
                HeaderText="Notes"
                SortExpression="Notes" />
            <asp:BoundField DataField="Opponents"
                HeaderText="Opponents"
                SortExpression="Opponents" />
        </Fields>
    </asp:DetailsView>
    <asp:SqlDataSource ID="SqlDataSource1" runat="server"
        ConnectionString="<%$ ConnectionStrings:WroxUnited %>"
        SelectCommand="
            SELECT *
            FROM [Fixtures]
            WHERE ([FixtureID] = @FixtureID)">
        <SelectParameters>
            <asp:QueryStringParameter
                DefaultValue="1"
                Name="FixtureID"
                QueryStringField="FixID"
                Type="Int32" />
        </SelectParameters>
    </asp:SqlDataSource>
</asp:Content>
```

6. Test the page by running it. By default, game number 1 will be displayed. In your browser's address bar, try changing the URL from . . . `/WroxUnited/Fixtures-One.aspx` by adding a querystring to make . . . `/WroxUnited/Fixtures-One.aspx?FixID=3` and click the GO button of your browser (as shown in Figure 7-38).

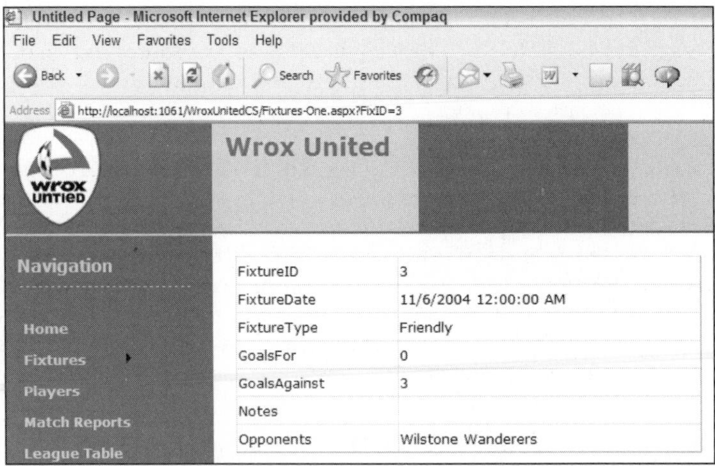

Figure 7-38

How It Works

First, you disabled paging because with only one record in the stack, there is no need for navigation. Then you revised your `SelectCommand`. Even though you already have your `SqlDataSource` control configured, you can restart the wizard and modify the control. This eliminates the possibility of introducing typos by editing in Source View.

In prior exercises, you did not use the WHERE button and so VWD built for you a `SelectCommand` that returned all of the records. In the Add WHERE Clause step, you selected a column (a field) that was going to be scanned for matches. You wanted your matches to be exact, so you selected the = operator. Then you selected a source of `QueryString`. This means that the value of which fixture to display (the parameter) can be found in the querystring. Under parameters properties, you set the name of the value in the querystring to be `FixID`. Don't forget to click the Add button in the Add WHERE Clause window — it is easy to overlook.

VWD keeps an eye on the data source control for each data-bound control. When you finish your revision to the data source control, VWD warns you that you better synch up any data-bound controls using that source. You can also do that synch explicitly by clicking the Refresh Schema button of the smart task panel.

All of these changes left the page ready to accept an ID of a game in the querystring. The value must have the name of `FixID`. Your data source will take that value (or `1` if there is no `FixID`) and use that in the `SelectCommand` to find the records with a matching `FixtureID`. Only that game will be shown. When you test the page, you only have to remember the syntax to attach a value to a URL. After the page name, type a question mark to begin parameters. Then type the parameter name, an = sign, and the parameter's value.

Multiple Data Controls Working Together

The previous section described a crude way to use parameters by typing them into the URL. The enlightened way is to use one data-bound control to create the parameters for another data-bound control. These are called *ControlParameters*. This section demonstrates two very common cases. In the first case, a `DropDownList` control determines which record or records to display in a `GridView` control. In the second case, a selection in a `GridView` control determines the record for which the page should show more fields in a `DetailsView` control. These are called *master-child scenarios*. A selection in a master data-bound control establishes the value for a `WHERE` clause in the data source control of the child data-bound control. In almost all cases, there must be separate data source controls for the master and child data-bound controls.

In the master control, you only need one special property. If the master control is a `ListBox` or `DropDownList` control, the `AutoPostBack` property must be set to `True` so that when a selection is made from the master, ASP.NET 2.0 will invoke a refresh of the page and the resulting change in the record will be shown in the child control. Keep in mind that `ListBox` and `DropDownList` controls have two field parameters. The first is the field to display (the `DataTextField` property), and the second is the field that is used in page code (the `DataValueField` property). This allows a last name, for example, to be displayed to the user in the list box but the more useful value of, for example, PlayerID to be used in SQL statements. If the master control is a `GridView`, you can open its smart task panel and choose

Enable Selection to get VWD to build a new column with select buttons for each record. When clicked, ASP.NET will react to the selection of that record, as you will see.

In the child control, you must set a parameter into the `WHERE` clause of the child control's data source control. In the previous section, you set the parameter to a field of the querystring using the Add WHERE Clause dialog box of the Configure Data Source Control wizard. You can use the wizard again, but this time when you get to the Add WHERE Clause panel, you set your column equal to a value from a control (not a querystring). The wizard presents a list of controls from which you can select. Within the selecting control, you determine which value to use, normally the SelectionValue.

In the following Try It Out, you practice two combinations of controls. In the first, you use a `GridView` selection to show additional fields in a `DetailsView` control. In the second, you use a `DropDownList` control to show only certain records in a `GridView`.

Try It Out Multiple Controls Working Together

1. Now you will build your final version of `Fixtures.aspx`. Create a folder named **OldPages** and move your existing `Fixtures.aspx` to this retirement home. Because the steps are so quick and easy (and it is a good review), you will start your final Fixtures page from scratch. Add a new item to the site named `Fixtures.aspx` using the Master page with C# code in a separate file. Switch to Design View.

2. Open Database Explorer and navigate to WroxUnited.mdf⇨Tables⇨Fixtures. Select only the fields for `FixtureID`, `FixtureDate`, and `Opponents` (using Ctrl+Click) and drag them to the page. VWD will crank for a few seconds and then give you a `GridView` with its smart task panel open. Choose Enable Selection as shown in Figure 7-39. Note that VWD has already added the column of Select buttons.

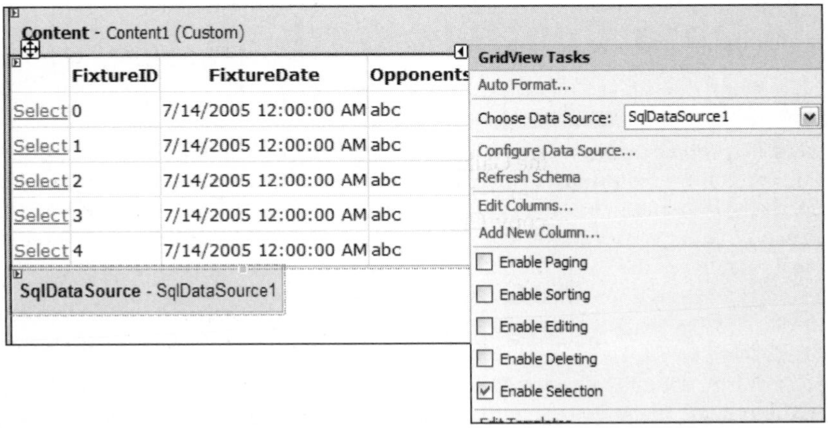

Figure 7-39

3. Go to the bottom of the content holder and drag a `DetailsView` control from the Toolbox. Choose a data source of New, configure the database with an ID of `SqlDataSource2`, and continue using the connection string named WroxUnited that you've used throughout this chapter. Specify to get data from the Fixtures table, but this time select only the FixtureID and Notes fields.

4. Click the WHERE button and select the column of `FixtureID`. Set the operator to = and select Control from the Source drop-down list (see Figure 7-40).

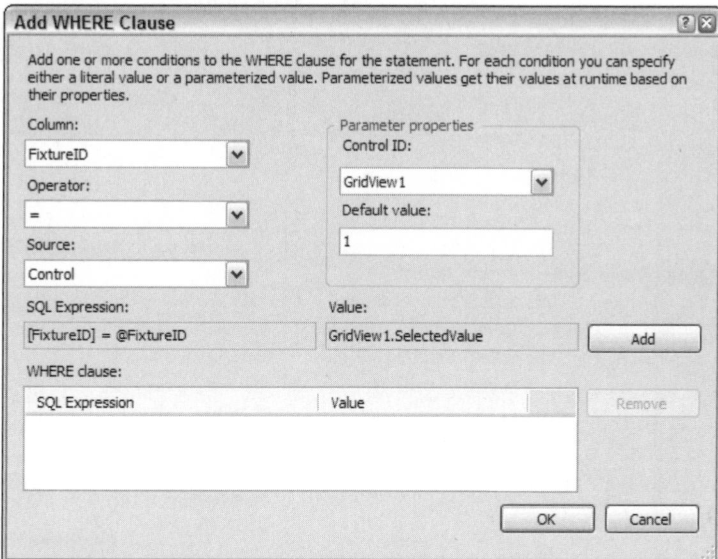

Figure 7-40

5. In the parameter properties, set the `ControlID` to `GridView1` and the default value to `1`. Don't forget to click the Add button (not done yet in Figure 7-41). Click OK, Next, and then the Test Query button (a value of 1 is fine), and finally, click the Finish button.

6. Make the `DetailsView` control wider (through the Properties pane or by dragging the right edge). Save and view it in your browser (see Figure 7-41). Select various matches from the `GridView` and see their notes below the `GridView` in the `DetailsView` control.

7. Now shift gears to work on the Gallery page. You want to only show pages from one match. In Solution Explorer, select `Gallery-All.aspx` in the root, copy it to the clipboard and paste it back into the root to make a copy. Change the name from `Copy of Gallery-All` to `Gallery.aspx`.

8. Open `Gallery.aspx`, and add a few line breaks and then a `DropDownList` box to the top of the page. Configure its data source to a new source of type Database and name it **SqlDataSource2**. Use the `WroxUnited` connection string and from the Fixtures table, select the `FixtureID`, `FixtureDate`, and `Opponents`.

9. Click ORDER BY and sort on `FixtureDate` ascending. Click OK and Next. Then test the query and click Finish. This brings you back to the Choose a Data Source window.Display (for now) the Opponents and set the value to `FixtureID`. Click OK. While the `DropDownList` control is still selected, turn on Enable AutoPostBack from the smart task panel.

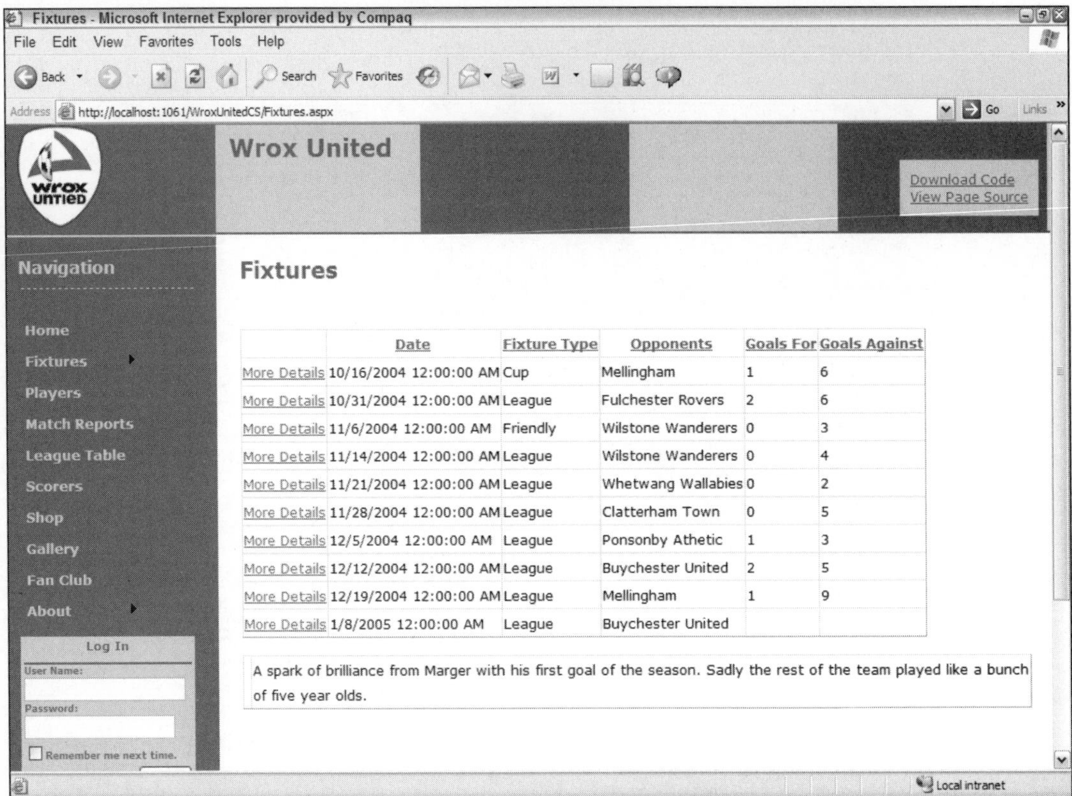

Figure 7-41

10. Open the smart task panel for the `DataSourceControl1` (used by the `DataList`) and start its Configure Data Source wizard. Step through to the `WHERE` clause. Set the Column of `FixtureID` to equal a control with the `ControlID` of `DropDownList1` and a default value of `1`. Don't forget to click the Add button and then click OK. Continue by clicking Next, and then test query (a parameter value of 1 is fine) and click Finish. When you are prompted to reset the templates for the `DetailslView` control, answer No. You will see the result shown in Figure 7-42 in your browser (albeit all the photos to-date have been from game 1).

Your code should look like the following in Source View:

```
<%@ Page Language="C#" MasterPageFile="~/site.master" AutoEventWireup="true"
CodeFile="Gallery.aspx.cs" Inherits="Gallery_All" Title="Untitled Page" %>
<asp:Content ID="Content1" ContentPlaceHolderID="mainContent" Runat="Server">
    <h2>
        Match Images</h2>
    TIO - Multiple Controls - Gallery<br />
    <br />
```

```
    <asp:DropDownList ID="DropDownList1" runat="server"
        AutoPostBack="True"
        DataSourceID="SqlDataSource2"
        DataTextField="Opponents"
        DataValueField="FixtureID">
    </asp:DropDownList>
    <asp:SqlDataSource ID="SqlDataSource2" runat="server"
        ConnectionString="<%$ ConnectionStrings:WroxUnited %>"
        SelectCommand="SELECT [FixtureID], [FixtureDate], [Opponents]
            FROM [Fixtures] ORDER BY [FixtureDate]">
    </asp:SqlDataSource>
    <br />
    <br />
    <asp:DataList ID="DataList1" runat="server"
        DataKeyField="PictureID"
        DataSourceID="SqlDataSource1"
        RepeatColumns="3"
        RepeatDirection="Horizontal">
        <ItemTemplate>
            FixtureID:
            <asp:Label ID="FixtureIDLabel" runat="server"
                Text='<%# Eval("FixtureID") %>'>
            </asp:Label>
            PictureID:
            <asp:Label ID="PictureIDLabel" runat="server"
                Text='<%# Eval("PictureID") %>'></asp:Label><br />
            <asp:Image ID="Image1" runat="server"
                ImageUrl='<%# Eval("PictureURL", "~/MatchImages/{0}") %>' /><br />
            <asp:Label ID="NotesLabel" runat="server"
                Text='<%# Eval("Notes") %>'></asp:Label><br />
            UploadedByMemberName:
            <asp:Label ID="UploadedByMemberNameLabel" runat="server"
                Text='<%# Eval("UploadedByMemberName") %>'>
            </asp:Label><br /><br />
        </ItemTemplate>
    </asp:DataList><asp:SqlDataSource ID="SqlDataSource1" runat="server"
        ConnectionString="<%$ ConnectionStrings:WroxUnited %>"
        SelectCommand="SELECT [PictureID], [FixtureID],
            [UploadedByMemberName], [Notes], [PictureURL]
            FROM [Gallery] WHERE ([FixtureID] = @FixtureID)">
        <SelectParameters>
            <asp:ControlParameter ControlID="DropDownList1"
                DefaultValue="1"
                Name="FixtureID"
                PropertyName="SelectedValue"
                Type="Int32" />
        </SelectParameters>
    </asp:SqlDataSource>
</asp:Content>
```

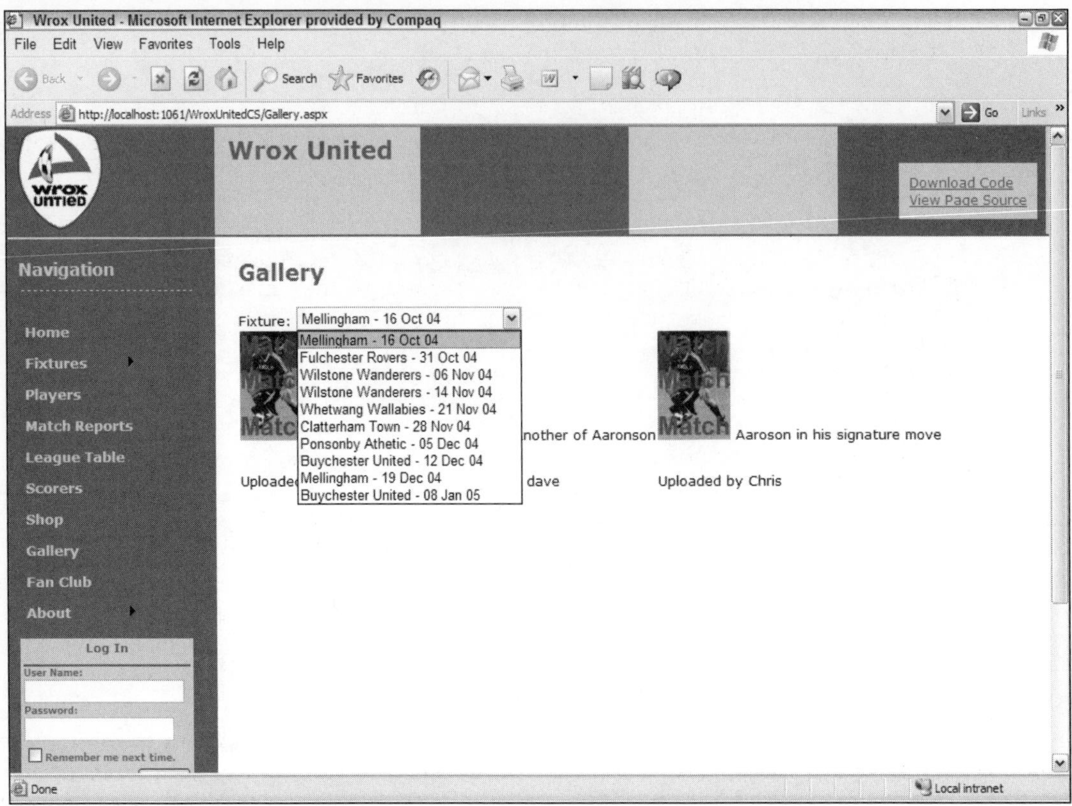

Figure 7-42

11. You'll finish up with a trick to resolve the problem of the user not knowing which match to select in the `DropDownList` when the same opponent is listed several times. Change the `SelectCommand` of the `DropDownList` data source control (`SqlDataSource2`) and the `DataTextField` of the `DropDownList` as follows:

```
<asp:DropDownList ID="DropDownList1" runat="server"
    DataSourceID="SqlDataSource2"
    DataTextField="FixtureCombo"
    DataValueField="FixtureID"
    AutoPostBack=true >
</asp:DropDownList>

<asp:SqlDataSource ID="SqlDataSource2" runat="server"
    ConnectionString="<%$ ConnectionStrings:WroxUnited %>"
    SelectCommand="SELECT [FixtureID], (Opponents + ' - ' + CONVERT(varchar,
FixtureDate, 6)) As FixtureCombo  FROM [Fixtures] ORDER BY [FixtureDate]">
```

How It Works

Both of these pages are logical extensions of what you did in earlier exercises. As before, you changed the `SelectCommand` (using VWD's Configure Data Source wizard) so that there is a `WHERE` clause that gets its value from a parameter. In the previous Try It Out, the parameter came in with the querystring, but on these two pages, the parameter comes from another control.

In the first case, the `GridView` filled the parameter with the ID of the record for which the Select button was clicked. That value was then used by the data source control in its `WHERE` clause. An important (and frequently overlooked) step is to set the `DropDownList` control to `AutoPostBack`.

In the final step, you wanted to display more than one field in the `DropDownList` control. You can achieve that goal by using a SQL statement that creates a new field by concatenating values from existing fields. The following code brings together the opponent's name, the literal text of spaces, a hyphen, and a converted format of the game date to create a field called `FixtureCombo`:

```
        SelectCommand="SELECT [FixtureID], (Opponents + ' - ' + CONVERT(varchar,
  FixtureDate, 6)) As FixtureCombo  FROM [Fixtures] ORDER BY [FixtureDate]">
```

Note how a plus sign (+) is used between each section of the string of text. The opponent value comes from the database in a form ready to use. The `FixtureDate` also comes from the database, but it comes in a date format that is not what you want. So you convert it to a type called `varchar`, which is a string of characters. You then put together the two parts with a dividing section of text that consists of a space, a hyphen, and another space.

Working with XML Data

XML has solidified as the standard format for information on the web. XML files (or streams of data) are self-describing (each value has a label) and hierarchical in that every item of data has a parent except the top-most tag. Typically, an XML file will have its highest-level tags that merely state the kind of information held, such as Players. Then there would be a set of tags called "player" for each member of the team. Within there would be further, lower-level tags describing that player. Each item is called a node, for example, one player. Additionally, XML is case-sensitive. XML files can be created, read, and revised using ASP.NET 2.0. In the following Try It Out, you create an XML file using VWD.

The league has issued a few changes to Wrox United's 2007 schedule:

Game Number	Date	Home	Visitor
1	2007, October 21	Wrox United	Clatterham
2	2007, October 22	Mellingham	WroxUnited
3	2007, October 22	Wrox United	Fulchester

Try It Out Creating XML Data

1. Right-click the root of your site, add a new item of the type XML file, and name it **Schedule2007**. Normally you would store an XML file in `App_Data`, but for this exercise that creates some rights problems when viewing the file in your browser.

2. At the beginning of the file, VWD will automatically add the tag for the XML version. Go to the end of the file and type <Games>. Notice that VWD automatically adds the closing tag for <Games>. These tags are the highest level and describe the entire contents of the XML file.

3. Now you will create a node for the first game. Inside the <Games> tags, create a <Game> tag (note that this is singular). Now add **Number="1"** inside the opening <Game> tag as per the code listing after the next step.

4. Inside the <Games> tag, add three pairs of child tags with values for the team names and the date as follows:

```
<Games>
  <Game Number="1">
    <Date>2007/10/21</Date>
    <Home>WroxUnited</Home>
    <Visitor>Clatterham</Visitor>
  </Game>
</Games>
```

5. Add the other two games in the same manner and save the file. The additional games will be as follows (for the sake of completeness, the first game is included again):

```
<Games>
  <Game Number="1">
    <Date>2007/10/21</Date>
    <Home>WroxUnited</Home>
    <Visitor>Clatterham</Visitor>
  </Game>

  <Game Number="2">
    <Date>2007/10/22</Date>
    <Home>Mellingham </Home>
    <Visitor>WroxUnited</Visitor>
  </Game>

  <Game Number="3">
    <Date>2007/10/22</Date>
    <Home>WroxUnited</Home>
    <Visitor>Fulchester</Visitor>
  </Game>
</Games>
```

6. If you run the file the XML, data will be sent to the browser, and most browsers can render a simple presentation (see Figure 7-43). Try it, noting that there is no ASP.NET 2.0 involvement yet.

How It Works

You saw in this exercise that you start with a top-level node named <Games>. Then, being careful not to make typos in the case, you added a node for the first game. The data for that game was organized in two ways. The number of the game was placed in the <Game> tag as an attribute. But you chose to place the date and competitors in separate tags at a lower level than the <Game> tag. After running the file, you saw how your browser handles a raw XML file. In the next section, you see what ASP.NET 2.0 can do with that information.

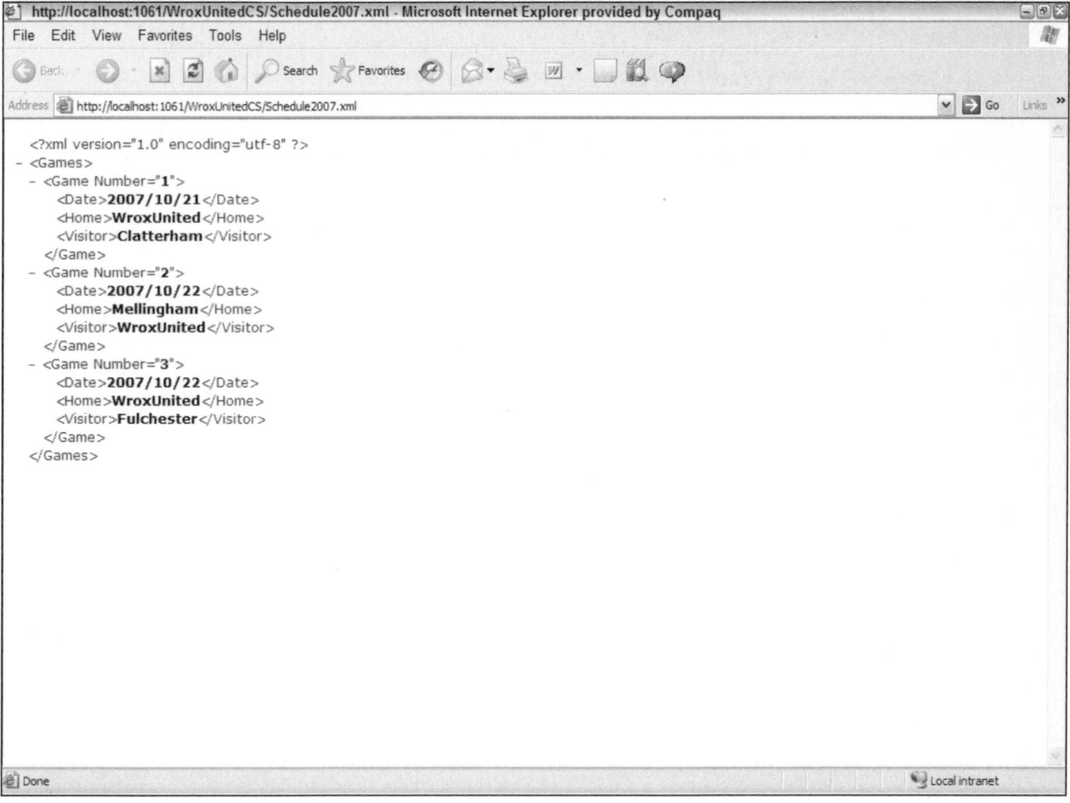

Figure 7-43

Reading XML Data

Because XML data is organized as a hierarchy, ASP.NET 2.0 provides alternate data source and data-bound controls from those you used with tabular data earlier in the chapter. The XML data source control provides the data source control for most cases. The key property that must be set in this control is the name of the XML database file.

ASP.NET 2.0 supports rendering of tree data with three data-bound controls named `TreeView`, `Menu`, and `SiteMapPath`. The `TreeView` is a little tricky to set up, as you will see, but then it does its job just fine. The `TreeView` control is fine for any XML data. The `Menu` control is designed only for its named purpose. The `SiteMapPath` control renders differently depending on the page that is currently opened. Chapter 2 presented more on this navigation control.

VWD offers a handy way to identify which pieces of data should appear in its rendering. The tool is called the `TreeViewDataBindings` Editor and it can be opened from the `TreeView` control's smart task panel, as you will practice in the following exercise.

In the following Try It Out, you create a display of the games scheduled for 2007 at the bottom of the `Fixtures.aspx` page.

Try It Out Reading XML Data

1. Open `Fixtures.aspx` in Design View and drag a `TreeView` control (in the navigation section of the Toolbox, shown in Figure 7-44) to the bottom of the page.

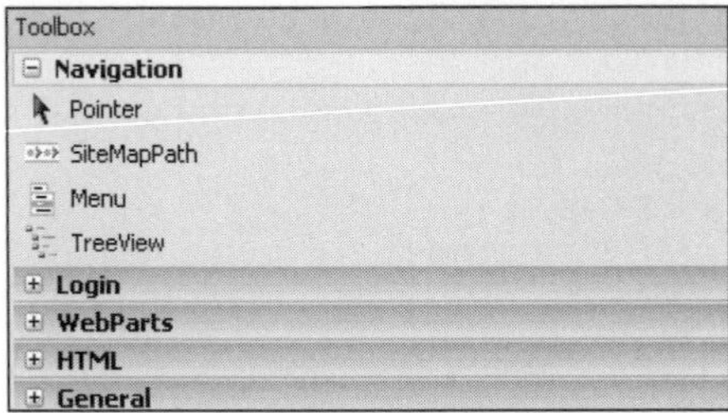

Figure 7-44

2. On the smart task panel, select Choose Data Source and select New. Note that this time you have different choices for a data source. You want to use an XML file (see Figure 7-45).

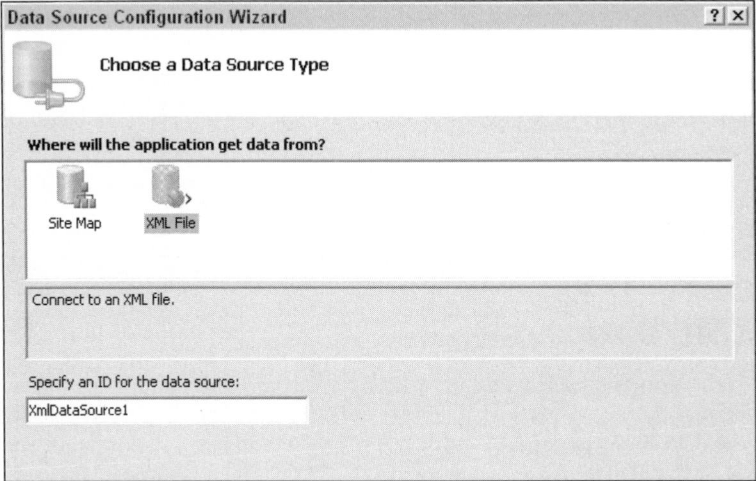

Figure 7-45

3. Specify an ID of **Schedule2007XML** and then in the next dialog box, set the Data File by browsing to the `Schedules2007.XML` file that you created. For now, leave the Transform and XPath boxes in the wizard blank, and just click OK. Run the page in your browser (see Figure 7-46) and look at the tree at the bottom of the page. The page is rendering the names of the nodes but not the data of the nodes. Close the browser.

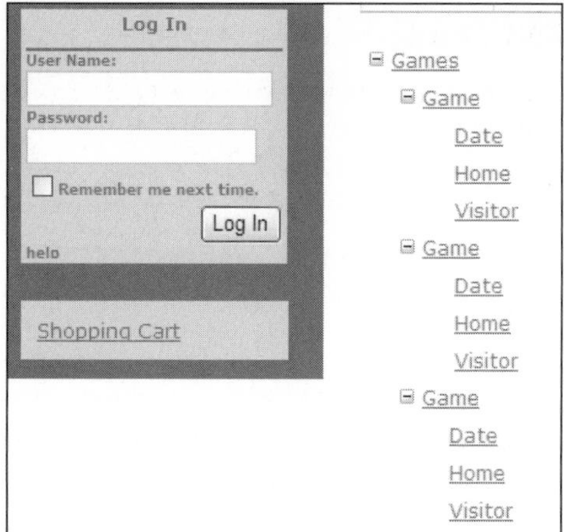

Figure 7-46

4. In Design View, select the `TreeView` control, open its smart task panel, and click Edit Treenode Data Bindings. Select Game in the top left (the singular Game, not the plural Games) and click Add (see Figure 7-47).

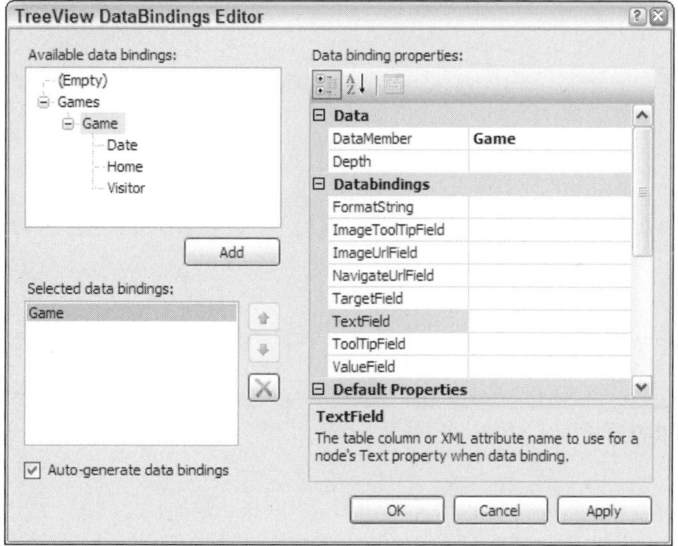

Figure 7-47

5. In the Properties window, set the `TextField` to `Number`. Staying in the DataBindings editor, select Home, click Add, and set its `TextField` to `#InnerText` because you want to display the text between the `<Home>` and `</Home>` tags on the page. Repeat the setting of `#InnerText#` for the Date and Visitor data. Save and view in your browser as in Figure 7-48.

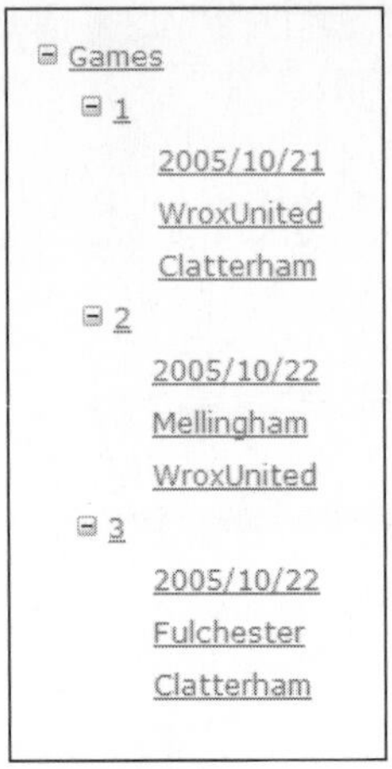

Games
1
2005/10/21
WroxUnited
Clatterham
2
2005/10/22
Mellingham
WroxUnited
3
2005/10/22
Fulchester
Clatterham

Figure 7-48

How It Works

In the first step, you found the `TreeView` control in the Navigation panel of the Toolbox. After dragging it to the page, you can set its source of data the same way that you do for other data-bound controls, by using the Choose Data Source in the smart task panel. But in the case of a `TreeView`, you want to use a hierarchical source, so you pick the XML file you made in the last exercise.

As you observed in the first run of the page, by default you only get the generic names of the nodes, not the actual data. The data is specified by using the `TreeViewDataBindings` Editor. You can add (or remove) tags to which you want data rendered. After a field is added, you go to the right side and select its `TextField` property. If you have data within a tag, such as Number within the `<Game>` tag, then the name of that data will show up without a number sign. If the data is between an opening and closing tag, such as `<Home>WroxUnited</Home>`, the `TextField` option will be set to `#InnerText`.

Binding Syntax

In this book, you have taken advantage of VWD's features to build code and thus spent little time examining the code that was built for you. But it is worth understanding code that actually brings together the data source controls and the data-bound controls. Within a template for a `GridView`, `DataList`, `Repeater`, `DetailsView`, or `FormView`, you see the following code:

```
<asp:DataList ID="DataList1" runat="server"
  DataSourceID="SqlDataSource1"
     <ItemTemplate>
      <asp:Label ID="FixtureIDLabel"
         runat="server"
         Text='<%# Eval("FixtureID") %>'
         BackColor="Yellow"></asp:Label>
    </ItemTemplate>
  </asp:DataList>
```

The shaded line instructs the page to bind the control named `FixtureIDLabel` to the field named `FixtureID` in the data source `SqlDataSource1`. This method (a request for a specific behavior), named `Eval()`, actually performs the connection between one field in the data source control and a rendering mechanism in the data-bound control. Two similar methods exist: `Eval()` is for read-only, and `Bind()` allows both read and write (and is covered in Chapter 8). Within templates, VWD will write code to specifically employ these methods. But if there is no templating, the binding is implied and will not appear in the code.

Summary

ASP.NET 2.0 greatly eases the use of data on a web page by encapsulating most of the code into easy-to-use controls. In this chapter, you learned that data source controls and data-bound controls work together. The former provides a connection to an information source, and the latter renders that information onto a page. ASP.NET 2.0 ships with four data source controls — `SqlDataSource`, `AccessDataSource`, `XMLDataSource`, and `SiteMapDataSource` — each optimized to work with a particular type of data. This chapter focused primarily on the `SqlDataSource` control, because it can be used with any database that can understand SQL statements. A fifth data source control, `ObjectDataSource`, is used for custom-designed business objects.

After describing the basics of data source and data-bound controls, the chapter drilled down into the specifics of how to use them on your pages, specifically covering the following topics:

- How to use the `GridView`, `DataList`, and `Repeater` controls to display tabular data
- How to use the `DetailsView` and `FormView` controls to display single records
- How to use the `ListBox` and `DropDownList` controls to display a selection of records
- How to use the `TreeView`, `SiteMapPath`, and `Menu` controls to display tree data

Additionally, this chapter covered the use of templates and wizards when setting up data source and data-bound controls. Recall that a template is a space into which you can drag various fields or other controls. When they are in a template, these controls can be bound to the record currently shown by the template.

Most data-bound controls offer templates. These spaces can hold many kinds of controls that can be data-bound, including labels, text boxes, and images. All of the bound controls within a template will have their information revised when the user moves from record to record. To change a template, you select the control and switch to Template Editing mode. After making your changes, be sure to click the smart task panel's End Template Editing to revert to normal mode.

Data-bound controls can be configured to display only a portion of the records. This behavior can be set statically by a value in a `WHERE` clause of the `SELECT` command of the data source control. The restriction of records can also be set dynamically. The parameter can come from a querystring or another data-bound control. For example, the selection in a `DropDownList` (master control) can be used as the parameter of a `WHERE` clause that limits the records shown in a `GridView` (child control).

Reading and displaying data is half of the data story. The other half is getting information to flow in the opposite direction. Chapter 8 looks at how to get information from users and write it to your data store.

Exercises

1. Describe the general capabilities of data source and data-bound controls.
2. Which data-bound controls render data in tables?
3. Compare and contrast the `DetailsView` and `FormView` controls.
4. Describe how a `GridView` control can limit its records to only those that match a player's name selected in a `DropDownList` of last names.
5. Which data source control is best suited for the `Menu` or `SiteMapPath` data-bound controls?

Writing Data

In Chapter 7, you learned how to read data from a database and present it on a page. In this chapter, you study the reverse: how to gather data from a user and write it to a database. When this book refers to *writing*, it means three kinds of operations: the creation of new records, changing existing records, and deleting records. The pattern is the same for all three, and the setup is made quite easy with the internal functionality of the data source and data-bound controls, as well as the auto-typing features of VWD. As a bonus, this chapter discusses transferring files from the browser to the server and then wraps up with an exercise that integrates several techniques from Chapter 6 through this one.

Introduction to Writing Data

ASP.NET 2.0 uses two groups of controls to work with data, as previously discussed in Chapter 7. Data source controls provide a connection to a source of data and enable certain behaviors, such as reading and writing to the data source. Data-bound controls provide a user interface on the page that can take advantage of the data source control capabilities. For the most part, the controls are mix-and-match. A `DropDownList` can use a `SqlDataSource`, `XMLDataSource`, or `AccessDataSource` control. Conversely, a `SqlDataSource` control can have its output rendered by a `GridView`, `DetailsView`, `DataList`, or `DropDownList` data-bound control. Having noted that flexibility, data controls are optimized for either tabular (relational) or hierarchical (tree) data.

Data controls are optimized for one of two ways to organize information, as discussed in Chapter 7. The first type is relational and the second is hierarchical. Although there can be some crossover in functionality, the division of the controls is described in the following table.

	Relational	Hierarchical
Data Source Controls	`SQLDataSource`	`XmlDataSource`
	`AccessDataSource`	`SiteMapDataSource`
	`ObjectDataSource`	

Table continued on following page

	Relational	Hierarchical
Data-bound Controls	`GridView`	`TreeView`
	`DataList` and `Repeater`	`Menu`
	`DetailsView` and `FormView`	`SiteMapPath`

Both data source and data-bound controls have functionality (like writing to a database) built into their code and you can specifically turn on any or all of those behaviors. For example, in Chapter 7 you enabled paging and sorting. Most of this chapter discusses how to turn on the writing behaviors.

Before diving into details, let us clarify some terminology surrounding writing data. First, writing actually means *changing* data, as opposed to just reading it. That means that writing includes changes to existing records, creating new records, and deleting existing records. ASP.NET 2.0 uses some industry-standard language for control properties. Changing an existing record is called an `UPDATE`, and creating a new record is called an `INSERT` or `INSERT INTO`. `DELETE` means removing an entire record from the database. Note that if you want to delete one value from an existing record (for example, the date of birth of one player), you would `Update` that player's record with a change of the birth date value from a date to `NULL`. The term `SELECT`, which you used in the last chapter, means reading data (no changes). ASP.NET 2.0 controls add three terms that are used to accept a user's actions. `NEW` means to switch to a view of a control that allows the user to enter data for a new record. This action would be followed by `create`, which actually sends the SQL `INSERT INTO` instruction to the database. And last, `EDIT` means switch to a view wherein the user can change a record's data. That would be followed by a click on `UPDATE` to actually execute the updating instruction.

Options for Writing Data

Not all data controls support writing. Of the data source controls, all support writing data except for the `SiteMapDataSource`. But among the data-binding controls, there are more limitations. The selection lists (`DropDownList` and `ListBox`) do not support writing. The new ASP.NET 2.0 data-bound controls support the best methods of writing data: `GridView`, `DetailsView`, and `FormView`. However, `GridView` can only update existing records, not create new records. `DataList` and `Repeater` can be used to write data, but because they are older controls, in many cases they must use the older ASP.NET 1.1 techniques.

> `GridView` **does not support the creation of new records. But** `GridView` **can easily open a** `DetailsView` **control (as you practiced in Chapter 7) and that** `DetailsView` **can create a new record.**

DataKeyNames

When you enable some types of data writing, VWD will add a property to the data-bound control named `DataKeyNames`. The purpose is to hold both old and new values of a field so that the writing can be performed correctly. To understand this role, imagine that you have a table of comments about Wrox United games named MatchReports. In the table you have as the first field (as most tables do) a field that contains an ID number unique to each row. You call it MatchReportID, and it gets values of 1, 2, 3, and so forth, as fans send in reports about matches. Now say that there was a mix-up and the administrator has to change the ID of a report from 20 to 19. When the administrator makes the change, he starts by selecting which record to change. ASP.NET 2.0 will store that record's ID value in a parameter, just like it did in Chapter 7 when you used a `GridView` as a master control. Next, the administrator changes the value of the ID field. When he sends that command to the database, it will look something like the following:

```
UPDATE MatchReports SET MatchReport=19 WHERE MatchReport=@MatchReportID
```

Notice that there is the name of the field to change (MatchReportID) and the new value (19). That command also holds an identification of which record to change, something like `WHERE MatchReportID=@MatchReportID`. But there is a conflict because you have two potential values that could go into `@MatchReportID`: the old one as saved by the `GridView` (the value of 20) and the new one that the administrator entered (the value of 19).

`DataKeyNames` solves this problem by creating a dictionary that keeps two values for fields in its list. One value is old and one is new. When a writing command is issued to a database, ASP.NET uses its smarts to supply the new value from `DataKeyNames` for the `SET` part of the command and to use the old value from `DataKeyNames` for the `WHERE` part of the command. It would be wasteful and slow to load up the `DataKeyNames` dictionary with every field, particularly because most fields will not raise conflicts. VWD automatically adds to the `DataKeyNames` those fields that are structured as unique in the database. You can add others, but VWD usually gets it right. In summary, `DataKeyNames` holds names of fields for which ASP.NET 2.0 must remember both old and new values. When using VWD, you rarely have to change `DataKeyNames`.

Changing Existing Records

The capability to change an existing record can be turned on with two simple steps using VWD. When you create a data source control, you go through a panel in the wizard that asks you to select the table and columns (see Figure 8-1).

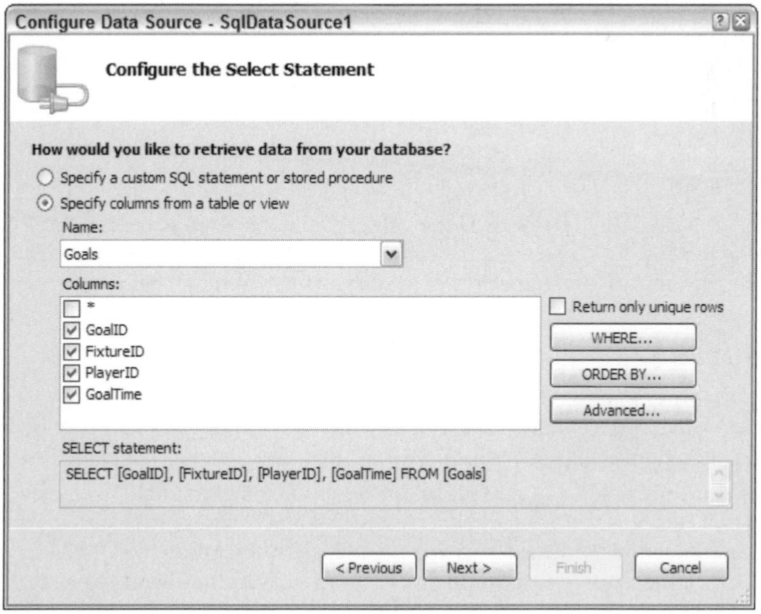

Figure 8-1

There is also an Advanced button that gives you the option to tell VWD to generate INSERT, UPDATE, and DELETE statements (see Figure 8-2). This simple step enables the UPDATE behavior of the data source control. Also, checking Use optimistic concurrency will reduce conflicts of two updates simultaneously on a busy web site.

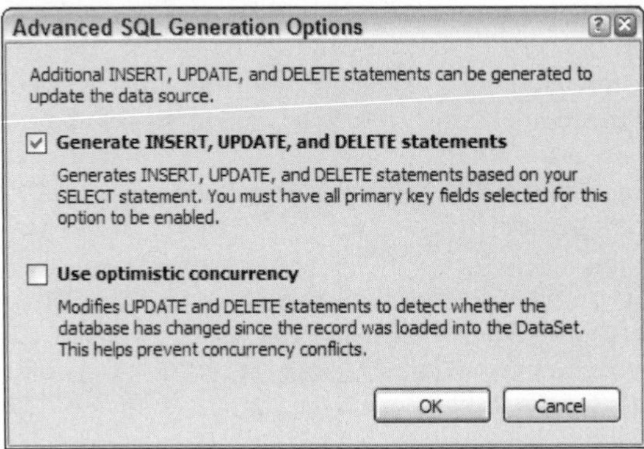

Figure 8-2

VWD takes care of all the work for you, fast and without error (we wish we could say the same for the Wrox United strikers). Two changes are made to the data source control. First, an UPDATE statement is added, similar to the following (INSERT and DELETE statements are also added, but those are discussed later):

```
<asp:SqlDataSource ID="SqlDataSource1" runat="server"
...
UpdateCommand= "UPDATE [MyTable]
        SET [Field1] = @Field1, [Field2] = @Field2
        WHERE [Field1] = @Field1>
...
 </asp:SqlDataSource>
```

The UPDATE statement indicates that you want to change an existing record. You provide the table holding the record (MyTable):

```
UpdateCommand= "UPDATE [MyTable]
```

Then you provide a set of field names and the values you want them to contain. ASP.NET 2.0 generally does not specify those values directly in the command; rather, it uses a reference to a parameter that holds the value. References to parameters begin with an at symbol (@) before the parameter's name, as shown here:

```
        SET [Field1] = @Field1, [Field2] = @Field2
```

Note the WHERE clause at the end, which specifies which record to modify. The following syntax says to change the record in the database for which the Field1 value matches the value held in the Field1 parameter:

```
        WHERE [Field1] = @Field1
```

You know that the value to match is from the parameter because you use @ before the field name, which directs ASP.NET 2.0 to get the value from the parameters list. Without the `WHERE` clause, the update would change *all* of the records to have the new values the user entered.

VWD also adds a set of tags to the data source control to create the `UPDATE` parameters. ASP.NET 2.0 automatically fills these with the values that currently exist in the table. When the user makes a change to the data-bound control, ASP.NET 2.0 intelligently substitutes in the new value. The exception is for unique fields such as identifiers, in which case ASP.NET 2.0 keeps both the old and new values in the `DataKeyNames` dictionary as discussed in the introduction to this chapter.

Parameters (of any type) are not controls. They are tags *within* data source controls.

`<ControlParameters>` can hold values in the same way as `<UpdateParameters>`. Whereas `<UpdateParameters>` hold the values that the data source control read from the existing record, `<ControlParameters>` hold values that the user enters or selects from controls other than the data-bound control that is changing the data. For example, you may be changing the date in a `GridView`, but you want the date to come from a selection in a `Calendar` control. You encountered `<Control Parameters>` in Chapter 7 when you created pages with a master-child relationship, and you will see examples in context of writing data later in this chapter.

An optional property can be added to a data source control: `ConflictDetection="Compare AllValues"`. Conflict detection implements the `DataKeyNames` solution to avoid two users updating the same record at the same time.

In a data-bound control that implements updates, you see two changes as well that are needed to move from a read-only control to a control that can update records (highlighted in the following code listing). First is the addition of a property for `DataKeyNames`. Second is in the list of fields, where you see the following new "field" added. Called a `CommandField` because it offers the user a button that will execute a command, it is only a field in the sense that ASP.NET 2.0 will create a field-like rendering for the button on the data-bound control:

```
<asp:DetailsView ID="DetailsView1" runat="server"
        AutoGenerateRows="False"
        DataKeyNames="FixtureID"
        DataSourceID="SqlDataSource1" Height="50px" Width="125px">
    <Fields>
      <asp:BoundField DataField="FixtureID"
        HeaderText="FixtureID" InsertVisible="False"
        ReadOnly="True" SortExpression="FixtureID" />
      <asp:BoundField DataField="FixtureDate"
        HeaderText="FixtureDate" SortExpression="FixtureDate" />
        <asp:CommandField
        ShowEditButton="True"
        ShowInsertButton="True" />
        </Fields>
 </asp:DetailsView>
```

For example, the preceding code would contribute toward a `DetailsView` as follows in Figure 8-3 with the Edit and New buttons at the bottom of the data-bound `DetailsView` control.

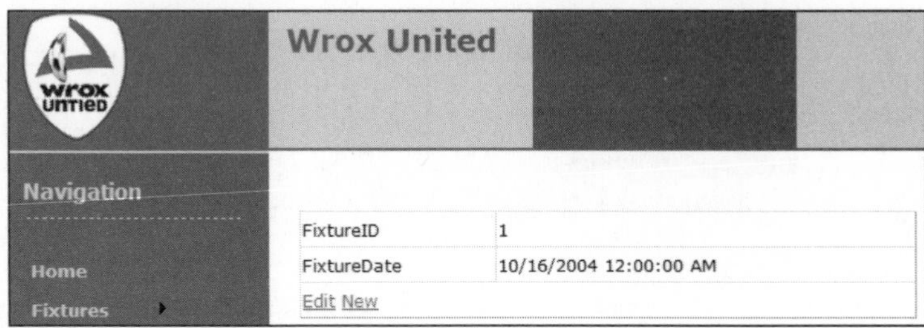

Figure 8-3

The following small tag enables all of the functionality in the data-bound control to update records. This tag will render itself as a button labeled EDIT on a `DetailsView` or a column of EDIT buttons in a `GridView`. It will also automatically hide itself and substitute buttons for Update and Cancel when the control is in edit mode:

```
<asp:CommandField ShowEditButton="True"
```

A common problem is to attempt to update a record with invalid data. For example, in the box for Goals Against, a user may enter a bit of text or a date. When the data controls send this to the database, an error will arise because the database is configured to limit values in a GoalsAgainst field to be integers. The problem can be solved in several ways, two of which are aspects of ASP.NET 2.0. First, you try to eliminate user-typed input whenever possible. For example, for the user to enter values for GoalsAgainst a football team, you could offer a list box with options from 1 to 10 (maybe 1 to 20 for Wrox United). The second technique is to use the ASP.NET 2.0 validation controls, which are covered in Chapter 15. As a rule of thumb, anything that a user types should be run through a validation control before it is sent to the database. This policy greatly reduces the susceptibility to a SQL injection attack.

The preceding directions explain the steps to turn on editing at the time you create a control. You can still turn on this feature using VWD after the control is on a page. Open the Common Tasks panel for the data source control and click Configure Data Source. You walk through the wizard again, but with choices filled in as per the existing state. It is easy to click the Advanced button and add the extra commands. Then go back and open the Common Tasks panel for the data-bound control and enable the Editing feature.

In the following Try It Out, you practice the technique to enable updating data in a `GridView` and a `DetailsView` control by changing data for fixtures (games). You will be building on the `Fixtures.aspx` page you created in Chapter 7 that had a `GridView` with a child control of a `DetailsView`.

Try It Out — Updating Existing Records

1. In VWD, open the chapter web site at `C:\BegASPNET2\Chapters\Begin\Chapter08`, and open the `Fixtures.aspx` page in Design View.
2. Add the remainder of the fields to the `GridView` and its `SqlDataSource`. Start with the smart task panel of `DataSource1` and click Configure Data Source. Click Next to go past the connection and then add all of the fields in the checklist. Click Next and Finish. Select the `GridView1`

control, open its Common Tasks panel, and click Edit Columns. Select the `FixtureType` field and then click the Add button. Repeat for the other fields that are not selected, and click OK to end editing. Enable Editing and, if not already enabled, enable Selection.

3. Select the `SqlDataSource2` control (used by the `DetailsView`), open its Common Tasks panel, and click Configure Data Source. Make sure you select WroxUnited for the connection. On the Configure Select Statement screen, select the option to specify the columns from a table or view, select the Fixtures table, and select all columns individually (not the *).

4. Click the Advanced button, and on the Advanced window, turn on both options. Click OK to close the window, then click Next and Finish to close the configuration wizard. As always, accept the refresh of the data keys if offered.

5. Select the `DetailsView` data-bound control and open its Common Tasks panel. Enable Editing. Click Edit Fields and, as in the `GridView`, select the remaining fields and click Add for each. Close the panel. With these simple changes, you have enabled editing of fixtures in both the `GridView` and `DetailsView`.

6. You will make one final change. VWD is overzealous in creating the `WHERE` clause for the `UpdateCommand`. By default, VWD added a check of every field prior to updating. You can be confident that if you match the `FixtureID`, you have the right record. So in Source View, modify the `UpdateCommand` of `SqlDataSource2` (be sure you pick number 2) to delete the shaded section in the following code — you may have to scroll the Source window to see the `UpdateCommand`. Your line breaks may be different — we modified the listing for clarity. Be sure that the command still ends with the `">` characters:

```
UpdateCommand="UPDATE [Fixtures]
 SET
 [FixtureDate] = @FixtureDate,
 [FixtureType] = @FixtureType,
 [GoalsFor] = @GoalsFor,
 [GoalsAgainst] = @GoalsAgainst,
 [Notes] = @Notes,
 [Opponents] = @Opponents
 WHERE
 [FixtureID] = @original_FixtureID
  AND [FixtureDate] = @original_FixtureDate
  AND [FixtureType] = @original_FixtureType
  AND [GoalsFor] = @original_GoalsFor
  AND [GoalsAgainst] = @original_GoalsAgainst
  AND [Notes] = @original_Notes
  AND [Opponents] = @original_Opponents
">
```

7. Run the page in your browser. In the `GridView` control, try clicking Edit and changing the name of an opponent as in Figure 8-4. Then do the same in the `DetailsView` control as shown in Figure 8-5.

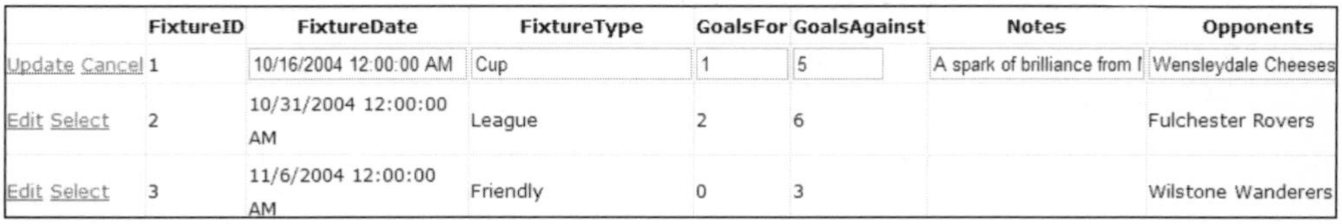

	FixtureID	FixtureDate	FixtureType	GoalsFor	GoalsAgainst	Notes	Opponents
Update Cancel	1	10/16/2004 12:00:00 AM	Cup	1	5	A spark of brilliance from I	Wensleydale Cheeses
Edit Select	2	10/31/2004 12:00:00 AM	League	2	6		Fulchester Rovers
Edit Select	3	11/6/2004 12:00:00 AM	Friendly	0	3		Wilstone Wanderers

Figure 8-4

Figure 8-5

How It Works

ASP.NET 2.0 has again made all of this easy by including the functionality of updating within the data controls. To enable updates in the data source control, you checked off the option to include `INSERT`, `UPDATE`, and `DELETE` commands. This is more than you need for now (although you will use the `INSERT` and `DELETE` later in this chapter). VWD built two changes to the data source control that enable it to perform updates on data. First is the addition of an `UpdateCommand` as follows:

```
<asp:SqlDataSource ID="SqlDataSource1" ...
UpdateCommand="UPDATE [Fixtures] SET [FixtureDate] = @FixtureDate, [FixtureType] =
@FixtureType, [GoalsFor] = @GoalsFor, [GoalsAgainst] = @GoalsAgainst, [Notes] =
@Notes, [Opponents] = @Opponents WHERE [FixtureID] = @original_FixtureID">
```

VWD then added a set of parameters that will hold the values you will use for updates, as shown in the following code. Note that the `FixtureID` is saved in two parameters (the first and last). The first is the new value, if the user enters one. The second is named `original_FixtureID` and will hold the original value so it can be used in the `WHERE` clause to match which record to change:

```
<UpdateParameters>
    <asp:Parameter Name="FixtureDate" Type="DateTime" />
    <asp:Parameter Name="FixtureType" Type="String" />
    <asp:Parameter Name="GoalsFor" Type="Int16" />
    <asp:Parameter Name="GoalsAgainst" Type="Int16" />
    <asp:Parameter Name="Notes" Type="String" />
    <asp:Parameter Name="Opponents" Type="String"  />
    <asp:Parameter Name="original_FixtureID" Type="Int32" />
</UpdateParameters>
```

In the `GridView` control, you added the single property of displaying the Edit button in a column:

```
<asp:GridView ID="GridView1" ...
    <Columns>
        <asp:CommandField ShowSelectButton="True" ShowEditButton="True" />
```

The procedure was almost the same for the `DetailsView`. You modified the `SqlDataSource2` control to enable updates by adding an `UpdateCommand` and a set of update parameters. However, VWD is more conservative with DetailsView and provides original_ parameters for all fields and compares all fields in the WHERE clause. You excised those extra comparisons and just relied on matching the FixtureID.

Adding New Records

Adding new records, known in SQL parlance as INSERT or INSERT INTO, is almost as easy as changing an existing record. The main difference is that the GridView does not support adding a new record, which will be considered shortly.

As discussed previously, four changes must be made to the data controls. First, in the data source control you have the Advanced button in the Create New Data Source wizard. A click there and a check on Generate INSERT, UPDATE, and DELETE gave you all three of the SQL statements. That created two additions to the data source control. The first is the InsertCommand itself. The second is the set of INSERT parameters. (Actually, commands and parameters were also created for UPDATE and DELETE, but it is INSERT that is of interest to us in this section.)

In the data-bound control, you enable inserting with a check box on the data-bound control's Common Tasks panel. Two changes result. The first is in the <asp:commandfield> where you now have the ShowInsertButton. This will co-exist with the ShowEditButton and ShowDeleteButton if they have been selected. The ShowInsertButton enables the functionality to add new records. As with the other CommandField buttons, ShowInsertButton automatically hides itself and displays other buttons (Insert and Cancel) when the control switches to INSERT mode.

GridView is a special case because it does not directly support the addition of new records. The most common path is to display existing records in the GridView and create a button on the GridView that goes to a DetailsView (which can be on the same page or a second page). The DetailsView can then open in INSERT mode, ready to accept the values for the new record. The option to open in INSERT mode is set by the DefaultMode property of the data-bound control.

As in editing, constraints on data are acceptable. For example, if you were adding a new match report, the fixture must match an existing fixture. You can't comment on a match that did not happen. As with editing, you can decrease these conflicts by giving users a list of possible options instead of typing. If they must type, then run the values through a validation control.

In this Try It Out, you add the INSERT capability to the Fixtures.aspx page. You cannot insert new records in a GridView, so this exercise only affects the DetailsView control.

Try It Out — Inserting a New Record

1. Open VWD and your Fixtures.aspx page in Source View and scroll down to the SqlDataSource2 control (the data source for the DetailsView control). Observe that in the last exercise when VWD added the capability to update a record, it also added similar tags for insert and delete operations. Therefore, in the data source control the insert behavior is already enabled.
2. Select the DetailsView control, open its Common Tasks panel, and enable inserting, as shown in Figure 8-6.

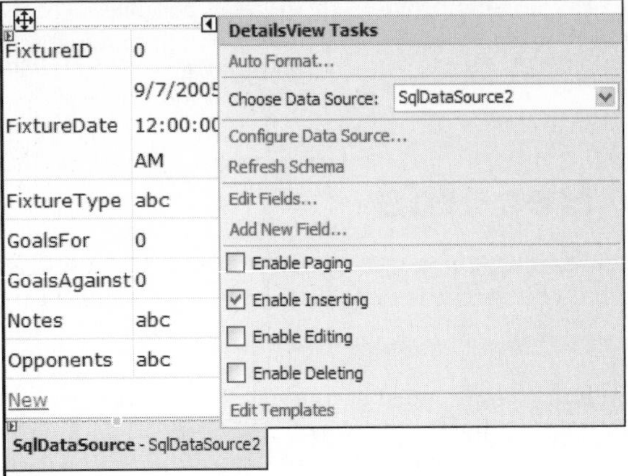

Figure 8-6

3. In the Properties window, find DefaultMode (see Figure 8-7) and change its value to Insert.

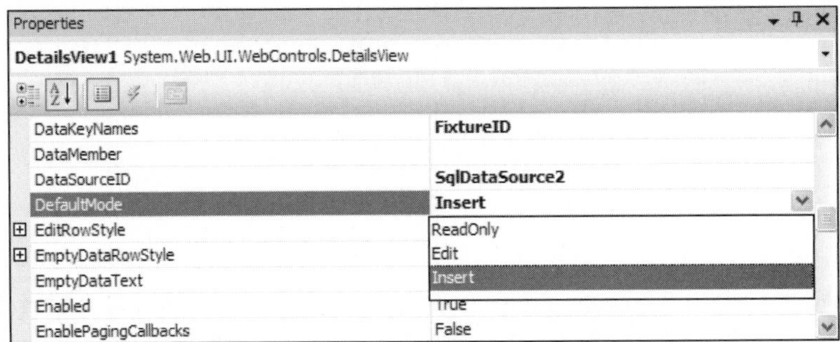

Figure 8-7

4. Save and view in the browser (see Figure 8-8). Try adding a new fixture and refresh the page.

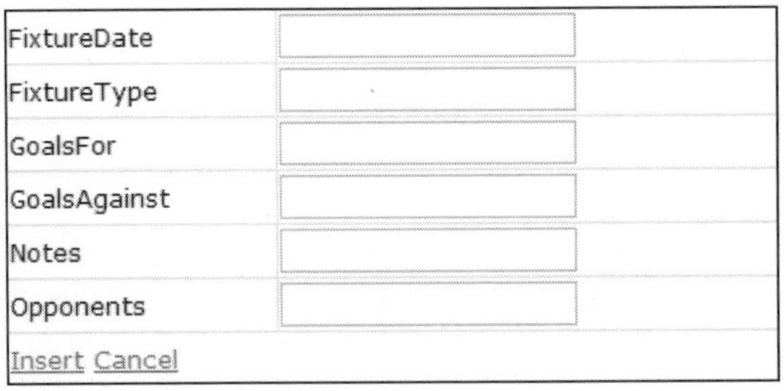

FixtureDate	
FixtureType	
GoalsFor	
GoalsAgainst	
Notes	
Opponents	
Insert Cancel	

Figure 8-8

5. Try entering some nonsense data, such as a date of **99/99/2006**. Note how the error is not, at this point, handled very gracefully. Chapter 15 looks at handling errors.

How It Works

Many of the tags for this process were created in the previous exercise when you configured the data sources and VWD offered the Advanced button with options to create INSERT, UPDATE, and DELETE commands. It may have seemed like an overwhelming number of tags at first, but you can now see how the pattern of a command plus a set of parameters enables a data-writing function.

Specifically, you are using the InsertCommand of the SqlDataSource2 that supports the DetailsView. That command relies on the set of InsertParameters, as shown in the following code. Note that there is no need for a WHERE clause because you do not need to identify an existing record upon which to carry out the action:

```
<asp:SqlDataSource ID="SqlDataSource2" ...
InsertCommand="INSERT INTO [Fixtures] ([FixtureDate], [FixtureType], [GoalsFor],
[GoalsAgainst], [Notes], [Opponents]) VALUES (@FixtureDate, @FixtureType,
@GoalsFor, @GoalsAgainst, @Notes, @Opponents)"
...
        <InsertParameters>
            <asp:Parameter Name="FixtureDate" Type="DateTime" />
            <asp:Parameter Name="FixtureType" Type="String" />
            <asp:Parameter Name="GoalsFor" Type="Int16" />
            <asp:Parameter Name="GoalsAgainst" Type="Int16" />
            <asp:Parameter Name="Notes" Type="String" />
            <asp:Parameter Name="Opponents" Type="String" />
        </InsertParameters>
...
</asp:SqlDataSource>
```

ASP.NET 2.0 handles INSERT operations in a way that is very similar to the UPDATE operations you did in the previous section. When you select the option in the Advanced dialog box, VWD builds a SQL INSERT INTO statement with a set of parameters that can hold the data entered by the user. When you enable INSERT on the data-bound control, VWD adds the CommandField button for adding a new record. All the rest of the code is taken care of by Microsoft, hidden from your view in the data controls. The only trap to remember is that inserting new records is available in DetailsView and FormView, but not GridView.

Deleting Records

By now you have a good feel for how writing data works and can anticipate that the procedure for deleting a record is similar. In the data source control, you must include the DELETE command, which can be automatically generated in the Advanced button of the control's Configure New Data Source dialog box. That button will also create a set of DeleteParameters. But there are differences. For example, the DeleteParameters will be used to make an exact match for deletion in the WHERE clause, but they will not be used for changing information in the record.

As discussed before, there are some hazards when writing data and these are particularly true for deleting. The first is the human error of deleting the wrong record. More sophisticated systems respond to a request to delete by actually moving the record to a Deleted table. That gives a chance for recovery, at least until the Deleted table is purged. Discussions of this strategy are common in database texts and are not difficult to implement in ASP.NET 2.0. A second problem is when the user attempts to delete a record that the database has blocked from deletion. That block is most often the result of another record being dependent on the record that was to be deleted. For example, a table of orders would have a field for the ID of a customer that placed an order. If you delete that customer, you are left with a value in the Orders table that points to nowhere. In this case, the database will return an error.

In this Try It Out, you enable the capability to remove a match from the list of fixtures.

Try It Out — Deleting an Entire Record

1. Continue using VWD with `Fixtures.aspx` in Design View. Both of the data source controls already have the `DeleteCommand` and a set of `DELETE` parameters.

2. Select the `GridView` control, open its Common Tasks panel, and select Enable Deleting (see Figure 8-9), which adds the following shaded line to the `GridView` control. That code also adds the Delete command fields in Figure 8-9.

```
<asp:GridView ID="GridView1" runat="server"
...
   <Columns>
       <asp:CommandField
         ShowEditButton="True"
         ShowSelectButton="True"
         ShowDeleteButton="True" />
...
   </Columns>

</asp:GridView>
```

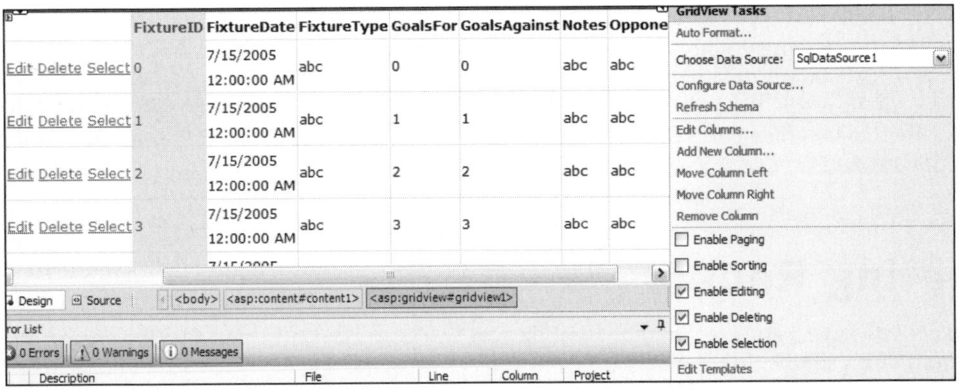

Figure 8-9

3. Select the `DetailsView` control, open its Common Tasks panel, and select Enable Deleting. Go to the `DetailsView`'s Properties window and change the DefaultMode back to ReadOnly.

4. As before, when VWD creates a `DetailsView` with deleting, it is overly cautious in checking fields to match up the correct record to delete. The original `DELETE` statement is shown in the following code. (Be sure you are looking at `SqlDataSource2`, the one for the `DetailsView`.) Delete the shaded portion. Double-check that the `DeleteCommand` still ends with a double quote:

```
DeleteCommand="DELETE FROM [Fixtures] WHERE [FixtureID] = @original_FixtureID
AND [FixtureDate] = @original_FixtureDate
AND [FixtureType] = @original_FixtureType
AND [GoalsFor] = @original_GoalsFor
AND [GoalsAgainst] = @original_GoalsAgainst
AND [Notes] = @original_Notes
AND [Opponents] = @original_Opponents
"
```

5. Save the page and test it in your browser. It should look like Figure 8-10.

Edit Delete Select	8	12/12/2004 12:00:00 AM	League	2
Edit Delete Select	9	12/19/2004 12:00:00 AM	League	1

FixtureID	1
FixtureDate	10/16/2004 12:00:00 AM
FixtureType	Cup
GoalsFor	1
GoalsAgainst	5
Notes	A spark of brilliance from Marger with his first goal of the season. Sadly the rest of the team played like a bunch of five year olds.
Opponents	Mellingham
Edit Delete New	

Figure 8-10

Note that if you try to actually delete a fixture you will get an error message. Many other aspects of the site rely on the list of fixtures, so deleting one will leave those data hanging without a fixture. This situation is called a *reference constraint* as mentioned in the error.

How It Works

The pattern is the same as for other means of changing data. The data source control must have a `DeleteCommand`. When you checked the option in the Advanced step of the Configure Data Source wizard, VWD created the `DeleteCommand` for you. VWD also created a set of `DeleteParameters` that will be used by the `WHERE` clause to identify the record to delete. As with `UPDATE`, VWD tries to match every field in the `DeleteParameters` list for `DetailsView`. This may be necessary in some cases, but for now a simple match of the `FixtureID` is sufficient.

You then enabled deleting on the data-bound control, which instructed VWD to add a `CommandField` of the type Delete to the data-bound control. The term "field" here is a little odd because there is no connection to a field in the data table, but it is an addition to the data-bound control that is rendered similarly to a field.

One thing you may have noticed while running through the exercises in this chapter is that you have two ways of showing and editing the fixtures: `GridView` and `DetailsView`. When you edited data in one, the changes weren't reflected in the other. To get around this, you need to add code to the data source controls, and although you only need a single line of code, it has to be entered in several places. This is because there are several ways the data can change: you can insert new fixtures, edit existing fixtures, or delete fixtures. Each of these causes the `SqlDataSource` control to raise an event, and it is within that event that you have to rebind the data for the other control.

The code for this is shown here:

```
protected void SqlDataSource1_Deleted(object sender,
System.Web.UI.WebControls.SqlDataSourceStatusEventArgs e)
  { DetailsView1.DataBind(); }

protected void SqlDataSource1_Inserted(object sender,
System.Web.UI.WebControls.SqlDataSourceStatusEventArgs e)
  { DetailsView1.DataBind(); }

protected void SqlDataSource1_Updated(object sender,
System.Web.UI.WebControls.SqlDataSourceStatusEventArgs e)
  { DetailsView1.DataBind(); }

protected void SqlDataSource2_Deleted(object sender,
System.Web.UI.WebControls.SqlDataSourceStatusEventArgs e)
  { GridView1.DataBind(); }

protected void SqlDataSource2_Inserted(object sender,
System.Web.UI.WebControls.SqlDataSourceStatusEventArgs e)
  { GridView1.DataBind(); }

protected void SqlDataSource2_Updated(object sender,
System.Web.UI.WebControls.SqlDataSourceStatusEventArgs e)
  { GridView1.DataBind(); }
```

You can see that there are three events for each control. The `Deleted` event is raised after a record is deleted, the `Inserted` event is raised after a record is added, and the `Updated` event is raised when a record is updated. Even through you are using a `GridView` control to display one set of data, and a `DetailsView` control for the other, the events look the same because it is the `SqlDataSource` control that raises the event. For the `GridView`, which is bound to `SqlDataSource1`, the `DetailsView` needs to be refreshed, so the `DataBind()` method is called on the `DetailsView`, which instructs it to re-fetch the data. A similar procedure is done for the events of `SqlDataSource2`, which is used by the `DetailsView`, but this time the `DataBind()` method is called on the `GridView1` control. It's a simple procedure — when data in one control changes, you refresh the data in the other control.

Uploading Pictures

ASP.NET 2.0 offers an easy way to upload pictures (or other files) from the browser to the server. Although not strictly a database issue, the topic is covered here. The toolbar offers the FileUpload tool, which can be added to the page to produce a text box with a browse button. You, as the designer, must also add a button to give the user the capability to actually execute the upload.

In the button's click code, the simplest option is shown in the following code. The file that the user indicated (either by typing or browsing) will be transferred to the server:

```
FileUpload1.SaveAs(FileUpload1.FileName);
```

But this code is too simplistic because the file will be plopped into the root of the web site. You can add a literal string to be appended in front of the file name that will direct the file into an appropriate folder on the server. Note that when you open the page in your browser you can view the source, but the path on your server is not revealed. The following code places the file in MyImageFolder:

```
using System.IO

string  ImagesFolder = "MyImageFolder";
string  savePath;
string  saveFile;

savePath = Path.Combine(Request.PhysicalApplicationPath, ImagesFolder);
saveFile = Path.Combine(savePath, FileUpload1.FileName);
FileUpload1.SaveAs(saveFile);
```

When the `FileUpload.SaveAs` method is invoked, ASP.NET 2.0 creates an object named `FileUpload.PostedFile` with several properties about the operation. The most obvious are `FileName` and `ContentLength`. So if you create a label named `Label1` you can display in its text the name of the file that was uploaded as follows:

```
FileUpload1.SaveAs(saveFile);
Label1.Text = FileUpload1.PostedFile.FileName;
```

What if the user clicks the button without first selecting a file? You can avoid this problem with an `IF THEN` statement as follows (code structures such as `IF THEN` are explained in Chapter 9):

```
    // If a file was selected, then upload the file
    if (FileUpload1.HasFile)     // perform the upload
    {
      FileUpload1.SaveAs(saveFile);
                               // Displays status of success
      Label1.Text ="Your file was uploaded successfully.";
    }
    else                       // probably no file selected
    {
       // Display status of failure
      Status.Text = "You did not specify a file to upload.";
    }
```

Other errors can occur, so you should encase the `FileUpload` method in an error-catching routine as follows:

```
    protected void ButtonUsingTryCatch_Click(object sender, EventArgs e)
    {
        string ImagesFolder = "MatchImages";
        string savePath;
        string saveFile;

        if (FileUpload1.HasFile)
        {
            try
            {
                // perform the upload
                savePath = Path.Combine(Request.PhysicalApplicationPath,
ImagesFolder);
```

```
                saveFile = Path.Combine(savePath, FileUpload1.FileName);
                FileUpload1.SaveAs(saveFile);
                // Displays status of success
                StatusLabel.Text = "Your file was uploaded successfully.";
            }
            catch(Exception exUpload)
            {
                // display status of error
                StatusLabel.Text = exUpload.Message;
            }
        }
        else  // probably file was not selected
        {
            // Display status of failure
            StatusLabel.Text = "You did not specify a file to upload.";
        }
```

In the following Try It Out, you give users a way to add pictures to the gallery.

Try It Out Uploading Files — Basic

1. Using VWD, create a new page named **GalleryUpload.aspx** using the Web Form template. As you have with most pages up to this point, use the `site.master` as the Master page, use Visual C#, and enable the option to place the code on a separate page.
2. In Design View, add a `FileUpload` control from the Toolbox and a `Label` control that will have an ID of `FileUploadReport` with an empty `text` property. Also add a `button` control with the `text` property set to `"Upload"`.
3. Double-click the button to go to its code. Add the following shaded code to the `Sub`:

```
using System;
using System.IO;
using ...

public partial class GalleryUpload : System.Web.UI.Page
{
    protected void Button1_Click(object sender, EventArgs e)
    {
        string ImagesFolder = "MatchImages";
        string savePath;
        string saveFile;

        if (FileUpload1.HasFile)
        {
            try
            {
                // perform the upload
                savePath = Path.Combine(Request.PhysicalApplicationPath,
ImagesFolder);
                saveFile = Path.Combine(savePath, FileUpload1.FileName);
                FileUpload1.SaveAs(saveFile);
                // Displays status of success
                FileUploadReport.Text = "Your file was uploaded successfully.";
            }
            catch(Exception exUpload)
```

```
            {
                // display status of error
                FileUploadReport.Text = exUpload.Message;
            }
        }
        else  // probably file was not selected
        {
            // Display status of failure
            FileUploadReport.Text = "You did not specify a file to upload.";
        }
    }
}
```

4. Save the page and view it in your browser (see Figure 8-11). You probably won't have pictures of the hapless Wrox United fumblers, but you can try uploading any jpeg or gif you have on your hard drive.

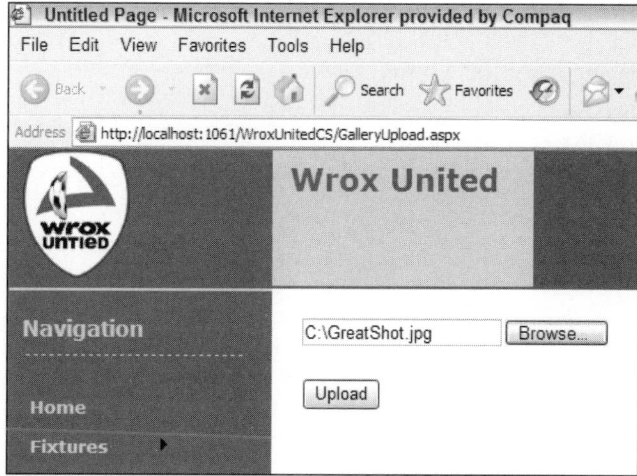

Figure 8-11

How It Works

The `FileUpload` control itself is a simple drag-and-drop. The browsing capability is built in. However, there is no built-in means to execute the upload. So you added a button to fire the `SaveAs` method of the `FileUpload` control. That method needs an argument specifying where to put the file on the server. You hard-coded a literal for the path and then appended the name of the file the user entered into the `FileUpload` control.

You have done some embellishments beyond the basic control. The `FileUpload` control has a handy property called `HasFile`. When there is a valid file name in the text box, the `HasFile` property will be `TRUE`. The `IF` statement determines whether the user actually typed or browsed to a file to upload. If not, the code hops down to the `ELSE` statement to display an error message. Other things could go wrong, like the Wrox United webmaster (even more hapless than the team) changes the name of the folder in which to store images. So you encapsulated the execution of the `SaveAs` within a `Try...Catch` block.

Improving the Upload of Pictures

You finish this chapter with an improvement to the page that uploads photos and, in the process, review some ideas from this chapter and Chapters 6 and 7. You will add a feature that creates an entry in the database table of photos when a photo is uploaded. In other words, you will both upload the file and create a new record. The following few paragraphs give an overview of your tasks and the Try It Out gives exact directions.

Start by using the Data Explorer to take a look at the structure of the Gallery table as in Figure 8-12. Each record represents an image a fan has uploaded, with fields for the fan's name, URL of the picture file, date, and opponent.

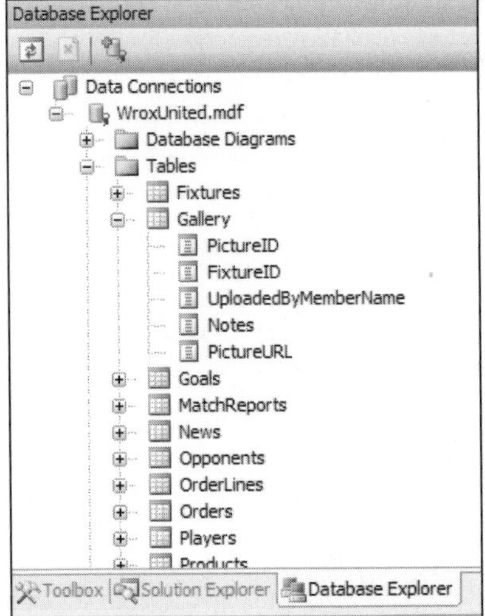

Figure 8-12

Now you need to add inputs to the page to get the information you need for the fields of the Gallery table. Whenever possible, avoid letting users type information. In this case, the number of matches is reasonably small, so you will create a `ListBox` control for that input. The `SelectCommand` that provides data for the `ListBox` will display the date of the match to the user. The `FixtureID` will be the `ListBoxValue`. You will also want to gather the user's name and comments with text boxes. The page will end up looking like Figure 8-13.

Now the trick will be inserting a new record into the table. You do this by setting up a `SqlDataSource` control that is enabled for inserting. But you do not need to render any data, so this data source control will not have a data-bound control. Built into the `SqlDataSource` is the `Insert` method, which you can invoke from your button-click code.

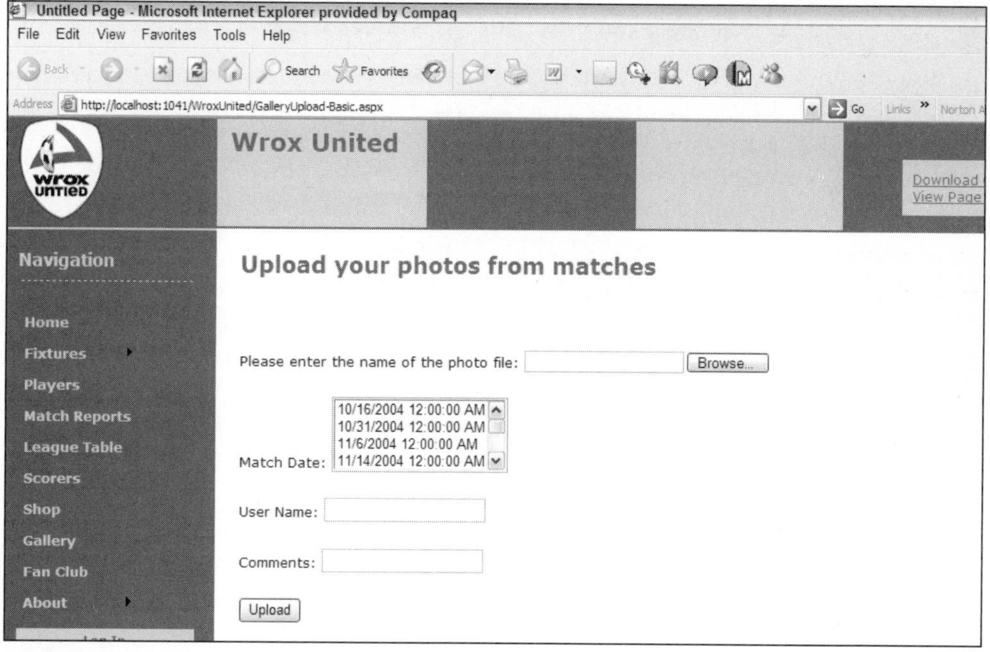

Figure 8-13

In this Try It Out, you enhance the gallery upload so that it performs the upload of the image file and then creates a record for the image file in the Gallery table.

Try It Out Uploading Files with Record Creation

1. Using VWD, open the Solution Explorer and make a copy of the `GalleryUpload.aspx` pages following these instructions. Find in the file list, but do not open, the `GalleryUpload.aspx` page. Right-click it and select Copy. Right-click the root of the site and select Paste. Now find the nascent file that named `Copy of GalleryUpload.aspx`. Rename it **GalleryUpload Enhanced.aspx**. This procedure ensures proper copying and renaming of the associated code file.

2. Working with `GalleryUploadEnhanced.aspx` in Design View, move the insertion bar (cursor) below the `FileUpload` control, add a `ListBox`, and from the smart task panel, click Choose Data Source. Select a new data source, use a database source, and name the control `SqlData SourceFixtures`. Use the WroxUnited connection string and set it to display from the Fixtures table only the `FixtureID` and `FixtureDate` fields, ordered by date ascending. After finishing the Wizard, you can set the `ListBox` properties to display the date and field for the value to `FixtureID` (see Figure 8-14).

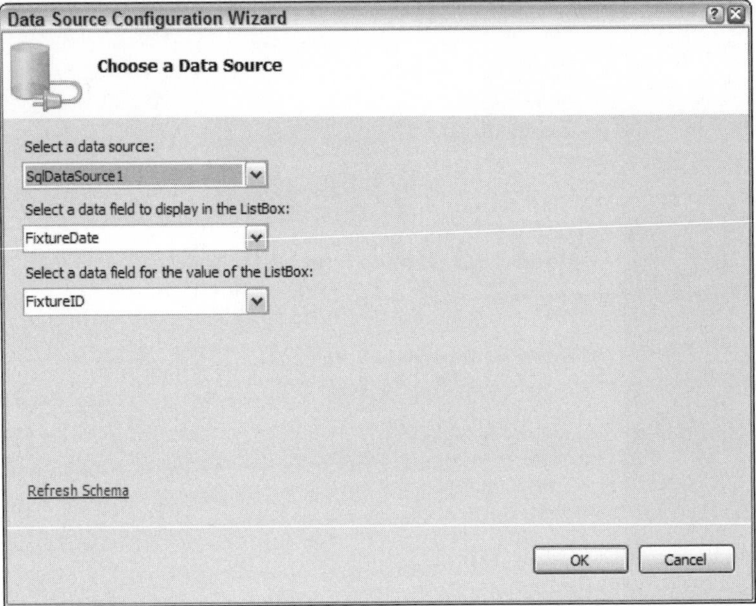

Figure 8-14

3. Add to the page two `TextBox` controls for the fan's name and notes about the picture. In the Properties window, set the ID of the boxes to `TextBoxMemberName` and `TextBoxNotes`. Give them some labels with text that identifies what the user should type in the box.

4. Add a second `SqlDataSource` to the page that you will configure to create the record in the Gallery table for the new uploaded photo. Name it **SqlDataSourceCreateGalleryRecord**. Using its smart task panel, configure the data source and choose the WroxUnited connection string. Use the Gallery table and select all of the fields. In the Advanced panel, check the creation of the `INSERT`, `DELETE`, and `UPDATE` commands. Click the Next and Finish buttons. If you want, switch to Source View and delete the commands and parameters for the `UPDATE` and `DELETE` functions. They will not be used, so deleting them cleans up the code to make maintenance easier, but they don't interfere if you want to leave them. Be careful not to delete any end-of-property double quotes or any end-of-tag > symbols.

5. Switch to Source View and find the set of `<InsertParameters>`. Modify them so that they come from the four input controls, as per the shaded lines in the following listing of the entire .aspx page's code:

```
<%@ Page Language="C#" MasterPageFile="~/site.master" AutoEventWireup="false"
CodeFile="GalleryUpload-Enhanced.aspx.cs" Inherits="GalleryUpload" title="Untitled
Page" %>
 <asp:Content ID="Content1" ContentPlaceHolderID="mainContent" Runat="Server">
     <h2>Upload your photos from matches</h2>
     <br /><br />Please enter the name of the photo file:
     <asp:FileUpload ID="FileUpload1" runat="server" />
     <br /><br />
     Match Date:
     <asp:ListBox ID="ListBox1" runat="server"
         DataSourceID="SqlDataSource1"
         DataTextField="FixtureDate"
```

```
            DataValueField="FixtureID">
        </asp:ListBox>

        <asp:SqlDataSource ID="SqlDataSource1" runat="server"
                ConnectionString="<%$ ConnectionStrings:WroxUnited2 %>"
                SelectCommand="SELECT [FixtureID], [FIxtureDate] FROM [Fixtures]">
            </asp:SqlDataSource>

        <br /><br />
        User Name: <asp:TextBox ID="TextBoxMemberName" runat="server"></asp:TextBox>
        <br /><br />
        Comments: <asp:TextBox ID="TextBoxNotes" runat="server"></asp:TextBox>
        <br /><br />
        <asp:Button ID="Button1" runat="server" Text="Upload" /><br />
        <asp:Label ID="FileUploadReport" runat="server"></asp:Label><br />

        <asp:SqlDataSource ID="SqlDataSource2" runat="server"
            ConflictDetection="CompareAllValues"
            ConnectionString="<%$ ConnectionStrings:WroxUnited2 %>"
            InsertCommand="INSERT INTO [Gallery] ([FixtureID], [UploadedByMemberName],
Notes], [PictureURL]) VALUES (@FixtureID,@UploadedByMemberName,@Notes,@PictureURL)"
            OldValuesParameterFormatString="original_{0}" >
            <InsertParameters>
                <asp:ControlParameter Name="FixtureID"
                    ControlID="ListBox1"
                    PropertyName="SelectedValue"
                    Type="Int64" />
                <asp:ControlParameter Name="UploadedByMemberName"
                    ControlID="TextBoxMemberName"
                    PropertyName="Text"
                    Type="String" />
                <asp:ControlParameter Name="Notes"
                    ControlID="TextBoxNotes"
                    PropertyName="Text"
                    Type="String" />
                <asp:ControlParameter Name="PictureURL"
                    ControlID="FileUpload1"
                    PropertyName="FileName"
                    Type="String" />
            </InsertParameters>
        </asp:SqlDataSource>
 </asp:Content>
```

6. Now you just need to modify the `GalleryUpload-Enhanced.aspx.cs` code page (shown here). In Design View, double-click the Upload button and add the following shaded line of code:

```
using System;
using System.IO;
...
    protected void Button1_Click(object sender, EventArgs e)
...
            try
...
            catch(Exception exUpload)
```

```
            {
                // display status of error
                FileUploadReport.Text = exUpload.Message;
            }
            SqlDataSourceCreateGalleryRecord.Insert();
        }
        else  // probably file was not selected
        {
...
```

7. Save the page and test it in your browser by uploading any picture (you can use My Pictures/Samples) along with picking a match and your name and a comment. Figure 8-15 shows the screen prior to clicking the Upload button.

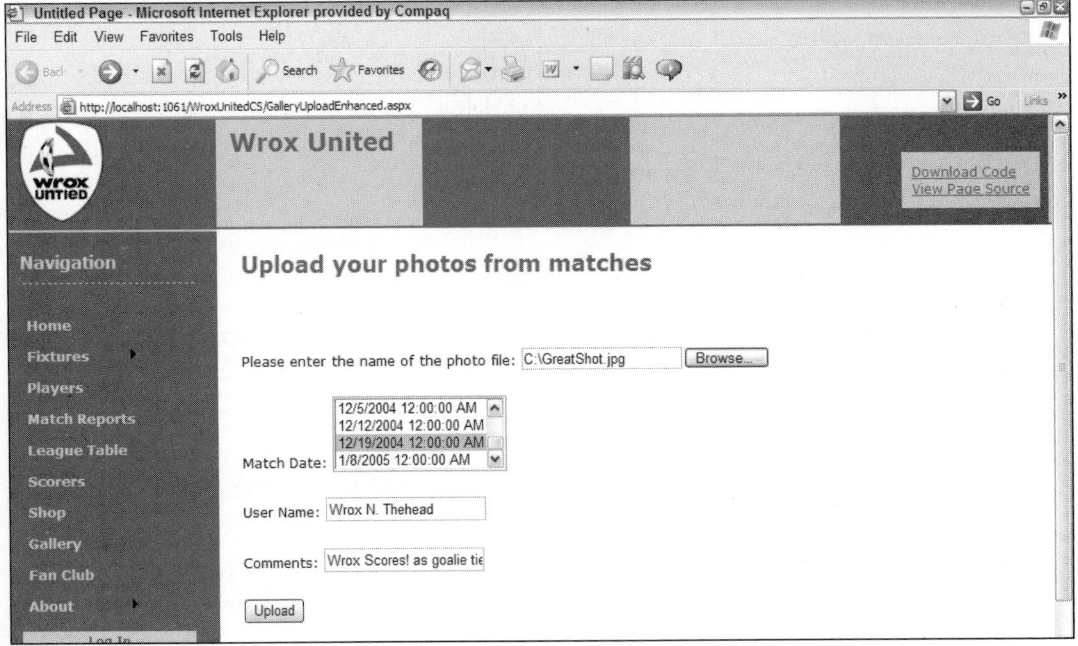

Figure 8-15

8. Confirm your success by closing the browser, returning to VWD, opening the Database Explorer, and expanding WroxUnited and then Tables. Right-click Gallery and select Show Table Data. Observe your new record as in the bottom line of Figure 8-16.

Gallery: Quer...OXUNITED.MDF)

PictureID	FixtureID	UploadedByMe...	Notes	PictureURL
1	1	lou		aaronson.jpg
2	1	lou	asdfasdfadf	aaronson.jpg
3	1	lou	asdfasdfadf	aaronson.jpg
4	1	lou	foo	aaronson.jpg
5	1	lou	another good one	aaronson.jpg
6	1	dave		aaronson.jpg
7	1	dave	test	aaronson.jpg
8	1	dave		aaronson.jpg
22	9	Wrox N. Thehead	Wrox Scores! (As opponents' goal keeper ties his shoe.)	Sunset.jpg
NULL	NULL	NULL	NULL	NULL

Figure 8-16

How It Works

The objective here was to create a new record in the Gallery table whenever a user uploaded an image. You started by setting up inputs so the user could enter data needed for the record. The `ListBox` offered a choice of games and two `TextBox` controls took in the user's name and notes. In order to populate the `ListBox`, you created a `SqlDataSource` that picked up two fields from the Fixtures table.

In order to create a new record, you need to add a `SqlDataSource` control that holds the `INSERT` functionality. When you asked VWD to add commands for insert, you got a lot, and it wasn't what you wanted. You deleted the commands and parameters for `SELECT`, `UPDATE`, and `DELETE` because you won't use them. Then within `<InsertParameters>`, you changed to use the input controls as sources.

Last, you wanted to actually tell the `SqlDataSource` to perform the insert of a new record. You did that with a single line of code in the `Button_Click` event that invoked the `Insert()` method.

This enhanced page brings together several ideas from the last few chapters. You used code in an event (Chapter 6) to catch problems with the `FileUpload` and to invoke the data source control's `Insert()` method. You read from a database (Chapter 7) to stock the `ListBox`. And, last, you wrote to a database (in this chapter) to create a new record to represent the uploaded picture.

Summary

Writing data includes creating entire new records (called inserting), changing values in existing records (updating), and removing entire records (deleting). Both data source and data-bound controls contain code for behavior to write to databases. This chapter explained how to turn on and use these behaviors.

Most, but not all, data controls support writing. Selection lists (`DropDownList` and `ListBox`) do not support writing. `GridView` can update and delete, but not insert. `DetailsView` or `FormView` are ideal for all forms of writing.

Any database front-end that updates data can run into problems when a value is simultaneously changed and needed for identifying a unique record. ASP.NET 2.0 manages a dictionary of old and new values. The fields to be included in the dictionary are listed in the `DataKeyNames` property of the data-bound control.

The pattern for inserting, updating, and deleting is to make three changes to the data controls. In the data source control, you must add the appropriate command with the value of a valid SQL statement. You must also include a set of parameters that feed values into the SQL statement. In the data-bound control, you must include a `CommandField` of the type equal to the writing operation you want to perform. All three of these changes are made through VWD with check-offs in wizards or the Common Tasks panels.

The parameters can be a little tricky until you gain some experience. Simple parameters will hold the existing values that came from the database. `ControlParameters` will hold values that were entered by the user into controls other than the data-bound control that holds the parameter. Reference to a value in a parameter is made in a command by placing an at symbol (@) before the parameter's name. Parameters are organized into sets for each kind of writing command. So when performing an `INSERT`, ASP.NET 2.0 will look up values in the parameter set within `<InsertParameters>`.

Keep in mind two caveats when writing data:

- Writes can lead to logical and organizational errors. For example, your database administrator will not let you delete a customer if that customer has an order (otherwise the order would be shipped to a non-existent customer). It behooves you to limit your user requests and then also be prepared to handle a rejection from your database.
- Writing commands opens your data to a number of types of attacks. Whenever possible, present the user with a list of options rather than allowing typed input. When typing is absolutely necessary, use the ASP.NET 2.0 validation controls.

The capability to transfer files from the user to the server enhances many business objectives. A single, simple control provides the functionality to identify a file. However, the actual transfer requires the use of a button to actually execute the uploading behavior. As demonstrated in the final exercise, that button can also trigger the execution of writing behavior in a data source control that has no data-bound control. The data source control can use control parameters to gather values and create an insert in a table.

Over the last eight chapters you have seen how powerful ASP.NET 2.0 can be with the use of practically no code. You have solved many common business scenarios such as logging on, personalization, and working with data. But in some more advanced cases, you will be forced to write custom code, and for those techniques, carry on to Chapter 9.

Exercises

1. Enabling the capability to write to a database requires changes to the properties of a data source control, a data-bound control, or both?
2. Describe the difference between an `asp:Parameter` and an `asp:ControlParameter`.
3. What problem does the `DataKeyNames` property solve?
4. A page needs to delete the date of birth value from one record. Which command should be used?
5. What tags must be added to a page to allow a `GridView` to create new records?

9

Code

You're now getting to the stage where the site is getting more features, and you need to start learning more about code. Some of the code used in previous chapters might not have been explained fully — that's because what the code was doing was more important than the actual code itself. It's not that the code wasn't important, but rather that the technique being taught was the key; understanding how the actual code worked could come later. Now it's time to learn about the basics of writing code, what makes good code, and how you put all that code together.

In particular, this chapter looks at the following topics:

- What data types and variables are and how they are used
- How you make decisions in your code
- How you repeat lines of code
- What object-oriented programming means and why it's important
- How to think about structuring your code so it's well organized and easy to maintain
- How one of the new language features in ASP.NET 2.0 eases working with collections of objects

There's a lot to cover, and although some of it might sound difficult, it's actually quite easy. You start with finding out about data types.

Variables and Data Types

When you use applications, you don't really care how the application stores your data, just that it does. As a programmer, however, you have to think about this. What sort of data is the user entering? Is it text, numbers, dates, or something else? This matters because how you store data internally in your application affects not only how you deal with the data, but also what you can do with that data. To store data internally, *variables* are used (variables are simply names, used to store information during code), and variables have types; there is a type for each type of data. For example, there is a data type called `string`, unsurprisingly used for *strings*, or text data. There is a data type called DateTime for dates and times, an Integer data type for whole numbers, and a Decimal or Double data type for floating-point numbers. Each has different characteristics. The int type can only store integer numbers, and trying to store any other type of data into an int will raise an exception. Likewise, the DateTime data type can only store dates and times. Following is the full list of data types:

- bool is used to store either true or false. The default value is false.
- byte is used for a single byte of data. This can be a single character or a number from 0 to 255. The default value is 0.
- char is used for two bytes of data. This can be a character or a number from 0 to 65,535. Because it is bigger than a byte, char can store double-byte characters like those used by foreign character sets such as Chinese. The default value is 0.
- DateTime is used to store a date and time. The default value is 0:00:00 (midnight) on January 1, 0001.
- decimal is used for decimal values. It supports up to 29 significant digits and is therefore the most accurate type for financial numbers. The default value is 0.
- double is used for floating-point numbers. Unlike the decimal data type, double has a smaller range and is less accurate. However, it is also faster in use, so it is the preferred data type for floating-point numbers unless a great depth of precision is required. The default value is 0.
- int is used for whole numbers between –2,147,483,648 and 2,147,483,647. The default value is 0.
- long is used for whole numbers between –9,223,372,036,854,775,808 and 9,223,372,036,854,775,807. The default value is 0.
- Object is used to represent objects. The default value is null.
- sbyte is used to hold whole numbers between –128 and 127. The default value is 0.
- short is used for whole numbers between –32,768 and 32,767. The default value is 0.
- float is used for floating-point numbers that don't require the full size of a double. The default value is 0.
- string is used for storing text (or string) data. The default value is null in C#.
- uint is the unsigned equivalent of an int. Because it is unsigned it can only store positive numbers, giving a range of 0 to 4,294,967,295. The default value is 0.
- ulong is the unsigned equivalent of a long. Because it is unsigned it can only store positive numbers, giving a range of 0 to 18,446,774,073,709,551,615. The default value is 0.
- ushort is the unsigned equivalent of a short. Because it is unsigned, it can only store positive numbers, giving a range of 0 to 65,535. The default value is 0.

Having different data types allows the type to provide features that only that type requires. For example, the DateTime type allows dates to be manipulated, the individual parts of the date or time to be extracted, and so on. Also, data types allow you to choose the most efficient way of storing data, so if you need to store a really long number, you would use a long. A long takes up more room in memory than a short, so if you only ever needed to store numbers between 1 and 100, you wouldn't use a long. In essence, the data type you choose depends not only on the type of data, but also its size.

Common Language Runtime Types

This may seem confusing, but there are different names for the same data types. This is because there are data types that the language uses, and data types that the *Common Language Runtime* (CLR) uses. Simply put, the CLR is the system that actually makes .NET run. You don't need to know much about it now, although it's definitely worth learning about as you become more experienced. The reason that the CLR has data types and the language has data types is that the CLR is common to all languages in .NET. Whether you use Visual Basic .NET, C#, or even COBOL .NET, underneath you are using the CLR. However, languages have history (apart from C#, which was new for .NET, but C# has a C and C++ base in terms of the language syntax), and so have data types of their own. For compatibility reasons, it makes sense to keep these specific language types. This enables users of the language to work with familiar data types, and the compiler takes care of using the actual CLR data type.

For much of what you do, you'll use the language data types, but there are times when you need to know what CLR data type a language data type maps onto, and the following table shows this.

CLR Type	Visual Basic Type	C# Type
`Boolean`	`Boolean`	`bool`
`Byte`	`Byte`	`byte`
`Char`	`Char`	`char`
`DateTime`	`Date`	`DateTime`
`Decimal`	`Decimal`	`decimal`
`Double`	`Double`	`double`
`Int32`	`Integer`	`int`
`Int64`	`Long`	`long`
`Object`	`Object`	`Object`
`SByte`	`SByte`	`sbyte`
`Int16`	`Short`	`short`
`Single`	`Single`	`float`
`String`	`String`	`string`
`UInt32`	`UInteger`	`uint`
`UInt64`	`ULong`	`ulong`
`UInt16`	`UShort`	`ushort`

When you look at converting between data types, you'll see why it might be important to know the underlying data type.

What Are All Those Curly Brackets and Semicolons For?

These are covered in more detail later in the chapter, but you'll see a brief explanation now so you understand what you are seeing. The first thing to note is that in C#, a line of code only ends when the semicolon character (;) is reached. This means that you can spread the code line across multiple physical lines to make it easier to read, or so it doesn't scroll off the end of the window.

The next thing to know is that the code blocks are surrounded by curly brackets ({}), which define the start and end of the code block. There will be lots more on these later in the chapter, explaining when these are required, but for now just know that they are part of the language. The term *curly brackets* is often used to differentiate them from parentheses of square brackets.

The other really important thing to know about C# is that it is case-sensitive. In Visual Basic .NET it doesn't matter what case you use, and IntelliSense will correct the language keywords. In C#, however, what you type is what you get, so a common cause of errors is simply mistyping—you know, when you mistakenly hit the Caps Lock key instead of the Shift or Tab key.

Declaring Variables

There is a specific syntax for creating variables, which requires the data type and name. The name is up to you, but it's always best to use a sensible name, something that represents what the variable holds. To define a variable you use the data type followed by the variable name, like so:

```
DataType VariableName;
```

Replace the `VariableName` and `DataType` with your requirements:

```
string FirstName;
string LastName;
int Age;
DateTime Birthday;
```

Here you see sensible names for the variables: there are two `string` types to hold the first and last names, an `int` to hold the age, and a `DateTime` to hold the birthday. In some documents and books, you might see a prefix on the variable name, giving an indication of its data type. For example, the names and ages might be declared like so:

```
string strFirstName;
string sLastName;
int iAge;
DateTime dBirthday;
```

Here `str` or `s` has been used as a prefix for `string` types, `i` for `int` types, and `d` for `DateTime` data types. You may find this technique useful when learning how to use variables and data types, although it isn't generally recommended and has dropped out of favor. A correctly named variable should give a good indication of its data type. Having said that, there are times when some form of prefix is useful, and you'll see this when you look at classes later in the chapter.

Assigning Values

After you declare a variable, you can assign values to it, and this is simply a matter of setting the variable equal to the required value. The syntax for this is as follows:

```
variable = value;
```

This says give the variable named on the left of the equals sign the value on the right of the equals sign. For example:

```
FirstName = "Arthur";
LastName = "Arbuthnot";
Age = 24;
```

As you can see, string values are enclosed in quotation marks, whereas numeric values aren't.

Variables can also be initialized when they are declared, like so:

```
string FirstName = "Arthur";
string LastName = "Arbuthnot";
int Age = 24;
DateTime Birthday = new DateTime(1980, 22, 10);
```

These examples show the assignment using literal values, but you can also assign values to other variables or objects. For example, in ASP.NET pages, it's very common to assign values from user-entered data, perhaps from a text box:

```
FirstName = FirstNameTextBox.Text;
LastName = LastNameTextBox.Text;
```

Or vice versa:

```
FirstNameTextBox.Text = FirstName;
LastNameTextBox.Text = LastName;
```

The `TextBox` control has a property called `Text` that contains the text value, so you are simply copying that value into the `string` variable, or copying the string value into the property. This is fine for `string` types, but extra work needs to be done if the variable isn't a `string` type. For example, allowing a user to enter his age would require a text box and an `int` type variable. However, you can't assign the values of differing types — you need to convert them.

Data Conversion

Visual Basic .NET provides some automatic conversion of data types, but C# doesn't provide this facility, and you have to explicitly convert variables between data types. Explicit conversion makes it clear exactly what your code does, a useful point when you (or others) look at your code later. There isn't a single syntax for converting between types, but there is a lot of commonality in the different methods.

Converting to string values is the simplest, because every data type has a `ToString` method. For example, to convert age to a `TextBox` you could use the following:

```
AgeTextBox.Text = Age.ToString();
```

For the `bool` type the conversion method is the same, but the string value will be either `true` or `false`.

Converting from a string value to another type is slightly different, because there aren't methods on the `string` type to do this automatically. Instead you have to use a separate class to perform the conversion.

Converting Data Types Using the Framework Classes

There are two ways to convert from string values to other types using the framework classes, and it's worth mentioning both in case you see them in code. The first is to use the `Parse` method that most data types supply. For example, to convert a number held in a `TextBox` control into an `int` data type, you could do this:

```
int Age;
Age = int.Parse(AgeTextBox.Text);
```

What's happening here is that the `Parse` method *parses* the value passed to it—that is, it reads the value, checks that it is an integer value, and converts it into an integer. The value to be converted is the value from the `Text` property of the `AgeTextBox` control, which is a string. So the string is passed into the `Parse` method, which converts it into an integer and returns the integer, which in turn is assigned to the `Age` variable.

All of the data types, apart from `Object`, support the `Parse` method, which means that even though you may be using a different data type, the syntax is the same. For example:

```
double ANumber;
ANumber = Double.Parse(NumberTextBox.Text);
```

The second way to perform data conversion is to use the `Convert` class, which converts between types. It's a very flexible class because it can convert between all types, but it requires knowledge of the CLR type. For example, the preceding example using an integer could be written as follows:

```
int Age;
Age = Convert.ToInt32(AgeTextBox.Text);
```

For the double example, this would be:

```
double ANumber;
ANumber = Convert.ToDouble(NumberTextBox.Text);
```

In use there is no difference between the `Convert` class and the data type class when converting types. The only reason for using the `Convert` class is that it makes code easier to convert to another language. This was important when writing the Wrox United web site, but may not be important to you if you intend to stick with one language.

Converting Data Types with Casting

Another way of converting between types is by *casting*. Instead of explicitly converting the type, the value is forced into another type. Casting doesn't work in the same way as converting, and isn't always suitable. For example, you can't use casting to convert from strings to numbers. You can, however, use casting to convert between similar types. For example, you could cast between a `double` and an `int` by using the following code:

```
double MyDouble = 123.456;
int MyInteger;
MyInteger = (int)MyDouble;
```

The last line in this code example shows the actual cast — the use of the data type surrounded by parentheses — the `(int)` bit. This tells the compiler to take the value of the `MyDouble` variable and convert it to an integer type, which has the effect of just removing all of the digits after the decimal point. It doesn't change the `MyDouble` variable at all — that is still a `double` and still retains the original value.

One thing you should be aware of is that casting may change the value of the variable. In the preceding example this is obvious, because changing a floating-point number into an integer will lose the values after the decimal point. Converting between a `long` and an `int` isn't so obvious, but may result in changes. Because an `int` has a range half that of a `long`, if the value in the `long` exceeds that of the `integer`, the value will be shortened when converted.

Explicit Conversion

You may see another form of conversion, but not realize it's actually a conversion:

```
float num = 18.3f;
```

This follows the usual form of declaration but has an `f` on the end. The reason for this is that 18.3 is taken as a `double`, so you would get a compiler error saying that a `double` cannot be implicitly converted to a `float`. Adding the `f` to the end of `18.3` does an explicit conversion.

Null Values

All data types have default values, but there is also the concept of a null value. This doesn't usually affect the standard types, and is more common on custom or complex types. It simply means that the object doesn't exist. For example, consider a method that returns a `DataSet` object, filled with data from a database. What happens if, while fetching the data, there is some sort of error? There will probably be an exception thrown (these are covered in Chapter 15), but the method still might return, only there's no data for you — the value returned might be null.

In C# the null value is represented by the keyword `null`. You look at how you test for null values later.

Working with Strings

When working with strings, it's useful to know that the `string` class has a great number of methods that allow you to manipulate those strings, and any variable that is a string therefore has the ability to use those methods. You won't go into all of them here, instead concentrating on some of the most common ones.

One of the most common requirements is being able to strip blank spaces (or white space as it's sometimes called) from the beginning or end of strings. This is useful when taking input from a user and is especially important when trying to compare two string values. For example, consider the following code fragment:

```
string Name1 = "Dave";
string Name2 = "Dave      ";

if (Name1 == Name2)
```

The `if` test would result in `false`, because the strings aren't the same — `Name2` has spaces at the end. Three methods can help here: `TrimStart` removes spaces from the start of the string, `TrimEnd` removes spaces from the end of a string, and `Trim` removes spaces from both the start and end of a string. If the preceding code were modified to include `Trim`, the result would be `true`:

```
string Name1 = "Dave";
string Name2 = "Dave      ";

if (Name1.Trim() == Name2.Trim())
```

Both strings have been trimmed, so the `if` test would return `true`. The strings have only been trimmed as part of the comparison, though; the strings haven't been modified themselves. Consider this code:

```
string Name1 = "Dave";
string Name2 = "Dave      ";

if (Name1.Trim() == Name2.Trim())
{
  // this would return true
}

if (Name1 == Name2)
{
  // this would return False
}
```

You can see that using `Trim` only affects that one instance, unless the underlying variable is changed:

```
string Name1 = "Dave";
string Name2 = "Dave      ";

Name1 = Name1.Trim();
Name2 = Name2.Trim();

if (Name1 == Name2)
{
  // this would return True
}
```

Now that `Name1` and `Name2` have been reassigned with the trimmed values, subsequent comparisons work. The key point here is that using string methods only affects that particular use of the string, and the string variable will only be changed if assignment is done.

Another situation that can occur when comparing strings, especially those supplied by user input, is mismatched case. What if the user has the Caps Lock key on? Two methods help with this: `ToLower`, which converts the string to lowercase, and `ToUpper`, which converts the string to uppercase. For example:

```
string Name1 = "dave";
string Name2 = "DAVE";

if (Name1 == Name2)
```

This code would fail because the strings are different, even though we know them to mean the same thing. To get around this, you can change the case:

```
string Name1 = "dave";
string Name2 = "DAVE";

if (Name1.ToLower() == Name2.ToLower())
```

Now the test would succeed because the values being compared are lowercase.

Plenty of other string methods exist, some of which are described here:

- `EndsWith` returns `true` if the string ends with a given string. For example:

```
if (MyString.EndsWith("ate"))
```

- `StartsWith` returns `true` if the string starts with a given string. For example:

```
if (MyString.StartsWith("wha"))
```

- `IndexOf` returns the position within the string of a given character or string, or `-1` if the item isn't found. For example:

```
if (MyString.IndexOf("abc") > 0)
```

- `Insert` inserts a string at a given position. For example, to insert the string `new words` at position `5` you would use this:

```
MyString.Insert(5, "new words");
```

- `LastIndexOf` returns the last position within the string of a given character or string. This is similar to `IndexOf` but is useful for finding the last instance of a character.

- `PadLeft` and `PadRight` perform the opposite of `Trim`, allowing you to pad strings to a given length. The padding defaults to a space but can be any character. For example, to pad a string to a total of 15 characters, you would use the following:

```
MyNewString = MyString.PadLeft(15)
```

- `Remove` removes a section of a string. For example, to remove five characters starting at position 4, you would use this:

```
MyNewString = MyString.Remove(4, 5);
```

- Replace replaces characters within the string. For example, to replace abc with def you would use this:

```
MyNewString = MyString.Replace("abc", "def")
```

- SubString returns a portion of a string. For example, to return five characters starting at position 4, you would use this:

```
MyNewString = MyString.SubString(4, 5);
```

For a full list of string methods, you should consult the documentation. The String type has a couple of properties, but the only one you will probably use is Length, which returns the number of characters within the string.

Working with Dates

In C#, you can place dates as literals into your code, but one problem with this is that it has to be in the MM/DD/YYYY format, which can be confusing if you are in a country that doesn't use that format. For example, take the date 03/05/2005—does this represent March 5 or May 3? You could easily assume the format, but that leads to potential errors.

Instead of using literals to initialize dates, C# uses the DateTime object to create a new instance on a date, like so:

```
DateTime Birthday = new DateTime(2005, 3, 5);
```

The parameters are in year, month, and day order, and because you have IntelliSense (or at least the documentation if you aren't using VWD), you know what the order should be. If required, the individual parts of the date can be accessed like so:

```
int day = Birthday.Day;
int month = Birthday.Month;
int year = Birthday.Year;
```

There are other properties such as DayOfWeek and DayOfYear, as well as ones for dealing with the time and parts of the time. You can find more information about these additional properties in the documentation.

Dates behave just like numeric variables in that they allow addition, subtraction, and comparison. For example, you can add a number of days using the AddDays method:

```
NewDate = Birthday.AddDays(18);
```

There is also a Subtract method that subtracts one date from another. However, this method doesn't return a Date type, but rather a TimeSpan, which is a data type used to define spans of time. For example:

```
DateTime Date1 = new Date(2005, 3, 10);
DateTime Date2 = new Date(2005, 3, 5);
TimeSpan Difference;

Difference = Date1.Subtract(Date2);
Label1.Text = Difference.ToString();
```

This code creates two dates, March 10 and March 5, and then declares a variable of type `TimeSpan`, which will hold the difference between the dates. The difference is calculated by using the `Subtract` method of the date — because the `Date1` variable is a `Date` type the `Subtract` method can be used, and `Date2` is passed into this method. The result is that `Date2` is subtracted from `Date1`, and in this case the result would be 5.00:00:00, which represents 5 days, 0 hours, 0 seconds, and 0 milliseconds.

Now that you have a good base of knowledge to work with, the following Try It Out has you work with simple data types.

Try It Out Working with Simple Types

1. Open the directory for the Chapter 9 samples, called `Chapter09` and located under the directory where you placed the sample code.
2. Create a new Web Form called `SimpleTypes.aspx`. Remember to make sure it uses a separate file for the code.
3. Drag three text boxes, three labels, and a button onto the page, so it looks like Figure 9-1. Make sure the `TextBox` and `Label` controls are in order, so `TextBox1` is at the top, followed by `TextBox2`, and then `TextBox3`.

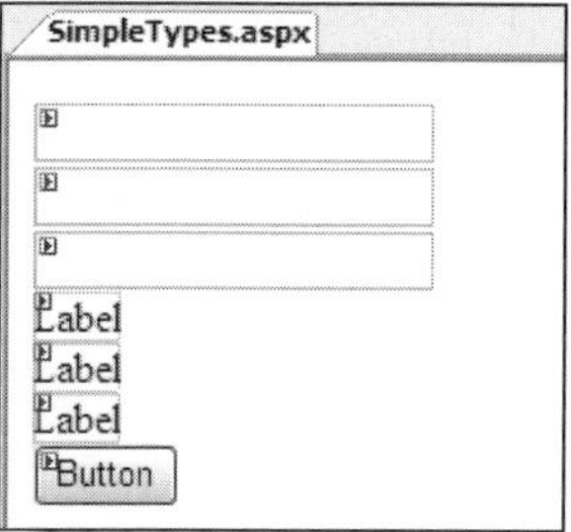

Figure 9-1

4. Double-click the button to create the code-behind file and button click event, and add the following code into the event procedure:

```
Label1.Text = TextBox1.Text + TextBox2.Text;
Label2.Text = DateTime.Parse(TextBox3.Text).ToString("dd MMM yyyy");
Label3.Text = DateTime.Parse(TextBox3.Text).ToString();
```

5. Save both the Web Form and the code-behind file, and set the Web Form to be the start page (right-click the page in the Solution Explorer).
6. Press F5 to run the page and enter **3** into the first text box, enter **4** into the second text box, and enter **12/2/05** into the third text box.
7. Press the button and observe the results. On a machine configured with UK regional settings, you'll see Figure 9-2.

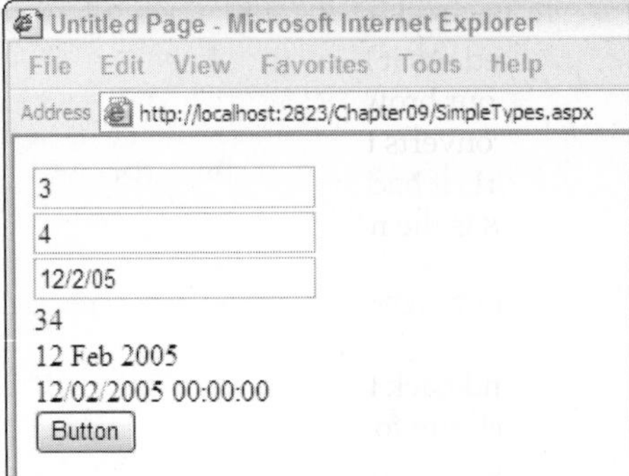

Figure 9-2

With the regional settings set to USA, Figure 9-3 will appear.

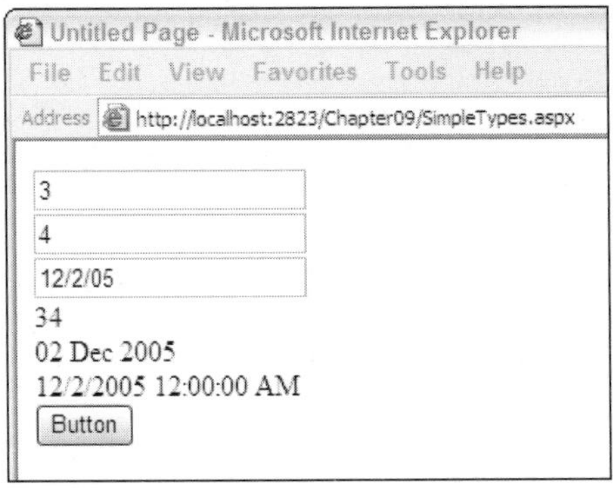

Figure 9-3

How It Works

There are two points to note about this page. The first is that the numbers you entered into the text boxes haven't been added as you might expect, and the second is that the date format changes depending upon the regional settings.

Take a look at the numbers first:

```
Label1.Text = TextBox1.Text + TextBox2.Text;
```

The code seems obvious, just adding two numbers, but you have to remember that the `Text` property of the `TextBox` control returns a string. For strings, the addition operator (+) means concatenation, so it simply joins the strings. To add the strings, you would have to convert them to numbers first, like so:

```
Label1.Text = Convert.ToInt32(TextBox1.Text) + Convert.ToInt32(TextBox.Text);
```

Here the `Convert` class is used to convert the text to numbers, so when the addition is done, the values are numbers.

For the dates, you have to consider the regional settings of the machine that the web server is running on — this is where the code is executed. As it happens, when running the VWD web server, the machine processing the pages is the same as your browser, but on a real web site, this isn't the case. So take a look at what the code does. The first line converts the value from the text box into a `DateTime` type by using the `Parse` method, and then it converts it back into a string. The `ToString` method has an explicit format, where `dd` is the day number, `MMM` is the month name, and `yyyy` is the year:

```
Label2.Text = DateTime.Parse(TextBox3.Text).ToString("dd MMM yyyy");
```

The reason for converting to a date and back to a string is to show that parsing the date is system-dependent. So if you are writing a web site for a company that uses a different date format from yours, the results you see may not always be what you expect.

The final line of code shows what the default `ToString` method does:

```
Label3.Text = DateTime.Parse(TextBox3.Text).ToString();
```

This simply shows the date and time. Notice that this displays the same value for the date regardless of the regional settings. The time is shown differently but again that's because of the regional settings on the machine. You might like to experiment with your regional settings to see how the output differs. If you do this, you will need to stop the VWD web server before rerunning the application; you can do this by selecting the icon in the task tray and clicking Stop from the right mouse-button menu.

One thing you might like to experiment with is what happens if you either leave a text box empty or enter the wrong data type (for example, entering a string into the third text box for conversion to a string). Depending on what you enter, you might see a different range of exceptions, a topic that is covered in more detail in Chapter 15.

Working with Arrays and Collections

Arrays and collections are two sides of the same coin, because they both provide ways of storing multiple copies of data types. For example, consider having to store several names, perhaps the authors of this book. You could store them in individual strings, but then what if you wanted to print them all? You'd need a statement for each variable. With an *array* or a *collection*, you need only one variable for multiple items. You can think of arrays as cells in a spreadsheet. A *single dimensional* array is a single row, with multiple cells, and a *multi-dimensional* array is multiple rows, each with multiple cells. Instead of cells, the term *elements* is generally used, and the *index* is the number of the element (the row or column number to continue the spreadsheet analogy).

Single Dimensional Arrays

Arrays are declared in much the same way as variables, but with the addition of square brackets after the variable type. For example:

```
string[] Names;
```

This declares a string array called `Names`, but it's an empty array — it doesn't actually create any spaces for the array elements. To do this, you use the `new` keyword, so to store five names you would change the declaration to the following:

```
string[] Names = new string[5];
```

One thing to note is that the index for arrays starts at 0. So this array has 0, 1, 2, 3, and 4, which gives five entries. The bounds of the array are 0 to 4.

Accessing array values, either to read or assign values, follows the same rules, with the addition of the square brackets. Within the square brackets, you put the index number of the element required. For example:

```
Names[0] = "Dave";
Names[4] = "Dan";
NameTextBox.Text = Names[4];
```

In this example, `Dave` is the first entry and `Dan` is the fifth entry. The entries between will be empty because no values have been set for them.

Trying to access an element that doesn't exist (anything above 4 in this example) will generate an exception with the message "Index was outside the bounds of the array."

Arrays can also be dynamically sized when declared:

```
string[] Names = {"Dave", "Chris", "Chris", "John", "Dan"};
```

Here the array has five elements with the first being assigned to `Dave`, the second to `Chris`, and so on. The curly brackets enclose the list of items for the array.

Multi-Dimensional Arrays

Arrays aren't limited to one dimension, so you can replicate that spreadsheet type of storage. For example, to use an array to store first and last names, you could do this:

```
string[,] Names = new string[5, 2];
Names[0,0] = "Dave";
Names[0,1] = "Sussman";
Names[1,0] = "Chris";
Names[1,1] = "Hart";
...
Names[4,0] = "Dan";
Names[4,1] = "Maharry";
```

Here the declaration separates the dimensions by a comma. The number of elements in each dimension is included in the variable declaration, so the first dimension has five elements (0–4), and the second has two (0–1). This gives you storage like so:

	0	1
0	Dave	Sussman
1	Chris	Hart
	...	
4	Dan	Maharry

A 4-by-4 array (four rows, four columns) would be declared as follows:

```
string[,] MyArray = new string[3, 3];
```

Adding another dimension is as simple as adding a comma and another number. So a three-dimensional array, with four elements in each dimension would be:

```
string[,,] MyArray = new string[3, 3, 3];
```

Like single dimensional arrays, multi-dimensional ones can also be initialized at declaration time:

```
string[,] Names = {{"Dave", "Sussman"}, {"Chris", "Hart"}};
```

Like the single dimension, curly brackets are used to surround the entries, but there are two sets of brackets, one for each dimension: the outer set for the first dimension, and the inner set for the second. The first names, `Dave` and `Chris`, are placed in the first dimension, and the last names, `Sussman` and `Hart`, are placed in the second dimension. So this is the same as:

```
string[,] Names = new string[2, 2];
Names[0,0] = "Dave";
Names[0,1] = "Sussman";
Names[1,0] = "Chris";
Names[1,1] = "Hart";
```

Which style you use is a matter of personal preference, because there's no real difference between them.

Collections

Another way of storing multiple items is to use collections. Collections differ from arrays in that they are always dynamically allocated, which makes them more suitable for situations where the amount of data changes frequently. There are different collections for different purposes, stored in the `System.Collections` namespace (more on namespaces later), including the following:

- `ArrayList` provides a general collection for objects.
- `Hashtable` provides storage for key/value pairs. A key/value pair is simply the storage of values, which can then later be identified by a key. In array terms, the key is the index of the array element, but a `Hashtable` allows the key to be non-numeric.
- `Queue` provides a first-in, first-out collection, which means that items are taken off the queue in the same order in which they were placed onto it, just like a real queue — the person who arrives first gets served first.

- `SortedList` provides ordered storage for key/value pairs.
- `Stack` provides a last-in, first-out collection, where items are taken off the stack in the reverse order in which they were placed onto it. Think of a stack of plates — the last one put onto the stack is the first off.
- `StringCollection` provides a collection of strings.

There are other collections, but these are the ones you'll probably use most frequently. Data is added to collections by calling an `Add` method, the parameters of which depend upon the collection being used. For the `StringCollection`, you simply supply the string to be added. For example:

```
StringCollection Names = new StringCollection();
Names.Add("Dave");
Names.Add("Chris");
```

To access the entries, you use the same method as an array:

```
NameTextBox.Text = Names[0];
```

This would return `Dave`, because the names are added in numerical order.

A `HashTable` is different because the index isn't numerical, but rather string-based. With a `StringCollection`, the index is a number, and it is assigned automatically, in order of the items added. With a `HashTable`, you have to specify the key as well as the item you want to add. For example:

```
HashTable Names = new Hashtable();
Names.Add("Dave", "Sussman");
Names.Add("Chris", "Hart");
```

In this example, the first parameter is the key, and the second is the value, which leads to them being called key/value pairs. You can also add entries without using the `Add` method:

```
Names["John"] = "Kauffman";
```

There's no real difference between using and not using the `Add` method, although it's best to use `Add` if only because it clarifies what is being done. Without the `Add` method, the code looks more like an assignment, so you aren't completely sure whether a new item is being added or if an existing one is being modified.

To access the entries you use the key:

```
NameTextBox.Text = Names("Chris")
```

One important point about using `HashTables` is that the keys must be unique. So in the preceding example, a `HashTable` wouldn't really be suitable for storing the author names, because two of the authors have the same first name. So this code would fail:

```
HashTable Names = new Hashtable();
Names.Add("Chris", "Ullman");
Names.Add("Chris", "Hart");
```

An exception would be raised on the second `Add` line, because the key has already been used.

Collections, and arrays for that matter, aren't only useful for storing native types such as strings or integers. They can also be used to store custom classes, which you will look at later in the chapter. The following Try It Out, however, puts your knowledge of arrays and collections to use.

Try It Out Working with Arrays and Collections

1. Create a new Web Form, called `ArraysCollections.aspx`.
2. Add a `TextBox`, a `Button`, a `ListBox`, and another `TextBox` to the form.
3. For the text boxes, set the `TextMode` property to `MultiLine`, the `Columns` property to `50`, and the `Rows` property to `5`. When finished, it should look like Figure 9-4.

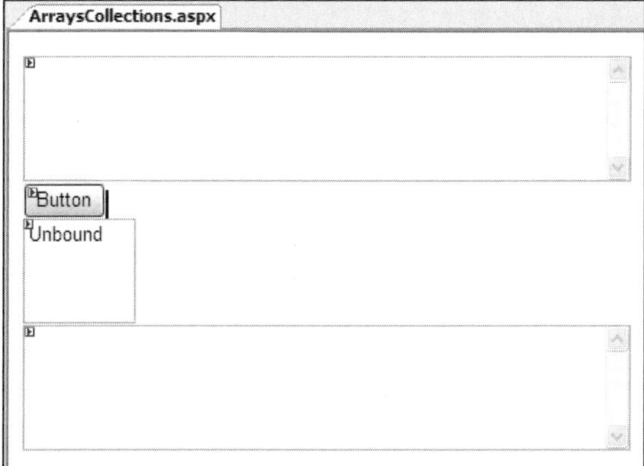

Figure 9-4

4. Enter the following code into the `Click` event for the button:

```
string splitChars = " ";
string[] words;

words = TextBox1.Text.Split(splitChars.ToCharArray());

ListBox1.Items.Clear();
for (int wordIndex = words.Length - 1; wordIndex >= 0; wordIndex--)
{
  ListBox1.Items.Add(words[wordIndex]);
}

string paragraph = string.Empty;
foreach (ListItem word in ListBox1.Items)
{
  paragraph += word.Value + " ";
}

TextBox2.Text = paragraph;
```

5. Save the files, and set `ArraysCollections.aspx` as the start page.
6. Press F5 to run the page and enter **Wrox United are the best** into the first text box.
7. Press the button and you will see the screen shown in Figure 9-5.

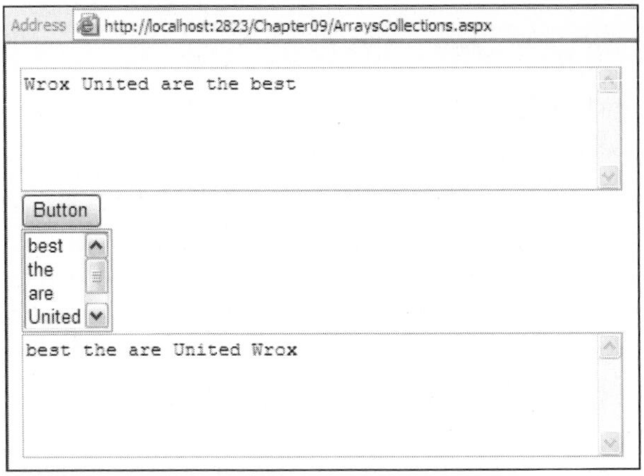

Figure 9-5

You can see that the sentence in the first text box has been split into its component words, those words have been entered into the list box in reverse order, and then the words have been combined into the second text box. The following section explains how this works.

How It Works

The first two lines of the code simply define variables. The first, `splitChars`, is a string containing the characters that will be used to split the sentence, and the second, `words`, is an array of strings:

```
string splitChars = " ";
string[] words;
```

Next, the sentence entered into the text box is split into an array, using the `Split` method. Although it looks like `Split` is a method of the `Text` property, remember that the `Text` property returns a `String`— so `Split` is a method of the `String` class. The parameter passed into the string is not the `splitChars` variable itself, but `splitChars` converted to a character array (using the `ToCharArray` method). This is because a character array is the required type for the `Split` method, which allows a great deal of flexibility in splitting strings:

```
words = TextBox1.Text.Split(splitChars.ToCharArray());
```

At this stage, the `words` array now contains a separate entry for each word in the sentence, ready for addition into the list box. Before the words are added to the list, the existing `Items` collection is cleared, which stops the list from getting ever bigger if the button is clicked multiple times. Then you loop through the words array, but loop backwards, adding each word into the list:

```
ListBox1.Items.Clear();
for (int wordIndex = words.Length - 1; wordIndex >= 0; wordIndex--)
```

```
{
  ListBox1.Items.Add(words[wordIndex]);
}
```

Don't worry too much about the exact syntax of the looping—you get to that later in the chapter.

After the words are in the list, they can be removed again, into another string. This has an initial value that might seem unusual—`String.Empty`—but this is quite a common thing for initializing strings:

```
string paragraph = String.Empty;
```

`String.Empty` is a special value that indicates that the string is empty. This is different from a string assigned to `""`, which has a value, albeit a string of zero length that doesn't contain any characters. The reason for having a distinction between a zero-length string and an empty string is that it allows you to detect whether the string has been set or changed from its initial value. One of the reasons for declaring an initial value is that without it you get a warning in VWD, but on a later line, indicating that the `paragraph` variable is being used before it has been set. In this case, it doesn't matter, but reducing warnings in VWD means it's easier to spot warnings and errors that do matter.

Now loop through the `Items` collection of the list box, and the `Items` collection contains `ListItem` objects. The `Value` of each `ListItem` is simply appended to the paragraph string, along with a space:

```
foreach (ListItem word in ListBox1.Items)
{
    paragraph += word.Value + " ";
}
```

Finally, the paragraph is displayed in the second text box:

```
TextBox2.Text = paragraph;
```

This may seem an overly lengthy way to reverse the words in a sentence, but the point of the exercise is to show that there are different ways of working with arrays and collections.

Deciding Whether to Use Arrays or Collections

There are pros and cons of using both arrays and collections, and the decision of which to use can sometimes be confusing. In general, if the number of elements isn't going to change, an array is best—it's efficient and fast, and it provides easy access to the elements. If you need to change the number of elements, or insert elements between others, then a collection is best.

Both arrays and collections can, like some of the data objects, be used for data binding. For example, the Wrox United shop could have a list of delivery methods in a drop-down list:

```
string[] delivery = {"Post", "Courier", "International"}
DeliveryDropDownList.DataSource = delivery;
DeliveryDropDownList.DataBind();
```

Here the array is simply used as the source to which to bind the list. Collections can also be used in this manner. Data binding was covered in Chapter 7.

Enumerations

Enumerations are a custom data type where the value can be one of a number of values. This is easier to see with an example, so take a look at the `Calendar` control. This is a complex control and has many properties to allow its look to be changed, one of which is the `DayNameFormat` (see Figure 9-6).

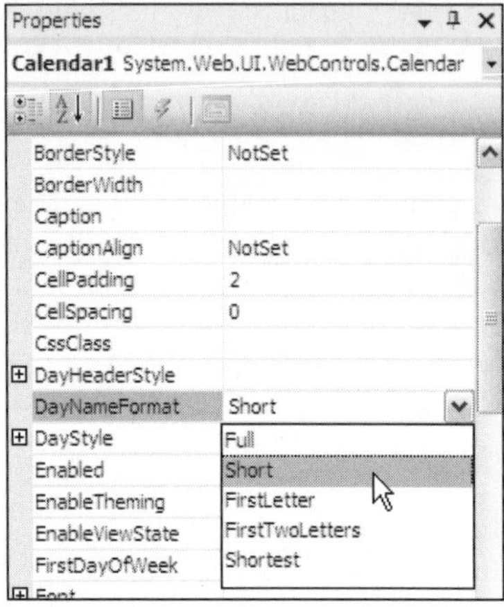

Figure 9-6

The format must be one of five values — Full, Short, FirstLetter, FirstTwoLetters, and Shortest — and no other, so there needs to be a way of ensuring only these values can be selected. This is where enumerations come in because enumerations restrict the variable to a set of known values. The syntax for creating an enumeration is as follows:

```
public enum EnumerationName
{
  enumeration values
}
```

What this does is declare a new type, with the name of the type being whatever name you give it as `EnumerationName`. This type is a special type where the values can only be one of those in the supplied list. For example, the `DayNameFormat` is an enumeration, which has been created like so:

```
public enum DayNameFormat
{
  Full,
  [Short],
  FirstLetter,
  FirstTwoletters,
  Shortest
};
```

The values used in the enumeration are separated by a comma. Because this is a new type, it can be used in variable declarations:

```
DayNameFormat dayFormat;
dayFormat = DayNameFormat.FirstLetter;
```

This declares a new variable of the enumeration type — `DayNameFormat`. Then it assigns a value to the variable, and the value assigned is one of the defined values. This shows as the enumeration name and value separated by a period. What's great is that you get IntelliSense, so you can pick from a list of the known values when assigning the variable.

Enumerations provide a way to have a human-readable value associated with a number. In the preceding example, no numbers are explicitly assigned, so they are created automatically, starting at 0. So here, `Full` would be `0`, `Short` would be `1`, and so on. The `Short` value was enclosed within square brackets when it was declared because `Short` is also a data type. Using the square brackets tells .NET that this is the custom name rather than the data type. If you don't want to use the default numbers for the values, you can specify them yourself. For example:

```
public enum DeliveryType
{
  Post,
  Courier = 4,
  International
};
```

Here, the `Post` would be `0` and the `Courier` has an explicit value of `4`. Because `International` doesn't have an explicit value, automatic numbering starts again, at the last number used, so it would have a value of `5`.

Enumerations are used when you need to allow one of a limited number of values for a selection. It's used extensively in the ASP.NET server controls to allow only selected values, often allowing the behavior to change. The `TextBox`, for example, has a `TextMode` property that can be one of `SingleLine`, `MultiLine`, or `Password`. How the `TextBox` is displayed changes depending on which value is selected. When creating code yourself, for the day-to-day running of an application, there is perhaps less use for enumerations (the Wrox United site doesn't use any `Enums`), but they can be useful, perhaps when you're building central libraries of code.

Constants

Constants are another way to provide a human-readable form for values, but unlike enumerations, constants are a single value only and as their name suggests, they are constant and never change. This is useful for situations where you need to use a fixed value. Using a constant means you can give that value a name and use the name throughout the code. The value is defined once, meaning it is easy to change, and because the readable name is used throughout the code, the code becomes more maintainable.

Even if the value is only used once, it's sensible to use constants because they provide a way to centralize this type of fixed value. The syntax for a constant is as follows:

```
private const Type ConstantName = Value;
```

`const` is what defines this as a constant, and `private` is how visible the constant is — you look at this later in the chapter. The rest of the declaration is just like any other variable, the difference being that the value is constant, and therefore cannot be changed.

For example, in the Wrox United web site there is a shopping cart to store items bought from the shop. Members of the fan club receive a 10% discount, so this value is stored as a constant:

```
private const single MemberDiscountPercentage = 0.1;
```

When the total price of the order is calculated this constant can be used, just like any other variable:

```
MemberDiscount = SubTotal * MemberDiscountPercentage;
Total = SubTotal - MemberDiscount;
```

You look at the implementation of the shopping cart later in the chapter.

Statements

Statements are where the real action of code is, allowing you to control the program. You have seen many statements in code already in the book, and at the time it wasn't convenient to explain what they meant or how they worked. Now is that time, because statements are what drive your code. Statements are what allow you to structure your code, to make decisions, and to repeat actions a number of times. For example, to make a decision, you use the `if` statement, which can be used to allow the code to react to external criteria. Take the Wrox United checkout page, where members of the fan club receive a discount. This is done with a decision, which goes something like this:

```
if (person is a member of the fan club)
{
  give that person a discount
}
```

The `if` is the C# statements that test a condition—or ask a question. Think of the program as a person deciding what to do. The code within the curly braces is the code that is run if the condition is true.

For repeating tasks, there are statements called loops, and there are different types of loops for different tasks. Some (`for`) repeat a fixed number of times, whereas others (`while`) repeat until a condition is met, or while a condition is true.

Before conditions and loops can be examined in more detail, some other topics need to be covered.

Operators

The first thing to look at is *operators*, which are how values are manipulated. If you can remember back to your math lessons in school, this will be familiar. You've already seen the assignment operator, the equals sign (=), in action earlier in the chapter, and this simply assigns a value to a variable. The next several sections discuss how the remaining operators allow you to carry out predefined operations.

Concatenation

Concatenation is used to join strings. For example, consider if you had the first and last names in a multidimensional array (as shown when you looked at arrays), and you wanted to have a single variable with the full name. You would use the concatenation operator, the plus sign (+), to do this:

```
string FullName;
FullName = Names[0,0] + Names[0,1];
```

This takes the last name and joins it to the end of the first name. However there is no space separating them, so the code could be:

```
FullName = Names[0,0] + " " + Names[0,1];
```

Now you have two concatenations taking place. First a space is added and then the last name. You could have also used another form of the assignment operator:

```
FullName = Names[0,0];
FullName += " ";
FullName += Names[0,1];
```

The use of += simply says take the variable on the right of the assignment and append to it the contents on the left. This also works with arithmetic operators, which are the subject of the next section.

Arithmetic Operators

Arithmetic operators allow you to perform arithmetic on variables: addition, subtraction, and so on. The following table displays the arithmetic operators:

Operator	Action
+	Addition
-	Subtraction
*	Multiplication
/	Division
%	Modulus

The standard mathematical operators are easy to understand — they add, subtract, multiply, and divide in the way you'd expect:

```
int n1 = 6;
Single n2 = 14.3;
double n3;

n3 = n1 + n2;              // results in: 20.3
n3 = n2 - n1;              // results in: 8.3
n3 = n1 / n2;              // results in: 0.41958
n2 = n1 * n2;              // results in: 85.8
```

Modulus divides two numbers and returns the remainder. One of the classic uses for this is to test if a number is odd or even:

```
int n1;

n1 = 1 % 2;              // results in: 1
n1 = 2 % 2;              // results in: 0
n1 = 3 % 2;              // results in: 1
n1 = 14 % 2;             // results in: 0
```

So if a number `% 2` is 0, then it's even.

Like concatenation, operators can be combined with assignment. In order to add 1 to a number, you can do this:

```
int n1 = 4;
n1 = n1 + 1;
```

This says take `n1`, add 1 to it, and assign that value back to `n1`. Remember that assignment works by taking the value on the right of the = and assigning that to the variable of the left of the =. This works even if the variable being assigned is on the right because the right side is calculated first. An alternative to this is to combine operators:

```
int n1 = 4;
n1 += 1;
```

This has the same result as the first example although it looks very different. In fact it's just a shortcut that allows the addition operator to be combined with the assignment. It simply says take the `n1` variable and add 1 to it. The other arithmetic operators can be used in the same way.

The subtraction operator is also used for negation, like so:

```
int n1;
int n2;

n1 = -3;
n2 = -n1;                    // results in: 3
```

Negation can be used on any numeric type.

Comparison Operators

Comparison is how decisions are made in code. You'll find out about the mechanism of that in due time, but for now, all you need to know is that the operators define what comparison is made. The comparison operators are shown in the following table:

Operator	Action
<	Less than
<=	Less than or equal to
>	Greater than
>=	Greater than or equal to
==	Equal to
!=	Not equal to

Comparison always involves an *expression* — the term for all operators and operands involved in the comparison. The result of a comparison expression is a Boolean value — it is either `true` or `false`. You look at the mechanics of using expressions in decisions in a while, but these operators work just like the ones you've already seen. If you have two variables, `n1` with a value of `4` and `n2` with a value of `5`, the following could be used as expressions:

```
n1 > n2                    // results in: false
n2 > n1                    // results in: true
```

For numbers, the comparison is obvious, but for other data types it might not be. Dates, for example, work in a similar way, but the test is whether one date is earlier or later than another. For example:

```
DateTime d1 = new DateTime(2005, 10, 1);  //  1 October 2005
DateTime d2 = new DateTime(2004. 1, 2);   //  2 January 2004

d1 > d2                                 // results in: true
```

The greater than operator tests to see if the first date is later than the second, so the result is `true`. For equality tests, two ==s are used together:

```
if (d1 == d2)
```

The same comparison operators are used with objects, but with objects, you check to see if two object references point at the same object. The `!=` operator does the opposite, checking to see if two object references point at different objects. This is useful when you're dealing with objects, and many of the scenarios where this is used are covered in later chapters. However, it's worth showing an example here. Because the concept of databases has already been covered, we can use that in this example. When you use the data controls on pages, you get a lot of functionality by just dropping a control onto a page and setting a few properties, but there are occasions where you need to explicitly deal with a database, and this becomes truer as you gain experience and write more complex applications. The checkout for Wrox United is one case, where the items from the shopping cart are written to the database. For this a `SqlConnection` object is used, which provides a way to connect to a specific database. For example:

```
SqlConnection conn = new SqlConnection(" . . .");
conn.Open();

// insert the checkout items

conn.Close();
```

This code fragment opens a database connection, inserts the checkout items, and then closes the connection. However, if there is an error when opening the connection, the `conn` variable wouldn't contain an active connection, so the `Close` would fail. This is where object tests are used, so the `Close` could be modified to the following:

```
if (conn != null)
  conn.Close();
```

If an error occurs, `conn` wouldn't be assigned a value and would be `null`, so `conn` is tested before being closed. If it is not `null`, the connection can be closed. You'll learn more about this topic in Chapter 15.

Logical Operators

Logical operators allow the combination of expressions. The operators are as follows:

Operator	Actiond
`&&`	True if both sides of the expression are true.
`||`	True if either side of the expression is true, or if both sides of the expression are true.
`^`	True if only one side of the expression is true.
`!`	Negates the expression.

All except `!` require two expressions, in the following form:

```
LeftExpression Operator RightExpression
```

The following table should make the result more obvious.

Operator	LeftExpression	RightExpression	Result
`&&`	true	true	true
	true	false	false
	false	true	false
	false	false	false
`||`	true	true	true
	true	false	true
	false	true	true
	false	false	false
`^`	true	true	false
	true	false	true
	false	true	true
	false	false	false

One important thing to know about testing expressions is that when you have multiple expressions, not all of them might be evaluated because expression testing can stop if one of the expressions can guarantee a result. For example, consider the following code:

```
string Name = "Dave";

if (Name == "Dave" || Name == "Dan")
{
  // name is either Dave or Dan
}
```

Here, `Name` is first checked to see if it is `Dave`. It is, so the second expression (the check for `Dan`) is never done — it's not needed because it won't affect the result. For example, imagine instead of a simple test for a name, you called a function that updated a database:

```
if (User.IsInRole("Admin") && UserAudit("Admin")) Then
  ' user is an admin and their details have been updated
End If
```

This would only call the `UserAudit` function if the user is in the `Admin` role. Using `&&` means that if the first part of the test fails, there is no point evaluating the second part, so it is never run.

Another time when this is useful is when you need to see if a property of an object has a value — you only want to check if the object actually exists, not if it is set to `null`. For example, consider the following code, where data is fetched from a database and then some action needs to be performed only if some rows were returned:

```
SqlDataReader rdr;
rdr = DataLayer.GetProducts();

if (rdr != null && rdr.HasRows)
```

Assume that the database access fails for some reason, and `rdr` is set to a null value — that is, `null`. First the check for `null` is done, and this test returns `false` — `rdr` is `null` — and because it is `false`, the second test isn't done. There's no need because the first is `false` and the entire expression can never be `true`.

Operator Precedence

Operators aren't limited to just one or two expressions, and they can be combined in a multitude of ways. Before doing this, however, you need to understand that there is an order of precedence, so the result you get might not be what you expected. This is the same as the order of preference you learned in math all those years ago. Consider this simple expression:

```
1 + 2 * 3
```

This returns 7 because multiplication has a higher precedence than addition. You can use parentheses to force a change in order:

```
(1 + 2) * 3
```

This returns 9 because the expression in parentheses is evaluated first. It's always a good idea to include parentheses in your expressions because it makes your intentions clear, and this is certainly a good thing when you (or someone else) looks at your code later.

If you don't use parentheses, the order of precedence is as follows, in descending order:

- Unary negation (-)
- Multiplication and division (*, /)
- Modulus (%)
- Addition and subtraction (+, -) and string concatenation (+)
- Arithmetic bitshift (<<, >>)
- Comparison (=, <>, <, <=, >, <=)
- Negation (!)
- Conjunction (&&)
- Disjunction (||, ^)

This chapter hasn't covered all of these operators because some of them you won't use very often, or they are used in more advanced techniques. They were included in the preceding list just so that you know where they fit into the order.

Decisions

Decisions are how you make code react to data, usually from a database or user input. You've already seen plenty of decisions throughout the book, and in this chapter, logical operators covered how expressions play an important part of the decision-making process. Decisions can be made in two ways, and which way you use depends on the number of values an expression can be. For example, if an expression can return one of two values (`true` or `false`), the `if` statement is used. If the decision is a selection among a number of choices (perhaps the delivery method from the Wrox United shop), the `switch` statement is used.

Single Selections

Single selections are based on the `if` statement, which always has two parts. The first is the expression being tested, which will result in a `true` or `false` value, and the expression is always contained with parenthesis. The second is the block of code to be executed if the expression is `true`. The syntax is as follows:

```
if (condition)
  // code to run if condition is true
```

This syntax is suitable if there is only one line of code to run if the condition is `true`. If there are multiple lines of code, you need to enclose the lines of code within curly brackets. For example:

```
if (condition)
{
  // code to run if condition is true
  // more code to run
  // yet more code
}
```

The preceding two examples test a single condition and only run code if the condition is `true`. It is important to understand that the multiple lines of code to be run must be enclosed within curly brackets — the indentation doesn't have anything to do with the actual code run. For example, consider the following:

```
if (User.IsAuthenticated)
  MemberDiscount = 0.01;
  JoinFlag = true;
```

In the preceding code, if the `IsAuthenticated` property of the `User` object is true, then the `MemberDiscount` is set to `10%`. Even though the `JoinFlag` line is indented the same as the member discount line, it is not part of the `if` statement — `JoinFlag` will always be set to `true`, whether or not the user is authenticated. In effect, this code is as follows:

```
if (User.IsAuthenticated)
  MemberDiscount = 0.01;
JoinFlag = true;
```

To ensure that both lines are part of the `if` statement, they should be enclosed within curly brackets:

```
if (User.IsAuthenticated)
{
  MemberDiscount = 0.01;
  JoinFlag = true;
}
```

Some people use these curly brackets even if they only have a single line of code to be run for the `if` statement. It doesn't slow the code down at all, and it does make your intentions explicitly clear. For example:

```
if (User.IsAuthenticated)
{
  MemberDiscount = 0.01;
}
JoinFlag = true;
```

Another form of selection is as follows:

```
if (condition)
  // code to run if condition is true
else
  // code to run if the condition is false
```

This tests a single condition but has code for both the true and false situations. This is only suitable if both the `true` and `false` pieces of code have a single line to run, but the use of the curly braces can be used in either of the code blocks:

```
if (condition)
{
  // code to run if condition is true
  // more code to run
}
else
  // code to run if the condition is false
```

Alternatively, you could write the following:

```
if (condition)
  // code to run if condition is true
else
{
  // code to run if the condition is false
  // more code to run
}
```

Yet another way you could write it is as follows:

```
if (condition)
{
  // code to run if condition is true
  // more code to run
}
else
{
  // code to run if the condition is false
  // more code to run
}
```

All of these examples show an either/or situation, with just two blocks of code. For multiple tests, you can use the following:

```
if (condition)
  // code to run if condition is true
else if (condition1)
  // code to run if condition1 is true
else
  // code to run if no conditions were true
```

There can be any number of `else if` conditions.

Consider Wrox United, where the club sends out a newsletter, but only to those fan club members who have ticked the check box when they entered their details. The user settings are stored in the `Profile` object, which was shown in Chapter 5:

```
if (Profile.Mailings == true)
  // send the newsletter to this person
```

This is a simple case, where there is only one expression being tested, and one set of code to run.

If some code needs to be run when the expression is `false`, the `else` statement can be used:

```
if (Profile.Mailings == true)
  // send the newsletter to this person
else
  // don't send the newsletter
```

The `else` and `if` statements can be used together to choose among several different expressions. For example:

```
if (Profile.IsNewUser)
  // send introductory mail
else if (Profile.Mailings == true)
  // send the newsletter to this person
else
  // don't send the newsletter
```

In this example, the expressions first check to see if the member is a new user — that is, if they have only just joined and haven't had any mailings yet. If so, the introductory mail is sent. If the first expression is `false`, that is they aren't a new user, then the next expression is checked — do they require mailings? If so, then that code block is run, and if none of the expressions are `true`, the `else` block is run. If a condition tests true, the appropriate code block is run and no more conditions are tested — the `if` statement ends.

Multiple Selections

For selections where the expression can be one of a number of possible answers, the `if` statement can become unwieldy. For example, consider the Wrox United shop where you can buy a range of branded merchandise. Currently items are sent using the standard postal service, but what if the club wanted to offer different delivery methods, perhaps by way of a drop-down list:

```
string[] delivery = {"Next Day Post", "3 Day Post", "Courier", "International"};
DeliveryDropDownList.DataSource = delivery;
DeliveryDropDownList.DataBind();
```

Maybe the data is from an array, or more likely from a database where the delivery type and associated cost are both included. When the total price is calculated, though, different action needs to be taken — perhaps to instruct the packing department which box type to use, or maybe to interface directly with the delivery company's tracking system. Using the `if` statement would result in the following code:

```
string del = DeliveryDropDownList.SelectedValue;
if (del == "Next Day Post")
  // pack in a normal box and stick lots of stamps on it
else if (del == "3 Day post")
  // pack in a normal box and stick one stamp on it
else if (del == "Courier")
  // pack in a courier specific box and book a pickup
Else
  // pack in a large create and take to the freight company
```

You can see that all those `else if` statements and the layout make this hard to read. In situations like this, it's best to use the `switch` statement, which would turn the preceding code into the following:

```
switch (DeliveryDropDownList.SelectedValue)
{
case "Next Day Post":
  // pack in a normal box and stick lots of stamps on it
  break;

case "3 Day post":
```

```
    // pack in a normal box and stick one stamp on it
    break;

  case "Courier":
    // pack in a courier specific box and book a pickup
    break;

  default:
    // pack in a large create and take to the freight company
    break;
  }
```

This code is much neater, easier to read, and less error prone. It works in a similar way to the previous example, where the expression is on the first line — the selected value from the drop-down list. This is then compared to each of the values in the `case` statements, starting at the top and working down. The first match causes the code block under that `case` statement to be executed, and all other `case` statements are ignored. If there is no match, the code block under the `default` statement is run.

The `switch` statement allows matching multiple selections or ranges. The syntax for this is as follows:

```
switch (condition)
{
case test1:
case test2:
  // code to run if condition matches test1 or test2
  break;

case test3:
case test4:
case test5:
  // code to run if condition matches test3, test4, or test5
  break;

default:
  // code to run if the condition matches no tests
  break;
}
```

In this syntax, the same block of code will be run for tests 1 and 2, as will the same code for tests 3, 4, and 5. Anything that doesn't match these tests will run the code under the default section.

Loops

Loops provide a way to repeat actions, either a fixed number of times or until some condition is met. The decision of which loop to use depends on whether you know in advance how many times you need to loop, or whether some external factor influences this. For example, when a `DataReader` object provides a way to read through some records from a database, this has a `Read` method that returns `false` when there are no more records. This is a case of not knowing in advance the number of times you need to loop.

The while Loop

To perform looping until some condition is met, you can use the While or Do loops, both of which are dependent upon an expression. Take the While loop first, using the case of data from a database:

```
SqlConnection conn = new SqlConnection("...");
SqlCommand cmd = new SqlCommand("SELECT * FROM Products", conn);
SqlDataReader rdr = cmd.ExecuteReader();

while (rdr.Read())
{
  // do something with the data record
}
rdr.Close();
```

Ignore the SQL statement, because it's not that important for this example. All that's important is that a number of records will be returned when the SQL command is run. This statement is simple — the while loop continues execution of its code block while the condition is true. The Read method returns true if it has a record, and false if it doesn't, so this loop continues until there are no more records. So, the first time the while statement is encountered, the expression is tested. If it is true, the code in the while block is executed, and when the closing curly bracket (}) is encountered, the loop starts again, testing the expression once more. This continues until the expression is false, in which case, processing continues with the statement after the closing curly bracket. This happens regardless of the initial value of the condition, so if the condition is initially false, the contents of the loop are never executed.

If you need to stop processing a loop, that is, break out of it in the middle, you can use the break statement. For example:

```
while (rdr.Read())
{
  if (rdr["ItemCost"] < 0)
    break;
}
```

Like the if statement, while can be used without curly braces if the code to be run consists of only a single line. For example:

```
while (rdr.Read())
  Console.WriteLine(rdr["Column1"].ToString());
```

Because the code block only consists of a single line, no brackets are needed. However, this could be written as follows:

```
while (rdr.Read())
{
  Console.WriteLine(rdr["Column1"].ToString());
}
```

Brackets would be needed if multiple lines were to be run within the code:

```
while (rdr.Read())
{
  Console.WriteLine(rdr["Column1"].ToString());
  Console.WriteLine(rdr["Column2"].ToString());
}
```

The `while` loop tests the condition before the loop starts, which means that the code block for the loop might never get executed. To guarantee at least one execution, you can use the `do` loop with the condition at the end:

```
do
  // loop contents
while (condition);
```

Or if you need multiple lines run, you use the following:

```
do
{
  // loop contents
}
while (condition);
```

Because the condition is not tested until after the loop contents have been executed the first time, this type of loop is not suitable for use with a `DataReader` object. For example, you cannot do this:

```
do
{
  if (rdr["ItemCost"] < 0)
    break;
}
while (rdr.Read());
```

Although this is perfectly valid, the code will fail unless `Read` has already been called. The reason for this is that when a `DataReader` object is first opened, it doesn't point at the first record, but rather before it. So the act of calling `Read` moves to the first record. In the preceding code, if no `Read` has been called, the access to `rdr["ItemCost"]` will fail because there will not be a valid record.

The for Loop

The `for` loop is useful when the number of iterations is known, and is most often used when counting through numeric values or performing some action a set number of times. For example:

```
for (int counter=0; counter < 10; counter++)
  ' loop code
```

The syntax for this is as follows:

```
for (starting condition; test condition; counter change)
```

The starting condition sets the starting point of the loop. It can include the variable declaration, but it doesn't have to (although this does affect the scope of the variable — a topic you'll be seeing later in the "Variable Scope and Lifetime" section). For example, consider the following loop:

```
for (int counter=0; counter < 10; counter++)
```

This loop is equivalent to the following loop:

```
int counter;
for (counter=0; counter < 10; counter++)
```

The loop will continue while the test condition is true, so the preceding examples will loop while the `counter` variable is less than 10. The counter change section changes the `counter` value. In the examples, it adds one each time around the loop (remember that `++` is a shortcut for adding 1 to a variable). Loops can go down as well as up. Here the `counter` starts at 10 and decreases by 1 every time around the loop (`--` subtracts 1 from a variable) — the loop will stop when `counter` reaches 0:

```
for (int counter=10; counter > 0; counter--)
```

Like the `while` and `do` loops, `for` loops can be exited during processing:

```
for (int counter=0; counter < 10; counter++)
{
  // loop code

  if (SomeFunction(counter))
    break;

  // loop code
}
```

Here, if `SomeFunction` returns `true`, the loop is executed directly. Any code below the `break` statement is ignored.

The foreach Loop

The `foreach` loop is used for looping through collections or arrays and has a variety of uses, and unlike the `for` loop, you don't need to know in advance the number of times the loop will run. Regardless of what you're looping through, the syntax is the same:

```
foreach (Type LoopVariable in Collection)
{
  // code to run in loop
}
```

The parts of this are as follows:

- `Collection` is the object containing the items to be looped through. It doesn't have to be a collection (from `System.Collections`), but it can be an array.
- `LoopVariable` is the name of the variable that will be assigned to each individual entry from `Collection`.
- `Type` is the data type of `LoopVariable`.

For example, consider the following code that loops through a string array:

```
string[] Names = {"Dave", "Dan", "Chris", "Chris", "John"};
string AllNames;

foreach (string Name in Names)
  AllNames += Name + " ";
```

This first creates an array of names, plus a variable to hold all of the names concatenated. When the loop starts, `Name` is assigned to the first entry in the array, `Dave`, and this is appended to the `AllNames` variable. The next time around the loop, `Name` is assigned to the next entry in the array, `Dan`, and so on. When all items in the array have been processed, the loop ends.

Like the `for` statement, there is a second form of this loop where the loop variable is declared outside of the loop:

```
string Name;
foreach (Name in Names)
  AllNames += Name + " ";
```

For the purposes of the loop, this is exactly the same as declaring the variable in the loop itself, but it does affect the scope of the variable (more on that in the "Variable Scope and Lifetime" section).

Collections and lists are used a lot in .NET programming, so `foreach` is very useful. In Wrox United, `foreach` is used as part of the shop, when the checkout is reached (this is `Checkout.aspx`). The shop allows you to buy multiple items, and these are put into a shopping cart — this is a custom object called `Cart`, which contains a collection of `CartItem` objects. You look at the creation of the shopping cart later, but when you check out, the items in the cart need to be added to the database, and because it is a collection, `foreach` is ideal.

This chapter won't go into the checkout function in complete detail, but here's what you have:

- A `ShoppingCart` object that contains the cart. This is stored in the `Profile` as `Cart` (the profile is covered in Chapter 5).
- A collection of `CartItem` objects. This is stored as the `Items` property of the `ShoppingCart`.

To iterate through the items in the cart, you could use the following code:

```
foreach (CartItem item in Profile.Cart.Items)
{
}
```

Each time through the loop, `item` would contain the actual item from the cart. When the user proceeds to the checkout, you need to do the following:

- Create an order in the database, adding it into the `Orders` table.
- Loop through the items in the cart and add each item to the `OrderLines` table.

This sounds like a lot of work, and is actually quite a lot of code (around 80 lines, including comments), but it is really simple. It builds on some of the data techniques discussed in Chapter 8, and though those aren't covered in detail here, the code should be familiar. Here's where the actual items from the cart are added to the database:

```
cmd.CommandText = "INSERT INTO OrderLines(OrderID, ProductID, Quantity, Price) " +
                  "VALUES (@OrderID, @ProductID, @Quantity, @Price)";
cmd.Parameters.Clear();
cmd.Parameters.Add("@OrderID", SqlDbType.Int);
cmd.Parameters.Add("@ProductID", SqlDbType.Int);
cmd.Parameters.Add("@Quantity", SqlDbType.Int);
cmd.Parameters.Add("@Price", SqlDbType.Money);

cmd.Parameters["@OrderID"].Value = OrderID;
foreach (CartItem item in Profile.Cart.Items)
{
  cmd.Parameters["@ProductID"].Value = item.ProductID;
  cmd.Parameters["@Quantity"].Value = item.Quantity;
  cmd.Parameters["@Price"].Value = item.Price;

  cmd.ExecuteNonQuery();
}
```

The first line simply sets the SQL statement used to insert the items, and the following lines create the parameters and set the `OrderID`. The object `cmd` is a `SqlCommand` object, with an associated connection. Within the loop, the details of each `item` are copied to the parameters, and then the query is executed — this occurs for each order item, so the SQL statement happens each time. After all of the items have been added to the database, the `Items` collection of the shopping cart is cleared.

Give all of this looping and testing a try, by working out how well Wrox United is doing. The following Try It Out has you loop through the fixtures to see how many goals have been scored and how many games have been won, lost, or drawn.

Try It Out Looping and Making Decisions

1. Create a new Web Form called **Decisions.aspx** and set this as the start page. Remember to place the code in a separate file when you create the Web Form.
2. Add six labels and some text, so the page looks like Figure 9-7. You can just type the text directly onto the page, and make sure you add the labels in top to bottom order, so `Label1` is at the top and `Label6` is at the bottom.

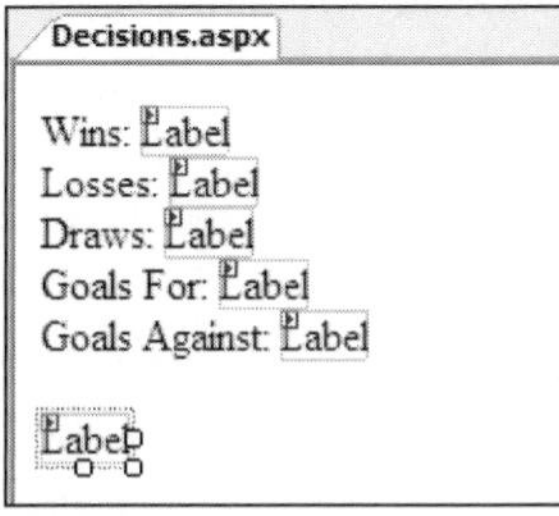

Figure 9-7

3. View the code file for the page, and at the top of the file add the following two `using` statements (don't worry about what these are — they're covered later in the "Namespaces" section):

```
using System.Data;
using System.Data.SqlClient;
```

4. Create the `Page_Load` event procedure by double-clicking the form in design view. In the `Page_Load` event, add the following code (remember you can copy it from the finished samples if you don't want to type it all):

```
SqlConnection conn = new
  SqlConnection(ConfigurationManager.ConnectionStrings[
  "WroxUnited"].ConnectionString);
SqlCommand cmd = new SqlCommand("select * from Fixtures", conn);
SqlDataReader rdr;

int wins = 0;
int losses = 0;
int draws = 0;
int goalsFor = 0;
int goalsAgainst = 0;
int winRatio;

conn.Open();
rdr = cmd.ExecuteReader(CommandBehavior.CloseConnection);

while (rdr.Read())
{
  goalsFor += Convert.ToInt32(rdr["GoalsFor"]);
  goalsAgainst += Convert.ToInt32(rdr["GoalsAgainst"]);

  if (goalsFor > goalsAgainst)
    wins++;
  else if (goalsFor < goalsAgainst)
    losses++;
  else
    draws++;
}

Label1.Text = wins.ToString();
Label2.Text = losses.ToString();
Label3.Text = draws.ToString();
Label4.Text = goalsFor.ToString();
Label5.Text = goalsAgainst.ToString();

if (losses == 0)
{
  Label6.Text = "No losses - a perfect season.";
  return;
}

winRatio = Convert.ToInt32((wins / losses) * 10);

switch (winRatio)
```

```
{
  case 0:
    Label6.Text = "No wins. Relegation is a certainty.";
    break;
  case 1:
  case 2:
    Label6.Text = "Less than 20%. Very poor.";
    break;
  case 3:
  case 4:
  case 5:
    Label6.Text = "Under half. Could do better.";
    break;
  case 6:
  case 7:
    Label6.Text = "Winning more than losing. Excellent.";
    break;
  default:
    Label6.Text = "A high ratio - near the top of the table.";
    break;
}
```

5. Modify the `web.config` file, changing the `<connectionStrings/>` section so that it is the same as the one for the Wrox United site. You can copy this section from `web.config` in the Wrox United site to save the typing — it's the section that looks like this:

```
  <connectionStrings>
     <add name="WroxUnited" connectionString="Data Source=.\SQLEXPRESS;
AttachDbFilename=|DataDirectory|WroxUnited.mdf;Integrated Security=True;User
Instance=True"/>
  </connectionStrings>
```

6. Save the files and run the page to see Figure 9-8.

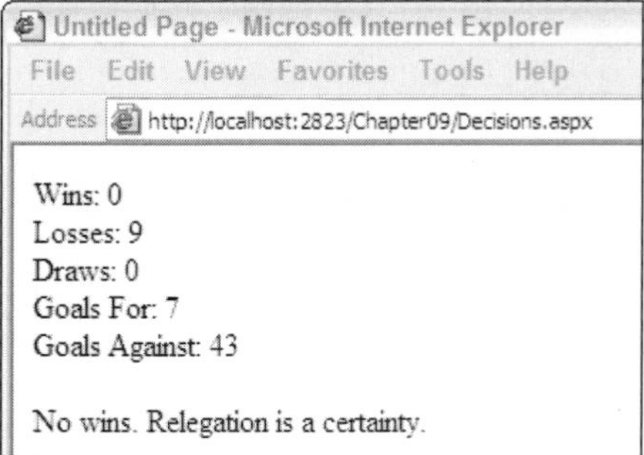

Figure 9-8

The output isn't spectacular, but it's the code that's interesting, so take a look at how it works.

How It Works

First you have the variable declarations, starting with a connection to the database, a command to fetch the fixtures, and a reader to iterate through the fixtures:

```
SqlConnection conn = new
  SqlConnection(ConfigurationManager.ConnectionStrings[
  "WroxUnited"].ConnectionString);
SqlCommand cmd = new SqlCommand("select * from Fixtures", conn);
SqlDataReader rdr;
```

Next you have the variables to hold the counts of the wins, losses, draws, and goals scored, and the win ratio:

```
int wins = 0;
int losses = 0;
int draws = 0;
int goalsFor = 0;
int goalsAgainst = 0;
int winRatio;
```

After the variables are declared, the database is opened and the data fetched:

```
conn.Open();
rdr = cmd.ExecuteReader(CommandBehavior.CloseConnection);
```

With the data reader full of data, the loop is started; the `Read` method returns a Boolean value of `false` when it has read the last record. This will continue until there are no more records:

```
while (rdr.Read())
{
```

Within the loop, the totals are incremented, the values from the reader being converted into integers before being used to increment the totals:

```
  goalsFor += Convert.ToInt32(rdr["GoalsFor"]);
  goalsAgainst += Convert.ToInt32(rdr["GoalsAgainst"]);
```

Now comes the first decision, incrementing the number of wins, losses, and draws:

```
  if (goalsFor > goalsAgainst)
    wins++;
  else if (goalsFor < goalsAgainst)
    losses++;
  else
    draws++;
}
```

After the loop has finished, the totals can be displayed in the labels:

```
Label1.Text = wins.ToString();
Label2.Text = losses.ToString();
```

```
Label3.Text = draws.ToString();
Label4.Text = goalsFor.ToString();
Label5.Text = goalsAgainst.ToString();
```

The ratio of wins to losses needs to be counted next (despite the fact that given the team's performance you can almost assume this will be 0). However, before doing the calculation, you need to ensure that the number of losses isn't 0, otherwise a division-by-zero exception would occur. So if the number of losses is 0, a message is displayed and `Return` forces the `Page_Load` event handler to exit:

```
if (losses == 0)
{
  Label6.Text = "No losses - a perfect season.";
  return;
}
```

If the team has lost at least one match, the ratio is calculated — this will be a number between 0 and 10 to represent the percentage groups:

```
winRatio = Convert.ToInt32((wins / losses) * 10);
```

Now the message can be displayed depending on the win ratio. Remember that the `case` statements are tried in the order in which they are declared, so the `default` will match a win ratio of higher than 80%:

```
switch (winRatio)
{
  case 0:
    Label6.Text = "No wins. Relegation is a certainty.";
    break;
  case 1:
  case 2:
    Label6.Text = "Less than 20%. Very poor.";
    break;
  case 3:
  case 4:
  case 5:
    Label6.Text = "Under half. Could do better.";
    break;
  case 6:
  case 7:
    Label6.Text = "Winning more than losing. Excellent.";
    break;
  default:
    Label6.Text = "A high ratio - near the top of the table.";
    break;
}
```

All of these statements, the loops and decisions, are fairly simple on their own, but together they show you the power of what code can do. You can build up functionality with more and more statements, as the complexity of your applications requires.

The next section introduces the topic of namespaces, a fundamental way in which code can be arranged.

Namespaces

Namespaces are a way to logically group related code. A *namespace* is simply a name, and that name can include periods to provide grouping. For example, the namespace for the data handling code of ADO.NET is in `System.Data`, whereas the SQL Server-specific code is in `System.Data.SqlClient`. All of the .NET data types you saw earlier are in the `System` namespace. Namespaces can also be created for your own code, so for the Wrox United code the namespace is `Wrox.Web`. This is defined in the classes within the App_Code directory.

Namespaces are important for several reasons:

- Grouping related code means it's easier to find related items. For example, if you want to find all of the data handling code, you know it's located within the `System.Data` namespaces. This can be useful when using the documentation.
- Namespaces provide more readable code, because if the namespace is known, only the data type is required to define a variable. For example, consider declaring a `SqlConnection` object without having the namespace known to the program:

```
System.Data.SqlClient.SqlConnection conn;
```

  This requires more typing as well as being hard to read. However with the namespace known, this can be reduced to:

```
SqlConnection conn;
```

- Namespaces allow both the compiler and IntelliSense to find the variable types.

To use a namespace, you use the `using` statement:

```
using System.Data;
using System.Data.SqlClient;
```

You can test to see if this is working by taking these lines out of the sample in the previous Try It Out. See what happens in the code editor — IntelliSense attempts to indicate a problem, and you'll receive a compiler error if you try to run the page.

Within your code, you can declare namespaces by use of the `Namespace` statement — you place this around your classes. For example:

```
namespace Wrox.Web
{
  // class goes here
}
```

You can use the same namespace in multiple files, so you can split your code into physical files (a file for each class is a good idea), and the namespace spans those classes. The namespace is logical and not physical — it isn't restricted to a single file.

Now that you know how code works and how it can be organized, you can move onto the subject of classes, a topic that underlies the whole of .NET.

Working with Classes

Object orientation sounds complex and scary, one of those things people tell you that you have to master before you become a proper programmer. Ignore them — there's no such thing as a proper programmer, it's a term that doesn't really mean anything. Object orientation is worth learning though, and it will make you a better programmer — everyone can be a better programmer, and this is just one step along the ladder. It's important not to worry about this topic, because object orientation is actually quite simple. It can get complex, but at the basic level, it's easy to get into and doesn't require a degree in rocket science (unless you work at NASA, in which case knowledge of astrophysics might be useful).

Throughout the book you've already seen plenty of objects. In fact, everything you've seen has been an object: the ASP.NET controls are objects, data access is done via objects, ASP.NET pages are objects, and even the data types are objects. This is one of the underpinnings of .NET — everything is an object. The following paragraphs define a few terms so you can see how these fit in with the existing objects and new objects you create.

First is the difference between objects, classes, and instances. A *class* is a template for an object; it defines what the object will be able to do — think of it as a cookie cutter, defining the shape of the cookie. An *object* or *instance* is a class that's been created — it's the actual cookie, after it's freed from the cutter. Look at these terms with an example using `SqlConnection`:

```
SqlConnection conn;
```

This defines the variable `conn` as being of type `SqlConnection`. As it stands, however, this isn't usable, because it just defines the type of object — the object doesn't yet exist. You've only defined the shape of the cookie cutter, and haven't actually cut the cookie. To create the cookie, create an instance of the object:

```
conn = new SqlConnection();
```

This can also be done at declaration time:

```
SqlConnection conn = new SqlConnection();
```

Use of the `new` keyword creates the instance, and after it is created, the object becomes usable.

The *properties* of a class define the characteristics of that class. For example, the `SqlConnection` object has a property called `ConnectionString`, which defines the details of the database being connected to. Another property is `State`, which indicates what state the connection is in (open, closed, and so on):

```
if (conn.State == ConnectionState.Open)
{
  // The connection is open
}
```

The *methods* of a class define the actions that can be performed, so for the `SqlConnection`, you can `Open` or `Close` it:

```
conn.Open();
```

The *events* of a class provide the user of the class with information about the status. For example, `SqlConnection` has two useful events: `InfoMessage` and `StateChange`. The first is *raised* (or *fired*) when SQL Server returns a warning or some informational message, and the second is raised when the `State` is changed, such as when the connection is closed.

Creating Classes

You can create classes in ASP.NET pages, but if you are creating the class for a special purpose, it's best to use a separate file and location. The best place for these is in the `App_Code` directory, a special directory into which class files can be put. Using this directory enables you to keep your class files together, as well as having them automatically compiled by ASP.NET. You look at creating this later, but for now take a look at the structure of a class. The syntax is as follows:

```
[Accessor] class ClassName
{
  // class contents
}
```

The `ClassName` can be anything you want, but like variable naming, it's best to use something sensible. For example, the shopping cart item is a class called `CartItem`, and the cart itself is called `ShoppingCart`.

The `Accessor` defines the accessibility of the class; that is where the class can be seen from. This can be one of the values detailed in the following table:

Accessor	Description
`public`	No access restrictions.
`private`	The class is only accessible from within its declaration context.
`protected`	The class is only accessible from within its own class or derived classes.
`internal`	The class is only accessible from within the assembly that contains it.
`protected internal`	The class is only accessible from within its own class, a derived class, or its containing assembly.

It's best not to worry too much about these for the moment. As a general rule, if you create a class that's going to be used in ASP.NET pages you should use `public`. So your shopping cart is as follows:

```
public class ShoppingCart
{
}
```

Constructors

The *constructor* is a special method that runs when the class is instantiated, and it allows you to set the initial state of the class when it's created. The constructor is always named the same as the class. For example, the shopping cart with the constructor is highlighted here:

```
public class ShoppingCart
{
  private DateTime _dateCreated;
  private List<CartItem> _items;

  public ShoppingCart()
  {
    _items = new List<CartItem>;
    _dateCreated = DateTime.Now;
  }
}
```

What this constructor does is create another object — a new `List` of `CartItem` objects. This is what the cart items are stored in — it's a collection of `CartItem` objects (you look at this in more detail in the "Generics" section). After that's created, the initial creation date is set. You could use this `ShoppingCart` class like so:

```
ShoppingCart cart = new ShoppingCart();
```

This would create a new instance, and you'd know that the items collection had also been created, ready for you to add items.

The `CartItem` class shows another aspect of constructors — overloading:

```
public class CartItem
{
  private double _lineTotal;
  private double _price;
  private int _productID;
  private string _productImageUrl;
  private string _productName;
  private int _quantity;

  public CartItem
  {
  }

  public CartItem(int ProductID, string ProductName,
    string ProductImageUrl, int Quantity, double Price)
  {
    this._productID = ProductID;
    this._productName = ProductName;
    this._productImageUrl = ProductImageUrl;
    this._quantity = Quantity;
    this._price = Price;
    this._lineTotal = Quantity * Price;
  }
}
```

Here there are two constructors. The first, with no parameters, does nothing, and the second accepts parameters containing the details for an item being bought. Don't worry too much about the specific syntax of the parameters, because they're examined in detail during the discussion of methods. The important point to note is that the constructor is overloaded — that is, there are two of them. You can have overloaded constructors (and methods) as long as the *signature* differs. A signature is what defines the uniqueness of a constructor or method — this includes its name, its return type, and the type and order of the parameters. Because these two constructors have different signatures, they are both allowed.

Having two constructors means the class can be created in two ways. Either with this:

```
CartItem item = new CartItem();
```

Or with this:

```
Cartitem item = new CartItem(1, "Scarf", "images\scarf.jpg", 1, 4.95);
```

The first constructor would create an empty cart item, ready for you to fill in the details, and the second constructor creates a cart item with the details already filled in. These details are passed in as parameters within the parentheses, and these get mapped to the parameters declared in the `New` method.

Properties

Properties are used to control the characteristics of a class, or to expose to users of the class some internal values. For example, consider the `CartItem` class — if the first constructor is used, how would the details of the item being bought be set? The variables can't be accessed directly because they are `private`, so they can't be seen outside of the class. Properties are the answer, and these would be created in the following manner:

```
public class CartItem
{
  private double _lineTotal;
  private double _price;
  private int _productID;
  private string _productImageUrl;
  private string _productName;
  private int _quantity;

  public int ProductID
  {
    get
    {
      return _ProductID;
    }
    set
    {
      _productID = value;
    }
  }
}
```

Break this down and look at the parts. First you have the definition of the property itself, by use of `public` followed by the data type and the name of the property. So it's like a variable declaration, but it contains some content as well—`public` means it's going to be accessible outside of the class, which is exactly what you want. In fact, it's the reason for creating the property in the first place, to make the internal variable accessible.

Next comes the bit that allows read access to the property—the `get` section (often called the *getter*), which simply returns the value of the internal private variable:

```
    get
    {
      return _ProductID;
    }
```

`get` is a special keyword that allows the property to be read. When you access a property like this, the `get` part of the property is run:

```
int pid = item.ProductID;
```

Next is `set` section. The `set` (or *setter* as it's sometimes called) allows the property to be written to, and the value being written is held in the `value` variable, which is a special variable that is automatically defined:

```
    set
    {
      _productID = value;
    }
  }
```

To set a property value, you do this:

```
item.ProductID = 123;
```

When this is executed, the `set` part of the property is run. In this case, the value of `123` would be automatically assigned to the `value` variable before the `set` part of the property is run. Remember that C# is context-insensitive, meaning that lines can be combined. For example, you might see properties defined like this:

```
public int ProductID
{
  get {return _productID;}
  set {_productID = value;}
}
```

Here all parts of the `get` have been combined onto one line, as have all parts of the `set`. This has no effect on the code apart from readability.

These forms of defining properties are the same for all properties, with only the name and data type changing. For example, a property for the product name would be:

```
public string ProductName
{
  get
  {
    return _Productname;
  }
  set
  {
    _productName = value;
  }
}
```

With these `ProductID` and `ProductName` properties in place, the `CartItem` could be used like so:

```
CartItem item = new CartItem();

item.ProductID = 1;
item.ProductName = "The WroxUnited Scarf"
```

This would create the class and set the properties. When setting these properties the setter part of the property is called, and the value to be set (`1` in this case of the `ProductID`) is passed into the setter as the variable `value`.

To read from the properties, you could do the following:

```
IDTextBox.Text = item.ProductID.ToString();
NameTextBox.Text = item.ProductName;
```

The first line reads from the property, converting to a string, because the `Text` property of the `TextBox` is a `string` type. When the property is accessed, the getter is called, which simply returns the value from the internal variable. For the `ProductID`, this is an `int`, but the `ProductName` property is a `string`, so no conversion is required.

Read-Only Properties

If you want to provide read-only access to a property, and not allow the user of the class to update the property, you can make it read-only, like so:

```
public int ProductID
{
  get
  {
    return _ProductID;
  }
}
```

Only the getter section of the property is included, so this automatically becomes a read-only property, and the value cannot be set. This is exactly what the `LineTotal` property of the `CartItem` does:

```
public double LineTotal()
{
  get
  {
    return _quantity * _price;
  }
}
```

Here you can see that you don't even have a `private` variable. The value returned is simply a calculation.

Because the property is read-only, the value cannot be set, and trying to do so will generate a compile error.

Write-Only Properties

Making a property write-only follows a similar procedure to read-only, except only the setter part of the property is used:

```
public int ProductID()
{
  set
  {
    _productID = value;
  }
}
```

With this definition, trying to read from the property would result in a compile error.

Properties Versus Public Variables

While you've been reading the text on properties, you might have been wondering why they are used. Why not just make the internal variables public? Well, you could easily do this:

```
public class CartItem
{
  public int ProductID;
  public string ProductName;
  public string roductImageUrl;
  public int Quantity;
  public double Price;
  public double LineTotal;
}
```

This would work, but is not a good idea because it breaks one of the rules of object orientation—*abstraction*. (There are other rules of object orientation, but they aren't pertinent to this particular topic.) This means that you should abstract functionality, thus hiding the inner workings of the class. The reason for working this way is that it allows you to change how the class works internally without changing how it's used. For example, consider `LineTotal`, which is the `Quantity` multiplied by the `Price`. You have to have some way of calculating the total, and if you use a `public` variable, then where do you put the calculation? It could be done in the constructor, but what about the blank constructor that just creates an empty item? Would you have the user of the class calculate the total, or provide some other function to do it? Neither is a good solution.

Abstraction means that you are providing a simple, guaranteed way to access the functionality of the class, and that the user doesn't have to know about how the class works. You're using properties to hide the internal storage—those private variables are the internal storage, and the properties are just a way for users of the class to access the internal variables.

Abstracting the internal storage with properties enables you to handle the problem of a line total, because the property accessor does the calculation for you. In fact, using this type of abstraction means you could store the internal state of the `CartItem` in any way you pleased, without having to change the code that uses `CartItem`.

There are no strict rules on naming for the private variables that actually store the property values, but an underscore as a prefix is commonly used, as well as a different case. So your property would be `LineTotal`, whereas the internal private variable is `_lineTotal`.

Methods

Methods are the actions of a class, what you use to get the class to perform a task. The `CartItem` class is purely for storage, has no actions, and therefore contains no methods (although technically the constructor is a method). The shopping cart, however, contains methods, because you need to do things like insert, update, and delete items.

Methods fall into two types: those that return a value and those that don't. The first form is useful for performing an action and then returning some result, perhaps whether the action succeeded or not. The second is useful when you don't need a value from the action.

The syntax for a method as follows:

```
[Accessor] DataType FunctionName([parameters])
{
  return value
}
```

The syntax is the same whether or not you are returning a value. If you aren't returning a value, you use the data type of `void`,which is a special data type for methods that simply tells ASP.NET that no value is being returned from the method.

Like classes, the `Accessor` defines the visibility of the method. Use `public` for methods that are visible from everywhere, and use `private` for a method that is used only by the class. Methods accept an optional parameter list, much like constructors.(You'll look at the ins and outs of parameters in more detail soon.)

The difference between a method that returns a value and one that doesn't is minimal. The first difference, as mentioned, is that you use the `void` type for a method that doesn't return a value. Use the shopping cart and examine the methods, starting with deleting items, because that's the simplest:

```
public void DeleteItem(int rowID)
{
  _items.RemoveAt(rowID);
  _lastUpdate = DateTime.Now;
}
```

Here the method takes a single parameter—the index of the row to be deleted. This index is then passed into the `RemoveAt` method of the `_items` collection, which is the collection that stores the cart items. When the item has been removed, the last update time is set. The method could be called like so:

```
Profile.Cart.DeleteItem(2);
```

This would remove the third row. (Remember that arrays and collections start at 0.)

Inserting items into the cart is done with the `Insert` method:

```
public void Insert(int ProductID, double Price, int Quantity,
  string ProductName, string ProductImageUrl)
{
  CartItem NewItem = new CartItem();
  NewItem.ProductID = ProductID;
  NewItem.Quantity = Quantity;
  NewItem.Price = Price;
  NewItem.ProductName = ProductName;
  NewItem.ProductImageUrl = ProductImageUrl;
  _items.Add((CartItem) NewItem);
  _lastUpdate = DateTime.Now;
}
```

This routine accepts five parameters, one for each part of the item (the ID, the price, and so on). Within the routine, a new `CartItem` is created, and the properties are set to the values of the parameters. After all of the parameters are set, the item is added to the `_items` collection and the time is updated.

One problem with the `Insert` method is that it could be called multiple times for the same product, which would result in multiple items in the cart. It would be more sensible to see if the item is already in the cart, and if so, simply add one to the quantity. To do this, you need to search through the collection looking for an item with the same `ProductID`, so a function has been created to do this:

```
private int ItemIndexOfID(int ProductID)
{
  int index = 0;

  foreach (CartItem item in _items)
  {
    if (item.ProductID == ProductID)
      return index;
    index++;
  }
  return -1;
}
```

Here the function accepts the `ProductID` as a parameter and returns an `int`. Within the function, the `_items` collection is looped, and if the `ProductID` of an item matches the supplied `ProductID`, the `return` statement is used to return the index. If the loop ends without having found a match, `-1` is returned. Notice that this function is marked as `private`.That's because it's not going to be used from outside the class.

The `Insert` method can now be changed to the following:

```
public void Insert(int ProductID, double Price, int Quantity,
  string ProductName, string ProductImageUrl)
{
  int ItemIndex = this.ItemIndexOfID(ProductID);
  if (ItemIndex == -1)
  {
    CartItem NewItem = new CartItem();
    NewItem.ProductID = ProductID;
    NewItem.Quantity = Quantity;
    NewItem.Price = Price;
    NewItem.ProductName = ProductName;
    NewItem.ProductImageUrl = ProductImageUrl;
    _items.Add((CartItem) NewItem);
  }
  else
  {
    _items[ItemIndex].Quantity++;
  }
  _lastUpdate = DateTime.Now;
}
```

The method still accepts the same parameters, but the first thing it does is call the private `ItemIndexOfID` to get the index number of the current product. If the index is `-1`, it didn't already exist in the collection and is added. If it does exist, the `Quantity` is increased.

Referencing Internal Variables

There are two ways to access the private internal variables within properties and methods of a class. You can use only the variable name, as shown here:

```
public string ProductName
{
  get
  {
    return _Productname;
  }
  set
  {
    _productName = value;
  }
}
```

Alternatively, you can use an object reference, with the keyword `this`, which means the current instance of the class. For example:

```
public string ProductName
{
  get
  {
    return this._Productname;
  }
```

```
    set
    {
      this._productName = value;
    }
  }
```

There's no real difference between these two uses of internal variables, and you'll see both forms used in help files and examples.

Shared Methods and Properties

With the classes you've seen so far, you have to create an instance of them before they can be used. For certain classes, this can be an overhead that's not really required. For example, consider a class called `Tools` that provides a range of utility methods, one of which is `Log`, to log exceptions:

```
public class Tools
{
  public void Log(string ErrorMessage)
  {
    // log the error
  }
}
```

You could use this class like so:

```
Tools u = new Tools();
u.Log("An exception occurred");
```

The object instance only exists for the purpose of calling the `Log` method. There are no properties to set, so it seems a bit of a waste to have to create the instance, especially if it's only going to be used once. To get around this, you can create shared class members (sometimes called *static* members). For example:

```
public class Tools
{
  public static void Log(string ErrorMessage)
  {
    // log the error
  }
}
```

The introduction of the `Shared` keyword means that a class instance is no longer required, allowing the method to be called like so:

```
Utils.Log("An exception occurred");
```

When you're dealing with utility classes, shared methods are extremely useful. You'll see how the logging features can be implemented in Chapter 15.

Inheritance

Inheritance is another of the key features of objected-oriented software, and works just like real life, where you inherit properties and behavior from your parents. Inheritance can get quite complex, so this section covers only the basics to give you an understanding of what inheritance is and how it works, especially as it's used in all code-behind files. The essentials of inheritance are that one class (the base class) can be inherited by another (the subclass), in which case the subclass automatically has the same methods and properties as the base class. But the subclass can change the behavior if it needs to, or add to it.

ASP.NET uses inheritance as part of its standard programming model, and you probably already have seen this in action. For example, consider a `Default.aspx` Web Form, which would have the following in it:

```
<%@ Page Language="C#" CodeFile="Default.aspx.cs" Inherits="_Default" %>
```

Here you can see the `Inherits` keyword being used, telling you that when the Web Form is compiled, it should inherit its features from the class `_Default`. This class is in the code-behind file:

```
partial class _Default : System.Web.UI.Page
{
   . . .
}
```

Within the code file, inheritance uses the colon (`:`) to separate the class from the class it is inheriting from. So in the preceding example, `_Default` is the new class and `System.Web.UI.Page` is the class being inherited from (which is the base class). This means that the `_Default` class will contain all of the properties and methods that the `System.Web.UI.Page` contains. One thing to notice is the `partial` keyword, which tells the compiler that this class is split across multiple files: the Web Form and the code-behind file.

The following exercise has you use some simple (and rather contrived) examples to show how inheritance works.

Try It Out Classes and Inheritance

1. Create a new class in the `App_Code` directory called **Vehicles.cs**. If the `App_Code` directory doesn't exist, you can create this directory by selecting the top item in the Solution Explorer and using the right mouse button to select Add Folder and then App_Code Folder, as shown in Figure 9-9.

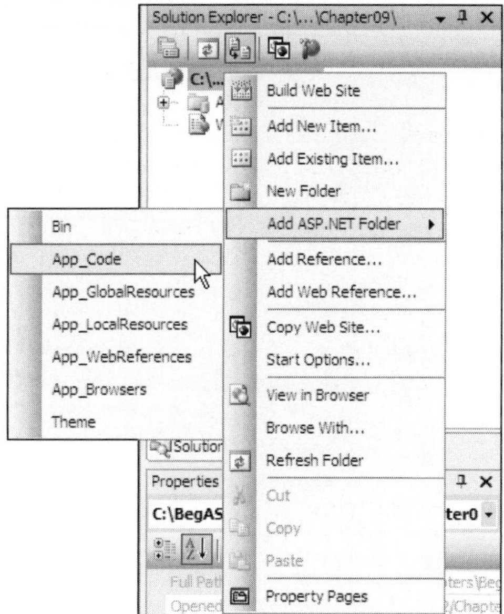

Figure 9-9

2. Delete the existing template class, and create a new one called **Vehicle**, which has properties called `Wheels` and `TopSpeed`, and a method called `Warning`:

```
public class Vehicle
{
  protected int _wheels;
  protected int _topSpeed;
  protected string _warningSound;

  public int Wheels
  {
    get {return _wheels;}
    set {_wheels = value;}
  }

  public int TopSpeed
  {
    get {return _topSpeed;}
    set {_topSpeed = value;}
  }

  public virtual string Warning()
  {
    return _warningSound;
  }
}
```

3. Create another class, in the same file, called **Car**:

```
public class Car : Vehicle
{
  public Car()
  {
    _wheels = 4;
    _topSpeed = 150;
    _warningSound = "Honk";
  }
}
```

4. Create another class, called **Bike**:

```
public class Bike : Vehicle
{
  public Bike()
  {
    _wheels = 2;
    base.TopSpeed = 30;
    _warningSound = "Ring Ring";
  }
}
```

5. Create another class, called **Skateboard**:

```
public class Skateboard : Vehicle
{
  public Skateboard()
  {
    _wheels = 4;
    _topSpeed = 15;
  }
}
```

6. Between the closing bracket of the constructor and the closing bracket of the class, type the following:

```
Public override
```

7. Press the space bar to see that a little helper tip pops up (see Figure 9-10).

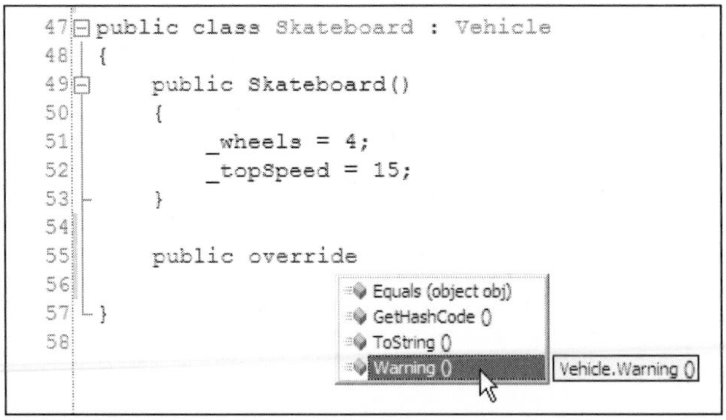

```
public class Skateboard : Vehicle
{
    public Skateboard()
    {
        _wheels = 4;
        _topSpeed = 15;
    }

    public override
                      Equals (object obj)
                      GetHashCode ()
}                     ToString ()
                      Warning ()        Vehicle.Warning ()
```

Figure 9-10

8. Select the `string Warning()` entry and press Enter See how the function is created for you. Delete the existing return line and add a new one:

```
public override string Warning()
{
  return "No warning - you'll have to shout yourself";
}
```

9. Save and close the class file.

10. Create a new Web Form called **Inheritance.aspx**. Add three buttons and three labels, so it looks like Figure 9-11. Make sure the `Label` next to `Wheels` is `Label1`, the `Label` next to `Speed` is `Label2`, and the `Label` next to `Warning` is `Label3`. You can use the `Text` property of the buttons to change the text shown on them.

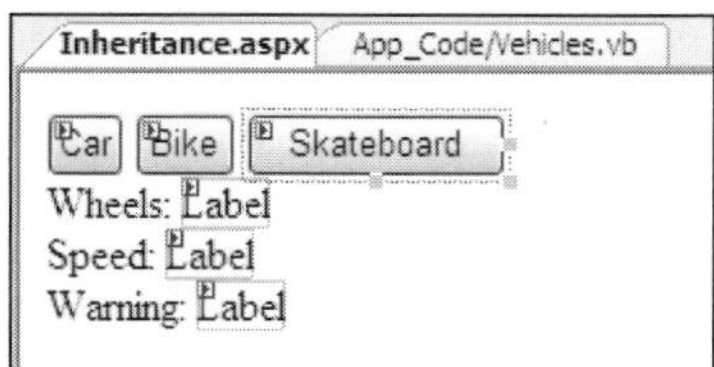

Figure 9-11

11. Create an event handler for the `Click` event for the `Car` button:

```
protected void Button1_Click(object sender, System.EventArgs e)
{
  Car myTransport = new Car();
  Label1.Text = myTransport.Wheels.ToString();
  Label2.Text = myTransport.TopSpeed.ToString();
  Label3.Text = myTransport.Warning();
}
```

12. Create an event handler for the `Bike` button:

```
protected void Button2_Click(object sender, System.EventArgs e)
{
    Bike myTransport = new Bike();
    Label1.Text = myTransport.Wheels.ToString();
    Label2.Text = myTransport.TopSpeed.ToString();
    Label3.Text = myTransport.Warning();
}
```

13. Create an event handler for the `Skateboard` button:

```
protected void Button3_Click(object sender, System.EventArgs e)
{
    Skateboard myTransport = new Skateboard();
    Label1.Text = myTransport.Wheels.ToString();
    Label2.Text = myTransport.TopSpeed.ToString();
    Label3.Text = myTransport.Warning();
}
```

14. In the Solution Explorer, right-click `Inheritance.aspx`, and from the menu, select Set As Start Page.

15. Press F5 to run the page. Click the three buttons and notice what is displayed in the labels.

How It Works

To see how this works, start with the `Vehicle` class. This is similar to what you've seen before, but with a few subtle differences. One of the private variables, `_warningSound`, is not set anywhere—don't worry about that, it's deliberate, and will be used in other classes. Also the private variables are declared as `protected`, meaning that other classes in the same file will be able to access them. This class will be the base class that other classes inherit from. The other difference is that the `Warning` method has a new keyword on it—`virtual`:

```
public virtual string Warning()
{
  return _warningSound;
}
```

A `virtual` method means that inheriting classes can override the method and provide their own implementation. Take a look at the inheriting classes, starting with the `Car`:

```
public class Car : Vehicle
{
  public Car()
  {
    _wheels = 4;
    _topSpeed = 150;
    _warningSound = "Honk";
  }
}
```

This defines a new class, but in the line after the class name, it specifies the class to be inherited from. This means the `Car` automatically has the properties and methods of the base class. The base class hasn't set any values so the car has a constructor to do this, which uses the private variables declared by the base class. It can access those variables because they've been declared as `Protected`.

The `Bike` class is slightly different:

```
public class Bike : Vehicle
{
  public Bike()
  {
    _wheels = 2;
    base.TopSpeed = 30;
    _warningSound = "Ring Ring";
  }
}
```

The way it inherits is the same, but setting the properties is different. For the number of wheels, instead of using the private variable of the base class, the property of the class is used. Even though the current class doesn't define the Wheels property itself, it does have a Wheels property because it is inherited from the base class. For the top speed, the property of the base class is called directly; the keyword base refers to the base class. There is no property for the warning sound, so the private variable is used directly.

All of these methods are acceptable, and you'll see all three used in various pieces of documentation, books, or online tutorials. In general, it's best to use the properties, because that fits with the object-oriented principles discussed earlier.

The Skateboard class is different:

```
public class Skateboard : Vehicle
{
  public Skateboard()
  {
    _wheels = 4;
    _topSpeed = 15;
  }

  public override string Warning()
  {
    return "No warning - you'll have to shout yourself";
  }
}
```

The constructor sets the values for _wheels and _stopSpeed, but not the warning message. The big difference is that the Warning property is overridden, meaning that instead of using the Warning method from the base class, the Skateboard class is defining its own Warning method. This is called *polymorphism*, and allows different classes to have the same methods and properties but with different behavior.

Using these classes is simple:

```
Car myTransport = new Car();
Label1.Text = myTransport.Wheels.ToString();
Label2.Text = myTransport.TopSpeed.ToString();
Label3.Text = myTransport.Warning();
```

This creates the new class and accesses the properties and the methods. Whatever the class type created, you can see that the same properties and methods are available. Even though these classes don't define the properties themselves, inheritance means they have the properties. The same applies to the methods, where the Car and Bike don't define the methods, but the Skateboard does, overriding the existing implementation and providing its own.

Variable Scope and Lifetime

Although it is related to variables, the discussion of scope and lifetime has been left until now because it affects all of the other topics discussed in this chapter. The term *scope* means the degree to which a variable is accessible to other code, and the scope affects the lifetime. You've seen how Private and Public affect the visibility of methods and properties, but may not realize that visibility of variables depends on where they are declared. To make this easier, have a look at some code:

```
public class Class1
{
  private int _variable1;

  private void Method1()
  {
    int variable2;

    _variable1 = 1;
    variable2 = 3;
  }

  private void Method2()
  {
    _variable1 = 2;
  }
}
```

The `variable1` variable _ is declared within the class, outside of any methods, so it can be accessed from any methods and properties. On the other hand, `variable2` is declared within the `Method1` method, so it can only be accessed within `Method1` — no other methods or properties would be able to use it. This is called a *local variable.*

The same rules apply to variables declared within code blocks. For example:

```
int number1;
if (number1 == 15)
{
  int number2;
  number2 += 15;
}
```

Here `number1` is declared outside of the `if` block, and can therefore be used within it. But `number2` is declared within the code block, so it cannot be used outside of the code block. The same rules apply to other code blocks such as loops.

The `foreach` loop also has this:

```
foreach (CartItem item in Cart.Items)
{
}
```

The variable item is declared within the statement itself, but follows the same rule: it can only be accessed from within the loop. Trying to access it outside of the loop would generate a compile error.

Generics

Generics refers to classes and methods that work uniformly on values of different types. Generics are often discussed as an advanced topic, and though some of it is advanced, some of it is simple and easy to use. In fact, one feature of generics is used in the shopping cart. Remember how the cart consists of two classes: the `CartItem` and the `ShoppingCart`, which uses the `CartItem` as a collection.

Many of the collections discussed early in the chapter provide storage for objects — the `Object` being a type. Because they are designed to work with a data type of `Object`, collections can in fact store any data type. However, when you take items out of a collection, they often need to be converted from the `Object` data type to their native data type. This involves extra coding and reduces performance. Another problem results because collections can store any data type, which means you can store any data type in them. If you had a collection to store the `CartItem` objects, you could in fact store strings, numbers, dates, and so forth in the same collection. For example, you could do this:

```
List _items = new List();
CartItem item = new CartItem( . . .);

_items.Add(item);
_items.Add("this isn't a cart item");
_items.Add("65");
```

When you take items out of the collection, you have no idea what data type it is unless you track which objects you put into the list.

To get around this problem, use generics, or more specifically generic collections. These are stored in the `System.Collections.Generic` namespace, and the one the shopping cart uses is the `List`:

```
private List<CartItem> _items;
```

This simply states that `_items` is a `List`, but a list of only `CartItem` objects. So now you do this:

```
List<CartItem> _items = new List<CartItem>;
CartItem item = new CartItem( . . .);

_items.Add(item);
```

But because the list is of a specific data type, you can't do this:

```
_items.Add("this isn't a cart item");
_items.Add("65");
```

Both of these lines would generate compile-time errors. Whenever you need a collection of custom classes, it's always a good idea to use generic collections, because they improve the readability of your code, reduce the potential for errors, and provide performance improvements over the standard collections.

Summary

This chapter covered a lot of ground, but it was necessary. Although the rich controls in ASP.NET 2.0 provide a way to create web applications with less code than previous versions, you can't get away without coding completely. So you've learned the fundamentals of coding and what you need to control your program. Specifically, this chapter covered the following topics:

- You looked at variables and data types, and how to work with the different data types, seeing that data types have different features. You also looked at arrays and collections, as a way of storing groups of variables.
- The control of programs is by way of decisions and loops, which use expressions and operators as part of the decision process. You saw how there are different ways to perform both decisions and loops, depending on the requirements.
- You looked at classes, and how they have constructors, properties, and methods. You didn't look at events explicitly, but like the controls you use on Web Forms, custom classes can have them if required.
- You took a brief look at generics, and saw how they help produce type-safe code and improve code readability and performance.

The next chapter examines componentization, and discusses the use of code-behind files and standalone classes from the design and structure perspective rather than what the code actually means.

Exercises

1. Create a class and shared method (called `DeliveryDate`) to calculate a delivery date given the date of an order. All deliveries should be made within three days of the order.
2. Continuing from Exercise 1, modify the `DeliveryDate` method to take into account that deliveries do not happen on the weekend.
3. Modify the `DeliveryDate` method to take into account that an order takes three working days to process. So orders falling on a Wednesday will be delivered on the following Monday, and orders from Thursday will be delivered on the following Tuesday.
4. For each of the following Boolean expressions, say for what integer values of `A` each of them will evaluate to `True` and when they will evaluate to `False`:

    a. NOT A=0

    b. A > 0 OR A < 5

    c. NOT A > 0 OR A < 5

    d. A > 1 AND A < 5 OR A > 7 AND A < 10

    e. A < 10 OR A > 12 AND NOT A > 20

Componentization

Programming has been through several distinct phases in its history and has moved a long way from its humble beginnings where punch-cards dashed with holes were placed into mechanical readers. Early programs on PCs were often just sequential lines of Do A, Do B, Do C kinds of commands. If you wanted to repeat a section of the code, you were left with the option of going Do A, Do A, and Do A or encasing it in a loop and telling the PC to Do A 20 times. This quickly made code repetitive and unwieldy. Worse than that, it made it hard to follow, even for the people who had written it. To follow the flow from the beginning of a program to the end was as difficult as following the path of one thread of spaghetti on a plate in a mound of food. In fact, it became commonly known as spaghetti-coding.

Over the past 20 years, there has been a move away from this kind of coding to a more object-based approach. This is where you break down the design of an application into a series of objects, and then any time you require an object, you just call it whenever you need it. This process is known as *componentization*. This is the creation of small objects, or components, that are self-contained parcels of code that have specific functions and are only called by the main application when needed. You looked at objects in Chapter 9 and saw how they could be mapped onto real-life counterparts to make coding less abstract. However, objects didn't totally solve the problems with spaghetti-coding.

Classic ASP suffered from this malaise as well, and despite having a whole series of objects such as `Response`, `Request`, and `Server`, and also allowing users to create their own objects, ASP pages are still a nightmare to debug and follow if they get too big. In fact, three main problems can be highlighted, the first being that HTML code and ASP code tended to be dumped in the same page together, despite having completely different purposes. HTML manages the structure of the page, whereas ASP is concerned with what the page does. The second problem is that with any kind of data handling in a page, there are two different purposes being dealt with, the connecting to and management of data stores, and the reading and writing of the data itself to a data source. The third problem is that of code-reuse, how users could easily create portable objects that could be called from within the code over and over, and how they could end up reducing the amount of code needed.

With ASP.NET 1.x, these problems were partially addressed; however, the solutions weren't perfect. ASP.NET 2.0 delivers the most comprehensive set of solutions to these problems. At the design previews, the ASP.NET development team openly boasted that ASP.NET 2.0 meant a 70% reduction of code in your pages. This chapter looks at the following topics:

- ❑ Separation of code and content
- ❑ Code-behind
- ❑ Data layers
- ❑ User controls

You've already looked at a lot of the new controls that are designed for every aspect of a web site, but now you're going to dig behind the scenes and see how ASP.NET 2.0 also makes life easier for the developer with separation of code from content, data layers, and user controls.

The Separation of Code from Content

The funny thing with most text books that you pick up about a new technology is that they'll quite happily tell you what was wrong with the old one, but not a lot about shortcomings in the new. Time and time again you'll probably come across a variation on the same theme: the code of the page should be separated from the style and design of the page. It happened in HTML, it happened in classic ASP, and it still happened to some extent in ASP.NET 1.x, although with a little care and effort it was possible to eliminate. With each new release you get a bit closer to achieving that lofty ambition. Before describing what ASP.NET 2.0 can offer to improve upon this, you need to know the answer to the question, "What is the separation of code from content, and why do you need to do it?"

Let's start with the first part, but first, we'll digress a little. In most walks of life, it's possible for a person to wear many hats at the same time, thus you'll find builders who can do carpentry, actors who think they can write, bus drivers who think they could drive a racing car; the list goes on. The truth is while most people's skills are spread across a fairly wide area, they're only likely to be able to specialize or be an expert in one or two areas at most. With programming, it's common to find designers, administrators, and programmers lumped in together. In fact, in recent years "web site developer" has become a bit of an insult, meaning someone who can't really design, can't really program, and would struggle to administer a database as well. In fact, I've seen several job advertisements where the time-honored "time wasters need not apply" has been replaced by the 21st-century version "web developers need not apply!"

You might well be thinking at this point, "Hang on, I want to be a web developer. What's wrong with that?" Well behind the seeming insult is a more serious point: A web developer is usually the person who has to spread him- or herself thinly across three related but really quite different disciplines. The old cliché "jack of all trades, master of none" springs to mind. One of the reasons why they've had to do this is because the technologies involved (in this case ASP) have forced all three disciplines into one web page. So within your ASP page, you would have to place the controls, have to implement the design, and have to stick the code to make it work, and that code would more likely than not reference the database. Classic ASP was very easy to learn and pick up and hence people could get away with doing this kind of thing, but the truth is a lot of early ASP sites were very ugly, took ages to access the database, and were quite often buggy.

Consider this scenario: What happens if your boss tells a designer to change the font on the web site, while telling the developer to add a search text box to the front page to search on the contents of the site? In times gone by, both people would be scrambling for the same page to make the alterations. Worse still, the designer could do his version of `index.asp`, while the programmer could do his, and therefore neither version would please the boss. Even if they did it sequentially, quite often the programmer would mess up the pristine design, or the designer would break a vital piece of code. I'm not intending to patronize either job; this has honestly happened on projects I've worked on. It therefore makes more sense to have two different versions of the same page. And it makes sense to let the designer with his graphic design and art qualifications do the interface of the web site, with the programmer at the back end connecting all the bits of the site and making them work.

This is where separating the code from the content comes in. In this fictitious scenario, you'd probably use Cascading Style Sheets to get around the problem. However, you'd still have the problem of the separating the design from the code. In other words, the positioning of the ASP.NET controls would still be the responsibility of the programmer. ASP.NET 2.0 goes beyond the separation of code from content.

The Separation of Code from Design

So far you've read about two distinct areas in ASP.NET 2.0, the first being the HTML code and ASP.NET controls, which you can see in this sample page:

```
<html>
<head>
</head>
<body>
<form runat="server">
<aspnet:label id="label1" runat="server" text="Enter your name:"><aspnet:label>
<aspnet:textbox id="textbox1" runat="server"></aspnet:textbox>
<aspnet:button id="button1" runat="server" text="submit">
</form>
</body>
</html>
```

The second is the actual code, which is placed within the `<head>` tags of the first:

```
<script language="C#">
private void Page_Load(object sender, EventArgs e)
{
 if (Page.IsPostback==true)
 {
    Label1.Text = "Hello" + textbox1.Text;
 }
}
</script>
```

This layout is known as the *single-file* scenario. This chapter uses the term "single-file" when talking about putting the code within `<script>` tags on the page. The first section of code in the single-file sample page is purely concerned with the design and structure of the page. For example, you could move the label and textbox and button around, and the program would still work perfectly. However, if you altered the order of the second section of code, everything would come to a jarring halt.

Worse still, behind the scenes the single-file scenario actually created far more work than was necessary. A second scenario is a little sidebar that displays a shopping basket as you browse around the site. How would you do it? Would you have to add this code to every single page? If you added it to every page, would you have to update every single page, every time you made a change? A sensible strategy of separating content from code, data from code, and being able to reuse the code is obviously needed. So let's start by looking at the first point in this three-pronged strategy.

Code-Behind

Code-behind is simply a separate code file linked to your Web Form or .aspx page. You place all of your HTML tags and ASP.NET controls in the .aspx page, and you have a separate page "behind" this page that contains all of the code that is normally contained within the <script> blocks for the page. So to answer the designer/developer dilemma, your designer can update the .aspx page, while your developer can update the code-behind page.

Code-behind pages are very easy to use. Like their .aspx counterparts, they are composed of pure text and can be viewed in Visual Web Developer, Notepad, or any text editor. The .aspx is the centerpoint, and the code-behind is like an attachment. In Visual Web Developer, code-behind pages are not created until they are needed, although when you select a Create Web Site option, a Default.aspx page and the corresponding code-behind Default.aspx.cs are created automatically. However, for any further pages that you create, only the .aspx page is added, unless you check the Place Code in Separate File option, which is unchecked by default.

This runs contrary to what happens in Visual Studio .NET 2005, where when you create a new Web Form, a new code-behind file is automatically created at the same time.

The code is stored in a separate file, which is identified by a .cs suffix or (if you're using VB.NET) a .vb suffix. So if you created a Default.aspx page, the code-behind file for that page would be called Default.aspx.cs. Not all languages in the .NET Framework support the code-behind model, most notably J#, but the two main languages that most developers use and the only two considered in this book both use code-behind.

The Page Directive

You've already met the Page directive in Chapter 5 when you learned about the idea of using inheritance with the .NET Framework, to inherit certain features from classes. The Page directive also refers to where your separate code-behind file is stored. Look at the same directive and the same attributes again, but this time from a slightly different angle:

```
<%@Page Language="C#" CodeFile="Default.aspx.cs" Inherits="_default"%>
```

You're interested in two particular attributes of `Page`:

- `Inherits`: This attribute tells you which class you want to inherit from. It's vital that the `Inherits` attribute matches a class in the code-behind file.
- `CodeFile`: This attribute specifies the name of the code-behind file. Typically you would expect the code-behind file to be kept in the same folder, but it's possible to keep it separate and specify a URL inside this attribute as well.

If you want to use code-behind, you must include these two attributes at all times. If you want to add a code-behind file manually to an .aspx file, then after you've added these two attributes, next you need to create the code-behind file itself.

Partial Classes

You can check the contents of a typical code-behind file by creating a new ASP.NET web site and then viewing the contents of `Default.aspx.cs`, which is created automatically. You will see the following three lines:

```
partial class _Default : System.Web.UI.Page
{
    ...
}
```

Any code you create should be placed within a *partial class*. Although this section won't go into partial classes too much, it is necessary to talk a little about them. In the last chapter, you saw classes as being cookie cutters that define the shape of the cookies. So what is a partial class? Half a cookie cutter? Well in some ways, yes is the answer. If you've played around with ASP.NET 1.x at all, you'll have noticed that there was a lot more than just three lines of code in the code-behind file, in the section marked Web Form Designer Generated Code. In the previous version of ASP.NET, if you stuck your control in the page, under certain conditions your code-behind file didn't always see it. Partial classes mean that at compilation time, your code-behind file and the Web Form are now merged into one class file, thus making sure this kind of scenario didn't happen. It also means you only need these three lines of code to make it work. So your code-behind file is one half of the cookie cutter and the Web Form is the other half, and together they make the whole. Let's leave that analogy before it gets squeezed any more.

Event Handlers/Functions

You place the code in the partial class; however, this is not quite enough to make it work. The code also should be placed within an event handler or a subroutine or function of some sort. All code in ASP.NET is run in reaction to an event of some sort. If you don't actually place your code in an event handler, you'll probably need a call to your subroutine or function placed within an event handler. The most common one is the `Page_Load` event handler that occurs when the page is first loaded:

```
private void Page_Load (object sender , EventArgs e ) {
 ...
}
```

Of course you don't have to type this in — if you double-click the page in Design View, the `Page_Load` event handler will be added for you. This is just another good reason for using Visual Web Developer. In previous versions of this book, we've used humble Notepad as our editor to make changes to the code. This isn't because we endorse a firmly Luddite/anti-progress view of the world, but because Notepad made no changes to our HTML code (unlike the majority of HTML editors), and because it is something everybody with a version of Windows automatically had. With code-behind, things become slightly more complex, in that you have two files that basically refer to the same page (see Figure 10-1). You can still of course manage them via Notepad, but the features in Visual Web Developer make it much easier to manage the two separate pages (and see them as connected entities).

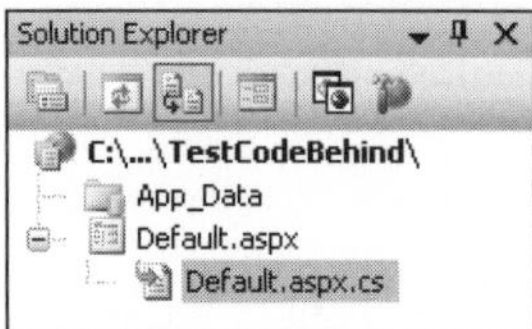

Figure 10-1

Of course, you might think, well why not stick with Notepad and also stick with the single-file model? The following list reiterates some of the advantages of using code-behind files:

- Separation of the content (user interface) from the code. It is practical to have a designer working on the markup while a programmer writes code.
- Better security, because code is not exposed to the designers or others who are working only with the page content.
- Code can be easily reused for multiple pages.

However, this doesn't mean that code-behind is always the perfect solution to all your problems. Using a single file for your code and content is still the more sensible option within some scenarios:

- Single-file is best suited for pages where the code consists primarily of event handlers for the controls on the page.
- Where there is little code, it can be easier to view a single-file page because both the code and the HTML are in the same place.

There are also some reasons of convenience to consider as well, namely single-file pages are easier to send to another programmer because there is only one file, they're easier to rename, and managing files is slightly easier, because the page is self-contained in a single file, and there are therefore fewer pages to manage. Generally, though, you really should be placing your code in a separate code-behind file, because the advantages outweigh the disadvantages for the most part.

Creating a Code-Behind File

That's enough talk. In the next Try It Out, you get down to the business of creating an incredibly simple code-behind file that interacts with a sample page containing `TextBox`, `Button`, and `Label` controls.

You'll see how you can manipulate all of these controls in the same way as you might expect to when using a single file.

Try It Out Creating a Code-Behind File

1. Open VWD and create a new web site called **TestCodeBehind** in the Chapter directory (`C:\BegASPNET2\Chapters\Begin\Chapter10`).

2. Go to Solution Explorer and click the plus symbol (+) next to `Default.aspx` to expand the tree to reveal the file `Default.aspx.cs` (refer to Figure 10-1).

> **Again, `Default.aspx` is the only file that has the code-behind file automatically created for you. If you create another Web Form, you must make sure to check the Place Code in a Separate File option, which is unchecked by default.**

3. Go back to the `Default.aspx` file and add two `Label` controls, a `TextBox` control, and a `Button` control, as shown in Figure 10-2.

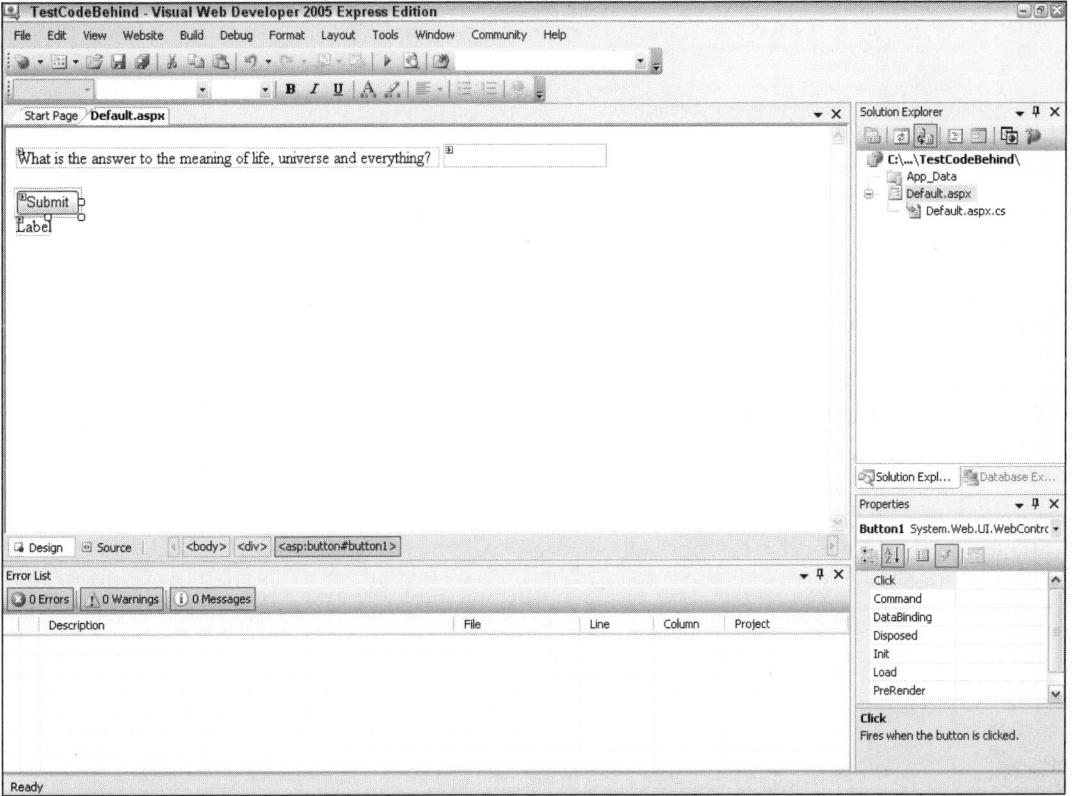

Figure 10-2

Adjust the source HTML to read as follows:

```
    <asp:Label ID="Label1" runat="server" Text="What is the answer to the meaning of
life, the universe and everything?:"></asp:Label>
    <br /><br />
    <asp:TextBox ID="TextBox1" runat="server"></asp:TextBox>
    <br /><br />
    <asp:Button ID="Button1" runat="server" Text="Submit" />
    <br /><br />
    <asp:Label ID="Label2" runat="server" Text=""></asp:Label>
```

4. Go back to Design View and double-click anywhere on the background of `Default.aspx` other than on the controls. Doing so will open up into the code-behind file, shown in Figure 10-3.

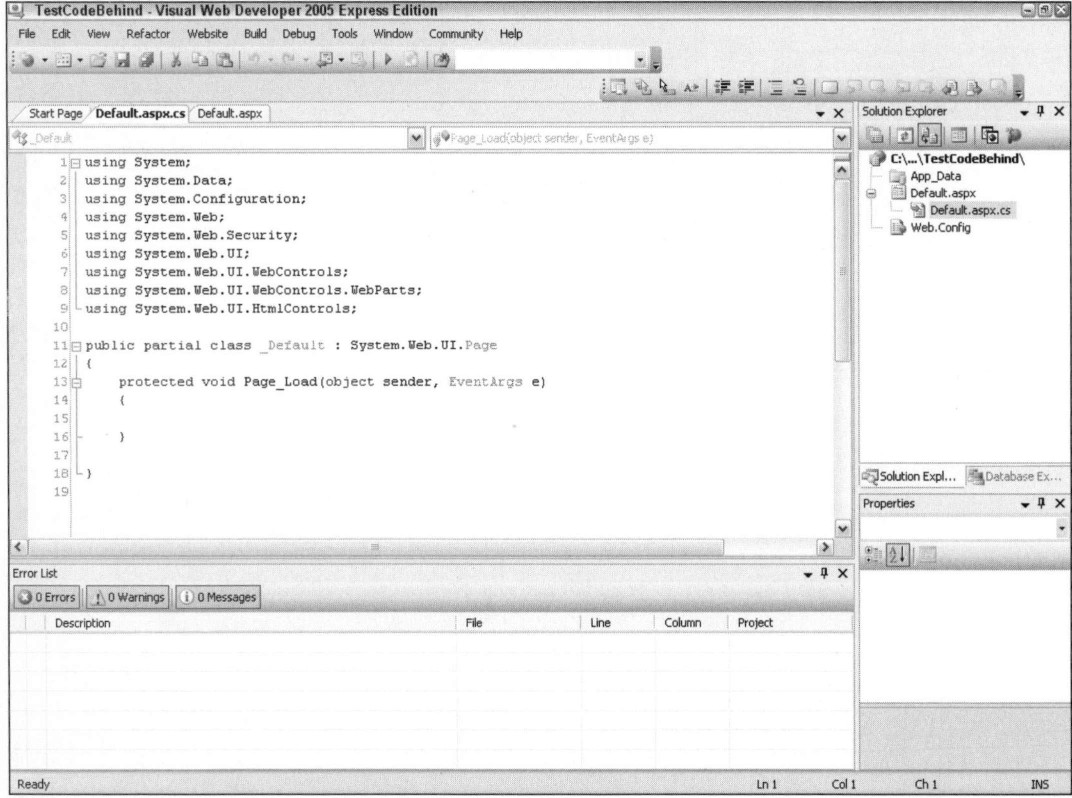

Figure 10-3

5. Add the following code to the `Page_Load` event handler:

```
        if (Page.IsPostBack)
        {
            if (TextBox1.Text == "42")
                Label2.Text = "So you read Douglas Adams as well...";
            else
            {
```

```
                Label2.Text = "No, I'm not sure that's it";
            }
        }
```

6. Click the green arrow to run it. You may get a textbox asking whether or not to add a new Web.config file or run without debugging. Click the former.
7. Enter a value or lengthier sentence into the text box, as shown in Figure 10-4.

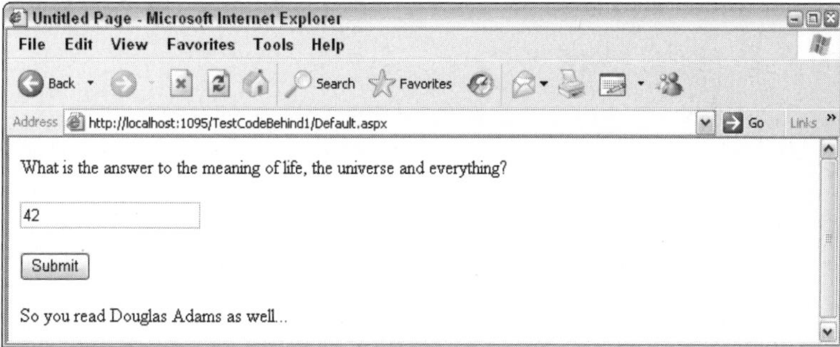

Figure 10-4

How It Works

It all seems very simple — instead of putting your code within `<script>` tags, you place it within a separate page, connected by the `Page` directive tag. Indeed, if you check at the top of the Source View for `Default.aspx`, you can see that the following was already created:

```
<%@Page ... CodeFile="Default.aspx.cs" Inherits="_Default" %>
```

This refers to the code-behind file `Default.aspx.cs`. There the following code is run when the `Page_Load` event is called (when the page is viewed). This is just the normal kind of code talked about in Chapter 9:

```
                 if (Page.IsPostBack)
        {
                if (TextBox1.Text == "42")
                    Label2.Text = "So you read Douglas Adams as well...";
                else
                {
                    Label2.Text = "No, I'm not sure that's it";
                }
          }
```

It says if the page has been posted back (submitted), check the contents of the `TextBox` control. If it equals `42`, then you have your correct answer, and you set the `Label2` control's `Text` property accordingly. If the contents of the `TextBox` control do not equal `42`, you display a different answer (`"No, I'm not sure that's it"`).

However, there is a bit more going on beneath the covers, namely the method by which your code is compiled.

Compilation in ASP.NET 2.0

Compilation is another one of those subjects that this book doesn't go into in depth, because you don't need to know too much about it. However, you should be aware of its presence. When you submit your Web Form to the server, your Web Form and ASP.NET pages first have to be translated into a language the server can understand. This is known as *compilation*. You can see how this process works in .NET 2.0 in Figure 10-5.

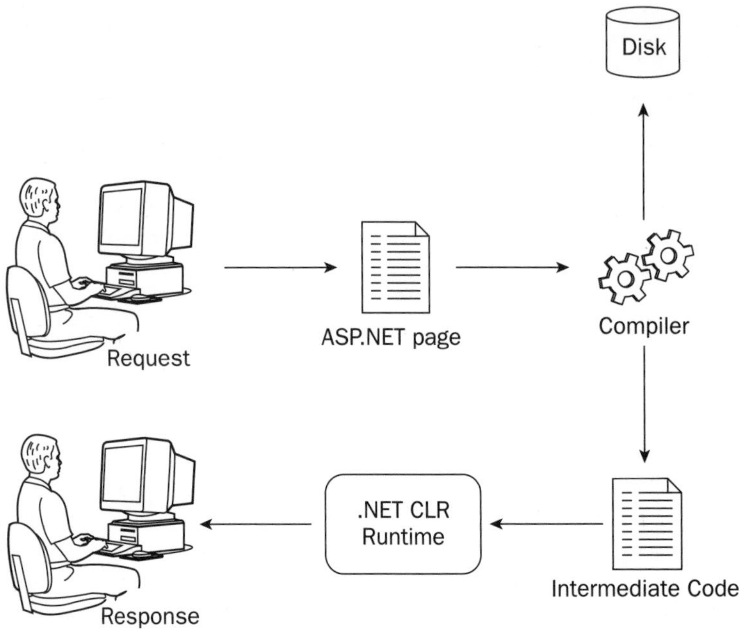

Figure 10-5

The compiler changes your code into something known as *intermediate code*, or Microsoft Intermediate Language (MSIL). This language is something that is independent of any PC it is run on. The .NET CLR (Common Language Runtime) is able to take this intermediate code and change it into executable code that it can run and provide output for. The output is then sent back to the user as a response. (There's actually a bit more to this process, as you'll see in Chapter 14.)

During the process of compilation, your pages are approved syntactically, so if you've made any typos such as the following, they will be spotted at compile time:

```
if (Paige.IsPostBack)
```

Your code can be compiled in two ways:

- **Pre-Runtime Compilation:** The "normal" way (or the "old way," — the default way in ASP.NET 1.1). Code-behind files are compiled into an assembly and stored in the `\bin` directory. Web Forms and .aspx pages are compiled when needed.

- **Full Runtime Compilation:** Code-behind files and any other associated code can now be placed in the `App_Code` folder. ASP.NET 2.0 will then create and maintain references to the assembly that is generated from these files at runtime.

> **There is actually a third option called deployment pre-compilation, which is for full compilation of your project prior to deployment. You'll learn a little more about this in Chapter 16.**

The App_Code Folder

If you create an `App_Code` folder in your project, any code you place in that project will automatically be compiled when you run the project. It's a far more robust solution than the old `\bin` folder used by ASP.NET 1.x, and for that reason you should use it for any code other than code-behind. The reason you should not use it for code-behind is that it is easier in VWD to keep your code files attached to the page they are related to; otherwise viewing them could be a pain.

So not only can you organize your code and in which pages it is placed, but ASP.NET 2.0 dictates a different structure for ordering where those pages are placed.

Data Layers

You've looked at how code and content can be successfully separated, but there is a third dimension to our discussions, namely that of the data. Throughout this book, we've paused to reflect briefly on various aspects of the history of the Internet and the Web, while trying to keep you away from a huge lecture on the entire subject. However, another quick history lecture is in order here to help you understand the purpose of the next ASP.NET 2.0 feature.

Two-Tier Applications

Rather than rewinding too far back, let's jump in halfway. When HTML started getting beyond the universities, it became necessary to provide something more than just static text and images. One of the first ways in which web pages were made dynamic was to enable them to access a database. The browser was one tier, and the database was the second tier. In this scenario, the browser dealt with rules about the business or application and user interface.

> **The term *business rules* is used to encompass any part of the application logic that isn't the user interface or the database. If the application isn't being used for a business, then the term *application logic* might be more applicable, although they mean the same thing.**

The data retrieval and manipulation was performed by another separate database application, such as SQL Server or Microsoft Access. It would handle the data storage and retrieval device for the application. These two-tier applications were also commonly know as *client-server* applications. A typical client-server application is depicted in Figure 10-6.

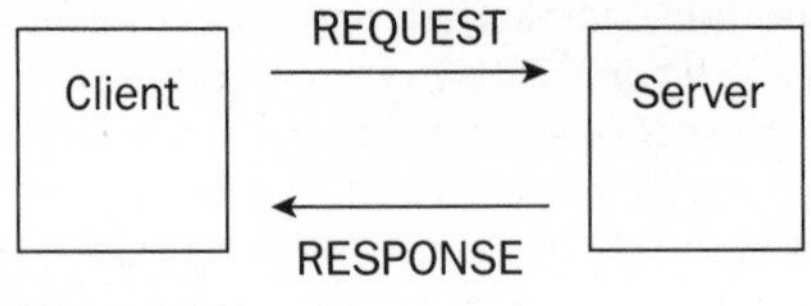

Figure 10-6

The other popular variation on the two-tier application saw the business rules (application logic) being executed on the database system. Such applications would commonly use *stored procedures* to manipulate the database (or in some cases triggers). A stored procedure is a query that is stored on the database. It can be called by the client application and then run on the server. It would contain rules about the business as well. For example, if you had a league table on Wrox United that awarded three points for a win and one point for a draw, then in the database query, it would somehow have to record that when one side scores more goals than another side, it is worth three points. This is a business rule. It doesn't matter to the database how many points you add on to the win; however, your league table would fail to work properly if you added two or five points for a win.

Three-Tier Applications

The big difference with three-tier applications is that business rules are no longer located on either the client or the database. They are stored and run on a system in between the client and the server. The advantage of this is that the business rules server can ensure that all of the business processing is done correctly. There is now a third layer interface, business rules and data. The introduction of the data tier is illustrated in Figure 10-7.

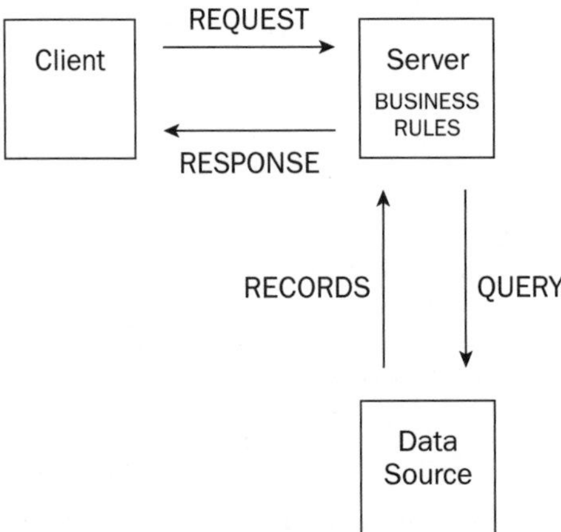

Figure 10-7

In a three-tier application, the client never accesses the data storage system directly. You can make changes to the business rules and this would mean you could change any part of the system without having to alter the other two parts. As the three different sections of the application communicate via interfaces, and as long as the interface between the code and application front-end remains the same, the internal workings of each part can be changed without affecting the rest of the application. The advantages of doing this are similar to those for keeping code and content separate. Typically, a database is managed by a database administrator (DBA), and it might even be managed by a separate company. The web developer as jack-of-all-trades would previously have been required to know the intimate workings of the database, when really they shouldn't be interfering there at all. So this brings you to the end of your little excursion, because you can now look at a new feature in ASP.NET 2.0 that allows you to separate your applications more simply into three tiers.

What's New in ASP.NET 2.0

In ASP.NET 2.0, you are no longer restricted to binding only to data controls. You can also bind to separate business controls via the `ObjectDataSource` control.

Using the ObjectDataSource Control

The new ASP.NET `ObjectDataSource` control enables you to declaratively bind data controls such as the `GridView`, `DataList`, and `DropDownList` controls to a separate business control or a data component. Previously, you could only bind the controls directly to a database. This new development enables the separation of your business rules from your content and your data.

`ObjectDataSource` is a more difficult control to explain than a `GridView` or `DropDownList` control, so rather than wasting excessive verbiage, it's quicker to show you exactly what the `ObjectDataSource` control does in an example. You're actually going to do two examples to show it in action. In the first example, you'll see how to create a data component to return a list of players from the Players table. This Try It Out is split into two sections: the first section where you create the `ObjectDataSource` itself and the second where you bind the `ObjectDataSource` control to a `GridView` control. The resulting output will be completely non-editable. In the second example, you'll use the Try It Out to create a data component that can not only read from the Wrox United database but also write data to it. You'll create and bind the data component in this same example that will make it quite lengthy.

The data component that you create in both examples will consist of an XSD schema file (.xsd). This file describes the data you require and defines which methods will be used to read and write data. This doesn't require any code or knowledge of XML schemas because when you run the application, the .xsd file is compiled for you and performs all of the tasks needed.

Start by creating the data component for the read-only example.

Try It Out — Creating the Data Component

1. Open Visual Web Developer and select Open Web Site. From the `C:\BegASPNet2\Chapters\Begin\Chapter10` folder, select `ObjectDataSource` and click OK.
2. In Solution Explorer, right-click the name of your web site, select Add ASP.NET Folder, and select `App_Code`.
3. Right-click the `App_Code` folder and select Add New Item from the list.
4. From the Visual Studio installed templates, click DataSet.
5. Rename the DataSet **ods.xsd** and click Add.
6. VWD starts the TableAdapter Configuration Wizard. (Be patient here, because this one really does take a while to kick in.) When the wizard finally arrives, select ConnectionString (Web.config) from the drop-down list (see Figure 10-8) and click Next.

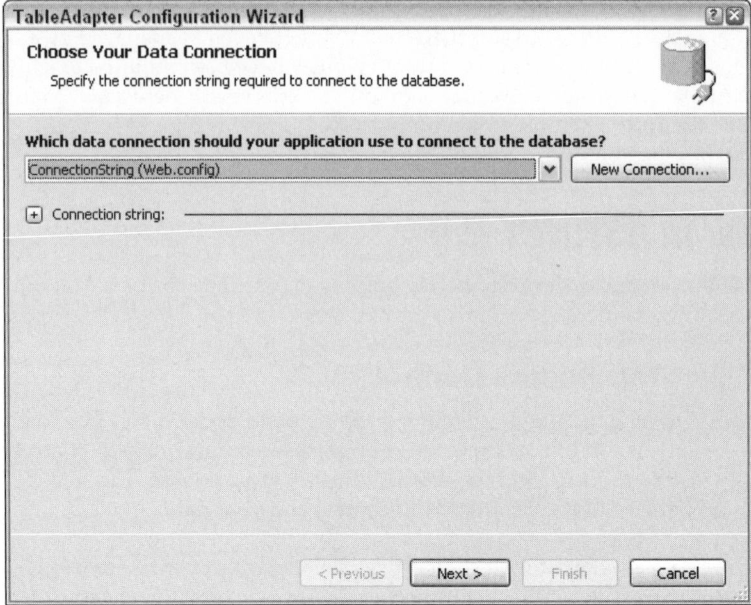

Figure 10-8

7. Next you get a page where you can choose to use SQL statements or stored procedures. Select the Use SQL statements radio button (as shown in Figure 10-9) and click Next.

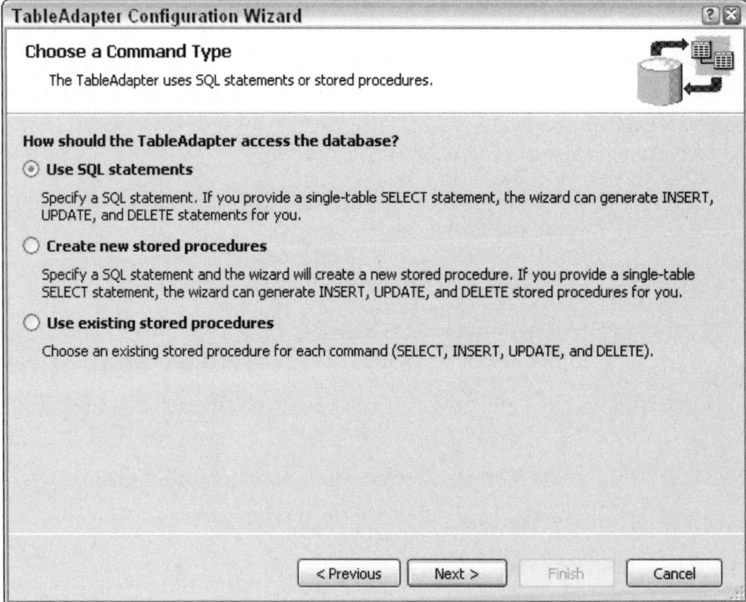

Figure 10-9

8. On the next wizard screen, you can define the SQL statement. Type the following SQL statement into the "What data should be loaded into the table" area of the dialog box:

```
SELECT PlayerID, FirstName, LastName, Position, DateJoined, DateLeft FROM Players
```

9. After entering the SQL statement, click Next. You can now define which methods the component will expose. Uncheck the Fill a DataTable check box and make sure that the Return a DataTable check box is checked (see Figure 10-10). In the Method name box, type **GetPlayers**. This method is used later to retrieve the data. Uncheck the final check box.

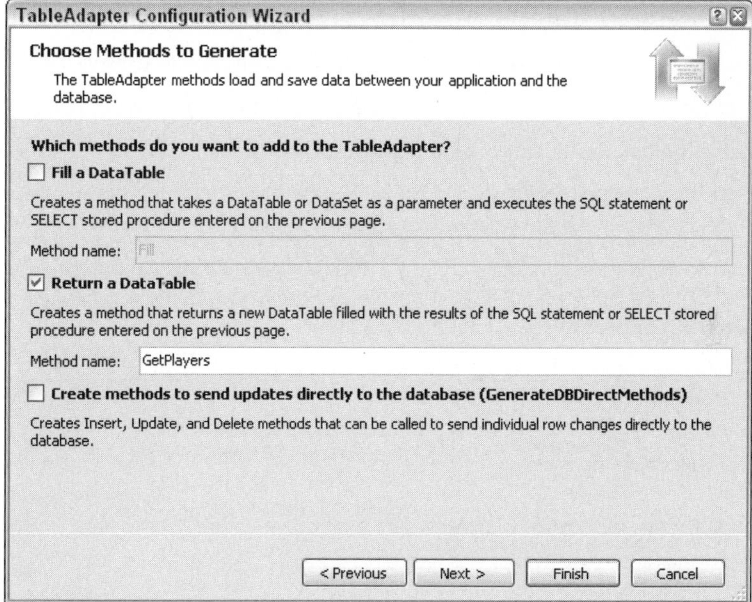

Figure 10-10

10. Click Finish. In Figure 10-11, you can see the data component in the designer. It shows both the data you selected and the method you created.

Figure 10-11

11. Save the data component and close the component designer.

12. Select Build➪Build Web Site to compile the component. (Note that this won't produce anything viewable.)

How It Works

The data component is now usable as a data source within a Web Form. You've used the wizard to create the component for you, to select the fields from the database, and also to name the method by which you want to be able to call this component.

Thenext step is to bind to this component. To do this, you can create and configure an `ObjectDataSource` control. You can then add controls, such as the `GridView` control, to the page and bind them to the data source control.

Try It Out Binding to the ObjectDataSource Control

1. Open the `Default.aspx` from Solution Explorer and switch to Design View.
2. Open the Toolbox and from the Data section drag an `ObjectDataSource` control onto the page.
3. Select the Toolbox again, and from the Data section drag a `GridView` control onto the page.
4. Click the black arrow in the top-right corner of the `ObjectDataSource` control. The Common Tasks box appears with the words "Configure Data Source." Click this.
5. In the dialog box that appears, there is a single drop-down list asking you to choose your business object (see Figure 10-12). There should only be one, the `odsTableAdapters.PlayersTableAdapter`. Select it and click Next.

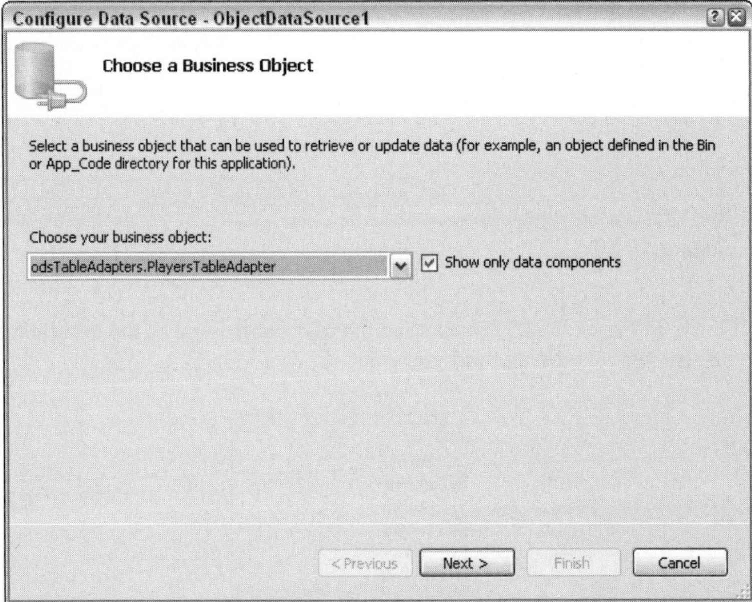

Figure 10-12

6. On the next screen (shown in Figure 10-13), under the Select tab in the Choose a method drop-down box, the `GetPlayers(), returns PlayersDataTable` method is displayed. Select it and click Finish (the other methods are automatically picked for you).

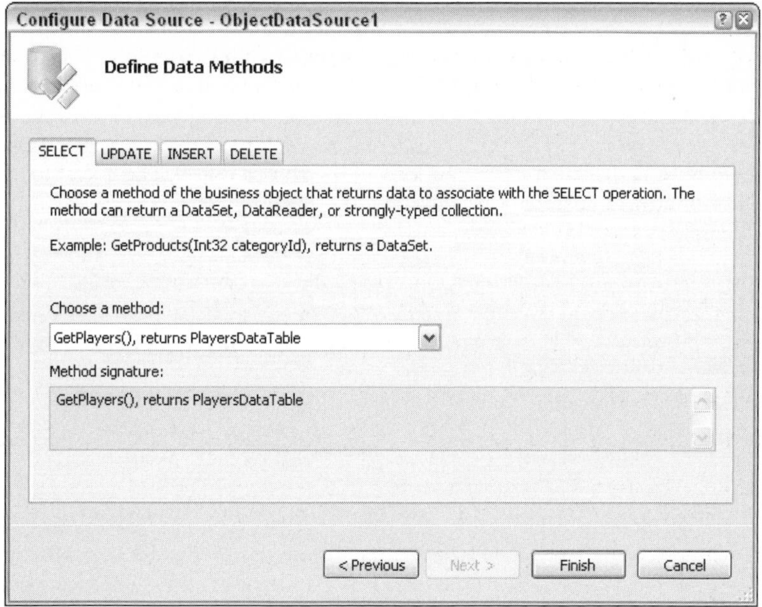

Figure 10-13

7. Click the black arrow on the top-right corner of the `GridView` control and from the Choose Data Source list that appears, select `ObjectDataSource1`. The Grid will update in Design View.

8. Open the Properties window and check that the `DataKeyNames` property is set to `PlayerID`.

9. Run the application, and you will see Figure 10-14 in your browser.

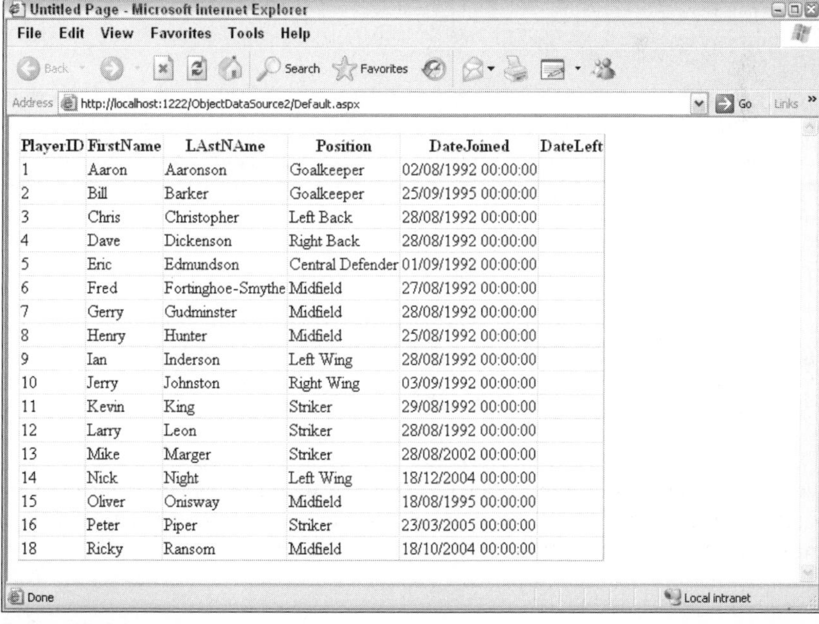

PlayerID	FirstName	LAstNAme	Position	DateJoined	DateLeft
1	Aaron	Aaronson	Goalkeeper	02/08/1992 00:00:00	
2	Bill	Barker	Goalkeeper	25/09/1995 00:00:00	
3	Chris	Christopher	Left Back	28/08/1992 00:00:00	
4	Dave	Dickenson	Right Back	28/08/1992 00:00:00	
5	Eric	Edmundson	Central Defender	01/09/1992 00:00:00	
6	Fred	Fortinghoe-Smythe	Midfield	27/08/1992 00:00:00	
7	Gerry	Gudminster	Midfield	28/08/1992 00:00:00	
8	Henry	Hunter	Midfield	25/08/1992 00:00:00	
9	Ian	Inderson	Left Wing	28/08/1992 00:00:00	
10	Jerry	Johnston	Right Wing	03/09/1992 00:00:00	
11	Kevin	King	Striker	29/08/1992 00:00:00	
12	Larry	Leon	Striker	28/08/1992 00:00:00	
13	Mike	Marger	Striker	28/08/2002 00:00:00	
14	Nick	Night	Left Wing	18/12/2004 00:00:00	
15	Oliver	Onisway	Midfield	18/08/1995 00:00:00	
16	Peter	Piper	Striker	23/03/2005 00:00:00	
18	Ricky	Ransom	Midfield	18/10/2004 00:00:00	

Figure 10-14

How It Works

You started by creating an instance of an ObjectDataSource control. To give it its functionality, you attached it to the GetPlayers() method that was specified in the data component. The GetPlayers() method was created in the previous Try It Out. This method returns the results of the SQL statement, available as a DataTable object. The DataTable object is an object that the GridView (and indeed all data controls) can bind to. If you go back and look at the source that has been created, you can see the source for the two controls you added to your form.

```
<div>
        <asp:ObjectDataSource ID="ObjectDataSource1" runat="server"
OldValuesParameterFormatString="original_{0}"
            SelectMethod="GetPlayers" TypeName="odsTableAdapters.PlayersTableAdapter">
        </asp:ObjectDataSource>

    </div>
        <asp:GridView ID="GridView1" runat="server" AutoGenerateColumns="False"
DataKeyNames="PlayerID"
            DataSourceID="ObjectDataSource1">
            <Columns>
                <asp:BoundField DataField="PlayerID" HeaderText="PlayerID"
InsertVisible="False"
                    ReadOnly="True" SortExpression="PlayerID" />
                <asp:BoundField DataField="FirstName" HeaderText="FirstName"
SortExpression="FirstName" />
                <asp:BoundField DataField="LastName" HeaderText="LastName"
SortExpression="LastName" />
                <asp:BoundField DataField="Position" HeaderText="Position"
SortExpression="Position" />
                <asp:BoundField DataField="DateJoined" HeaderText="DateJoined"
SortExpression="DateJoined" />
                <asp:BoundField DataField="DateLeft" HeaderText="DateLeft"
SortExpression="DateLeft" />
            </Columns>
        </asp:GridView>
```

The GridView control binds each of the fields in the dataset to a column in a table on the display. The ObjectDataSource takes five attributes. The ID and runat attributes are standard, the OldValuesParameterFormatString is set to the original setting, the SelectMethod attribute specifies the name of the actual method, and the TypeName specifies the PlayersTableAdapter. These are all the instructions needed to be able to bind the return PlayersTable to the GridView control. The final display looks the same as a normal GridView control—it's only the plumbing underneath that has routed your data from the ObjectDataSource control that is different.

The Wrox United ObjectDataSource

This data so far has been static. So as mentioned previously, in this next Try It Out, you go one further and use the ObjectDataSource control to be able to edit and update your squad's details. In the Admin section of the Wrox United site, there is a page called EditSquad.aspx, which is used to change the players' details. However, it uses the SqlDataSource control for the details. This can be replaced with an ObjectDataSource control. It has insert, update, select, and delete methods that map neatly to the methods in a simple class.

Try It Out — The Wrox United ObjectDataSource

1. Open the Wrox United application from the chapter samples (`C:\BegASPNET2\Chapters\Begin\Chapter10\WroxUnited`) in Visual Web Developer.
2. Right-click the `App_Code` folder and select Add New Item from the list.
3. From the Visual Studio installed templates, click DataSet.
4. Rename the DataSet **wroxunited.xsd** and click Add.
5. VWD starts the TableAdapter Configuration Wizard. (As before, be patient here.) When the wizard finally arrives, select wroxunited (Web.config) and click Next.
6. When you get the page where you can choose to use SQL statements or stored procedures. select the Use SQL statements radio button and click Next.
7. On the next wizard screen, you can define the SQL statement. Type the following SQL statement into the "What data should be loaded into the table" area of the dialog box:

```
SELECT PlayerID, FirstName, LastName, Position, PictureURL, DateJoined, DateLeft
FROM Players
WHERE PlayerID = @PlayerID
```

8. After entering the SQL statement, click Next. You can now define which methods the component will expose. Uncheck the Fill a DataTable check box and make sure that Return a DataTable check box is checked. In the Method name box, type **GetPlayers**. This method is used later to retrieve the data. Make sure the final check box, "Create methods to send update directly to the database," is checked.
9. Click Next and then click Finish. Save the data component, and close the component designer.
10. Select Build⇨Build Web Site to compile the component.
11. Open the Admin folder of WroxUnited and open the `EditSquad.aspx` file.
12. In Design View, scroll down, select the second `SqlDataSource` control, `DetailsDataSource` (shown in Figure 10-15), and delete it.
13. From the Data Section of the Toolbox, drag an `ObjectDataSource` control where the `SqlDataSource` used to be.
14. Click the black arrow at the top right of the `ObjectDataSource` control, and from the Common Tasks menu, select Configure Data Source.
15. In the opening dialog box, select `wroxunitedTableAdapters.PlayersTableAdapter` and click Next.
16. In the Select tab, select the `GetPlayers(Int32 PlayerID), returns PlayersDataTable` method from the drop-down list box and click Next.
17. In the Define Parameters dialog box, select Control from the Parameter Source drop-down list box. Select `GridView1` in Control view. The parameters on the left of the dialog box will now show `GridView.SelectedValue`. Click Finish.

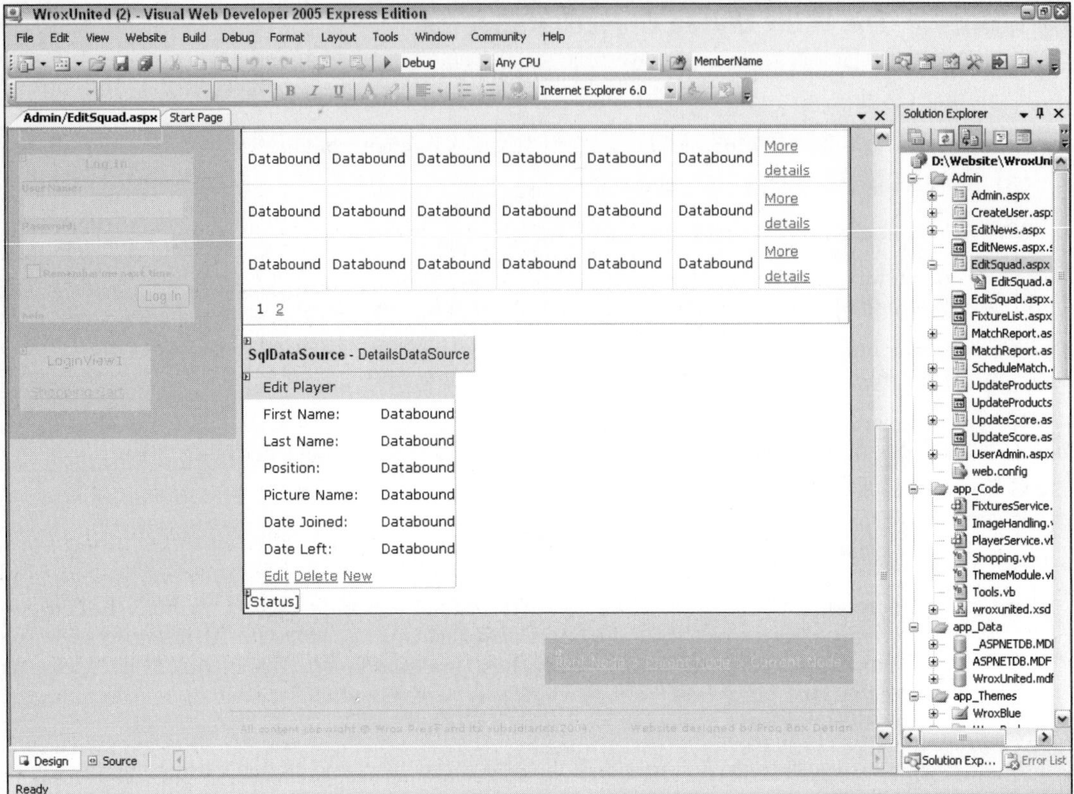

Figure 10-15

18. Right-click the `ObjectDataSource` control in Design View and select Properties.

19. In the Properties window, change the `(ID)` property so that it reads `"DetailsDataSource"`.

20. Open `EditSquad.aspx.cs` and amend the code in the procedure parameters to read as follows in the three subs:

```
protected void DetailsDataSource_Updated(object sender ,
System.Web.UI.WebControls.ObjectDataSourceMethodEventArgs e)
{
  ...
}
protected void DetailsDataSource_Inserted(object sender ,
System.Web.UI.WebControls.ObjectDataSourceMethodEventArgs e)
  ...
}
protected void DetailsDataSource_Deleting(object sender , As
System.Web.UI.WebControls.ObjectDataSourceMethodEventArgs e)
{
  ...
}
```

21. Save and close the file.
22. Run the application, log in as an administrator (**dave\dave@123**), and navigate to the `EditSquad.aspx` page. It works in the same way as before except that you are now using an `ObjectDataSource` control.

How It Works

You haven't changed much between this and the previous example. You built a data component, and you then added an `ObjectDataSource` control into the `EditSquad.aspx` page. You added methods for the Update, Insert, and Delete methods via the wizard. The code that provided your functionality in the classes was already in existence—all you had to do was change the references from the `SqlDataSource` control to the `ObjectDataSource` control. Then you ran it, and the WroxUnited application was able to use the `ObjectDataSource` instead.

User Controls

Your final problem is that of making your code easy to reuse, and this is addressed by *user controls*. Again, these existed in ASP.NET 1.x, but this is something that also has been improved upon in ASP.NET 2.0. So what are user controls? Well in a nutshell, user controls are reusable Web Forms. They've been through several name changes and evolutions from scriptlets to pagelets, before arriving at user controls. They can be thought of as mini-scripts, mini-pages, or pages within your pages, but however you choose to think of them, the key is that they can be called up as many times as you need them.

If you browse the Wrox United site, you can see several examples of user controls, and one, the `News` control, is visible on the front page. In fact, if you look at the front page (shown in Figure 10-16), it is a multitude of components garnered from different sources.

The `News` control is a user control, the `Login` control is an ASP.NET control, the shopping cart is a link to a user control, and the menu is derived from the site master, which itself is an ASP.NET control. So the entire site front page and design is reusable. If you click the Shopping Cart link, you will see the second user control, shown in Figure 10-17.

And there are a couple more user controls in the administrative section of the site too, but you get the idea that these controls can be used in multiple pages, or called from different places, and rather than having to cut and paste the code individually each time, you can just call on this one section of code over and over again. One question you might have is how do they differ from the normal ASP.NET server controls, such as the `TextBox` control or the `Login` control that you looked at earlier?

Very little is the answer. The main difference is that you have to provide the code behind the control yourself, whereas ASP.NET server controls come fully functional out of the box. You can add properties to user controls and set them as attributes, just like you would with a normal ASP.NET server control.

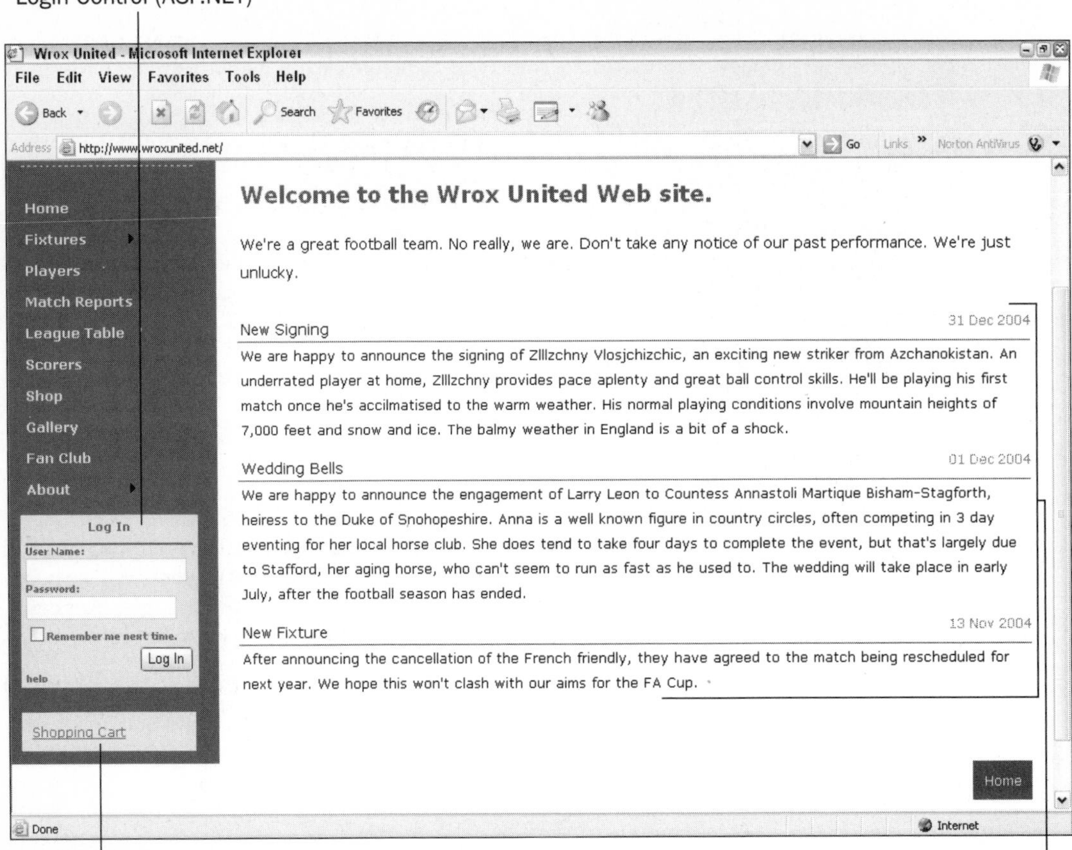

Figure 10-16

So why isn't everything an ASP.NET server control? Well, ASP.NET 2.0 ships with a multitude of controls designed for the most common scenarios and situations. ASP.NET 2.0 adds greatly to the number of server controls. For example, in ASP.NET 1.1 if you wanted a `Login` control, you had to stitch together a username text box, a password text box, a button, and a label for messages within a panel, so you had to create this as a user control. In version 2.0, the `Login` control comes as a server control. However, it just isn't possible to anticipate everything that a user might want or need. Therefore, it makes sense to have the flexibility to create your own.

If you view the source code in Internet Explorer for the home page (`Default.aspx`) in WroxUnited.net, you'll see no indication that a user control has been used — it's all HTML elements and some occasional script, which is just as it should be. If you were using a Flash plug-in or a Java applet, you would see some indication with an `<object>` tag or on older browsers, possibly an `<embed>` tag. So there's no worry about extra download time being taken either.

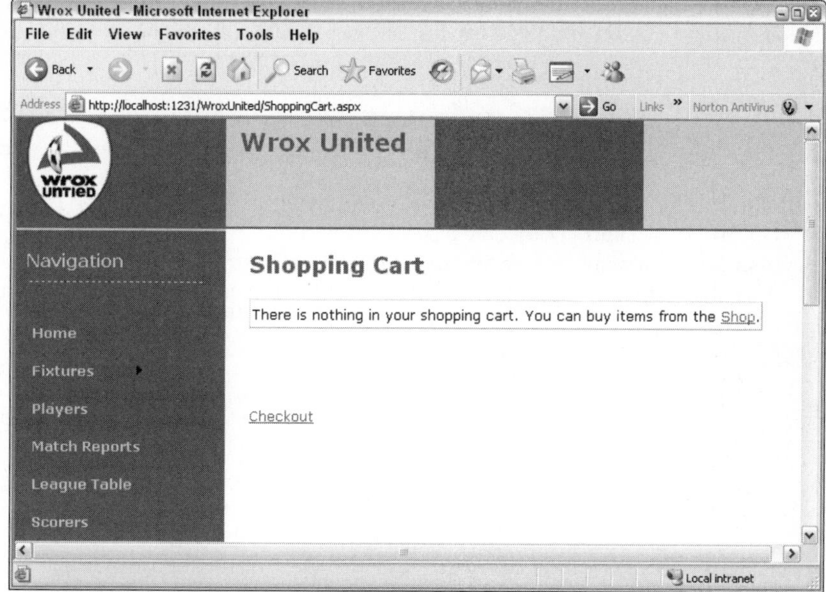

Figure 10-17

If you look at the actual page that is sent to the server, you can see the user control is included with two simple lines of code that highlighted here (this source code page is available for download at www.wrox.com):

```
<%@ Page Language="C#"  Trace="false" MasterPageFile="~/site.master"
AutoEventWireup="true" codefile="Default.aspx.cs" Inherits="_Default" %>
<%@ Register TagPrefix="uc1" TagName="News" Src="News.ascx" %>
<asp:Content ID="Content1" ContentPlaceHolderID="mainContent" Runat="server">

    <h2>Welcome to the Wrox United Web site.</h2>
    <p>We're a great football team. No really, we are. Don't take any notice
    of our past performance. We're just unlucky.</p>

    <uc1:news id="News1" runat="server" ItemsToShow="3"></uc1:news>

</asp:Content>
```

This page starts giving you some clues as to how user controls work.

User Control Structure

User controls are stored in separate files with a separate .ascx extension. Any time you see this extension, you know that you are dealing with a user control. To create a user control, you need to add a `@Register` directive to the top of your Web Form identifying where you can find your user control:

```
<%@Register TagPrefix="WroxUnited" TagName="MyControl" %>
```

You need to add a new tag specifying where the control will go on your page. It consists of the `TagPrefix`, followed by a colon, followed by the `TagName`, an ID, and the now familiar `runat=server` attribute:

```
<WroxUnited:MyControl id="mycontrol1" runat="server">
</WroxUnited:MyControl>
```

Lastly, you need to specify the user control itself in a separate .ascx file. Unlike Web Forms, you don't need to specify extra `<html>` and `<body>` tags, because the contents of this control will be added to the body of the containing main page. In fact, all you need to have is the controls that you want to include. For example, you could include the controls from the code-behind example used earlier in the chapter:

```
    <asp:Label ID="Label1" runat="server" Text="What is the answer to the meaning
of life, the universe and everything?:"></asp:Label>
    <asp:TextBox ID="TextBox1" runat="server"></asp:TextBox>
    <br /><br />
    <asp:Button ID="Button1" runat="server" Text="Submit" />
    <br />
    <asp:Label ID="Label2" runat="server" Text=""></asp:Label>
```

Of course, user controls can have code-behind files as well, just like Web Forms:

```
public void Page_Load( object sender,  System.EventArgs e)
  {
             if (Page.IsPostBack)
       {
            if (TextBox1.Text == "42")
                Label2.Text = "So you read Douglas Adams as well...";
            else
            {
                Label2.Text = "No, I'm not sure that's it";
            }
        }
```

This control can then be bolted into your web pages wherever you specify the `@Register` directive and add a tag for the control.

A Simple User Control

In the next Try It Out, you're going to start by creating a trivial "Hello World"-style user control to get you used to the idea of including them in your pages. This code does no more than encapsulate the code-behind from the first example you created in the chapter as a user control. You'll see how you can place the user control in one web page, and then in a second web page.

Try It Out Creating a Simple User Control

1. Open VWD and create a new ASP.NET web site called **SimpleUserControl** in the chapter directory (`C:\BegASPNET\Chapters\Begin\Chapter10`).
2. In Solution Explorer, right-click the web site and select Add New Item. Select Web User Control, enter the name **SimpleUserControl.ascx**, and check the Place Code in Separate File option, as shown in Figure 10-18.

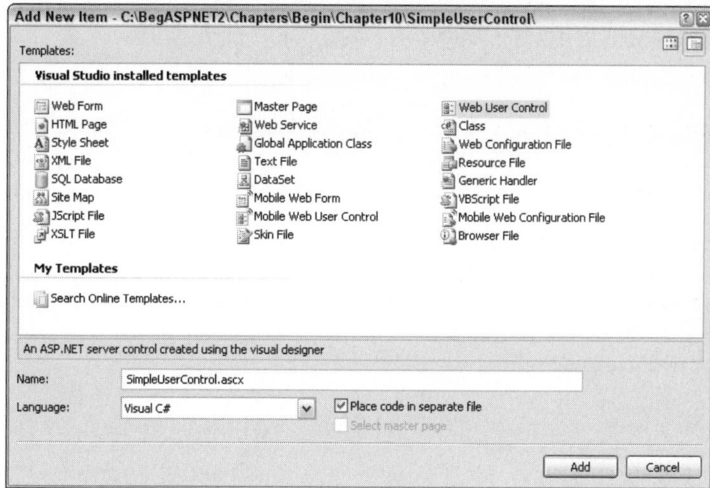

Figure 10-18

3. Now you need to add the controls to the page. Again, drag two `Label` controls, a `TextBox` control, and a `Button` control, as shown in Figure 10-19.

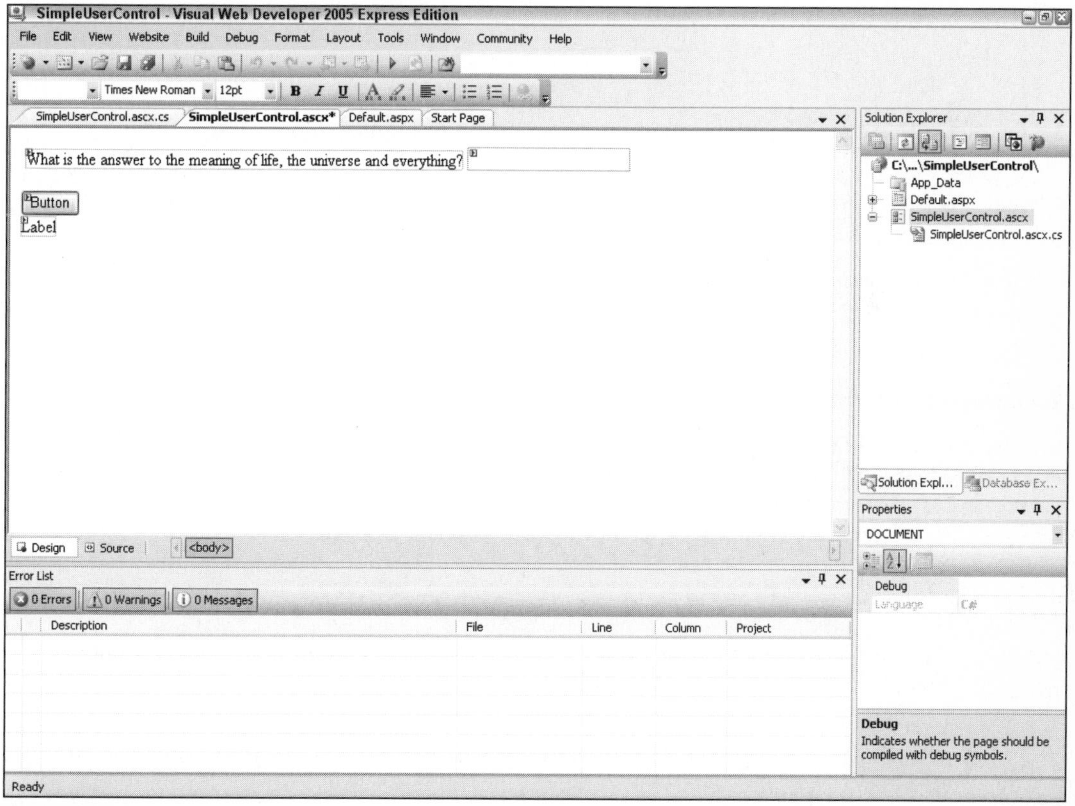

Figure 10-19

You can cut and paste the relevant code from the first Try It Out in this chapter into Source View if you still have it at hand:

```
<asp:Label ID="Label1" runat="server" Text="What is the answer to the meaning of
life, the universe and everything?:"></asp:Label>
    <asp:TextBox ID="TextBox1" runat="server"></asp:TextBox>
    <br /><br />
    <asp:Button ID="Button1" runat="server" Text="Submit" />
    <br />
    <asp:Label ID="Label2" runat="server" Text=""></asp:Label>
```

4. Double-click the page again and this time, add the following code-behind to `SimpleUserControl.ascx.cs`:

```
public partial class SimpleUserControl : System.Web.UI.UserControl
{
    protected void Page_Load(object sender, EventArgs e)
    {
      if (Page.IsPostBack)
      {
         if (TextBox1.Text == "42")
            Label2.Text = "So you read Douglas Adams as well...";
         else
         {
            Label2.Text = "No, I'm not sure that's it";
         }
      }
    }
}
```

5. Next you need to add this control to a page. From Solution Explorer, drag `SimpleControlUser.ascx` into Design View for `Default.aspx` (see Figure 10-20).
6. Click the green arrow to run `Default.aspx`. It works in exactly as it did in the first Try It Out of this chapter, as evidenced in Figure 10-21.
7. Go to Solution Explorer and right-click the project. Select Add New Item and add a new Web Form to the page called **secondpage.aspx**.
8. Go to Design View and drag `SimpleUserControl.ascx` into this page. Next, go to Solution Explorer and right-click `secondpage.aspx` and select Set As Start Page.

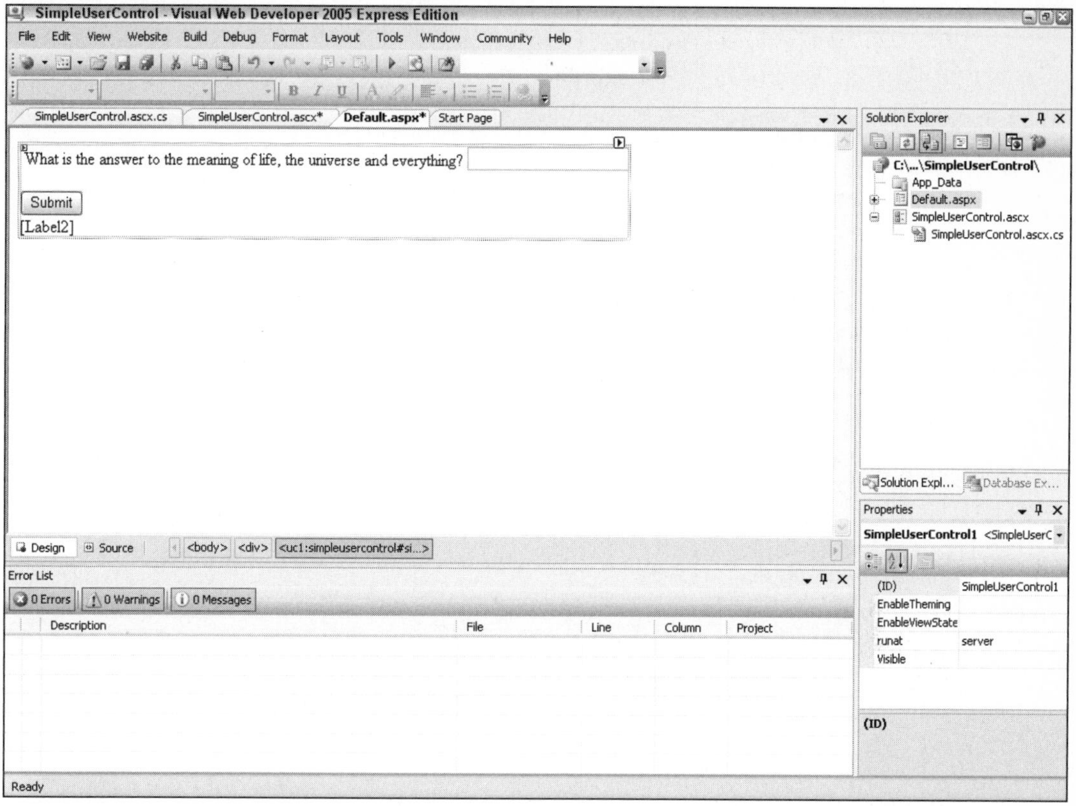

Figure 10-20

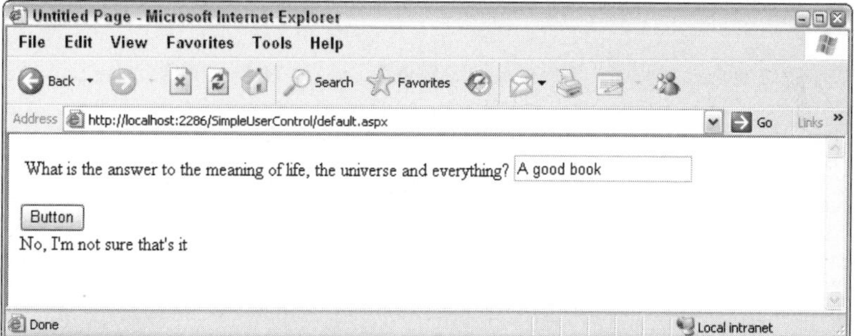

Figure 10-21

9. Run the project again. You should see what appears in Figure 10-22. Your control has been successfully duplicated with no extra lines of code being required.

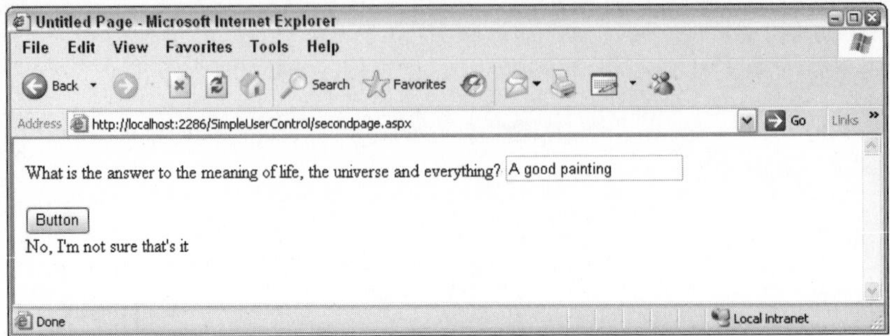

Figure 10-22

How It Works

This hopefully shows you just how easy it is to reuse code in your pages. If you go to `Default.aspx` and view the source, you will see the following:

```
<%@ Page Language="C#" AutoEventWireup="false" CodeFile="Default.aspx.cs"
Inherits="_Default" %>
<% Register Src="SimpleUserControl.ascx" TagPrefix="uc1"
TagName="SimpleUserControl" %>

<!DOCTYPE html PUBLIC "-//W3C//DTD XHTML 1.1//EN" "http://www.w3.org/TR/xhtml11/
DTD/xhtml11.dtd">

<html xmlns="http://www.w3.org/1999/xhtml" >
<head runat="server">
    <title>Untitled Page</title>
</head>
<body>
    <form id="form1" runat="server">
    <div>
    <uc1:SimpleUserControl id="SimpleUserControl1 runat="server" />
    </div>
    </form>
</body>
</html>
```

The highlighted lines of code are the only two lines that have been added to the original source code. The first registers the user control and specifies a tag prefix of `uc1` (short for "user control one") and a `TagName` of `SimpleUserControl`. The control is then inserted into the page along with an `id` attribute and a `runat=server` attribute.

There's nothing to stop you from copying this tag and pasting it again and again in the page, although it might make your page a little illogical, with several versions of the user control. Note that this example got you to cut and paste the old code from the code-behind page. This was quite deliberate because this was the old way of transferring replicated code. Each time you wanted to transfer the code, you would cut and paste it manually. Not only is cutting and pasting more labor-intensive, but it is also far more prone to mistakes, because if you altered the code in one page, it would need to be altered in all of the rest. With user controls, any changes you need to make can just be made to the .ascx file and the .ascx.cs file themselves, and then every time the user control is called, it automatically uses the new code.

The Wrox United News User Control

You're now going to move onto a more complex user control, and one that is used on the Wrox United web site. You're going to re-create the `News` control that you find on the main Wrox United site. This control scans the News table, selects the most up-to-date stories, and displays them on the front page, with the most recent being displayed first.

Before you launch into the coding, it's worth saying a little bit about why we chose to make this a user control, while other bits and pieces we chose not to. A `News` control is something that is going to be common on many web sites (although technically speaking, user controls shouldn't be used across several applications — as you will see at the end of this chapter — because there is something better served for that purpose). It is also something that will quite likely be called upon at several places throughout the application (although you only call upon it once within the Wrox United application), and the principle will remain the same throughout — it will display a list of articles in order, with the most recent first. Of course, not all things you will design on this site will be suitable for reuse and for creating as user controls, but the `News` control is a content delivery mechanism and content is the driving force behind most web sites. In the following Try It Out, you create your own `News` user control and drop it into your own blank page.

Try It Out — Using the News Control

1. Open Visual Web Developer and select Open Web Site. From the Chapter10 folder (`C:\BegASPNET\Chapters\Begin\Chapter10`), select `WroxUnitedNewsControl` and click OK.

2. Go to Visual Web Developer and right-click the top item in Solution Explorer. Select Add New Item and select Web User Control. Type **NewsUserControl.ascx** in the Name text box. Make sure the Place Code in Separate File check box is selected, as shown in Figure 10-23.

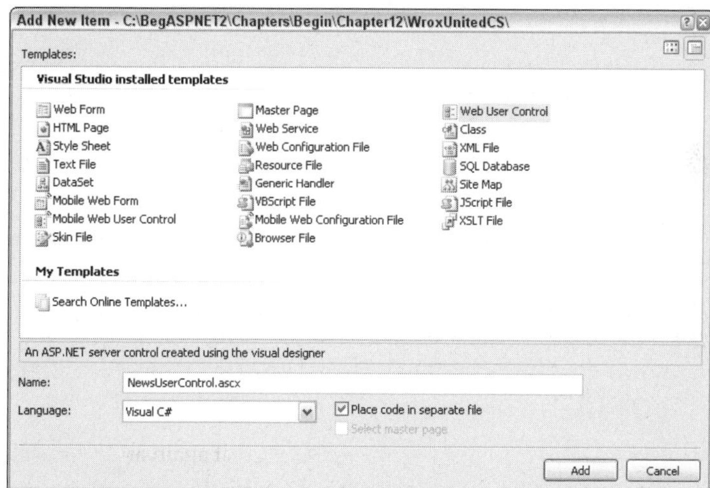

Figure 10-23

3. Go to Design View and drag a `SqlDataSource` control from the Data section of the Toolbox menu. Don't, however, click to configure the Data Source from the Common Tasks box that appears.

4. From the Data section of the Toolbox menu, add a `Repeater` control below the `SqlDataSource` and select `SqlDataSource1` to be the `Repeater`'s Data Source (see Figure 10-24).

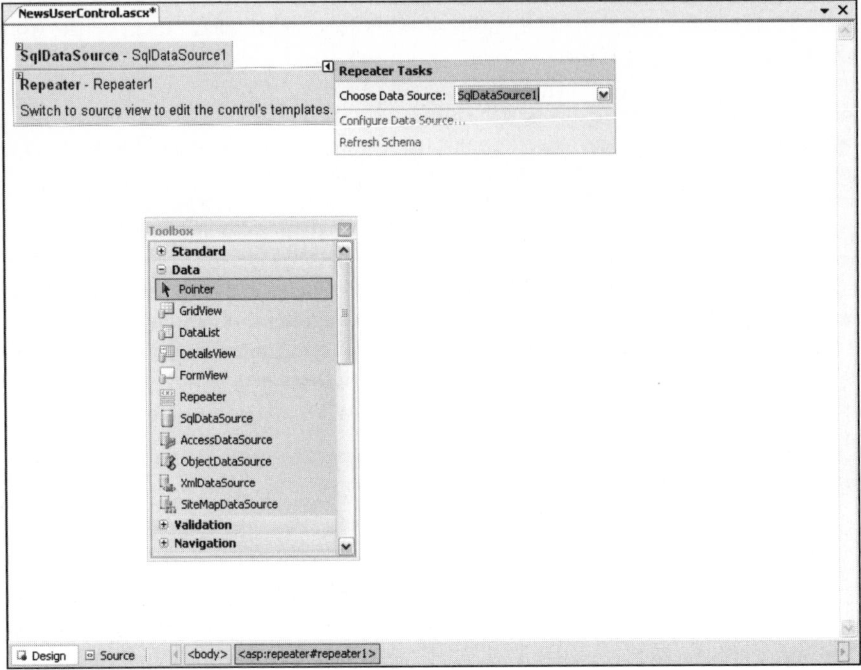

Figure 10-24

5. Add the template to the HTML. With the `Repeater` control, you have to switch to Source View to add the template. Switch to Source View and add the following code:

```
<asp:Repeater ID="Repeater1" Runat="server" DataSourceID="SqlDataSource1">
    <ItemTemplate>
        <div class="newsItem">
            <span class="newsDate"><%#Eval("DateToShow", "{0:dd MMM yyyy}")%>
            </span>
            <span class="newsTitle"><%#Eval("Title")%></span>
        </div>
        <span class="newsContent">
            <%#Eval("Description") %>
        </span>
    </ItemTemplate>
</asp:Repeater>
```

6. Still in Source View, add the following to the `SqlDataSource`:

```
ConnectionString="<%$ConnectionStrings:WroxUnited%>"
```

This contains the connection string information that you will need for this example.

7. Go to the code-behind file and add the following code for an `ItemsToShow` property, which governs how many items are shown on the screen at the same time:

```
public partial class NewsUserControl : System.Web.UI.UserControl
{
    private int _itemsToShow = 5;
     public int ItemsToShow
     {
        get
         {
            return _itemsToShow;
         }
        set
        {
            _itemsToShow = value;
        }
     }
```

8. Add the following code directly underneath the code you previously added:

```
private void Page_PreRender(object sender, System.EventArgs e)
    {
        string sel   = string.Format("SELECT Top {0} * FROM [News] WHERE DateToShow
<= '{1}' ORDER BY DateToShow DESC", _itemsToShow,
DateTime.Now.ToString("yyyy/MM/dd"));
//Make sure above is all on one line.
        SqlDataSource1.SelectCommand = sel;
    }
```

9. Go to Solution Explorer and create a new Web Form called **NewsDisplay.aspx**. Go to Design View and drag your `NewsUserControl.ascx` into the Web Form.

10. Run it—it's fairly raw without any styles, but you will see five news items, as shown in Figure 10-25.

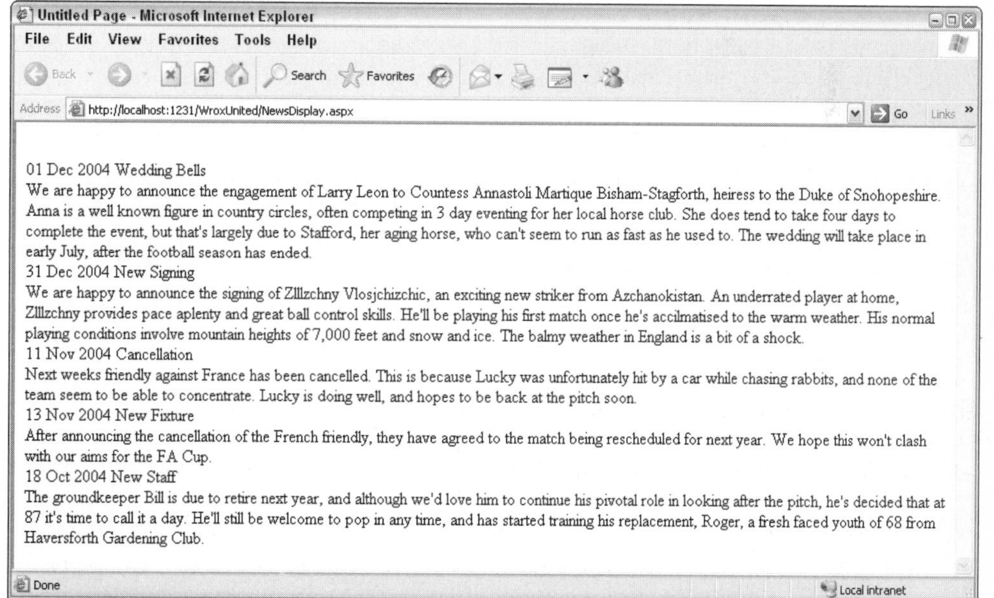

Figure 10-25

11. Go back to Source View and add an `ItemsToShow` attribute, and set it to **2**:

```
<div>
 <uc1:NewsUserControl id="NewsUserControl1" runat="server" ItemsToShow="2">
 </uc1:NewsUserControl>
</div>
```

12. Save the page and run it again, and you will see the output shown in Figure 10-26. If you want to improve the "rough and ready" look of this control, as we have, drag the `site.css` file from the templates folder in the directory into the aspx file to apply the style sheet.

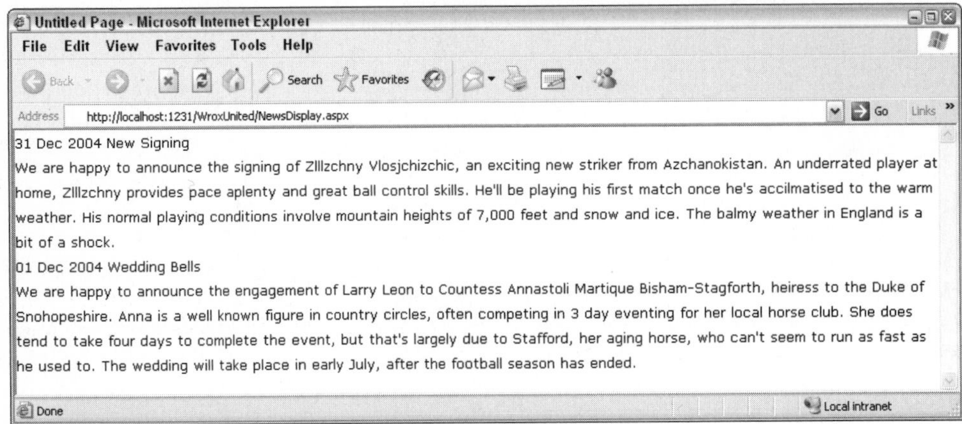

Figure 10-26

How It Works

You have a `News` control that not only can you drop in any page (it is used on the front page of the Wrox United site), but also enables you to configure the number of items shown via a single attribute. The following code has been created in the user control, a `SqlDataSource` control that queries the news table together with a `Repeater` control that displays each of the news items:

```
<%@ Control Language="C#" AutoEventWireup="false" codefile="News.ascx.cs"
Inherits="NewsControl" %>
<asp:SqlDataSource id="SqlDataSource1" Runat="server"

    ConnectionString="<%$ ConnectionStrings:WroxUnited %>">
</asp:SqlDataSource>

<asp:Repeater ID="Repeater1" Runat="server" DataSourceID="SqlDataSource1"
        <ItemTemplate>
        <div class="newsItem">
            <span class="newsDate"><%#Eval("DateToShow", "{0:dd MMM yyyy}")%>
            </span>
            <span class="newsTitle"><%#Eval("Title")%></span>
        </div>
        <span class="newsContent">
            <%#Eval("Description") %>
        </span>
    </ItemTemplate>
</asp:Repeater>
```

It's the code-behind that provides the main functionality. Once again, the relationship between the code-behind and the main control is shown. You added an `ItemsToShow` property to the code-behind and exposed it as a public property. This has the effect of creating an attribute that you can set via the Web Form:

```
private int _itemsToShow = 5;
    public int ItemsToShow
    {
       get
        {
           return _itemsToShow;
        }
       set
       {
           _itemsToShow = value;
       }
    }
```

You set the default to `5`, so if the attribute isn't set, you automatically display five items instead. The property enables you to both get and set the separate values.

The code that occurs in the `Pre_Render` event enables you to display the contents of the control. This is similar to the `Page_Load` event, except it occurs just before the controls on a page are rendered. Because you want to display these at the last possible moment, you place two statements here. The first one provides a SQL statement that selects the top news items ordered by date, and restricted by the `_itemsToShow` variable that you created at the top of the class:

```
string sel   = string.Format("SELECT Top {0} * FROM [News] WHERE DateToShow <=
'{1}' ORDER BY DateToShow DESC", _itemsToShow,
DateTime.Now.ToString("yyyy/MM/dd"));
//Make sure above is all on one line.
        SqlDataSource1.SelectCommand = sel;
```

The second statement sets this SQL to the `SelectCommand` property of your data source, and this restricts the number of items shown by your user control.

Composite Controls

You've looked at how user controls are nested inside pages, but it doesn't stop there. You can nest user controls inside user controls. These are known as composite controls. If you consider a scenario where you require a group of user controls, such as a `News` control, a `Login` control, and a `Fixture viewer` control. Rather than having to place references to these controls separately each time, you could place them in a single user control and use that control instead. This further enhances the code-reuse within the application.

Assemblies and Custom Server Controls

.NET also provides the capability to pre-compile code components into a central location that can be accessed from anywhere within the site. These components, like user controls, can contain one or more classes. However, the crucial difference is that ASP.NET uses the compiled *assemblies* rather than the code inside the component itself at runtime (in other words, the component isn't compiled at the same time as the main application, but rather has to be done beforehand). .NET assemblies can use any of the .NET-compliant languages, and the assemblies are compiled into .dll files. These .dll files are then placed within the `App_Code` folder, and can be used by ASP.NET as part of the program.

Custom server controls are a specific version of assemblies. You have already seen how ASP.NET provides such controls as `TextBox`, `Label`, `CheckBox`, and radio button controls to aid in the development of user interfaces. Although the vast majority of server controls should cover you for most situations, and also the fact that in ASP.NET 2.0, there is an even wider range of server controls, there are still times when you might need to create controls that extend the user interface still further. Custom controls are controls that generate a visible user interface. If you consider that when ASP.NET was created, the ASP.NET server controls are actually just custom controls that someone at Microsoft has already created for you and distributed with ASP.NET 2.0. A main difference between user controls and custom controls is that user controls are intended to be confined to the application they were created for, whereas custom controls can be used with any application. Hence they are pre-compiled into assembly files, making them more portable. They also inherit from the `System.Web.UI.Control` namespace rather than the namespace specific to the application. Typical examples of custom controls include `TreeView` controls and custom file open dialog boxes for a particular file type.

The creation of custom controls is something you have to worry about less now, given the vast amount of controls provided with ASP.NET 2.0, and for that reason they are not covered in this book.

For in-depth discussion of custom controls, consult Professional ASP.NET 2.0 by Bill Evjen, et al, from Wrox Press.

Summary

This chapter has taken a slightly more theory-heavy slant than previous chapters, because the only way developers can learn their trade well is by learning the best practices. This chapter has been all about componentization and code reuse. You have looked at four strategies for these. The first was the use of code-behind. The main reason for using code-behind is to separate the web page's design, style, and user interface from the main structure and the code of the web site. The second was using the `ObjectDataSource` control to create a separate business layer and data layer in your application. This was the next step, separating your application into an interface, a business rules layer, and a data layer. Third was the idea of centralizing all of our data access code into one component that could be deployed across different applications. Finally, you looked a user controls and how the use of user controls promotes code-reuse.

Although this chapter delved a lot into theory, it also taught you the way you should code and the techniques you should employ. Good applications are ones that contain as little code as possible, that don't repeat the same code and ultimately run quicker, have fewer bugs and are easier to maintain, and are possibly even easier for the end-user to use. The next chapter examines another new feature in ASP.NET 2.0, that of profiles and roles.

Exercises

1. Create a new web site and a new page called **CodeBehind.aspx** with a single label, but making sure that you don't check the box marked Placed Code in a Separate File. Now create a code-behind file manually for that page that displays the content of the label.

2. How would you go about adding an image to accompany each news item? Note that it shouldn't display if there is no news image present for that article.

11

Roles and Profiles

In Chapter 4, you learned how ASP.NET handles simple user accounts, how access to a site can be controlled on a user-by-user basis, and how to group users into roles and control access to a site through the use of roles. Using the ASP.NET Web Site Administration Tool, you have the ability to define user accounts, administer roles, and set security permissions all in one central location. This chapter revisits the concept of roles and looks at how accounts and roles are used in Wrox United. You also learn how to control program logic and flow based on which roles the current user is a member of, all using code.

Additionally, because you should now feel comfortable working with .NET code, this chapter takes you on a tour of user profiles. The user profiles that you can create in ASP.NET can store additional information on a user-account-by-user-account basis; for example, a user's favorite football team or favorite color. You'll recall that, in Chapter 5, the concepts of styling controls and pages using central themes were discussed; in this chapter, one of the items you'll be adding to user profiles is the preferred theme to use for a specific web site.

In this chapter, you learn how to:

- Manage site accessibility on a role-by-role basis in code
- Use roles effectively in a site, using the Wrox United site as an example
- Employ user profiles to store additional information about a user
- Work with profiles in code to store and apply favorite themes to a site

This chapter revisits Wrox United and introduces the Fan Club page to the site. In this page, you'll learn how to display different content depending on which role a user is a member of, and how to update a user's profile. You'll also make use of the powerful `LoginView` control, which simplifies the process of displaying different content dependent on role membership.

The Importance of Roles

A *role* is a key concept to understand when you do any work on a system that involves user accounts. In any organization, user accounts are likely to be assigned to roles that relate to the type of user account. For example, if you look at the local user accounts set up on your PC, you will find lists of different types of groups; for example, users, power users, and administrators. In a simple Windows domain-based network, you may find that all corporate users are members of the Domain Users role. Certain user accounts in a network may be members of a different group — for example, your system administrators may be members of the Domain Administrators group, enabling them to administer the users in the company domain. Figure 11-1 displays the groups available to a fairly basic Windows XP installation; each user account can be a member of zero or more groups.

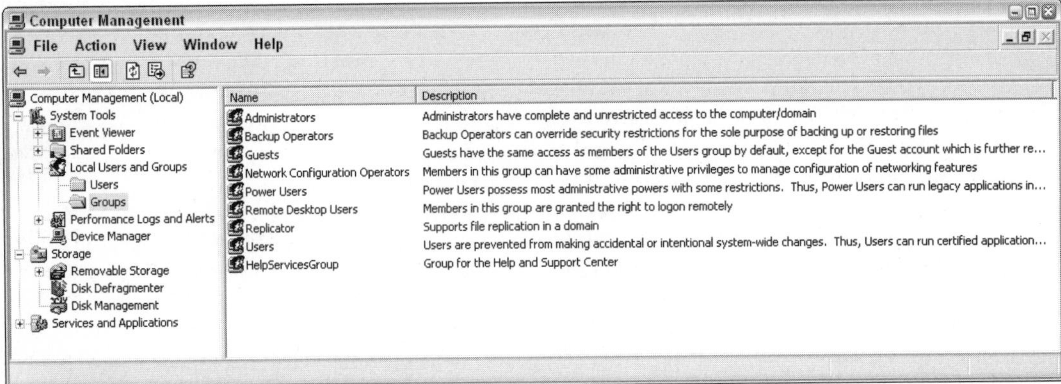

Figure 11-1

Because each user account can be a member of more than one group, if required, Figure 11-2 shows an example of an account on the same machine.

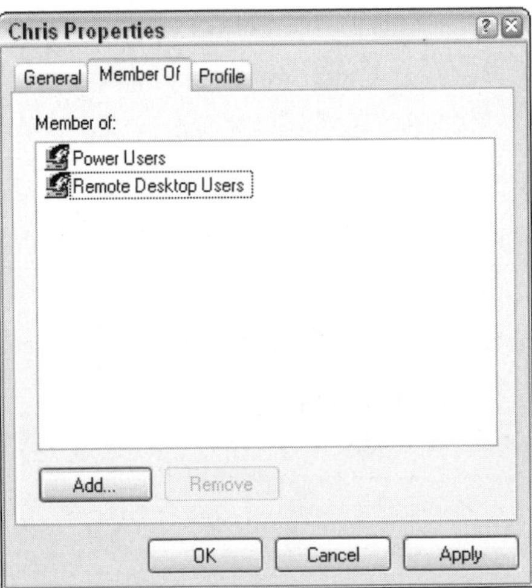

Figure 11-2

Notice that the user displayed here is a member of both the Power Users and Remote Desktop Users groups. This means that the user (called Chris) can log in via a Remote Desktop session (if remote connections are allowed), and can perform most day-to-day administration tasks, with some restrictions, required on the computer.

The ability to group users into related roles simplifies the process of administration. If my administrator wanted to grant a specific permission to all the members of the development team at the office where I work, he could either assign those permissions to each one of the 12 user accounts individually, or he could add us all to a "Developers" role, and grant that one permission to the role. It's a simple and logical way to work, and you will almost always have to consider which roles a user is a member of when you develop an application.

One of the most important roles you will come across is that of the Administrator. An Administrator can pretty much do anything to an application or a system. For this reason, you can rejoice in the ability to log in as an Administrator to fix a problem that can only be fixed with a specific set of permissions. However, you need to be very aware of permissions when you develop applications because it's potentially dangerous from a security perspective. Code running with full privileges can modify a system to the point where the system is completely destroyed — you don't want to end up deleting the entire contents of your Windows directory, or formatting your hard drive accidentally.

The best practice to adopt is that of lowest-privilege. Start with a low-privilege user account and add only those permissions that are required by the application. The default settings in ASP.NET mean that the code that runs ASP.NET web applications will have a limited set of privileges by default, and IIS6 (the web server provided with Windows Server 2003) is locked down tight when you first install it, so you have to actually enable ASP.NET when you install it just to run ASP.NET web applications. That doesn't mean that you can sit back and keep running as an administrator the whole time — try logging in as a user who is only a member of Power Users, or, better still, the Users group, and test your code regularly. Never assume that an application is working without having tested it as a completely different user.

Introducing Roles in Wrox United

In the full Wrox United application, you'll recall that roles have been configured to enable different levels of access to the site. Each user account that is defined has a different level of access, whether it's as a site administrator or a fan club member. Time to recap a little on what you achieved in Chapter 4. If you open up the Wrox United application source in VWD and select Website⇨ASP.NET Configuration, you'll see the list of current users, the list of roles, and you can explore each user account to see their roles. Figure 11-3 shows the list of roles defined in the preconfigured Wrox United application.

> *These screenshots were taken from the user configuration stored in the* `C:\BegASPNET2\Chapters\Begin\Chapter11` *version of the site, though the configuration is the same in the full version of the site.*

So, that's a total of five different roles. If you look at the users defined in the application, you'll find that there are seven different users: ChrisH, ChrisU, Dan, Dave, Jim, John, and Lou. Because users can be members of more than one role, and roles can have more than one member, that's quite a few possible combinations. Clicking the Manage link shown next to each role in Figure 11-3 displays all members of a role. Figure 11-4 displays the list of FanClubMembers.

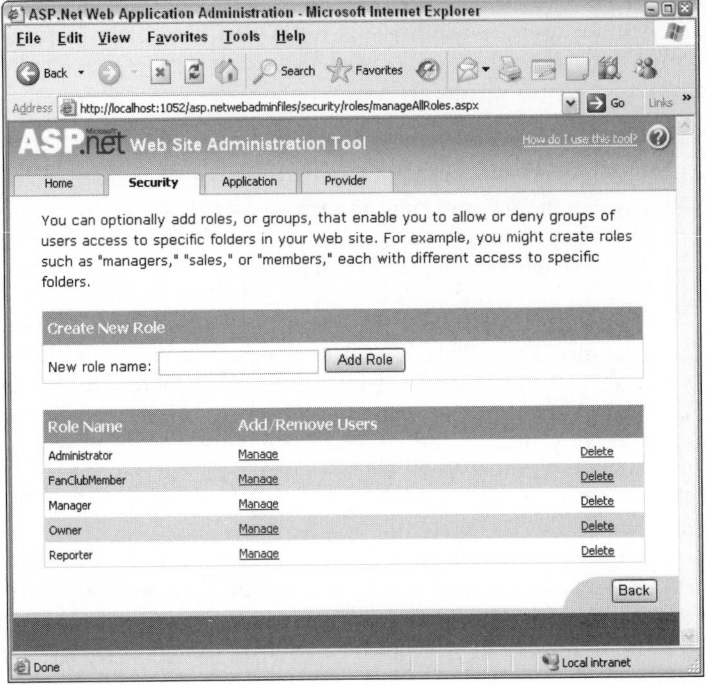

Figure 11-3

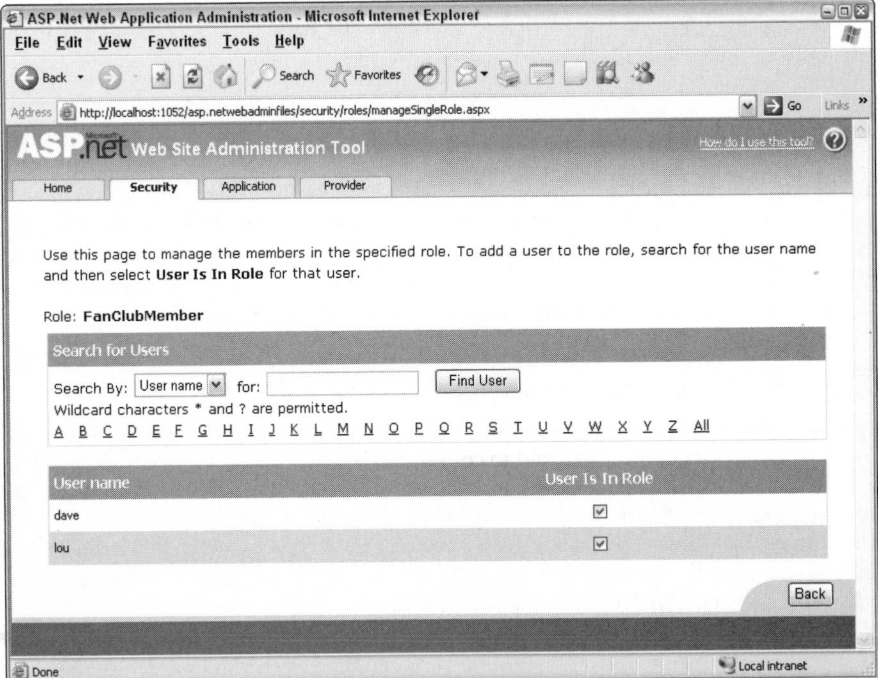

Figure 11-4

You can continue to explore each of the user accounts and roles to see who is a member of each group, so you can discover the following (among other things):

- ChrisH, ChrisU, Dave, and John are reporters.
- Dave is a member of all groups; hence he's the "super user" (who can access all areas of the site, which is great for testing).
- Lou is only a member of the Fan Club; hence she is the only true fan of the team.
- Dan's the team's manager and Jim's the owner.

After digging through the site configuration, in the Access Rules section, you'll also recall that the Admin section of the site was restricted so that only site administrators could enter that part of the site. Additionally, the Fan Club was restricted so that only members could see the fan club–specific links available in the fan club section.

In the next example, you get to use this configuration and try it out for yourself. The Fan Club for Wrox United is a good place to start.

In the following Try It Out, you build the skeleton for the Fan Club page and see how different users will see a different version of the page, depending on whether they are logged in, and, if the user has logged in, the current user's identity.

Try It Out The Wrox United Fan Club

1. Open up the chapter version (in `C:\BegASPNET2\Chapters\Begin\Chapter11\WroxUnited`) of the Wrox United application and run the site by pressing Ctrl+F5.
2. Log in to the site as Lou, using the password **lou@123**. There is a link to the Fan Club (`FanClub.aspx`) in the menu on the left (shown in Figure 11-5), and to the two subpages: `FanClubMatchReport.aspx` and `FanClubPictures.aspx`.

   At the moment, the pages are looking a bit empty, so it's time to start adding some code.
3. Open `FanClub.aspx` in Visual Web Developer and switch to Design View.
4. Drag a `LoginView` control onto the page, as shown in Figure 11-6.
5. Rename the control **FCLoginView**.

   You're going to create three different views on this page:

   - **AnonymousTemplate:** Anonymous visitors will be asked to purchase a Fan Club membership before they can access the fan club pages.
   - **Administrator/Manager/Owner/Reporter:** All logged-in users who are not members of the Fan Club will be told to contact the administrator of the site to gain access to the fan club.
   - **FanClubMembers:** Members of the Fan Club will be able to change their passwords and to update their profiles (you add this part later in the chapter).

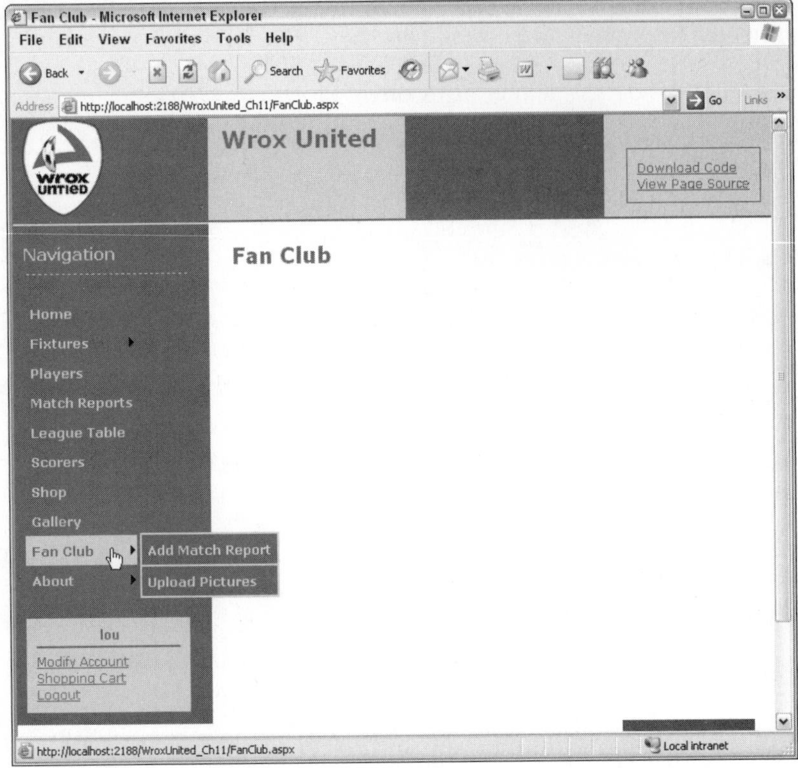

Figure 11-5

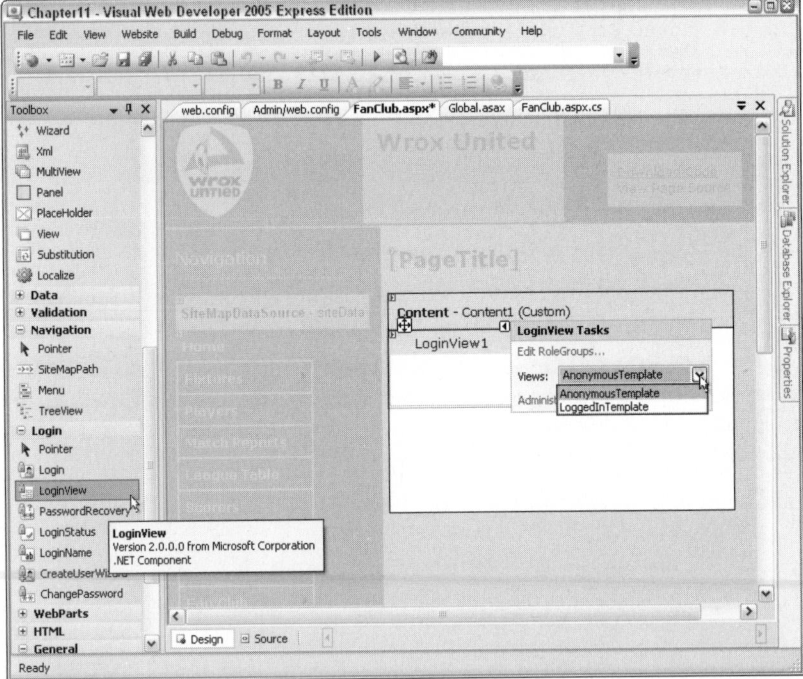

Figure 11-6

6. In the Common Tasks box of the `LoginView` control (the flyout highlighted in Figure 11-6), click the Edit RoleGroups link. In the dialog box that appears (shown in Figure 11-7), you can enter the details for the two custom role groups. Click the Add button to add a new group, and then click the ellipsis next to the Roles property on the right and enter **FanClubMember** in the dialog box that appears.

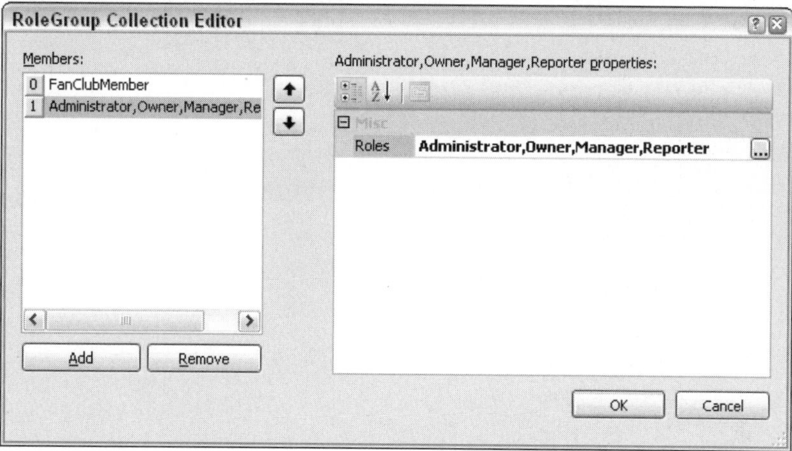

Figure 11-7

7. Repeat the process and enter **Administrator**, **Owner**, **Manager**, and **Reporter**, each on separate lines in the pop-up, as depicted in Figure 11-8.

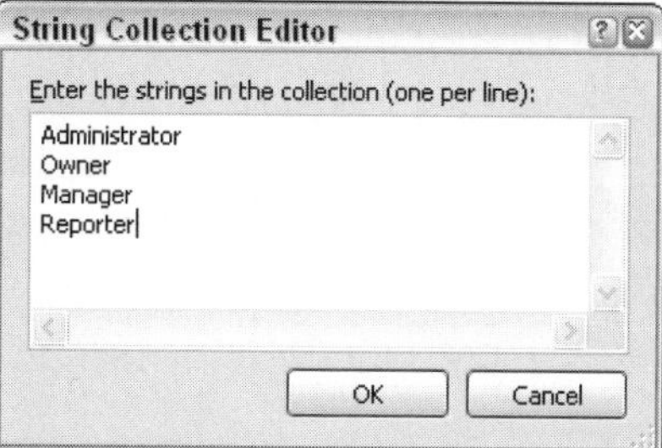

Figure 11-8

8. Click OK to close the dialogs and you'll be returned to the Design View for the page.

9. Back in the Common Tasks box of the `LoginView` control (refer to Figure 11-6), select the AnonymousTemplate from the View drop-down and enter just a few words of text in the body of the control (see Figure 11-9).

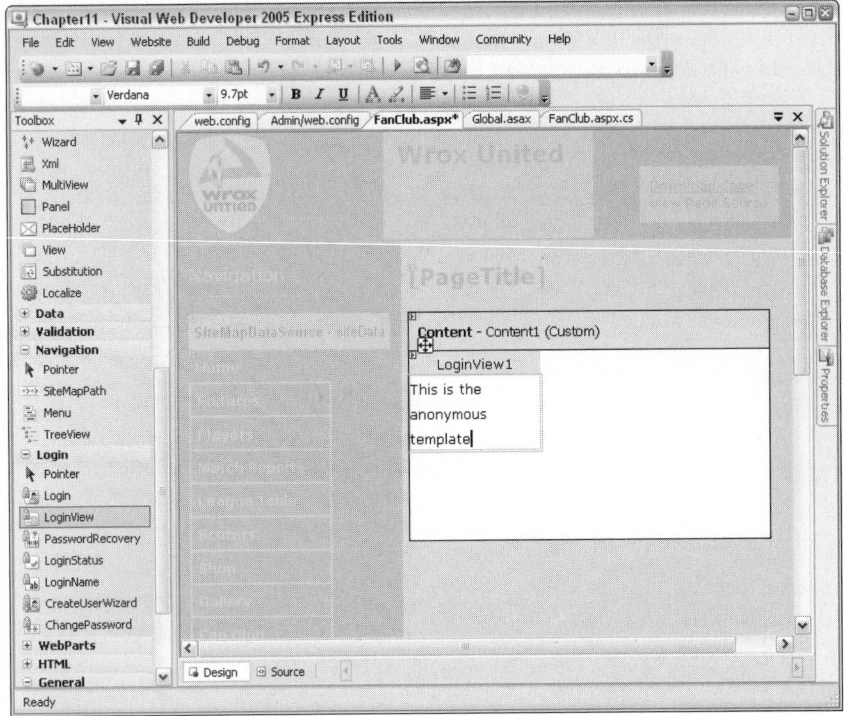

Figure 11-9

When you return to Source View, you will now see the following code:

```
<%@ Page Language="C#" MasterPageFile="~/site.master" AutoEventWireup="false"
CodeFile="FanClub.aspx.cs" Inherits="FanClub" Title="Fan Club" %>
<asp:Content ID="Content1" ContentPlaceHolderID="mainContent" Runat="Server">
  <asp:LoginView ID="FCLoginView" runat="server">
    <RoleGroups>
      <asp:RoleGroup Roles="FanClubMember">
      </asp:RoleGroup>
      <asp:RoleGroup Roles="Administrator,Owner,Manager,Reporter">
      </asp:RoleGroup>
    </RoleGroups>
    <AnonymousTemplate>
      This is the anonymous template
    </AnonymousTemplate>
  </asp:LoginView>
</asp:Content>
```

10. Stay in Source View and enter the following lines of code — this will make sure you have some visible content displayed no matter who views the site:

```
<asp:LoginView ID="FCLoginView" runat="server">
  <RoleGroups>
    <asp:RoleGroup Roles="FanClubMember">
      <ContentTemplate>
        <p>
          Welcome back
          <asp:LoginName ID="FCLoginName" runat="server" />
          .</p>
        <p>
          There are always lots of exciting things happening with the fan club,
          most of which you already know from the email we regularly send out.
          One that hasn't made it to the email yet is the proposed end of season
          BBQ - a great excuse for a summer party (not that we really need an
          excuse). This will be open to all members of the public and tickets
          will be heavily discounted for fan club members as a thank you for all
          of the great support you've given the club. The date hasn't yet been
          set, but keep your eyes on your inbox for more details.
        </p>
      </ContentTemplate>
    </asp:RoleGroup>
    <asp:RoleGroup Roles="Administrator,Owner,Manager,Reporter">
      <ContentTemplate>
        To see the Fan Club features you need to be a member. As special users
        you get free entry to the fan club - talk to the admin people to get set
        up.
      </ContentTemplate>
    </asp:RoleGroup>
  </RoleGroups>
  <AnonymousTemplate>
    <p>
      The fan club provides a way for you to show your devotion to the club, and
      gains you exclusive privileges. You get discounts on match tickets and at
      the club store, as well as having the opportunity to meet up with
      like-minded fans.
    </p>
    <p>
      Membership to the Fan Club can be bought from
      the <a href="Shop.aspx"> Club Shop</a>. Once membership has been received
      we'll enable your account as a Fan Club Member.
    </p>
  </AnonymousTemplate>
</asp:LoginView>
```

11. Time to run the page and see how this works. Launch the site from VWD and, before you log in, go to the Fan Club page as an anonymous user. You should see the screen shown in Figure 11-10.

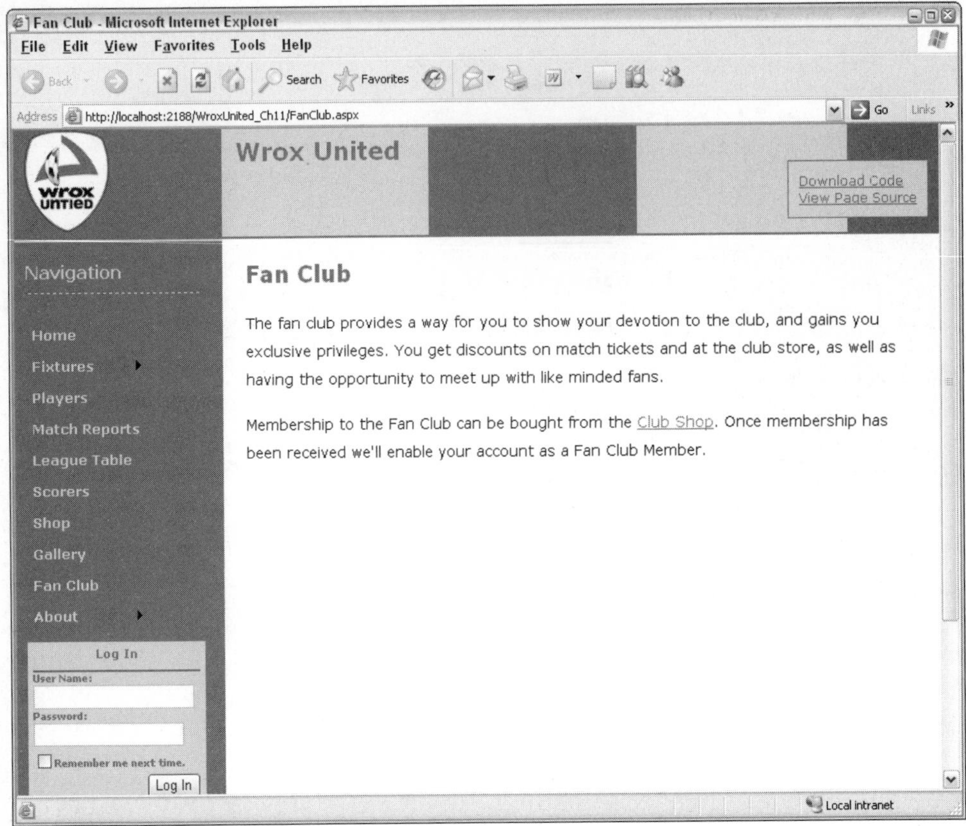

Figure 11-10

12. Log in to the site as **ChrisH**, using the password **chrish@123**. You will now see the screen in Figure 11-11.

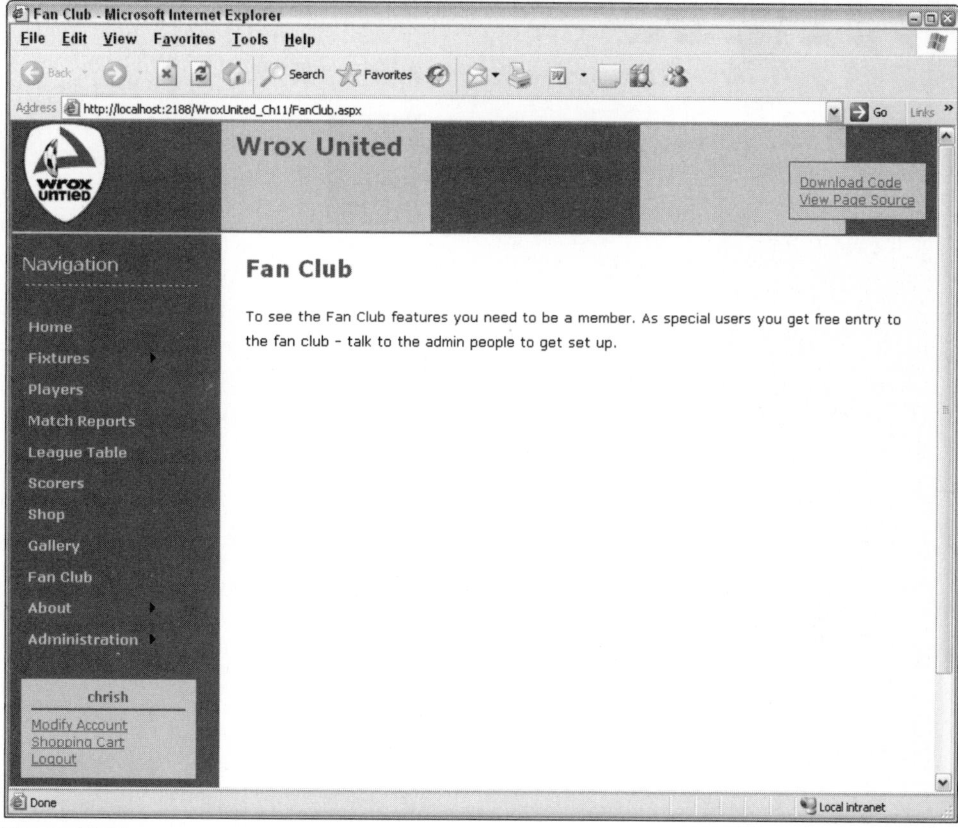

Figure 11-11

13. Log out, and then log back in as **Lou**, using password **lou@123**. You'll be presented with the welcome screen shown in Figure 11-12.

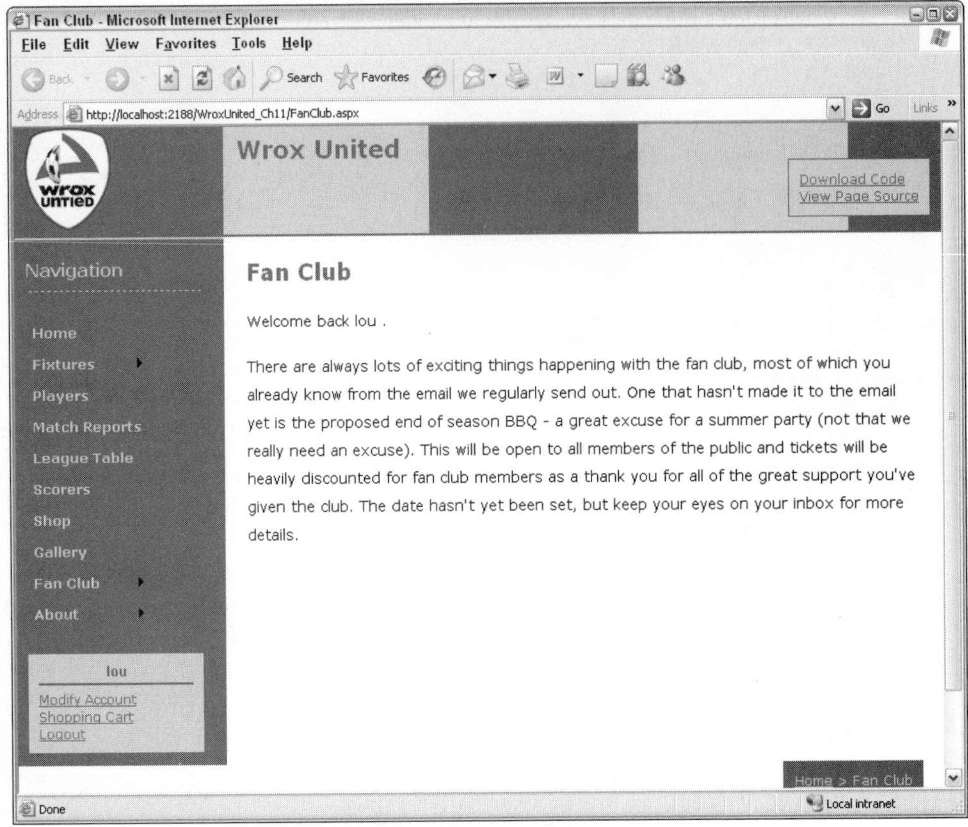

Figure 11-12

How It Works

The `LoginView` control, which you first met in Chapter 4, is a great way of displaying content that is directly related to the user who is currently viewing a page. In this example, you've added code so that three possible views are available of the Fan Club home page.

If the user is anonymous, the anonymous template is used:

```
<AnonymousTemplate>
  <p>
    The fan club provides a way for you to show your devotion to the club, and
    gains you exclusive privileges. You get discounts on match tickets and at
    the club store, as well as having the opportunity to meet up with like
    minded fans.
  </p>
  <p>
    Membership to the Fan Club can be bought from
    the <a href="Shop.aspx">Club Shop</a>. Once membership has been received
    we'll enable your account as a Fan Club Member.
  </p>
</AnonymousTemplate>
```

If the user has logged in, it's fairly safe to assume that he is a member of a group, and hence he will see a different page depending on which roles he belongs to:

```
<RoleGroups>
  <asp:RoleGroup Roles="FanClubMember">
    <ContentTemplate>
      <p>
        Welcome back
        <asp:LoginName ID="FCLoginName" runat="server" />
        .</p>
      <p>
        There are always lots of exciting things happening with the fan club,
        most of which you already know from the email we regularly send out.
        One that hasn't made it to the email yet is the proposed end of season
        BBQ - a great excuse for a summer party (not that we really need an
        excuse). This will be open to all members of the public and tickets
        will be heavily discounted for fan club members as a thank you for all
        of the great support you've given the club. The date hasn't yet been
        set, but keep your eyes on your inbox for more details.
      </p>
    </ContentTemplate>
  </asp:RoleGroup>
```

Fan Club members will see a custom page with some text. There's not a lot on here yet, but that will change later in this chapter when you learn about user profiles. These profiles can be used to store additional information about a user, so the fan club page will become a central place for site members to come so that they can modify their profiles.

If the user is a member of one of the other roles (Administrator, Owner, Manager, or Reporter), the user will see a different display:

```
  <asp:RoleGroup Roles="Administrator,Owner,Manager,Reporter">
    <ContentTemplate>
      To see the Fan Club features you need to be a member. As special users
      you get free entry to the fan club - talk to the admin people to get set
      up.
    </ContentTemplate>
  </asp:RoleGroup>
</RoleGroups>
```

If you wanted to extend this part of the site, perhaps you could include a button or a link that would fire an e-mail to the site administrator, indicating your interest in joining the fan club.

This example demonstrates how simple and easy it is to change the appearance of a page, depending on who is logged in to the site. There are some drawbacks to this technique, however, which you'll see when you look at extending the display for fan club members to show and edit their profile details.

You now know that you can change the display of a site by user roles. The next step is to lock down parts of the site by role, and work with role-level access to the site.

Configuring Page-Level Authorization

You control access to folders by managing general application access via the Web Site Administration Tool (see Figure 11-13). Previously (back in Chapter 4), you learned how to restrict access to the pages contained within the Admin folder to deny all unapproved users access to those pages.

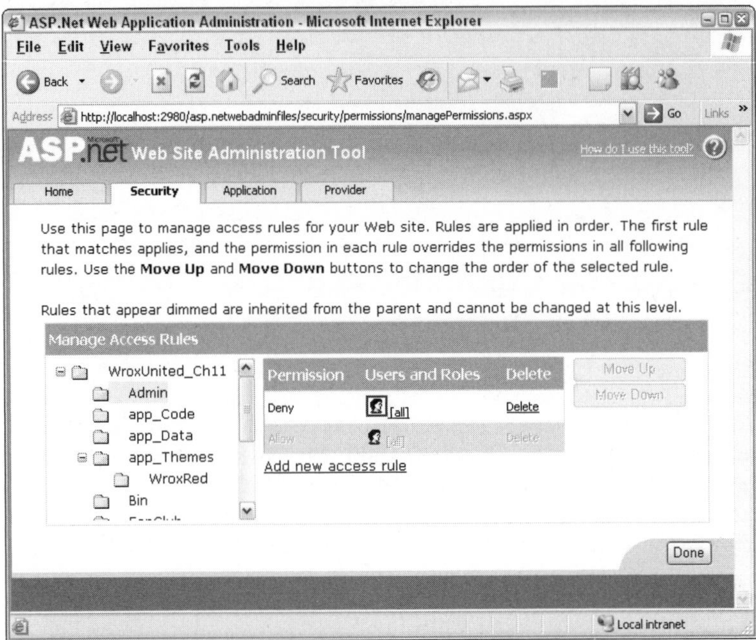

Figure 11-13

This general level of restriction is fine for hiding the contents of a directory, but configuring who can access each page is controlled in the `Web.config` file for each folder.

In the Admin folder, in the code for the full Wrox United application, you will find a `Web.config` file. The following statements appear in this file:

```
<system.web>
  <authorization>
    <deny users="*" />
  </authorization>
</system.web>
<location path="Admin.aspx">
  <system.web>
    <authorization>
      <allow roles="Reporter,Administrator,Owner,Manager" />
    </authorization>
  </system.web>
</location>
```

The first part of this extract reflects the setting applied in the site administration tool, denying all users access:

```
<deny users="*" />
```

The second part of the extract applies access permissions to a specific page — the `Admin.aspx` page, in this case. The users who are allowed to view the `Admin.aspx` page include anyone who is a member of any of the Reporter, Administrator, Owner, or Manager roles:

```
<allow roles="Reporter,Administrator,Owner,Manager" />
```

And so the pattern continues for the remainder of the configuration file, where access to each page is controlled by the configuration file, enabling access permissions to be set for each role against each page in the hierarchy.

Controlling Page Visibility

There may be some situations where you will want to allow a user to know of the existence of a page, even if the user is denied access to it. In this way, you can offer a link to users, but when they click that link, they are prompted to log in as a user with sufficient privileges before they can view the page. In order to achieve this, a `roles` attribute (see the shaded lines in the following code) can be added to the `web.sitemap` file, which ensures that a link will be visible to certain users to specified pages, even if the user is unable to view the content of the page itself. Here is an example:

```
<siteMapNode title="Administration" url="Admin/Admin.aspx"
            roles="Reporter,Owner,Manager,Administrator">
  <siteMapNode title="Edit News" url="Admin/EditNews.aspx"
              description="Edit club news"
              roles="Reporter,Owner,Manager,Administrator" />
  <siteMapNode title="Schedule Match" url="Admin/ScheduleMatch.aspx"
      description="Schedule a Match"
      roles="Manager,Owner" />
```

Notice that the `roles` attribute on the `Admin.aspx` page states that Reporters, Owners, Managers, and Administrators should be aware of the existence of the `Admin.aspx` page. Contrast this with the `ScheduleMatch.aspx` page, and you'll see that only Managers or Owners can see the link to be able to schedule matches.

If you log in to the site as ChrisH, you're a member of the Reporter role, so even if all access to all `Admin` pages is revoked, you will still see links to the `Admin.aspx` and `EditNews.aspx` pages, but you won't see a link to the `ScheduleMatch.aspx` page.

Because the `Web.config` file and the `roles` attributes in the `web.sitemap` work together to control both visibility and access, the best way to understand how they work together is to see them in an example.

For this Try It Out, make sure you are using the Chapter 11 version of the Wrox United code. The code supplied has been modified slightly for the purposes of this example. Also, make sure you close any open browser windows from the previous exercise, or your changes may not appear as expected.

Try It Out Configuring Visibility, Access, and Authorization

1. Take a look at the code in the `web.sitemap` file. This file contains the same code that is used in the live Wrox United application. The following is an extract from that file, highlighting the use of the `roles` attribute:

```
...
    <siteMapNode title="Fan Club" url="FanClub.aspx">
      <siteMapNode title="Add Match Report" url="FanClub/FanClubMatchReport.aspx"
                   description="Add a match report"
                   roles="FanClubMember" />
      <siteMapNode title="Upload Pictures" url="FanClub/FanClubPictures.aspx"
          description="Upload pictures or video of a match"
          roles="FanClubMember" />
    </siteMapNode>
...
    <siteMapNode title="Administration" url="Admin/Admin.aspx"
                 roles="Reporter,Owner,Manager,Administrator">
      <siteMapNode title="Edit News" url="Admin/EditNews.aspx"
                   description="Edit club news"
                   roles="Reporter,Owner,Manager,Administrator" />
      <siteMapNode title="Schedule Match" url="Admin/ScheduleMatch.aspx"
          description="Schedule a Match"
          roles="Manager,Owner" />
      <siteMapNode title="Edit Squad" url="Admin/EditSquad.aspx"
          description="Edit the players in the squad"
          roles="Owner" />
      <siteMapNode title="Update Score" url="Admin/MatchScore.aspx"
          description="Edit the score for a match in progress"
          roles="Reporter" />
      <siteMapNode title="Match Report" url="Admin/MatchReport.aspx"
          description="Upload or edit a match report"
          roles="Reporter" />
      <siteMapNode title="Shop" url="Admin/UpdateProducts.aspx"
                   description="Update products"
                   roles="Administrator" />
    </siteMapNode>
...
```

2. Take a look at the `Web.config` stored in the root of the Admin folder. Notice that no specific locations are defined in this file, hence the only permission currently active on that folder is to deny access to all users:

```
<?xml version="1.0" encoding="utf-8"?>
<configuration>
  <system.web>
    <authorization>
      <deny users="*" />
    </authorization>
  </system.web>
</configuration>
```

The result of these two configuration specifications is demonstrated if you run the site and log in, as Figure 11-14 shows using login ChrisH (password chrish@123).

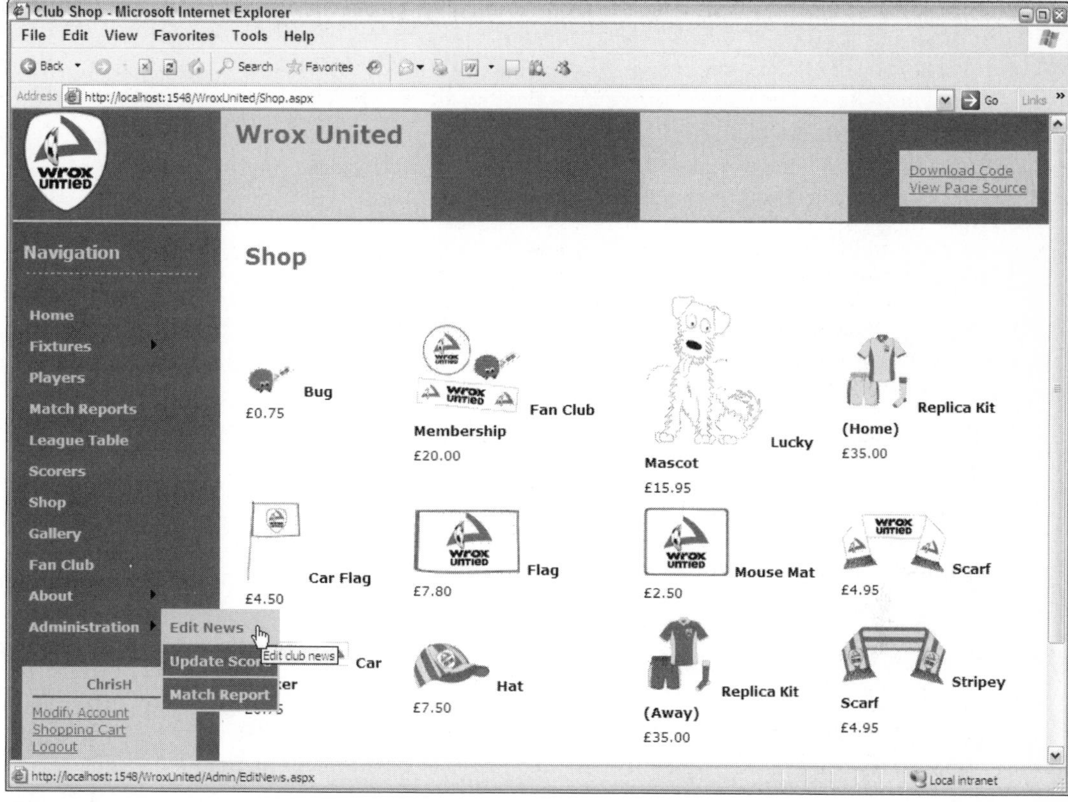

Figure 11-14

Chris is a reporter, so he can see the Administration link, and he can see the links to Edit News, Update Score, and Match Report. However, if he clicks any of those links, he goes straight back to the front page of the site — access has been denied.

3. Close your browser window before continuing — it's time to make some configuration changes. The next step is to allow access to certain resources in the Admin section of the site by role. Open the `Web.config` for the Admin folder and add just the following highlighted code:

```
<?xml version="1.0" encoding="utf-8"?>
<configuration>
  <system.web>
    <authorization>
      <deny users="*" />
    </authorization>
  </system.web>
  <location path="Admin.aspx">
    <system.web>
      <authorization>
        <allow roles="Reporter,Administrator,Owner,Manager" />
      </authorization>
    </system.web>
  </location>
</configuration>
```

4. Run the site again and log in as **ChrisH**.You will now be able to click the Administration link itself and see the `Admin.aspx` page, shown in Figure 11-15.

Figure 11-15

5. The only problem is that you still can't actually update scores or match reports until you add the remaining permissions. Close your browser window again before continuing because you'll be making further configuration changes.

6. Add the following code to complete the `Web.config` file for the Admin section — and notice that one of the permissions isn't quite correct:

```
...
   <location path="Admin.aspx">
    <system.web>
      <authorization>
        <allow roles="Reporter,Administrator,Owner,Manager" />
      </authorization>
    </system.web>
  </location>
  <location path="EditNews.aspx">
    <system.web>
      <authorization>
        <allow roles="Reporter,Administrator,Owner,Manager" />
```

```
      </authorization>
    </system.web>
  </location>
  <location path="MatchScore.aspx">
    <system.web>
      <authorization>
        <allow roles="Reporter" />
      </authorization>
    </system.web>
  </location>
  <location path="MatchReport.aspx">
    <system.web>
      <authorization>
        <allow roles="Reporter" />
      </authorization>
    </system.web>
  </location>
  <location path="EditSquad.aspx">
    <system.web>
      <authorization>
        <allow roles="Owner,Reporter" />
      </authorization>
    </system.web>
  </location>
  <location path="ScheduleMatch.aspx">
    <system.web>
      <authorization>
        <allow roles="Owner,Manager" />
      </authorization>
    </system.web>
  </location>
  <location path="UpdateProducts.aspx">
    <system.web>
      <authorization>
        <allow roles="Administrator" />
      </authorization>
    </system.web>
  </location>
  <location path="UserAdmin.aspx">
    <system.web>
      <authorization>
        <allow roles="Administrator" />
      </authorization>
    </system.web>
  </location>
  <location path="CreateUser.aspx">
    <system.web>
      <authorization>
        <allow roles="Administrator" />
      </authorization>
    </system.web>
  </location>
</configuration>
```

7. In the permissions for the `EditSquad.aspx` page, notice that the Reporter role has just been granted access. The `web.sitemap` page hasn't been modified, so see if you can guess what will be displayed when the page is run. Try it again, running the site and logging in as **ChrisH** once more and see what happens (see Figure 11-16).

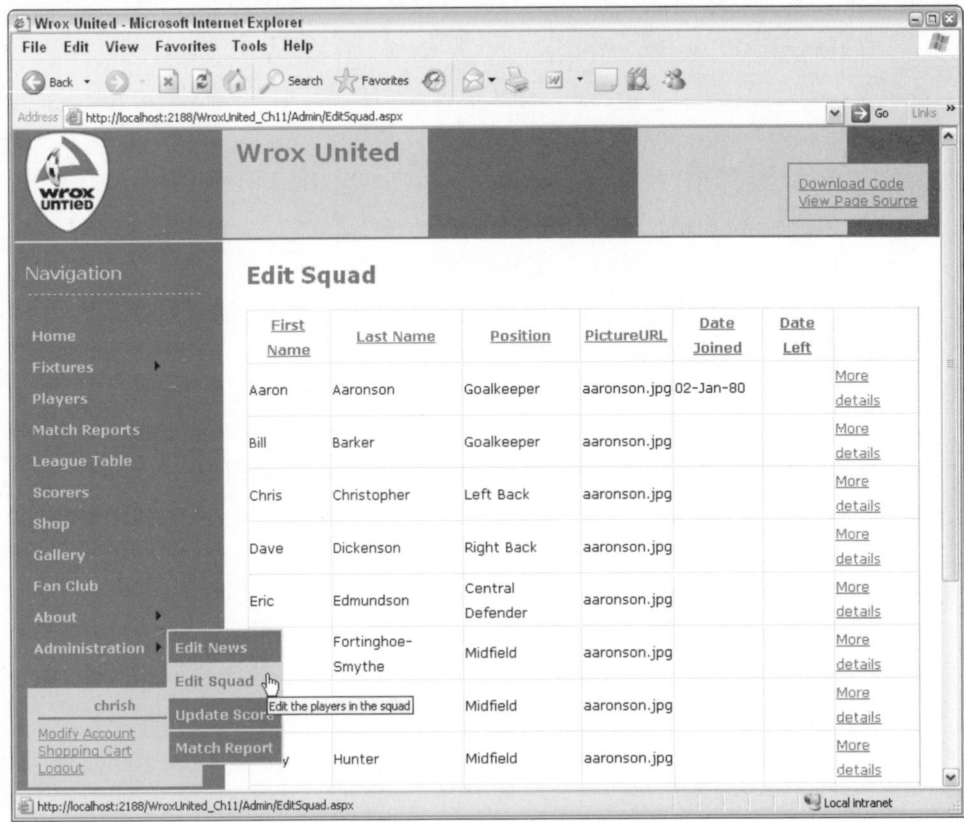

Figure 11-16

8. This is the final result — not only can you see the Edit Squad link, but you can actually go to the Edit Squad page and modify members of the squad. You need to make just one last change to fix this problem — after all, reporters aren't supposed to be able to modify membership of a team. Again, you also need to close the browser window before continuing so that your changes take effect as expected.

9. Open the Admin folder's `Web.config` file again and edit the following highlighted line:

```
<location path="EditSquad.aspx">
  <system.web>
    <authorization>
      <allow roles="Owner" />
    </authorization>
  </system.web>
</location>
```

10. Run the site again, and you will find that if you log in as any of the users who are only members of the Reporters role (ChrisH, John, or ChrisU), you will be able to view the Edit News, Update Score, and Match Report links and page content.

11. One last change to make. This time, modify the `web.sitemap` file as follows:

```
    <siteMapNode title="Match Report" url="Admin/MatchReport.aspx
                 description="Upload or edit a match report"
                 roles="Reporter" />
    <siteMapNode title="Shop" url="Admin/UpdateProducts.aspx"
                 description="Update products"
                 roles="Administrator, Reporter" />
  </siteMapNode>
```

12. Run the page one last time and log in as a Reporter. You will be able to see the link to the Shop page in the Administration section, but if you click the link, you will be taken straight back to the default page. Fix this by removing the Reporter role from the `SiteMapNode` for the `UpdateProducts.aspx` page.

How It Works

This example highlighted the somewhat delicate nature of keeping your `web.sitemap` and `Web.config` file data up to date with current business-case requirements. If you want to allow users to browse a site anonymously, a common configuration decision is to prompt users when it's time for them to log in, and then display a link that they will want to click but forcing them to authenticate before enabling them to view the page.

In this example, you saw that the settings for authorization will control which links are available to each user role. The `web.sitemap` file can then be used to display additional links to a user. These are links to content that the user doesn't have permission to access, to indicate that a facility exists (in this case, the Update Products facility in the Admin section) but that the user needs to log in as a sufficiently privileged user before the link will work.

Here's a look at the most important bits in the code. From the `Web.config` file for the Admin folder on the site, the shaded lines of code specify that only administrators can add or update products:

```
<location path="UpdateProducts.aspx">
  <system.web>
    <authorization>
      <allow roles="Administrator" />
    </authorization>
  </system.web>
</location>
```

Compare this with the addition to the `siteMapNode` that was made in the last part of the example:

```
<siteMapNode title="Shop" url="Admin/UpdateProducts.aspx"
             description="Update products"
             roles="Administrator, Reporter" />
```

This particular combination results in a Reporter being able to see a link, but being unable to access the contents of the link.

If the opposite is true, and the authorization level specified in the `Web.config` file contains more roles than the `web.sitemap` file, the authorization will take precedence. Hence, when you changed the permissions for the `EditSquad.aspx` page and logged in as a Reporter, the link appeared in the navigation menu, and the page could be accessed:

```
<location path="EditSquad.aspx">
  <system.web>
    <authorization>
      <allow roles="Owner,Reporter" />
    </authorization>
  </system.web>
</location>
```

Working with Roles in Code

Up to this point in the chapter, all of the customization that you looked at concerned the use of configuration files to lock down access to parts of the site based on user roles. In addition to these techniques, it's possible to work with roles programmatically in code. This technique has been employed to some extent in the process of applying discounts to shop prices for members of the Fan Club. Many other different methods exist that you can use for working with roles, but the most commonly used is the `IsInRole()` method.

The following code extract (which you will encounter again in Chapter 13) shows this in action:

```
public double MemberDiscount
{
  get
  {
    if (HttpContext.Current.User.IsInRole("FanClubMember"))
    {
      return (this.SubTotal * MemberDiscountPercentage);
    }
    return 0;
  }
}
```

This code resides within the `Shopping.cs` class file used when users purchase items from the shop. The important piece in this code is the statement that applies the discount to users who are members of the Fan Club, using the `User.IsInRole()` method call.

The `IsInRole()` method takes, as an input, a string that is the name of the role to test. As the name of the method suggests, the result will indicate whether or not the user belongs to the role, hence the return value for the method is either `true` (yes, the user belongs to the requested role) or `false` (no, the user is not a member of that role). This technique is used again as part of the shopping process:

```
if (Context.User.IsInRole("FanClubMember"))
{
  SubTotalLabel.Text = string.Format("Sub-Total:{0,35:C}", Profile.Cart.SubTotal);
  MemberDiscount.Text = string.Format("Member Discount:{0:C}", _
                                      Profile.Cart.MemberDiscount);
  DiscountPanel.Visible = true;
}
```

In this extract (from `ShoppingCart.ascx.cs`), the same test is made. There are slight differences between the two calls. The first employs the `HttpContext.Current` object:

```
if (HttpContext.Current.User.IsInRole("FanClubMember"))
{
...
```

The second call employs the `Context` object:

```
if (Context.User.IsInRole("FanClubMember"))
{
...
```

You don't really need to worry about why there is a difference between the two method calls in the context of this chapter, because the actual method that is being called is the same in both cases. However, in case you have a more inquisitive nature, here's what's going on.

In the first case, because the code lives within a separate class file (not a code-beside file for an aspx page or ascx user control), the code could theoretically be called by a different application entirely, outside of the web environment. When users request a web page, they do so within a context. This context will contain a small amount of information along with each request that the user makes, which is understood by the web server. If the user is anonymous, the server will know that the current context represents an anonymous user. If the user has logged in, this small bit of information indicates that the request has come from an authenticated user. The context of a logged-in user states that the request comes from a specific user ID, which ASP.NET can interrogate to find out which roles the user belongs to.

The current context is freely available to web pages and user controls, but classes need to be told a bit more information before they will compile. The actual context that's being used on the web page is the current context of the HTTP request, hence the class needs to have the `HttpContext.Current` version of the context, rather than the context that is available to all requests to a web page.

Enabling User Profiles

Enabling roles on a web site is a good way to open up or hide resources to users, and it also provides limited metadata about the users themselves. Just by being a member of the Reporters group, you can assume that John regularly attends matches and submits scores as they happen. However, this is very limited metadata, and it doesn't give you much more insight into who John is, or what he is interested in. This is where you can start to adopt ASP.NET's user profiles technology to store more information about a user.

For example, if you are a member of a web site that sells a wide variety of goods, you can buy goods from that site by creating a very basic user profile that validates your e-mail address, and can be used to process and track orders. However, on many shopping sites, you can take this "enrollment" process much further and supply additional information to your user account and say, "I like products like this." When you revisit the site, you may then find that the front page changes to show you more items that you are interested in buying, and less of those you're not so enamored with.

This sort of information can be used to extend a simple user account by creating a user profile for storing this additional information; hence you can specify that you have no interest in owning a PlayStation or Xbox, because you only play games on my PC, and the site will be less likely to show you offers related to PS2 or Xbox editions of games. Furthermore, the sales team behind the web site may send out targeted e-mails to customers who have expressed an interest in a certain type of product, with the aim of increasing sales.

One of the uses for user profiles is to create areas of a site that are tailored specifically to the currently logged-in user, giving that user a more personalized view of the site. This technique — called *personalization* — can be used to develop a My Site style area of a web site, where you can amend your own user profile settings, and view information directly relevant to you. In larger corporations, you'll find that the idea of a personalized area of a web or intranet application is quite commonly used — anyone who has ever used SharePoint Portal Server (or similar Portal-style application) will be familiar with the idea of a My Site area.

As far as SharePoint is concerned, the My Site area of a portal can be highly customized to display your calendar and inbox (linked to an Exchange server), or to store custom lists of links to areas of the portal that you may be interested in. Although you're not going to build anything as involved as this in this book, SharePoint Portal Server is one of the best examples of personalization, and doubtless the many other Portal-style applications available for purchase will offer similar levels of personalization.

ASP.NET 2.0 has some great tools available for developing simple profiles with relative ease, so in the next section of this chapter, you explore how these tools can be used to customize a site, and you look at how the Wrox United application uses profiles.

Building a Profile

There are two parts to building a profile. The first is to define what items you want to store. The second is to add functionality to a page to both add and edit information in a user profile.

To define which items you want to store in a profile, you add a list of items, and the type of data each item will contain, to the root `Web.config` file for a site. For example:

```
<profile enabled="true">
  <properties>
    <add name="MemberName"/>
    <add name="Name"/>
    <add name="Address"/>
    <add name="City"/>
    <add name="County"/>
    <add name="PostCode"/>
    <add name="Country"/>
    <add name="Mailings" type="System.Boolean"/>
    <add name="Email"/>
    <add name="Theme"/>
    <add name="Cart" serializeAs="Binary" type="Wrox.Commerce.ShoppingCart"
allowAnonymous="true"/>
  </properties>
</profile>
```

The list of profiles specified is actually the set of properties to be stored for all registered users of the Wrox United application. The default type of data to store is textual data (string data), so for those items without a specific `type` attribute, the data type is assumed to be `string`.

Two items on this list are not strings. The first is the `Mailings` property. This is a `Boolean` value (`true` or `false`) that can be used to store a simple choice. For example, does the user want to receive e-mail concerning the current news about the club or not? You can control the input for this value on a web page by simply including a check box that the user can click as a simple yes or no response to a question. This is an example of using a standard .NET type, and you could add profile properties using different types, such as storing an age in an `Integer`, or a date of birth in a `DateTime`.

The other non-string data type being used in this case is a custom type called `Wrox.Commerce.ShoppingCart`. This type is explained in more detail in Chapter 13. For now, you should know that this type will store details of the current user's shopping cart, so that if they fill the cart with items on one visit to the site, but choose not to purchase those items at that time, the data about the items stored in the cart will remain. In this way, when they next log in, the items are still in their cart. It also dictates whether anonymous users can fill a shopping cart. Because this is set to `true`, anyone coming to the site can fill a basket with items, so it's up to you to make sure that you create a profile for them when they check out. You'll come back to this point a bit later in this chapter in the "Managing Anonymous Shopping Carts" section.

> *A custom type is an object that has been defined by code to meet the requirements of a specific scenario. The code is contained in a class that has been developed to describe the properties and methods available to objects based on that particular type definition. For example, a* `String` *object has a* `ToString()` *method, but a* `DateTime` *object has* `ToString()`, `ToShortDateString`, *and* `ToLongDateString()` *methods, among others. You can write a custom type, like the* `ShoppingCart` *in this example, that has a specific set of properties and methods available, so a* `ShoppingCart` *object will have an* `Update()` *method and a* `SubTotal()` *method.*

To store some data in a profile, the following syntax can be used in a code file for a web page:

```
Profile.Name = "Chris Hart";
```

Or, similarly, you can use this syntax to use a value entered by a user to populate the `Name` information in the `Profile`:

```
Profile.Name = txtName.Text;
```

This will cause the profile to store whatever the user has entered as the value of a text box on a page. So, to retrieve a value from a profile and display it on a page, you use the opposite syntax:

```
txtName.Text = Profile.Name;
```

This is all quite simple. The next section looks at it in context.

Profiles in Wrox United

When it comes to employing profiles in a live site, you need first to create a definition for the profile properties, and then a page where you can add and edit the items in a user profile. On the Wrox United site, this is controlled on the Fan Club page, so take a look at how this page is constructed.

Earlier in this chapter, you built the skeleton for the `FanClub.aspx` page and made use of the `<asp:LoginView>` control to display different content depending on who is logged in to the page. In this Try It Out, you build on the code from earlier. You add code to the `FanClub.aspx` page, and use some settings from the `Web.config` file so that you can store details about each user in their profile.

Try It Out Using Profiles in Wrox United

1. Open the `Web.config` file from the root of the Chapter 11 version of the Wrox United application. Look at the bottom of the code and you will see the following:

```
<!--
  Define the user profile properties
-->
<profile enabled="true">
  <properties>
    <add name="MemberName"/>
    <add name="Name"/>
    <add name="Address"/>
    <add name="City"/>
    <add name="County"/>
    <add name="PostCode"/>
    <add name="Country"/>
    <add name="Mailings" type="System.Boolean"/>
    <add name="Email"/>
    <add name="Theme"/>
    <add name="Cart" serializeAs="Binary" type="Wrox.Commerce.ShoppingCart"
         allowAnonymous="true"/>
  </properties>
</profile>
  </system.web>
</configuration>
```

In the profile definition for Wrox United, you have specified that users can store their name, address details, whether they would like to receive mailings from the site, their e-mail address, and their favorite theme for the site. There is also a `Cart` property, which is used each time the user wants to purchase items from the store.

2. Add some code to the `FanClub.aspx` page so that users can both store new profile properties and view or edit existing properties. Open the page and add the following highlighted lines of code (there's quite a lot of code to add, but as you'll see, all you'll be doing is adding controls to the page and laying them out in a table):

```
<asp:LoginView ID="FCLoginView" Runat="server"
  OnViewChanged="FCLoginView_ViewChanged">
    <RoleGroups>
      <asp:RoleGroup Roles="FanClubMember">
        <ContentTemplate>
          <p>
```

```
    Welcome back
    <asp:LoginName ID="FCLoginName" runat="server" />
    .</p>
  <p>
    There are always lots of exciting things happening with the fan club,
    ...
    set, but keep your eyes on your inbox for more details.
  </p>
  <h3>
    User Settings</h3>
  <p>
    Your user details are shown below.</p>
  <asp:ChangePassword ID="ChangePassword1" runat="server">
  </asp:ChangePassword>
  <br />
  <table border="0">
    <tr>
      <td>Name:</td>
      <td><asp:TextBox ID="txtName" runat="server" Columns="30" />
          <asp:RequiredFieldValidator ID="rfv1" runat="server"
           ControlToValidate="txtName"
           Text="*" ErrorMessage="You must enter a value for your name" />
      </td>
    </tr><tr>
      <td>Address:</td>
      <td><asp:TextBox ID="txtAddress" runat="server" Columns="25" Rows="5"
           TextMode="multiLine" />
          <asp:RequiredFieldValidator ID="RequiredFieldValidator1"
           runat="server" ControlToValidate="txtAddress" Text="*"
           ErrorMessage="You must enter a value for the address" />
      </td>
    </tr><tr>
      <td>City:</td>
      <td><asp:TextBox ID="txtCity" runat="server" />
          <asp:RequiredFieldValidator ID="RequiredFieldValidator2"
           runat="server" ControlToValidate="txtCity"
           Text="*" ErrorMessage="You must enter a value for the city" />
      </td>
    </tr><tr>
      <td>County:</td>
      <td><asp:TextBox ID="txtCounty" runat="server" />
          <asp:RequiredFieldValidator ID="RequiredFieldValidator3"
           runat="server" ControlToValidate="txtCounty"
           Text="*" ErrorMessage="You must enter a value for the county" />
      </td>
    </tr><tr>
      <td>Postcode:</td>
      <td><asp:TextBox ID="txtPostCode" runat="server" />
          <asp:RequiredFieldValidator ID="RequiredFieldValidator4"
           runat="server" ControlToValidate="txtPostCode" Text="*"
           ErrorMessage="You must enter a value for the post code" />
      </td>
    </tr><tr>
      <td>Country:</td>
      <td><asp:TextBox ID="txtCountry" runat="server" />
```

```
                <asp:RequiredFieldValidator ID="RequiredFieldValidator5"
                 runat="server" ControlToValidate="txtCountry" Text="*"
                 ErrorMessage="You must enter a value for the country" />
            </td>
          </tr><tr>
            <td>Subscribe to email updates:</td>
            <td><asp:CheckBox ID="chkMailing" runat="server" /></td>
          </tr><tr>
            <td>Email:<br /></td>
            <td><asp:TextBox ID="txtEmail" runat="server" />
                <asp:RequiredFieldValidator ID="RequiredFieldValidator6"
                 runat="server" ControlToValidate="txtEmail"
                 Text="*" ErrorMessage="You must enter a value for the email" />
                <asp:RegularExpressionValidator ID="rev1" runat="server"
                 ControlToValidate="txtEmail"
             ValidationExpression="\w+([-+.']\w+)*@\w+([-.]\w+)*\.\w+([-.]\w+)*"
                 Text="*" ErrorMessage="Please enter a valid email address" />
            </td>
          </tr><tr>
            <td>Membership Alias:</td>
            <td><asp:TextBox ID="txtAlias" runat="server" />
                <asp:RequiredFieldValidator ID="RequiredFieldValidator7"
                 runat="server" ControlToValidate="txtAlias" Text="*"
                ErrorMessage="You must enter a value for the membership alias" />
            </td>
          </tr>
        </table>
        <br />
        <asp:ValidationSummary ID="vs" runat="server" DisplayMode="BulletList" />
        <br />
        <asp:Button ID="btnSaveChanges" runat="server"
          OnClick="btnSaveChanges_Click" Text="Save Changes" />
        <asp:Button ID="btnCancelChanges" runat="server"
          OnClick="btnCancelChanges_Click"
          CausesValidation="false" Text="Cancel Changes" />
      </ContentTemplate>
    </asp:RoleGroup>
...
  </RoleGroups>
...
</asp:LoginView>
```

3. You also need to add code to the `FanClub.aspx.cs` file so that the `btnSaveChanges` and `btnCancelChanges` buttons have event handlers that will run code each time they are clicked. Right-click `FanClub.aspx` and select View Code, and then add the following highlighted methods to the `FanClub.aspx.cs` file:

```
using System;
using System.Web;
using System.Web.UI.WebControls;

partial class FanClub : System.Web.UI.Page
{
```

```
    private void Page_Load(object sender, System.EventArgs e)
    {
      if (!Page.IsPostBack)
        DisplayProfileProperties();
    }

    protected void btnCancelChanges_Click( object sender,  System.EventArgs e)
    {
      DisplayProfileProperties();
    }

    protected void btnSaveChanges_Click( object sender,  System.EventArgs e)
    {
      Profile.Name = ((TextBox)FCLoginView.FindControl("txtName")).Text;
      Profile.Address = ((TextBox)FCLoginView.FindControl("txtAddress")).Text;
      Profile.City = ((TextBox)FCLoginView.FindControl("txtCity")).Text;
      Profile.County = ((TextBox)FCLoginView.FindControl("txtCounty")).Text;
      Profile.PostCode = ((TextBox)FCLoginView.FindControl("txtPostCode")).Text;
      Profile.Country = ((TextBox)FCLoginView.FindControl("txtCountry")).Text;
      Profile.Mailings = ((CheckBox)FCLoginView.FindControl("chkMailing")).Checked;
      Profile.Email = ((TextBox)FCLoginView.FindControl("txtEmail")).Text;
      Profile.MemberName = ((TextBox)FCLoginView.FindControl("txtAlias")).Text;
      Server.Transfer(SiteMap.CurrentNode.Url);
    }

    protected void FCLoginView_ViewChanged( object sender,  System.EventArgs e)
    {
      DisplayProfileProperties();
    }

    private void DisplayProfileProperties()
    {
      TextBox NameBox = (TextBox)FCLoginView.FindControl("txtName");

      if (NameBox != null)
      {
        ((TextBox)FCLoginView.FindControl("txtName")).Text = Profile.Name;
        ((TextBox)FCLoginView.FindControl("txtAddress")).Text = Profile.Address;
        ((TextBox)FCLoginView.FindControl("txtCity")).Text = Profile.City;
        ((TextBox)FCLoginView.FindControl("txtCounty")).Text = Profile.County;
        ((TextBox)FCLoginView.FindControl("txtPostCode")).Text = Profile.PostCode;
        ((TextBox)FCLoginView.FindControl("txtCountry")).Text = Profile.Country;
        ((CheckBox)FCLoginView.FindControl("chkMailing")).Checked = Profile.Mailings;
        ((TextBox)FCLoginView.FindControl("txtEmail")).Text = Profile.Email;
        ((TextBox)FCLoginView.FindControl("txtAlias")).Text = Profile.MemberName;
      }
    }
}
```

4. Run the site again and log in as **Lou**, password **lou@123**. Go to the home page for the Fan Club and you will see what is shown in Figure 11-17 at the bottom of the page.

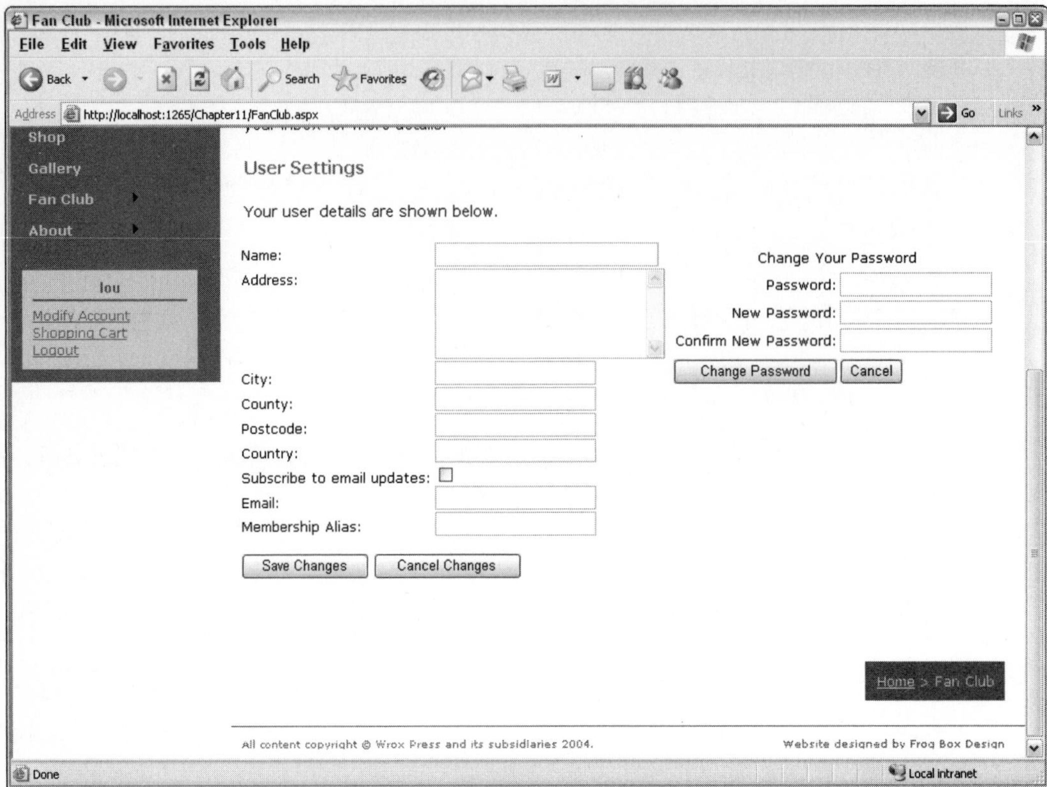

Figure 11-17

5. Enter some details and click the Save Changes button. If you log out and log back in again, you'll see that the information is saved, as shown in Figure 11-18.

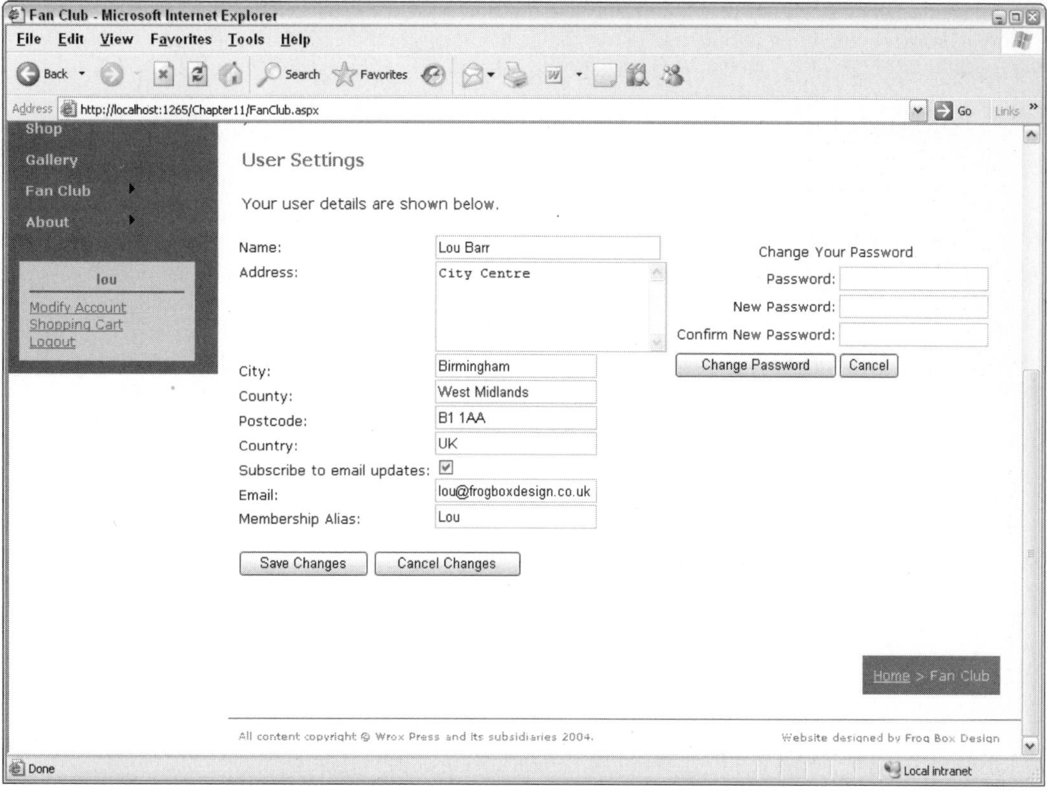

Figure 11-18

How It Works

The `Web.config` file contains the definition for each of the profile properties employed in the Wrox United application. These include (among others) the name of the user, the address, and the e-mail address. The capability to store data for each user in a profile is controlled by the code in the `FanClub.aspx` page.

When users update their profile by clicking the Save Changes button, the following code is run:

```
protected void btnSaveChanges_Click( object sender,  System.EventArgs e)
{
  Profile.Name = ((TextBox)FCLoginView.FindControl("txtName")).Text;
  Profile.Address = ((TextBox)FCLoginView.FindControl("txtAddress")).Text;
  Profile.City = ((TextBox)FCLoginView.FindControl("txtCity")).Text;
  Profile.County = ((TextBox)FCLoginView.FindControl("txtCounty")).Text;
  Profile.PostCode = ((TextBox)FCLoginView.FindControl("txtPostCode")).Text;
  Profile.Country = ((TextBox)FCLoginView.FindControl("txtCountry")).Text;
  Profile.Mailings = ((CheckBox)FCLoginView.FindControl("chkMailing")).Checked;
  Profile.Email = ((TextBox)FCLoginView.FindControl("txtEmail")).Text;
  Profile.MemberName = ((TextBox)FCLoginView.FindControl("txtAlias")).Text;
  Server.Transfer(SiteMap.CurrentNode.Url);
}
```

This code looks quite messy, and this is because of one very good reason. You've chosen to display these controls only on one view of the page using the `LoginView` control. Here's the syntax for storing just the name:

```
Profile.Name = ((TextBox)FCLoginView.FindControl("txtName")).Text;
```

The syntax used to essentially say "`TextBox.Text`" means "find me the control called `txtName`, and when you find it, treat it like a `TextBox` control, and then grab the data stored in its `Text` property and use that value to store in the profile." The similar syntax used against the `Mailings` profile property demonstrates this slightly differently:

```
Profile.Mailings = ((CheckBox)FCLoginView.FindControl("chkMailing")).Checked;
```

This time around, it's a case of "find me a control called `chkMailing`, treat it as a `CheckBox` control, and set the `Mailings` property of the profile to the value of the `Checked` property of the `CheckBox`."

After the profile has been populated with data, the code will then call a method, the `Server.Transfer` method, which will run the code that would run if the specified page were requested:

```
Server.Transfer(SiteMap.CurrentNode.Url);
```

The `Server.Transfer()` method stops the current page from executing, and runs the content on the specified page, which in this case is like reloading the current page again to refresh the current view of the page.

At several points in the page life cycle, the display of the profile properties is updated. For example, each time the view of the Fan Club changes, the following code is run:

```
protected void FCLoginView_ViewChanged( object sender,  System.EventArgs e)
{
  DisplayProfileProperties();
}
```

This calls the following method:

```
private void DisplayProfileProperties()
{
  TextBox NameBox = (TextBox)FCLoginView.FindControl("txtName");

  if (NameBox != null)
  {
    ((TextBox)FCLoginView.FindControl("txtName")).Text = Profile.Name;
    ((TextBox)FCLoginView.FindControl("txtAddress")).Text = Profile.Address;
    ((TextBox)FCLoginView.FindControl("txtCity")).Text = Profile.City;
    ((TextBox)FCLoginView.FindControl("txtCounty")).Text = Profile.County;
    ((TextBox)FCLoginView.FindControl("txtPostCode")).Text = Profile.PostCode;
    ((TextBox)FCLoginView.FindControl("txtCountry")).Text = Profile.Country;
    ((CheckBox)FCLoginView.FindControl("chkMailing")).Checked = Profile.Mailings;
    ((TextBox)FCLoginView.FindControl("txtEmail")).Text = Profile.Email;
    ((TextBox)FCLoginView.FindControl("txtAlias")).Text = Profile.MemberName;
  }
}
```

The convoluted syntax for retrieving the value of each control should be a bit more familiar from the code used earlier in this How It Works section, but there's one addition here. Notice that there is a test to see if the txtName text box exists on the currently visible version of the page:

```
TextBox NameBox = (TextBox)FCLoginView.FindControl("txtName");

if (NameBox != null)
{
```

So, if the txtName text box is visible (which it will be if the user is logged in as a member of the FanClubMember role), then the profile data is retrieved. If the user is anonymous, or is a member of other roles (and not the FanClubMember role), then the profile will not exist. To avoid errors at run-time, you don't want to try to retrieve data that does not exist, so this check is essential (just try removing it and accessing the page as an anonymous user to see the mess if you're not careful).

One last thing to consider before moving on — in the layout code (on FanClub.aspx), there were some controls that you may not be familiar with yet:

```
<table border="0">
  <tr>
    <td>Name:</td>
    <td><asp:TextBox ID="txtName" runat="server" Columns="30" />
        <asp:RequiredFieldValidator ID="rfv1" runat="server"
         ControlToValidate="txtName"
         Text="*" ErrorMessage="You must enter a value for your name" />
    </td>
  </tr><tr>
```

In the layout code, each TextBox control had a validation control next to it. In this example, the txtName TextBox had a RequiredFieldValidator control next to it, which will ensure that users fill in data for each of the required fields before saving profile changes. Essentially, the text box is marked as "Required," as the validator's name suggests. If no value is entered, there will be a small red asterisk displayed next to the text box.

You'll learn more about validation controls in Chapter 15, where you can see how they are used to minimize data entry errors and protect your code from malicious user input.

So, you've stored some simple data in a user profile. If you want to know where exactly this data is stored, you will find it in the AspNetDB.mdf database. Take a look in the aspnet_Profiles table and you will see that data, similar to Figure 11-19, is stored in your database.

In Figure 11-19, you can see that the Lou profile currently has some properties set, as you specified in the example. You will not need (or want) to edit this data, but it's useful to know where it's stored.

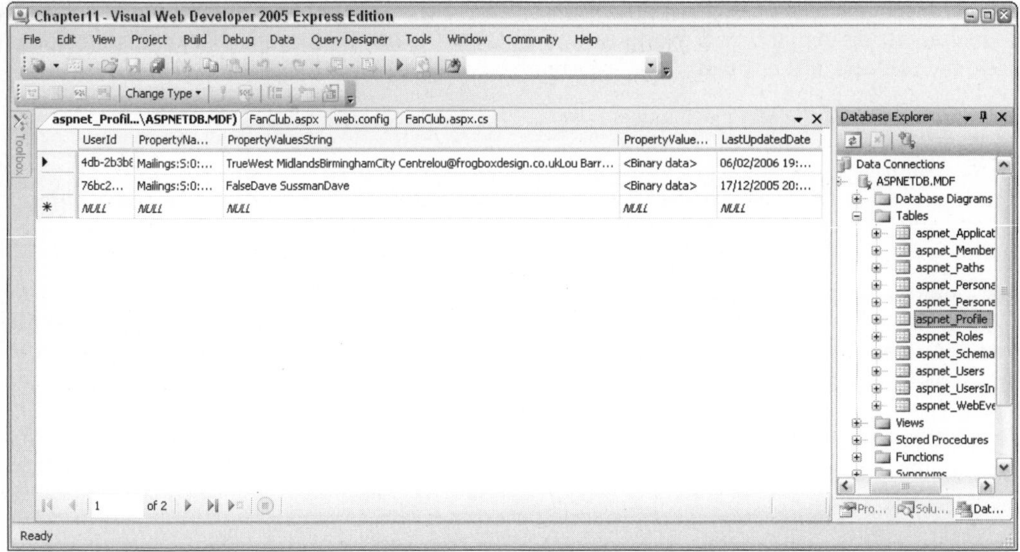

Figure 11-19

Storing Preferences

There's one last example that you can play with in this chapter, and that goes way back to the discussions you will recall from Chapter 5. In that chapter, along with page styling and CSS, you learned the concept of storing layout and style preferences in themes. These themes can be switched on a page-by-page basis as was discussed in that chapter. However, you can also store data about which theme a user may prefer to use for a site in a user profile, enabling users to personalize their viewing experience a bit more. In the following Try It Out, you have a go at including this functionality in the Wrox United application.

Try It Out Storing Theme Preference in Profiles

1. Add the following highlighted lines of code to the `FanClub.aspx` page:

```
</tr><tr>
  <td>Membership Alias:</td>
  <td><asp:TextBox ID="txtAlias" runat="server" />
      <asp:RequiredFieldValidator ID="RequiredFieldValidator7"
        runat="server" ControlToValidate="txtAlias" Text="*"
        ErrorMessage="You must enter a value for the membership alias" />
  </td>
</tr>
<tr>
  <td>Theme:</td>
  <td><asp:DropDownList ID="ThemeList" runat="server">
        <asp:ListItem Text="Default" Value="" />
        <asp:ListItem Text="Wrox Red" Value="WroxRed" />
        <asp:ListItem Text="Wrox Blue" Value="WroxBlue" />
      </asp:DropDownList>
  </td>
</tr>
```

2. The other piece of the puzzle is to add some code to store and retrieve the theme preference from the user's profile. Modify `FanClub.aspx.cs` to add the following highlighted lines of code to the `btnSaveChanges_Click` event handler:

```
protected void btnSaveChanges_Click( object sender,  System.EventArgs e)
{
  Profile.Theme =
    ((DropDownList)FCLoginView.FindControl("ThemeList")).SelectedValue;
  Profile.Name = ((TextBox)FCLoginView.FindControl("txtName")).Text;
  Profile.Address = ((TextBox)FCLoginView.FindControl("txtAddress")).Text;
  Profile.City = ((TextBox)FCLoginView.FindControl("txtCity")).Text;
  Profile.County = ((TextBox)FCLoginView.FindControl("txtCounty")).Text;
  Profile.PostCode = ((TextBox)FCLoginView.FindControl("txtPostCode")).Text;
  Profile.Country = ((TextBox)FCLoginView.FindControl("txtCountry")).Text;
  Profile.Mailings = ((CheckBox)FCLoginView.FindControl("chkMailing")).Checked;
  Profile.Email = ((TextBox)FCLoginView.FindControl("txtEmail")).Text;
  Profile.MemberName = ((TextBox)FCLoginView.FindControl("txtAlias")).Text;
  Server.Transfer(SiteMap.CurrentNode.Url);
 }
```

3. Modify the `DisplayProfileProperties` method to include the code that will retrieve and display the currently stored value for the `Theme` property from the user's profile:

```
private void DisplayProfileProperties()
{
  TextBox NameBox = (TextBox)FCLoginView.FindControl("txtName");

  if (NameBox != null)
  {
    ((DropDownList)FCLoginView.FindControl("ThemeList")).SelectedValue =
      Profile.Theme;
    ((TextBox)FCLoginView.FindControl("txtName")).Text = Profile.Name;
    ((TextBox)FCLoginView.FindControl("txtAddress")).Text = Profile.Address;
    ((TextBox)FCLoginView.FindControl("txtCity")).Text = Profile.City;
    ((TextBox)FCLoginView.FindControl("txtCounty")).Text = Profile.County;
    ((TextBox)FCLoginView.FindControl("txtPostCode")).Text = Profile.PostCode;
    ((TextBox)FCLoginView.FindControl("txtCountry")).Text = Profile.Country;
    ((CheckBox)FCLoginView.FindControl("chkMailing")).Checked = Profile.Mailings;
    ((TextBox)FCLoginView.FindControl("txtEmail")).Text = Profile.Email;
    ((TextBox)FCLoginView.FindControl("txtAlias")).Text = Profile.MemberName;
  }
```

At this stage, you've added all the required code to store the preference. The thing that's missing is the ability to actually switch the theme on the pages on the site.

4. Right-click the `App_Code` folder and add a new item. Select Class from the list of available templates, and call it **ThemeModule.cs**, as shown in Figure 11-20.

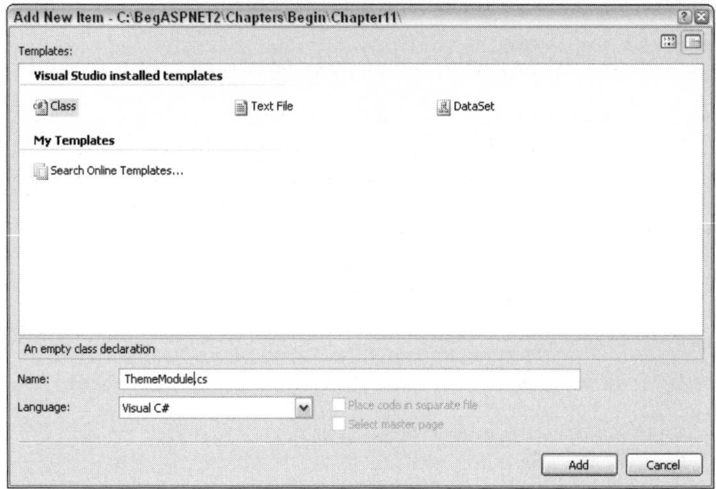

Figure 11-20

5. Enter the following code into the new Class file:

```
using System;
using System.Web;
using System.Web.UI;

namespace Wrox.Web.GlobalEvents
{
  public class ThemeModule : IHttpModule
  {
    public void Init(HttpApplication context)
    {
      context.PreRequestHandlerExecute +=
        new EventHandler(this.app_PreRequestHandlerExecute);
    }

    private void app_PreRequestHandlerExecute(object Sender, EventArgs E)
    {
      Page p = HttpContext.Current.Handler as Page;
      if (p != null)
      {
        ProfileCommon pb = (ProfileCommon)HttpContext.Current.Profile;
        p.Theme = pb.Theme;
      }
    }

    public void Dispose()
    {
    }
  }
}
```

6. Save the file. Open `Web.config` and add the following highlighted code, just below the `System.Web` node:

```
<system.web>
  <httpModules>
    <add name="Page" type="Wrox.Web.GlobalEvents.ThemeModule"/>
  </httpModules>
```

7. Run the page. You will see that there is now a drop-down box (shown at the bottom of Figure 11-21) on the page that enables you to select different themes to store in your user profile.

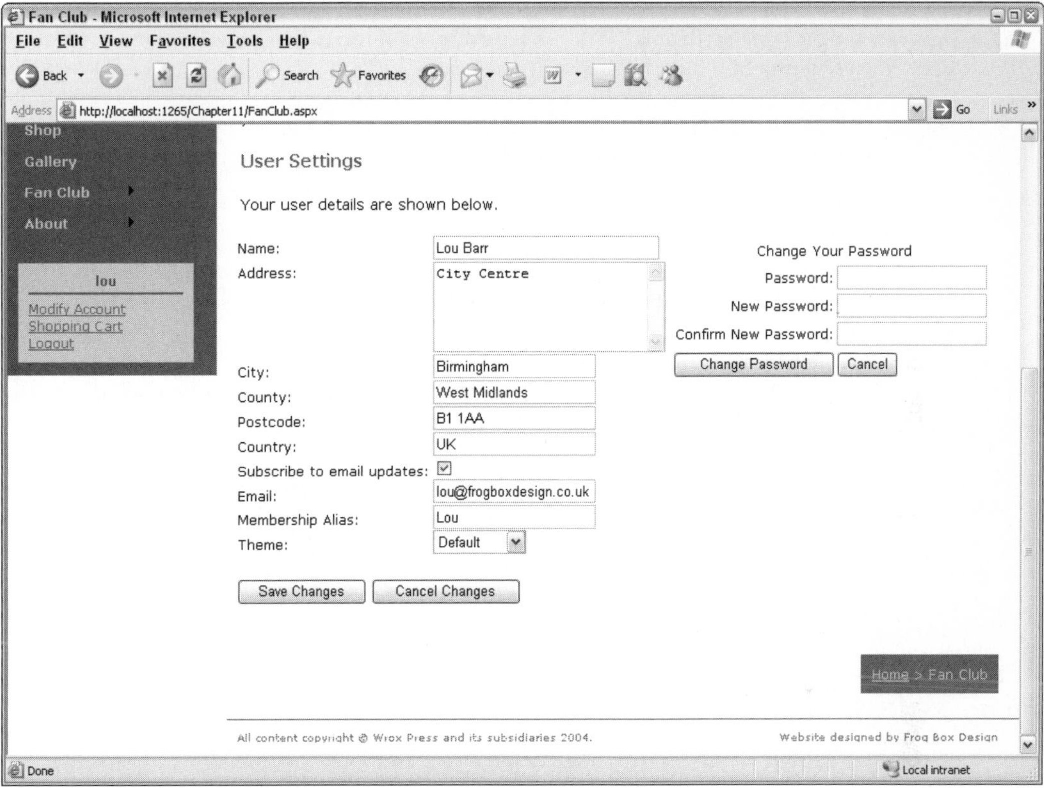

Figure 11-21

How It Works

In this example, you extended the basic `FanClub.aspx` page so that users can store their preferred theme in their profile. This facility is available only to registered members of the Fan Club.

Amending the layout code was a simple process of adding a `DropDownList` control to the page:

```
<asp:DropDownList ID="ThemeList" runat="server">
  <asp:ListItem Text="Default" Value="" />
  <asp:ListItem Text="Wrox Red" Value="WroxRed" />
  <asp:ListItem Text="Wrox Blue" Value="WroxBlue" />
</asp:DropDownList>
```

The value for the theme is stored as a simple string of text in the user's profile, and is set in the same way as any other profile setting:

```
Profile.Theme =

  ((DropDownList)FCLoginView.FindControl("ThemeList")).SelectedValue;
```

This code means "find me the `ThemeList` control; it's a `DropDownList`, so get me its `SelectedValue` property." In this case, the `DropDownList` control's `SelectedValue` property will be whatever the `Value` property for the selected item is set to, so, for example, if the user selected the item with the text "Wrox Red," the value stored would be `WroxRed`.

At this stage, the profile has been updated with the user's preference, but the last bit of this exercise gave the site the capability to apply the selected theme to each page. You used an `HttpModule` to do this.

> **An `HttpModule` contains code that is processed every time any page in an application is processed. The module can be enabled and disabled via the `Web.config` file. The module code can handle events that are raised each time a page is requested.**

In this case, the event that is intercepted is processed before the code on a page is processed, and the requested page's theme can be changed to match the theme specified in the user's profile.

This section of the code is getting to be quite advanced in terms of programming techniques. Don't worry if you don't fully understand how this works — you will encounter more code like this in Professional ASP.NET 2.0, so you can treat this as a taste of what you can expect when you start to unleash the full power of ASP.NET.

Take a look at the code in the `HttpModule` and see how it works:

```
using System;
using System.Web;
using System.Web.UI;

namespace Wrox.Web.GlobalEvents
{
  public class ThemeModule : IHttpModule
  {
```

The first part of the code in the file imports a few useful namespaces that contain classes you'll need later in the code. The `ThemeModule` class is configured to reside within the `Wrox.Web.GlobalEvents` namespace. Additionally, the `ThemeModule` class implements the `IHttpModule` interface, which turns this simple class into a class that can be used as an `HttpModule`, provided you then implement the required methods, because there are some specific methods that all `HttpModules` must implement in order to work correctly.

In this case, two methods have to be implemented: the `Init()` method and the `Dispose()` method. Here's the `Dispose()` method — because there's nothing that you need to do in this method, the empty method signature will just sit there in the file not bothering anyone:

```
public void Dispose()
{
}
```

Now compare that to the code in the `Init()` method:

```
public void Init(HttpApplication context)
{
  context.PreRequestHandlerExecute +=
    new EventHandler(this.app_PreRequestHandlerExecute);
}
```

The code within the method itself is a bit tricky to grasp at first. There's only one line to consider, which declares a new event handler. The event handler will run each time the current context is at the `PreRequestHandlerExecute` stage in the request life cycle — in plain English, that's pretty early in the request stage. This line of code means that each time the appropriate event fires, you can add an event handler that will be processed:

```
private void app_PreRequestHandlerExecute(object Sender, EventArgs E)
{
  Page p = HttpContext.Current.Handler as Page;
  if (p != null)
  {
    ProfileCommon pb = (ProfileCommon)HttpContext.Current.Profile;
    p.Theme = pb.Theme;
  }
}
```

This method handles that `PreRequestHandlerExecute` event. The first line in this method gets the currently requested page object so that you can interact with it:

```
Page p = HttpContext.Current.Handler as Page;
```

Notice the method used here to cast the current `Handler` object to a `Page` object type. This means that if the requested item is a page, the cast will be successful and the `p` object will contain an object reference to the requested page. However, if the item requested is not a page, the cast fails, and the `p` object is set to `NULL`.

As long as the `Page` object exists (and is not set to Nothing), you can then try to apply the theme to the page by obtaining the current profile properties and using that profile's `Theme` property:

```
if (p != null)
{
  ProfileCommon pb = (ProfileCommon)HttpContext.Current.Profile;
  p.Theme = pb.Theme;
}
```

Notice that the way casting is performed in this case (casting the current `Profile` object to type `Profile Common`) will throw an exception if the attempted cast fails. The only case when this would happen would be if you disabled profiles in the `Web.config` file, which would surely make this example a bit pointless. At the end of this method, the `Theme` property of the page is set to the value stored in the profile property called `Theme`.

Finally, there was a new section added to the Web.config file that enabled the HttpModule itself:

```
<system.web>
  <httpModules>
    <add name="Page" type="Wrox.Web.GlobalEvents.ThemeModule"/>
  </httpModules>
```

The <httpModule> section can be filled with many different modules that you may want to run. In this example, there is just one module — the ThemeModule. The ThemeModule class that was declared is added in the type attribute, along with the namespace that it resides in, so that .NET knows exactly which ThemeModule you want to run.

That's about it for this example. It's a tricky piece of code, but it's a neat way to make themes switch instantly on pages, and to stay switched for all pages on a site, because the module will run for each requested page on a site.

Managing Anonymous Shopping Carts

Earlier this chapter, the presence of the following profile property was briefly mentioned:

```
<profile enabled="true">
  <properties>
    <add name="MemberName"/>
     ...
    <add name="Cart" serializeAs="Binary" type="Wrox.Commerce.ShoppingCart"
                     allowAnonymous="true"/>
```

The allowAnonymous flag that is stored against the Profile.Cart value for each user session indicates that anonymous users can have a shopping cart. In this case, users may visit the site and neglect to log on, or they may be completely new to the site. The user will then happily fill up a basket with items, so it will be up to you to handle either switching the cart to an existing user when they log in, or creating a new profile when the anonymous user logs in and transferring the cart to the newly created user when the user attempts to check out.

There is code that handles this transition in the Global.asax file, which handles global events raised by the code. Here's the code as it is used in the Wrox United application:

```
void Profile_OnMigrateAnonymous(object sender, ProfileMigrateEventArgs e)
{
  // get the profile for the anonymous user
  ProfileCommon anonProfile = Profile.GetProfile(e.AnonymousID);

  // if they have a shopping cart, then migrate that to the authenticated user
  if (anonProfile.Cart != null)
  {
    if (Profile.Cart == null)
      Profile.Cart = new Wrox.Commerce.ShoppingCart();

    Profile.Cart.Items.AddRange(anonProfile.Cart.Items);

    anonProfile.Cart = null;
```

```
    }

    ProfileManager.DeleteProfile(e.AnonymousID);
    AnonymousIdentificationModule.ClearAnonymousIdentifier();
}
```

This code is examined in far more detail in Chapter 13, when you see exactly how the whole shopping experience works, but it's useful to understand that there are consequences when you log in as a user. The transferring of a shopping cart from one profile to another is the most important, because none of the other properties can actually be set for anonymous users.

Summary

This chapter delved deeper into the world of roles, and introduced the concept of user profiles for storing additional data about a user. The two technologies can sit happily side-by-side, and used together are a great way to control access to a site and for customizing the user experience.

In this chapter, you had a chance to take more control over the access permitted to users on a fully functional web application, including the following:

- Show or hide resources to selected user roles.
- Display different page content depending on which role views the page.
- Display links to selected pages, but prompt the user for more credentials for authorization.
- Store more information about users in their user profile.
- Store different types of data in a user profile, including the user's preference for site theme.

These techniques will be expanded in the upcoming chapters to form part of the shopping cart functionality built in to the Wrox United site.

Exercises

1. Create a new user account called **Admin**, and make this user a member of all groups. Log in to the Wrox United site as **Admin** and test to see whether you can access all of the different pages in both the fan club and the administration section.
2. Remove the Admin user from any role other than the Administrator role and test the site again. Ensure that you can access the following pages:
    - `Admin.aspx`
    - `EditNews.aspx`
    - `UpdateProducts.aspx`
3. The Admin user has had a request by a reporter out in the field — he's uploaded a score for a match, but the score has just changed. Unfortunately, the reporter's laptop has run out of battery, so he's asked the Admin user to update the score for him. Make sure that the Admin user can update the score of a match.

4. Add a field to the user profile for the Wrox United application called **DateOfBirth**. Give this property a data type of `System.DateTime`. Add an input field to the `FanClub.aspx` page so that users can update their date of birth. Note that you will need to convert the value entered in a text box to a `DateTime` value when you save the data — you might want to try the `DateTime.Parse()` function for this purpose. To retrieve the data, use the `Profile.DateOfBirth.ToShortDateString()` function.

Web Services

Web services have been "the next great thing" for a little too long now. They were originally introduced as part of the .NET Framework in its first incarnation (although they have been present in Java for a lot longer). Web services are a method of making information available in a standardized way that could be accessed by any developer's application over the Web. Web services can form a library or shared repository of information that could be anything from the latest weather forecast, a map of your local amenities, a mathematical function calculator, to the tracks and album cover of the CD that you just inserted into your CD-ROM drive. You should be aware, though, that a web service on its own isn't an application. Web services aren't rendered as web pages, or as executable files (`.exe`); they come completely shorn of a user interface. It's up to you as a developer to use them and integrate them into your applications. They are there to save you time and effort by reducing code duplication.

They can be used in one of two ways. You can create a web service that is exposed to the web, to share with other developers and other applications. Or you can search for a web service that can be added to your own application. (They are similar to plug-ins in that respect.) For example, if your application is a company web site and you want to include directions to company headquarters, rather than scan in a map, or attempt to hand-draw one in a graphics tool, why not use one of the web services that makes sections of maps available online?

The information contained in the web service is wrapped up as an XML document (in other words, plain text), so that worries about platform-specific concerns, such as whether you're accessing them on an old Windows 98 machine or a turbo-powered Powerbook, simply evaporate. Web services aren't really anything new either — components have been performing a similar trick for many years now. However, there are some crucial differences. Components had to be distributed by the developer, and they had to be downloaded and installed. These things alone meant that they tended to be tied to one platform. This isn't true of web services. A key word that emphasizes what web services offer is *standard*. Everything to do with web services is standardized: the method of transmission, the method used to wrap the web service up, the way the web service is defined, all have clear W3C standards associated with the technologies involved. And to make life much easier, all these standards are based on XML. So they're quick and easy to download, and even easier to use.

This chapter looks at the following:

- Introducing web services
- Consuming web services
- What happens in the typical life cycle of a web service
- Testing a web service
- Discovering a web service
- Creating and consuming an example web service that uses a parameter
- Creating a proxy — the old way of doing things
- Web service security

Looking at Web Services

The introduction alluded to the fact that web services haven't quite taken off in the way that was expected, and it's true and there are probably several reasons for that, but none that should stop you from using them. One is that developers and businesses don't like giving away their hard work for free. The truth is when businesses create a web service, it usually isn't for public consumption. It is for in-house use only, and even if it is available for the public to use, it is likely to come at a price. On the flip-side, with free web services, you have no guarantee that they will still be there in a week or a year's time, so it's no good basing a large application around them. So do you fork out for a web service and increase the cost of your application, or take a gamble that a particular service will still be in existence over the next few years? This dilemma isn't easily remedied.

Second is lack of education. People are still largely unaware of what web services can offer. I recently worked on a customer services application, which had to integrate with an existing contacts manager application and detect when the contacts manager was running and if it had loaded the latest customer information correctly. Rather than use a web service to make this information available, the client chose instead to write to the clipboard (especially awkward considering the users themselves might also be using the clipboard) and then my application had to periodically check the clipboard for the text to indicate that the contacts manager was running. As a result, the application was 20 times more complicated than it needed to be.

Third is the lack of a single killer application. Before you started this chapter, could you name five common examples of web services? The problem is that they're too good at the job they do, so they become practically invisible. Where is the Google or Internet Explorer of web services? I don't know, but you might just be using it unwittingly. A good web service should dovetail seamlessly into your application, and your user should never know it's there.

Last is the apparent learning curve required. With web services, it's easy to get drawn into listing the mass of technologies involved, and therefore easy to get confused about what you need to know. SOAP, WSDL, UDDI, and DISCO all play valid parts in the process of making a web service available. However, you don't need to know about any of these acronyms to be able to use a web service.

In fact, before you start creating a web service and learning what goes into them, it's a good idea to look at an example first.

Consuming a Third-Party Web Service

Consuming a web service is almost as easy as firing up your browser, typing in a URL of a web service, and pressing Return. Perhaps we're oversimplifying a little bit here, but if you browse to the URL of a web service endpoint, you will find that you can use it functionally, albeit without any graphical frills. An *endpoint* is the specific location where the web service can be accessed. So let's do exactly that. Because of the nature of the Web, sites are very often up and down. If you wanted to phone up a plumber on the other side of the city, you'd check your local phone directory for a number—but that plumber may or may not still be in business, and web services are just the same. Several good starting points are the following sites: `www.webservicex.net`, `www.webservicelist.com`, `www.webserviceoftheday.com`, and `www.wsiam.com`. All of these sites provide lists of web services you can browse. More alternatives are available, and if one of these sites is inoperable, another will be working.

There are plenty of possibilities to integrate web services into your example site. Wrox United chronicles the football fixtures, results, merchandise, and news of one soccer team. Now Wrox United isn't always the most successful soccer team in the league, and they're usually looking for an excuse on which to hang a particularly poor performance, such as the weather. It would be nice if you could stick a weather report on the bottom of your match reports, just so you know that if the goalkeeper claims the fifth and sixth goals slipped through his hands, maybe the 85-degree temperature would be a bit of a giveaway.

In the following Try It Out, you start by finding an example weather web service that is freely available.

Try It Out — Consuming an Example Web Service

1. To be able to access a web service, you need to locate an .asmx file (you'll learn what one of those is after you've finished this example). Figure 12-1 shows an example of a weather service at `www.webservicex.net/globalweather.asmx`.

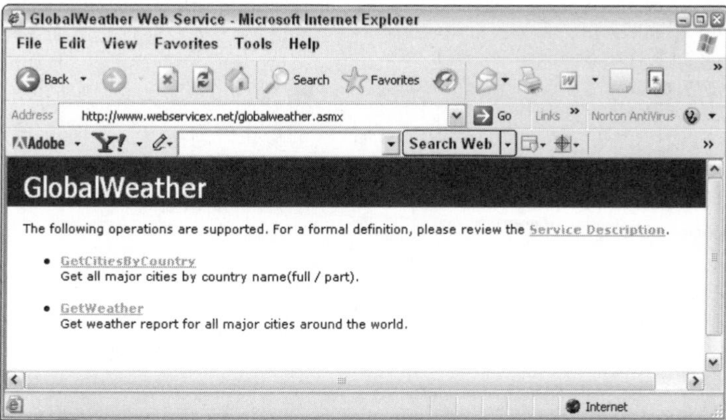

Figure 12-1

> **If for any reason this web service is giving an HTTP error 404, go back to any of the previous web service directories, type Weather into the search link, and use one of the example sites it returns. Most weather web services work the same way.**

2. There are two possible web services here. The format and style of this screen are the same for any .asmx web service file you browse. The link to the web service that gives you the weather forecast is called `GetWeather`. Click this link, and you'll arrive at a screen similar to Figure 12-2.

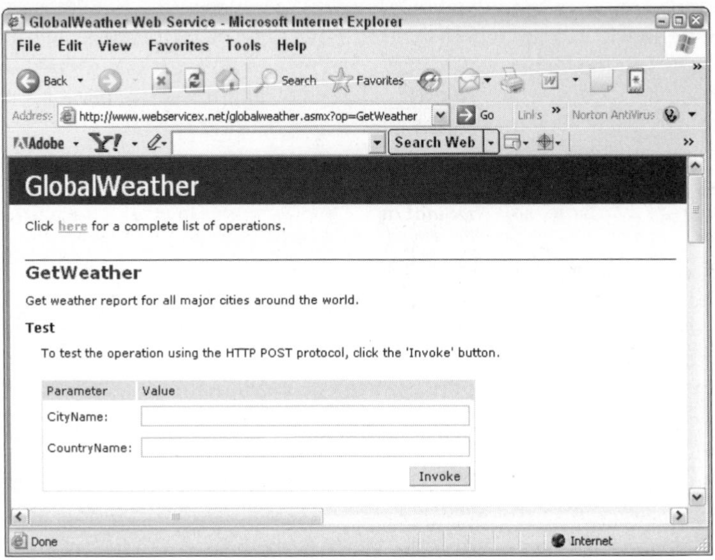

Figure 12-2

3. Supply the name of the city where you live, or closest to where you live, and the name of the country. Scroll down and look at the code (see Figure 12-3).

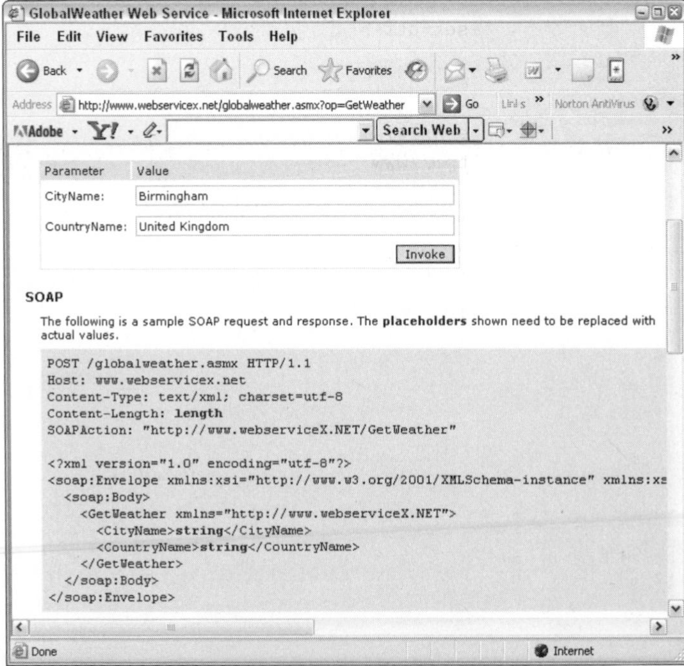

Figure 12-3

4. Click Invoke to get the result, shown in Figure 12-4. It will be customized to where you live and is dependent on the weather of the moment.

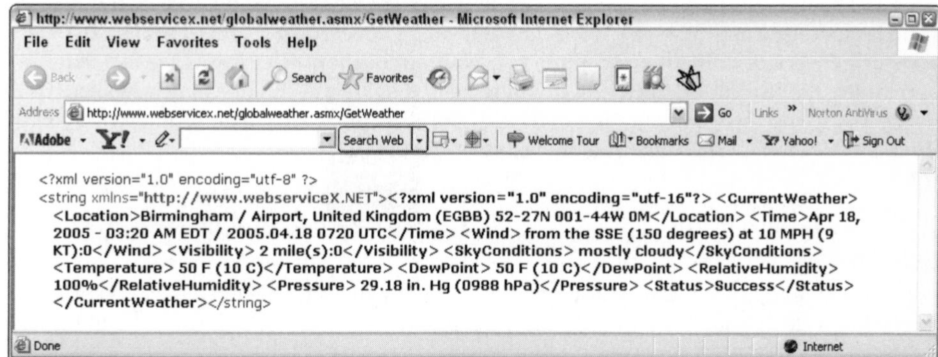

Figure 12-4

How It Works

You've just consumed a web service. The Wrox United application does not have the capability to do weather forecasting, so you looked elsewhere to get this service. By browsing to an .asmx file, you are able to use the web service, and supply input and get an answer tailored to your specifics. When you supplied the city name and country name, you probably noticed that your input was wrapped up in an XML document. This is the document broadcast to the server. Although the data can be wrapped up by three different methods, just look at the first on the page for now:

```
POST /globalweather.asmx HTTP/1.1
Host: www.webservicex.net
Content-Type: text/xml; charset=utf-16
Content-Length: length
SOAPACTION: "http://www.webserviceX.NET/GetWeather"

<?xml version="1.0" encoding="utf-16"?>
<soap:Envelope xmlns:xsi="http://www.w3.org/2001/XMLSchema-instance"
xmlns:xsd="http://www.w3.org/2001/XMLSchema"
xmlns:soap="http://schemas.xmlsoap.org/soap/envelope/">
  <soap:Body>
    <GetWeather xmlns="http://www.webserviceX.NET">
      <CityName>string</CityName>
      <CountryName>string</CountryName>
    </GetWeather>
  </soap:Body>
</soap:Envelope>
```

Your input is simply substituted for the words `string` in the highlighted code:

```
<GetWeather xmlns="http://www.webserviceX.NET">
  <CityName>Birmingham</CityName>
  <CountryName>United Kingdom</CountryName>
</GetWeather>
```

Of course one big drawback is that there isn't a user interface, so you're using a normal interface, and also all your code is returned as one large lump of XML. So it's not exactly something you'd stick into your application as it is, without your users getting confused. Also you'll see that the weather report is much too detailed for your match reports. Ideally you'd just want to be able to pick out, say, sky conditions and temperature and probably leave it at that. To be honest, a few other pitfalls exist that would make a weather service difficult to integrate into your application. Not least is the fact that the weather service extracts the current weather, and if you were to display this in your match reports, you'd need to make sure you saved the weather in the database alongside the match details, otherwise you'd be reading about Wednesday's match, and seeing Friday's weather.

Later in the chapter, you'll look at creating some web services for the Wrox United application, but for now you only need to understand that web services are freely available for very ordinary chores to all sorts of weird and wonderful things. If there is a URL with an .asmx file available, you can access and use the web service in a standard way. And if you can access and use the web service in this standard way, you can stick it in your application just as easily.

The Life Cycle of a Web Service

It's time to look at some theory behind what is happening here. This section strips down a web service to its basic essentials, which is a four-stage process. Following that, this section expands upon each stage, and talks a little bit about the technologies and standards used at each step.

The four-stage process of a web service is as follows (as detailed in Figure 12-5):

1. The client calls web service over a protocol.
2. The client sends the method to the server, which contains instructions on what is needed from the web service.
3. The server returns values and/or an acknowledgment that it has received the method.
4. The client gets the results and acts on the received information. This may involve calling the web service again, or a different web service, with the results received.

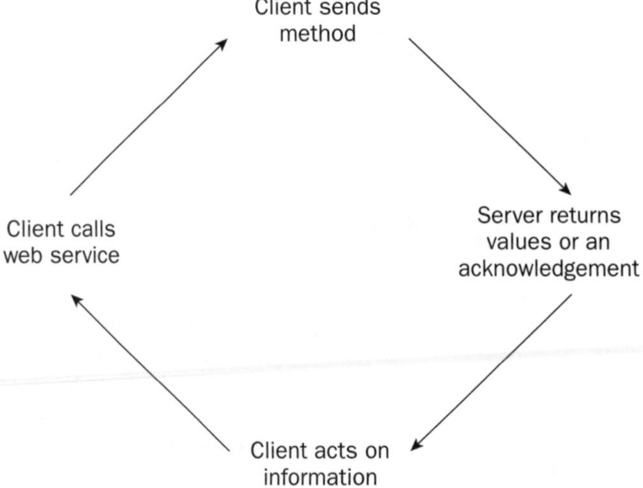

Figure 12-5

This can happen as a cyclical process, where information is sent and received, acted upon, and sent out again. In the next several sections, each step of the process is put under the magnifying class because with web services, there are usually quite a few interesting things going on.

Calling the Web Service

When you ran the first example and consumed the simple web service, you did so by typing a URL into a browser. However when you type the URL, you also specify the protocol that you are using (for example, `http://`). This is important, because web services are able to work over a multitude of protocols from SMTP (Simple Mail Transport Protocol) to HTTP (secure HTTP). However, using anything other than HTTP is beyond the scope of this book, and you can achieve plenty just using the HTTP protocol, but you shouldn't think that you are restricted in this way.

ASP.NET passes information backward and forward using the HTTP-Request/Response system. Any information is sent to the web service as part of the request, and the server will return anything from the web service as part of the response. Most commonly, you can transmit values to a web service via an HTML form and the standard HTML controls.

The request that is sent to the web service contains the following information:

- The web service's URL
- The fact that it is an HTTP request
- The amount of information being sent
- The type of document you want back from the web service
- Information about the client
- The date of the request
- The parameters you want to send to the web service

The browser collects the information from the form and wraps it up in a document ready for transmission. This process is called *serialization*.

Transmitting the Web Service

When you transmit the information required by the web service, as you've seen already, it is serialized in an XML document. This can be done in three different ways:

- `HTTP-GET` via the querystring
- `HTTP-POST` via the body of the form
- `SOAP` via the body of the form

You already know about the first two methods, so this section focuses on the last one. The phrase "serialized in an XML document" doesn't tell the whole story with `SOAP`. `SOAP` isn't just any type of XML, but a specific dialect specially created for the exchange of messages. `SOAP` used to stand for Simple Object Access Protocol, but these days it is commonly regarded as not standing for anything in particular. A message contained in `SOAP` is nothing more than a well-formed XML document or plain, vanilla text. So what exactly is `SOAP`'s purpose?

SOAP is a message template for sending requests and receiving responses to web services between the browser and the web service. Because the web relies on the HTTP protocol, it commonly excludes anything other than HTTP; so SOAP (XML) documents have to be sent as part of the HTTP data. SOAP will send a particular instruction such as "Get me a certain bit of information" wrapped in the HTTP, and then this information can be retrieved by the web service at the other end.

In the previous Try It Out, underneath the text boxes into which you entered the name of a city and country, you saw some example code. The example code took the three formats: HTTP-GET, HTTP-POST, and SOAP. The SOAP document looked like this:

```
POST /globalweather.asmx HTTP/1.1
Host: www.webservicex.net
Content-Type: text/xml; charset=utf-16
Content-Length: length
SOAPACTION: "http://www.webserviceX.NET/GetWeather"

<?xml version="1.0" encoding="utf-16"?>
<soap:Envelope xmlns:xsi="http://www.w3.org/2001/XMLSchema-instance"
xmlns:xsd="http://www.w3.org/2001/XMLSchema"
xmlns:soap="http://schemas.xmlsoap.org/soap/envelope/">
  <soap:Body>
    <GetWeather xmlns="http://www.webserviceX.NET">
      <CityName>string</CityName>
      <CountryName>string</CountryName>
    </GetWeather>
  </soap:Body>
</soap:Envelope>
```

The first thing to note is that the document was split into two sections. The first section is a set of HTTP headers that are used to communicate various aspects about your document. HTTP headers are also sent as a matter of course with HTML page requests so there's nothing new here. Take a brief look at the HTTP headers to see what they indicate.

The first line indicates that you are sending information via the HTTP-POST method. This might seem to immediately contradict the fact that you are using SOAP, but your SOAP message has to be sent as or in an HTTP request to allow it to get through to most web servers. It also specifies the endpoint of your service, globalweather.asmx. The next three lines of HTTP headers are pretty standard, but the final header, the SOAPACTION header, must be present; otherwise the message will be invalid. It's there to help the server decide whether it can let through a message's content.

The XML document is of greater interest. The opening line is the XML document header, standard to all XML documents. Then you have the structure of the document, which in SOAP will always have this structure. You have a SOAP Envelope tag that contains a SOAP Header and a SOAP Body.

The SOAP Header is optional and is missing from the code, but the SOAP Envelope contains some vital information in the attributes to help it make up the document. It contains three attributes that all provide namespace information: xsi, xsd, and soap. xmlns is short for XML namespace. At this level of programming, you really only want to know about the latter attribute, and this is because you use it to specify a prefix to your SOAP tags:

```
xmlns:soap="http://schemas.xmlsoap.org/soap/envelope/"
```

The prefix specified after the xmlns: attribute is soap, and this prefix is used in front of all the SOAP tags:

```
<soap:Envelope>
 <soap:Body>
 ... Web Service content here...
 <soap:Body>
<soap:Envelope>
```

All documents sent by `SOAP` will need to adhere to this structure. Inside the `SOAP:Envelope` attribute is the `SOAP:Body` tag. The `SOAP:Body` tag is always contained within the envelope and it contains the information that has been gleaned from the parameters and needs to be sent to the web service. Inside the `SOAP:Body` tags, you find at last the data you want to send:

```
<GetWeather xmlns="http://www.webserviceX.NET">
  <CityName>Birmingham</CityName>
  <CountryName>United Kingdom</CountryName>
</GetWeather>
```

The `GetWeather` tag is the web service, and the `xmlns` attribute outlines the location of the web service, which in this case is `www.webservicex.net`. Inside the `GetWeather` tag are two tags: `CityName` and `CountryName`. These are the two parameters that you originally supplied to the web service when you invoked it. These parameters have been serialized into a `SOAP` document, which itself is parceled up in the HTTP data and is now transmitted to the web service.

> **Rather than use the more common terminology *call*, the term *invoke* is used with relation to web services. If you check Dictionary.com, you will find the definition of invoke is to call upon a "higher system or power for assistance, support or inspiration." The higher power in this instance is of course the web service. I suppose it is used because the word call, of course, just doesn't paint the same picture.**

You're probably wondering why we're going into some quite esoteric detail about `SOAP` document structure. The answer is that if you want to supply data to the web service manually, it is going to have to have this structure involved. Also there is another important reason, which you will discover in the next sections.

Returning the Response

A web service doesn't have to return a response. It will most commonly return a response, but this isn't essential — it might be just enough to send some information to a database or to change an attribute on the server. Before a response of any sort can be returned, though, a few tasks must be accomplished by the web service.

Because the data has been serialized so that it can be transmitted across the web, it has to be *deserialized* first. This is just the process of obtaining the data (which in the previous example were the words "Birmingham" and "United Kingdom") from the XML and then executing the web service with this data. Of course the data isn't the only thing sent back as part of the response. You also get the following:

- A return address for the consumer
- The fact that this is an HTTP response and that there is no further action required
- A success or failure code
- Configuration information

One of two scenarios is possible: either a value needs to be returned, in which case the result has to be serialized once more in an XML document and sent back to the client, or there are no values that need transmitting back, in which case there will only be a success or failure code to indicate what has happened to your web service.

In the example, you might notice that the response isn't actually returned as a `SOAP` document, but one large XML string using the `HTTP-POST` protocol. This is because you sent your original call to the service as a `HTTP-POST` document, so the web service is just returning in like format. It is also possible to call your web service using `HTTP-GET`. As you might remember from Chapter 2, a call to the server using `HTTP-GET` involves adding a querystring to the URL and adding the parameters as querystrings. You can send the same request to the example web service as follows:

```
http://www.webservicex.net/globalweather.asmx/GetWeather?CityName=Birmingham&Coun
tryName=United%20Kingdom
```

Doing this will return exactly the same response as you saw in Figure 12-4.

This leaves the `SOAP` message template. To send and retrieve a document using `SOAP` requires a little more effort, and isn't possible via the endpoint without extra code. However, the information contained with a `SOAP` document retains structure, rather than being sent back as a convoluted jumble bundled in a `<string>` element:

```
HTTP/1.1 200 OK
Content-Type: text/xml; charset=utf-16
Content-Length: length

<?xml version="1.0" encoding="utf-16"?>
<soap:Envelope xmlns:xsi="http://www.w3.org/2001/XMLSchema-instance"
xmlns:xsd="http://www.w3.org/2001/XMLSchema"
xmlns:soap="http://schemas.xmlsoap.org/soap/envelope/">
  <soap:Body>
    <GetWeatherResponse xmlns="http://www.webserviceX.NET">
      <GetWeatherResult>
        <Location>Birmingham / Airport, United Kingdom (EGBB)
         52-27N 001-44W 0M</Location>
        <Time>Jul 12, 2005 - 05:20 AM EDT / 2005.07.12 0920 UTC</Time>
        <Wind> from the E (090 degrees) at 5 MPH (4 KT) (direction
         variable):0</Wind>
        <Visibility> greater than 7 mile(s):0</Visibility>
        <SkyConditions> mostly cloudy</SkyConditions>
        <Temperature> 64 F (18 C)</Temperature>
        <DewPoint> 59 F (15 C)</DewPoint>
        <RelativeHumidity> 82%</RelativeHumidity>
        <Pressure> 30.47 in. Hg (1032 hPa)</Pressure>
        <Status>Success</Status>
      </GetWeatherResult>
  </GetWeatherResponse>
   </soap:Body>
</soap:Envelope>
```

The first three lines are the HTTP header. However, this time the weather report results (which are different than what was shown in Figure 12-4 because it was done on a different day) are placed within the

<soap:Envelope> and <soap:body> elements. There is no <soap:header> element here—it's optional and you don't need one. If you examine the results, you will also see that the <string> element is missing, which leaves your document with its intended structure.

This doesn't answer one question, though: What happens if you didn't want to include all of the information that the web service had returned, and just wanted some particular bits and pieces? The weather web service returns all kinds of extraneous information, when all you were interested in were the sky conditions and temperature. It's certainly possible to extract items from a string, but you are better served by restricting what information the web service returns at source. To do this, you need to invest in the flexibility that a command-line prompt tool like wsdl.exe (a tool that comes as part of the .NET Framework) offers. And that requires a little extra work and is beyond the scope of this book.

Using the Response

After the client has received a response from the web service saying that either the response has succeeded or failed along with any data that was required, the cycle of your web service ends. The client in the test example received pure XML, and therefore displayed it as a normal XML document. Both HTTP-POST and HTTP-GET wrapped the response in a single string, which to be fair isn't a lot of use to you. This is why it is preferable to use SOAP, because the response would be returned in the same format as the request, and it would enable you to access individual items within the XML document more easily. However, because browsers use HTTP to transfer information, it would require a separate application to create a web service that uses the SOAP message template, and to be able to decipher the response sent via the SOAP message template.

When you consume a web service in the Wrox United application, it will be problematic when you get the whole document returned as one string, rather than individual elements, from which you can pick and choose. However, it is beyond the scope of this chapter to write a separate application to be able to send a web service request in the SOAP message template. We will instead settle for this imperfect state of affairs and try and use the information contained within the string as best we can. In the real world, we suggest that you use SOAP. For more details, look at http://msdn.microsoft.com/webservices/.

The Structure of Your Web Service

A web service has a particular structure that needs to be maintained whenever you create a new web service. This structure is pretty much unchanged between ASP.NET 1.x and ASP.NET 2.0, so if you have experience in the area, it should look familiar. Every web service you create must have basically four items (detailed in the following sections).

Processing Directive

At the head of any web service file, you need a directive, which essentially just lets ASP.NET know that this is a web service. The processing directive must always be the first line and it takes the following syntax:

```
<%@ WebService Language="language" Class="classname" %>
```

The directive is used to specify particular settings such as which language the web service is written in and where to find the class that defines the particulars of your web service. The class should be a separate file.

Namespaces

As with the rest of ASP.NET, occasionally you will need to specify other namespaces so that you can appropriate other classes and functions within your own web service. These namespaces are defined after the `@WebService` attribute in the file. In C#, four references are added as default, which are as follows:

```
using System;
using System.Web;
using System.Web.Services;
using System.Web.Services.Protocols;
```

These references are required as an absolute minimum, because they contain classes needed for web services to handle network connection issues and other related tasks.

Public Class

The class is simply a container for the web service, and the name of the class signifies the name of the web service:

```
public class Service : System.Web.Services.WebService
{    ...
}
```

The class name needs to correspond with the `class` attribute that is specified within the processing directive. Then for all other intents and purposes, it is just a normal object, albeit one that is exposed to the web. The trick with this web server, though, is that any calls to the object will look like they came from the same machine, and not via a foreign source.

Web Methods

To signify that a particular method (or property) is callable via the web, you need to add a `[WebMethod]` declaration. In ASP.NET 1.x, you could only expose methods to the web, but in ASP.NET 2.0, you can also expose properties.

The `[WebMethod]` declaration is the part that does all of the legwork. You can define one or more web methods, and not only that, you can make sure some web methods are publicly accessible, whereas others can have access to them restricted via the `protected` keyword. Though the syntax varies slightly between VB.NET and C# (VB.NET uses greater-than and less-than symbols, whereas C# uses square brackets to define the method call), they are both recognizably similar.

The syntax in VB.NET is as follows:

```
<WebMethod()> _
Public Function Hello (ByVal strName As String) As String
....
End Function
```

This defines a web method that accepts a string as a parameter and returns a string as a result, just like a normal function.

The syntax in C# is as follows:

```
[WebMethod]
public string Hello (string strName)
{
....
}
```

This also defines a web method that accepts a string as a parameter and returns a string as a result. If you don't want to expose a particular web method to the public, you simply remove the declaration.

Web methods also take parameters of their own. You can set the different attributes to modify the behavior of the web service. This allows you to customize the web service in several ways. For example, you can use the `CacheDuration` attribute to specify the number of seconds for which you want the `WebMethod` declaration to cache its results. When a consumer browses to the web service inside this allotted period, instead of the web service going back to retrieve the result, it gets a cached copy of the results instead.

In VB.NET, you can specify an attribute as follows:

```
<WebMethod(CacheDuration:=60)> _
Public Function Hello (ByVal strName As String) As String
....
End Function
```

In C#, you can specify an attribute as follows:

```
[WebMethod(CacheDuration=60)]
public string Hello (string strName)
{
....
}
```

You can specify multiple attributes by separating them with commas. The `Description` attribute allows you to specify a little detail about your web method, which can help potential consumers identify whether or not they want to use it.

In VB.NET, you can specify multiple attributes as follows:

```
<WebMethod(Description:="A web service that says hello to you", _
CacheDuration:=60)> _
Public Function Hello (ByVal strName As String) As String
....
End Function
```

In C#, you can specify multiple attributes as follows:

```
[WebMethod(Description="A web service that says hello to you",CacheDuration=60)]
public string Hello (string strName)
```

```
{
....
}
```

You can see the effect of adding a description to a web method in Figure 12-6. The text is displayed next to the web service so that in a list of web services, you would be able to differentiate between each one.

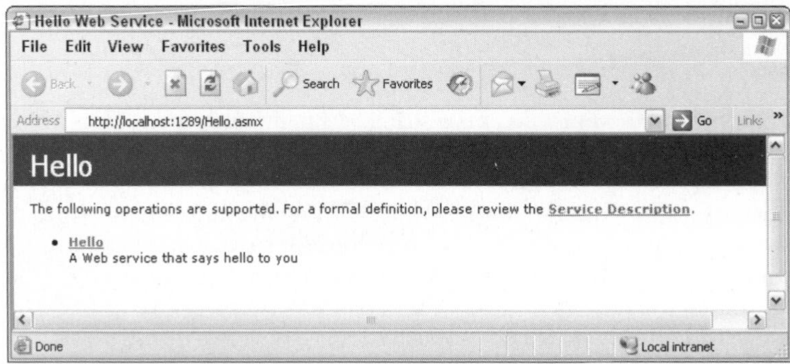

Figure 12-6

For more information on `WebMethod` attributes, go to `http://msdn.microsoft.com/library/default.asp?url=/library/en-us/cpref/html/frlrfsystemwebserviceswebmethodattributememberstopic.asp`.

Creating a Web Service

So far you've consumed a third-party web service and seen how you can send and receive responses via a standard interface provided from the .asmx endpoint. However, it isn't the .asmx file that is the web service — it just points you in the direction of the web service. As stated earlier, the Wrox United application doesn't provide weather forecasting, so you borrowed someone else's service. What happens, though, if you want to create your own web service?

In the past, creating a web service wasn't always as easy as it should have been. If you created ASP.NET 1.x pages with Notepad, you would find yourself delving around the murky world of the command prompt to compile the service, and having to create an application by hand with which to consume the service. Here you're only going to worry about creating a web service with which you can call and transmit the data.

In this Try It Out, you create an example web service that is able to return the list of results and fixtures from the Wrox United web site.

Try It Out — The Fixtures Web Service

1. With the Chapter12 solution (`C:\BegASPNET2\Chapters\Begin\Chapter12`) open, go to Solution Explorer and select the top line, which reads `C:\... \Chapter12`. Right-click it and select Add New Item.
2. A new dialog box appears. Make sure that the Language is set to Visual C#. Type the name **FixtureService.asmx**, select the Web Service option, and click Add, as shown in Figure 12-7.

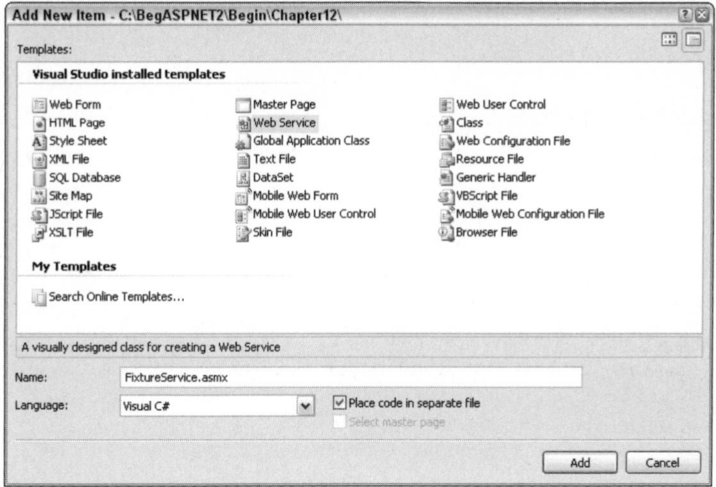

Figure 12-7

3. This creates a template web service from which to work. If it doesn't appear automatically, go to the `App_Code` folder in Solution Explorer and click `FixtureService.cs`, as shown in Figure 12-8.

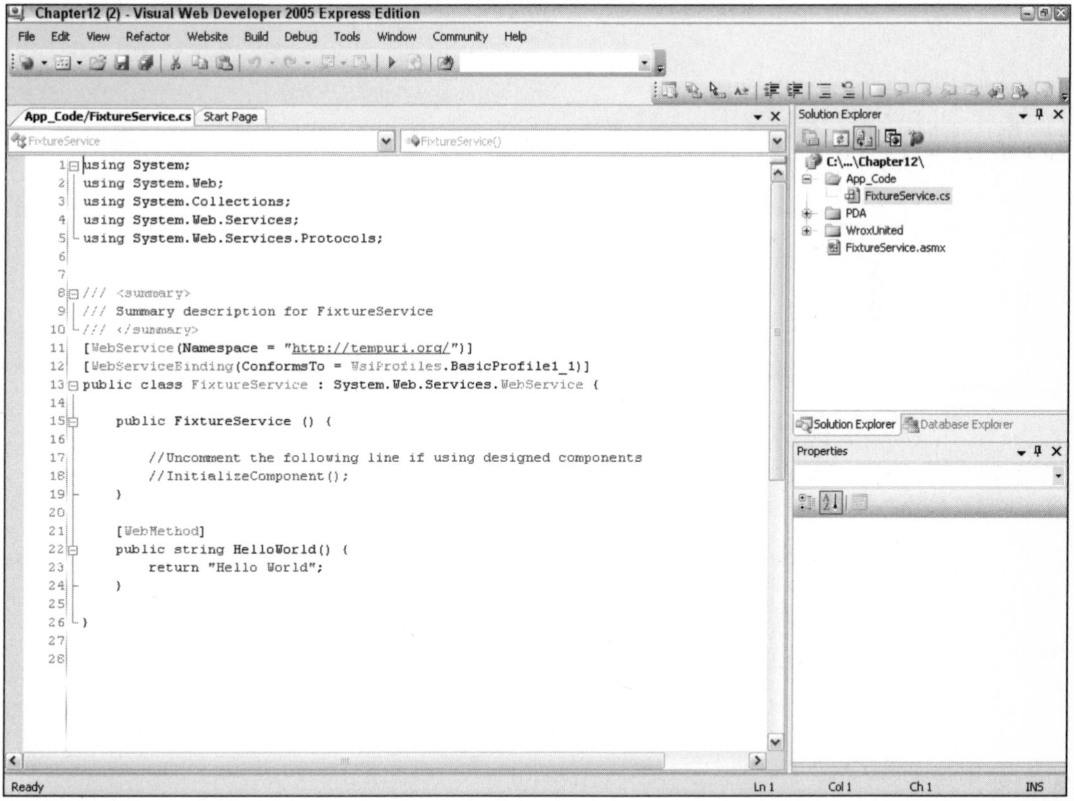

```
using System;
using System.Web;
using System.Collections;
using System.Web.Services;
using System.Web.Services.Protocols;


/// <summary>
/// Summary description for FixtureService
/// </summary>
[WebService(Namespace = "http://tempuri.org/")]
[WebServiceBinding(ConformsTo = WsiProfiles.BasicProfile1_1)]
public class FixtureService : System.Web.Services.WebService {

    public FixtureService () {

        //Uncomment the following line if using designed components
        //InitializeComponent();
    }

    [WebMethod]
    public string HelloWorld() {
        return "Hello World";
    }

}
```

Figure 12-8

4. Add the following lines to the list of namespaces at the top of the page:

```
using System;
using System.Web;
using System.Web.Services;
using System.Web.Services.Protocols;
using System.Data;
using System.Data.SqlClient;
using System.Configuration;
```

5. Remove the lines from `[WebMethod]` to `}` (because this is just a default test web service), and replace it with the following code:

```
    [WebMethod]
    public DataSet Fixtures()
    {
        SqlConnection conn = new
SqlConnection(ConfigurationManager.ConnectionStrings["WroxUnited"].ConnectionString
);
        SqlDataAdapter adapter = new SqlDataAdapter("SELECT FixtureDate, Opponents,
FixtureType, GoalsFor, GoalsAgainst FROM Fixtures ORDER BY FixtureDate", conn);
        DataSet ds = new DataSet();

        adapter.Fill(ds, "Fixtures");

        return ds;
    }

}
```

6. Change the namespace attribute at the top of the class to the following:

```
[WebService(Namespace="http://wroxunited.net/")]
```

7. Save this file.

How It Works

Inside your `[WebMethod]` declaration, you have a simple functionthat creates a connection using the connection string, and then creates a `SqlDataAdapter` and passes it the SQL to query the fixtures table:

```
public DataSet Fixtures()
    {
        SqlConnection conn = new
SqlConnection(ConfigurationManager.ConnectionStrings["WroxUnited"].ConnectionString
);
        SqlDataAdapter adapter = new SqlDataAdapter("SELECT FixtureDate, Opponents,
FixtureType, GoalsFor, GoalsAgainst FROM Fixtures ORDER BY FixtureDate", conn);
        DataSet ds = new DataSet();

        adapter.Fill(ds, "Fixtures");

        return ds;
    }
```

You create a dataset, and fill this dataset with the contents of the adapter (in other words, the result of your query) and then return the dataset as a result. You also had to add a couple of namespaces. This is because the `SqlDataAdapter` isn't accessible by default, and so to use it you have to add `System.Data` and `System.Data.SqlClient` to enable you to create a connection and to hook up to your SQL database. You also changed the default namespace from `http://tempuri.org` (the default namespace provided by Microsoft) to `http://www.wroxunited.net`, which is the URL of the Wrox United site.

There is nothing unusual about this function — it's actually the code that surrounds this function that is important. This is what you look at in the next section.

Testing Your Web Service

You've created your web service and taken a look at its structure, but you haven't actually done anything with it yet or tested it. Fortunately you already have tools at your disposal to test the web service. Being able to browse to the endpoint of your service enables you to try the web service out.

Try It Out Testing the Fixtures Web Service

1. When you created `FixtureService.cs` and placed it in the `App_Code` folder, it automatically created an endpoint (.asmx file) for you. Go to Solution Explorer and select `Fixture Service.asmx`. Right-click it and select View in Browser. You will see something similar to Figure 12-9.

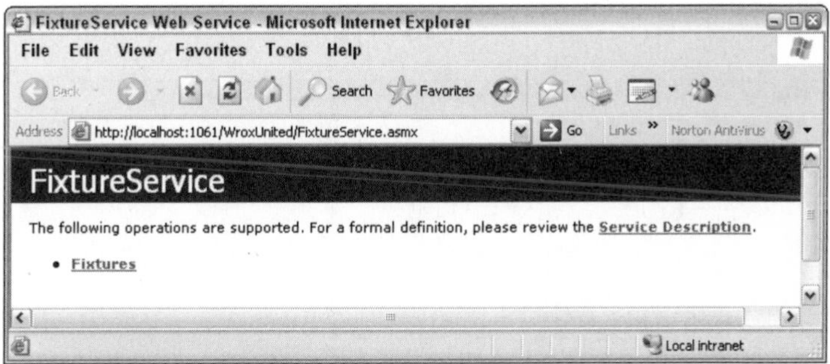

Figure 12-9

2. Click Fixtures, and you will arrive at a screen similar to the one displayed in Figure 12-10. From here you can test your service. Note that the service doesn't require any input.
3. Click Invoke and scroll down the screen until you see the XML depicted in Figure 12-11.

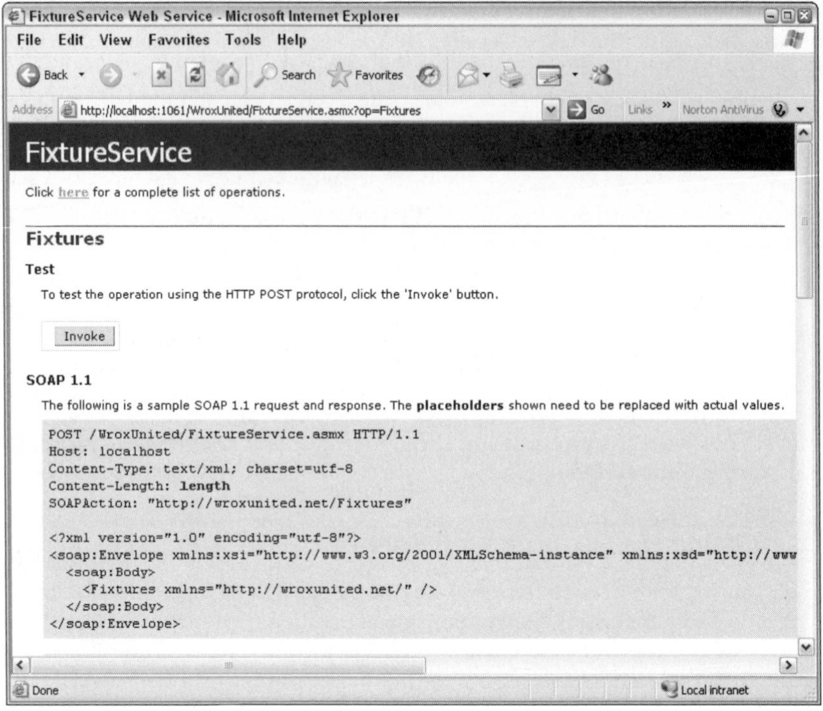

Figure 12-10

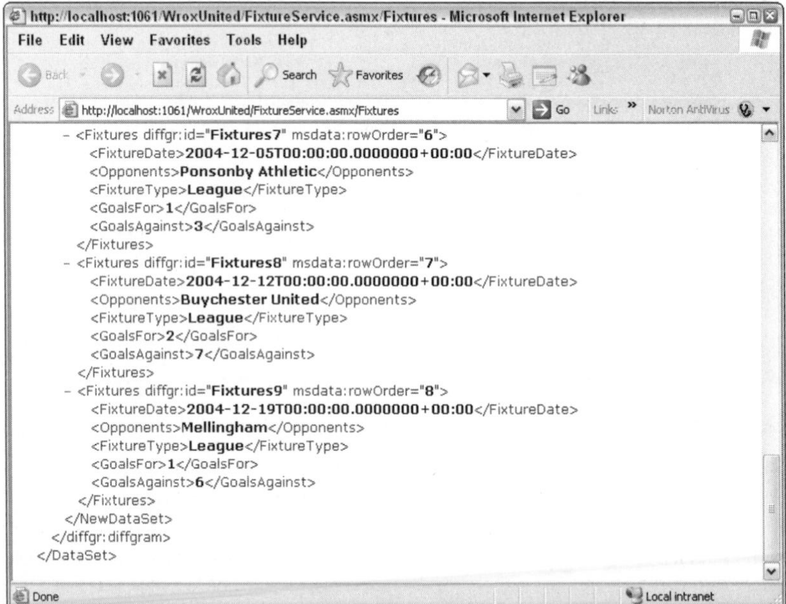

Figure 12-11

How It Works

You can see that the test has returned the fixtures and results of Wrox United's matches within the XML. The answers supplied are in pure text, so this is something that can be easily passed back and forth across the web. You started by going to the endpoint of the service and clicking the link. From the testing page, you clicked Invoke to produce the web service result in XML. This web service generated a set of fixtures from the class `FixtureService.cs` and the resulting dataset is rendered as a set of XML elements: `<FixtureDate>`, `<Opponents>`, `<FixtureType>`, `<GoalsFor>`, and `<GoalsAgainst>`.

The WSDL Contract

If you go back to the endpoint `FixtureService.asmx` and browse it again, you'll find a line with a link reading, "For a formal definition, please review the Service Description." If you click the Service Description link, you will see the page shown in Figure 12-12, which contains the WSDL.

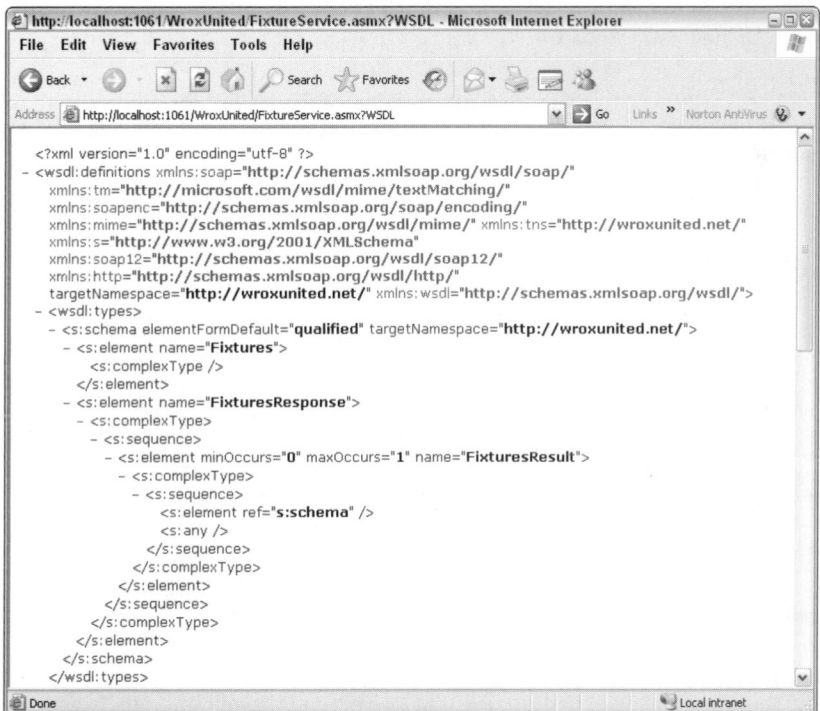

```
http://localhost:1061/WroxUnited/FixtureService.asmx?WSDL - Microsoft Internet Explorer
File  Edit  View  Favorites  Tools  Help
Address  http://localhost:1061/WroxUnited/FixtureService.asmx?WSDL

  <?xml version="1.0" encoding="utf-8" ?>
- <wsdl:definitions xmlns:soap="http://schemas.xmlsoap.org/wsdl/soap/"
    xmlns:tm="http://microsoft.com/wsdl/mime/textMatching/"
    xmlns:soapenc="http://schemas.xmlsoap.org/soap/encoding/"
    xmlns:mime="http://schemas.xmlsoap.org/wsdl/mime/" xmlns:tns="http://wroxunited.net/"
    xmlns:s="http://www.w3.org/2001/XMLSchema"
    xmlns:soap12="http://schemas.xmlsoap.org/wsdl/soap12/"
    xmlns:http="http://schemas.xmlsoap.org/wsdl/http/"
    targetNamespace="http://wroxunited.net/" xmlns:wsdl="http://schemas.xmlsoap.org/wsdl/">
  - <wsdl:types>
    - <s:schema elementFormDefault="qualified" targetNamespace="http://wroxunited.net/">
      - <s:element name="Fixtures">
          <s:complexType />
        </s:element>
      - <s:element name="FixturesResponse">
        - <s:complexType>
          - <s:sequence>
            - <s:element minOccurs="0" maxOccurs="1" name="FixturesResult">
              - <s:complexType>
                - <s:sequence>
                    <s:element ref="s:schema" />
                    <s:any />
                  </s:sequence>
                </s:complexType>
              </s:element>
            </s:sequence>
          </s:complexType>
        </s:element>
      </s:schema>
    </wsdl:types>
Done                                                    Local intranet
```

Figure 12-12

This is yet more behind-the-scenes work. WSDL is short for Web Services Description Language and it is an XML file that defines how the interaction between a web service and its consumer will occur. For example, WSDL states whether the web service uses `GET`, `POST`, or `SOAP`. The WSDL document defines whether the web service requires 0, 1, or 20 parameters, and defines how many you expect back. It can also specify that when, for example, a web service expects two specific parameters and returns a single value, what the names, order, and data types of each input and output value should be. With WSDL, all of the information necessary is present to begin using the web service functionality. WSDL is yet another standard managed by W3.org and you can find the standard details at `www.w3.org/TR/wsdl`.

At the head of the WSDL document is a declaration for the `<definitions>` element, which contains various namespaces, which make references to `SOAP`. Next up is the `<types>` element, which defines each of the data types that the web service expects to receive and return after its completion. The `<types>` element is written in yet another XML language, XSD (XML Schema Definition Language).

If you want to see a particular definition of a data type, you need to scroll down the screen and expand each node within Internet Explorer.

After the `<types>` element are various `<message>`, `<port type>`, and `<binding>` elements, which all refer to transmissions between the web service and consumer. The `WebMethod` message named FixtureService is contained in here, and various `SOAP` message structures are defined. In short, this file has everything needed to handle communication with your web service. And it was automatically created when you created your .asmx file.

Although you've consumed web services by browsing directly to the endpoint (the .asmx file), you haven't actually tackled how you'd go about including the web service's functionality within your own program, which is the purpose of the next section.

Web Service Discovery

Perhaps another reason why web services haven't been as successful as they might have been is that web service discovery has been a rather hit-and-miss affair. If you think back, you've created your extravagant rainfall-amount-cataloguing weather service, now how do you let people know about it? Stick it on your web site and hope the Google spiders will index it sooner rather than later? Stand down at your local shopping center with a placard around your neck? Web service discovery is like the process of locating any item on a search engine. You know roughly what you want to find; you just need to know the URL of where to find it. Web services are the same.

If you are the only person who needs to know about the web service, then it's a very simple affair — you just add a web reference in Visual Web Developer. When you add the web reference to the web site, it handles not only the process of compiling your web service for you, but also the process of discovering a web service. However, you first have to compile the web service. In prior incarnations of ASP.NET, creating a web service was a bit more fiddly than it is in ASP.NET 2.0, and it involved using the command-line prompt. You shouldn't need to drop down to a command prompt, though. Instead, you can simply use Visual Web Developer's IntelliSense feature to compile your web services for you. However, to make it available to a wider range of people, this is inadequate.

Two technologies are used in making web services available. The great thing is that you really don't need to know too much about either. This is because Visual Web Developer has a feature that makes the discovery of web services very straightforward: the Add Web Reference option. However, before you use it, the next sections take a brief look at the two technologies underlying web service discovery.

DISCO

DISCO is a colorful name that belies a rather more prosaic abbreviation — discovery. DISCO is a Microsoft technology that is generally used to make web services available on your local machine. To do this, you place information about the web service in a .disco document. This is an XML document that contains links to other resources that describe the web service, and can be thought of like an HTML file that contains human-readable documentation or a WSDL file.

Rather than having to worry about creating this yourself, Visual Web Developer takes care of this task for you when you add a web reference. It creates the .disco file from the .asmx endpoint file and generates a .DISCOMAP file, both of which are placed in the `app_WebReferences` folder. These documents can then be used with Visual Web Developer automatically to find your web service.

UDDI

UDDI goes beyond DISCO. It's like a giant directory of web services, and only four big companies that use web services keep one. Following the closure of Microsoft's UDDI registry (formerly at `http://uddi.microsoft.com`), the main one is IBM's `www-3.ibm.com/services/uddi/`. The registries aren't just restricted to the companies involved — you can publish your own web service details within these directories. The UDDI directory was intended to work in the same way as a phone directory, with white pages, yellow pages, and green pages. White pages contained the business details, yellow pages contained the classification of the business, and the green pages contained technical information about the web service. Because a lot of web services are created just for the businesses involved and not for general public use, these never took off in the way they were intended to. However, if you create a web service and you want to market it to the public, or give it away for free, then putting it in a UDDI repository is very simple. Just go to the previously mentioned URL and follow the registration instructions.

Once again, Visual Web Developer is closely integrated with UDDI, and you can browse different registries when you come to add a web reference to your web site, and add a service to the registry in this way.

Discovering Your Web Service

DISCO and UDDI are both technologies that go on behind the scenes, and though you can make use of both of them, you don't require any specialist knowledge to do so. More often than not, you'll probably just want to make use of a web service at a local level, within your application. In the following Try It Out, you see how you can go about discovering the fixture service that you have just added to your application, by adding a web reference to it.

Try It Out — Adding a Web Reference to Your Application

1. Staying within the WroxUnited web site solution, from Visual Web Developer select the Web Site⇨Add Web Reference option. You will see the screen shown in Figure 12-13.

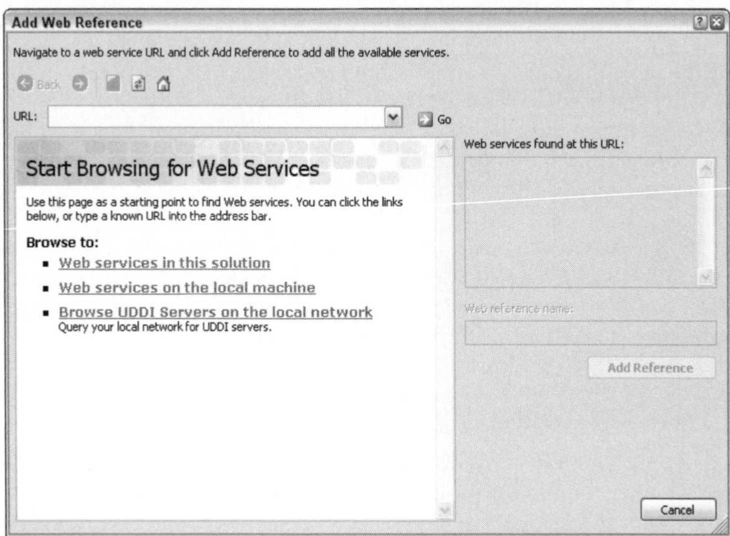

Figure 12-13

2. From here you can either browse to web services in your local application or on the local machine. You have already created a web service, so click Web Services in This Solution to arrive at the screen displayed in Figure 12-14.

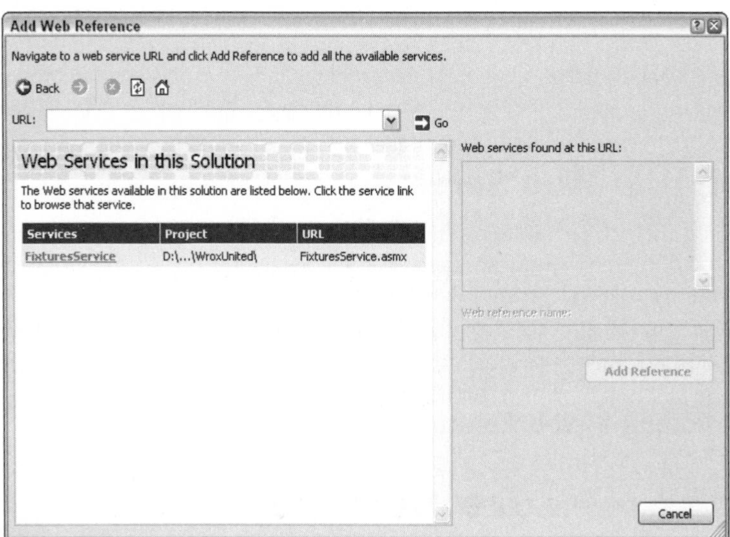

Figure 12-14

3. Only one web service should be in the solution so far, because you've only created one. Click the FixtureService link and you should be able to see a view of the web service .asmx file (see Figure 12-15).

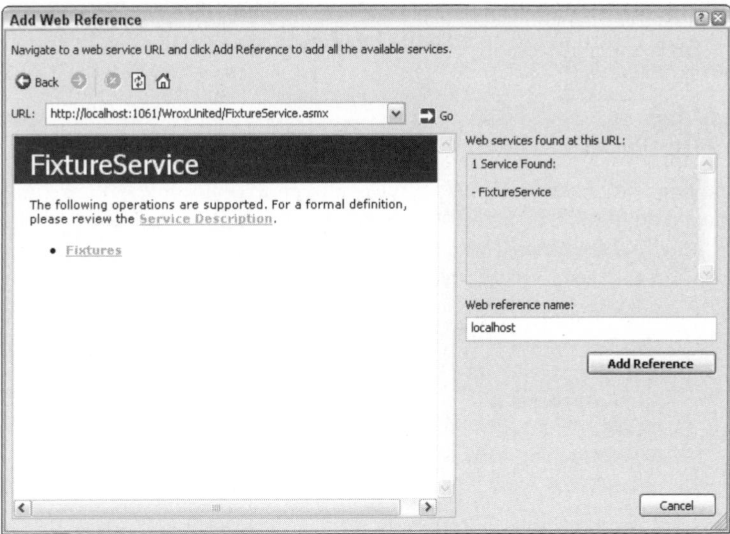

Figure 12-15

4. Click Add Reference. In Solution Explorer, you should see a folder called `App_WebReferences`, and underneath this folder, another folder, `localhost`, which contains three files, as shown in Figure 12-16.

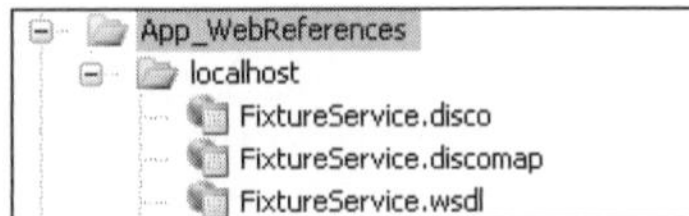

Figure 12-16

How It Works

You created the .disco and .wsdl files in this Try It Out automatically. The process of adding a web reference involved selecting a web service (there was only one to select) and adding a reference. The reference then appeared in the `App_WebReferences` folder. The .wsdl and .disco files were created at the same time. This means can access the web service from within your code. This is the ultimate point of your web service and you're almost there now.

Adding the Fixture Service to Your Application

The web service now exists as an object within your code that you can access and query the methods of, just like you would with any normal object. In fact, to your application, for all intents and purposes this is a local object. There is a sleight-of-hand going on here. What .NET Framework has done for you is to create a *proxy* object. This object acts like the web service and calls the methods on your behalf and actually passes the details to the web service.

This might sound quite complicated, but there really is no difference between creating this proxy object and creating a normal object. In the next Try It Out, you create a small page in your application that consumes your web service.

Try It Out Adding the Service to Your Application

1. Create a new Web Form in Visual Web Developer. In Solution Explorer, right-click the top line and select Add New Item. Select Web Form and call it **Consume.aspx**, as shown in Figure 12-17, making sure that the Place Code in Separate File box is checked. Also check the Select Master Page box. On the second page, select site.master as a Master page.

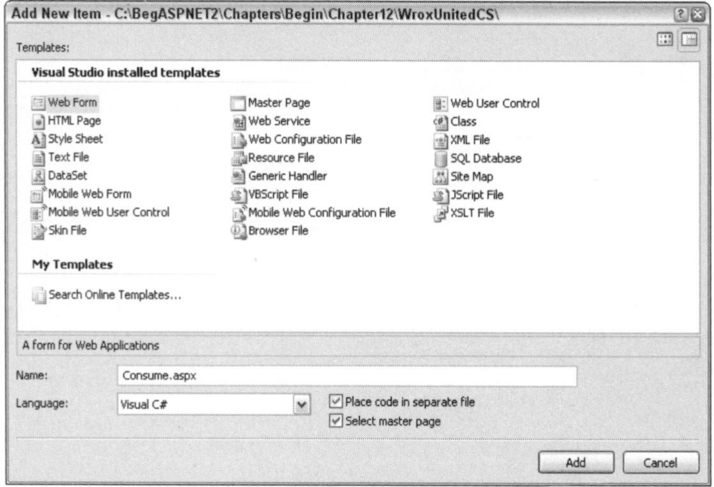

Figure 12-17

2. In Design View, add a single grid view tool to your new Web Form as in Figure 12-18.

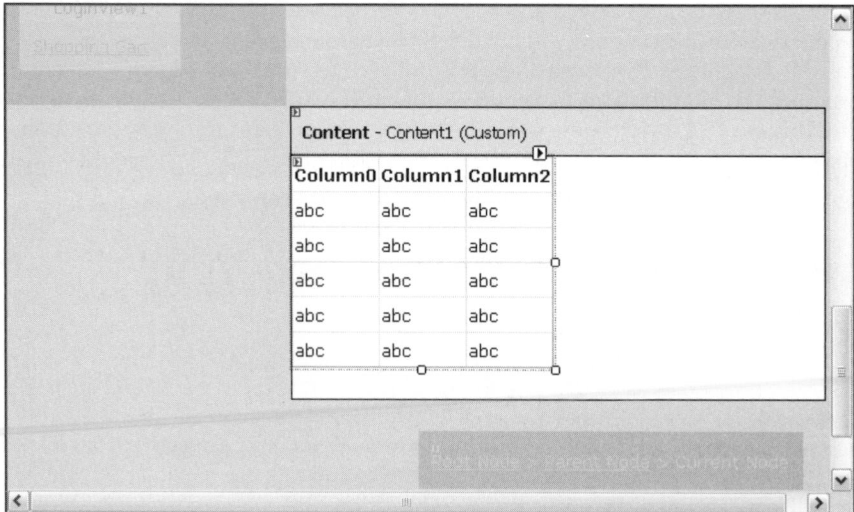

Figure 12-18

3. Click the page alongside the new grid, in the blank part of the content are to open `Consume.aspx.cs`'s `Page_Load` event and add the following code inside:

```
public partial class Consume : System.Web.UI.Page
{
    protected void Page_Load(object sender, EventArgs e)
    {        localhost.FixtureService wsConvert = new localhost.FixtureService();
                GridView1.DataSource = wsConvert.Fixtures();
        GridView1.DataBind();
    }
```

4. Save the page and view it in the browser. It will look like Figure 12-19.

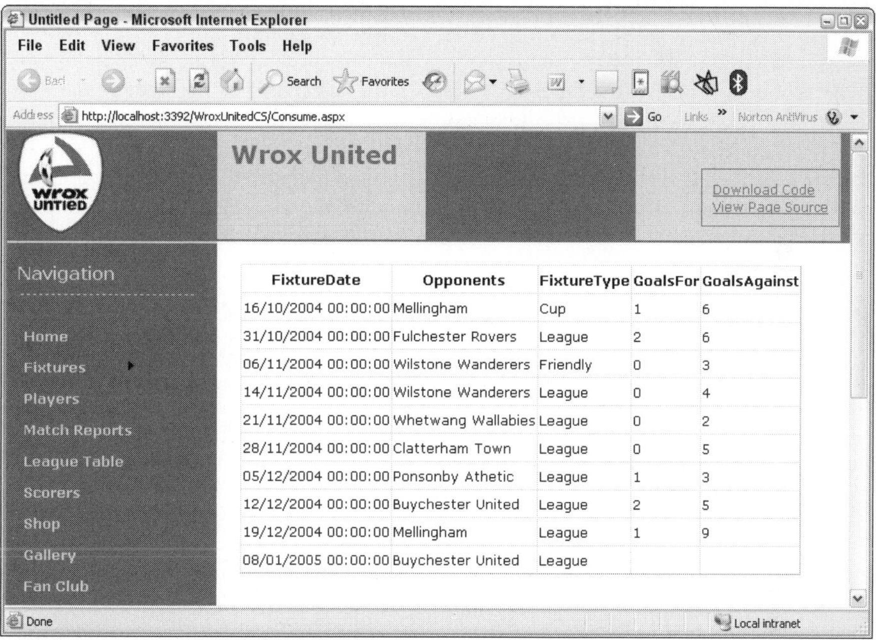

Figure 12-19

How It Works

The `GridView` control has created a table that has bound to the results and fixture provided by your fixtures web service. Only three lines of code were necessary in your final application to do this:

```
localhost.FixtureService wsConvert = new localhost.FixtureService();


 GridView1.DataSource = wsConvert.Fixtures();
 GridView1.DataBind();
```

First you created a proxy object from `localhost.FixtureService` called `wsConvert`. In the previous example, you created a `localhost` folder under your `App_WebReferences` folder, which contained the .wsdl and .disco files.

Next, you bound to the `Fixture` method of your new `wsConvert` proxy object, and then you bound to the `GridView` control. Your web service output is rendered in Grid View. You're now free to style and alter the presentation of the web service in any way you choose.

Putting It All Together

Here's a quick recap. We've separated out each step of creating, testing, discovering, and consuming a web service so far, and we might have created the illusion that there are a lot of separate steps to perform. This isn't really the case, because we've had to abstract out each step to explain what is going on. Now you can put them all together in one large, fluid example, and create a separate user control that you can place in any application.

One common feature of many sports sites is the capability to access league tables and show a miniaturized view of where your team is in the league, and though the Wrox United league table isn't huge (containing only eight teams), you can certainly create a web service that will show the team above and below Wrox United in the league. There are two provisos to this of course. One is that in the unlikely event that Wrox United is at the top of the league, you need to show the two teams underneath them. In the far more likely scenario that Wrox United is at the bottom, you should show the two teams above them instead. However, we'll leap those particular chasms when we get to them.

Try It Out Creating a League Table Mini View Web Service

1. Go to Solution Explorer, right-click the top line, select Add New Item, and then select the Web Service option. Change the name to **LeagueMiniView.asmx** and click OK.
2. Add the extra namespaces at the top of the page underneath the existing `using` statements:

```
using System.Data;
using System.Data.SqlClient;
using System.Configuration;
```

3. Remove the `HelloWorld()` method and add the following code to the `WebMethod` (note that the SQL string should all be on one line):

```
 [WebMethod]
    public DataSet ViewLeague()
         {
        SqlConnection conn = new
SqlConnection(ConfigurationManager.ConnectionStrings["WroxUnited"].ConnectionString
);
        string sqlstring;


sqlstring = "SELECT [OpponentID], [Name], [TotalGoalsFor], [TotalGoalsAgainst],
[TotalGoalsFor]-[TotalGoalsAgainst] AS [GoalDifference], [Points] FROM [Opponents]
Order By [Points] DESC, [GoalDifference] DESC, [TotalGoalsFor] DESC";

        SqlDataAdapter adapter = new SqlDataAdapter(sqlstring, conn);
        SqlDataAdapter adapter2 = new SqlDataAdapter(sqlstring, conn);

        DataSet ds = new DataSet();
        DataSet ds2 = new DataSet();
```

```
            int position=0;
        int offset;
        DataRowCollection rows;

        adapter.Fill(ds, "ViewLeague");
        rows = ds.Tables["ViewLeague"].Rows;

        for (int i = 0; i< rows.Count; i++)
        {
            if (rows[i]["Name"].ToString() == "Wrox United")
                {
                position = i + 1;
            }
        }

        if (position > 1 && position < rows.Count)
        {
            offset = position - 2;
         }
        else if (position == 1)
        {
            offset = position -1;
         }
        else
         {
            offset = position -3;
        }
        adapter2.Fill(ds2, offset, 3, "ViewLeague");

        ds2.Tables["ViewLeague"].Columns.Add("Position", typeof(int));
        rows = ds2.Tables["ViewLeague"].Rows;
        for (int i = 0;i< rows.Count;i++)
        {
            rows[i]["Position"] = offset + i + 1;
        }

        return ds2;
    }
```

4. Change the namespace from tempuri.org to wroxunited.net again, to `[WebService(Name space:="http://wroxunited.net/")]`.
5. Save this file.
6. You now need to create a page that can use this web service. Create a new web user control called **LeagueView.ascx** and add a `GridView` control to it. Double-click the LeagueView web user control in Design View and add the following code to `LeagueView.ascx.cs`:

```
public partial class LeagueView : System.Web.UI.UserControl
{
    protected void Page_Load(object sender, EventArgs e)
    {
        localhost.LeagueMiniView wsConvert = new localhost.LeagueMiniView();
        GridView1.DataSource = wsConvert.ViewLeague();
        GridView1.DataBind();
    }
}
```

7. Save the page. Add this control to `default.aspx` by changing that page's code as follows.

```
<%@ Register TagPrefix="wu" TagName="News" Src="News.ascx" %>
<%@ Register TagPrefix="wu" TagName="LeagueView" Src="~/LeagueView.ascx" %>
<asp:Content ID="Content1" ContentPlaceHolderID="mainContent" Runat="server">
    <h2>Welcome to the Wrox United Web site.</h2>
    <p>We're a great football team. No really, we are. Don't take any notice
    of our past performance. We're just unlucky.</p>
    <uc1:leagueview id="miniview" runat="server"></uc1:leagueview>
    <uc1:news id="News1" runat="server" ItemsToShow="5"></uc1:news>
</asp:Content>
```

8. Go to `default.aspx` and view it (see Figure 12-20).

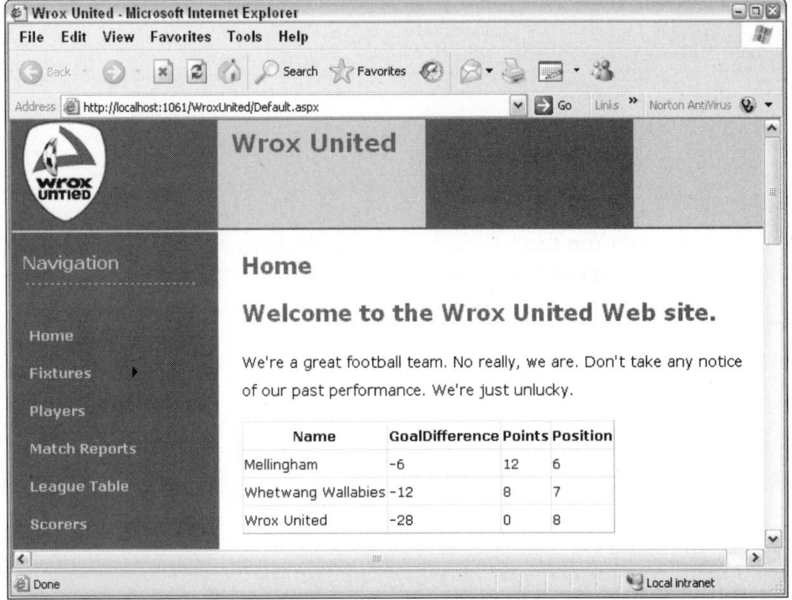

Figure 12-20

How It Works

Hopefully you will be getting a feel for this now. Although you could make the control a little more unobtrusive, the basic gist is there. Admittedly, it's a little repetitious, but should make it easier to remember. Once again your web service has returned a dataset. This time, the `WebMethod` has a lot more to do. You start by creating a function that returns your dataset:

```
public Function DataSet ViewLeague()
```

The first task within the function is to connect to the database. You use the predefined WroxUnited connection string to do this.

```
        SqlConnection conn = new
SqlConnection(ConfigurationManager.ConnectionStrings["WroxUnited"].ConnectionString
);
```

You then create the SQL that is needed to return your Mini-League table. You create two `SqlDataAdapters`, one to go with each SQL string. You need two, because one is a full table and the other is your mini-view of the same league table. `adapter2` contains your new shortened view of the table with only three teams, whereas `adapter` contains the full table:

```
sqlstring = "SELECT [OpponentID], [Name], [TotalGoalsFor], [TotalGoalsAgainst],
[TotalGoalsFor]-[TotalGoalsAgainst] AS [GoalDifference], [Points] FROM [Opponents]
Order By [Points] DESC, [GoalDifference] DESC, [TotalGoalsFor] DESC";

       SqlDataAdapter adapter = new SqlDataAdapter(sqlstring, conn);
        SqlDataAdapter adapter2 = new SqlDataAdapter(sqlstring, conn);
```

You then create two datasets, and create some variables to help you keep track of where you are in the datasets:

```
DataSet ds = new DataSet();
DataSet ds2 = new DataSet();
int position=0;
int offset;
DataRowCollection rows;
```

Next you fill the first adapter with the results of the first SQL query in `sqlstring1`, which returns the whole league table in order. You then iterated through this table, position by position, until you find an entry that matches `"Wrox United"`. You save that position into the variable position:

```
for (int i = 0; i< To rows.Count; i++)
{
    if (rows[i]["Name"].ToString() == "Wrox United")
        {
        position = i + 1;
    }
}
```

There are three scenarios here:

- The *golden* scenario: Wrox United is top, and you need to display the second and third place teams.
- The *doomsday* scenario: Wrox United is bottom and you need to display the two teams above them.
- The *usual* scenario: Wrox United is neither top nor bottom, but somewhere in between, in which case you display one team above them and one team below them.

Your first `if` condition deals with the case where the position isn't top or bottom of the league. You take 2 off the position (so if Wrox United is 5, this would be 3). Then you fill the `adapter2` with the `adapter2` starting at position `3`, and the number 3 indicates that there are three teams only. For example:

`Adapter2.Fill(`*name of dataset*`,` *position to start in dataset*`,` *number of rows*`,` *name of query*`);`.

So you say if the position isn't `1` and isn't last (you obtain the amount for last by counting the number of teams in the league), then you set the offset to the position minus 2 and pass that to the `adapter2.Fill` method at the end of the `if then` condition:

```
        if (position > 1 && position < rows.Count)
    {
            offset = position - 2;
         }
```

Of course if Wrox United has come in fifth, why are you starting with third? Surely that would display third, fourth, and fifth, when actually you intend to display fourth, fifth, and sixth. The answer is that when you filled your adapter, you started at row 0. The team that came first is 0, the team that came second is 1, and so on. So the preceding line to fill the adapter actually does return only three teams, and will return the teams in fourth, fifth, and sixth.

Your second condition deals with what happens if Wrox United is top. You check to see if the position is 1, you set the offset to `0, (1-1)`, and then you fill the adapter at the end of the `if` condition with the dataset starting at row 0, with the next three teams:

```
        else if (position == 1)
        {
            offset = position - 1;
         }
```

Last, you can deduce that if your team isn't first and also didn't finish between first and last, then they must be last. You set the offset variable accordingly, and fill your data adapter:

```
        else
        {
            offset = position - 3;
        }
        adapter2.Fill(ds2, offset, 3, "ViewLeague");
```

You then add a new column to your second dataset called `Position`, and you read in the positions for each team in your mini-table:

```
    rows = ds2.Tables["ViewLeague"].Rows;
        for (int i As Integer = 0; i< rows.Count;i++)
        {
            rows[i]["Position"] = offset + i + 1;
        }

        return ds2;
      }

    }
```

Having created the method that fuels your web service, you then need some way of being able to reference it. Because you have a dataset, you create a user control called `leagueview.ascx` and then add a `GridView` control to the user control and bind it to your web service.

The final step is to add a reference to your new user control to the Wrox United front page, so that it is displayed in the appropriate position. It is rather large and cumbersome, so you might choose to style it more and position it differently. This is left as an exercise for you to complete if you so desire, because any more code would distract from the already large code listings you have created.

Remote Web Services — PocketPC Application

This chapter has stressed that what makes web services so flexible is their capability to work across platforms. However, you've had to take that for granted, because not many people will have a Mac or Linux machine in addition to their own PC. There is one platform, though, that will be familiar to quite a few readers, and that is the PocketPC platform that runs on PDAs and other mobile technologies. Because we appreciate that not everyone will be able to use the following Try It Out, we will keep it relatively brief, but it demonstrates how your online reporters can supply updates to the Wrox United web site using just a web service with a PocketPC application on their PDA. Because you have already created the application that can submit data, all you need to do in this Try It Out is create a web service that will receive scores from reporters and alter the scores on the Wrox United site accordingly.

The extra bit of functionality that this Try It Out also includes is the ability to send parameters with the web service. This is just like sending parameter in a method, as you saw in Chapter 8.

To be able to run this Try It Out, you will need a piece of hardware capable of running PocketPC applications. This Try It Out was tested and run on a Dell AXIM PDA that was running PocketPC 2003. While we endeavor to make sure this application will work on all PDAs running PocketPC, due to the diverse nature of the PDA, we can make no such guarantees. If you don't have a PDA, you could try running it on an emulator instead.

Try It Out — Updating the Scores Web Service

1. Make sure you have a copy of the PocketPC application from `c:\BegASPNet2\Chapters\Begin\Chapter12\PDA`.
2. Open the `C:\BegASPNet2\Begin\Chapter12\WroxUnited` web site.
3. Go to Solution Explorer. Right-click the top line, select Add New Item, and then select the Web Service option. Change the name to **UpdateScore.asmx** and click OK.
4. Add the extra namespaces at the top of the page underneath the existing `Imports` statements:

```
using System.Data;
using System.Data.SqlClient;
using System.Configuration;
```

5. Add the following web method.

```
    [WebMethod]
    public void UpdateGoals(int FixtureID , bool GoalFor ,
      int PlayerID , int GoalTime )
 {
        SqlConnection conn = new
SqlConnection(ConfigurationManager.ConnectionStrings["WroxUnited"].ConnectionString
);
        conn.Open();
        SqlCommand cmd = new SqlCommand("usp_UpdateScore", conn);
        cmd.CommandType = CommandType.StoredProcedure;

        cmd.Parameters.Add("@FixtureID", SqlDbType.Int).Value = FixtureID;
```

```
        cmd.Parameters.Add("@GoalFor", SqlDbType.Bit).Value = GoalFor;

        cmd.ExecuteNonQuery();

        if (GoalFor)
        {
            Goal(FixtureID, PlayerID, GoalTime);
        }
    }
```

6. Add another web method underneath the previous one:

```
[WebMethod]
    public void Goal(int FixtureID, int PlayerID, int GoalTime )
 {
        SqlConnection conn = new
SqlConnection(ConfigurationManager.ConnectionStrings["WroxUnited"].ConnectionString
);
        conn.Open();
        SqlCommand cmd = new SqlCommand("usp_Goal", conn);
        cmd.CommandType = CommandType.StoredProcedure;

        cmd.Parameters.Add("@FixtureID", SqlDbType.Int).Value = FixtureID;
        cmd.Parameters.Add("@PlayerID", SqlDbType.Int).Value = PlayerID;
        cmd.Parameters.Add("@GoalTime", SqlDbType.Int).Value = GoalTime;

        cmd.ExecuteNonQuery();

    }
```

7. Change the namespace from `http//:tempuri.org` to `http://wroxunited.net`, once again in the line at the beginning of the definition of the web service:

```
[WebService(Namespace:="http://wroxunited.net/")]
```

8. Save this file.

9. Run the PDA application, add a scorer and goal details on the page, and hit the submit button (note that the PDA must have an active Internet connection for this to work). For example, in Figure 12-21, we've suggested adding Jerry Johnston at 90 minutes in the Wrox United versus Mellingham fixture.

10. Run the Wrox United site and go to the scorers link, which now shows the updated details where Jerry Johnston has been added to the scorers list, as shown in Figure 12-22.

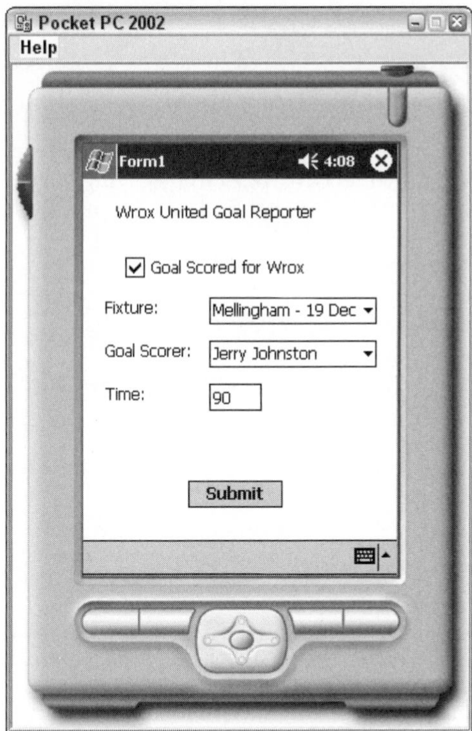

Figure 12-21

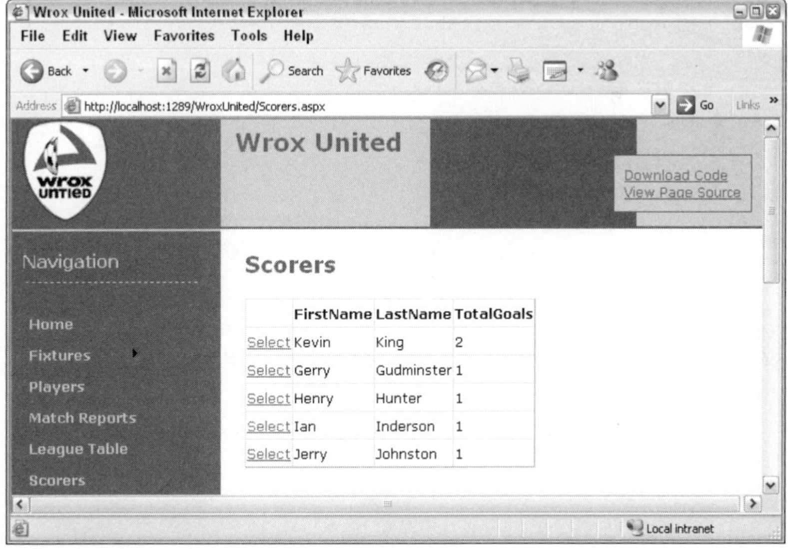

Figure 12-22

How It Works

In this Try It Out, you created two web methods as part of your web service. Which web method you use depends on whether Wrox United scored the goal or whether the goal was scored by an opponent. If Wrox United scored a goal, then you need to update the goal, the player who scored it, and the time it was scored. If the opposition scored it, then you only need to use two of the parameters to update the score in the database. To use the web service, you start by calling the `UpdateScore` method first and then you detect whether it is a Wrox United goal, and only if it is a Wrox United goal do you update the `Goal` method as well.

The `UpdateGoals` web method updates which side scored the goal and the `Score` method takes four parameters, shown in bold in the following code:

```
public Sub void UpdateGoals(int FixtureID, bool GoalFor, _
      int PlayerID, int GoalTime)
```

The web method creates a connection and a command, and sets the command type as stored procedure (stored procedures are discussed in Chapter 14):

```
SqlConnection conn = new
SqlConnection(ConfigurationManager.ConnectionStrings["WroxUnited"].ConnectionString
);
        conn.Open();
        SqlCommand cmd = new SqlCommand("usp_UpdateScore", conn);
        cmd.CommandType = CommandType.StoredProcedure;
```

You pass the parameters of the `FixtureID` and the whether the goal was for or against us and execute the query.

```
        cmd.Parameters.Add("@FixtureID", SqlDbType.Int).Value = FixtureID;
        cmd.Parameters.Add("@GoalFor", SqlDbType.Bit).Value = GoalFor;

        cmd.ExecuteNonQuery();
```

If the goal was for us, then you call the `Goal` web method with the `FixtureID`, the `PlayerID`, and the `GoalTime`:

```
        if (GoalFor)
        {
            Goal(FixtureID, PlayerID, GoalTime);
        }
```

The `Goal` web method updates the Wrox United goals and the `Score` method only takes three parameters, shown in bold here:

```
    public void Goal(int FixtureID, int PlayerID, int GoalTime )
```

These three parameters are the fixture number, the number of the player, and the timing of the goal. In the PDA application, you selected the `FixtureID` from a selection of possible fixtures (for example, Wrox United versus Ponsonby Athletic) rather than selecting `FixtureID 27` from a `DropDownList` control, and you selected the name of the player from a `DropDownList` control along with check box indicating if it was a goal for or against Wrox United. In the text box, you typed the time of the goal. These are passed to your web method.

This web method is very similar to the previous one in that it you create a connection and call a stored procedure, which will update the Wrox United database. It passes the three parameters and executes the query:

```
        SqlConnection conn = new
SqlConnection(ConfigurationManager.ConnectionStrings["WroxUnited"].ConnectionString
);
        conn.Open();
        SqlCommand cmd = new SqlCommand("usp_Goal", conn);
        cmd.CommandType = CommandType.StoredProcedure;

        cmd.Parameters.Add("@FixtureID", SqlDbType.Int).Value = FixtureID;
        cmd.Parameters.Add("@PlayerID", SqlDbType.Int).Value = PlayerID;
        cmd.Parameters.Add("@GoalTime", SqlDbType.Int).Value = GoalTime;

        cmd.ExecuteNonQuery();
```

Much of the work is done behind the scenes with the PocketPC application. However, as long as the Wrox United application makes the information available in a standard way (as was done here), then any application — whether a Windows application, a web application, or a PDA application — can use it via an Internet connection.

Web Service Security

This chapter's introduction mentioned that one of the reasons that web services' lack of adoption in some quarters may be due to the lack of ease with which they can be secured. If you create a web service, and you want to market it, then you need to be able to control and regulate access to the web service.

While certainly possible in ASP.NET 1.x, it wasn't the easiest of tasks and this is one area that has definitely been improved in ASP.NET 2.0. Also, as you've seen, the web service request and response is sent as XML documents (in other words, pure text), so if you're not sending via SSL, then anyone is able to intercept and steal the code. A couple of new facilities in ASP.NET 2.0 help you deal with this.

Encryption and Message-Based Security

Encryption is the process of scrambling the text containing your web service so that only the intended reader is able to decrypt it with the aid of a key. *Message-based* security was introduced in web services.

Message-based security allows you to hand your encrypted messages to anyone, and they won't be able to decrypt the encrypted data. If your message is modified, you will be able to detect that straightaway because the signature attached to the message will be invalid and you can throw those messages away. It works by encrypting the message at both request and response level and is defined in the web services WS-Security specification (a relatively new W3 specification detailing how to handle web services security).

Authentication and Access Controls for Services

Authentication is the process of checking to see if a particular user is who they claim to be. This is usually done by the common user ID and password entry. One way to secure a web service is to force anyone who attempts to use a service to have to supply credentials first. They have to supply a user ID and password, and if they don't they are refused access to the web service.

You can find more details at `http://msdn.microsoft.com/library/default.asp?url=/library/en-us/rsprog/htm/rsp_prog_soapapi_dev_6ne8.asp`.

Using both of these facilities is beyond the scope of this book. They are mentioned here because people would have previously disregarded web services for transferring sensitive and confidential information, but that no longer needs to be the case.

Summary

Web services are a massive subject that could command a whole book quite easily in their own right. We have been necessarily curt in our treatment of them to give you an idea of how they might be accessed and used within your own applications. As you saw at the beginning of this chapter, a web service is simply a functionality that can be remotely called over the web. However, the distinct advantage they enjoyed over other similar methods is that all information was sent and returned in the form of XML documents (and therefore text). Specifically, this chapter covered the following topics:

- The process of using a web service, which can be broken down into creating a web service, making the web service available for discovery, and ultimately consuming the web service.
- A lot of new technologies introduced in this chapter (fortunately Visual Web Developer handles them smoothly for us), including `SOAP`, which is a framework for exchanging messages and is used in the transmission of web services. A `SOAP` document is transmitted as part of the HTTP data. DISCO and UDDI are used to make the web service available so that people can see and use it.
- A proxy object within your code takes the place of the web service and allows you to access the different methods of the web service as though it were on the same PC.

Although each of these technologies has a role to play, they have been much hidden from us. The files and objects are created automatically for us, and the bottom line is that if you create a method or object, basically all you need to do is start a `[WebMethod]` with a few extra configuration details, and the rest is done for you.

The next chapter deals with e-commerce by showing you how to set up a shopping cart and how to shop for merchandise on Wrox United's web site.

Exercises

1. What is the role of `SOAP` in web services?
2. Create a web service that retrieves a Wrox United score whenever they've scored more than one goal.
3. Create a page that consumes the third-party weather forecast for Birmingham, United Kingdom. (Hint: You will also need to discover this service first.)

E-Commerce

This is the first version of this book that's ever dared to talk about e-commerce. This isn't because we've forgotten to, or because we think it's unimportant, but mainly because this is the first version of ASP.NET where it hasn't been too complicated to even think about. I must admit it's the one area as a developer that even I (or any developer) will tread very carefully. The reason is simple — money. When you're handling other people's money, you really must make every effort to ensure that nothing can go wrong. If not, you, or the company you work for, could be held responsible and personally liable for every penny lost or stolen.

If you're not frightened off by that rather stern introduction, then I must hasten to add that there has never been a better time for building e-commerce functionality into your applications. By *e-commerce* I'm using an all-embracing term, because e-commerce covers a multitude of features. In fact, it extends over the entire process of buying and selling an item on the web. If you consider what happens when you visit a site such as Amazon, with an intention to purchase something, there are several stages. First is the product catalog that displays the list of items from which you want to make a purchase. After you choose an item, it is moved into your shopping cart. You can continue shopping and add more items, and when you finish, you check out. After you check out, your order has to be processed. These kinds of questions have to be answered when order processing: Is your item in stock? How long will it take to order if it isn't? Where should it be delivered? Next comes the bit we all hate: getting the credit card out and supplying details, checking that the number is valid, and the dates. The whole transaction should be secure. Then you get a summary and maybe an e-mail containing the details of the sale. ASP.NET 2.0 introduces a terrific range of controls to help you build a workable e-commerce solution for any web site.

Of course it isn't possible to fully model every step of this process in just one chapter, and as with web services, entire books are devoted to this subject. Also, it isn't practical to set up a credit card–handling facility for the sake of testing one chapter. However, with the new components that ASP.NET 2.0 brings, you can create a product catalog, a shopping cart, and a checkout system; update the stock details and product catalog; get users to enter their details; and see how you would handle real credit card details. This should give you a strong overview of how you can add the capability to buy and sell items from your web site, and although it is something to be wary of and treated very seriously, it isn't something to be scared of adding, because ASP.NET 2.0 makes it simpler than ever before.

This chapter looks at the following:

- The typical process involved in an e-commerce transaction
- Creating a product catalog
- Creating a shopping cart and remembering which items you have in it
- Completing an e-commerce transaction and checkout
- What you need to do to process the order
- The considerations involved in credit card–handling
- Conducting secure transactions

The E-Commerce Pipeline

The once-common term *pipeline* is used to describe the whole e-commerce process, from browsing for particular products all the way through to having the product or products in your hand. Although the term has fallen out of the common vernacular slightly, it's one that we use here because it accurately reflects what is going on. Although different businesses may have different variations on the pipeline, it remains fundamentally similar for most web sites. A typical e-commerce pipeline might look like Figure 13-1.

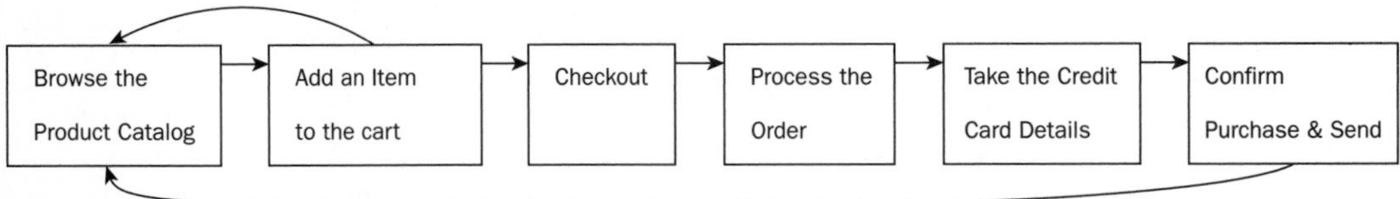

Figure 13-1

It's referred to as a pipeline because the next stage is dependent on the last and you have to pass the details through each stage. So like water flowing from a reservoir, through the pipes, to your faucet, here it's the same with the product. You select a product, you add that product to the shopping cart, you check out with that selected product, you get a total price for the product you want to purchase, you pay for the product, you get confirmation of that purchase, and then hopefully, the product is sent to you. At any stage of the pipeline, you must be able to halt the transaction, with the minimum of hassle. The only moment the transaction becomes irrevocable is when you hit Confirm Purchase. Even then, you should be able to return the product to the shop if you ordered the wrong one, or you just plain don't like it. However, although we're not going to go to quite to that extreme level of detail, you should get the idea.

The Wrox United web site already has a fully formed pipeline, and what you're going to do in this chapter is rebuild the pipeline from the ground up, step by step, right from the initial design, and learn about the decisions that need to be made as it is built. You should see that e-commerce isn't just about programming a solution, but it's about design, layout, and taking into account the customer's needs and requirements. This chapter spends a lot of time away from the programming "factory floor" talking about these needs, too.

The Product Catalog

This chapter starts at the beginning with the Product catalog. *Catalog* is the commonly accepted term for an online version of a store's brochure. It is the one rare occasion where jargon hasn't gotten involved to complicate matters, because the word describes perfectly what it does. Every e-commerce site depends upon its catalog—it's the place from which customers will pick and choose which items to buy, and place them in the shopping cart. Wrox United is no different in this respect.

The Structure of the Catalog

The first question should be, "What are we going to sell?" The Wrox United team, like most franchises, has its own range of branded items, and you want to make all of them available on the web site for the public to buy. The current Wrox United product range looks like this:

- Scarf (plain edition or striped edition)
- Car Sticker
- Lucky Mascot
- Large Flag (for the match)
- Fan Club Membership
- Replica Kit (Home and Away)
- Small Flag (for the car)
- Mouse Pad
- Hat
- Bug

Already you can see that there might be different categories of items that you might need to differentiate between in your catalog, such as a Home Replica Kit and an Away Replica Kit. However, the product range is small, boasting just 10 different items, so you can make the decision not to subdivide the catalog into different categories, because you should be able to display the details on just one page, and treat them all as individual items.

The Design of the Catalog

Having sorted out what you're going to sell, the next question is, "What should our customers want to see when they come to purchase an item?" Because there are only 10 items on display, you'll do your best to make sure that all of the items are displayed together on one page. That means cramming in a lot on just one page, so you can use a grid to lay them out and try to get away with not adding too much to the page.

For the Wrox United products, perhaps the absolute minimum you could offer is as follows:

- Product image
- Product title
- Price

Behind the scenes, you'll also need to make sure that you can uniquely identify each product you offer, so you'll need a product ID as well. When customers come to examine a product, they'll probably want to know a little more about it, such as a product description, but you can deal with this on a separate page dedicated to the item.

In addition to this, you could also consider a wider set of attributes that you might want listed for each product, such as how many products are currently in stock, how long they will take to deliver, the release date of the product, customer reviews and testimonials regarding how wonderful or appalling the product is, and even a cross-linking reference that mentions which other items customers purchased when they purchased this item.

For Wrox United, this is all complete overkill — there are only so many things you can say about a flag. However, you should be able to see that what you will require in the database will be specific to your particular business. For Wrox United, it's easy to settle on the aforementioned five fields (Image, Title, Price, Description, and for behind the scenes, the unique Product ID). Normally, the first stage would be to build or alter the database to add these categories, but all of them are already contained within the Products table of the database, so you don't need to add anything else to it. You've got a structure of the catalog and you've got a design, and a database that supports it, so you can proceed straight to the next stage and implement it.

Implementation of the Catalog

The product catalog actually breaks down into two pages: one is like an index of all the products in your catalog and the second is the page that shows particular details about the item. In this Try It Out, you start by building the product catalog.

Try It Out — Building an Index Page for the Catalog

1. Open Visual Web Developer and open the `C:\BegASPNET2\Chapters\Begin\Chapter13` web site. Open the blank `wroxshop.aspx` page.
2. First you'll add some controls. Drag a `SqlDataSource` control from the Data menu of the Toolbox into the Design View of the page, and click the smart tasks panel that appears (see Figure 13-2).
3. Click Configure Data Source from the Tasks panel, and select `WroxUnitedConnectionString` (which is already automatically configured, as indeed connection strings are for all databases within the `App_Data` folder), as shown in Figure 13-3.
4. Click Next and then from the Configure the Select Statement dialog box that appears, select the Products table and all of the fields contained within it, as shown in Figure 13-4.
5. Click Next. Test the query to make sure it retrieves the data and then click Finish, which takes you back to Design View.
6. Now you need to add a second control to your page. From the Data menu of the Toolbox, select the `DataList` control. Click the smart tag dialog box that appears. From the Choose Data Source drop-down list, select `SqlDataSource1`, as shown in Figure 13-5.

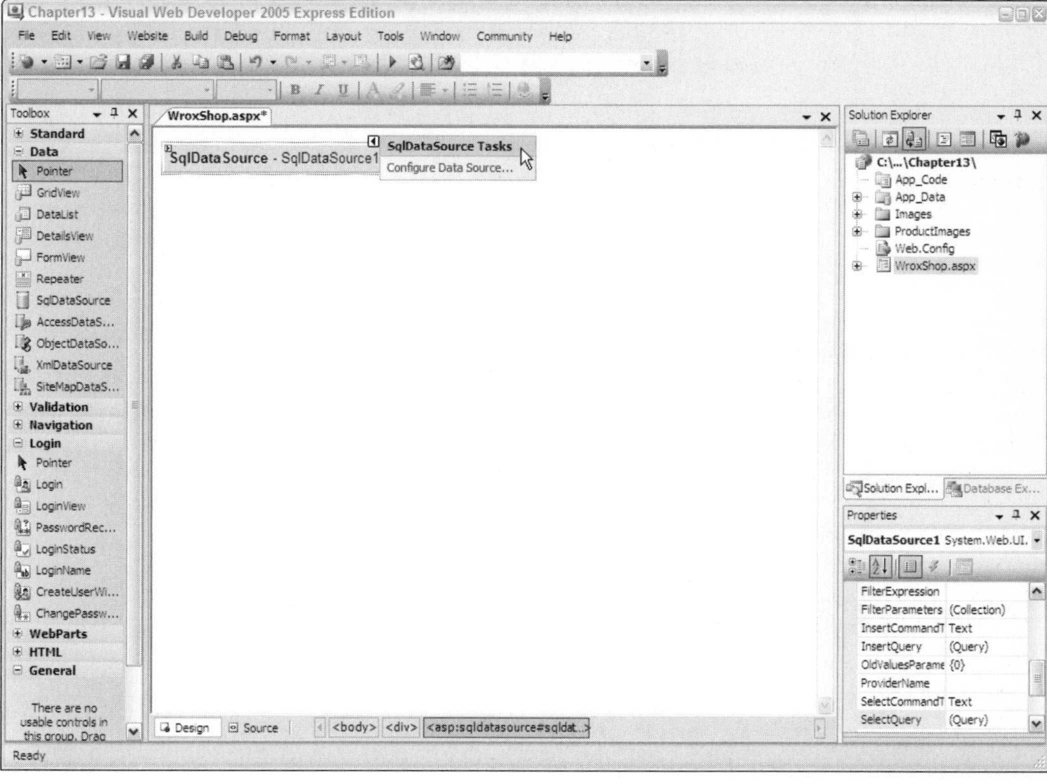

Figure 13-2

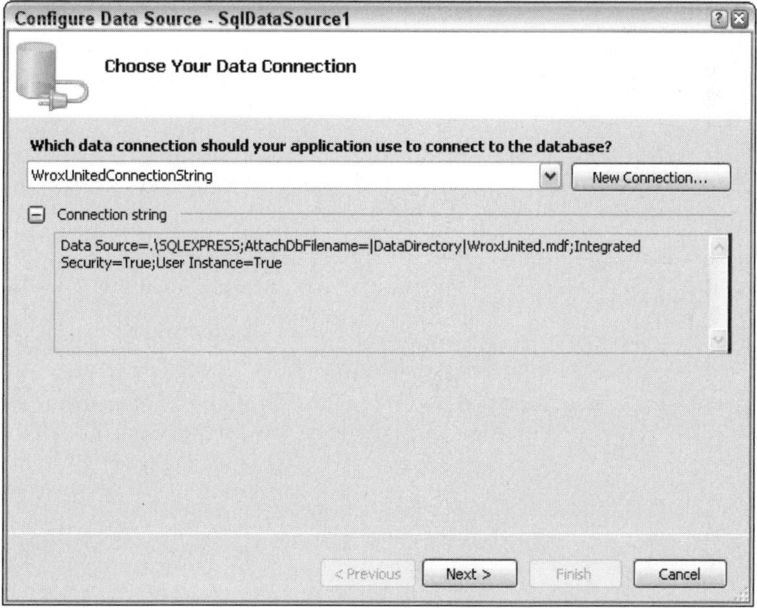

Figure 13-3

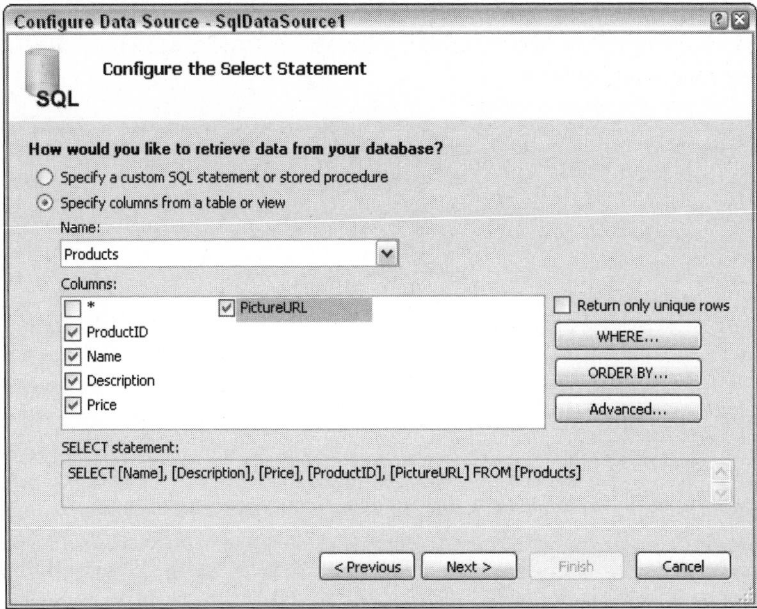

Figure 13-4

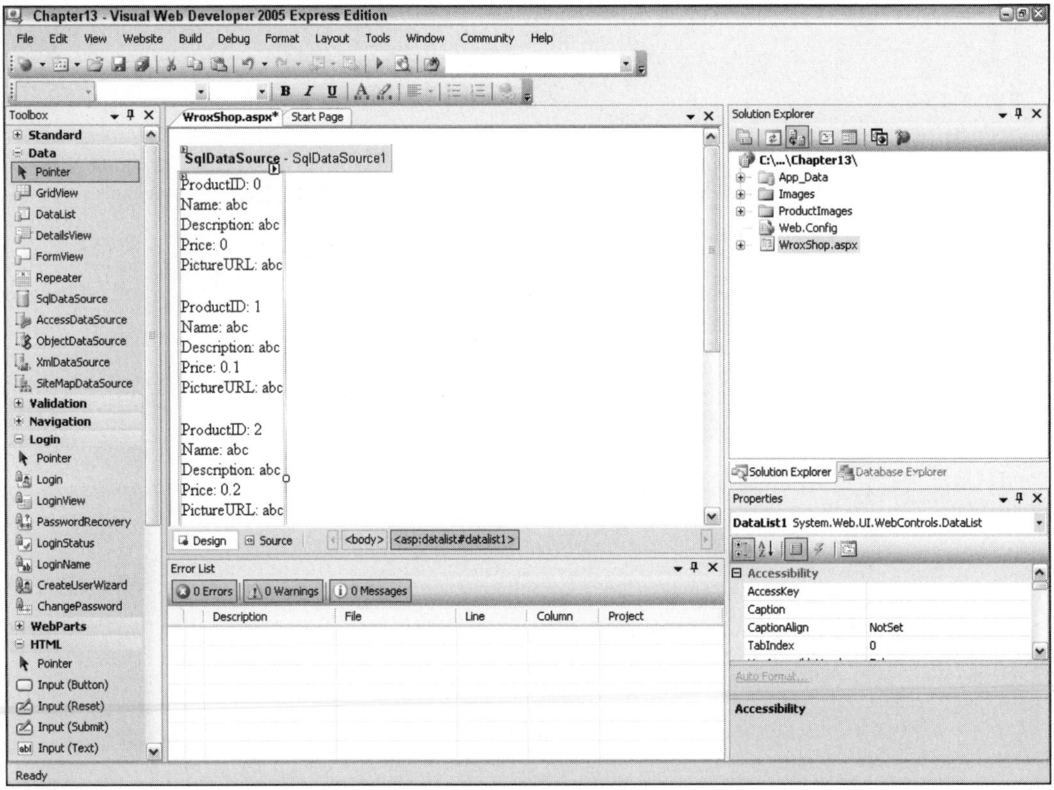

Figure 13-5

7. Click the smart tag dialog box above the `DataList` control and select Edit Templates. (Chapter 7 looked at the process of editing an ItemTemplate if you need a quick reminder.) Figure 13-6 shows your default layout.

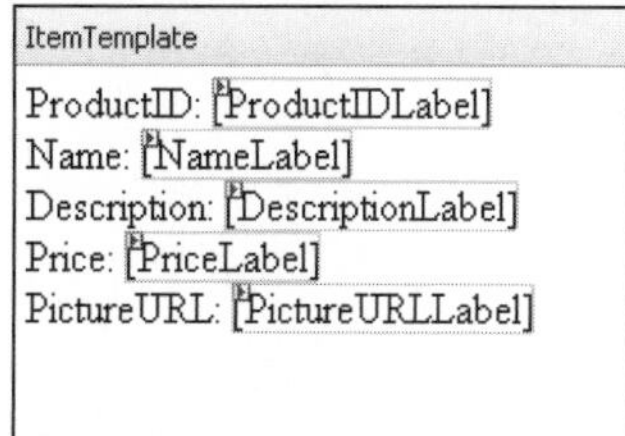

Figure 13-6

8. This ensuing layout needs a bit of refining to be suitable for displaying a catalog. First delete all of the explanatory text, such as Name and Description, using the Backspace key. Also, you don't need to display all of the items from the Products table — in fact, you only need a picture of the item, its price, and its name on the catalog page, as agreed on in the design. Delete the Product ID and Description and move the Picture URL to the top. You can drag and drop the `Label` controls to order them correctly, as shown in Figure 13-7.

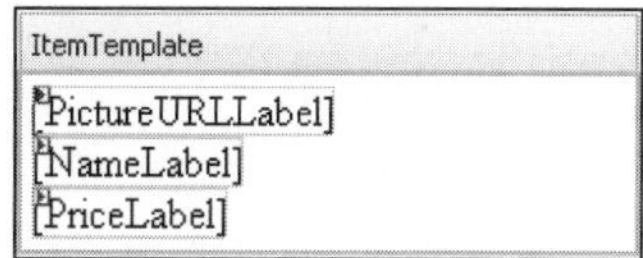

Figure 13-7

9. Delete the `PictureURL` label, because you want to display an image here rather than a label. Select `ImageButton` from the menu and drag it across to where the `PictureURLLabel` was. A red cross and the smart tag dialog box with the legend Edit Data Bindings should appear (see Figure 13-8). (You saw in Chapter 7 how to do this, but it delved directly into the code, whereas here you're using the wizard.)

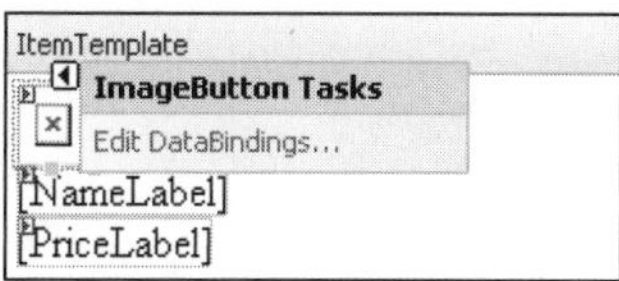

Figure 13-8

10. Select Edit Data bindings and then select the Custom binding radio button. Amend the Code expression box so that it reads as follows:

```
Eval ("PictureURL","ProductImages\\thumb_{0}")
```

Figure 13-9 shows how everything should look.

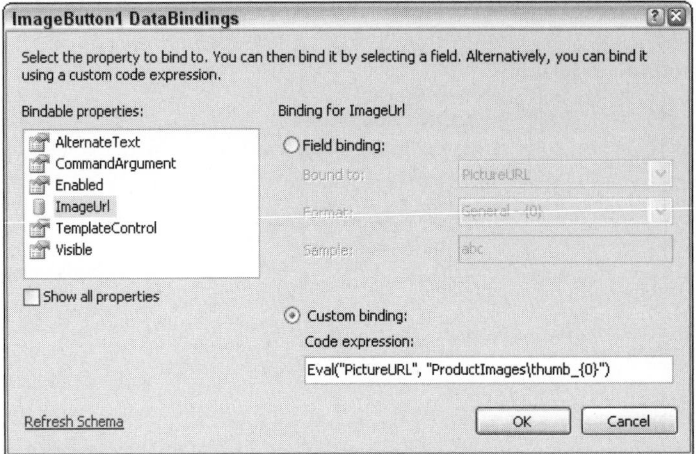

Figure 13-9

11. Click OK. Select the smart tag dialog box that appears next to `PriceLabel` and select Edit DataBindings (see Figure 13-10). This time select the `Text` property under Bindable properties, and select the Currency option from the Format drop-down list.

Figure 13-10

12. Click OK. You have a couple of final tasks to perform. Go to the smart tag dialog and select End Template Editing. Click the smart tag dialog box by the `DataList` control and select Property builder. Set the Columns to **4** and change the Direction from Vertical to Horizontal, as shown in Figure 13-11. Then click OK.

13. You've now finished the layout of the catalog. Run the project and view the catalog. It should look like Figure 13-12.

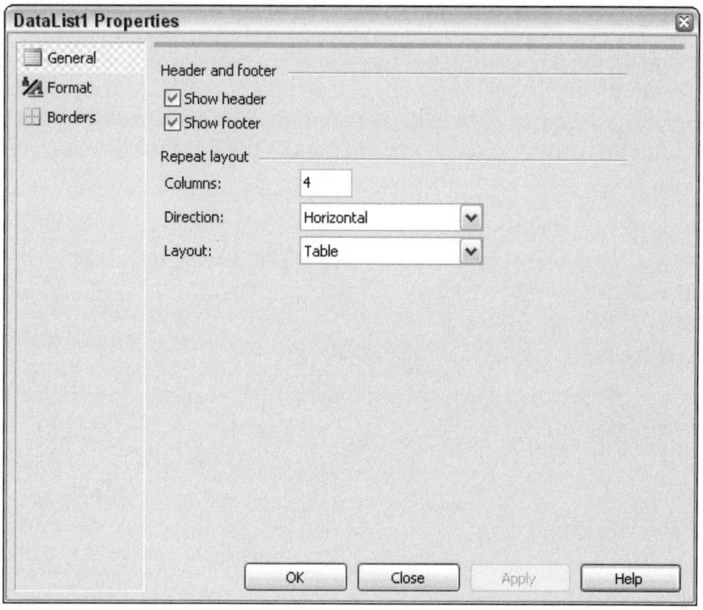

DataList1 Properties

General
Format
Borders

Header and footer
Show header
Show footer

Repeat layout
Columns: 4
Direction: Horizontal
Layout: Table

OK Close Apply Help

Figure 13-11

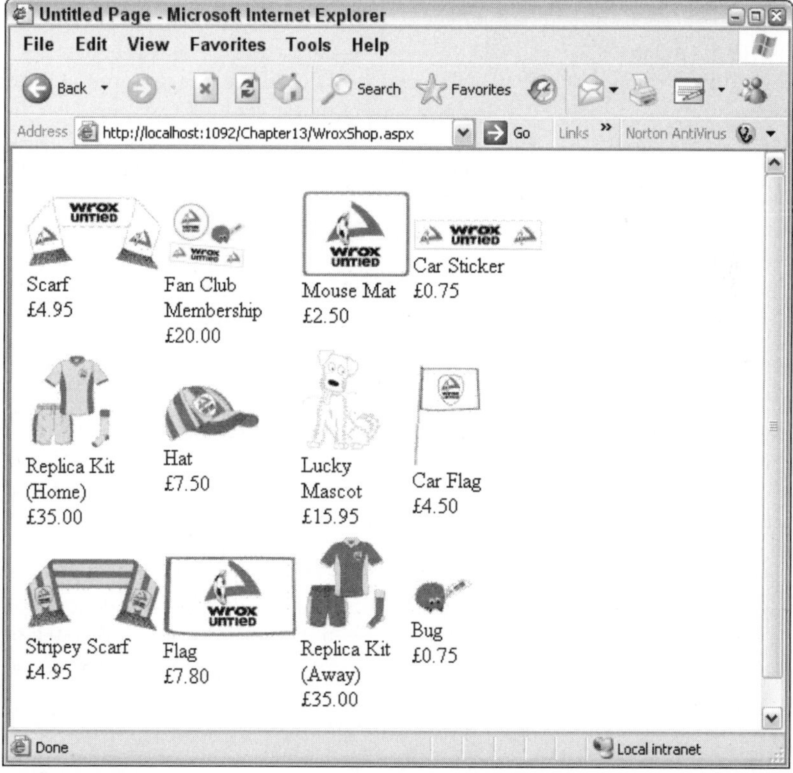

Figure 13-12

How It Works

You created a catalog that pretty much resembles the one on the Wrox United web site. You created your images as image buttons, which will eventually act as links to the individual product item page. If you click an image, it doesn't take you anywhere (yet), but in all other respects it is the same as the example site. In this Try It Out, two controls do the work. If you go back to Visual Web Developer and view the source for this page, you will see the following code:

```
<asp:SqlDataSource ID="SqlDataSource1" runat="server" ConnectionString="<%$
ConnectionStrings:WroxUnited %>" SelectCommand="SELECT [Name], [Description],
[Price], [ProductID], [PictureURL] FROM [Products]">
</asp:SqlDataSource>

<asp:DataList ID="DataList1" runat="server" DataKeyField="ProductID"
 DataSourceID="SqlDataSource1" RepeatColumns="4" RepeatDirection="Horizontal">
     <ItemTemplate>
          <asp:ImageButton ID="ImageButton1" runat="server" ImageUrl='<%#
           Eval("PictureURL", "ProductImages\\thumb_{0}") %>' /><br />
          <asp:Label ID="NameLabel" runat="server" Text='<%# Eval("Name")%>'>
          </asp:Label><br />
          <asp:Label ID="PriceLabel" runat="server" Text='<%# Eval("Price",
           "{0:C}") %>'></asp:Label>
     </ItemTemplate>
</asp:DataList>
```

The first control, `SqlDataSource1`, is the one that sources your catalog. The details of what is for sale in the Wrox United web site are stored in the Products table. It contains the connection string that enables you to connect to the database, as well as a `SelectCommand` attribute that specifies the SQL that will pluck the Name, Description, Price, ProductID, and the URL of the image from the Products table. The `SqlDataSource` on its own doesn't display anything, though. It needs the `DataList` to do this for it.

The `DataList` contains three controls as well as the formatting needed to display your catalog correctly. You started by replacing the `Label` control contained for `PictureURL` with an Image button. You did this because, if you hadn't, a label would just have displayed the text URL of the image, such as `ProductImages\Item1.gif`. Secondly, you chose an `ImageButton` in place of an image because you needed a link to the product item page. Rather than having to move or re-create this folder of product images, we placed it in the web site folder already, and all you had to do is reference it as follows:

```
Eval("PictureURL", "ProductImages\\thumb_{0}")
```

The data-binding expression has two parameters: the first is the name of the field from the Products table you want to bind to your image button and the second is the contents of the field itself (indicated by `{0}`). You altered the second parameter so that it pointed to the ProductImages folder. Then you placed `"thumb_"`, which indicates that you don't want to use a full-sized image, but instead, you want to usea thumbnail of the image for the catalog.

You used labels for the other two items in the catalog, because you only needed to display text, but for your price, you changed the format so that it displayed it in currency format as $0.00, rather than just 0.0000. Last, you altered the layout so that it displayed the items in a horizontal grid format, four across in each row.

The Product Item Page

In our design discussion, we talked about all the possible features you might want to add to a specific product page, but settled on only really needing an enhanced description of the product. Of course your item page shouldn't contain any less information about the product than the catalog, so you will need to display the name, image, and price in addition to the description. You add that to your web site in the following Try It Out.

Try It Out — Building a Product Page for the Catalog

1. Go to Solution Explorer, right-click the top item in it, and select Add New Item. Add a new Web Form and call it **WroxShopItem.aspx**.
2. Once again you need the `SqlDataSource` and `DataList` controls. In Design View, drag a `SqlDataSource` control from the Data section of the Toolbox.
3. Click the Configure Data Source flyout of the `SqlDataSource` control and select the `WroxUnitedUnitedConnectionString` from the drop-down list in the Choose your Data Connection dialog box that appears.
4. Click Next and, as with the previous Try It Out, select the Products table and select each of the items within it, as shown in Figure 13-13.

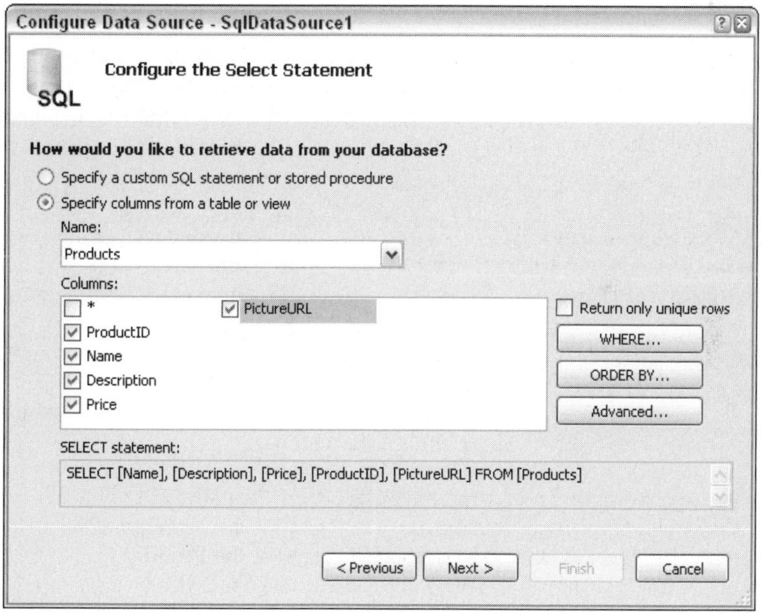

Configure Data Source - SqlDataSource1

Configure the Select Statement

How would you like to retrieve data from your database?

- Specify a custom SQL statement or stored procedure
- Specify columns from a table or view

Name: Products

Columns: * | ProductID | Name | Description | Price | PictureURL

Return only unique rows | WHERE... | ORDER BY... | Advanced...

SELECT statement:

SELECT [Name], [Description], [Price], [ProductID], [PictureURL] FROM [Products]

< Previous | Next > | Finish | Cancel

Figure 13-13

5. Click WHERE. You will be presented with the screen depicted in Figure 13-14. Select ProductID from the Column drop-down list; select QueryString from the Source drop-down list; and type in **ProductID** to the QueryString field, leaving the Default value blank. This step allows you to hone in on your single selected product. You use the filter clause to match the product ID of the selected product and therefore only show details about that particular product. Click Add.

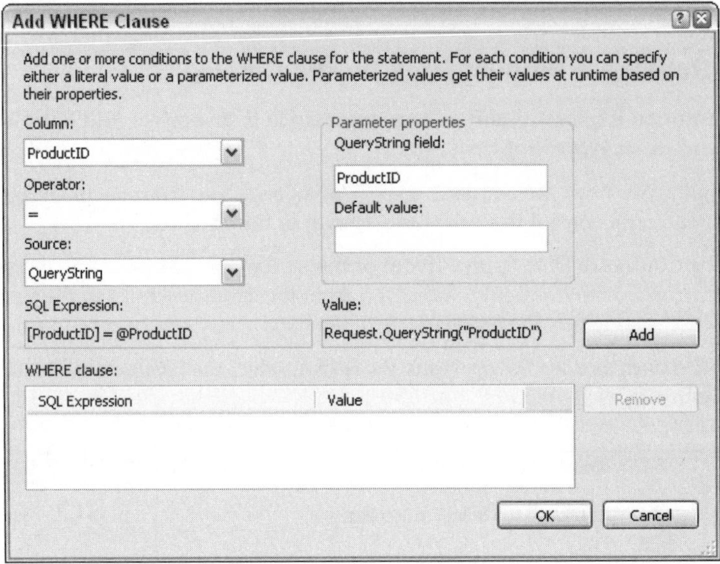

Figure 13-14

6. Click OK, and then click Next and Finish to return to Design View.

7. Add a `DataList` control, click Configure DataSource, and select `SqlDataSource1` from the Choose Data Source drop-down list.

8. Click Edit Templates from the list, and delete all the text alongside the labels. Move the `PictureURL` label to the top. This time, only remove the product ID label, so that it now looks like Figure 13-15.

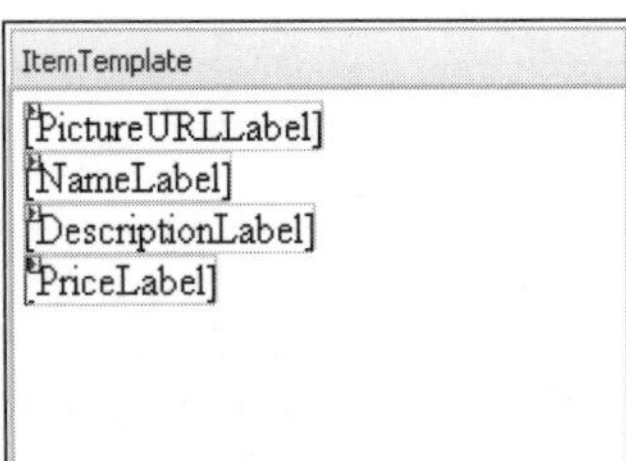

Figure 13-15

9. Right-click `PictureURLLabel` and select Properties. In the Properties window, change the Visible property to false. You're going to need the URL, but you don't want it displayed on the

screen. `PictureURLLabel` is used to provide the URL of where to find the image of your product; however, you don't want the actual URL text displayed, but rather the image itself.

10. In Design View, add an `Image` control from the Standard section of the Toolbox to the top of the controls.
11. Click the smart tag dialog box next to the `Image` control and select Edit Data Bindings.
12. In the dialog box that appears, click Custom Bindings and amend the text so that it reads as follows (which is slightly differently from the last Try It Out, because you want a full-sized version of the image, not a thumbnail):

```
Eval("PictureURL", "ProductImages\\{0}")
```

13. Click OK, and then go to Price Label and select the Edit Data Bindings option from the menu that appears when you click the black arrow. Enter the following code in the Custom Bindings drop-down list box:

```
Eval("Price", "{0:##0.00}")
```

> **This is slightly different from before, because you want to use the currency format. However, currency format adds a $ symbol, and you want to use this value in your code later, so you don't want to include the $ symbol in the label.**

14. Click OK. In Design View, select Hyperlink from the Standard section of the Toolbox menu and place it below the `DataList` control, as shown in Figure 13-16.

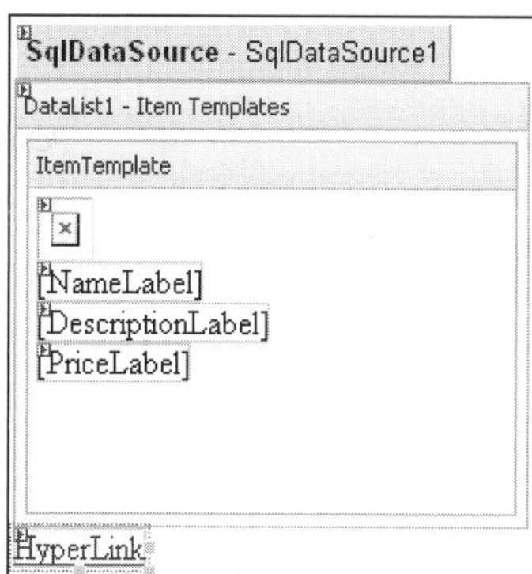

Figure 13-16

15. Right-click `HyperLink` and select the Properties option. Change the `Text` property so it reads **Return to Shop**, and change the `NavigateURL` property so that it reads **~/WroxShop.aspx**, as shown in Figure 13-17. Alternatively, you can click the ellipsis button in the NavigateURL property box and choose `wroxshop` from there.
16. Close the Properties window, and go to Design View in the first page you created (`WroxShop.aspx`).

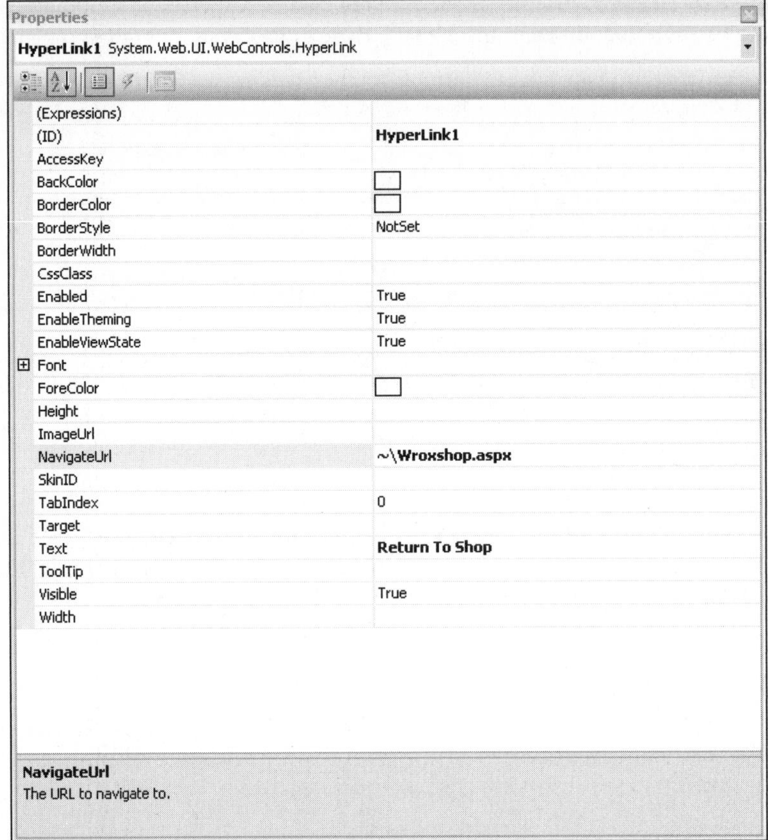

Figure 13-17

17. Select the `DataList` control underneath `SqlDataSource1`. From the smart tag dialog box, select Edit Templates⇨Item Template.

18. Go to the Image Button (the graphic with the red cross), click the smart tag dialog box, and select Edit Data Bindings.

19. Click Show All Properties and select PostbackURL. Check the Custom bindings and change it so that it reads as follows:

```
Eval("ProductID","WroxShopItem.aspx?ProductID={0}")
```

20. Click End Template Editing for both pages, run the application from `WroxShop.aspx`, and click the Scarf image. You should see what appears in Figure 13-18.

21. To get details about another product, click Return to Shop and go back and select the corresponding product image.

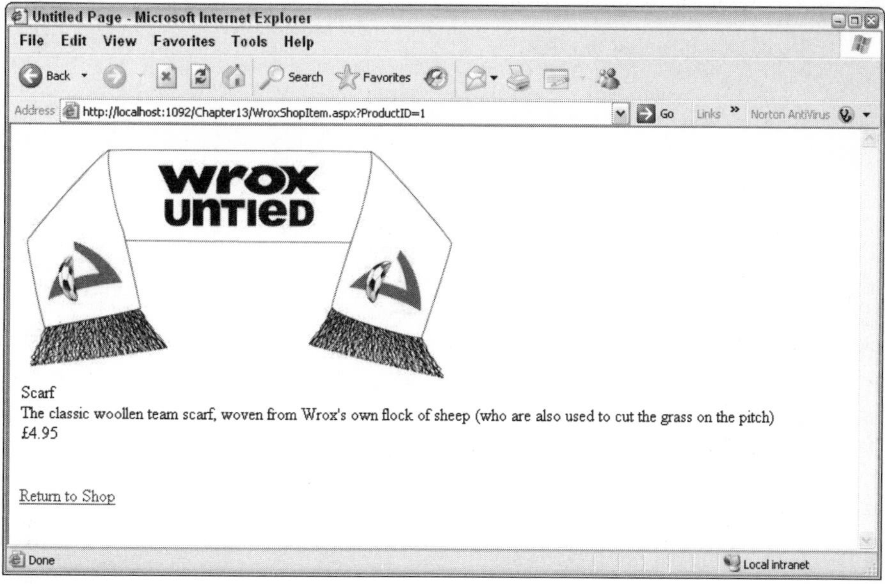

Figure 13-18

How It Works

The Product Item page is put together in much the same way as the Product Catalog, the main difference being that instead of all of the items being viewed, you only want to look at the details of a single item. If you view the source, you will see that it comprises the `SqlDataSource` and `DataList` controls:

```
<form id="form1" runat="server">
        <asp:SqlDataSource ID="SqlDataSource1" runat="server" ConnectionString="<%$
ConnectionStrings:WroxUnited %>"
         SelectCommand="SELECT DISTINCT [ProductID], [Name], [Description],
         [Price], [PictureURL] FROM [Products] WHERE ([ProductID] = @ProductID)">
            <SelectParameters>
                <asp:QueryStringParameter Name="ProductID"
                 QueryStringField="ProductID" Type="Int32" />
            </SelectParameters>
        </asp:SqlDataSource>
        <asp:DataList ID="DataList1" runat="server" DataKeyField="ProductID"
         DataSourceID="SqlDataSource1">
            <ItemTemplate>
                <asp:Label visible="false" ID="PictureURL"
Text='<%#Eval("PictureURL")%>' />
                <asp:Image ID="Image1" runat="server" ImageUrl='<%#
                 Eval("PictureURL", "ProductImages\\{0}") %>' /><br />
                <asp:Label ID="NameLabel" runat="server" Text='<%# Eval("Name")
                 %>'></asp:Label><br />
                <asp:Label ID="DescriptionLabel" runat="server" Text='<%#
```

```
                    Eval("Description") %>'>
                    </asp:Label><br />
                    <asp:Label ID="PriceLabel" runat="server" Text='<%# Eval("Price",
                    "{0:##0.00}") %>'></asp:Label><br />
                    <br />
                    <br />
                </ItemTemplate>
            </asp:DataList>
            <asp:HyperLink ID="HyperLink1" runat="server"
             NavigateUrl="~/WroxShop.aspx">Return to Shop</asp:HyperLink>
    </form>
```

The difference is that this time the `SqlDataSource`'s `SelectCommand` attribute has an extra `WHERE` clause:

```
SelectCommand="SELECT DISTINCT [ProductID], [Name], [Description],
[Price], [PictureURL] FROM [Products] WHERE ([ProductID] = @ProductID)"
```

This references a `ProductID` parameter. Underneath this element, the `SqlDataSource1` also contains a `SelectParameters` element, which specifies where you are going to get the parameter from:

```
<SelectParameters>
    <asp:QueryStringParameter Name="ProductID"
     QueryStringField="ProductID" Type="Int32" />
</SelectParameters>
```

These parameters are used to transfer the details about the item you have clicked. This is where the hidden ProductID comes into play. You haven't used it so far, but now you most definitely need it. Each item in your catalog has a unique identifier, this being ProductID. You collect ProductID when the image is collected and send it as a `QueryString` as follows:

```
http://localhost/Chapter13/WroxShopItem.aspx?ProductID=1
```

Then your second page (`WroxShopItem.aspx`) is able to pick that up and use it in the `WHERE` clause of the `SELECT` command of the `SqlDataSource` control to return the details of that single item. The `DataList` control of `WroxShopItem` is similar to the `WroxShop DataList` control. The are only two changes, the first being that instead of referencing the thumbnail version of the image, you just use the whole version of the image. Space is no longer such an essential here, because you don't have to worry about nine other items. The second change is that you have added the Description from the Products table as an extra label. You've also used the `PictureURL` from `PictureURLLabel` as a URL for your `<asp:Image>` control that you use to display the merchandise. Apart from that, it is business as usual.

You're actually quite a distance into this chapter and so far you haven't created anything totally specific to e-commerce. The problem is that without a catalog and a set of items, you have nothing to put into your cart. The order in which you create things is essential. Now that you have a catalog and the ability to browse specific items in the catalog, it's at last time to wheel out your shopping cart.

The Shopping Cart

The shopping cart is a simple enough control in principle, but until ASP.NET 2.0, it has been an awkward feature to create. The reason is this — how do you go about remembering which items are stored in the cart? The quick answer is state. State management, though, has never been quite as straightforward as it perhaps should be. Chapter 14 looks at sessions and state in detail, but we need to talk about it briefly here.

It's not a new feature and to be fair, it's been going on behind the scenes throughout this book, because every page contains a `ViewState` control that holds an encrypted version of each page's control contents. However, this is squared against the fact that the Internet is stateless, and every time you move from page to page, the web server acts like a goldfish — asking the same question, "Who are you?" So you must do the remembering for the web server.

Previously, in ASP.NET 1.1, you could go about remembering the items in the cart in one of two common ways. Either you could create a cart and stick the whole contents of the cart in a `Session` object, and lose the list of items every time someone logged out and back in again, or alternatively you could create a shopping cart item in the database, and then be tied to updating the database each time you added something to the cart. The advantage of the second approach is of course that if you lost your Internet connection suddenly when you came to log back in, you would still have the contents of the cart. This is particularly useful if you've just spent an hour assembling the weekly shop, only to have to endure your ISP's 0.01% downtime at that crucial point. Of course, the first approach could make use of cookies so that it could link back to your shopping cart if you logged on again, but then this would rely on a whole membership system, so you can see how suddenly your nice small shopping cart becomes a rather larger and more complex shopping cart and membership system.

ASP.NET 2.0 is able to take some of the advantages from both approaches (remembering the between connections) while leaving at home some of the awkwardness (constant database access, needing to log on as a member before you can use the shopping cart). It does this by making use of the new profiles features that you looked at in Chapter 11. You'll see how you can use this as you build your shopping cart control. First, though, you need to build the object that is going to form the foundations of your shopping cart's memory.

The Shopping Object

You're going to create an object that can store your items. You start again at the drawing board by creating a design. The first thing to mention is that your shopping object has to look after two things: the items in the cart and the cart itself. Therefore, you're going to need two objects:

- `CartItem`
- `ShoppingCart`

Both merit some more in-depth discussion as to what is required.

The CartItem Object

The `CartItem` object is easiest. Design is often just a case of sitting down with pen and paper and trying to imagine what you as a user would require from a site. A second option is to look at what everyone else is doing. However, it's probably best to stick to this order when brainstorming, because what you might require from a site might be unduly influenced by you looking at other vendors' sites. So you're going to have a quick think now. It doesn't matter if you don't get it absolutely right the first time, because you can amend it as you go along.

With your shopping cart, a good first stab would be the following list of attributes:

- A representation of the item
- The quantity of the item
- The price of the item
- The total price

For the representation of the item, you could quite easily use the title or the description of the item, but given that you have some thumbnail pictures at hand, it would be nice to use them as well. In your cart you will start with the name and a link to the image of the item purchased. The quantity and the price are both self-explanatory enough. However, the total price needs a little expanding. You could have a total price as shown in the following table.

Item	Quantity	Price
Scarf	2	$4.95
Bug	2	$0.75
Total Price		$11.40

It looks a little strange. That's because you're immediately totalling the $4.95 and the 75 cents, and they don't add up to make $11.40. So as well as the total price, it might be better to do it spreadsheet style and total the price and the quantity first and create a total for each line, as shown in the following table.

Item	Quantity	Price	Item Total
Scarf	2	$4.95	$9.90
Bug	2	$0.75	$1.50
Total Price			$11.40

Now add line total to the list of attributes you want to store. That's as much as you need for each `CartItem`, so let's move onto the `ShoppingCart`.

The ShoppingCart Object

The `CartItem` object was the easiest, because it's fairly static in its conception. Either you have a `CartItem` object or you don't, unless you prescribe to some sort of parallel universe theory where you can have both at the same time. However, computing is quite complicated enough already without parallel universes to think about, too. The reason the `ShoppingCart` object is more complex is because it will comprise one or several items in the cart. So you immediately need somewhere to store a stack of cart items in your object. Rather than a warehouse or a shopping trolley, you can use the collections talked about in Chapter 9 to do this.

This also raises other questions, namely how do you differentiate between different items in the cart, and how do you maintain some sort of order with them? The answer is to add an index, so that, for example, if you add a scarf and that is item 1 in the cart, and then you add a bug, that becomes item 2 in the cart.

Your cart will also need to deal with the set of possible actions that you can perform on the contents of the cart. Briefly the most common actions you might perform on a shopping cart are as follows:

- Adding an item to the cart
- Updating the information about an item in the cart
- Updating the total price of all of the items in the cart
- Deleting an item from the cart

You will need to handle these four actions. Last, because you are keeping a record of all of the items within the cart, it might be easier to move the total purchase price across to this object instead. This is just the kind of amendment we talked about earlier when creating a design. Better to discover it now, than when you've actually created it. So the things you are going to have built into your `ShoppingCart` object are the cart item collection; an index; the add, update, and delete actions; and a final total.

Now that you've got an outline of what you need to store, in this Try It Out you build the object to store it.

Try It Out Building the ShoppingCart Object

1. Go to Solution Explorer, right-click the top item, and select Add New Item. Choose Class and call it **Shopping.cs**.
2. Click Add. Visual Web Developer might inform you that you are attempting to add a class to an ASP.NET application and that it should be moved to the `App_Code` folder to be generally consumable. If so, then click Yes to accept this proposition.
3. Add the following code to create a shopping cart item object, called `CartItem`:

```
using System.Data;
using System.Web;
using System.Data.SqlClient;
using System.Collections.Generic;


namespace Wrox.Commerce
{
  [Serializable]
  public class CartItem
  {
    private int _productID;
    private string _productName;
    private string _productImageUrl;
    private int _quantity;
    private double _price;
    private double _lineTotal;

    public void New()
```

```
    {
    }

    public void New(int ProductID , string ProductName ,
      string ProductImageUrl , int Quantity ,
      double Price )
       {
      _productID = ProductID;
      _productName = ProductName;
      _productImageUrl = ProductImageUrl;
      _quantity = Quantity;
      _price = Price;
      _lineTotal = Quantity * Price;

    }

    public int ProductID
    {
      get
      {
        return _productID;
      }
      set
      {
        _productID = value;
      }
    }

    public string ProductName
    {
      get
      {
        return _productName;
      }
      set      {
        _productName = value;
      }
    }

    public string ProductImageUrl
     {
      get
      {
        return _productImageUrl;
      }
      set
      {
        _productImageUrl = value;
      }
    }

    public int Quantity
     {
      get
       {
```

```
            return _quantity;
          }
          set
          {
            _quantity = value;
          }
        }

        public double Price
        {
          get
          {
            return _price;
          }
          set
          {
            _price = value
          }
        }

        public double LineTotal
        {
          get
          {
            return _quantity * _price;
          }
        }

      }
    }
```

4. Underneath the `CartItem` class, add the following code to create the `ShoppingCart` object:

```
    [Serializable]
    public class ShoppingCart
    {
      private DateTime  _dateCreated;
      private DateTime  _lastUpdate;
      private List<CartItem> _items;

      public ShoppingCart()
      {
          if (this._items == null)
          {
              this._items = new List<CartItem>();
              this._dateCreated = DateTime.Now;
          }
      }

      public List<CartItem> Items
  {
        get
        {
          return _items;
```

```
        }
        set
        {
          _items = value;
        }
      }

      public void Insert (int ProductID , double Price,
                          int Quantity, string ProductName ,
                          string ProductImageUrl )
  {
        int ItemIndex  = ItemIndexOfID(ProductID);
        if (ItemIndex == -1)
         {
          CartItem
  NewItem = new CartItem();
          NewItem.ProductID = ProductID;
          NewItem.Quantity = Quantity;
          NewItem.Price = Price;
          NewItem.ProductName = ProductName;
          NewItem.ProductImageUrl = ProductImageUrl;
          _items.Add(NewItem);
        }
        else
        {
          _items[ItemIndex].Quantity += 1;

        }
        _lastUpdate = DateTime.Now;
      }

      public void Update(int RowID, int ProductID,                          int Quantity
  , double Price )
      {
        CartItem Item = _items[RowID];
        Item.ProductID = ProductID;
        Item.Quantity = Quantity;
        Item.Price = Price;
        _lastUpdate = DateTime.Now;
      }

      public void DeleteItem(int rowID )
      {
        _items.RemoveAt(rowID);
        _lastUpdate = DateTime.Now;
      }

      private int ItemIndexOfID(int ProductID  )
      {
        int index=0;
        foreach (CartItem item in _items)
          {
          if (item.ProductID == ProductID)
           {
            return index;
```

```
            }
            index += 1;
          }
          return -1;
        }

          public double Total
          {
          get
           {
            double t=0;

            if (_items == null)
            {
               return 0;
            }

            foreach (CartItem Item in _items)
            {
              t += Item.LineTotal;
            }

            return t;
          }
        }
        }
    }
```

5. Save this page. Unfortunately you can't do anything with the class until you come to instantiate an instance of the object, so there's nothing to see just yet.

How It Works

The `ShoppingCart` class provides you with an object that you can just insert into your code. You start by defining both objects as being in the `Wrox.Commerce` namespace. This means that you can insert them into any page by using the following reference at the top of a page:

```
<%@ Import Namespace = "Wrox.Commerce" %>
```

This reference enables you to make use of all of the properties and methods within the `ShoppingCart` object. There is a lot of code here within the object, so let's briefly skip through what is happening with each object inside the `ShoppingCart` object.

The `CartItem` is just a series of properties to store each of the cart attributes in. You define a set of private variables that represent each of the items in your `CartItem` object. In addition to the five previously mentioned, the `productID` is there so you can uniquely identify the type of item:

```
private int _productID;
private string _productName;
private string _productImageUrl;
private int _quantity;
private double _price;
private double _lineTotal;
```

The productID attribute is an integer, because it stores your unique identifier. The productName attribute is text, so you store that as a string. Next comes the productImageUrl attribute. Rather than store a physical image, you store a URL of the location where you can find that image (thus saving you from having to physically store the images in the database), which is also stored as text. The quantity attribute is stored as an int, because it is impossible to have a fraction of an item (Wrox United doesn't sell half a scarf, or a bug with two legs). The price attribute, however, is a representation of currency, so that requires a double data type because you will be dealing with fractions. The lineTotal attribute is made from quantity multiplied by price, so that must also be a double data type.

Each of these attributes must be both readable and writable, so you create a set of properties for each in this format, using the ProductID() property as an example:

```
public int ProductID
{
  get
  {
    return _productID;
  }
  set
  {
    _productID = value;
  }
}
```

Each of the properties takes this format with both Get and Set constructors, referencing the variables you defined at the top of the ShoppingCart definition. The only one that is any different is the LineTotal() property, which is a multiplication of the quantity and price properties. You don't want anyone to be able to alter this because you change it yourself, so it only has a get constructor:

```
public double LineTotal
{
  get
  {
    return _quantity * _price;
  }
}
```

That sums up the entire CartItem object. The ShoppingCart object is a little trickier. Because you are constantly updating your shopping cart, you need to keep a track of when it was created and when it was last updated. You start by defining a couple of variables that do this for you:

```
private DateTime  _dateCreated;
private DateTime  _lastUpdate;
```

These two variables store the time at which the ShoppingCart object was created and the time at which it was last updated. Next you create the collection. The collection is a List object and it contains a list of CartItem objects. The ShoppingCart constructor that you can call in your code is used to create a new instance of a shopping cart:

```
public ShoppingCart()
  {
      if (this._items == null)
```

```
            {
                this._items = new List<CartItem>();
                this._dateCreated = DateTime.Now;
            }
        }
```

You create a property called `Items` in which to store your `List` of `CartItems`:

```
     public List<CartItem> Items
    {
          get
          {
            return _items;
          }
          set
          {
            _items = value;
          }
        }
```

Then you come to your four actions, which you code as three methods (the two update actions are handled in one `Update` action). The first method insert requires all the information that your cart requires, namely `ProductID`, `Quantity`, `Price`, `ProductName`, and the `ProductImageUrl`:

```
    public void Insert (int ProductID , double Price,
                          int Quantity, string ProductName ,
                          string ProductImageUrl )
    {
          int ItemIndex  = ItemIndexOfID(ProductID);
          if (ItemIndex == -1)
           {
            CartItem
    NewItem = new CartItem();
            NewItem.ProductID = ProductID;
            NewItem.Quantity = Quantity;
            NewItem.Price = Price;
            NewItem.ProductName = ProductName;
            NewItem.ProductImageUrl = ProductImageUrl;
            _items.Add(NewItem);
          }
          else
          {
            _items[ItemIndex].Quantity += 1;
          }
          _lastUpdate = DateTime.Now;
        }
```

When you add a new item into the cart (the `Insert` method), you need to create an index to track this. If the index is –1, you know that item is not already present in the cart, and you need to create a new cart item with the accompanying `ProductID`, `Quantity`, `Price`, `ProductName`, and `ProductImageUrl` details. If it is present, you just need to add one to the quantity. Because you have just made the last update to the cart, you also need to record this in the `lastUpdate` variable and use the `DateTime.Now` function to record the current date and time.

The `Update` action is in fact just a recalculation of `Price`; as mentioned earlier. `Quantity` is the only item you can actually change when you update the cart details. (If you think about it, this makes sense, because you can't have the customers updating the price, product name, or description.) The quantity affects the price.

```
public void Update(int RowID, int ProductID,                    int Quantity ,
double Price )
    {
      CartItem Item = _items[RowID];
      Item.ProductID = ProductID;
      Item.Quantity = Quantity;
      Item.Price = Price;
      _lastUpdate = DateTime.Now;
    }
```

You identify the item again using the index. You read the `ProductID`, the `Quantity`, and the `Price` from the `CartItem` collection, and set it to the new `Quantity` for your chosen product. You update the time the cart was updated as well.

You've looked at the `Update` and `Insert` methods, so that just leaves the question of how customers can remove items from the cart. This is done via the `Delete` method. The `Delete` method is the simplest of the three — all you need to do is use the index to identify which item has been selected for deletion and remove it with the `RemoveAt` method. You also set the `_lastUpdate` variable to contain the current time, because you have just updated the cart by deleting an item from it:

```
public void DeleteItem(int rowID )
    {
      _items.RemoveAt(rowID);
      _lastUpdate = DateTime.Now;
    }
```

Under the `Insert`, `Update`, and `DeleteItem` methods is the `index` property. The `index` property is as follows:

```
private int ItemIndexOfID(int ProductID  )
    {
      int index=0;
      foreach (CartItem item in _items)
        {
        if (item.ProductID == ProductID)
         {
          return index;
        }
        index += 1;
      }
      return -1;
    }
```

The index, which is used to identify each item in the cart, stores each product's `Product` ID. If the first item in the cart was a scarf, then the first item in the index will contain the scarf's `ProductID`. If you haven't got a `ProductID`, you return `-1` instead to indicate that this product is not currently in the cart, and that you need to create a `CartItem` object for it.

The `Total` comes last:

```
public double Total
      {
      get
       {
        double t=0;

        if (_items == null)
        {
           return 0;
        }

        foreach (CartItem Item in _items)
        {
          t += Item.LineTotal;
        }

        return t;
      }
    }
  }
```

It's a fairly simple property too. If there are no items in your collection (you check this by seeing if it `Is Nothing`) then you don't have any arithmetic to do. Otherwise, you iterate through each `Item` in the `CartItem` collection, adding the `LineTotal` property for that item, and you return the total amount as the variable `t`.

The Profile

You have your `ShoppingCart` object, which will act as the memory of the shopping cart, but this still doesn't answer a key question—how are you going to keep this shopping cart if your user gets his Internet connection violently terminated? In fact, you've already looked at the solution to this in a previous chapter.

In Chapter 11, you looked at how you can create a user profile and how it can be used to create a particular personalized view of the site for any user who logs on to the site. In particular, you stored the member's name, address (including city, county, and country), e-mail, whether he wanted to receive mailings or not, and his particular theme of the site. It is via this capability that you can also store the `ShoppingCart` object. Rather than getting you to create the whole profile, we've already provided it in the ready-to-go application that is available for download from `www.wrox.com` for this chapter.

I can hear the wiseguys at the back now—so I see how to save the cart, but surely you still have to log in to get associated with your cart? That's where the wiseguys are wrong. Another great new feature of ASP.NET is the capability to track seemingly anonymous users via the personalization and profiling system. If the wiseguys had been paying attention in Chapter 11, they would have known that.

In Chapter 11, you saw how you could set up a template to handle anonymous users, and how you could also migrate the details from the anonymous person's shopping cart to the bona fide logged-in user's shopping cart. Now it's time to fill in the other jigsaw pieces. How does this fit into the overall shopping cart picture?

Well, you can set an attribute to track anonymous users so that even if they haven't logged in, and have their connection to the application terminated, then when they come back they will still have their shopping cart contents intact. This is all contained within the Web.config file, which you have already partially predefined for the application in this chapter, so that your e-commerce application makes use of changes introduced to the Wrox United site in Chapter 11, and therefore requires a minimal amount of extra code. You add that capability in the next Try It Out.

Try It Out Amending the Profile to Use the ShoppingCart Object

1. In the Chapter13 application, go to Solution Explorer and open the Web.config file. Scroll down to find the <profile> element and add the highlighted code:

```
<anonymousIdentification enabled="true"/>
<profile enabled="true">
   <properties>
         <add name="MemberName"/>
         <add name="Name"/>
         <add name="Address"/>
         <add name="City"/>
         <add name="County"/>
         <add name="PostCode"/>
         <add name="Country"/>
         <add name="Mailings" type="System.Boolean"/>
         <add name="Email"/>
         <add name="Theme"/>
         <add name="Cart" serializeAs="Binary"
              type="Wrox.Commerce.ShoppingCart"
              allowAnonymous="true"/>
   </properties>
 </profile>
```

2. Save Web.config.

How It Works

Because Web.config is used by your application, the simple act of saving any changes ensures that the update is immediately applied. You've added only two items. The first just switches on anonymous identification, which is switched off by default:

```
<anonymousIdentification enabled="true" />
```

The second is the cart definition:

```
<add name="Cart" serializeAs="Binary"
     type="Wrox.Commerce.ShoppingCart"
     allowAnonymous="true"/>
```

You use the type attribute to refer to the ShoppingCart object. You set the allowAnonymous attribute to true so that this particular property is tracked even when the user hasn't logged in. Last, there is a bit of technical detail in the serializeAs property, which needn't concern you. It simply enables you to make use of your ShoppingCart object. You can find more details about it at http://msdn2.microsoft.com/en-us/library/system.configuration.SettingsSerializeAsAttribute.aspx.

The Shopping Cart Control

Unfortunately, among the multitude of new controls, there is no predefined shopping cart control that you can use, so you are going to have to create one. However, what you can do is make use of some of the existing ASP.NET 2.0 controls and you can construct a shopping cart control that you can use in any application you build. In ASP.NET 2.0, the data handling features have taken a giant leap forward, and you can use the `GridView` control and some clever data-binding to create your shopping cart for you.

Before you rush into building the cart, though, it's worth thinking a little bit more about design. How are you going to access your cart? How are you going to display the items in it? The first question is easy enough to answer: You add a button to your product item page, which when clicked simply adds the item to the cart. However, where should you go then? Rather than going to your shopping cart, you probably want to return to your catalog. Shopping carts by nature should be unobtrusive—you don't want to be confronted with the contents of your cart every time you stick an item in, which is probably not conducive to impulse buying (and by inference profitable selling). It's much easier only to be confronted with the contents when you get to the checkout. So your system develops a structure like Figure 13-19.

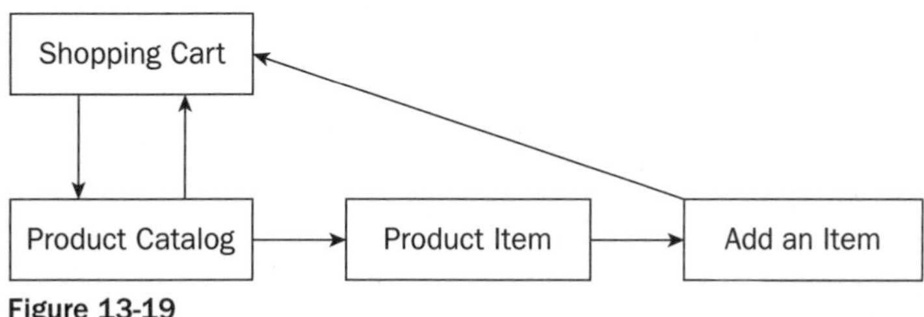

Figure 13-19

This diagram shows how you can navigate between the different parts of your application. You can move from the Product Catalog page, either to the shopping cart itself or to the Product Item page. From the Product Item page you can add an item, which in turn will appear in the shopping cart.

The second question, then, is about how you should display your shopping cart. If you were feeling extremely confident about the layout, you could probably have a little control pop up at the side that appeared in every page of the site, but because you don't want to have to spend a lot of time with the jigsaw puzzle of fitting things into your web site design, you'll just make the shopping cart a separate page that can be easily accessed via a separate link. You've already earmarked the `GridView` control to display the contents of your cart, so continue and build the next stage of your pipeline.

In this Try It Out, you create a user control, the `ShoppingCart` control, and then add it to a page. The user control is a lot more portable (you learned about them in Chapter 10 and how they help you to reuse code effectively).

Try It Out — Adding a Shopping Cart Control

1. Open Solution Explorer in Visual Web Developer. Right-click the top item and select Add New Item. Add a Web User Control and call it **ShoppingCart.ascx**.
2. In Design View, select the `GridView` control from the Data section of the Toolbox. Click the smart tag dialog box and select the Edit Columns option.

3. From the dialog box that appears, select one `TemplateField`, four `BoundFields`, and one `CommandField`, as shown in Figure 13-20. These will be used to represent the `ProductImage`, `ProductName`, `Quantity`, `Price`, and `LineTotal` (that is, quantity multiplied by price) of that particular item and a button to edit that item or to delete it from your shopping cart, respectively.

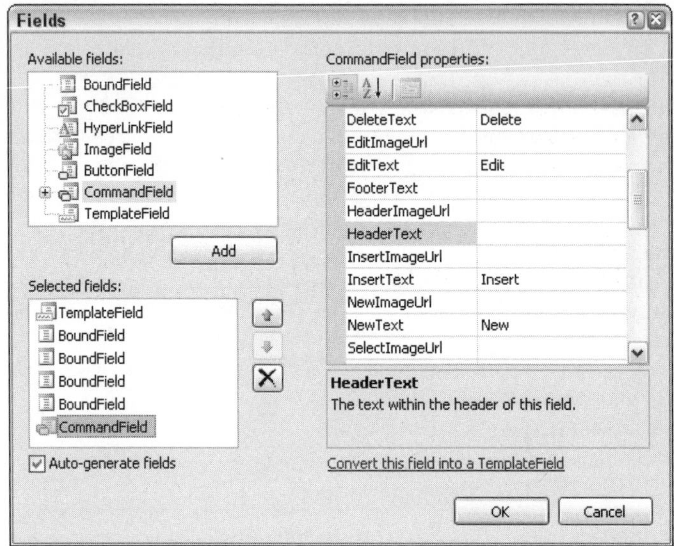

Figure 13-20

4. Select the `BoundFields` field and change the properties one by one in the Properties window as shown in the following table.

Don't click OK in between adding each item, which will take you back to Design View.

	DataField	HeaderText	ReadOnly	DataFormatString
Bound Field 1	`ProductName`	Product	True	
Bound Field 2	`Quantity`	Quantity	False	
Bound Field 3	`Price`	Price	True	{0:c}
Bound Field 4	`LineTotal`	Total	True	{0:c}

5. Go to the `CommandField` and set the `ShowEditButton` and `ShowDeleteButton` properties to `True`.

6. Click OK to go back to Design View. Click the smart tag dialog box, and select Edit Templates from the flyout that appears.

7. Now drop an `Image` control into the `ItemTemplate` and click the smart tag dialog box, as displayed in Figure 13-21.

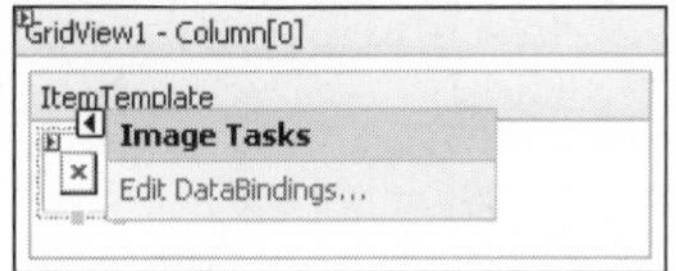

Figure 13-21

8. Select Edit Data Bindings and select `ImageUrl` from the Bindable properties. Add the following code to the Code Expression box:

```
Eval("ProductImageUrl", "~/ProductImages/thumb_{0}")
```

9. Return to Design View and select the smart tag dialog box on the `GridView` control. Select Edit Templates➪EmptyDataTemplate from the menu that appears. Type the following text directly into the `EmptyDataTemplate` (see Figure 13-22): **There is nothing in your shopping cart. You can buy items from the Shop.**

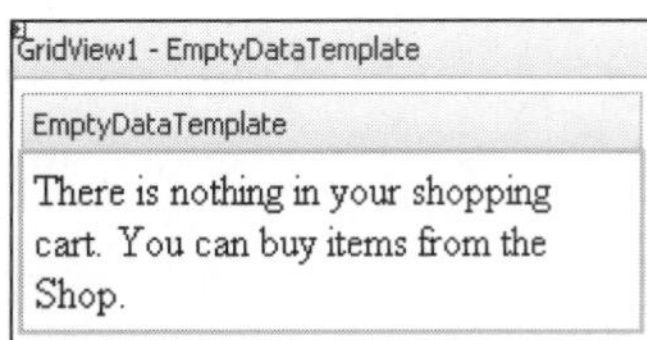

Figure 13-22

10. Return to Source view and add an anchor `<a>` tag around the Shop section as follows:

```
<a href="Wroxshop.aspx">Shop</a>.
```

This is the text that will be displayed when the user views a shopping cart with no items in it. You supply a link back to the main shopping page as well.

11. In Design View, and right-click the `GridView` control and select Properties. Enter the values shown in the following table.

Property	Value
(ID)	CartGrid
AutoGenerateColumns	False
DataKeyNames	ProductID

12. Right-click Solution Explorer and select Add a New Item. Select a Web Form and call the new item **ShoppingCartPage.aspx**. Note that this is an .aspx file now unlike the user control you have just created. This is the page that will host your user control.

13. In Design View, drag `ShoppingCart.ascx` onto the page, as shown in Figure 13-23.

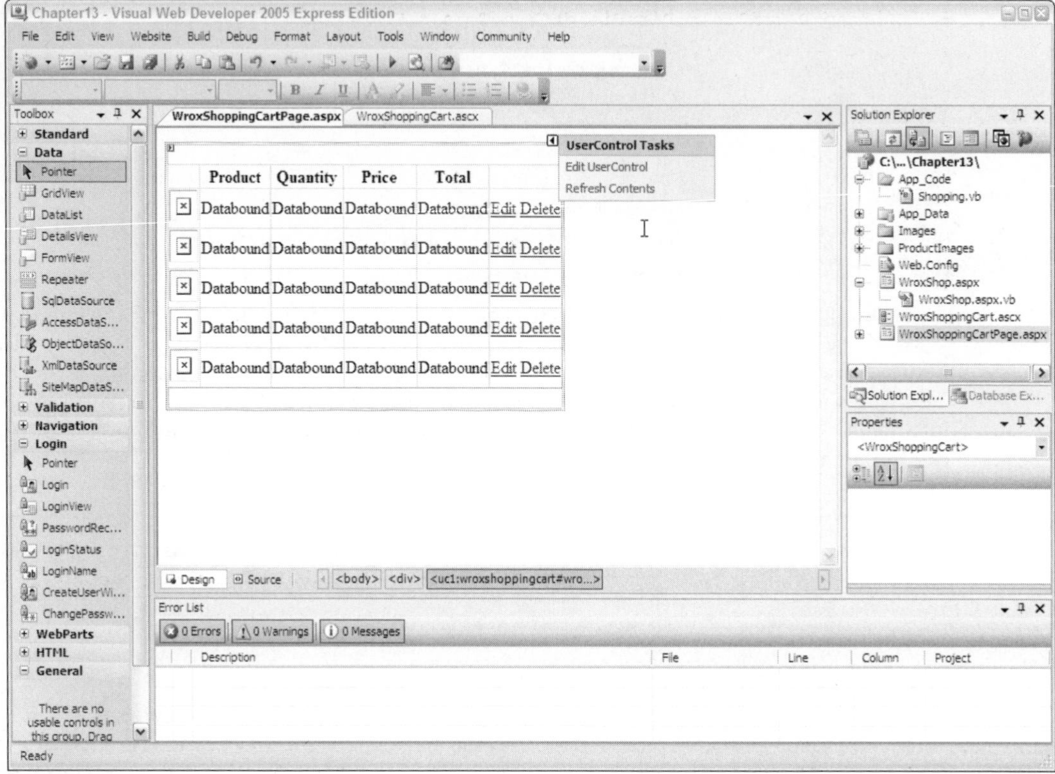

Figure 13-23

How It Works

This finishes the first stage of your `ShoppingCart` control. You created your control and you added a thumbnail image and fields to store the `Quantity`, `Price`, and `LineTotal` of the product, as well as a button enabling you to edit or delete your choices in the cart.

If you go to Source View, it will currently look as follows:

```
<asp:GridView ID="CartGrid" Runat="server" AutoGenerateColumns="False"
DataKeyNames="ProductID" >
      <Columns>
          <asp:TemplateField>
              <ItemTemplate>
                  <asp:Image id="ProductImage" Runat="server" ImageUrl='<%#
                   Eval("ProductImageURL", "~/ProductImages/thumb_{0}")%>' />
              </ItemTemplate>
          </asp:TemplateField>
          <asp:BoundField DataField="ProductName" HeaderText="Product"
           ReadOnly="True" />
          <asp:BoundField DataField="Quantity" HeaderText="Quantity" />
          <asp:BoundField DataField="Price" HeaderText="Price"
           DataFormatString="{0:c}" ReadOnly="True" />
```

```
            <asp:BoundField DataField="LineTotal" HeaderText="Total"
             DataFormatString="{0:c}" ReadOnly="True" />
            <asp:CommandField ShowEditButton="True"
             ShowDeleteButton="true"></asp:CommandField>
        </Columns>
        <EmptyDataTemplate>
           There is nothing in your shopping cart. You can buy items from the
           <a href="wroxshop.aspx">Shop</a>.
        </EmptyDataTemplate>
</asp:GridView>
```

This is all very familiar and close to what you supplied to the `DataList` controls in your Catalog and Item pages. You bind the `ProductImageURL` to an image in the `ItemTemplate`. You have several bound fields that will display text. The price fields have settings for the `DataFormatString` so that they display their values correctly as prices. However, there is one setting to note. In your bound fields, you made three of the four rows read-only. The `Quantity` row was left editable so that you can edit the contents of your cart.

You've also added an `EmptyDataTemplate` to display a message in the event that there is nothing in the cart. However, at the moment, you have no data source. In the Catalog and Item pages, you first created a `SqlDataSource` control and bound it to the `DataList` control. You haven't bound the ShoppingCart control to anything yet.

Automating the Shopping Cart

So far, so good, you have your `ShoppingCart` control fully designed. However, it doesn't do much at the moment. In fact, it doesn't do anything! If you want the cart to be responsive, you will need to add some code telling ASP.NET 2.0 what to do when something occurs. When you created your bound fields in the shopping cart, three of the four bound fields were read-only. The last one, Quantity, was left editable. This makes life simpler, because it means that you only need to anticipate what happens if someone changes the quantity of items within a particular row in the cart.

You will want to cater to four possible events, because there are four possible scenarios:

- **Editing the cart:** When you enter a new quantity.
- **Canceling an edit in the cart:** When you decide you don't want go with the quantity value you've changed.
- **Updating the cart:** When you want that new quantity to take effect.
- **Deleting items from the cart:** When you want to completely remove an item from the cart.

This will require some code-behind. You looked at code-behind in Chapters 9 and 10. Here your code-behind will be run directly in response to one of these four events occurring. So after you've updated the shopping cart, how do you associate that with a particular user? You've already created a profile — now all you need to do is to reference that profile within your code, via the `Profile` object.

Go ahead and add this code to your shopping cart in the next Try It Out.

Try It Out Automating the Shopping Cart

1. Go to your ShoppingCart control. Right-click `GridView` and select Properties. From the Properties window, select the lightning bolt button (the fourth one), as shown in Figure 13-24. This displays a list of events.

Figure 13-24

2. Double-click the `RowEditing` event. In Source View, a gap appears for the events. Add the following highlighted code to the events:

```
protected void CartGrid_RowEditing(object sender, GridViewEditEventArgs e)
    {  CartGrid.EditIndex = e.NewEditIndex;
  BindGrid();
}
```

3. Go back to Design View, right-click `GridView`, and select Properties. It should take you straight to `Events` this time. Double-click the `RowUpdating` event. Add the following highlighted code:

```
protected void CartGrid_RowUpdating(object sender, GridViewUpdateEventArgs e)
    {  TextBox QuantityTextBox =
    (TextBox)CartGrid.Rows[e.RowIndex].Cells[2].Controls[0];
  int Quantity = Convert.ToInt32(QuantityTextBox.Text);
  if (Quantity == 0)
  {
    Profile.Cart.Items.RemoveAt(e.RowIndex);
  }
  else
  {
    Profile.Cart.Items[e.RowIndex].Quantity = Quantity;
  }
  CartGrid.EditIndex = -1;
  BindGrid();
}
```

4. Go back to Design View. Right-click `GridView` and select Properties. Double-click the `RowCancelingEdit` event. Add the highlighted code:

```
protected void CartGrid_RowCancelingEdit(object sender, GridViewCancelEditEventArgs
e)
    {  CartGrid.EditIndex = -1;
  BindGrid();
}
```

5. In Design View, right-click `GridView` and select Properties. Double-click the `RowDeleting` event. Add the highlighted code:

```
    protected void CartGrid_RowDeleting(object sender, GridViewDeleteEventArgs e)
    {
  Profile.Cart.Items.RemoveAt(e.RowIndex);
  BindGrid();
}
```

6. From Design View, double-click the blank page surrounding the ShoppingCart control, and add the highlighted code to the Page_Load event:

```
protected void Page_Load(object sender, EventArgs e)
    {
    if (Profile.Cart == null)  {
      Profile.Cart = new Wrox.Commerce.ShoppingCart();
    }

    if (!Page.IsPostBack)
    {
      BindGrid();
    }
    if (Profile.Cart.Items == null)
     {
      TotalLabel.Visible = false;
    }
}
```

7. You may have noticed that you've also referenced a function called BindGrid() within all of these events. This function does the binding so that your shopping cart can display something. You need to add this code for BindGrid() underneath the functions within the code-behind as well:

```
private void BindGrid()
{
   CartGrid.DataSource = Profile.Cart.Items;
   DataBind();

   TotalLabel.Text = String.Format("Total:{0,19:C}", Profile.Cart.Total);
}
```

8. At the top of the page, add a reference to your ShoppingCart object:

```
using Wrox.Commerce;
```

9. Switch to Design View and drag a Label control onto the screen and place it under the GridView control. Right-click the Label control and select Properties. Delete the Text property and change the ID property to TotalLabel, as shown in Figure 13-25.

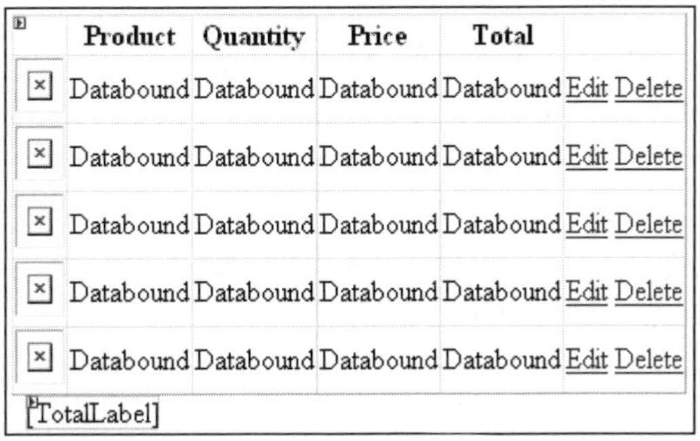

	Product	Quantity	Price	Total		
☒	Databound	Databound	Databound	Databound	Edit	Delete
☒	Databound	Databound	Databound	Databound	Edit	Delete
☒	Databound	Databound	Databound	Databound	Edit	Delete
☒	Databound	Databound	Databound	Databound	Edit	Delete
☒	Databound	Databound	Databound	Databound	Edit	Delete

[TotalLabel]

Figure 13-25

10. View the page `ShoppingCartPage.aspx`. You will see what appears in Figure 13-26.

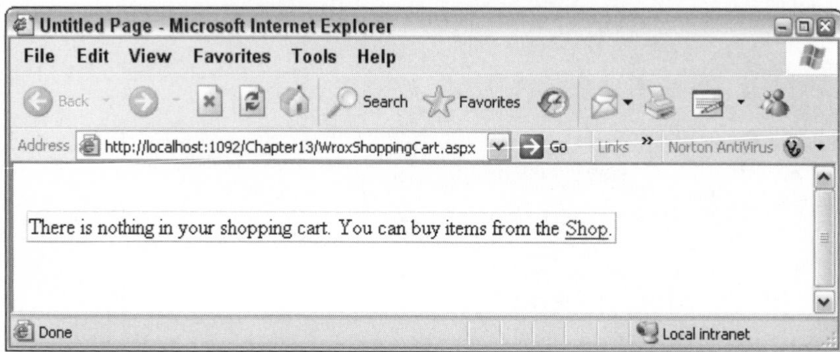

Figure 13-26

How It Works

For the first time you're able to browse your shopping cart, although you only get to view the `EmptyDataTemplate` at the moment. Your code, though, provides all of the necessary functionality to be able to use the cart properly. The `RowEditing` method allows you to store the ID of the Product you are editing to the index:

```
CartGrid.EditIndex = e.NewEditIndex;
BindGrid();
```

After this, you bind to the grid. The `RowCancelEdit` sets it back to the default of -1:

```
CartGrid.EditIndex = -1;
BindGrid();
```

This means that no row in the grid is currently selected. Once again you bind to the grid afterwards. Your `Delete` method removes the index number from the cart stored in the profile and binds to the grid:

```
Profile.Cart.Items.RemoveAt(e.RowIndex);
BindGrid();
```

The update first has to obtain the quantity figure from the text box, and then it converts it to an integer. If you've set the quantity to 0, then this acts the same as a delete, so you perform a `RemoveAt` to remove the `CartItem` object. Otherwise you simply re-adjust the quantity and reset the index to -1 and bind to the grid:

```
TextBox QuantityTextBox =
  (TextBox)CartGrid.Rows[e.RowIndex].Cells[2].Controls[0];
int Quantity = Convert.ToInt32(QuantityTextBox.Text);
if (Quantity == 0)
{
  Profile.Cart.Items.RemoveAt(e.RowIndex);
}
```

```
else
{
  Profile.Cart.Items[e.RowIndex].Quantity = Quantity;
}
CartGrid.EditIndex = -1;
BindGrid();
```

You need to consider two final sections of code. The first is the `BindGrid` function, which performs your data binding for you and is called by each of the events:

```
CartGrid.DataSource = Profile.Cart.Items;
DataBind();
TotalLabel.Text = String.Format("Total:{0,19:C}", Profile.Cart.Total);
```

It simply sets the `GridView` control's `DataSource` property to point to the Items collection of your particular profile and then sets the total for your cart.

The second second section of code to consider is the contents of the `Page_Load` event handler, which is fired whenever a page is started up:

```
if (Profile.Cart == null)
        {
            Profile.Cart = new Wrox.Commerce.ShoppingCart();
        }
        if (!Page.IsPostBack)
        {
            BindGrid();
        }
        if (Profile.Cart.Items == null)
        {
            TotalLabel.Visible = false;
        }
```

This basically says, "If the cart is empty, create an empty instance of the shopping cart (so that any subsequent calls to a non-existent cart don't fail)." It then says, "If the page hasn't been posted back, and is therefore the first time the user has seen the page, bind the grid," and it goes on to make the total label invisible if there is nothing in the cart and sets the format correctly for displaying the total as a currency. There is a distinction to be made here, between the first `IF` and third `IF` statement. The first `IF` statement will be triggered if the cart hasn't been created. The third `IF` will be triggered if the cart has been created but is empty (in other words, if someone has removed all the items from it). You have to be able to handle both scenarios when updating the cart in your profile.

The Add-to-Cart Facility

Your shopping cart is now fully functional in all but one respect. You can edit it and delete items from it, but you still can't add any items to it. This is because the adding of items needs to be done from a different page entirely.

The next part of your odyssey is to place an "add to cart" button, back on the previous Product Item page. In the following Try It Out, this will add the corresponding item to your cart every time a button is clicked. If you click it twice on two separate occasions, it will update the quantity for you.

Try It Out — Adding the Add to Cart Button

1. Open `WroxShopItem.aspx` in Visual Web Developer, go to Design View, and add an ImageButton, above the Return to Shop link. Via the Properties window, change the button name to **btnAddToCart**, and change the `ImageUrl` property to **"~/Images/AddToCart.gif"**, as shown in Figure 13-27.

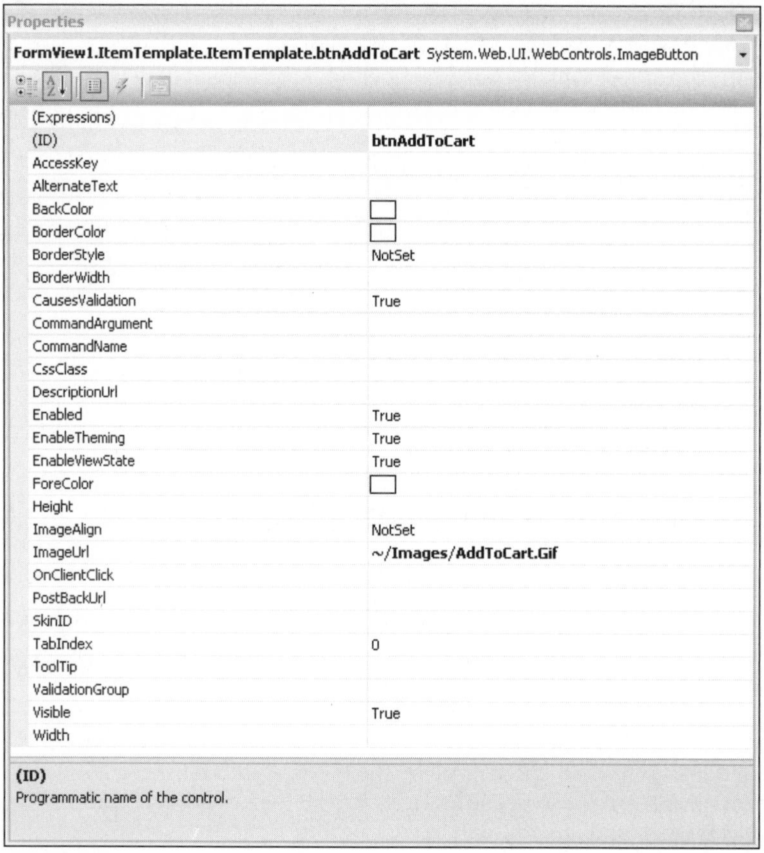

Properties

FormView1.ItemTemplate.ItemTemplate.btnAddToCart System.Web.UI.WebControls.ImageButton

Property	Value
(Expressions)	
(ID)	**btnAddToCart**
AccessKey	
AlternateText	
BackColor	
BorderColor	
BorderStyle	NotSet
BorderWidth	
CausesValidation	True
CommandArgument	
CommandName	
CssClass	
DescriptionUrl	
Enabled	True
EnableTheming	True
EnableViewState	True
ForeColor	
Height	
ImageAlign	NotSet
ImageUrl	**~/Images/AddToCart.Gif**
OnClientClick	
PostBackUrl	
SkinID	
TabIndex	0
ToolTip	
ValidationGroup	
Visible	True
Width	

(ID)
Programmatic name of the control.

Figure 13-27

2. Double-click the button and add the following code:

```
protected void btnAddToCart_Click(object sender, ImageClickEventArgs e)
    {
```

```
    double Price =
      double.Parse(((Label)DataList1.Controls[0].FindControl("PriceLabel")).Text);
    string ProductName  =
      ((Label)DataList1.Controls[0].FindControl("NameLabel")).Text;
    string PictureURL  =
      ((Label)DataList1.Controls[0].FindControl("PictureUrlLabel")).Text;
    int ProductID  = int.Parse(Request.QueryString["ProductID"]);


    if (Profile.Cart == null) {
      Profile.Cart = new Wrox.Commerce.ShoppingCart();
    }
      Profile.Cart.Insert(ProductID, Price, 1, ProductName, PictureURL);
      Server.Transfer("WroxShop.aspx");
}
```

3. Go back to `WroxShop.aspx` in Design View. Add a hyperlink button from the General section of the Toolbox. Right-click the link, select Properties, and change the properties listed in the following table.

Property	Value
`ID`	`ShoppingCartLink`
`NavigateURL`	`~/ShoppingCartPage.aspx`
`Text`	`View Shopping Cart`

It will now look like Figure 13-28.

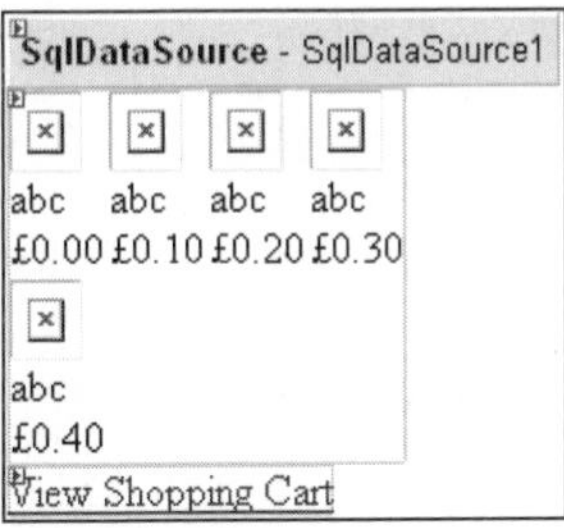

Figure 13-28

4. Give the shopping cart a test drive. Go to `WroxShop.aspx` and select the scarf, as shown in Figure 13-29.

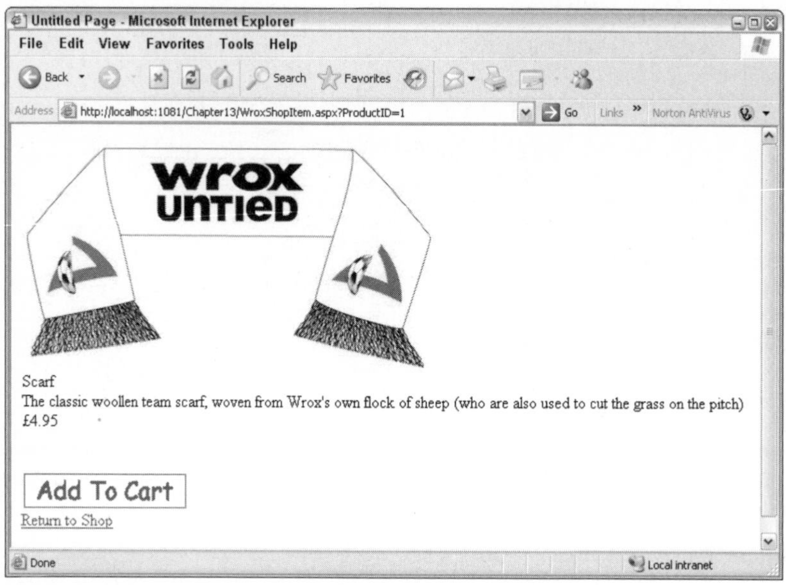

Figure 13-29

5. Click Add to Cart. This takes you back to the main shopping screen. Now click View Shopping Cart, and as you can see in Figure 13-30, your item has been added to the cart.

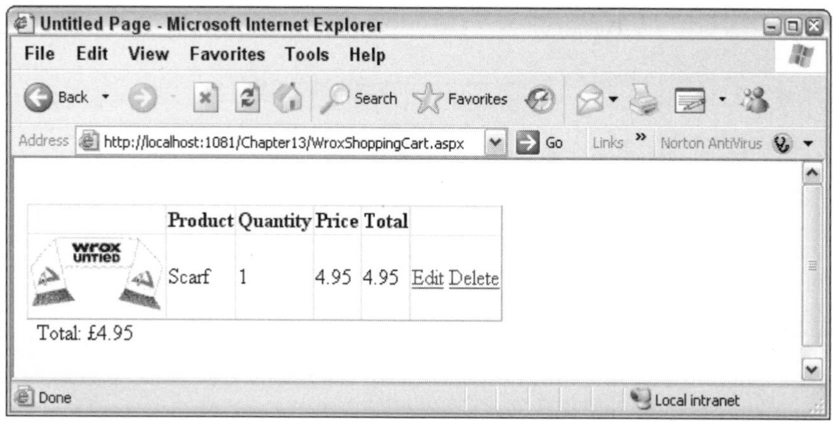

Figure 13-30

6. Click Edit to change the Quantity box into a text box that you can edit (see Figure 13-31).

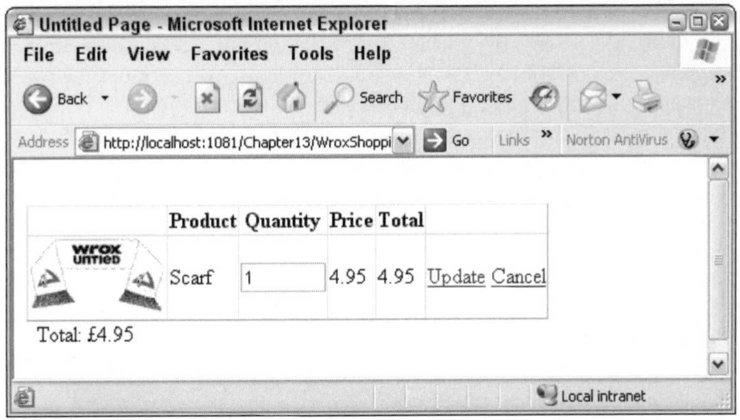

Figure 13-31

7. Type **2** and click Update. The totals are updated, as shown in Figure 13-32.

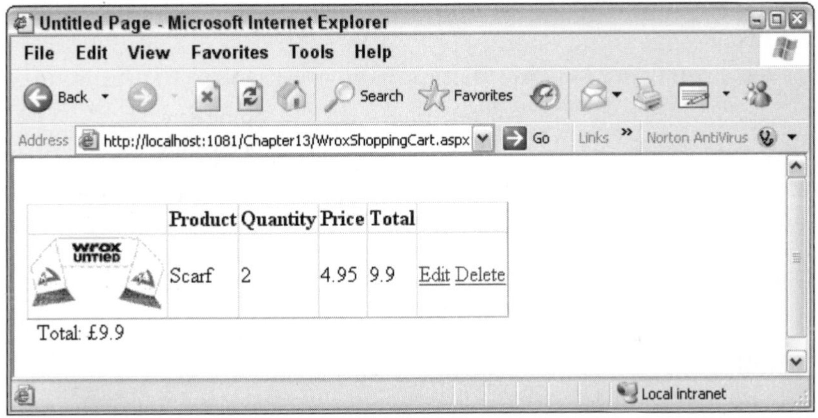

Figure 13-32

8. Click Delete. The item is removed from your cart.

How It Works

By adding two bits to the application in this Try It Out, you enabled the whole functionality of the shopping cart. You started by adding a button to the Product Item page and creating some code that ran when the button was clicked. The code handles the business of adding an item to your shopping cart. You start by getting the `Price`, `ProductName`, `PictureUrl` and `ProductID`:

```
double Price =
  double.Parse(((Label)DataList1.Controls[0].FindControl("PriceLabel")).Text);
string ProductName  =
  ((Label)DataList1.Controls[0].FindControl("NameLabel")).Text;
string PictureURL  =
  ((Label)DataList1.Controls[0].FindControl("PictureUrlLabel")).Text;
int ProductID  = int.Parse(Request.QueryString["ProductID"]);
```

This information has already been stored in the page. You use the `FindControl` method of a control to locate a control. The `DataList` control contains an item template, so you have to move into the controls collection of the `DataList` control to get at the `Label` controls. You can cast the contents of the control to text by prefixing them with the control type in brackets. So each of the three lines works like this. You declare a variable in which to store your item. You search the `DataList` control for your `Label` control using `FindControl`, and supply it with the name of the control you want to find. You convert the control from a "generic" control into a specific `Label` control. (Note that this only works if the control you are casting to actually is a `Label` control.) So for the `Price`, you search for the `PriceLabel` control's contents and you retrieve the `text` property of the label. There is actually another level of conversion required here. You want the price as a `double` data type, so you convert the text item you receive into a double and store it in the `double` data type. The `PictureUrlLabel` is the one you didn't delete in the second Try It Out of this chapter because we said you'd need it later. This is where you need it. Having stored the `Price`, `ProductName`, and `PictureURL`, you still need the `ProductID`. This can be located in the query string passed to the page:

```
int ProductID  = int.Parse(Request.QueryString["ProductID"]);
```

You check to see if a cart exists for this profile:

```
if (Profile.Cart == null) {
  Profile.Cart = new Wrox.Commerce.ShoppingCart();
}
  Profile.Cart.Insert(ProductID, Price, 1, ProductName, PictureURL);
  Server.Transfer("WroxShop.aspx");
}
```

If a cart doesn't exist, you create a new one. Then you need to insert a new item into your shopping cart along with the `ProductID`, `Price`, `ProductName`, `PictureURL`, and the quantity of 1:

```
Profile.Cart.Insert(ProductID, Price, 1, ProductName, PictureURL);
```

Last, you simply transfer the user back to the initial Product Catalog page:

```
Server.Transfer("WroxShop.aspx");
```

This stage can continue cyclically until the user either leaves the application or needs to check out.

Checkout

Checking out is perhaps the lengthiest stage of the whole process. The checkout process involves a number of considerations, not just the totalling up of the items and how much they cost, but also things like stock availability, getting the user's address and delivery details, obtaining and verifying payment for the items, and some sort of rounding up of the whole process.

Checkout is, in itself, a mini set of stages. If you're serious about implementing your own e-commerce process, it's worth checking some of the major e-commerce vendors (such as Amazon), seeing what they do in their checkout process, and asking is it quick and intuitive to use? A lot of time and effort has gone into producing checkout processes that can be completed in the minimum number of steps, with the minimum number of clicks.

In your design, consider checkout as comprising the following:

- Order processing
- Login
- Enter or get the address and delivery details
- Get the credit card details
- Finish

This is one part of the process that is impossible to model completely, without actually building a real, live, working e-commerce site. However, some considerations about each step are worth talking about.

Order Processing

The first step of the checkout process is to check whether or not the item is in stock. With a large retailer such as Amazon, not all of the items they carry will be sourced by them. They have a range of suppliers, and they often need to check with them first to see if a particular item is in stock. Hence you will find that some products will ship from Amazon within 24 hours, whereas others may take between four and six weeks. In reality there is often another pipeline (similar to Figure 13-33) going on here that has to be negotiated.

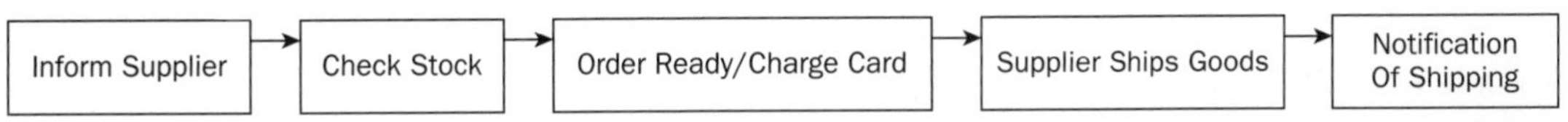

Figure 13-33

With Wrox United, you're not going to delve into this level of detail. You are going to assume that all goods are stored in the Wrox United warehouse, and after you've checked the stock level and they are in stock, they are good to be released for shipping.

Login

We've already mentioned that the Wrox United application uses one of ASP.NET 2.0's best features to keep track of the shopping cart, in that you don't have to physically log in to keep track of your shopping cart. However, when you come to checkout, you must log in, because you need to supply your address details and credit card information. You need to supply a login box and password to be able to authenticate your user's details. You will use the standard ASP.NET 2.0 login control to do this.

Address/Delivery Details

The address details are fairly easy to sort as well. One of two scenarios could occur. Either you have already captured the user's details and you can access the details that are stored with the profile, or if you don't have them on record, you must request that the user enter them into a series of text boxes. You can either use the Profile that was created in Chapter 11 and that stores these details, or you can store the details supplied in the text boxes by the user.

Credit Card Handling

Here you're going to cop out and not handle credit cards at all — you'll just add a small dummy section. This gives the impression that it isn't a major part of the e-commerce pipeline, but don't be fooled for a moment — it is of course critical to the success of the pipeline. For obvious reasons, you can't set up an actual credit card–handling facility. For starters, you don't have a physical product to sell. Fetching as the Wrox United kits undoubtedly would be, they only exist in cyberspace. So here we can't provide any code, but instead can quickly consider what you need to take into account when setting up a credit card–handling facility on your web site.

Credit card retailers first starting out need a merchant ID, usually supplied via their bank, which gives some sort of guarantee that the business is genuine. Most Internet businesses require the same thing. In the U.S., there are two ways to do this. The first is to provide all the processing and handling of credit cards yourself, and the second is to get someone else to do it on your behalf.

In-House Credit Card Transactions

Setting up credit card processing in-house is the ideal way to keep an eye on all your transactions, but it can be quite a slow and unwieldy process. You require an e-commerce ID (also known as a merchant number or as an Internet Merchant Account [IMA] in the UK) from a third party who can actually process the credit card details for you, meaning the third party can decide whether or not a particular credit card number is genuine. You will have to apply for an account with the third party and provide a lot of details that help establish your authenticity.

Obtaining an E-Commerce ID, Merchant Number, or IMA

In the U.S., you can go to one of the following web sites:

- **Verisign/CyberCash:** `www.icverify.com`
- **First Data/Card Service:** `www.cardservice.com`

In the UK, you can go to one of these web sites:

- **WorldPay:** `www.worldpay.co.uk`
- **DataCash:** `www.datacash.com`

For worldwide transaction processing, you can try PayPal (`www.paypal.com`), which accepts credit cards once you have set up a business account with them.

Payment Gateways

After you have your e-commerce ID, merchant number, or IMA, you still need another link in the chain, a way of communicating from a payment gateway to a bank. You should be able to use the same company you obtained an e-commerce ID from to do this. You supply the e-commerce ID to the bank, and they use it to track the money's movements to the gateway service and back again. These services usually come at a hefty price. If all this sounds too complex, you might want to consider the alternative.

Bureau Services

Because this is a beginner's book, it's probably safe to assume that the first site you start developing won't be a major store. More likely you'll be working on a small store (maybe your own) that perhaps won't really want to cover the risks and costs associated with having a system handling credit cards itself. In the early days of e-commerce on the web, there were a series of high-profile hacks. One notorious one was where all customers of a high-profile music store had their credit card details stolen when the database containing them was compromised. Rather than having to worry about all the risks from encrypting card details to storing them in a way to ensure their complete safety, it's easier to get someone else to do this for you. These are termed *bureau services*. When you get to the part of a site where you check out, instead of handling the details, you link to the bureau service's site, and they handle the whole process for you from then on.

Until relatively recently, bureau services were expensive propositions that required quite a large financial commitment on the part of the seller. Several years ago, I costed a small record label's ability to do this, and the cheapest I could find to provide an online store would have meant they would have to have sold several hundred CDs a month to cover the gateway fees alone. The rise of eBay has led to a massive rise in demand of people who want to handle their own sales instantly, so rather than having to wait for checks (which carry risk of both fraud and bouncing if the funds aren't present), or doing money transfers via banks or a third party such as Western Union, they want to be able to handle credit card transactions. In addition to that, they might only ever want to handle as little as 10 or 20 sales.

Two popular solutions supply this service, and can actually supply common components such as a shopping cart for you:

- **PayPal:** `www.paypal.com`
- **BTClick&Buy:** `www.btclickandbuy.com`

Other sites exist too. There are digital credit card services that specialize in micropayments when paying for small items such as single mp3s. It all depends on what you want to sell and how much you want to sell it for. If these two sites don't provide a solution that suits you, then look around for something more suited to your needs. If you want further details about how to handle credit card transactions, we suggest you read the details given on the sites mentioned in these sections.

Summarizing the Transaction

Typically, after you've completed your transaction, it would be good to receive a notification or receipt of what you've ordered. This is actually a relatively simple step of the process, but to e-mail somebody requires a working SMTP server, so for that reason alone, you aren't going to implement this step.

How You Intend to Checkout

Once again, you are governed by keeping things simple. What is the minimum you can boil down your checkout process to?

The five-stage process will be as follows:

- Login
- Delivery address
- Payment
- Confirmation of the order
- Finish

You will also need a breadcrumb to you to help you keep an eye on where you are in the whole checkout process. As mentioned at the beginning of the chapter, one priority is being able to abort the transaction at any point prior to confirming the purchase.

What you're not going to do is the stock handling (reducing items and keep track of stock levels) or sending a confirmation-of-order e-mail. The chapter is already big enough as it is and these things are arguably stretched over different disciplines to e-commerce. What you are going to do in the next Try It Out is create the final stages of the e-commerce pipeline.

Try It Out Checking Out

1. In Solution Explorer in Visual Web Developer, right-click the `C:\...\Chapter13` heading at the top and select Add New Item. Add a Web Form called **Checkout.aspx** and check the Place Code in Separate File box to ensure a separate code-behind file is created.

2. In Design View, from the Toolbox grab a `Wizard` control and drop it onto the page, as shown in Figure 13-34.

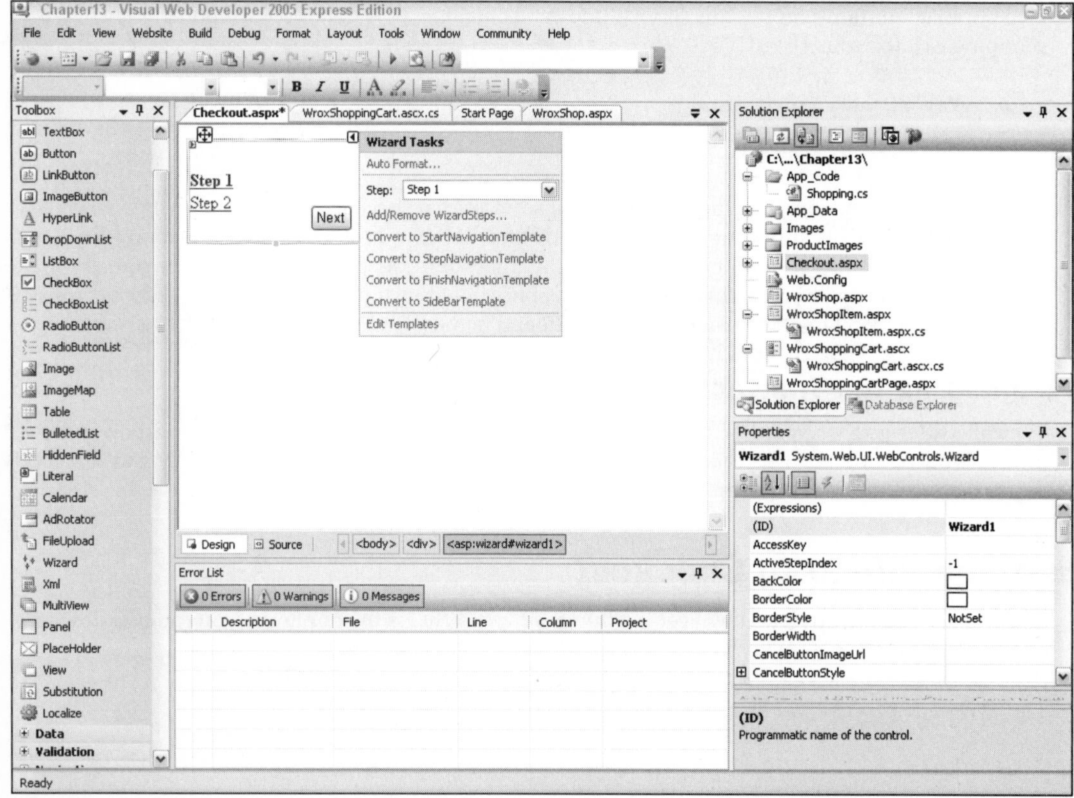

Figure 13-34

3. From the smart tag dialog box, select the Add/Remove wizard steps option.

4. In the dialog box that appears, you are going to add three extra steps. This is so you have five steps: one for login, one for address, one for credit card details, one to confirm the order, and one to finish the transaction. Start by clicking Add (see Figure 13-35) and entering **Step 3** next to Title. Then clicking Add again and enter **Step 4**. Click Add one more time and enter **Step 5**.

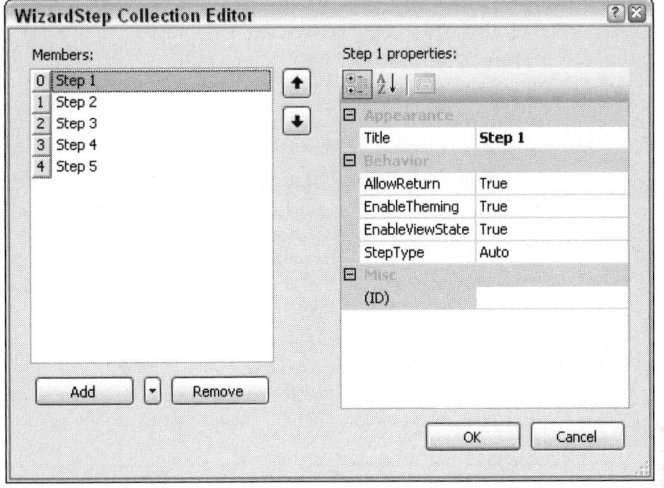

Figure 13-35

5. Go back and change the Title property in each so that it reads as shown in Figure 13-36.

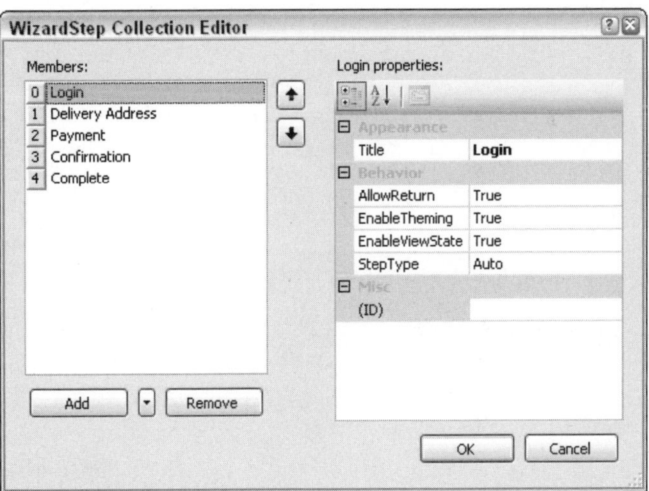

Figure 13-36

6. Click OK.

7. From the Login section of the Toolbox, drag a Login box into the `<asp:Wizard>` control, as shown in Figure 13-37.

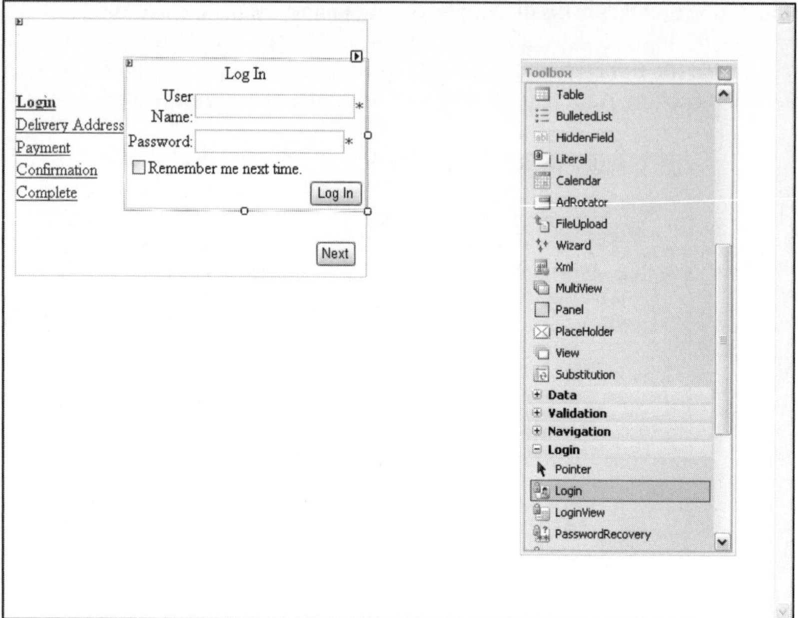

Figure 13-37

8. Click Source View. Add the following code to the Wizard step for Step 2 (Delivery Address):

```
<asp:checkbox id="chkUseProfileAddress" runat="server" autopostback="True"
  text="Use membership address"
  OnCheckedChanged="chkUseProfileAddress_CheckedChanged"></asp:checkbox><br />

<table border="0">
  <tr><td>Name</td><td><asp:textbox id="txtName" runat="server" /></td></tr>
  <tr><td>Address</td><td><asp:textbox id="txtAddress" runat="server" /></td></tr>
  <tr><td>City</td><td><asp:textbox id="txtCity" runat="server" /></td></tr>
  <tr><td>County</td><td><asp:textbox id="txtCounty" runat="server" /></td></tr>
  <tr><td>Postcode</td><td><asp:textbox id="txtPostCode" runat="server" />
    </td></tr>
  <tr><td>Country</td><td><asp:textbox id="txtCountry" runat="server" /></td></tr>
</table>
```

9. Add the following code to the Wizard step for Step 3 (Payment):

```
<asp:DropDownList id="lstCardType" runat="server">
  <asp:ListItem>MasterCard</asp:ListItem>
  <asp:ListItem>Visa</asp:ListItem>
</asp:DropDownList>
<br />
Card Number: <asp:Textbox id="txtNumber" runat="server"
  Text="0123456789" ReadOnly="True"/>
<br />
Expires:
<asp:textbox id="txtExpiresMonth" runat="server" columns="2" />
/
<asp:textbox id="txtExpiresYear" runat="server"  columns="4" />
```

10. Go back to Design View for Step 4 (Confirmation). Type the following:

```
Please confirm the amount you wish to have
deducted from your credit card.
```

11. Select `ShoppingCart.ascx` and drag it into the `Wizard` control above the text you have created, as shown in Figure 13-38.

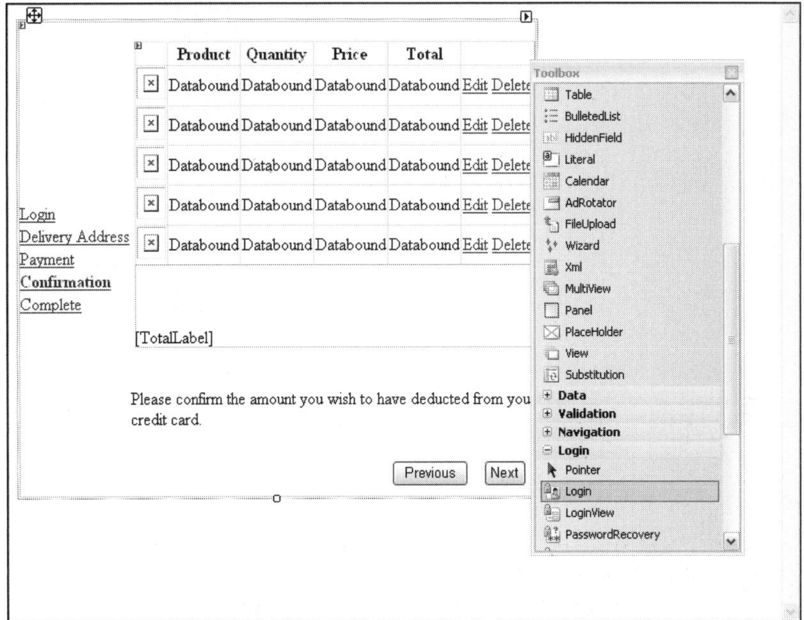

Figure 13-38

12. Click Complete and in Design View for Step 5 (Complete), type **Thank you for your order.**

13. Go to Source View and above the `<asp:Wizard>` control, add the following:

```
<asp:Label id="NoCartlabel" runat="server" visible="false">
There are no items in your cart. Visit the shop to buy items.
</asp:Label>

<div style="float:right">
  <asp:LoginView ID="LoginView1" Runat="server">
    <AnonymousTemplate>
      <asp:passwordrecovery id="PasswordRecovery1" runat="server" />
    </AnonymousTemplate>
  </asp:LoginView>
</div>
```

14. Above this code, add the following:

```
<%@ Import Namespace ="System.Data.SqlClient"%>
<%@ Import Namespace ="Wrox.Commerce"%>
```

15. Save the design.

16. Go to Solution Explorer, and select `checkout.aspx.cs`.

17. Add the following code-behind in place of whatever is already there:

```
using System;
using System.Data;
using System.Data.SqlClient;
using System.Configuration;
using Wrox.Commerce;
using System.Web.UI.WebControls;
using System.Web.Security;

public partial class Checkout : System.Web.UI.Page
{
    void Page_Load(object sender, EventArgs e)
    {

    if (!Page.IsPostBack)
    {
      if (Profile.Cart == null)
       {
        NoCartlabel.Visible = true;
        Wizard1.Visible = false;
      }

      if (User.Identity.IsAuthenticated)
      {
        Wizard1.ActiveStepIndex = 1;
      }
      else
      {
        Wizard1.ActiveStepIndex = 0;
      }
    }

  }

  protected void chkUseProfileAddress_CheckedChanged(object sender ,
    System.EventArgs e )
  {
    // fill the delivery address from the profile, but only if it's empty
    // we don't want to overwrite the values
    if (chkUseProfileAddress.Checked && txtName.Text.Trim() == "")
    {
      txtName.Text = Profile.Name;
      txtAddress.Text = Profile.Address;
      txtCity.Text = Profile.City;
      txtCounty.Text = Profile.County;
      txtPostCode.Text = Profile.PostCode;
      txtCountry.Text = Profile.Country;
    }

  }

  protected void Wizard1_FinishButtonClick( object sender,
System.Web.UI.WebControls.WizardNavigationEventArgs e)
```

```
  {
    // Insert the order and order lines into the database
    SqlConnection conn = null;
    SqlTransaction trans = null;
    SqlCommand cmd;

    try
    {
      conn = new
SqlConnection(ConfigurationManager.ConnectionStrings["WroxUnited"].ConnectionString
);
      conn.Open();

      trans = conn.BeginTransaction();

      cmd = new SqlCommand();
      cmd.Connection = conn;
      cmd.Transaction = trans;

      // set the order details
      cmd.CommandText = "INSERT INTO Orders(MemberName, OrderDate, Name, Address,
County, PostCode, Country, SubTotal, Discount, Total) " +
"VALUES (@MemberName, @OrderDate, @Name, @Address, @County, @PostCode, @Country,
@SubTotal, @Discount, @Total)";
      cmd.Parameters.Add("@MemberName", SqlDbType.VarChar, 50);
      cmd.Parameters.Add("@OrderDate", SqlDbType.DateTime);
      cmd.Parameters.Add("@Name", SqlDbType.VarChar, 50);
      cmd.Parameters.Add("@Address", SqlDbType.VarChar, 255);
      cmd.Parameters.Add("@County", SqlDbType.VarChar, 50);
      cmd.Parameters.Add("@PostCode", SqlDbType.VarChar, 15);
      cmd.Parameters.Add("@Country", SqlDbType.VarChar, 50);
      cmd.Parameters.Add("@SubTotal", SqlDbType.Money);
      cmd.Parameters.Add("@Discount", SqlDbType.Money);
      cmd.Parameters.Add("@Total", SqlDbType.Money);

      cmd.Parameters["@MemberName"].Value = User.Identity.Name;
      cmd.Parameters["@OrderDate"].Value = DateTime.Now;
      cmd.Parameters["@Name"].Value =
((TextBox)Wizard1.FindControl("txtName")).Text;
      cmd.Parameters["@Address"].Value =
((TextBox)Wizard1.FindControl("txtAddress")).Text;
      cmd.Parameters["@County"].Value =
((TextBox)Wizard1.FindControl("txtCounty")).Text;
      cmd.Parameters["@PostCode"].Value =
((TextBox)Wizard1.FindControl("txtPostCode")).Text;
      cmd.Parameters["@Country"].Value =
((TextBox)Wizard1.FindControl("txtCountry")).Text;
      cmd.Parameters["@SubTotal"].Value = Profile.Cart.SubTotal;
      cmd.Parameters["@Discount"].Value = Profile.Cart.MemberDiscount;
      cmd.Parameters["@Total"].Value = Profile.Cart.Total;

      int OrderID = Convert.ToInt32(cmd.ExecuteScalar());

      // change the query and parameters for the order lines
      cmd.CommandText = "INSERT INTO OrderLines(OrderID, ProductID, Quantity,
Price) " +
```

```
        "VALUES (@OrderID, @ProductID, @Quantity, @Price)";
      cmd.Parameters.Clear();
      cmd.Parameters.Add("@OrderID", SqlDbType.Int);
      cmd.Parameters.Add("@ProductID", SqlDbType.Int);
      cmd.Parameters.Add("@Quantity", SqlDbType.Int);
      cmd.Parameters.Add("@Price", SqlDbType.Money);

      cmd.Parameters["@OrderID"].Value = OrderID;
      foreach (CartItem item in Profile.Cart.Items)
      {
          cmd.Parameters["@ProductID"].Value = item.ProductID;
          cmd.Parameters["@Quantity"].Value = item.Quantity;
          cmd.Parameters["@Price"].Value = item.Price;

          cmd.ExecuteNonQuery();
      }

      // commit the transaction
      trans.Commit();

    }
    catch (SqlException SqlEx)
    {
      // some form of error - rollback the transaction
      // and rethrow the exception
      if (trans != null)
          trans.Rollback();

      CreateOrderErrorLabel.Visible = true;

      // Log the exception
      // Tools.log("An error occurred while creating the order", SqlEx)
      throw new Exception("An error occurred while creating the order", SqlEx);
    }
    finally
    {
      if (conn != null)
        conn.Close();
    }

    // we will only reach here if the order has been created sucessfully
    // so clear the cart
    Profile.Cart.Items.Clear();
  }

  protected void Wizard1_NextButtonClick( object sender,
System.Web.UI.WebControls.WizardNavigationEventArgs e)
  {
    if (e.CurrentStepIndex == 0)
    {
      System.Web.UI.WebControls.Login l = (Login)Wizard1.FindControl("Login1");

      if (Membership.ValidateUser(l.UserName, l.Password))
      {
```

```
            FormsAuthentication.SetAuthCookie(l.UserName, l.RememberMeSet);
            e.Cancel = false;
        }
        else
        {
          l.InstructionText = "Your login attempt was not successful. Please try
again.";
          l.InstructionTextStyle.ForeColor = System.Drawing.Color.Red;

          e.Cancel = true;
        }
      }
      else
      {
        if (!User.Identity.IsAuthenticated)
        {
          e.Cancel = true;
          Wizard1.ActiveStepIndex = 0;
        }
      }
    }

    protected void Wizard1_ActiveStepChanged( object sender,  System.EventArgs e)
    {
      if (!User.Identity.IsAuthenticated)
          Wizard1.ActiveStepIndex = 0;
    }

}
```

18. Open `ShoppingCartPage.aspx` and in Design View, add a hyperlink to the page. Right-click the link and change the properties as shown in the following table.

Property	Value
`ID`	`Checkout`
`Text`	`Checkout`
`NavigateURL`	`~/Checkout.aspx`

19. Run Wroxshop.aspx, add two scarves to your shopping cart, and click Checkout. Supply login details in the fields shown in Figure 13-39.

20. Click Next after you're logged in, and then either click your membership address or supply your address details (see Figure 13-40).

21. Click Next, and you'll arrive at the screen shown in Figure 13-41. This is your credit card handler — it doesn't require any user details.

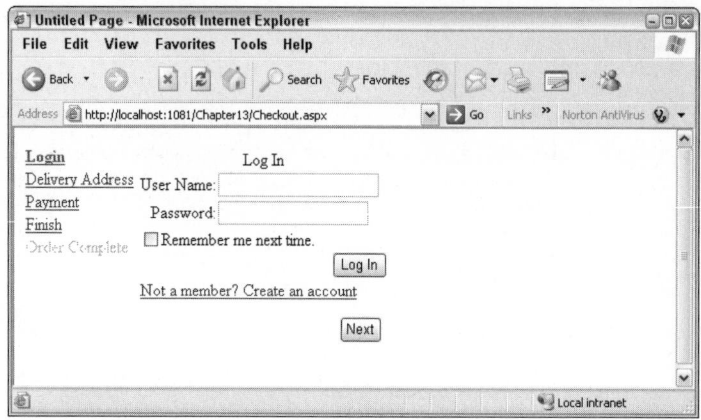

Figure 13-39

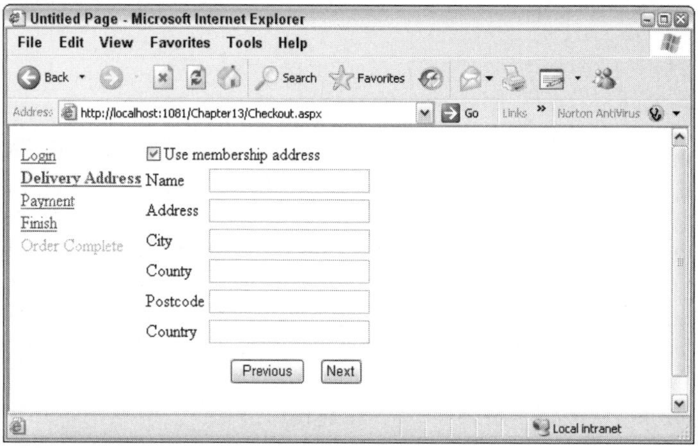

Figure 13-40

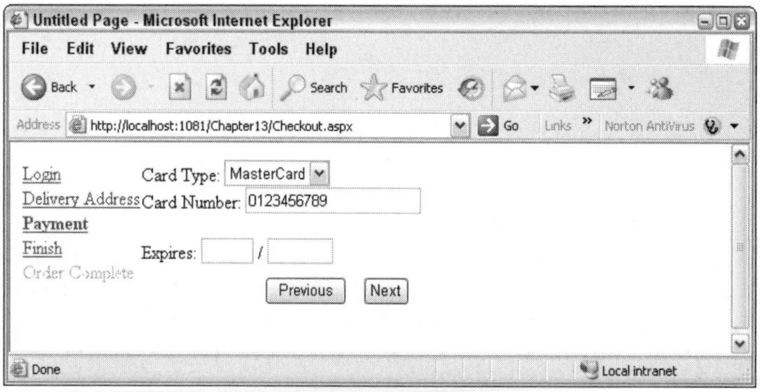

Figure 13-41

22. Click Next. On the last page (see Figure 13-42), you see a summary of the details.

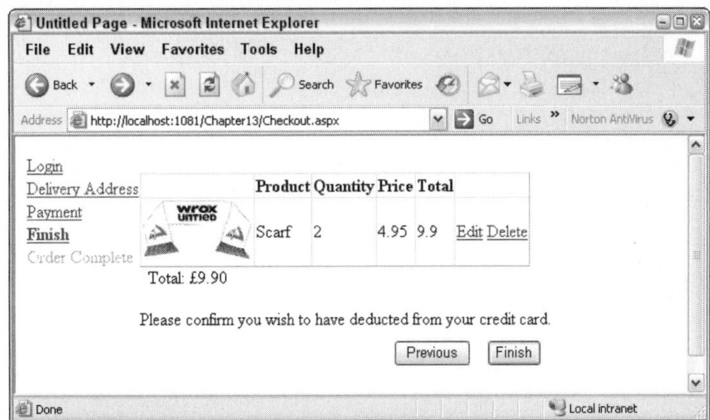

Figure 13-42

23. Click Finish to end the checkout.

How It Works

This completes your e-commerce pipeline. You started by creating the five stages of the checkout process using the `<asp:wizard>` control. The login stage used a `Login` control, and the delivery address used a check box and a series of text boxes to record the details. The payment stage took the credit card details via a drop-down list, which contained the type of credit card, and you had text boxes for the card number and expiration date. You didn't validate these details in any way. In the confirmation stage, you just inserted a copy of the shopping cart control, and the last step simply displayed a short thank you message.

You added a control `LoginView`, which contained your anonymous template:

```
<asp:LoginView ID="LoginView1" Runat="server">
    <AnonymousTemplate>
        <asp:passwordrecovery id="PasswordRecovery1" runat="server" />
    </AnonymousTemplate>
</asp:LoginView>
```

This displayed the password recovery control, which is displayed to aid any user who might have forgotten their password.

It was left to the code-behind to provide the meat of the example. When the page first loads, you check to see if there is anything in the cart. If there isn't, then you make the Wizard invisible and show the `nocartlabel`, which informs the user that there is nothing in the cart. The second check is to see if the user identity has been authenticated. This is a test of whether or not they have logged in. If they have logged in already, you jump them past the login stage, or else you have to get them logged in first:

```
void Page_Load(object sender, EventArgs e)
    {

    if (!Page.IsPostBack)
```

```
        {
          if (Profile.Cart == null)
           {
            NoCartlabel.Visible = true;
            Wizard1.Visible = false;
          }

          if (User.Identity.IsAuthenticated)
          {
            Wizard1.ActiveStepIndex = 1;
          }
          else
          {
            Wizard1.ActiveStepIndex = 0;
          }
        }

      }
```

The next procedure in the code is the code that responds to the check box being altered in Step 2, the delivery address. If this box is checked, you fill the text boxes with the details stored in the user's profile. Otherwise you leave them empty:

```
      protected void chkUseProfileAddress_CheckedChanged( object sender,
    System.EventArgs e)
        {
            // fill the delivery address from the profile, but only if it's empty
            // we don't want to overwrite the values
            if (chkUseProfileAddress.Checked && (txtName.Text.Trim() == ""))
            {
                txtName.Text = Profile.Name;
                txtAddress.Text = Profile.Address;
                txtCity.Text = Profile.City;
                txtCounty.Text = Profile.County;
                txtPostCode.Text = Profile.PostCode;
                txtCountry.Text = Profile.Country;
            }

        }
```

`NextButtonClick` is used to check whether the user has logged in successfully and can therefore progress to the next step of the Wizard. This step only comes into play if you are actually on the login stage at the time. You check to see if the user has been validated and, if not, you display an appropriate error message informing the user that they aren't able to log in this time. Otherwise you validate the user:

```
      protected void Wizard1_NextButtonClick( object sender,
    System.Web.UI.WebControls.WizardNavigationEventArgs e)
      {
        if (e.CurrentStepIndex == 0)
        {
          System.Web.UI.WebControls.Login l = (Login)Wizard1.FindControl("Login1");

          if (Membership.ValidateUser(l.UserName, l.Password))
          {
              FormsAuthentication.SetAuthCookie(l.UserName, l.RememberMeSet);
```

```
            e.Cancel = false;
          }
          else
          {
            l.InstructionText = "Your login attempt was not successful. Please try
again.";
            l.InstructionTextStyle.ForeColor = System.Drawing.Color.Red;

            e.Cancel = true;
          }
        }
        else
        {
          if (!User.Identity.IsAuthenticated)
          {
            e.Cancel = true;
            Wizard1.ActiveStepIndex = 0;
          }
        }
      }
```

`FinishButtonClick` contains perhaps the longest set of code, but it isn't as daunting as it looks. This is where you write the user's order to the database. You have to be able to roll this back if a mistake has occurred. You start by creating a connection string, and you create a transaction. Then you read in all of the details supplied in the checkout process into parameters. There are a lot of them! You have the member name, the delivery address, the credit card details, and the whole shopping cart total:

```
  protected void Wizard1_FinishButtonClick( object sender,
System.Web.UI.WebControls.WizardNavigationEventArgs e)
  {
    // Insert the order and order lines into the database
    SqlConnection conn = null;
    SqlTransaction trans = null;
    SqlCommand cmd;

    try
    {
      conn = new
SqlConnection(ConfigurationManager.ConnectionStrings["WroxUnited"].ConnectionString
);
      conn.Open();

      trans = conn.BeginTransaction();

      cmd = new SqlCommand();
      cmd.Connection = conn;
      cmd.Transaction = trans;

      // set the order details
      cmd.CommandText = "INSERT INTO Orders(MemberName, OrderDate, Name, Address,
County, PostCode, Country, SubTotal, Discount, Total) " +
"VALUES (@MemberName, @OrderDate, @Name, @Address, @County, @PostCode, @Country,
@SubTotal, @Discount, @Total)";
      cmd.Parameters.Add("@MemberName", SqlDbType.VarChar, 50);
      cmd.Parameters.Add("@OrderDate", SqlDbType.DateTime);
```

```
        cmd.Parameters.Add("@Name", SqlDbType.VarChar, 50);
        cmd.Parameters.Add("@Address", SqlDbType.VarChar, 255);
        cmd.Parameters.Add("@County", SqlDbType.VarChar, 50);
        cmd.Parameters.Add("@PostCode", SqlDbType.VarChar, 15);
        cmd.Parameters.Add("@Country", SqlDbType.VarChar, 50);
        cmd.Parameters.Add("@SubTotal", SqlDbType.Money);
        cmd.Parameters.Add("@Discount", SqlDbType.Money);
        cmd.Parameters.Add("@Total", SqlDbType.Money);

        cmd.Parameters["@MemberName"].Value = User.Identity.Name;
        cmd.Parameters["@OrderDate"].Value = DateTime.Now;
        cmd.Parameters["@Name"].Value =
  ((TextBox)Wizard1.FindControl("txtName")).Text;
        cmd.Parameters["@Address"].Value =
  ((TextBox)Wizard1.FindControl("txtAddress")).Text;
        cmd.Parameters["@County"].Value =
  ((TextBox)Wizard1.FindControl("txtCounty")).Text;
        cmd.Parameters["@PostCode"].Value =
  ((TextBox)Wizard1.FindControl("txtPostCode")).Text;
        cmd.Parameters["@Country"].Value =
  ((TextBox)Wizard1.FindControl("txtCountry")).Text;
        cmd.Parameters["@SubTotal"].Value = Profile.Cart.SubTotal;
        cmd.Parameters["@Discount"].Value = Profile.Cart.MemberDiscount;
        cmd.Parameters["@Total"].Value = Profile.Cart.Total;

        int OrderID = Convert.ToInt32(cmd.ExecuteScalar());
```

After you've written the data into the Orders table, you need to create an order in which you write into the OrderLines table. This contains an order ID, the product ID, the quantity, and the price. After this, you commit the transaction:

```
        // change the query and parameters for the order lines
        cmd.CommandText = "INSERT INTO OrderLines(OrderID, ProductID, Quantity,
  Price) " +
          "VALUES (@OrderID, @ProductID, @Quantity, @Price)";
        cmd.Parameters.Clear();
        cmd.Parameters.Add("@OrderID", SqlDbType.Int);
        cmd.Parameters.Add("@ProductID", SqlDbType.Int);
        cmd.Parameters.Add("@Quantity", SqlDbType.Int);
        cmd.Parameters.Add("@Price", SqlDbType.Money);

        cmd.Parameters["@OrderID"].Value = OrderID;
        foreach (CartItem item in Profile.Cart.Items)
        {
            cmd.Parameters["@ProductID"].Value = item.ProductID;
            cmd.Parameters["@Quantity"].Value = item.Quantity;
            cmd.Parameters["@Price"].Value = item.Price;

            cmd.ExecuteNonQuery();
        }

        // commit the transaction
```

```
    trans.Commit();

  }
```

The next part is the exception handler. If there is any kind of database error, you have to roll back the exception and write it to the error log. Exception handling is explained in more detail in Chapter 15. This code is specifically tailored to handle SQL errors and will cause an error in the application:

```
  catch (SqlException SqlEx)
  {
    // some form of error - rollback the transaction
    // and rethrow the exception
    if (trans != null)
        trans.Rollback();

    CreateOrderErrorLabel.Visible = true;

    // Log the exception
    // Tools.log("An error occurred while creating the order", SqlEx)
    throw new Exception("An error occurred while creating the order", SqlEx);
  }
```

Last, you close the connection and you clear the cart profile of the items if the transaction has been successful:

```
  finally
  {
    if (conn != null)
      conn.Close();
  }

  // we will only reach here if the order has been created sucessfully
  // so clear the cart
  Profile.Cart.Items.Clear();
```

There is also a failsafe step that checks to see if you have jumped in the Wizard. Normally this will be under the direction of the program — in other words, you check to see if the user has logged in and jump them forward one step. However, it's possible that an unscrupulous user might have jumped into this procedure halfway through, or that the procedure has accidentally "forgotten" the login details (normally caused by the session variable being lost — this might happen if ASP.NET restarts halfway through the Wizard). In this case, you check to see if the user has logged in, and if you have no record of them (in other words, they aren't authenticated), then you jump them back to the login dialog:

```
    protected void Wizard1_ActiveStepChanged( object sender,  System.EventArgs e)
    {
      if (!User.Identity.IsAuthenticated)
          Wizard1.ActiveStepIndex = 0;
    }
  }
```

The checkout process is a lengthy one, but it is the most essential part. If you get this wrong, you will never get any orders!

Secure Transactions

You might be forgiven for thinking that you're missing one vital part of the process. How do you ensure that your transaction isn't compromised and that credit card details aren't left wide open to the ether? Of course the nature of the HTTP protocol is exactly that, you send text across to the web server and you receive text back again. There's nothing to stop anybody out there from listening and recording your details.

Fortunately, there is a two-pronged attack with which you can ensure transactions are secure and that the credit card details and other confidential information are not compromised:

- **Encryption:** You must *encode*, or scramble, the information that is sent to the web server and received back from the web server. The web server has a public key, and users will have a private key that enables them to decode the information. Only having the public key and the private key together will allow you to encrypt the message. The web server will have a public key and its own private key at the other end. To encrypt messages, you use a secure communications protocol. Either Secure Sockets Layer (SSL) or Secure HTTP (S-HTTP) would provide this functionality. You can specify encryption methods and whether to use SSL on a connection in the `Web.config` file.
- **Certificates:** To guarantee that the site you are dealing with at the other end is reputable, it can be certified by a Certificate Authority. Verisign (`www.verisign.com`) is perhaps the most common Certificate Authority. The authority is paid a yearly fee by the e-commerce vendor and in return, the authority performs checks on the business to prove that it is legitimate. These checks are then recorded in the form of a certificate. You can browse particular sites' certificates during the checkout process. To make your site trustworthy, you should go about obtaining a certificate from a Certificate Authority.

You're not going to implement any of these features on the Wrox United site for reasons of practicality, but if you want to implement an e-commerce solution, you must make use of encryption and certificates.

What Else Can You Do?

Having gone this far in the chapter, you probably deserve a cup of tea and a sit down. However, while you're enjoying your well-earned brew, this would be a good time to get your thinking cap on and have a think about what else you could add to the shop. An e-commerce site is like a community and can continually evolve as your site evolves — you shouldn't think that you've done everything possible with it. The following list outlines some things to consider as your e-commerce site evolves:

- **Improving the product catalog:** You can show how many products are currently in stock, how long they will take to deliver, and the release date of a product. You can add customer reviews or testimonies to how wonderful or appalling the product is, and add a cross-linking reference that mentions which other items a customer bought when they purchased a particular item.
- **Improving membership tracking and personalization:** Add a member discount, record credit card details, and mail out special offers related to past purchases (so if a customer bought a replica kit in 2004, when the 2005 version comes out, it might be good to e-mail them).

- **Improving the shopping cart:** Make the shopping cart visible at all times.
- **Improving the checkout process:** Make the checkout process simpler so that it can be achieved in as few clicks as possible.

Summary

Hopefully this rather intense chapter hasn't scared you away. E-commerce is a lengthy and complex process — however, the new features of ASP.NET 2.0 make it approachable and possible to program for the first time without weeks of heartache and stress. Although e-commerce isn't something to be taken lightly, it is something that can be added to an application with a little bit of thought and careful work.

This chapter started by describing the e-commerce pipeline, which is outlined as follows:

- Select an item from the catalog
- Put the item in the shopping cart
- Check out with the item or items
- Supply address details
- Pay for the item
- Confirm the transaction

You started by creating a design for your product catalog and then you built a Catalog page. From the catalog you allowed the user to hone in on particular items, and you did this via a Product Item page. Neither of these items specifically required the use of the shopping cart, so you held off creating one. They just queried the database and displayed the relevant details. However, without these pages, you would not be able to shop effectively.

With a catalog working, you could add the cart. The cart consisted of two objects: the `CartItem` object (one for each item selected by the user from the catalog and the `ShoppingCart` object, (which contained a bundle of `CartItem` objects). To enable the shopping cart, you added `Insert`, `Update`, and `Delete` methods, which allowed you to put things into, change the amount of, and remove items from your shopping cart. Last, you connected the shopping cart to your catalog by creating an Add an Item button to your Product Item page.

Next you created a checkout process that handled the login, the confirmation of the delivery address, and the credit card details, and finished the procedure. Although you couldn't handle the card details with the application, you learned about the various options offered. Finally you learned how to make the transactions secure and some ways to extend and improve the e-commerce procedure in Wrox United.

Exercises

An e-commerce site could potentially offer many extra features. In these exercises, you're going to focus on just one. Some fan sites offer the capability for their members to purchase items at a reduced price, a membership discount. How would you go about implementing it? Each question is about a stage of the implementation and together they will give you this functionality.

1. The member discount is something that is applied to the shopping cart as you add items to the cart. What do you need to add to the `ShoppingCart` object to make sure it can store a discount of 10% for fan club members? You can assume that you can detect a fan club member with the property `HttpContext.Current.User.IsInRole("FanClubMember")`.

   Hint: You will need to create a subtotal as well.

2. How can you display the member discount details on the Shopping Cart page so that only a fan club member will see them?

Performance

Throughout the book you've learned a range of techniques to help you build web sites, and really concentrated on the possibilities regarding what controls and code you can use to produce great functionality for your site. One thing you haven't looked at, though, is how to make your site perform as well as it possibly can. After all, it doesn't matter how great your site looks — if it performs badly, it fails. Internet users are an impatient lot and expect sites to be fast.

Although performance should be addressed throughout the design and building of a site, this isn't always practical, especially for the beginner. So this chapter revisits some of the earlier pages to see how they can be improved, and discusses the techniques that can be used to create the best performing sites.

In particular, this chapter looks at the following:

- How to design and test for performance
- The techniques to use in ASP.NET pages and data handling to ensure the fastest possible pages
- What caching is and how it can be used

Let's start with the things you can do to either existing code or new code that you write.

Simple Techniques

Several simple things are easy to do and provide good performance, as well as being good design techniques and aiding future development work and maintenance. After all, writing applications isn't just about getting the best from them now, but also getting the best from them in the future.

Being able to fix and update web applications easily is just as much a part of development as producing the application in the first place. This section on simple techniques looks at the following:

- How to dispose of resources after they are no longer required
- How to ensure connecting to a database is done in the best possible way
- How using stored procedures can improve data access performance
- How to use generics to improve performance of collections
- How session state can be minimized to allow less processing to be done by ASP.NET
- How view state can be tuned to reduce the amount of data sent to and from the web server

This section starts with object disposal.

Object Disposal

In performance terms, certain things are expensive; that is, they can lead to performance problems. The reason for this is that objects need resources to manage them, resources such as CPU and memory. The fewer of these resources used, the less work the server is doing, which in turn leads to more pages for more users. If the use of these resources can be minimized, the site will perform better, and part of that minimization is to make sure you only use the resource for as little time as possible.

In general, objects that use expensive resources like the file system, graphics, or databases should be disposed of as soon as they are no longer needed. The only exception is database connections in ASP.NET applications, as discussed in the "Database Connections" section later in the chapter. Disposal of objects frees up resources, such as files and memory, allowing the web server to perform more efficiently. By default, resources are disposed of automatically by the Garbage Collector, but it is possible to improve performance by taking control of object disposal yourself, and you can do this in two ways. You can either use a standard pattern for creating the resource, using it, and then disposing of it, or you can use the `using` statement. This section looks at both methods, because you'll see both in documentation.

In the Wrox United site, one area where this is used is for images. Certain users have permission to upload images. Administrators can upload new images for the shop, the owner and coach can upload player pictures, and reporters and fan club members can upload match pictures. Part of this upload process involves creating a thumbnail image, which uses the `Image` object, something that should be disposed of as soon as it's no longer required. Disposal is necessary for two reasons. The first is because the image is a file-based resource, and the file may be required by other pages, so making sure you don't have any connection to it means it's available for others — the sooner you remove it, the sooner someone else can access it. The second reason for disposal is because images take memory, so disposing of the image means the memory is freed and available for other processes.

The routine for creating thumbnails is in the `ImageHandling.cs` file, in the `App_Code` directory, and is a simple class with a single shared method (actually, there are two methods, but one is only required as part of the image handling and isn't actually used).

The general structure of this code is to create a new `Image` object from an existing image stored on disc. Then a new `Image` object is created using the `GetThumbnailImage` method, which specifies the new width and height. It's pretty simple, but it involves two `Image` objects, so it requires two lots of disposal. The next section looks at how this routine works using the two ways of resource disposal.

Disposal with try/catch

To dispose using the `try/catch` methods you follow this simple pattern:

```
try
{
  // create resource
}
catch()
{
  // handle exception
}
finally
{
  // dispose of resource
}
```

Your image code using this pattern is as follows:

```
public static void GenerateThumbnail(string SourceImagePath,
                                     string TargetImagePath)
{
  short newHeight;
  short newWidth;
  Image sourceImage = null;
  Image targetImage = null;

  try
  {
    sourceImage = Image.FromFile(SourceImagePath);

    newHeight = short(sourceImage.Height * 0.25);
    newWidth = short(sourceImage.Width * 0.25);

    Image.GetThumbnailImageAbort abort1 = new
          Image.GetThumbnailImageAbort(ImageHandling.ThumbnailCallback);
    try
    {
      targetImage = sourceImage.GetThumbnailImage(newWidth, newHeight,
                                                  cb, IntPtr.Zero);
      targetImage.Save(TargetImagePath, Imaging.ImageFormat.Gif);
    }
    catch (Exception ex)
    {
      // log exception
    }
    finally
    {
      if (targetImage != null)
        targetImage.Dispose();
    }
  }
  catch (Exception ex)
  {
```

```
        // log exception
      }
      finally
      {
        if (sourceImage != null)
          sourceImage.Dispose();
      }
    }
```

You can immediately see this is a little hard to read. There are two `try/catch` blocks, one within the other. The outer one is for `sourceImage` — the original image. This is loaded from a file using `Image.FromFile`, and then the new width and height are calculated using the `Height` and `Width` properties of the source image — the new height and width are 25% of the original. After the new size is defined, a callback variable (`cb`) is created in case there is an error during the creation of the thumbnail — the `GetThumbnailImage` method will call the callback if an error occurs. We're not actually handling any errors because we decided that it isn't critical if thumbnails aren't generated. If you have an application where it is critical to know about these errors, you could log the error in the callback routine.

The inner `try/catch` block then surrounds `targetImage`, which is generated from `sourceImage` using `GetThumbnailImage` with the new width and height. This creates a new image based on the new size. After it is generated, `targetImage` is then saved to a file as a GIF image.

The `finally` blocks of each `try/catch` check that the `Image` object exists before disposing of the object, by calling the `Dispose` method.

Disposal with Using

The `using` statement makes the preceding code much simpler, as shown here:

```
public static void GenerateThumbnail(string SourceImagePath,
                                     string TargetImagePath)
{
  using (Image sourceImage = Image.FromFile(SourceImagePath))
  {
    short newHeight = (short) Math.Round((double)(sourceImage.Height * 0.25));
    short newWidth = (short) Math.Round((double)(sourceImage.Width * 0.25));
    Image.GetThumbnailImageAbort abort1 = new
          Image.GetThumbnailImageAbort(ImageHandling.ThumbnailCallback);
    using (Image targetImage = sourceiMage.GetThumbnailImage(newWidth, newHeight,
                                           abort1, IntPtr.Zero))
    {
      targetImage.Save(TargetImagePath, ImageFormat.Gif);
    }
  }
}
```

You can immediately see how much easier this is to read, as well as how much more sense it makes. The `using` statement created the resource, which is then automatically disposed of when the trailing brace (`}`) of the code block is reached. The syntax for the `using` statement is as follows:

```
using (resource)
{
  // code that uses the resource
}
```

What happens is that when the trailing brace (}) is reached, the resource is disposed of immediately—there's no waiting for the Garbage Collector to dispose of it. In the code you have the following:

```
using (Image sourceImage = Image.FromFile(SourceImagePath))
```

This is similar to declaring variables, in that it declares a variable, `sourceImage`, and assigns it a value. Unlike variable declaration though, the variable is disposed of as soon as the trailing brace is reached. So as soon as the trailing brace is done, the `sourceImage` variable is gone. In fact, because its scope is defined as part of the `using` statement, `sourceImage` isn't accessible outside of the `using` code block.

You only need to explicitly dispose of resources if they are deemed expensive resources, such as files (images, text files, and so forth) or graphics resources that use lots of memory. Normal variables and objects, even those you might think take a lot of memory such as a `DataSet`, should not be disposed of explicitly.

Database Connections

Fetching data from a database can be done automatically by way of the data source controls, or manually though the objects in the `System.Data` namespaces. One of these objects applies to connecting to a database—for SQL Server or SQL Server Express, that object is the `SqlConnection`. In general, databases are limited to the number of connections they can have. Each connection takes resources and may stop another application from connecting, so these should be used as sparingly as possible, and only kept open for as short a time as possible. The general rule is to open the connection as late as possible, fetch the data, and close the connection as soon as possible, disposing of the connection once done. The `Using` statement is excellent for this:

```
using (SqlConnection conn = new SqlConnection(". . ."))
{
  // code that uses the connection
}
```

Here the `using` statement keeps track of the connection object, `conn`, which is closed and disposed of when the trailing brace is reached.

In general, if you are manually creating connections, you should dispose of them as soon as you are finished. If you are using the data source controls, object disposal is handled automatically for you.

Stored Procedures

In the examples you've seen so far in this book, the data has been fetched either using a data source control such as the `SqlDataSource` or using code, where a `SqlCommand` or `SqlDataAdapter` were used. In all cases, the command that fetched the data, the SQL, was entered directly, such as:

```
SELECT [ProductID], [Name], [Description], [Price], [PictureURL] FROM [Products]
```

Now there's nothing intrinsically wrong with this—it's a standard SQL statement that works fine. However, it's not the fastest way to fetch data, because the database has to work out exactly how it is going to fetch the data when the command is executed. This involves creating what's known as an execution plan—a plan of how the SQL is going to be executed, how tables are to be joined if there are multiple tables, which indexes to use, and so on, and it does this every time. After the plan has been created, the stored procedure is also compiled and the compiled copy is the one that is executed.

A much better solution would be to work out the execution plan and store it for subsequent use. So when a query is executed, the plan is ready and doesn't need recalculating. You can do this by way of *stored procedures*, which are a way of wrapping up SQL into an easily manageable form. It's a bit like a procedure or a function in that the SQL to be executed can be wrapped in a stored procedure and the stored procedure name used to execute it. Consider this `SqlDataSource`:

```
<asp:SqlDataSource id="SqlDataSource1" runat="server"
  ConnectionString="<%$ConnectionStrings:WroxUnited%>"
  SelectedCommand="SELECT [ProductID], [Name], [Description], [Price], [PictureURL]
FROM [Products]"
</asp:SqlDataSource>
```

Using a stored procedure, the code would look like this:

```
<asp:SqlDataSource id="SqlDataSource1" runat="server"
  ConnectionString="<%$ConnectionStrings:WroxUnited%>"
  SelectedCommand="usp_Products"
  SelectCommandType="StoredProcedure"
</asp:SqlDataSource>
```

From the code perspective, this is already better for two reasons: it makes the code neater and easier to read; and it abstracts the SQL into a central place, the database. Having the SQL in the database is good because it's the natural place for it — it's code that deals directly with the tables and columns. It also means your code is easier to manage because you know that all of the SQL is in one place. A sensible naming scheme means stored procedures are easy to locate — we've used the naming scheme of `usp_` followed by the name of the table. The prefix `usp_` is a common one and denotes User Stored Procedure — many of system stored procedures that SQL Server provide are prefixed by `sp_`, so adding the `u` makes it obvious which procedures are ours and which are the server's. The other addition when using stored procedures is the `SelectCommandType` attribute, which tells the `SqlDataSource` that the command being issued is a stored procedure, rather than a textual SQL statement.

The syntax for creating a stored procedure is as follows:

```
CREATE PROCEDURE ProcedureName
AS
  SqlStatement
```

`ProcedureName` is the name of the procedure (`usp_Products`) and `SqlStatement` is the SQL statement that will be run when the stored procedure is called. So, how do you actually go about creating stored procedures, and what exactly do they contain? You give this a go in the following Try It Out.

Try It Out   Creating and Using Stored Procedures

1. In the WroxUnited VWD application for this chapter (`Chapters/Begin/Chapter14/WroxUnited`), load the `Shop.aspx` file and change the `SelectCommand` to **usp_Products**.

2. Add the following new attribute to the `SqlDataSource`:

```
SelectCommandType="StoredProcedure"
```

3. Save the file.
4. Select the Database Explorer tab and expand `WroxUnited.mdf`, which will appear under Data Connections (see Figure 14-1).

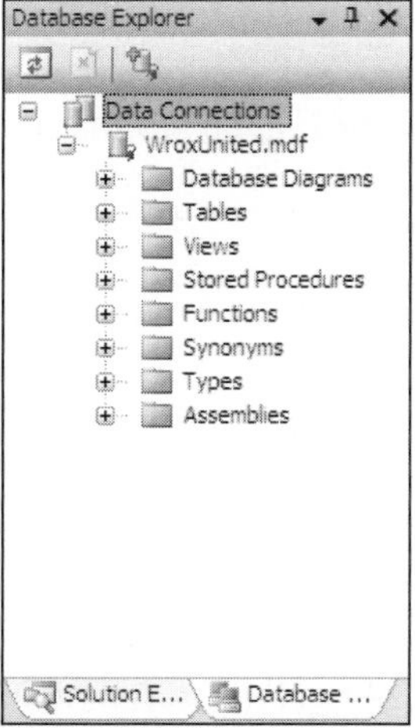

Figure 14-1

5. Right-click Stored Procedures and select Add New Stored Procedure from the menu.
6. Modify the procedure so that it looks like this:

```
CREATE PROCEDURE dbo.usp_Products
AS
  SELECT ProductID, [Name], Description, Price, PictureURL
  FROM Products
  ORDER BY [Name]
```

7. Save and close the procedure.
8. Right-click `WroxUnited.mdf` and select Close Connection from the menu. This ensures that when you run the application, you don't receive an error telling you that the data file couldn't be opened because it is in use by another process.
9. On the Wrox United web site, navigate to the Shop page to confirm that the page displays as you expect it to. You'll see no change from the user perspective, because stored procedures are a programming concept, and apart from speed, have no impact on what the user sees.

How It Works

The first thing to look at is the stored procedure itself:

```
CREATE PROCEDURE dbo.usp_Products
AS
```

```
SELECT ProductID, [Name], Description, Price, PictureURL
FROM Products
ORDER BY [Name]
```

So you can see that the name of your stored procedure is `usp_Products`. The `dbo` part indicates the owner of the procedure, and in this case the owner is `dbo` — a synonym for the database owner. Anything after the `AS` statement is the actual procedure itself, and yours simply consists of a `SELECT` statement. In fact, this is the same `SELECT` statement that was generated by VWD when the `SqlDataSource` was created, with the addition of an `ORDER BY` clause to order the results by the product name. This is a good way to combine the ease of data source controls with stored procedures — let the designer create the control, and then copy the SQL statement into a stored procedure and use the procedure name in the data source control. The column `Name` is wrapped within square brackets because `Name` is a keyword within SQL. The stored procedure works without the brackets, but using them tells SQL Server that this use of `Name` is a column, and saves SQL Server having to work that out on its own.

The procedure name starts with `usp_` for usability and historic reasons. You don't want your stored procedure to have the same name as the table, but keeping the table name is useful, because it helps to identify which stored procedures are related to which tables. In SQL Server, the system-stored procedures start with `sp_` (an acronym for stored procedure), so using that as a prefix would confuse your stored procedures with the system ones. So `usp_` (an acronym for user stored procedure) is generally used instead. This isn't a requirement, but you'll find that it is a common practice.

SQL is both case and context insensitive, meaning no line continuation characters are required.

In the ASP.NET page, the SQL statement has been replaced by the name of the stored procedure. By default, the `SqlDataSource` control expects a SQL statement, so when using a stored procedure, you have to add the `SelectCommandType` attribute, setting its value to `StoredProcedure`. This tells ASP.NET that the command isn't a SQL statement to be executed, but that the named stored procedure should be used instead.

Modifying Stored Procedures

To modify a stored procedure, you open it (double-click or right-click and select Open from the menu) from within the Database Explorer, where you will be presented with the following:

```
ALTER PROCEDURE dbo.usp_Products
AS
  SELECT ProductID, Name, Description, Price, PictureURL
  FROM Products
  ORDER BY Name
```

Notice that `CREATE PROCEDURE` has been replaced with `ALTER PROCEDURE`. The `CREATE` statement is only used when creating stored procedures, and subsequently `ALTER` is used. After you've completed your changes, perhaps changing the columns being selected, you can just save the file, and the procedure in the database will be updated. In fact, just the matter of saving a new query changes `CREATE` to `ALTER`.

Stored Procedure Names

In addition to using the `usp_` prefix, you may want to use a consistent naming scheme for your stored procedures. For example, a procedure that returns all rows from a table could simply have the prefix plus the table name, or perhaps be `GetTableName`, `usp_Products` or `usp_GetProducts`. For a procedure that returns on a single row, the single form would work well: `usp_GetProduct`, or `usp_GetProductByID`. Stored procedures that modify data should include the modification type: `usp_InsertProduct` or `usp_UpdateProduct`. Alternatively, place the table name before the action: `usp_ProductInsert`, `usp_ProductUpdate`, or `usp_ProductGet`. This latter scheme means that all procedures related to the same table will show together in the procedure list, while the former scheme means that procedures are grouped by their action. There's no single way of doing this, and it's really just a matter of preference, but pick one scheme and stick to it, so that you can find procedures easily.

Using the Query Builder

If you don't want to use the copy-and-paste method for creating SQL statements, you can use the Query Builder. You can access this when creating or modifying a stored procedure by selecting the Insert SQL item from the right mouse menu—just right-click anywhere in the stored procedure editor window to get the menu. You first see a window where you select the table (see Figure 14-2).

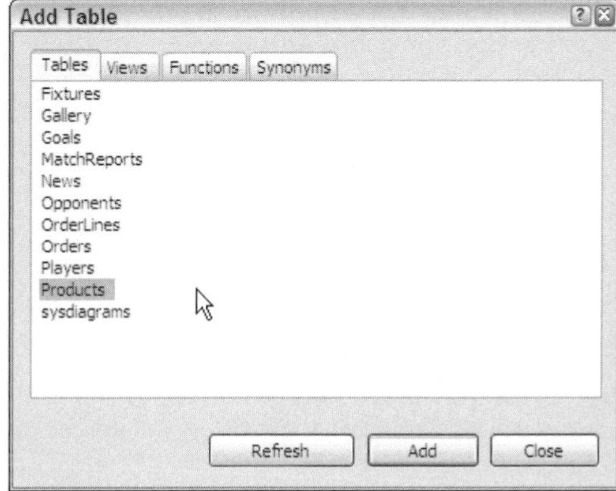

Figure 14-2

You can double-click a table to add it, or select the table and use the Add button. When you have selected your table and closed the window, you see the Query Builder, shown in Figure 14-3.

The Query Builder is an excellent way of learning SQL, because it presents you with an easy-to-understand graphical way of designing queries, and shows the actual SQL statement. When the Query Builder is closed, the SQL is inserted into the stored procedure. It doesn't update the existing SQL but inserts the new SQL instead.

If you want to use the Query Builder to edit the existing SQL in a stored procedure, you need to place the cursor within the SQL block when editing the procedure—this block is outlined in blue—and select the Design SQL Block from the right mouse menu. When you select this option, the Query Builder comes up right away with the existing SQL in place.

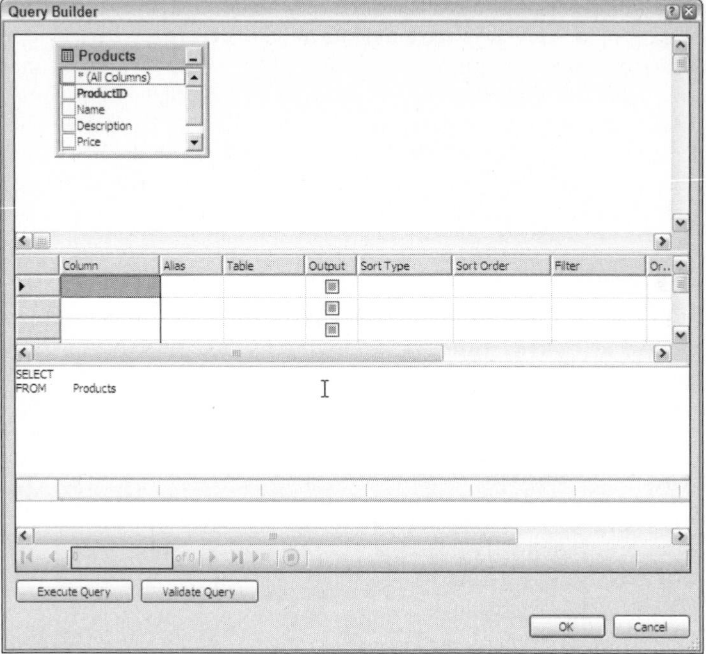

Figure 14-3

Modifying Data and Parameters

The query and stored procedure shown earlier only fetch data, but three other types of queries can be run: updates, inserts, and deletes. Just like `SELECT` queries, these update queries can also be converted into stored procedures. As an example, take a look at the administrative Edit News page, where the second `SqlDataSource` is defined like so:

```
<asp:sqldatasource id="SqlDataSource2" runat="server"
  ConnectionString="<%$ ConnectionStrings:WroxUnited %>"
  SelectCommand="SELECT * FROM [News] WHERE [NewsID] = @NewsID"
  UpdateCommand="UPDATE [News] SET [DateToShow] = @DateToShow, [Description] =
@Description, [PictureURL] = @PictureURL, [Category] = @Category, [Title] = @Title
WHERE [NewsID] = @NewsID"
  InsertCommand="INSERT INTO [News] ([DateToShow], [Description], [PictureURL],
[Category], [Title]) VALUES (@DateToShow, @Description, @PictureURL, @Category,
@Title)"
  DeleteCommand="DELETE FROM [News] WHERE [NewsID] = @NewsID"
  OnDeleted="SqlDataSource2_Deleted"
  OnInserted="SqlDataSource2_Inserted"
  OnUpdated="SqlDataSource2_Updated">
```

The important parts are the `SelectCommand`, `UpdateCommand`, `InsertCommand`, and `DeleteCommand` attributes, which define the SQL used when fetching and modifying data. There are also a number of parameters, which provide the mapping from the ASP.NET controls to the queries:

```
<DeleteParameters>
  <asp:Parameter Type="Int32" Name="NewsID"></asp:Parameter>
</DeleteParameters>
<UpdateParameters>
  <asp:Parameter Type="DateTime" Name="DateToShow"></asp:Parameter>
  <asp:Parameter Type="String" Name="Description"></asp:Parameter>
  <asp:Parameter Type="String" Name="PictureURL"></asp:Parameter>
  <asp:Parameter Type="String" Name="Category"></asp:Parameter>
  <asp:Parameter Type="String" Name="Title"></asp:Parameter>
  <asp:Parameter Type="Int32" Name="NewsID"></asp:Parameter>
</UpdateParameters>
<SelectParameters>
  <asp:ControlParameter Name="NewsID" Type="Int32" ControlID="GridView1"
PropertyName="SelectedValue"></asp:ControlParameter>
</SelectParameters>
<InsertParameters>
  <asp:Parameter Type="DateTime" Name="DateToShow"></asp:Parameter>
  <asp:Parameter Type="String" Name="Description"></asp:Parameter>
  <asp:Parameter Type="String" Name="PictureURL"></asp:Parameter>
  <asp:Parameter Type="String" Name="Category"></asp:Parameter>
  <asp:Parameter Type="String" Name="Title"></asp:Parameter>
</InsertParameters>
```

When you're converting these queries to stored procedures, the parameters can remain the same, because the stored procedures will still require information to be passed into them. So in the next Try It Out, you convert this page and see how the parameters and other queries work.

Try It Out Modifying Data and Parameters

1. Open the `Admin\EditNews.aspx` page and find the `SqlDataSource2` control.
2. In the Database Explorer, expand the `WroxUnited.mdf` file and add a new stored procedure (select the Stored Procedures item in the Database Explorer and from the right mouse menu select Add New Stored Procedure).
3. Delete the existing contents of the new stored procedure and replace them with the following:

```
CREATE PROCEDURE dbo.usp_NewsByID
  @NewsID int
AS
  SELECT * FROM News
  WHERE NewsID = @NewsID
```

   You can copy and paste the SQL from `EditNews.aspx` if you like. If copying the SQL, you don't have to worry about the square brackets — these were placed around column names when the data source control was created and ensure that the column names are not interpreted as keywords. Because none of the columns in this procedure are the same as keywords, it doesn't matter if you have the square brackets or not.

4. Save and close the procedure.

5. Create another new procedure, replacing the default text with the following code:

```
CREATE PROCEDURE dbo.usp_NewsUpdate
  @DateToShow datetime,
  @Description text,
  @PictureUrl varchar(50),
  @Category varchar(50),
  @Title varchar(50),
  @NewsID int
AS
  UPDATE News
  SET DateToShow = @DateToShow, Description = @Description,
      PictureUrl = @PictureUrl, Category = @Category,
      Title = @Title
  WHERE NewsID = @NewsID
```

6. Save and close the procedure.
7. Create another new procedure, replacing the default text with the following code:

```
CREATE PROCEDURE dbo.usp_NewsInsert
  @DateToShow datetime,
  @Description text,
  @PictureUrl varchar(50),
  @Category varchar(50),
  @Title varchar(50)
AS
  INSERT INTO News(DateToShow, Description, PictureUrl, Category, Title)
  VALUES (@DateToShow, @Description, @PictureUrl, @Category, @Title)
```

8. Save and close the procedure.
9. Create another new procedure, replacing the default text with the following:

```
CREATE PROCEDURE dbo.usp_NewsDelete
  @NewsID int
AS
  DELETE FROM News
  WHERE NewsID = @NewsID
```

10. Save and close the procedure.
11. In the Database Explorer, close the database connection by right-clicking `WroxUnited.mdf` and selecting the Close Connection menu item.
12. In `EditNews.aspx` change the SQL commands to their appropriate stored procedures, using the following table as a guide.

Command	Stored Procedure
SelectCommand	usp_NewsByID
UpdateCommand	usp_NewsUpdate
InsertCommand	usp_NewsInsert
DeleteCommand	usp_NewsDelete

13. Add the following attributes to SqlDataSource2:

```
SelectCommandType="StoredProcedure"
UpdateCommandType="StoredProcedure"
InsertCommandType="StoredProcedure"
DeleteCommandType="StoredProcedure"
```

14. Save the page and run the application to prove that the page still works as expected. (like the previous example, you won't see anything different when running the application). To edit the news items, you'll have to be a user in one of the following roles: Reporter, Owner, Manager, or Admin. You can find out login details by using the "help" link on the login box when not logged in to the site, but you can use dave, dan, jim, chrish, chrisu, or john.

How It Works

From the first example you can see that the SQL statements in the data source control have been replaced by names of stored procedures, and the appropriate CommandType attributes are set to indicate this. The stored procedures are different from the one used in the first example, though, so take a look at some of the specifics, starting with the one to fetch a row to be edited:

```
CREATE PROCEDURE dbo.usp_NewsByID
  @NewsID int
AS
  SELECT * FROM News
  WHERE NewsID = @NewsID
```

The first thing to notice is that there is an extra line between the CREATE PROCEDURE and the AS statement. This is where parameters are placed and is very similar to parameters for methods, as discussed in Chapter 9. In this case, you have a parameter called @NewsID, whose data type is an int (an integer). Parameters in SQL are always preceded by the at symbol (@). The value for this parameter is supplied in the same way as if this SelectCommand were a SQL statement, by the SelectParameters:

```
<SelectParameters>
  <asp:ControlParameter Name="NewsID" Type="Int32"
    Control="GridView1" PropertyName="SelectedValue"></asp:ControlParameter>
</SelectParameters>
```

The value of the Name attribute is passed through into the @NewsID parameter of the stored procedure. Within the procedure, the parameter is used to restrict the rows returned, so only rows where the NewsID matches the value of the @NewsID parameter are returned.

The same technique applies for the other stored procedures. For example, to update a news story, the following stored procedure is used:

```
CREATE PROCEDURE dbo.usp_NewsUpdate
  @DateToShow datetime,
  @Description text,
  @PictureUrl varchar(50),
  @Category varchar(50),
  @Title varchar(50),
  @NewsID int
AS
```

```
UPDATE News
SET DateToShow = @DateToShow, Description = @Description,
    PictureUrl = @PictureUrl, Category = @Category,
    Title = @Title
WHERE NewsID = @NewsID
```

There are more parameters here, each separated by a comma. The data types are also slightly different from what you might expect, because SQL handles strings differently from .NET. For example, the `Description` and `PictureUrl` are both a `String` type in .NET, but there are two data types used in SQL. This is because SQL allows for strings of a fixed maximum length (in which case the `varchar` data type is used with the maximum in parentheses) or for unlimited strings (in which case the `text` data type is used). `varchar` only defines the maximum length for the string, and doesn't necessarily store that much data. For example, `PictureUrl` is declared as `varchar(50)`, but if the `PictureUrl` only contains 10 characters, then only 10 characters are stored. There is another data type for handling strings, `char`, which does store all characters. So if `PictureUrl` was declared as `char(50)` and only 10 were used, what is stored is the actual string followed by 40 spaces. Those spaces would be automatically added when the string was inserted into the database and would remain when the data is fetched, which means you might have to truncate your data when displaying it. Unless you are storing a string that you know is fixed (three-character currency codes for example), then a `varchar` data type is best.

We don't have time to go into more detail on the SQL itself, because it's really outside the scope of what we cover in this book. The important thing to remember is that using stored procedures improves performance as well as centralizing data access statements.

For more on SQL, get a copy of *Beginning SQL*, by Paul Wilton and John Colby, and for more on database access in ASP.NET, see *Beginning ASP.NET 2.0 Databases* by John Kauffman. Both books are by Wrox Press.

Strongly Typed Collections

Chapter 9 briefly mentioned generics as a way to improve code in a number of areas: readability, reducing errors, and performance. We're not going to go into much detail about generics — it's a wide topic — but it does have an impact on performance, especially in regard to collections. So it's worth reiterating the differences between a normal collection and a generic one. Take the standard `ArrayList` as an example, which can be used like this:

```
using System.Collections;

ArrayList myList = new ArrayList();
myList.Add("abc");
myList.Add("def");

String s = (string)myList[0];
```

Now there's nothing wrong with this code — it works fine and is probably used in lots of web sites, but it's not the most efficient way to store a list of strings. This is because the `ArrayList` stores objects, so when a string is placed into the list, it is converted to an `object` data type. Likewise, when you're fetching data from the list, it needs to be converted back to its native type. This conversion between types is an overhead.

With a generic collection, the overhead is avoided because the collection is automatically of the correct type. Instead of an `ArrayList`, a generic `List` can be used:

```
using System.Collections.Generic;

List<string> myList = new List<string>;
myList.Add("abc");
myList.Add("def");

string s = myList[0];
```

When declaring the `List`, you set the type of object it contains within angle brackets — in this case `string`. When objects are added to the list, they don't need to be converted because the list is only storing strings. Similarly, no conversion is required when you're reading a value from the list. As a result, there's a performance improvement when adding data and fetching it.

The added benefit of generic collections is that you can't store anything other than the defined type in them. This reduces potential error situations, because attempted storage of the wrong data type will result in a compiler error.

Session State

Chapter 6 explained the stateless nature of web sites, and that without programming they forget information between requests. The ASP.NET controls retain information about their state, and the Profile retains information about a user, but there is no storage of data about a session, unless this is coded into the application. The session can be described as the time spent browsing a site, from the moment you first start browsing to the moment you close your browser. That's an important point, because once the browser closes the session ends — if you start browsing after closing the browser, you have a new session.

In previous versions of ASP.NET, many things that are now part of the framework had to be coded, and the session was often used for temporary storage of items such as user details, shopping carts, and so on. With the Profile storing user preferences and the Membership services storing user details, the need for session storage has been reduced. Membership is covered in Chapter 4, and the Profile is covered in Chapter 11, so refer to those chapters for details of what is stored.

This is important to know because session state takes resources, both the processor and memory, and if it's not required then why have it there? By default, the session is enabled for read and write access, but this can be disabled if your application is never going to use session state. You can do this in the application configuration file (`Web.config`), by using the `sessionState` element:

```
<sessionState mode="Off" />
```

This turns off session state, which will save valuable resources.

If session state is required, but none of the pages need to update it, then it can be made read-only (or turned off for pages) by changing the `enableSessionState` attribute of the `pages` element in `Web.config`:

```
<pages enableSessionState="ReadOnly" />
```

The values can be `False` to turn off session state, `True` to enable it, and `ReadOnly` to make it read-only. The `ReadOnly` property can also be applied to the `Page` directive on individual pages as follows:

```
<%@ Page enableSessionState="ReadOnly" %>
```

It should be noted that for low-user sites, turning off session state probably won't make much difference, but it could have an impact on a high-performance site with a large number of active users. You should also make sure that developers know that session state is turned off for a site, otherwise they may try to code for it when it isn't available.

View State

The way ASP.NET server controls retain their state is a great boon for the programmer and makes construction of web sites far easier than it used to be. The retention of state is called the *view state* and is stored within a hidden control on the page, so no extra programming is needed. This does, however, come with a downside, and that downside is that the size of the page increases, which in turn leads to a slower-loading page. The advantages of view state outweigh the disadvantages, but it's useful to understand how it works. Take a look at the Wrox United home page, which contains many controls. There are some links at the top, a menu and the login and shopping cart on the left, and then the main content, which consists of the news. All of these are handled by controls, and only the central content is specific to the individual page — the rest is supplied by the Master page, and therefore appears on every page.

This is important from the performance perspective because the view state for the menu is 2780 bytes. That might not seem like a lot, but it's sent on every page request and returned on every postback. Plus that's just the menu control; others have view state too. Essentially any control that participates in postback will probably have view state and thus the more controls, the more view state.

Like session state, view state can also be disabled, both at the page and control level, using the `EnableViewState` attribute. To enable this for all controls on a page (or the Master page) you modify the `Page` directive as follows:

```
<%@ Page EnableViewState="False" %>
```

For controls, the attribute is the same. For example, the menu control in `site.master` could have view state disabled like so:

```
<asp:Menu id="MyMenu" runat="server"
  EnableViewState="False" />
```

The menu continues to work as before, but now it has no view state so the page has more than 2000 bytes less to transmit every time. This technique can be applied to other controls, especially those such as grids or lists. One case is the Players page (`players.aspx`), which uses a `DataList` to show the player details, and has no interaction. Turning off view state for this control reduces the page size by another 2700 bytes.

In fact, many of the controls don't actually need view state, and those that interact with the page might be able to have view state disabled. This is different from previous versions of ASP.NET where disabling view state stopped some controls from working. View state can be disabled for the entire application in a similar way to session state, by modifying the `pages` element in the `Web.config` file:

```
<pages enableViewState="false" />
```

If this was done, you could then turn on view state for those controls that need it.

Later in the chapter, you'll look at how you can find out how large controls are and how much view state they store. But first, the next section looks at how you can use code to improve performance.

Pages and Code

Many techniques can be used in code to help with performance, from a simple use of framework classes to a properly architected application. Some techniques will only come from experience, some will only be relevant to certain applications, and some are things you should generally know.

One thing you should know is the .NET Framework class library. You don't have to know it inside out, nor remember all of the classes, but it's a good idea to familiarize yourself with the classes and namespaces. It's definitely worthwhile spending some time just browsing through the reference documentation, getting a feeling for what's possible. For example, many string handling routines are built right into the `String` object, and there are data type conversion classes, collections for storing multiple copies of objects, and so on.

Data Binding and Postback

If you aren't using data source controls for your data binding, one thing you should make sure you do is to only bind when you need to. Data binding involves fetching the data from the database (and as previously mentioned, data access is expensive) and binding each row and column from the data to the rows and columns in a control. There's no point doing all of that data access and binding unless it's absolutely necessary. For example, consider the following code:

```
protected void Page_Load(object Sender, EventArgs e)
{
  GridView1.DataSource = SomeCollection;
  GridView1.DataBind();
}
```

This simply binds a `GridView` control to a collection of data (the data is irrelevant for this discussion), but remember that if the page has buttons that post back, then the `Page_Load` event is run every time, so the data is bound every time. If the grid isn't going to change, and it retains its state, why rebind it? Using the `IsPostBack` property can avoid this:

```
protected void Page_Load(object Sender, EventArgs e)
{
  if (!Page.IsPostBack)
  {
    GridView1.DataSource = SomeCollection;
    GridView1.DataBind();
  }
}
```

Now the grid is only bound the first time the page is loaded. This may seem like an obvious point, but you'd be surprised how easy it is to forget. Remember that database access is relatively expensive—it consumes both time and resources.

If you are updating data and you do need to rebind the grid after a postback, you can bind in the button event as well, after the data has been changed. What you don't want to do is bind the grid in when the page loads, update the data, and then rebind the grid again.

Object References

One standard performance optimization is the use of references to objects or items in collections. For example, imagine you are processing some user input, perhaps a name, entered into the text box with an ID of NameTextBox. You have to work with the entered name in several places in some code, so you do this:

```
ValidateName(NameTextBox.Text);
UpdateDatabase(NameTextBox.Text);
DisplayName(NameTextBox.Text);
```

You can see that the `Text` property of the name is referenced three times. What happens if you realize the user could have entered leading and trailing spaces, but that your routines need these stripped off? You might be tempted to just trim the spaces each time, like so:

```
ValidateName(NameTextBox.Text.Trim());
UpdateDatabase(NameTextBox.Text.Trim());
DisplayName(NameTextBox.Text.Trim());
```

A much better solution is to only reference the name once, storing the value in a local variable as follows:

```
string Name = NameTextBox.Text.Trim();

ValidateName(Name);
UpdateDatabase(Name);
DisplayName(Name);
```

Not only is this easier to read, but it's also more efficient—you're performing the `Trim` once, and only referencing the `Text` property once.

In general, this technique should be used wherever you reference objects properties, or call methods, several times. There's probably very little performance improvement for referencing a `Text` property a few times, but it does sometimes aid readability, and it would certainly improve performance in a high-volume site. Consider the search box on Amazon—how many times a day does that get used?

StringBuilder Versus String Concatenation

Joining strings is a common occurrence and the technique most people use is *concatenation*, like so:

```
string FirstName = "Bill";
string LastName = "Barker";
string FullName = FirstName + " " + LastName;
```

Here the plus sign (+) is used to join strings. The `FullName` is created from the `FirstName`, a space, and then the `LastName`. With just these three strings, trying to improve performance probably isn't worthwhile, but when more strings are added, there is a significant overhead. The reason is that strings are immutable, which means that after they are created, they can never be changed. For example, consider creating a mail message to send to new members of the Wrox United fan club:

```
string Message = "Dear " + MemberName +
  ". Welcome to the Wrox United Fan Club. As a member you'll" +
  " receive regular newsletters to keep you up-to-date with the" +
  " activities of the club, special discounts in the club store," +
  " advance notice of special events, and many more exciting freebies.";

EmailMessage.Body = Message;
```

This is fine as it stands because most of this is literal strings — that is, text within quotation marks. When literal strings are concatenated, the compiler will join them so there is no overhead. But what if the strings are user-supplied? For example, you might have the following code, where the strings are taken from a Web Form:

```
string Address = AddressLine1.Text + AddressLine2 + AddressLine3 +
AddressLine4.Text + AddressLine5.Text;
```

This also is fine, and despite what you might read elsewhere, this is still very efficient because the compiler knows how many strings there are and can optimize the code for you. We've mentioned these two scenarios because certain books and articles explicitly state that this code is very inefficient — ignore them, because the code is fine. Where you might have a performance problem is when the number of strings is large (more than 10) or unknown. For example, imagine a string being built from some rows in a database (returned as a `SqlDataReader`, `rdr`), where you might have the following code:

```
string str;
while (rdr.Read())
  str += rdr.GetString(0);

return str;
```

This loops while the reader has some data and appends the data from column `0` to the string variable `str`. As it stands, this is very inefficient because the compiler doesn't know how many strings there will be, so it cannot perform any optimization. Although this looks innocuous, you have to remember that strings are immutable, so after they are created, they are never changed. The preceding code, therefore, doesn't really append one string to another — it actually creates a new string made up from the two being appended. This new string is then assigned to `str`, and this happens each time through the loop. To improve performance, the `StringBuilder` class can be used, which is in the `System.Text` namespace:

```
using System.Text;

StringBuilder sb = new StringBuilder();
while (rdr.Read())
  sb.Append(rdr.GetString(0));

return sb.ToString();
```

When the `StringBuilder` object is created, it allocates a buffer of memory, and as strings are appended to it using the `Append` class, the buffer gradually fills up. When full, another chunk of memory is allocated, ready for more strings, so memory allocation happens infrequently and in chunks. This is far more efficient than appending strings to each other where the memory allocation happens for each string.

In general, you should use a `StringBuilder` object where you are appending a large number of strings, or where the number of strings is unknown.

Picking the Right Collection

Numerous collections exist and at first glance some seem just as good as others, but you need to carefully consider the use of the collection to ensure optimal performance. The following list describes the collections and what their best uses are:

- The `ArrayList` dynamically resizes as items are added and is best used to store custom object types when the data changes frequently — for example, when you are performing frequent inserts and deletes.
- The `HashTable` is a collection of pairs of data (a key and a value) and is best suited for data that doesn't change frequently. It is especially useful for data that is queried often.
- The `ListDictionary` should only be used to store small amounts of data, generally fewer than 10 items.
- The `NamevalueCollection` is a sorted collection of keys and values and is best for data that is already sorted. It is efficient for data that frequently changes or needs to be queried often.
- The `Queue` provides first-in, first-out storage, so it should be used when sequentially ordered data is required.
- The `SortedList` stores keys and values in a sorted order. This makes adding data slow, because existing items need to be rearranged to ensure the new item is in the correct order. A `SortedList` is best for data that doesn't change often.
- The `Stack` provides first-in, first-out storage, so it should be used when sequentially ordered data is required.
- The `StringCollection` is a strongly typed `ArrayList`, so it is useful for storing strings in an arbitrary order, and for strings that change frequently.
- The `StringDictionary` is a strongly typed `HashTable`, so it is useful when strings need to be stored and those strings don't change often.

Using the correct collection not only improves performance but also reduces the potential for errors. For example, if you need to store strings, use a `StringCollection` or a `StringDictionary`, because they only store strings — trying to store another data type results in a compiler error, so your code is protected against storage of incorrect types. A generic list will always be faster than its non-generic equivalent.

Now it's time to turn away from the coding aspects of performance and look toward a feature that ASP.NET provides for us. Although coding and configuration is still required, it's not the code itself that will improve performance — rather, it is ASP.NET itself.

Caching

Caching is the term given to keeping a copy of something for later use, and provides a way of avoiding resource-intensive operations. For example, we've already talked about databases being expensive in terms of performance, but there's no real way to avoid them with data-driven sites. So what you can do is minimize database access by fetching data and storing it elsewhere (but not another slow resource such as a file). Another type of caching can just involve operations that don't need to be done multiple times — storing the result of that operation saves having to redo it when required.

Caching can be used in many ways, but luckily ASP.NET has made some of these easier.

Page Caching

You already know that ASP.NET pages are compiled, but you probably haven't thought much about it. After all, it works, so what's the big deal? Well, knowing how it works means you can understand how page caching works, and means you can use it effectively. The following set of diagrams show how the compilation works and how it affects caching. Figure 14-4 starts with the first request of a page, which is compiled and stored on disk in intermediate language — this isn't a fully compiled executable, but is a shortened source code format. The .NET runtime then compiles the intermediate code, which executes, and the result of that execution is the HTML that is returned to the browser.

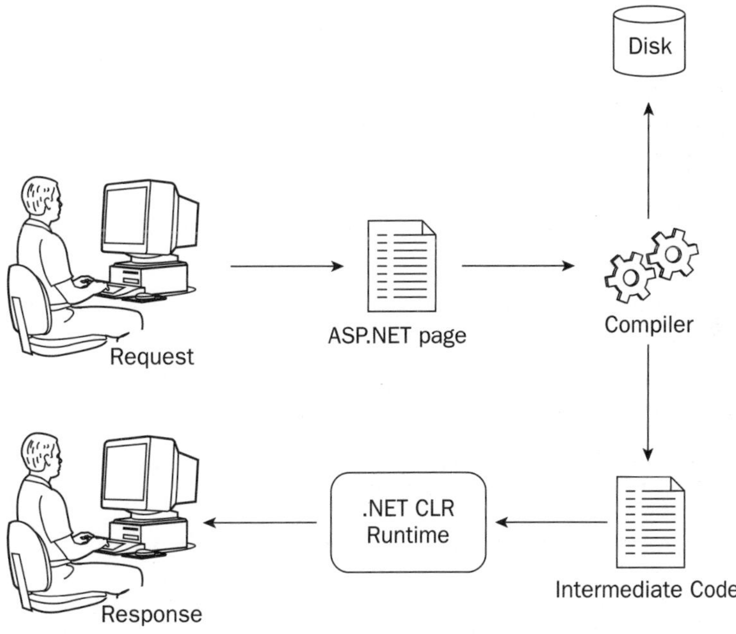

Figure 14-4

The second time the page is requested (see Figure 14-5), assuming the source hasn't been changed, the intermediate code is still available, so the compilation stage is bypassed.

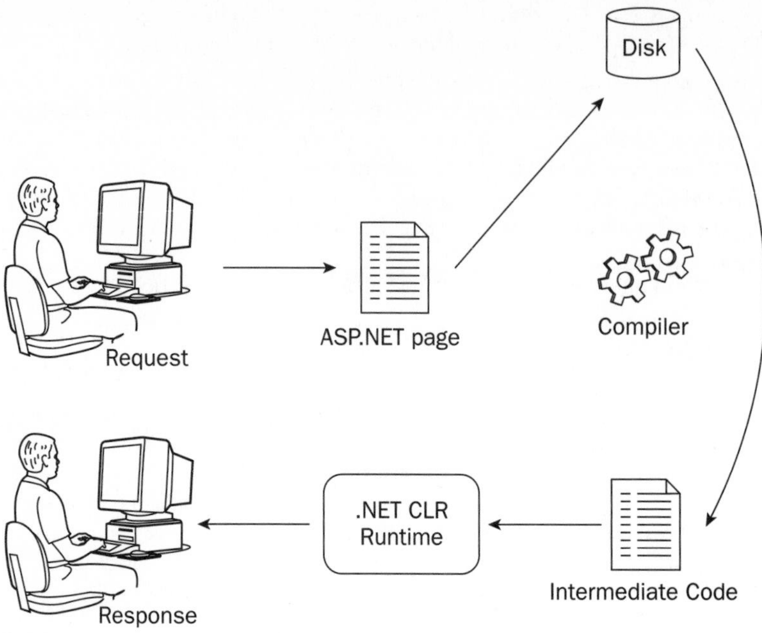

Figure 14-5

Already we have an improvement, just by the intermediate code being cached. What can also happen is that the page output can be cached, if designed as part of the page. When the intermediate code is compiled, the HTML is not only returned to the browser, but it is also stored on disk, as shown in Figure 14-6.

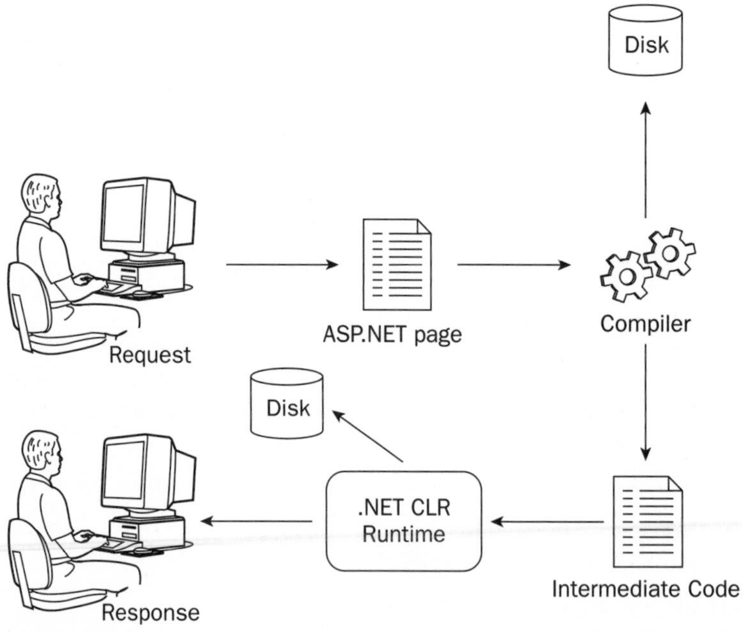

Figure 14-6

Now you have a great situation, because subsequent requests for the page simply get the HTML from the cache. All areas of compilation are avoided, as illustrated in Figure 14-7.

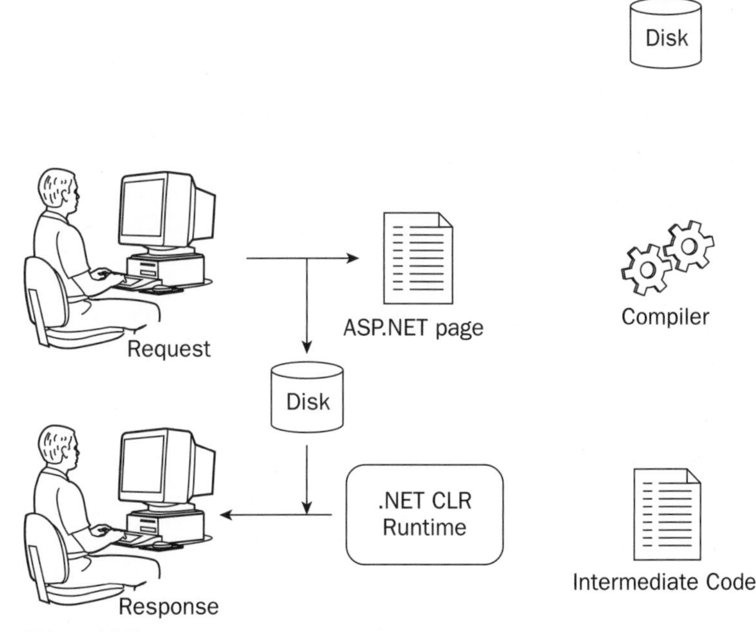

Figure 14-7

Now take a look at how you can implement this type of caching.

Output Caching

Output caching is the simplest of the page caching techniques shown in the previous section, whereby the entire page is cached. Give this a go in the next Try It Out to see how easy it is.

Try It Out Output Caching

1. In VWD, open `History.aspx`.
2. As the first line in the content, above the existing `h1` element, add the following:

```
<div class="boxFloatRight"><%=DateTime.Now%></div>
```

3. Save the file and run the application, navigating to the History page under the About menu. Notice the time to the right of the title, and press F5 to refresh the page. Press F5 several times, noting that the time is updated.
4. Close the browser. In VWD, edit the `History.aspx` page again, adding the following line, near the top of the page, underneath the `@Page` directive:

```
<%@ OutputCache Duration="30" VaryByParam="none" %>
```

5. Save the file and re-run the application. Try pressing F5 several times and notice that now the time isn't updated. Wait at least 30 seconds and refresh the page again — notice that the time has changed.

How It Works

Output caching works as shown in Figures 14-4 through 14-7. The `OutputCache` directive tells ASP.NET that after the output of the page has been created, it is to be stored in the cache. The `Duration` is the time in seconds that the page is to remain in the cache — any requests within those 30 seconds are served from the cache. After the 30 seconds are up, the cached page expires and is removed from the cache. The next request will re-execute the page, whereupon it is placed into the cache again. (The `VaryByParam` attribute is discussed in a just a bit.)

The `div` displaying the current time shows the time the page was executed. So the first time you request the page, the current time is shown, because this is when the HTML is generated. But because the HTML is cached, subsequent views of the page receive the cached HTML, which of course has the time fixed. It's only when the page is removed from the cache that it's re-executed and the time updated.

The advantage of this system is that pages that are used frequently will be often cached, whereas pages that aren't used often get discarded from the cache.

The `VaryByParam` attribute dictates whether any external influences affect how the page is cached. Setting the value to `none` means that nothing affects the caching — only one copy will be cached. However, what about pages that allow selections and fetch data based on those selections? One example is the Fixtures page, which can either show past fixtures or future fixtures, depending on a value passed in as part of the querystring. If `VaryByParam="none"` is used, only one copy of the page would be cached, so the first Fixtures page requested would be cached. Say two people view the fixtures one after another, and that the first view is for future fixtures, which would be cached. If the second person requests past fixtures, he or she would be returned the cached page, which was for future fixtures. In fact, with this model, the past fixtures wouldn't be viewable until the first page was evicted from the cache.

To get around this, `VaryByParam` can be set to the name of the querystring variable, which means that a copy of the page would be cached for each different value of the variable. This could be implemented in the Fixtures page simply by adding the following cache directive:

```
<%@ OutputCache Duration="30" VaryByParam="type" %>
```

The two menu entries for fixtures have the following as their URLs:

```
Fixtures.aspx?type=future
Fixtures.aspx?type=past
```

Now when two people request the different fixture pages, two copies are stored in the cache, one for each type.

Fragment Caching

Fragment caching enables portions of a page to be cached while the rest of the page remains dynamic. This is ideal for those pages that contain a mixture of static and dynamic content, and is achieved by having the content that is to be cached contained within a user control. The user control then uses the `OutputCache` directive to dictate how it should be cached, in the same way that pages use it:

```
<%@ Control OutputCache Duration="30" VaryByParam="none" %>
```

When the user control is placed on the page, only the content for the user control will be cached, allowing the rest of the page to remain dynamic.

This is useful for pages where the data is very dynamic and changing often and you don't want the page cached, but there is some content (perhaps from a database) that doesn't change often and can be cached.

Post Cache Substitution

Post cache substitution is the opposite of fragment caching, where the page is cached but a portion of the page is dynamic. This is achieved with the `Substitution` control, which works differently from other forms of caching. You still use the `OutputCache` directive on the page to determine the caching, but the `Substitution` control is simply a placeholder into which the content is to be placed, and this content has to be created manually. The `Substitution` control has a property called `MethodName` that indicates a function that will return a string of data to be substituted into the cached page. For example, the page would be as follows:

```
<%@ Page CodeFile="PCS.aspx.cs" Inherits="PCS" %>
<%@ OutputCache Duration="30" VaryByParam="none" %>
<html>
  <form runat="server">
    <div class="boxFloatRight"><%=DateTime.Now%></div>
    <asp:Substitution id="sub1" runat="server" MethodName="Substitute" />
  </form>
</html>
```

The code-behind would be as follows:

```
partial class PCS : System.Web.UI.Page
{
  static string Substitute(HttpContext myContext)
  {
    return "Date fetched on " + DateTime.Now.ToString();
  }
}
```

When this page is run, it will be cached, so the `div` with the date and time will remain the same. But each time the page is requested, the `Substitute` method will be called, so the data that it returns will not be cached. Here's how it works.

The first time the page is requested by a user, the normal caching regime is applied — the page will be placed into the output cache. However, because there is a `Substitution` control on the page, the output cache keeps a note of the `MethodName` (for each `Substitution` control if there is more than one on the page). When the page is next requested, instead of being returned directly from the cache, the method detailed in `MethodName` is called, which changes the contents of the `Substitution` control. At this point, it is integrated with the copy of the page in the output cache and returned to the user. In this case, you get the benefit of output caching but with the flexibility of dynamic content.

What's interesting about post cache substitution is that it's available to you if you write custom controls, meaning you can drop controls onto a page that automatically display up-to-date content irrespective of whether or not the page is cached. The `AdRotator` control works like this, so if you place an `AdRotator` onto a page, the ads will always be updated even if the page is cached. This works because within the `AdRotator` code there is a post cache substitution that is dependent on the file that stores the ads. When the `AdRotator` is on a page and that page is rendered, the `AdRotator` always checks the cache because that's what the post cache substitution does. If the ad's file hasn't changed, the cache entry will still be present, but if the file has changed, the cache entry will have been removed, so the ad's file is re-read. With the `AdRotator` you get the benefits of caching but without the problem of stale ads — an important consideration if customers are paying for ad space.

Designing for Performance

This is the vaguest area of the book, because much of the topic varies upon the particular application. There are general techniques that can be used, but some specific things depend on your site. For example, you wouldn't want to go to extreme lengths to extract the last ounce of performance from an intranet site with only 50 users. Sure, make it perform as best as you can, but sometimes there are trade-offs that aren't really justified. Is it worth spending a week of your time to gain an extra couple of seconds? Possibly, but not always.

When designing for performance, you have to think ahead and answer the following questions:

- **How many people are going to use the site?** For an intranet site, you'll have a fixed number of users — the employees in the company. For an Internet site, the user base is unlimited. More users mean more resources will be required on the web server.
- **How much page interaction is there going to be?** Do the pages just fetch and display data, or will the user be answering questions, making selections, and so on? You obviously want your pages to respond quickly whichever the interaction type, but for the latter, shaving off those extra seconds might be worthwhile.
- **Can any of the pages be pure HTML?** If there is no reason for having an ASP.NET page, then don't. HTML and ASP.NET pages can interact, and HTML pages are faster because they don't require processing by ASP.NET. Also, when you're using Internet Information Server 6 on Windows Server 2003, HTML pages are particularly fast because of the way in which they are stored and processed by the web server.
- **How much database access will there be?** This may affect how you configure some of the caching options shown earlier.

One thing you have to be aware of is what ASP.NET does and what the web server does. For example, in Chapter 4 you looked at security and saw how to protect sites and pages so that only certain users can access them. This security only works for ASP.NET pages and not HTML pages, so you have to weigh any performance improvements you might gain from HTML pages against the security implications. If you have pages that need to be secure, then they need to be ASP.NET pages, even if they don't contain any dynamic content. Using ASP.NET pages also allows you to take advantage of other aspects of ASP.NET, such as Master pages, themes, and navigation. Alternatively, you can configure Internet Information Server so that HTML pages are processed by ASP.NET as well as ASP.NET pages. This brings the addition of security, but at the loss of performance.

Generally, you should use the topics shown in this chapter, such as stored procedures and caching. There are other things that you shouldn't do, though, such as allowing users to free-search on a large database—it's inevitable that users will at some stage try to query for more data than they really need, causing a slow-down on the database and a slow-loading page. This they'll complain about. You may think it's their fault for running that query, but in reality, it would be your fault (or rather the designer of the application, which may not be you). You can avoid this situation by designing the application so this sort of long-running query isn't possible, or that if it is necessary, you ensure your database tables are indexed adequately.

Web Server Hardware and Software

This is always a controversial topic, but the physical platform shouldn't be ignored. Though it's easy to throw more hardware at the problem of poor performance, spending money is never the entire solution, nor is it always possible—the bean counters who control the money often can't see the justification or just don't have the money. But that shouldn't mean it's not a valuable topic to think about, and act on if possible. You don't necessarily have to spend a lot on hardware to benefit. Swapping your processor for a faster one is a choice many people would consider, but it could be a waste—not only is it relatively expensive (a new motherboard might also be required, as well as the expense of the processor), but it also might not be required. Memory, on the other hand, is nearly always a cost-effective upgrade. Memory is cheap, and a web server with lots of memory will perform better than one with little memory—there's more memory for the web server to work with plus more available for caching.

The software also shouldn't be ignored. Windows Server 2003 uses Internet Information Server 6 and in a like-for-like situation will generally perform better than version 5 (on Windows Server 2000). There are obvious licensing costs involved, but if you have the option, IIS6 is a worthwhile upgrade.

Testing Performance

How do you go about testing the performance of applications? Perhaps you want to test a new application or an application you've inherited, and you want to see if it's performing to its best ability. A number of techniques and tools are available that you can use, not all of them computer-based. One of them is just natural common sense, and this involves being realistic about your expectations, and the expectations of the web site users. For example, if you were creating an application that showed a picture gallery, you'd expect there to be some delay because pictures can be large and take time to load. But the aforementioned free database query is another matter—you understand the complexities involved, but your users may not, and they'll expect all queries to return with the same speed.

One of the first things you need to do is establish a *baseline*.tThis is the set of expectations and numbers that detail how the site performs currently: how fast pages are returned to the user, the number of pages served within a time period, and so on. This is important, because without any numbers you have no accuracy—you're in the realms of guesswork. With numbers, you can make changes and see whether they improve performance (more pages served over a given timeframe means more users). The following sections look at some simple ways of getting these numbers.

Tracing

The simplest method is to use ASP.NET *tracing*, and though it is not designed as a performance tool, it can be used to gain a great deal of understanding into how your pages are performing. One of the primary uses for tracing is to help with debugging, and you'll look at that in detail in the next chapter, but for now you can concentrate on its use for analyzing performance.

Tracing works by a simple configuration change, either in the page or in `Web.config`, which instructs ASP.NET to output additional information at the bottom of the page. You do this in the following Try It Out.

Try It Out Tracing

1. From the Wrox United web site in VWD, open the `Shop.aspx` file (it's in the main directory).
2. Add the `Trace` attribute to the `Page` directive (it doesn't matter where in the `Page` directive it goes):

```
<%@ Page Language="VB" Trace="True" MasterPageFile="..."
```

3. Save the file and run the application. You'll see something resembling Figure 14-8. You may see more or less depending on your screen resolution.

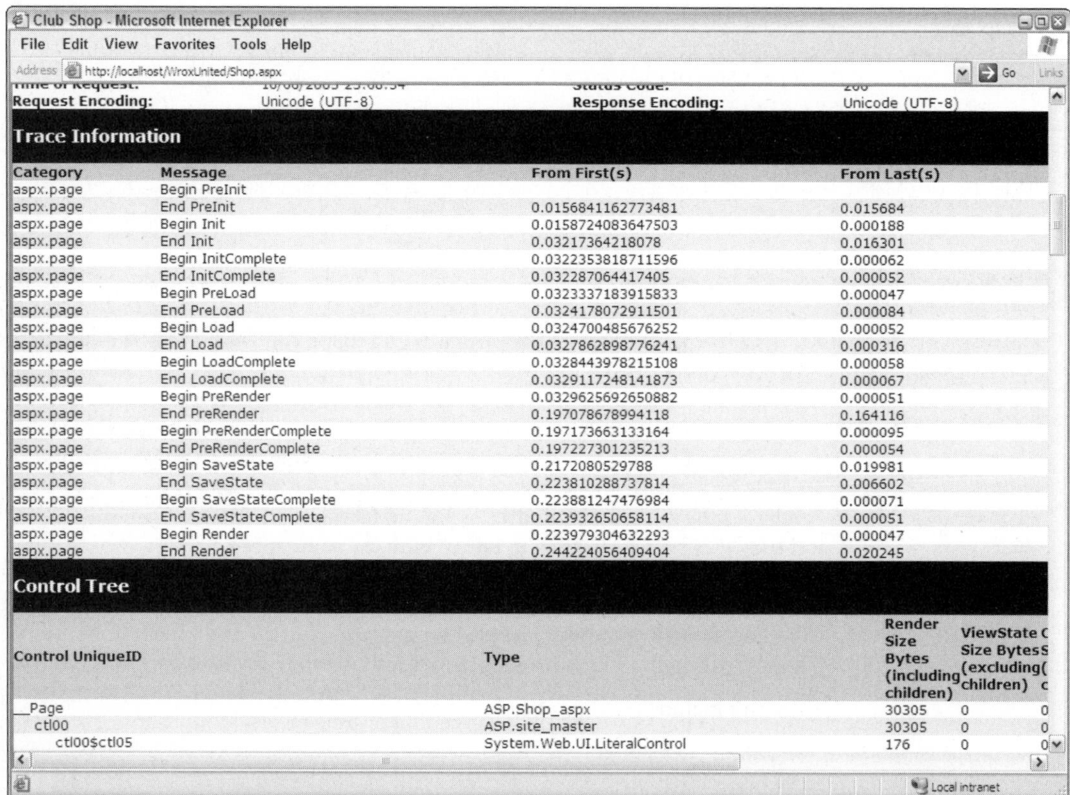

Figure 14-8

How It Works

It's not so much how it works as what it does, adding several pages worth of information to the end of the page. Chapter 15 looks at some of these sections in more detail, but for now let's concentrate on the Trace Information and the Control Tree.

The Trace Information shows four columns:

- **Category:** The category of the message. All messages generated by ASP.NET for the page have the page name as the category.
- **Message:** An individual trace message. By default, some of the ASP.NET events are shown, with two messages for each, one for the start of the event and one for the end.
- **From First(s):** The time in seconds since the first message was displayed.
- **From Last(s):** The time in seconds since the last message was displayed.

Immediately you can see that you have some rough performance information, because the total time taken to render the page is shown in the From First column for the End Render method (shown in the Message column). In general, this isn't a great guide to performance, but the trace information can help you narrow down slow-running areas when you realize you can add your own messages. This is achieved with the `Write` method of the `Trace` class. For example:

```
Trace.Write("My Category", "My Message");
```

This means you can wrap sections of code within trace statements to see which perform poorly. Chapter 15 looks at the tracing in more detail.

The second section that is of use for performance analysis is the Control Tree, which shows all of the controls on the page as a hierarchical list. Earlier in the chapter, we talked about view state and how minimizing it meant that less was being sent to the browser, and it's this section that allows you to see the view state. There are five columns:

- **Control UniqueID:** The unique ID of the control on the page. This will differ from the ID you've given a control, because it is a combination of the supplied ID plus the IDs of parent controls.
- **Type:** The data type of the control. You can clearly see from this that all content, even straight text, is converted to a control.
- **Render Size Bytes (including children):** The size, in bytes, of the control. For the entire page, which shows as `__Page`, the first control in the Control Tree section, this tells you the size of the page.
- **ViewState Size Byes (excluding children):** The size, in bytes, of the view state for this control. Note that this doesn't include child controls.
- **ControlState Size Bytes (excluding children):** The size, in bytes, of the control state for this control. Note that this doesn't include child controls.

For performance purposes, it's the numbers that are useful. The render size indicates the size of the controls, so you can see if controls are outputting more code than necessary. The view state can be turned off in many areas, further reducing the size of the page (which in turn reduces the time taken to render it).

The control state can't be turned off, but in general, controls use very little control state so this shouldn't be taken as a performance issue.

Tracing only gives rudimentary information about the performance of a site, but it's a useful starting point for analyzing pages. What it doesn't tell you is how well a site performs as a whole, or when multiple people access it. For that you need specialist tools.

Stress Testing Tools

Stress testing is the term given to running an application under high load, with lots of users. You could try to persuade lots of people to access the site, but that's not generally practical, so tools are used to simulate multiple users. Stress testing tools work by accessing pages continuously for a defined period of time, and recording the statistics for those pages. This gives accurate data on how a site performs under stress, and because the tools can take into account things such as certain pages being accessed more than others, the data is very accurate. Another great feature is that some of these tools can read existing web log files and build a stress test from them, which means they are using real-life data to perform testing.

A detailed look at stress testing tools is outside the scope of this book, but if you want to look into this in more detail, Visual Studio 2005 comes with a stress testing tool. If you're working in a corporate environment, you might already have all of the tools you need. You can find a scaled-down version of the Visual Studio tool from the Microsoft Download site at `www.microsoft.com/downloads`. Search for "Web Application Stress Tool." The related resources on the download page point to documents showing how this tool works.

One very important change to make before running any stress tests is to turn off debugging, so make sure that the `debug` attribute is either removed from a page or is set to `False`:

```
<%@ Page debug="False" ... %>
```

In the `Web.config` file, you should also ensure that the `debug` attribute of the `compilation` element is set to `false`:

```
<compilation debug="false" ... />
```

The importance of this cannot be over-emphasized, because an application with debugging will perform slower than one without. This is because the .NET runtime tracks debug code, and ASP.NET doesn't batch compile pages. It also creates additional temporary files. All of these can have a significant impact on performance tests.

Performance Monitor

Another area that's really too detailed to go into here is that of performance counters, which can be viewed from the Performance Monitor tool in the Windows Administrative Tools folder. These enable you to measure all sorts of statistics about the workings of your computer, including the CPU usage, the amount of memory being used, and so on. There are also groups and counters for ASP.NET so you can see how well ASP.NET is performing. For more details on performance monitoring, see the "Performance Counters for ASP.NET" topic in the ASP.NET documentation for more details.

Summary

This chapter looked at a variety of topics that will help your web sites perform to their best ability. It started by looking at some SQL issues, such as database connections and stored procedures, and showed how they not only will help with performance, but also make your code easier to read and maintain. The latter of these is worthwhile achieving on its own, so these techniques really are useful. Additionally, this chapter covered the following topics:

- Generic collections, which you won't encounter too many times as a beginner, but should certainly strive to use as you grow in expertise. Generics, as a specific area of programming, offer much more that just the collections, but these alone bring great benefits such as readability and improved performance.
- Session state and view state, showing how both can be turned off to reduce the amount of processing that ASP.NET needs to do when running pages.
- Binding, object references, concatenation, and collections. All of these are topics that will make you think about your code as you design and write it. Stepping back and thinking about code is often a good exercise because it makes you think about the site as a whole.
- Caching, which is an easy thing to implement, yet brings great performance improvements. Caching can happen at many levels, from ASP.NET to the database, and all reduce the amount of work required to create pages. Caching should be used wherever data isn't changing frequently.
- A brief look at design and testing, to see what you have to think about and how you go about seeing if your site can perform faster.

The next chapter looks at what happens when things go wrong, examining things like debugging and error handling.

Exercises

1. Convert the two shop pages, `Shop.aspx` and `ShopItem.aspx`, from using SQL statements to stored procedures.
2. Add caching to the `ShopItem.aspx` page, so that the page is cached. Note that you need to take into account that this page shows different products, so the cache needs to be varied by the product being shown.

Dealing with Errors

This chapter covers another topic that you need to think about during the whole of site construction — how to deal with errors. In many ways, this chapter could fit at the beginning of the book, because it's highly likely you'll get errors as you work through the book. What this chapter covers could be useful, but some of what's discussed here uses code and depends on other chapters, so we've left it until now.

It's a fact that you will get errors when creating applications, and that's okay. We all make mistakes, so this is nothing to be ashamed of or worried about. Some will be simply typing mistakes and some will be more complex, maybe due to lack of practice, but these go away with time. So what this chapter looks at is a variety of topics covering all aspects of handling errors. In particular, it examines the following:

- How to write code so that it is error proof
- What exceptions are and how they can be handled
- How to centrally handle exceptions
- How to use debugging and tracing to work out where errors are occurring

The first section looks at how to bulletproof code.

Defensive Coding

Defensive coding is all about anticipation — working out what could possibly go wrong and coding to prevent it. One of the precepts of defensive coding is that you should never assume anything, especially if user input is involved. Most users will be quite happy to use the site as intended, but hackers will search for ways to break into sites, so you have to do anything you can to minimize this risk.

Being hacked isn't the only reason to code defensively. A coding bug or vulnerability may not be found by a user, but by yourself or a tester. Fixing this bug, then, involves resources — perhaps a project manager, a developer to fix the bug, or a tester to retest the application, all of which take time and money. Also, any change to the code leads to potential bugs — there may not be any, but there's always the possibility. As you add code to correct bugs, the original code becomes more complex, and you occasionally end up with imperfect solutions because you had to code around existing code.

So what can you do to protect your code? Well, there are several techniques to defensive coding.

Parameter Checking

The first of the defensive coding techniques is checking the parameters of methods. When writing subroutines or functions, you should never assume that a parameter has a valid value — you should check it yourself, especially if the content originates from outside of your code. Take the code for the shopping cart for an example — this is in `App_Code\Shopping.cs`. One of the methods of the cart allows the item to be updated, like so:

```
public void Update(int RowID, int ProductID,
                  int Quantity, double Price)
{
  CartItem Item = _items[RowID];

  Item.ProductID = ProductID;
  Item.Quantity = Quantity;
  Item.Price = Price;
  _lastUpdate = DateTime.Now;
}
```

This is fairly simple code, but it does no checking on the parameters that are passed in. The reason for this is that the code that uses this gets the parameter values from the database before passing them in. So although you can say that the code is okay, what happens if this code is reused in another project? What happens if someone circumvents the calling code to pass in an incorrect price, one lower than that stored in the database? Or more simply, what if the `RowID` passed in is invalid? With this as an example, you could modify the code like so:

```
public void Update(int RowID, int ProductID,
                  int Quantity, double Price)
{
  if (RowID < _items.Count)
  {
    CartItem Item = _items[RowID];

    Item.ProductID = ProductID;
    Item.Quantity = Quantity;
    Item.Price = Price;
    _lastUpdate = DateTime.Now;
  }
}
```

You've now protected this against an incorrect `RowID`, so no errors will occur when this method is called. It's a simple check, ensuring that the ID of the row to be updated isn't larger than the number of rows.

In general, you should always check incoming parameters if the method is a public one — that is, it is called from outside the class. If it's a method that isn't accessible from outside of the class (`private` or `protected`), then this is less important because you're probably supplying those parameters yourself, although this doesn't necessarily mean the parameters will be correct—you might get the values from elsewhere before passing them into the method.

Avoiding Assumptions

In addition to checking parameters, you should avoid assumptions in your code. For example, consider an example that I actually had just now while formatting this document, where there was an error in my own code (yes, shocking isn't it?). I have VBA macros in Word to perform formatting for the styles of the book, one of which is for the grey code block. It's a generic routine that accepts three strings, which are the Word styles to use for the first line, the intermediate lines, and the last line, as shown here:

```
Private Sub FormatParas(First As String, Middle As String, Last As String)

    Dim iRow As Integer

    Selection.Paragraphs(1).Style = First
    For iRow = 2 To Selection.Paragraphs.Count - 1
        Selection.Paragraphs(iRow).Style = Middle
    Next
    Selection.Paragraphs(iRow).Style = Last

End Sub
```

This code uses Word objects to format paragraphs and assumes that there will be more than one paragraph, which seems sensible because each line is a separate paragraph and there is a separate macro to format code that is only a single line. The code works by setting the first paragraph in the selection to the style defined by `First`. For subsequent lines (line two downward), the `Middle` style is used, and for the final line, `Last` is used as the style. However, if there is only one paragraph in the selection, the `For...Next` loop doesn't run (`Selection.Paragraphs.Count` being `1`), but it does set `iRow` to `2`. The final line fails because `iRow` is `2` and there is only one paragraph in the selection. I failed in this code because I didn't defend it against user failure (me being the user in this case), where the selection was only a single paragraph.

The corrected code is as follows:

```
Private Sub FormatParas(First As String, Middle As String, Last As String)

    If Selection.Paragraphs.Count = 1 Then
        Selection.Paragraphs(1).Style = Last
        Exit Sub
    End If

    Dim iRow As Integer

    Selection.Paragraphs(1).Style = First
    For iRow = 2 To Selection.Paragraphs.Count - 1
        Selection.Paragraphs(iRow).Style = Middle
    Next
    Selection.Paragraphs(iRow).Style = Last

End Sub
```

With this code, a check is made for the number of paragraphs before the loop is done, and if there is only a single paragraph, no looping is done.

This is a surprisingly common occurrence — errors made because of simple assumptions. This particular code has been in use for several years without failure, but today, although it was user error that caused the problem, the failure is in the code for not protecting itself. The dumb user (me) had what looked like multiple paragraphs, but because of soft carriage returns in fact had only one. So the user was wrong, but the code didn't protect against it.

Query Parameters

If you build your applications using the wizards and data source controls, then you won't run into this problem, because the generated SQL statements contain parameters. But if you manually construct SQL, or inherit an application, you may see code like this:

```
string SQL = "SELECT * FROM Products " +
             "WHERE ProductID=" + Request.QueryString["ProductID"[
```

Or like this:

```
string SQL = "SELECT * FROM Employee " +
             "WHERE LastName='" + LastName.Text + "'"
```

Both of these dynamically construct a SQL statement, concatenating strings. The first uses a value from the `QueryString`, the second from a `TextBox`. The problem here is that there's no validation on the user input, so it's easy to perform what's known as *SQL injection*, where rogue SQL statements are injected into existing ones. With the second example, if the user enters a last name, the SQL would be as follows:

```
SELECT * FROM Employee WHERE LastName='Paton'
```

However, the user could enter the following:

```
Paton' OR 1=1 --
```

This would turn the SQL into the following:

```
SELECT * FROM Employee WHERE LastName='Paton' OR 1=1 --'
```

The first thing to know is that `--` is a comment in SQL, so the trailing quote is ignored. The SQL statement matches any `LastName` that is `Paton`, which is the intended match, but also the `1=1` statement, which will always be true. The result is that all employees would be shown, which is definitely not the intended purpose. This is mild, however, compared to the user who enters the following:

```
Paton' ; DROP TABLE Employee -
```

The SQL statement is now as follows:

```
SELECT * FROM Employee WHERE LastName= 'Paton' ; DROP TABLE Employee --'
```

The SELECT statement works as expected, but there's now a second SQL statement — the semicolon separates statements in SQL. So the query runs, and then the table is dropped — no more employees. Serious trouble. This could easily have been any other SELECT statement to find out more information about the database, or even dropping the entire database.

The solution to SQL injection is to use parameters, because these automatically prevent this type of attack. If you're using stored procedures, which you should be, then parameters are required for passing information into the procedure, but when you're building SQL dynamically, you can still use parameters. So if you were running a SqlCommand, you could do this:

```
string SQL = "SELECT * FROM Employee WHERE LastName=@LastName"
SqlCommand cmd = new SqlCommand(SQL, conn);

cmd.Parameters.Append("@LastName", SqlDbType.VarChar, 50);

cmd.Paramaters["@LastName"].Value = LastName.Text;
```

Here @LastName is the parameter name, and because the value is assigned via the parameter, no SQL injection can take place. This is because ADO.NET protects against SQL injection attacks when using parameters — the values passed into parameters are checked for specific content that would signify an attack.

Validation

We've already mentioned that any user input is automatically suspicious, and one of the things that can be done to mitigate the risk is to validate that input, stopping the user from entering bad input in the first place. This is good for two reasons: first, it means the code is safer, and second, users won't have to deal with potentially confusing error messages. They might still get messages telling them that their input is incorrect, but at least they won't get an obscure error message because your code failed.

To help with this problem, there is a suite of five validation controls with ASP.NET 2.0 that can check user input before it even gets to your code:

- RequiredFieldValidator: Ensures that a field is not left empty.
- CompareValidator: Compares the entered text with a value, or with another control.
- RangeValidator: Ensures the entered text is within a specified range.
- RegularExpressionValidator: Matches the entered text against a regular expression.
- CustomValidator: Runs custom code to validate the entered text.

These are standard ASP.NET controls that are placed on the page, generally alongside the control they are validating. There is also a ValidationSummary control that allows display of error messages in one place. You add these in the following Try It Out.

Try It Out — Validation Controls

1. In VWD, in the Wrox United project for this chapter (C:\BegASPNET2\Chapters\Begin\Chapter15\WroxUnited), open FanClub\FanClubMatchReport.aspx.

2. Find `FormView1` and find `TextBox1` in the `<EditItemTemplate>`. Between `TextBox1` and the `<br />`, add the following:

```
<br />
<asp:RequiredFieldValidator id="rfv1" runat="server"
  ControlToValidate="TextBox1"
  Text="You haven't entered the report!" />
```

3. Do the same for the `<InsertItemTemplate>` — enter exactly the same code between `TextBox1` and the `<br />`.

4. Save the file and run the application, logging in as a fan club member (use **Dave** or **Lou** as the user — the passwords are **dave@123** and **lou@123**).

5. Select the Add Match Report from the Fan Club menu, pick a match, and select the Add New Report link.

6. Don't enter any text in the text area, but press the Save New Report link. You'll see an error message, shown in Figure 15-1.

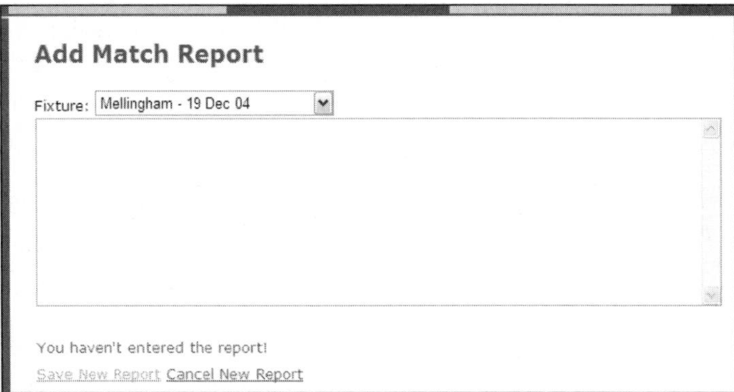

Figure 15-1

7. Enter some text and save the report.

8. Click the Add New Report link again to add another report.

9. Don't enter any text, but click the Cancel New Report link instead. Notice that the error message is displayed again. You can't cancel unless some text has been entered, so let's correct that.

10. Stop the application and, back in VWD, edit the page. Find `btnCancelReport` (a `LinkButton` that is in both the `<EditItemTemplate>` and `<InsertItemTemplate>`), and for both occurrences, add the following attribute:

```
CausesValidation="False"
```

11. Save the file and repeat steps 5 and 6. Notice that you can now cancel even if no text has been entered.

How It Works

This works because the validation control is linked to the text box and won't allow the page to be posted back to the server until some text has been entered. Here's a look at the validator in more detail:

```
<asp:RequiredFieldValidator id="rfv1" runat="server"
  ControlToValidate="TextBox1"
  Text="You haven't entered the report!" />
```

The two properties you're interested in are the `ControlToValidate` and the `Text`. The first is what links the controls — in this case, it's `TextBox1` that the validator will check. If no text is entered, the contents of the `Text` property are displayed. If text has been entered, the validator does nothing and no output is shown.

Validation occurs whenever a control would cause the page to be posted back to the server — this could be a `Button`, a `LinkButton`, and so forth, but what's important to note is that by default no postback occurs because the validation is done client-side in the browser. This means that the user sees a responsive display without that refresh that can be so annoying. However, you don't want the validation to take place when you're trying to cancel an edit — if you're canceling, it doesn't matter whether there's anything in the text box. By default, all means of posting back cause validation to occur, but by setting the `CausesValidation` property to `False` for the cancel link, no validation takes place.

> **Validation should always be done server-side, but can optionally be done client-side as well. You should never rely solely upon client-side validation, because it's easy for hackers to post data directly to a page, bypassing the client-side validation. The default settings in ASP.NET 2.0 are for both client- and server-side validation.**

Validating Multiple Controls

The previous example showed how to validate a single control, with the error message shown directly by the control. However, there are times when you want to validate several controls, and in these cases, it's not always sensible to have the error message presented directly by the control. For example, you might have a grid of data, or the data you are editing might be neatly aligned. Under these circumstances, you might not want to have the message displayed, because it would change the layout of the screen. However, you probably still want some form of indication as to which editable field failed the validation, as well as having the full error message displayed somewhere. For that, you use the `ValidationSummary` control. The following Try It Out shows how this can be done.

Try It Out — The ValidationSummary Control

1. Open `FanClub.aspx` and add `RequiredFieldValidator` controls between the end of the text boxes and the `</td>`. You'll need the following validators:

```
<asp:RequiredFieldValidator id="rfv1" runat="server"
  ControlToValidate="txtName"
  Text="*" ErrorMessage="You must enter a value for your name" />
<asp:RequiredFieldValidator id="rfv2" runat="server"
  ControlToValidate="txtAddress"
  Text="*" ErrorMessage="You must enter a value for the address" />
```

```
<asp:RequiredFieldValidator id="rfv3" runat="server"
  ControlToValidate="txtCity"
  Text="*" ErrorMessage="You must enter a value for the city" />
<asp:RequiredFieldValidator id="rfv4" runat="server"
  ControlToValidate="txtCounty"
  Text="*" ErrorMessage="You must enter a value for the county" />
<asp:RequiredFieldValidator id="rfv5" runat="server"
  ControlToValidate="txtPostCode"
  Text="*" ErrorMessage="You must enter a value for the post code" />
<asp:RequiredFieldValidator id="rfv6" runat="server"
  ControlToValidate="txtCountry"
  Text="*" ErrorMessage="You must enter a value for the country" />
<asp:RequiredFieldValidator id="rfv7" runat="server"
  ControlToValidate="txtEmail"
  Text="*" ErrorMessage="You must enter a value for the email address" />
<asp:RequiredFieldValidator id="rfv8" runat="server"
  ControlToValidate="txtAlias"
  Text="*" ErrorMessage="You must enter a value for the membership alias" />
```

For example, the `Name` would be:

```
<tr>
  <td>Name:</td>
  <td><asp:TextBox id="txtName" runat="server" />
      <asp:RequiredFieldValidator id="rfv1" runat="server"
        ControlToValidate="txtName"
          Text="*" ErrorMessage="You must enter a value for the name" />
  </td>
</tr>
```

2. After the validator for the e-mail address, add the following:

```
<asp:RegularExpressionValidator id="rev1" runat="server"
  ControlToValidate="txtEmail"
  Text="*" ErrorMessage="Please enter a valid email address" />
```

3. Switch the page into Design View and select the `LoginView` control, `FCLoginView`. From the Common Tasks menu, select RoleGroup[0]–FanClubMember from the Views list (see Figure 15-2). This will show the controls in the RoleGroup for users in the FanClubMemberRole.

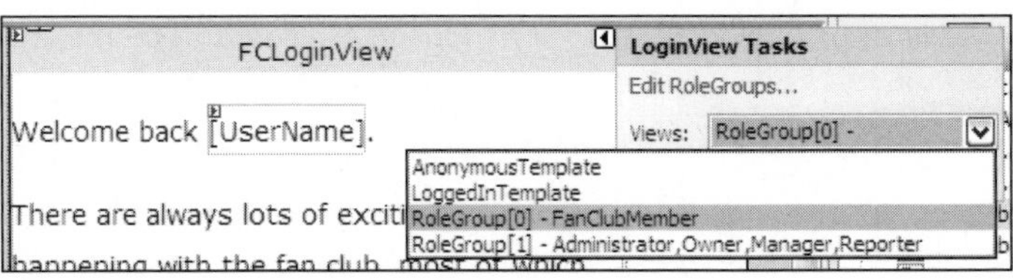

Figure 15-2

4. Scroll down the page to find the RegularExpressionValidator — this is the right-hand validator next to the Email text box. Select this validator, and in the Properties area, click the `ValidationExpression` property. Then click the button that appears, as shown in Figure 15-3.

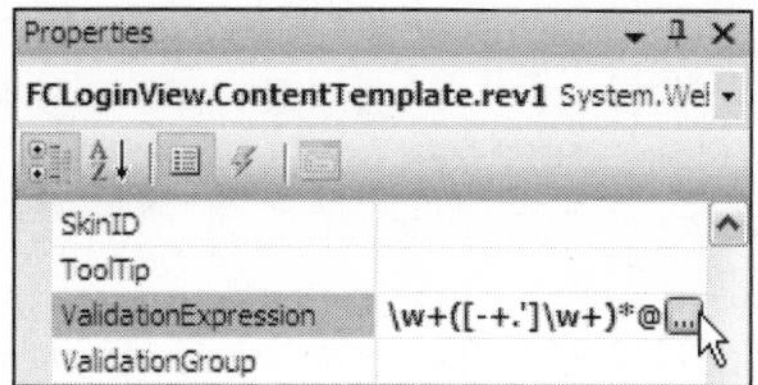

Figure 15-3

5. The window that appears is the Regular Expression Editor, which comes pre-filled with a selection of common expressions. Select Internet E-mail Address and click OK, and the selected expression will be filled into the `ValidationExpression` property.

6. Switch the page back to Source View, and before the `Button` (`btnSaveChanges`), add the following:

```
<asp:ValidationSummary id="vs" runat="server" DisplayMode="BulletList" /><br />
```

7. Save the file and run the application. Log in as either **Dave** (using the password **dave@123**) or **Lou** (using the password **lou@123**), and navigate to the Fan Club home page.

8. Add text to the fields, but leave the City and Email fields blank. Click the Save Changes link and you'll see Figure 15-4.

Name: Dave
Address: here
City:
County: everywhere
Postcode: somewhere
Country: UK
Subscribe to email updates:
Email: myemail
Membership Alias: Dave
Theme: Default

- You must enter a value for the city
- Please enter a valid email address

Figure 15-4

9. Enter some text into the Email field, but make sure it isn't a valid e-mail address. Click the Save Changes link again and notice how the error message has changed.

10. Delete the text from the Name field and press the Tab key to move to the next field. Notice that as soon as you tab out of the field, a red star appears next to the field, indicating an error.

How It Works

Several differences exist between this example and the first one where you used only one `RequiredFieldValidator`. In this example, there are several, each for different fields, as well as other validation controls. One thing you may have noticed about the required field validators is that no error message was displayed alongside the fields they are validating. That's because the `Text` property was set to `*` — just a simple marker to indicate an error in the field. The `Text` property is displayed inline — that is, wherever the validator is placed. The `ErrorMessage` property is used wherever the error is displayed, and in this case, that is shown by the `ValidationSummary`.

The `ValidationSummary` is fairly obvious in its purpose, because it simply displays in one location all error messages from validators. This allows the validators to be discrete, showing just a simple asterisk to mark the field in error without causing displacement on the screen, but still to have a full error message. The `DisplayMode` for the summary can be a list, bulleted list, or a paragraph.

The other validator used was the `RegularExpressionValidator`, which checks the entered text against a regular expression — this is a format for defining character sequences. If you want to use regular expressions for other fields, such as postal codes, then the Regular Expression Editor has some expressions. Otherwise, you can find many others at `www.regexlib.com/`, which has a searchable database of expressions freely available. You may have noticed that the Email field had two validators: one to ensure some text was entered, and one to ensure that the entered text was valid. Both validate the same control because they both have their `ControlToValidate` property set to `txtEmail`. You can mix and match the other validators in the same way, which gives great flexibility in ensuring that entered data is correct.

The other thing you may have noticed was that tabbing from field to field also showed the asterisk, but not the error message in the summary. Because validation is being done client-side, the client script knows that text is required for a field, so if the field is left empty, it can signal an error. But because the summary is intended to show all errors, this isn't filled in unless a postback is tried. So you get the best of both worlds — dynamic error handling with full error messages.

Exception Handling

Exception handling is the term given to anything out of the ordinary that happens in your application — exceptional circumstances. Although handling exceptions is part of defensive coding, there's a difference between programming for things that could quite easily go wrong, or are even expected to go wrong, such as incorrect passwords, and those things over which you have no control. For example, consider what happens if you can't connect to the database. How would you handle that situation? Now it's likely that there's nothing you can really do in your application, because it may well be dependent upon the database, but you still don't want your users to see an ugly error message. Instead, you want to display your own message, maybe letting them know that there is a problem and they can try again later.

The trick is to have a strategy, to work out in advance what you're going to do when something goes wrong.

What Are Exceptions?

Exceptions are a range of classes, all deriving from the same base class called `Exception`. Many different exceptions exist, such as `FileNotFoundException`, which would occur when trying to access a file that doesn't exist; and `SqlException`, which would occur when there is a database problem.

At some stage while working through the examples in the book, you may have seen something like Figure 15-5.

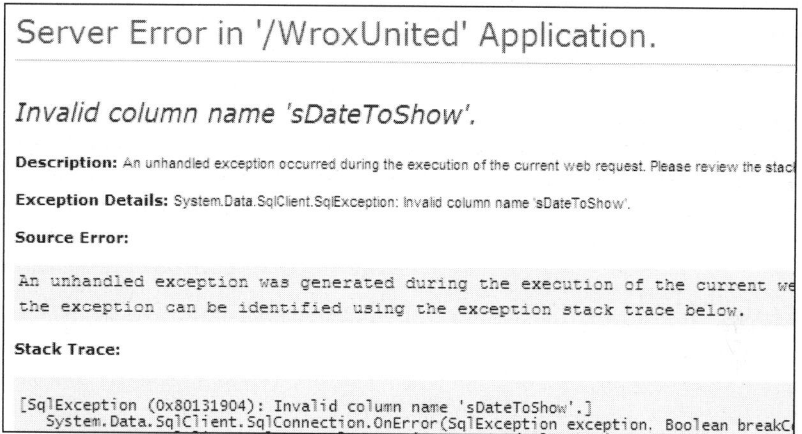

Figure 15-5

This occurred because of an incorrect SQL statement — one of the column names was wrong. This sort of exception is unlikely to get out into a live application, but other exceptions are, so you need to learn how to trap them.

The Exception Object

The `Exception` object is the base class for all exceptions and defines the base properties that all exceptions have. These properties are explained in the following table.

Property	Description
`Data`	A collection of key/value pairs that provide additional details about the exception.
`HelpLink`	The link to the help file that contains a description of the exception.
`InnerException`	The underlying exception that caused the problem.
`Message`	Text that describes the exception.
`Source`	The name of the application or object that caused the problem.
`StackTrace`	The trace of method calls that lead up to the problem.
`TargetSite`	The method that threw the current exception.

One thing that that you might notice is that there is an `InnerException` property. This allows exceptions to be stacked, which is useful when you have layers of code. For example, an underlying part of the .NET Framework may raise an exception, but that might be wrapped within another exception to provide more information.

Other exceptions might define additional properties to describe the specifics on the exception. For example, `SqlException` also defines the properties described in the following table.

Property	Description
`Class`	The severity of the error, as defined by SQL Server.
`Errors`	A collection of `SqlError` objects detailing the problem.
`LineNumber`	The line number within the SQL or stored procedure where the problem occurred.
`Number`	The error number.
`Procedure`	The name of the stored procedure where the problem occurred.
`Server`	The name of the SQL Server machine.
`Source`	The name of the data provider.
`State`	The error code from SQL Server.

You can see that when exceptions occur, you have a certain amount of information regarding the problem, but if you use the correct type of exception, you get more information. This is discussed later in the chapter.

How to Trap Exceptions

Trapping exceptions is crucial to maintaining control of your application, and is done with `Try Catch` statements. This is easiest to understand through an example, using some code you saw earlier in the book (Chapter 14) — the code that generates thumbnails for uploaded images:

```
public static void GenerateThumbnail(string SourceImagePath,
                                      string TargetImagePath)
{
  using (Image sourceImage = Image.FromFile(SourceImagePath))
  {
    short newHeight = (short) Math.Round((double)(sourceImage.Height * 0.25));
    short newWidth = (short) Math.Round((double)(sourceImage.Width * 0.25));
    Image.GetThumbnailImageAbort abort1 = new
          Image.GetThumbnailImageAbort(ImageHandling.ThumbnailCallback);
    using (Image targetImage = sourceiMage.GetThumbnailImage (newWidth, newHeight,
abort1, IntPtr.Zero))
    {
      targetImage.Save(TargetImagePath, ImageFormat.Gif);
    }
  }
}
```

At the moment, this code doesn't protect itself in any way, but you can add both defensive coding and exception handling. The source image, for example, must exist before it can be converted, so that can be checked first, but the target image doesn't exist, so you need to protect against some problem when saving it. Here's how the code could look:

```
public static void GenerateThumbnail(string SourceImagePath,
                                      string TargetImagePath)
{
  if (!File.Exists(sourceImage))
    return;

  using (Image sourceImage = Image.FromFile(SourceImagePath))
  {
    short newHeight = (short) Math.Round((double)(sourceImage.Height * 0.25));
    short newWidth = (short) Math.Round((double)(sourceImage.Width * 0.25));
    Image.GetThumbnailImageAbort abort1 = new
          Image.GetThumbnailImageAbort(ImageHandling.ThumbnailCallback);
    using (Image targetImage = sourceiMage.GetThumbnailImage(newWidth, newHeight,
                                          abort1, IntPtr.Zero))
    {
      try
      {
        targetImage.Save(TargetImagePath, ImageFormat.Gif);
      }
      catch(Exception ex)
      {
        Tools.Log("ImageHandling.GenerateThumbnail", ex);
      }
    }
  }
}
```

The first thing to note is the defensive coding for the source image. This uses the `Exists` method of the `File` class to see if the file exists, and if it doesn't, you simply exit silently. The exception handling is wrapped around the saving of the target file and follows this general principle:

```
try
{
  Place the code here that you need to trap exceptions for
}
catch (Exception ex)
{
  Place the code here to handle the exception
  This could be displaying a tidy message or logging the exception
}
```

In the code, `targetImage.Save` is the line that could potentially cause an exception. It might not be possible to save the file for a variety of reasons: an incorrect file name, permissions, and so on. If an exception does occur, execution immediately transfers to the `Catch` block, so any lines within the `Try` that were after the line in fault would not be executed.

The `catch` block is interesting because there can be more than one of them. For example:

```
try
{
  code to read from a database
}
catch (SqlException sqlEx)
{
  A SQL exception, so something is wrong with the database
}
catch (Exception ex)
{
  Any other error
}
```

When there is more than one `catch` block and an exception occurs, the exceptions are compared in the order in which they are declared. So if an exception was raised, it would be tested to see if it was a `SqlException`, and if it was, the `SqlException` `catch` block would be run. If the exception wasn't a `SqlException`, the next one down would be tried until a match was found or until the closing brace (`}`) of the `try` code block was reached. Because all exceptions ultimately inherit from `Exception`, this is the last chance saloon — the default exception if you will.

It's important that when you're using multiple `catch` blocks, you place the most granular first. For example, in the previous code example, consider if this had been done:

```
try
{
  code to read from a database
}
catch (Exception ex)
{
  Any other error
}
catch (SqlException sqlEx)
{
  A SQL exception, so something is wrong with the database
}
```

Even if a `SqlException` was raised, it would never be trapped because the `catch` for `Exception` would trap it. This is because `Exception` matches all exceptions, which is why you should always place it last when using multiple `catch` blocks.

There is also another part to `try catch`, which is the `finally` block. This is optional, and is a block of code that always runs, whether or not an exception is raised. Again, this is easier to see as code:

```
try
{
  code to read from a database
}
catch (Exception ex)
{
  Code to handle the exception
```

```
}
finally
{
  This code will always run
}
```

What happens here depends on whether an exception is raised. If not, then all of the lines of code in the `try` block are run, followed by the code in the `finally` block. If an exception is raised, the appropriate `catch` block is run, followed by the `finally` block. This gives you a chance to perform any clean-up operations that might be required. A typical example of this is when you're performing some database action, and you want to close the database connection whether or not an exception was raised:

```
SqlConnection conn;

try
{
  conn = new SqlConnection(" . . . ");
  conn.Open();

  // do some database action
}
catch (Exception sqlEx)
{
  // log the exception
  Tools.Log("A database exception occurred", sqlEx);
}
finally
{
  if (conn != null)
    conn.Close();
}
```

In this code, the connection is declared outside of the `try` block, allowing it to be referenced from within all code blocks (such as the `catch` and `finally` blocks). In the `finally` block, you don't just automatically close the connection because the exception might have been raised when trying to open the connection, so the connection object (`conn`) might not have a value. So `conn` is first checked to see if it has a value, and only then is it closed.

The following Try It Out gives you a better feel for how it can be used. You're going to update the Checkout page for the Wrox United shop to ensure that any database errors are handled gracefully and that they don't leave the database in an inconsistent state.

Try It Out Trapping Exceptions

1. In the Wrox United application for the chapter, open the code file for `Checkout.aspx` and move to the `Wizard1_FinishButtonClick` event. This is the event that runs when the checkout wizard has finished collecting information from the user and will move the order from the shopping cart into the database.
2. Add the following variable declaration at the top of the method:

```
SqlTransaction trans = null;
```

3. Modify the first few lines after the variable declarations so it looks like the following code — the new lines to add are shaded:

```
try
{
  conn = New SqlConnection( . . . );
  conn.Open();

  trans = conn.BeginTransaction();

  cmd = New SqlCommand();
  cmd.Connection = conn;
  cmd.Transaction = trans;
  . . .
```

4. You need to do the same at the end of the method, so modify the code to look like this:

```
      cmd.ExecuteNonQuery();
    }

    trans.Commit();
  }
  catch (SqlException SqlEx)
  {
    if (trans != null)
      trans.Rollback();

    CreateOrderErrorLabel.Visible = true;
    return;
  }
  finally
  {
    if (conn != null)
      conn.Close();
  }

  Profile.Cart.Items.Clear();
}
```

5. To ensure that the exception is seen in practice, there actually needs to be some error, so you'll force one by making the SQL statement incorrect. Change the SQL statement that inserts into the `Orders` table to insert into `no_Orders`:

```
cmd.CommandText = "INSERT INTO no_ORDERS(MemberName ...";
```

6. Save the file and run the application.

7. Go to the shop and add some items to your cart and then go to the Checkout page. Step through the checkout wizard. After clicking the Finish button, you'll see the message stating that an error has occurred. Although it says that the administrator and shop know about this, you'll be coding those bits later in the chapter.

How It Works

The code to trap any database exceptions is fairly straightforward, but you've added something else to ensure the integrity of the database, and this is a *transaction*. A transaction, in database terms, ensures that either all commands succeed or none of them do. The problem is that an order is being created in the Orders table and the items being ordered are created in the Order Items table. So at least two commands are being run, one for each table, but there will be a command for each order line. With any database operation, there is a chance of failure, and you need to ensure that both operations succeed, inserting the data into the Orders and Order Items table. You wouldn't want the order to be created but no order items, nor would you want the reverse. Both are problems. With only an order line, the system thinks that an order is there, but there are no items. The reverse means there would be order lines, but no corresponding order, and thus no way to access those order lines.

Wrapping all of these commands within a transaction means that the order and order lines are not only directly written to their tables, but they are also placed in a transaction log, a special table handled by the database. If there are no problems during the transaction, it is committed and all is as expected. If there are problems, however, the transaction is *rolled back*, which means that the rows that were added as part of the transaction are removed. So there are only two outcomes—all rows are added, or none are added. This means that an exception will leave the database in a consistent state, as it was when the transaction started. (It's a bit like time travel, but without all those weird states of seeing your parents when they were your age.)

Look at the code to see how this fits in with the exception handling. You saw the creation of this code in Chapter 13, when looking at e-commerce and the creation of the checkout process, but the explanation of the exception handling was postponed until this chapter.

The first thing is the declaration of a new variable, of type `SqlTransaction`:

```
SqlTransaction trans = null;
```

It is assigned an initial value of `null` to avoid potential runtime errors. In your code, this isn't a problem, but if you remove `= null` from the declaration and recompile the application, you can see that VWD displays an error stating "Use of unassigned local variable 'conn'" The reason is that the compiler cannot be sure that the variable will have an assigned value, so it gives a warning. You'll see where this assigned value of `Nothing` comes in later.

After the declaration, the code is wrapped within a `Try Catch` block:

```
try
{
  conn = New SqlConnection( . . . );
  conn.Open();
```

After the connection is open, a transaction is started. This gives you the marker point for the database commands, and it's to this state of the database that you will roll back if an exception occurs. The `BeginTransaction` method of the `SqlConnection` returns a `SqlTransaction` object, so later in the code, this can be used to commit or rollback the database changes:

```
  trans = conn.BeginTransaction();
```

With the transaction created, it is then assigned to the command using the `Transaction` property:

```
cmd = New SqlCommand();
cmd.Connection = conn;
cmd.Transaction = trans;
```

Now that the transaction has been assigned, the code can insert the required data into the tables. After that has happened, the transaction can be committed:

```
trans.Commit();
```

That's all the code for a successful operation, but if there is a problem, the exception needs to be caught:

```
catch (SqlException SqlEx)
```

Within the `catch` block, the transaction needs to be rolled back because some problem arose. But, before the transaction can be rolled back, the `trans` object needs to be checked to see if it contains a value. Remember that when the `SqlTransaction` object was declared, it was given a value of `null`. Within the `try` statement, the first lines of code create and open a connection, and these two lines of code could raise an exception. If that happened, the `SqlTransaction` object wouldn't have been created, so the `trans` variable would still have its default value of `null`. That's why the compiler gives an error and why the default value is set. So you only want to roll back the transaction if it was actually started, in which case the `trans` variable would not be `null`:

```
if (trans != null)
  trans.Rollback();
```

After the transaction has been rolled back, an error message is displayed, by simply making a `Label` control visible. After this is done, you can return from the method:

```
CreateOrderErrorLabel.Visible = true;
return;
```

Before you return, though, the connection needs to be closed, and this needs to be done whether or not an exception occurred, so a `finally` block is used. Remember that the `finally` block is always run. Like the transaction, the connection also has an initial value of `null`, and this is used to ensure that there is a connection before you try to close it:

```
finally
{
  if (conn != null)
    conn.Close();
}
```

The final thing to do is to clear the items from the cart, because they've now been added to the Orders and Order Items tables:

```
Profile.Cart.Items.Clear();
```

You can see that in use, the `try catch` block is quite simple, and that in conjunction with transactions, it allows the integrity of the database to remain. Displaying an error on the screen to let users know a problem occurred is a good thing, but the site administrators also need to know, so the next section looks at how these details could be logged to a file.

Logging Exceptions

Trapping exceptions is good, but you generally need to log them somehow. After all, if things go wrong you really want to know about it. Logging can be performed in many ways, with the log file being written to a variety of places, including a database table, the Event Log (either under Application events or a custom log), and a log file. There are advantages and disadvantages to all forms of logging. For example, you might not be able to write to the Event Log, because you might not have permission. Or if you can write to the Event Log, how would you then view the entries? Most web servers are tightly guarded and viewing the Event Log might not be allowed. The advantage of the Event Log is that exceptions are contained along with other application errors.

This section looks at the log file option, because it provides an easy way to log exceptions. A simple text file is used to store details of exceptions, showing the time and the details of the exception. Each exception is appended to the existing file, or if no file exists it will be created. Although you are using a log file, the technique works for the other ways of logging; the difference is simply where you log the exception. In the following Try It Out, you modify the exception code you added to the checkout.

Try It Out Logging Exceptions

1. In the Wrox United application for the chapter, open the code file for `Checkout.aspx` and move to the `Wizard1_FinishButtonClick` event.
2. In the section where the `SqlException` is caught, modify the code so that it looks like this:

```
catch (SqlException SqlEx)
{
  if (trans != null)

  trans.Rollback();

  Tools.Log("An error occurred while creating the order", SqlEx);

  CreateOrderErrorLabel.Visible = true;
  return;
```

3. Save the file.
4. In the `App_Code` directory, create a new class called **Tools** (right-click App_Code and select Add New Item).
5. In the new `Tools.cs` class file, add the following `Imports` statements at the top of the file:

```
using System.IO;
using System.Web;
```

6. Within the `Tools` class, add the following methods:

```
public static void Log(string Message)
{
  Log(Message, null);
```

```
  }

  public static void Log(string Message, Exception Ex)
  {
    string fileName = Path.Combine(
        HttpContext.Current.Request.PhysicalApplicationPath, "WroxUnited.log");

    using (StreamWriter logFile = new StreamWriter(fileName, true))
    {
      logFile.WriteLine("{0}: {1}", DateTime.Now, Message);
      if (Ex != null)
        logFile.WriteLine(Ex.ToString());
      logFile.Close();
    }
  }
```

7. Save the file and run the application. Log in, add some items to the shopping cart, and then follow the checkout procedure. When you finish the checkout, the screen will say that an error occurred.
8. Navigate to the directory in which the web site is running and open `WroxUnited.log`. You'll see the exception details logged.
9. Don't forget to change the SQL statement back to a correct one after you've run this example. Just remove the `no_` from the table name:

```
cmd.CommandText = "INSERT INTO ORDERS(MemberName ...";
```

How It Works

The first code modification was to log the exception from within the `Catch` block in the Checkout page:

```
Tools.Log("An error occurred while creating the order", SqlEx);
```

This calls the `Log` method of the `Tools` class, passing into it a string describing the problem, and the exception `SqlException` object. The `Log` method is a `static` method, so you didn't have to create an instance of the `Tools` class.

The exception will now be logged, so the logging class is created. This is a class file and is placed in the `App_Code` directory, which means that it will automatically be compiled. Within the `Tools` class, the first thing that is done is to add some namespaces:

```
using System.IO;
using System.Web;
```

`System.IO` is required because that is where the file handling routines are stored, and `System.Web` will allow you access to details of the current web site.

Next is the routine that trapped the exception, where the following was added:

```
Tools.Log("An error occurred while creating the order", SqlEx);
```

This calls the `Log` method of the `Tools` class, passing in an error message and the exception. Notice that it wasn't necessary to create an instance of the `Tools` class. Because the class is just a container for simple methods, those methods have been made `static`, so a class instance isn't required (`static` methods were explained in Chapter 9). The code for these is fairly simple, too, and shows a good case of overloaded methods.

The first method accepts a single argument, the error message to log. It doesn't actually do any logging itself, but calls another `Log` method, passing the message into that. It also passes `null` as a second parameter:

```
public static void Log(string Message)
{
  Log(Message, null);
}
```

The second method, also called `Log`, is where the real work is done. This method accepts two parameters. The first is the error message, and the second is an `Exception` object:

```
public static void Log(string Message, Exception Ex)
```

Next, the file name needs to be worked out. This can be placed in any suitable location, but keeping it in the home directory of the web site is a good idea. The path for that directory can be retrieved by the `PhysicalApplicationPath` property of the current `Request`. However, because this code isn't within an ASP.NET page, but is a class, the `Request` property isn't directly available. To get access to it, `HttpContext.Current` is used — this is the context of the current HTTP request that the ASP.NET page is running under.

The full file name needs to contain both the path and the file, so these are combined using the `Combine` method of the `Path` class. This will append a directory separator (the \ symbol) if one is required:

```
string fileName = Path.Combine(
    HttpContext.Current.Request.PhysicalApplicationPath, "WroxUnited.log");
```

When the full file name is available, the file can be opened, and for this a `StreamWriter` is used:

```
using (StreamWriter logFile = new StreamWriter(fileName, true))
```

Streams can be of different types, such as memory, but passing in the `fileName` parameter when the `StreamWriter` is created enables you to write directly to a file. The second parameter, `true`, indicates that data should be appended to the file, rather than a new file being created (which is the default). The `using` statement ensures that the reference to this file is disposed of when the code block is closed — this frees up the file resource as soon as it is no longer used, a technique that should always be followed.

After the file is opened, the `WriteLine` method is used to write data to the file:

```
logFile.WriteLine("{0}: {1}", DateTime.Now, Message);
```

`WriteLine` is an interesting method, because it can take many parameters. It always takes at least one parameter, but there can be others. The first parameter is the string to be written, but you want the current date and time, plus the message to be written as well. Rather than concatenating a string with these details, they can be added as parameters and placeholders used in the string to identify where they should go. The placeholders are identified by a number within curly braces, so `{0}` will be replaced by the current date and time, and `{1}` will be replaced by the message.

After the main message has been written to the file, the exception, passed into the `Log` method as a parameter, is tested. If it is not `null`, then an exception has been passed in, so this is also written to the file. The `ToString` method of the exception is used to get the descriptive text of the exception:

```
if (Ex != null)
  logFile.WriteLine(Ex.ToString());
```

The file is closed when all of the details have been written to the file:

```
logFile.Close();
```

After the `using` code block is ended, the file resources will be freed:

```
    }
}
```

At the end of this procedure, there is a `Log` method that can be called in two ways. The first way is as follows:

```
Tools.Log("error message");
```

The second way is like this:

```
Tools.Log("error message", exception);
```

This sort of overloaded method brings extra flexibility, because it allows you to use the same routine for different types of logging. If there's no exception, you use a different form of the `Log` method.

One thing you might have noticed is that the second parameter of the `Log` method is of type `Exception`, but when this method was called, a variable of type `SqlException` was passed in. This is acceptable because `SqlException` is derived from `Exception` Temember in Chapter 9 where inheritance was covered? `SqlException` inherits from `DbException`, which inherits from `ExternalException`, which inherits from `Exception`. It seems a long chain of inheritance, but that doesn't matter for parameter methods; as long as the type passed into a parameter ultimately derives from the type declared in the parameter, there will be no compilation errors. The types are compatible.

Mailing Exceptions

Log files are a great way to store exceptions, but they are generally passive—you have to go and look at them. A more active option for dealing with exceptions is to have them mailed to someone, perhaps the web site administrator. This is easy to achieve in ASP.NET 2.0, because classes are built in for sending mail messages, and these live in the `System.Net.Mail` namespace. Here's some code that could be used in addition to, or instead of, the file logging:

```
public static void SendMail(string Message, Exception Ex)
{
  using (MailMessage msg =
    new MailMessage("website@wroxunited.net", "admin@wroxunited.net"))
  {
    msg.Subject = "WroxUnited.net Web Site Error";
    if (Ex == null)
      msg.Body = "There was an error on the website";
    else
      msg.Body = Ex.ToString();

    SmtpClient client = new SmtpClient("MyMailServer");
    client.UseDefaultCredentials = true;
    client.Send(msg);
  }
}
```

Two classes are in use here. The `MailMessage` class defines the message to be sent — the constructor sets the "from" and "to" addresses for the message, and the `Subject` and `Body` properties set the subject line and the contents. The second class is the `SmtpClient`, the constructor of which defines the name of the mail server. Setting `UseDefaultCredentials` to `true` allows the ASP.NET code to connect to the server using Windows network credentials. Finally, the `Send` method actually sends the mail.

You can configure some of these properties in the web configuration file, `Web.config`, which is where you can also set authentication settings if they are required for connection to the mail server:

```
<configuration xmlns="http://schemas.microsoft.com/.NetConfiguration/v2.0">
<system.net>
  <mailSettings>
   <smtp deliveryMethod="Network">
    <network
      defaultCredentials="False"
      host="MyMailServer"
      password="MyPassword"
      port="25"
      userName="MyUserName"
      from="website@wroxunited.net"/>
   </smtp>
  </mailSettings>
 </system.net>
</configuration>
```

The properties for configuring mail are fairly simple. Setting `defaultCredentials` to `false` ensures that the user name (`userName`) and password (`password`) specified are used to connect to the e-mail server (`host`), and `from` sets the e-mail address of whom the e-mail is from. The `port` number has to do with TCP networking — e-mail uses port number 25, and you don't need to know any more about ports apart from that number.

Sending mail isn't just for notifying administrators of exceptions, and you can use it for all sorts of things. The security framework will use these settings when it sends forgotten passwords if users request them.

You could use the e-mail code instead of, or in conjunction with, the logging to a file. For example, you could have the following:

```
Tools.Log("My error message", SqlEx);
Tools.SendMail("My error message", SqlEx);
```

This would perform both actions, but it includes repeated code — the error message. An alternative would be to add the e-mail code into the `Log` method, but that would always send the e-mail, which might not be required. A better option might be to only send an e-mail if required, perhaps adding another parameter to the `Log` method to indicate if the e-mail is to be sent:

```
Tools.Log("My error message", SqlEx, true);
```

The `Log` method could then have the following code:

```
public static void Log(string Message, Exception Ex,
                       bool SendEmailMessage)
{
  if (SendEmailMessage)
    SendEmail(Message, Ex);

  // rest of logging code
}
```

This gives a combination of the passive reporting to a log file, and the active, which lets the administrator know of problems as they occur.

Raising Exceptions

You've seen that you can trap exceptions, but you can also raise your own exceptions. One use for this is that you can use the same exception handling mechanism to deal with custom errors as you use for .NET errors. However, this comes with a warning, in that you should still adhere to the rule of only using exceptions for exceptional circumstances. If you can handle the problem gracefully without using exceptions, you should do so.

To raise an exception, you use the `Throw` statement. For example:

```
throw new Exception("exception description");
```

You can also pass in an underlying exception:

```
throw new exception("exception description", ex);
```

If you are within a `Catch` block, you can also re-throw the existing exception by just calling the `Throw` statement on its own. You'll see how this can be used a little later when handling exceptions globally is discussed.

Exceptions Best Practices

Using exceptions is good practice, but the following rules should be adhered to when dealing with exceptions:

- You should only catch an exception if you actually expect the exception. This doesn't mean that it will happen, but that it could. A database failure is a good example, because these aren't unheard of. If you can understand why an exception would occur and you know how to deal with it, then that's a good case for catching it.
- Dealing with the exception doesn't mean that you know how to cure it, but that something can be done. For example, in the Checkout page modified earlier in the chapter, catching `SqlException` was necessary to allow the use of transactions so the database wouldn't be left in an inconsistent state. That is dealing with the exception, even if there is nothing that can be done about the underlying problem.
- As a general rule, it's a good idea to avoid catching only the base `Exception`. Because this is the base class for all exceptions, it's not narrow enough in its focus.
- If you are performing database work, catch the appropriate exception (`SqlException` for SQL Server).

Global Exception Handling

Handling exceptions where they happen is both good and bad. In the Checkout page, the exception had to be dealt with locally because of the transaction, but in many cases, you might want some form of centralized exception handling. You also might want some way to handle exceptions not trapped elsewhere. The Checkout page is again a good example, because there is handling for `SqlException`, but not for anything else. What happens if some other exception occurs? This is an important point because it really isn't sensible to put `Try Catch` around every piece of code just in case an exception might occur. In fact, that would be bad practice because it would make the code hard to read and isn't required.

The way global exception handling is managed is with the `Global.asax` file, which contains code for the application. In this case, the term *application* has a special meaning, because code in `Global.asax` responds to application-level events. These are events that are raised at specific points during the running of the application, events that are raised by ASP.NET. `Global.asax` is a code-only page, and has no user interaction.

Several events are contained in the `Global.asax` page:

- `Application_Start`: Raised when the application first starts. This will be when the first user accesses the site and should be used to set any initial start conditions.
- `Application_End`: Raised when the application stops.
- `Session_Start`: Raised when a user starts a session. This will be when the user starts accessing the site for the first time, and will include the time when a user closes the browser window and opens it again.

- `Session_End`: Raised when a user session ends. This isn't when the browser window is closed, because sessions have a timeout — if there is no user activity within that time, the session ends.
- `Application_Error`: Raised when an unhandled error occurs.
- `Profile_OnMigrateAnonymous`: Raised when an anonymous user logs in, and allows migration of any Profile properties. (The Profile was covered in Chapter 11.)

As you can see, the event you're interested in is the `Application_Error` event, which is where you can add code to centrally handle untrapped exceptions. You see how the `Application_Error` event can be used in the following Try It Out.

Try It Out — Handling Global Errors

1. Using Windows Explorer, navigate to the web site directory, `C:\BegASPNET2\Chapters\Begin\Chapter15\WroxUnited`, and have a look at `WroxUnited.log`.
2. In the Wrox United application, open the `global.asax` file.
3. Add the following code to the `Application_Error` event procedure:

```
Exception ex = Server.GetLastError();

Tools.Log("An unhandled error was caught by Application_Error", ex);
```

4. Save the file.
5. Open `checkout.aspx.cs` and move to the `Wizard1_FinishButtonClick` event.
6. Comment out the code that logs the error and replace it with the following:

```
throw;
```

7. To ensure that the exception is seen in practice, there actually needs to be some error, so you'll force one by making the SQL statement incorrect. Change the SQL statement that inserts into the `Orders` table to insert into `no_Orders`:

```
cmd.CommandText = "INSERT INTO no_ORDERS(MemberName ...";
```

8. Save the file and run the application.
9. If there are no items in your cart, go to the Wrox United shop and add some items. Otherwise, proceed to the Checkout page. Step through the checkout wizard. After clicking the Finish button, you'll be switched back to VWD stating that an error has occurred. Press F5 to continue.
10. Using Windows Explorer, navigate to the web site directory, `C:\BegASPNET2\Chapters\Begin\Chapter15\WroxUnited`, and check the `WroxUnited.log` file (or you can press the refresh button in the Solution Explorer, and the new file will appear). You'll notice that the exception has been logged. Check the last error and see that it states that an error was caught by `Application_Error`. Also notice that the next line states that an `HttpUnhandledException` was thrown, followed by details of the `SqlException`.
11. Delete `WroxUnited.log` and switch back to the `Checkout.aspx.cs` code.
12. Change the `throw` statement to this:

```
throw new Exception("An error occurred while creating the order", SqlEx);
```

13. Run the application again and follow the same procedure to generate the error.
14. Open WroxUnited.log again and look at the details. First there is the HttpUnhandledException, then Exception with the text you added, and then the SqlException.

How It Works

The first thing to understand is that the Application_Error in global.asax is raised when any unhandled error occurs. In this event, in your code you need to find out what the error was that caused the event to be raised, and for that you use the GetLastError method of the Server object. This returns an exception object, which is passed into the Log method to log the error. So if you had a Try Catch block around your code, how was it that you got to the Application_Error event? It's because you re-threw the error using the Throw statement — although you handled the initial SqlException, the re-thrown exception wasn't handled.

The important thing to note about what happened is that the exception is wrapped in another exception — an HttpUnhandledException. All exceptions you get from within Application_Error will be like this. The actual SqlException is shown because in the Log method, you used ToString to write out all of the details of the exception. If you didn't want the HttpUnhandledException shown, you could use the InnerException property of the exception:

```
Exception ex = Server.GetLastError().InnerException;
```

When the exception is logged, now it would only show the actual exception that was unhandled.

In the second case, you used the following:

```
throw new Exception("An error occurred while creating the order", SqlEx);
```

This throws a new Exception, but passes into that the actual exception that caused the problem. So you've wrapped the original exception within your own — a useful technique if you need to store more details than are available in the original exception. Here you are just detailing that the problem arose when an order was being created.

Don't correct the SQL statement. You'll need the incorrect statement in a later exercise when you look at debugging.

In general, using this simple code in Application_Error and logging exceptions to a file means that you always have details of problems that occur during the normal running of a site. You can use the stack trace (more on this later) to see exactly where the problem was, and you don't have to rely on users telling you what they think the problem was (the two very rarely match).

Custom Error Pages

One problem with the error handling code shown so far is that the user still sees a confusing message. Ideally, you'd like to present the user with something less shocking than a stack trace (a list of the methods called so far, which you'll look at later), for two very good reasons. First, a stack trace is not what users need to see—if something has gone wrong, then they need to see a clear description, explaining that it wasn't their problem, and that something is being done about it. Second, showing a stack trace gives away a lot of information about your site, details that can be used by hackers. Even if your site is secure, they could cause unnecessary slowdowns as they try to hack the site.

In addition to exceptions, there are other types of errors that aren't nice for a user to see. For example, what if you rename a page but don't update the links to it, or perhaps the user types in the wrong name for a page? In these cases, you'd see the 404—the error number that indicates a page could not be found. ASP.NET applications can be configured to redirect the user to other pages, depending on the type of error.

Configuring Custom Error Pages

Configuration of custom error pages is done in the `Web.config` file using the `customErrors` section. For example:

```
<customErrors mode="On" defaultRedirect="customError.aspx">
  <error statusCode="404" redirect="missingPage.aspx" />
</customErrors>
```

The `mode` attribute can be one of the following:

- `Off`: The ASP.NET error details are always shown, even if a custom error page exists.
- `On`: The custom error is always shown, and the ASP.NET error details are never shown.
- `RemoteOnly`: The ASP.NET error details are only shown to local users, meaning users logged on locally to the machine. For remote users (everyone else using the site), one of two things is shown: a default page telling the user that an error has occurred, but without showing any error details, or a custom error page if one exists.

The values of `On` or `RemoteOnly` should be used for a live site, whereas `Off` can be used for debugging purposes.

The `defaultRedirect` attribute defines the page that is shown if an unhandled error occurs.

The `error` element details specific errors and the page to redirect to if that error occurs. In this case, the `statusCode` is `404`, which means a missing page, so the user will be redirected to `missingPage.aspx` if the page they are looking for cannot be found. This enables you to have detailed pages for individual errors, so you can help the user correct the problem. The missing page example could explain that the page cannot be found and perhaps get users to check that they typed the correct URL.

In the following Try It Out, you create your own custom error page.

Try It Out Custom Error Pages

1. In the Wrox United application for the chapter, open `Web.config` and add the following within the `<system.web>` section:

```
<customErrors mode="On">
  <error statusCode="404" redirect="missingPage.aspx" />
</customErrors>
```

2. Save the file.

3. Create a new Web Form called **missingPage.aspx**, making sure that the code isn't placed in a separate file, but that you pick the `site.master` file for the Master page.

4. Within the `<asp:Content>` controls, add the following text:

```
We're sorry but the page you were looking for cannot
be found. It's probably hiding behind the couch. We'll
tell the Web site administrator to go and fetch it.
```

5. Save the file and run the application.

6. Navigate to a page that doesn't exist—perhaps `abc.aspx`. You'll need to type this page into the address bar of the browser. Notice that the text you entered is displayed rather than the normal message for a missing page.

How It Works

The working of this is quite simple, because when custom errors are enabled, ASP.NET intercepts the errors. What it does depends on how you've configured the `customErrors` section. In this case, the `mode` has been set to `On`, which means that custom errors will always be shown—this is required because you are logged on to the machine locally, so `remoteOnly` wouldn't work.

You've also configured a custom page for the `statusCode` of `404`, so whenever a page cannot be found, ASP.NET doesn't show the normal error message but instead redirects to the custom error page. This technique makes your site friendlier to use, which means that if an error does occur, the user isn't left with a frightening error message, but is presented with something more reassuring. Also, because this is an ASP.NET page, you could make the error message more helpful. For example, you could check the name of the file the user was looking for and see if something similar exists on the site, perhaps by looking up the pages in the SiteMap or from a database. You could then either take the user to the nearest matching page, or present them with a list of possible matches.

Error pages can be combined with logging to give very proactive feedback of problems within the site. For example, sites often expand or change, and the names of pages sometimes change, but you might forget to change a link to the changed page. If a user clicks a link on your site and that page isn't found, then sending an e-mail to the site administrator is very useful—the page in error can be quickly corrected so that no other users see the problem.

Debugging and Tracing

Controlling how errors are shown to the user is only part of the story when developing web sites, and tracking down those errors is just as important. Ideally, errors should be found during development and testing, and in many ways the job of testing is just as development. Many companies, Microsoft included, have teams of testers running through development projects, shaking out those errors.

As a developer, you are bound to make mistakes, ranging from simple typing errors to more complex coding problems. The typing problems are usually easy to track down because they often cause compilation errors, but runtime errors can be more problematic. Tracing and debugging are the two main techniques used to find errors.

Using ASP.NET Tracing

You first looked at tracing in Chapter 14. It is the technique of adding code to your pages, for a few reasons: for debugging purposes, to output values of variables, or simply to find out where in your code certain things happen. The great thing about ASP.NET tracing is that not only is it extremely simple to do, but it's also easily configurable and doesn't require tracing code to be removed if you don't want the trace information shown. What's also great is that you get a wealth of additional information about the page, which can be useful for both debugging purposes and for learning about ASP.NET.

Tracing Individual Pages

Tracing can be turned on for individual pages by adding the `Trace` attribute to the `Page` directive:

```
<%@ Page Trace="true" %>
```

On its own, this outputs a great deal of information about the page, but you can also add your own output using the `Trace` class, which has methods to write output to the trace log:

```
Trace.Write("my information")
```

The following Try It Out shows tracing in action.

Try It Out — Page-Level Tracing

1. In the Wrox United application for the chapter, open `Checkout.aspx` in Source View.
2. Add the `Trace` attribute to the `Page` directive:

```
<%@ Page Trace="True" ... %>
```

3. Save the file and run the application.
4. Add some items from the shop to your shopping cart and navigate to the Checkout page, where you'll see that the bottom of the page has lots of information added. You might have to scroll down the page to see all of the information.
5. Switch back to VWD and open the code file for the Checkout page.
6. At the top of the `Page_Load` event, add the following line of code:

```
Trace.Write("In Page_Load");
```

7. Before the check to see if the user is authenticated, add the following:

```
Trace.Write("In page_Load", User.Identity.IsAuthenticated.ToString());

if (User.Identity.IsAuthenticated)
...
```

8. Save the page and run the application, again navigating to the Checkout page.
9. Scroll the page down so you can see the Trace Information section, as shown in Figure 15-6.
10. Here you can see that the output from the `Trace.Write` statements is mixed with the output that ASP.NET puts into the trace. Take a look at how this works and what information the trace output produces.

Trace Information

Category	Message
aspx.page	Begin PreInit
aspx.page	End PreInit
aspx.page	Begin Init
aspx.page	End Init
aspx.page	Begin InitComplete
aspx.page	End InitComplete
aspx.page	Begin PreLoad
aspx.page	End PreLoad
aspx.page	Begin Load
	In Page_Load
In Page_Load	True
aspx.page	End Load
aspx.page	Begin LoadComplete
aspx.page	End LoadComplete

Figure 15-6

11. Edit `Checkout.aspx` again and set the `Trace` attribute to `False`:

```
<%@ Page Trace="False" %>
```

12. Save the page and run the application, again navigating to the Checkout page. Notice that the trace information is gone from the page, even though the `Trace.Write` statements are still in the code.

How It Works

The first thing to look at is what all of this trace information is, and what it is useful for. There are many sections, as detailed in the following table.

Section	Contains
Request Details	Details of the request, such as the status code.
Trace Information	The flow of page events, showing the category, message, and time from the first to last byte of information sent to the browser.
Control Tree	The hierarchy of controls in the page.
Session State	Any session variables in use.
Application State	Any application variables in use.
Request Cookies Collection	The cookies stored for the current site.
Response Cookies Collection	Any cookies set during the page processing.
Headers Collection	The HTTP headers.
Response Headers Collection	Any headers set during the page processing.
Form Collection	Contents of the form.
QueryString Collection	Any querystring parameters for the request.
Server Variables	The HTTP server variables.

All of this information is useful, although some sections are more useful than others. The Control Tree, for example, clearly shows the hierarchy of controls. You saw this in Chapter 14 when you looked at performance, but it's also useful for understanding how the page is made up from the hierarchy of controls. At the top is the `Page` object, beneath that the Master page, and then controls within the Master page. This continues with all of the page objects, and shows the unique name of the control as well as its type.

The Trace Information section shows the events in the order in which they are raised, so it is great for seeing exactly when things happen. Without any trace information of your own, the standard page events are shown, and anything you write is slotted into its correct space. So take a look what you actually did:

```
protected void Page_Load(object sender, System.EventArgs e)
{
  Trace.Write("In Page_Load");

  if (!Page.IsPostBack)
  {
    if (Profile.Cart == null)
    {
      NoCartlabel.Visible = true;
      Wizard1.Visible = false;
    }

    Trace.Write("In Page_Load", User.Identity.IsAuthenticated.ToString());
    if (User.Identity.IsAuthenticated)
      Wizard1.ActiveStepIndex = 1;
    else
      Wizard1.ActiveStepIndex = 0;
  }
```

In the first statement, you used `Trace.Write` to output a single string, which is displayed in the Message column. With the second `Trace.Write`, you passed in two parameters, and in this case, the first becomes the Category and the second becomes the Message. You can put trace statements anywhere within your code, and the output will be displayed in the Trace Information section, so it's a great way to simply see what's happening in your code. There is a also a `Warn` method of the `Trace` class, which outputs in the same way as `Write`, but the content is in red. This is useful for picking out statements within the trace output.

The other thing you may have noticed is that by changing the value of the `Trace` attribute at the top of page to `False`, no trace output is displayed. You didn't have to remove the `Trace.Write` statements from the code, because these are simply ignored if tracing isn't enabled. This is great during development, because you can liberally sprinkle `Trace.Write` statements throughout your code to give you a good understanding of the program flow, and you can turn on or off the tracing without having to remove or comment out these statements.

Tracing All Pages

Although tracing in individual pages is useful, what's great is being able to control tracing for the entire application. This is done with a configuration setting in `Web.config`, within the `<system.web>` section:

```
<trace enabled="True" />
```

When the `enabled` attribute is set to `True`, tracing is enabled for the application, but the output isn't shown in the pages. Instead, it is stored for viewing by way of a special URL — `Trace.axd` — which doesn't point to a physical file, but is instead interpreted by ASP.NET. You give application tracing a go in the next Try It Out.

Try It Out Application-Level Tracing

1. In Source View in `Checkout.aspx`, remove the `Trace` attribute from the `Page` directive at the top of the page.

2. Open `Web.config` and add the following within the `<system.web>` section:

```
<trace enabled="True" />
```

3. Save the file and run the application, navigating to the Checkout page.

4. Within Internet Explorer, select File➪New➪Window (or press Control+N) to launch a new window from the same site.

5. In the address bar, change `Checkout.aspx` to **Trace.axd** and press Enter. You should see something like Figure 15-7.

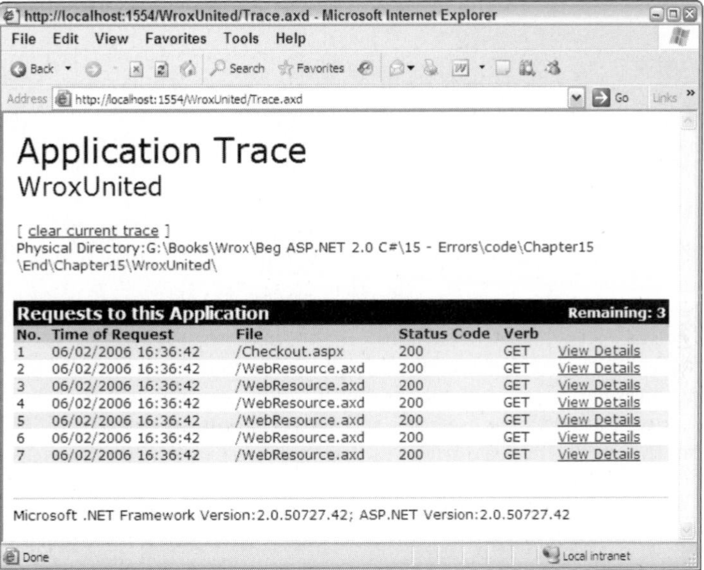

Figure 15-7

6. Click the View Details link on the `Checkout.aspx` line, and you will see the trace page you've already seen. Notice that it contains the two pieces of data that were added to `Checkout.aspx` in the `Page_Load` event.

How It Works

The working of this is simple: by enabling the trace element in `Web.config`, you are instructing ASP.NET to keep track of the trace information, but not to show it in the page. When you navigate to `Trace.axd`, ASP.NET recognizes this special URL, and instead of returning the standard 404 error page (or a custom page if you have one configured), it returns a list of pages that have been accessed in the application. Clicking the View Details link displays the trace information for that page.

The `<trace>` element has several attributes in `Web.config`, as described in the following table.

Attribute	Description
`enabled`	Indicates whether or not application tracing is enabled. The default value is `False`.
`localOnly`	When set to `True`, this ensures that `Trace.axd` is only accessible from the local machine. `True` is the default value, and stops remote users of the site from accessing the trace information.
`mostRecent`	Indicates whether or not the most recent trace requests are kept. The default is `False`, which keeps the first n items, where n is determined by the `requestLimit` attribute. If this is `True`, then the most recent n items are kept.
`pageOutput`	When this is set to `True`, the trace output is shown in the actual page, as well as being stored for show by `Trace.axd`. The default is `False`, although this doesn't affect pages that have tracing enabled on them directly.
`requestLimit`	The number of trace requests to store.
`traceMode`	Indicates the order in which the trace requests are shown. The default is `SortByTime`, where the order is time-based, but this can also be `SortByCategory`, where the requests are shown alphabetically.

The greatest thing about application tracing is that it can be invaluable in finding bugs in a running system. You can edit pages to add `Trace.Write` and turn on application tracing — the trace information will be stored, but the users won't see any of it. You can then examine the trace details to help diagnose any problems.

Using the Debugger

The tracing features of ASP.NET 2.0 provide a great way to trace the flow of the application, but probably the most important weapon in your coding arsenal is the debugger. This allows you to halt the application while it is running, examine variables, and step through the code line by line. The debugger is built into Visual Web Developer and Visual Studio 2005, so you don't have to run a separate application — you simply run the application from the development tool. The best way to learn debugging is to actually use it, as you do in the following Try It Out.

Try It Out — Debugging

1. In the Wrox United application for the chapter, open `Checkout.aspx.cs`.

2. In the `Page_Load` event, place the cursor on the line that checks to see if the cart has a value:

```
if (Profile.Cart == null)
```

3. Set a breakpoint on this line. You can do this in one of three ways. The first is by selecting the Toggle Breakpoint option from the Debug menu. The next is by pressing F9, and the last is by clicking the gray border at the left of the line of code:

4. Whichever method you use, this is a toggle, so performing the same action again removes the breakpoint. When a breakpoint is set, the gray border will show a red circle and the line will be highlighted, as shown in Figure 15-8.

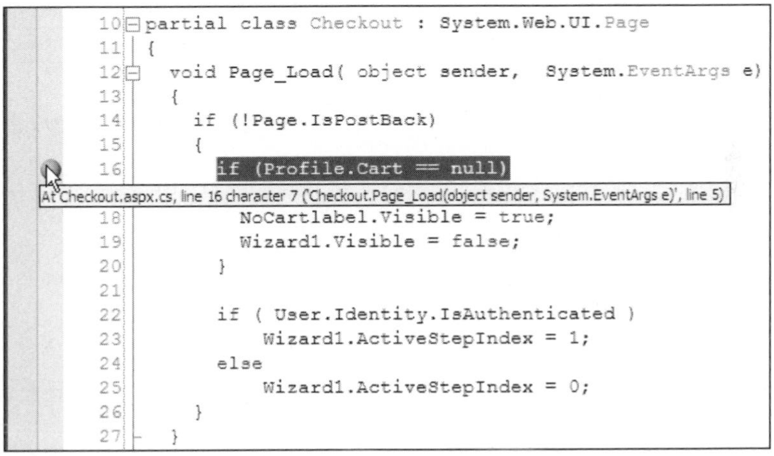

```
partial class Checkout : System.Web.UI.Page
{
  void Page_Load( object sender,  System.EventArgs e)
  {
    if (!Page.IsPostBack)
    {
      if (Profile.Cart == null)
At Checkout.aspx.cs, line 16 character 7 ('Checkout.Page_Load(object sender, System.EventArgs e)', line 5)
        NoCartlabel.Visible = true;
        Wizard1.Visible = false;
      }

      if ( User.Identity.IsAuthenticated )
          Wizard1.ActiveStepIndex = 1;
      else
          Wizard1.ActiveStepIndex = 0;
    }
  }
```

Figure 15-8

5. Scroll down to the `Wizard1_FinishButtonClick` event, and place a breakpoint on the following line:

```
foreach (CartItem item in Profile.Cart.Items)
```

6. Run the application from VWD or VS and navigate to the Checkout page. The page will not display — you'll see that you are stopped in the debugger (see Figure 15-9).

7. Press F5, or select Continue from the Debug menu. The page now appears.

8. Add some items to the shopping cart and then navigate to the end of the Checkout page again. When the breakpoint is reached, press F5, and you'll see the error message shown in Figure 15-10.

   You've hit an exception so the debugger halts. This is because of a change to the checkout code you did earlier, where you had an incorrect SQL statement so that you could force an exception.

```
partial class Checkout : System.Web.UI.Page
{
  void Page_Load( object sender,  System.EventArgs e)
  {
    if (!Page.IsPostBack)
    {
      if (Profile.Cart == null)
      {
        NoCartlabel.Visible = true;
        Wizard1.Visible = false;
      }

      if ( User.Identity.IsAuthenticated )
          Wizard1.ActiveStepIndex = 1;
      else
          Wizard1.ActiveStepIndex = 0;
    }
  }
```

Figure 15-9

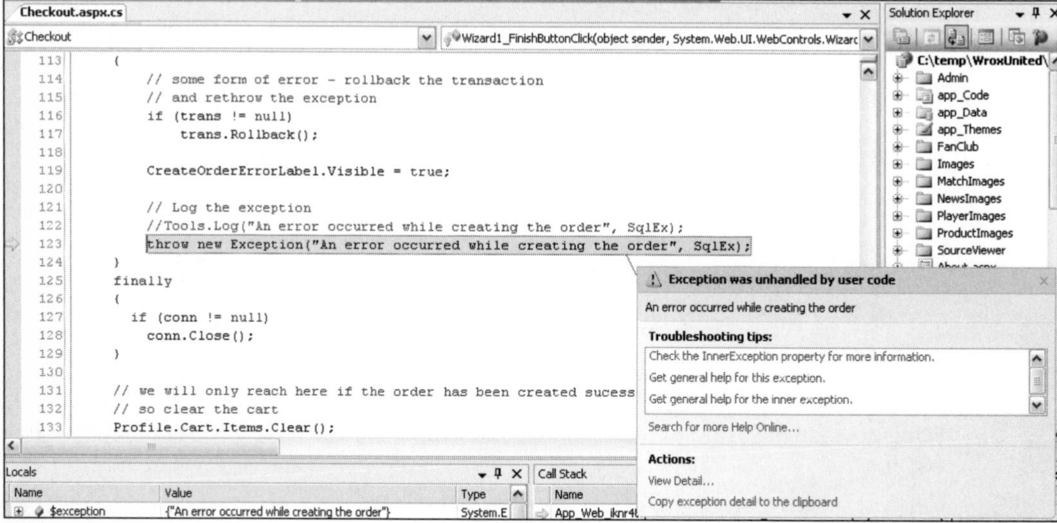

Figure 15-10

9. Click the View Detail link to show the details of the exception. Click the plus sign (+) to expand the details (see Figure 15-11), and you'll see that the exception shows your custom text and that there is an InnerException.

10. Click this open to show the original exception, in that there isn't a table called `no_Orders`. This isn't something that can be corrected while running the application, so you need to stop debugging.

11. From the Debug menu, select Stop Debugging, or press Shift+F5.

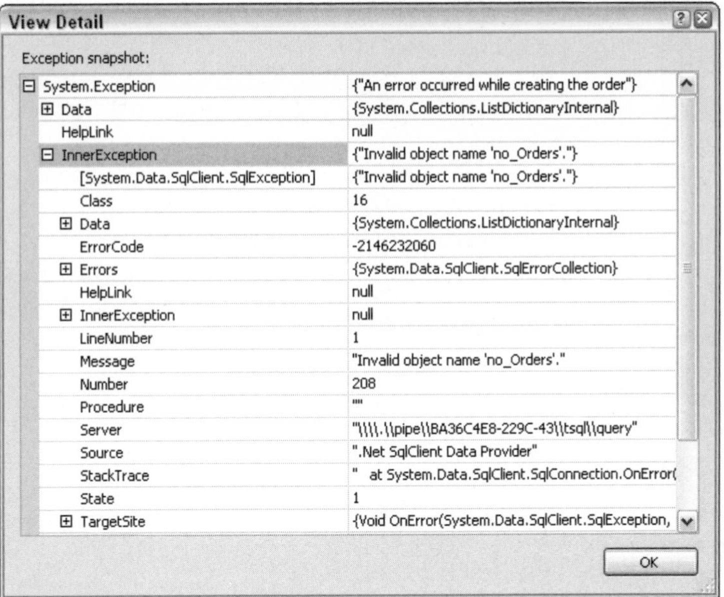

Figure 15-11

12. Edit the code to correct the error, changing `no_Orders` back to `Orders`:

```
cmd.CommandText = "INSERT INTO ORDERS(MemberName ...";
```

13. Run the application again, and navigate to the Checkout page again, making sure you have logged in and there are at least three items in your shopping cart.

14. When the breakpoint is reached in `Page_Load`, press F5 to continue.

15. Continue through the checkout process, noticing that the breakpoint doesn't get hit when you click the Next button. The breakpoint in `Page_Load` will only be reached the first time the page is loaded because the code block in which the breakpoint is set is only when `IsPostBack` is `false`.

16. When you get to the end of the checkout process, click Finish, and another breakpoint will be reached, as shown in Figure 15-12.

17. From the Debug menu, select Step Over, or press F10. Notice that execution moves to the next line.

18. Keep pressing F10 until you get to the line that sets the `@Quantity` parameter. Notice how execution moves to the next line each time you step.

19. Hover the cursor over the item of `item.Quantity`, and you'll see the tooltip showing the value of the variable.

20. Without moving the currently active line, hover the cursor over the item of the `foreach` line. You'll see another tooltip, but this time there isn't a value. That's because this is a complex type, a `CartItem`, but notice that there is a little plus sign on the left.

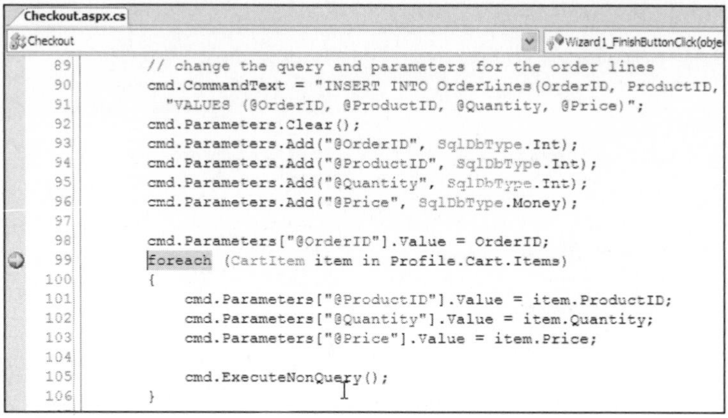

```
Checkout.aspx.cs
Checkout                                    Wizard1_FinishButtonClick(obje
        // change the query and parameters for the order lines
        cmd.CommandText = "INSERT INTO OrderLines(OrderID, ProductID,
          "VALUES (@OrderID, @ProductID, @Quantity, @Price)";
        cmd.Parameters.Clear();
        cmd.Parameters.Add("@OrderID", SqlDbType.Int);
        cmd.Parameters.Add("@ProductID", SqlDbType.Int);
        cmd.Parameters.Add("@Quantity", SqlDbType.Int);
        cmd.Parameters.Add("@Price", SqlDbType.Money);

        cmd.Parameters["@OrderID"].Value = OrderID;
        foreach (CartItem item in Profile.Cart.Items)
        {
            cmd.Parameters["@ProductID"].Value = item.ProductID;
            cmd.Parameters["@Quantity"].Value = item.Quantity;
            cmd.Parameters["@Price"].Value = item.Price;

            cmd.ExecuteNonQuery();
        }
```

Figure 15-12

21. Hover over or click the +, and the properties (both public and private) are shown for the item (see Figure 15-13).

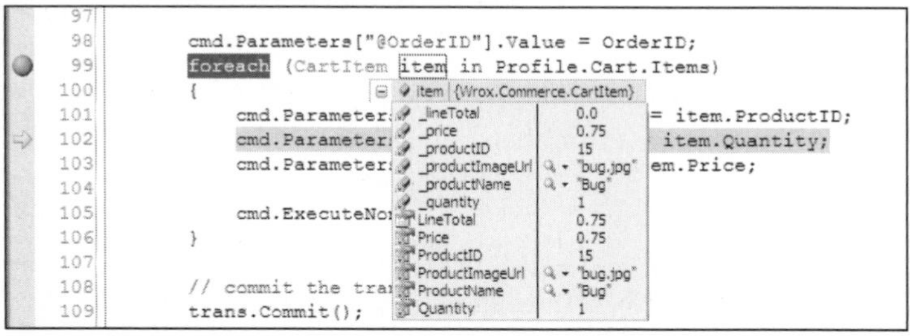

```
        cmd.Parameters["@OrderID"].Value = OrderID;
        foreach (CartItem item in Profile.Cart.Items)
        {
            cmd.Parameter   item {Wrox.Commerce.CartItem}     = item.ProductID;
            cmd.Parameter     _lineTotal         0.0             item.Quantity;
            cmd.Parameter     _price             0.75          em.Price;
                              _productID         15
                              _productImageUrl   "bug.jpg"
            cmd.ExecuteNo     _productName       "Bug"
        }                     _quantity          1
                              LineTotal          0.75
                              Price              0.75
        // commit the tra     ProductID          15
        trans.Commit();       ProductImageUrl    "bug.jpg"
                              ProductName        "Bug"
                              Quantity           1
```

Figure 15-13

22. From the Debug menu, select Step Into, or press F11. This will step into the line of code, opening up the code for the shopping cart, in the property `get`, as depicted in Figure 15-14.

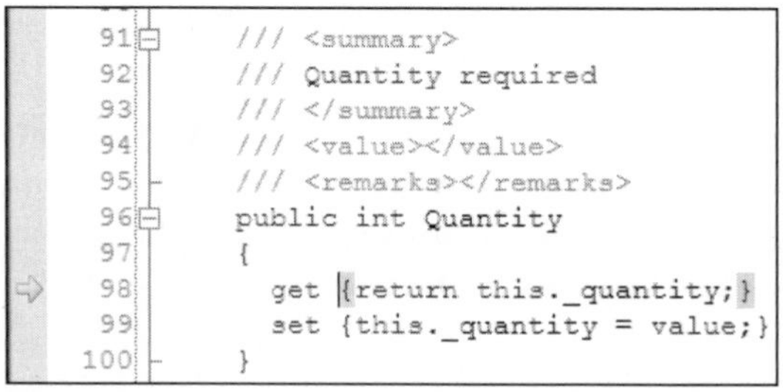

```
    /// <summary>
    /// Quantity required
    /// </summary>
    /// <value></value>
    /// <remarks></remarks>
    public int Quantity
    {
      get {return this._quantity;}
      set {this._quantity = value;}
    }
```

Figure 15-14

23. Keep pressing F11 until you are back into the checkout code.

24. Right-click the `trans.Commit()` line, and select the Run To Cursor option. Notice how all intermediate code is run, but that the next line is the `trans.Commit()` line.

25. From the Debug menu, select Delete All Breakpoints, or select Control+Shift+F9.

26. Press F5 to continue the code, and you'll be back in the browser.

How It Works

Debugging works because VWD controls the interaction of code. Normally the code runs without interruption, but a breakpoint tells VWD to suspend code at the appropriate line. And because VWD is in control, its debugging capabilities enable you to view variables, step through code line by line, and so on. Stepping through code is further enhanced by the fact that you can step into code called from the current routine. In this example, you stepped from the code in `Checkout.aspx.cs` into `Shopping.cs`, enabling you to follow the program flow line by line.

Debugging is extremely useful for not only tracking down problems in code, but also for understanding the flow of code. You can use it to understand which methods are called, the order in which they are called, and what code does in those methods. It's a practical skill that will make you a good programmer, so it's worthwhile spending time getting used to the debugger.

It's worth pointing out the difference between the various actions of the debug toolbar. These are summarized in the following table. An empty entry for the shortcut key means that there is no default key for that action.

Toolbar Icon	Shortcut Key	Description
	F5	Run the application if it currently isn't running, or continue running the application if it is currently paused at a breakpoint.
		Pause the running of the application.
	Shift+F5	Stop debugging the application.
	Ctrl+Shift+F5	Restart the application.
		Show the next statement, which highlights the next statement to be executed.
	F11	Step into a method. If the current line contains a method or property from another class, then stepping into that method will load the code file for the class and allow stepping through the code for the method or property.
	F10	Step over a method. If the current line contains a method or property from another class, then stepping over will execute the line without allowing stepping through the the code for the method or property.

Table continued on following page

Toolbar Icon	Shortcut Key	Description
	Shift+F11	Step out, which steps out of the current method or property. This is useful if you have stepped into a method but don't want to continue stepping though the lines. Stepping out will take you back to the calling routine.
Hex		Hex display, which displays the output in hexadecimal.
		Show the output window, which shows the actions VWD or VS take during debugging.

It's worth getting used to using both the buttons and the shortcut keys because it makes debugging quicker.

During the debugging exercise, you saw how you could hover the cursor over a variable to see the contents of that variable. But the viewing of variables is not just restricted to hovering the cursor over them, because there are special debugging windows that help with this. One of these is the Locals window (see Figure 15-15), which shows the local variables for the current procedure.

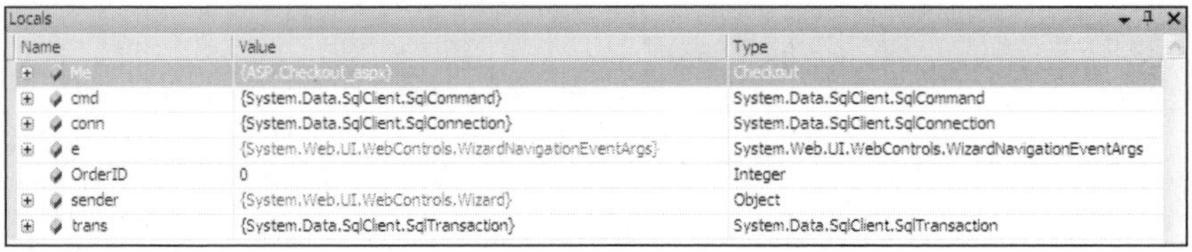

Name	Value	Type
Me	{ASP.Checkout_aspx}	Checkout
cmd	{System.Data.SqlClient.SqlCommand}	System.Data.SqlClient.SqlCommand
conn	{System.Data.SqlClient.SqlConnection}	System.Data.SqlClient.SqlConnection
e	{System.Web.UI.WebControls.WizardNavigationEventArgs}	System.Web.UI.WebControls.WizardNavigationEventArgs
OrderID	0	Integer
sender	{System.Web.UI.WebControls.Wizard}	Object
trans	{System.Data.SqlClient.SqlTransaction}	System.Data.SqlClient.SqlTransaction

Figure 15-15

Here you have all of the local variables, and those that are complex types can be expanded to show the properties.

The Watch window allows you to watch variables. When in Debug mode, you can highlight a variable, right-click it and select Add Watch from the menu. The use of the Watch window is the same as the Locals window, the only difference being that the Watch window only shows variables that you choose.

The Call Stack shows the current stack trace, which is the hierarchy of methods — which methods have been called from other methods. You can see the Call Stack at the bottom right of the screen when you are debugging. For example, in the shopping cart code, the stack trace displayed in Figure 15-16 might be shown.

Here the highlighted line is the current line of code, and you can see that it is the `Quantity` property of the `CartItem` (`get_Quantity` is shown because this is actually how the underlying code works; showing it is the `Get` part of the property). The second line shows the method that called this `Quantity` property, and this is `Wizard1_FinishButtonClick`.

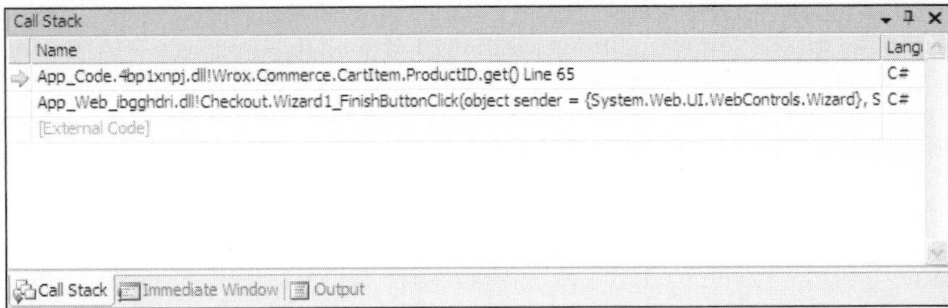

Figure 15-16

There are other windows, but Locals, Watch, and Call Stack aree the most common, and to get the best from the debugger you really have to practice. It's worth experimenting just to get a feel for how the debugger works, and the sort of things that are possible.

Summary

It may seem odd that we've had a whole chapter on the negative aspects of building web sites, but ultimately this will make you a better developer. After all, possessing knowledge is all well and good, but knowing how to cope with problems that arise is just as important. So this chapter looked at defensive coding, where you must take a pessimistic attitude. This takes the view that your code should be as robust as possible, not making assumptions about anything, such as parameters passed into methods. This is especially true when you're dealing with SQL statements that take data from the user, so you looked at how to replace the building of a SQL statement using concatenation with `SqlParameter` objects to prevent hacking attacks.

Another part of defensive coding is the use of validation controls, which provide a simple way to ensure that data entered by users is correct. Because these controls give both client- and server-side validation, users get a great experience because the validation notifies them of problems before posting back to the server.

Additionally, this chapter discussed the following topics:

- Exceptions, where you learned how to cope with the unexpected (cue the inquisition leaping in from off frame — "Nobody expects the exception" — apologies to the Monty Python team) Dealing with exceptions is a tricky business, and should be limited to those situations where you can gracefully recover from the problem. One of the key tenets is that you should always leave the application in a stable state when recovering from exceptions.
- Handling exceptions globally or at least how to manage their details globally, with the `global.asax` file. You saw that for both trapped and untrapped exceptions, the details can be centrally logged, ensuring that you always know of errors wherever they happen with the application.

- Tracing and debugging, and how you can track down problems within code. Tracing gives the capability to write the status of the running code, with the capability to switch the trace output on and off without affecting the trace statements themselves. Debugging delves into the code in more detail, enabling you to step through the code as it runs. These are the key techniques of learning how to find errors.

You're very nearly at the end of the book, and a lot of material has been covered. The final chapter looks at topics that will lead you from the book content to further learning and at topics of how to move forward with the knowledge you have. It also covers how to deploy your application so that it can be hosted by an ISP, allowing your great code to be seen by the whole world.

Exercises

1. Add defensive coding to the `GenerateThumbnail` method of the `ImageHandling` class stored in the `App_Code` directory.
2. Add validation controls to the Checkout page, the part that accepts the delivery address. There is a check box to copy the address from the membership details of the user, but there is nothing to ensure that all of the fields are filled in.
3. Use the debugger.

Deployment, Builds, and Finishing Up

It's been a long journey since you started this book by building a quick example web site, and then starting to build your full-fledged Wrox United application. You now have a web site that uses e-commerce to take customer details and credit card numbers, displays up-to-the-minute content, allows users to view (and listen to) multimedia, and references a multitude of data sources, all within the course of 15 chapters. This is the kind of thing that could have taken six months in the past and a whole team of developers. However, it doesn't end here. I'm often tempted at the end of a project to put my feet up and say, well I've done all the hard work, it's all smooth sailing now. However, I have been painfully disabused of this notion on more than one occasion. Even if you're confident of the extremely unlikely scenario of your application having no bugs and being simple to maintain, and your client never having any further questions to ask or features to add, you still have to deploy your site. Visual Web Developer has a feature that allows you to copy your web site from a local folder to a remote location, and you'll make use of that in this chapter.

After you've deployed your site, what next? If you succeed in becoming a professional developer, you will undoubtedly talk to plenty of companies who will set the final deadline as the day you deliver the working code to them. If you pencil in another project the day after this deadline, you might end up getting into trouble when you find yourself required back on site at your old project because something breaks down or doesn't work in the way it was intended. Testing is often completely overlooked by both companies and developers. Chapters 14 and 15 talked about various ways for testing your code as you create it, but testing your code after you've deployed the site should also feature in your timeline. If possible, you should also test it alongside your proposed user base. Even if everything goes fine, you should be prepared to maintain this site, make adjustments, and make sure that the site owners can run it in your absence.

And lastly, what should you do next after reading this book? Do you run out and apply for a set of developer jobs? Or do you have to go out and buy another book? You'll get a thorough grounding in what you should be looking to do next.

This chapter discusses the following topics:

- ❑ Deploying your site
- ❑ Testing and maintaining your site
- ❑ Where to now?

Site Deployment

Site deployment is the process of installing your site on the customer's machine and making your site available and accessible to the outside world — in other words, broadcasting it to the masses. In the first versions of ASP, and indeed with any pure HTML site, the idea of deployment went little beyond "parcel up all your files in a zip file, and unzip them to the correct folder on the site." For simple sites, this approach still works, but for more complex ones, you're asking for trouble if you follow this method and expect no problems.

One of the weaknesses of Visual Web Developer is that, unlike Visual Studio.NET, there isn't a special deployment wizard that can wrap all the different bits and pieces into a single installation file. However, there is an option in VWD that allows you to take your existing web site and publish the web site on a remote machine. There is also a second method that can be used if you prefer, which you learn about later in the chapter.

Before you do that, you should make sure you have everything necessary to ensure your site will work on another machine by compiling a checklist.

Checklist

Here's a simple checklist of common things you would normally expect to feature in a typical deployment:

- ❑ **HTML and CSS files:** Your design and structure.
- ❑ **ASPX files:** Your main pages.
- ❑ **ASPX.VB or ASPX.CS files:** The code-behind files.
- ❑ **ASCX and ASCX.VB/.CS files:** The user controls.
- ❑ **Database files (.MDB or .MDF):** The back end of the site.
- ❑ **Image files (.JPG, .GIF, .PNG):** Easily forgotten but vital to the sites working.
- ❑ **Multimedia files:** Includes both video and audio files.
- ❑ **XML files:** .XML and .XSD files.
- ❑ **Third-party components or controls:** ActiveX controls, Java applets, or such like.
- ❑ **License files:** Required to make your components work.

Quite often you will find that despite your best intentions, files can become spread out across folders all over your machine. It's a great idea to centralize them first and even try to deploy them on another local machine of your own if you have one.

Compiling and Running Your Application

The next step is to make sure that your site actually compiles and runs. In Chapter 15, you looked at simple reasons why a site might not compile, and there is no point in deploying a site that doesn't compile. Also be aware that even if your site happily compiles on your machine, it might not compile or run on your host's or client's machine. You must make sure that things like local references are changed so that file references are specific to the new machine and that the requisite components are installed. This is the most likely reason for your code failing on your host's machine. The best way to do this is to place any machine-specific information within the `Web.config` file and then reference it from inside the `appSettings`, as discussed in Chapter 2. Then you can change any information in the `Web.config` file without affecting your application.

Say, for example, you put a reference to a folder in the `<appSettings>` section of `Web.config` and add a `key` and a `value` attribute as follows:

```
<appSettings>
...
<add key="WroxUnited" value="C:\Program Files\Wrox United" />
...
</appSettings>
```

You can then access these values from your code as follows:

```
string WroxULocation =
System.ConfigurationManager.Configuration.AppSettings["WroxUnited"];
```

Of course, you will probably be faced with a scenario where you want to have a reference to a local file and also a reference to that same file in a location on your remote server. In this case, you can place a reference to both locations in `Web.config`. Here `LOCALHOST` is the active file location:

```
<appSettings>
  <!-- LOCALHOST -->
  <add key="WroxUnited" value="C:\Program Files\Wrox United" />
...
  <!-- REMOTE
  <add key="WroxUnited" value="D:\Websites\Wrox United" />
  -->

</appSettings>
```

All you need to do then is uncomment the `REMOTE` settings and comment out the `LOCALHOST` settings instead. In this way, no code needs to change. Make sure you comment which of the locations is local and which is remote, because it might not be entirely obvious to anyone else who uses the code. If you have reason to change the location of the file, you only have to change it once in `Web.config` and not every time it is mentioned within your code.

This doesn't just stop with remote file locations, but also with connection strings. If you are using a local database to test your code, you will have to change the connection settings as well. Your local database might use SQL Express, but your main server might be SQL Server 2005 — once again, no extra code is needed, it can just be worked by commenting the line out:

```
<ConnectionStrings>
  <!-- LOCALHOST -->
  <add key="WroxUnitedConnectionString" value="Data
Source=.\SQLEXPRESS;AttachDbFileName=|Data Directory|\WroxUnited.mdf;Integrated
Security=True;User Instance=True;" providername="System.Data.SqlDataClient"/>
...
  <!-- REMOTE
  <add key="WroxUnitedConnectionString" value=" Data
Source=MainSQLServer;AttachDbFileName=|Data Directory|\WroxUnited.mdf;Integrated
Security=True;User Instance=True;User ID=auser;Password=56gTR4£s "
providername="System.Data.SqlDataClient" />
  -->

</ConnectionStrings >
```

`LOCALHOST` in this example is the active string. If you changed the provider name, you could pass connection strings to other databases such as Access or MySQL or even Oracle.

Publishing the Site

After you're sure that everything is ready and everything compiles, you can use Visual Web Developer to publish your web site for you. There isn't much more to say on the subject — it's literally easier to go ahead and do it.

Try It Out — Publishing the Wrox United Web Site

1. Open the chapter copy of WroxUnited (`C:\BegASPNET2\Begin\Chapter16\WroxUnited`) and select the Web Site⇨Copy Web Site option (see Figure 16-1).

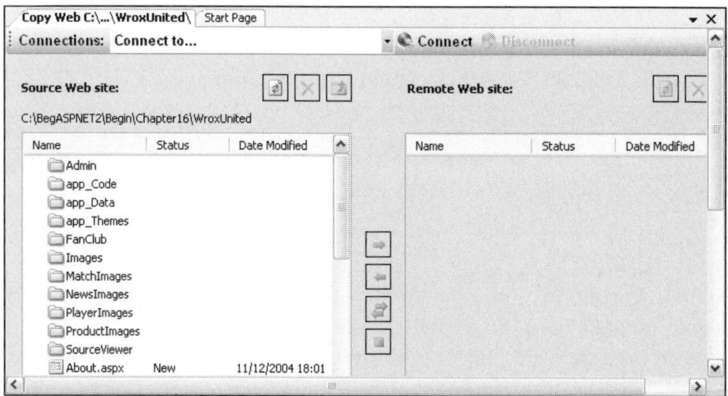

Figure 16-1

2. Click the Connections: Connect To box and enter **WroxUnited2** into the text box, as shown in Figure 16-2.

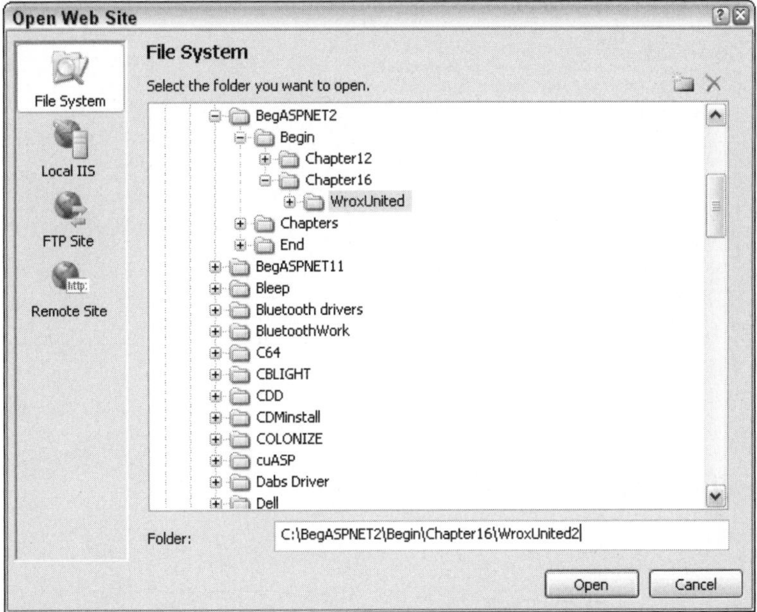

Figure 16-2

Notice that to actually deploy to a remote site, you need to select the Remote Site icon on the left-hand menu and then supply the URL or IP address of the location of the site, possibly entering relevant user ID and password details in along the way. It is unfortunately not possible to supply test web space for readers to deploy their sites to.

3. Click Open and click Yes when asked whether you would like to create a new folder.

4. Select all the files, as shown in Figure 16-3.

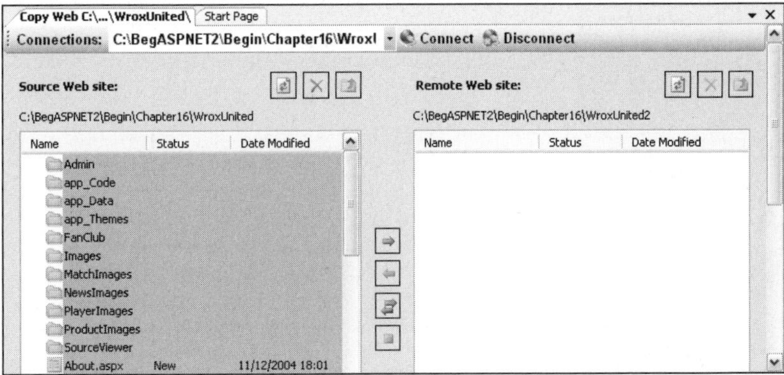

Figure 16-3

5. Click the blue single right-arrow button to copy the files across (see Figure 16-4).

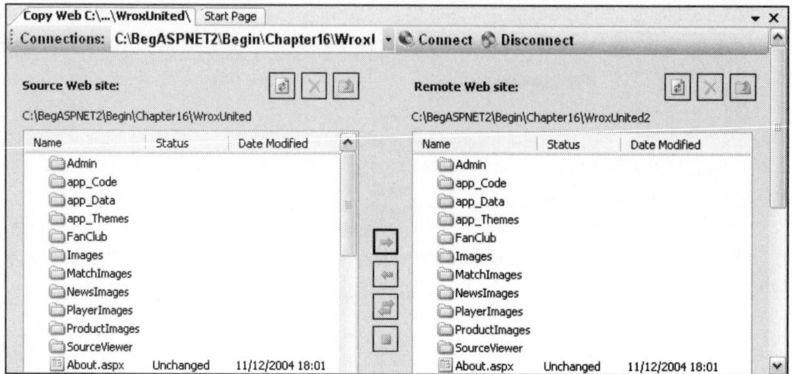

Figure 16-4

6. Close the web site down, by selecting Close Project from the File menu.
7. Select Open➪Web Site and select WroxUnited2.
8. Run the new web site. It should look like the old one (see Figure 16-5).

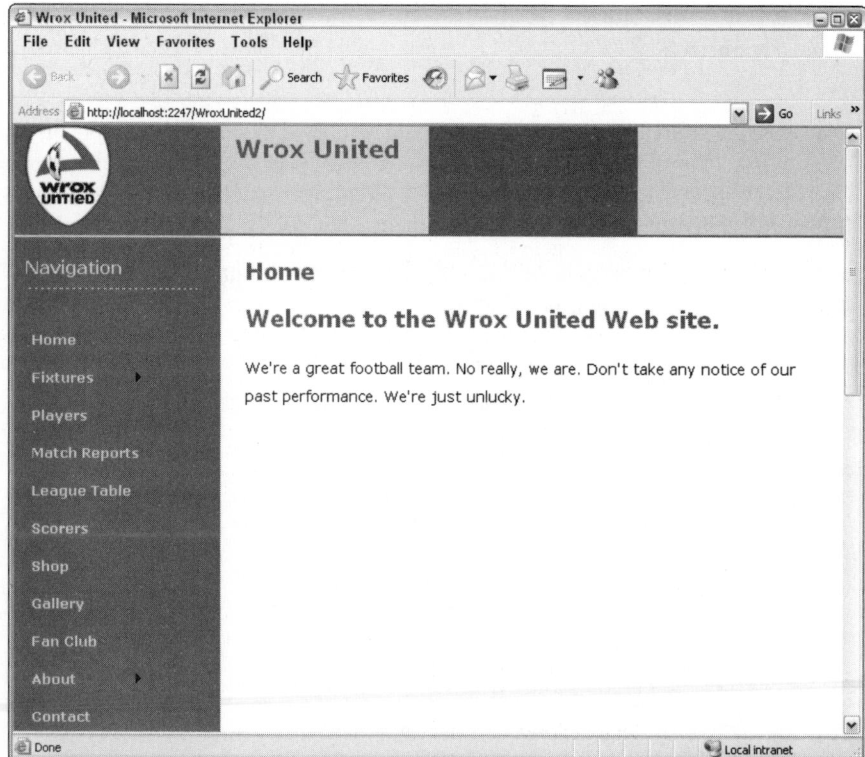

Figure 16-5

How It Works

In this Try It Out, you used the Copy Web Site option of Visual Web Developer to produce a complete, identical copy of the Wrox United site on your local machine. This mirrors the way in which you would go about deploying a web site to a remote location. In fact, if you have a remote machine that is also running ASP.NET 2.0, try deploying the Wrox United site on it yourself.

There really is very little to the physical act of deployment. The problems you may encounter are either caused by elements in your application that are locked in to your current setup (such as referencing files on a C:\ drive, when the host uses E:\ instead) or if you attempt to copy files into a folder or location where some files already exist. In this case, a blue question mark will appear next to the offending file in the left-hand dialog box, and you will get a dialog box (see Figure 16-6) that asks you whether you want to copy over the existing file.

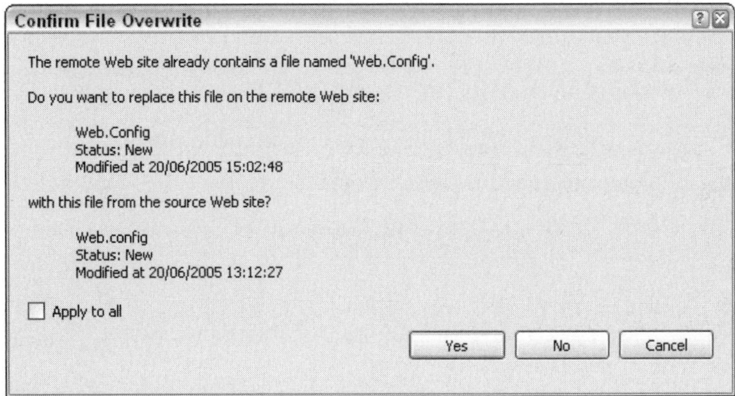

Figure 16-6

Before .NET, if you needed to install a component or control, this would require copying your component to the appropriate folder and registering that component via some ugly low-level tools we don't want to talk about here. In .NET, to install the component all you had to do was to copy the component's file into the bin folder of your application, which occasionally had some unexpected and unpleasant side-effects; however, in .NET 2.0 dropping components into the App_Code folder is all you need to do to be able to start using the component immediately. If you use third-party components (that is, separate executables), these should be installed separately.

XCOPY Deployment

There is a second way to deploy applications in .NET, if you don't have Visual Studio.NET. This is known as XCOPY deployment. This is a command-line tool that can be used to copy your site from one location to another. It takes a number of options, as detailed here:

- **/ E** copies folders, subfolders, and files, including empty ones.
- **/ H** copies both hidden files and system files in addition to the unhidden and non-system files.
- **/ I** specifies that the destination is a folder and to create the folder if it does not already exist.

- **/K** keeps all of the existing file and folder attributes such as read-only, which would otherwise be lost.
- **/O** retains all of the security-related permission ACLs (Access Control Lists — rules for who gets access to a particular resource) of the file and folders.
- **/R** overwrites files marked as read-only.

All you need to do is provide the location of where you want to copy the web site from and where you need to copy the web site to, and along with the relevant options, it will copy everything that you need. So typing in the following command would copy all files and folders to the WroxUnited3 folder:

```
XCOPY C:\BegASPNET2\Begin\Chapter16\WroxUnited
C:\BegASPNET2\Begin\Chapter16\WroxUnited3 /E
```

You can see how this works in the following Try It Out.

Try It Out   Publishing Wrox United Using XCOPY

1. Click Start⇨Run and type **CMD** to bring up the command prompt.
2. Type the following command and press Enter:

```
XCOPY C:\BegASPNET2\Begin\Chapter16\WroxUnited
C:\BegASPNET2\Begin\Chapter16\WroxUnited3 /E
```

3. You are presented with the screen shown in Figure 16-7, and asked whether the target is a file name or directory. Press d because it is a directory. XCOPY will now copy all the files over.

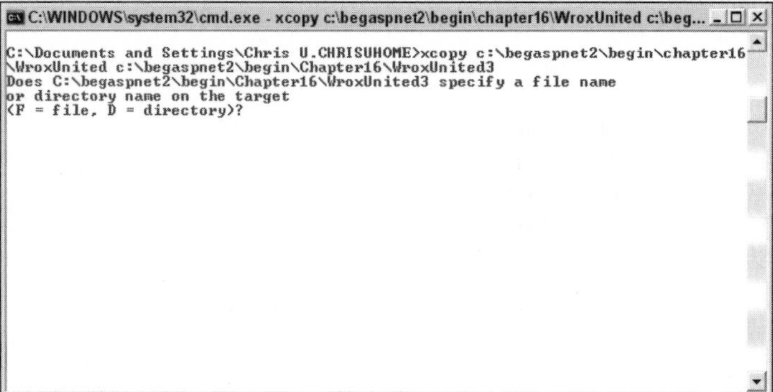

Figure 16-7

4. Close the command prompt.
5. Open Visual Web Developer, choose File⇨Open⇨Web Site, and select WroxUnited3.
6. Run the new web site. It should look just like the last one (see Figure 16-8).

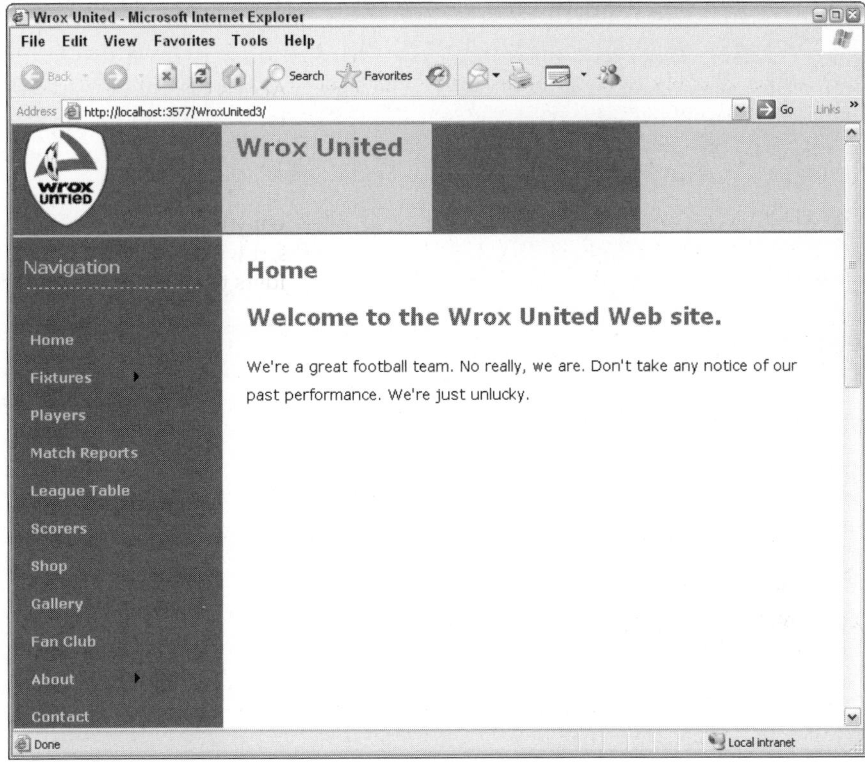

Figure 16-8

How It Works

The XCOPY option works in the same way as the Copy Web Site option in Visual Web Developer. It copies all of the files from one location to another. There are two main differences, however. The first difference is that you don't need Visual Web Developer installed, which is useful if you have been forwarded a web site from someone else in a zip file and want to, say, install it locally, test it, and then deploy it. The second difference is that because it is a command-line tool, it gives you more options on which files to copy and which files not to copy, with settings like /R to overwrite existing files that are marked as read-only.

Common Problems Encountered When Deploying a Site

You shouldn't have any problems with the physical act of deployment itself. However, what happens if you correctly copy all of the files over, install all of the relevant components, and install the third-party ones, and deployment still doesn't work?

With a fairly new technology, it's harder to compile a definitive list of problems, bugs, and glitches the user might experience — these things were put together from years of user frustrations. However, on our travels in the beta versions of ASP.NET 2.0, we came across a couple of gotchas that could break your site, which are worth talking about now.

Enabling App Data Permissions

If you are getting errors whenever the user runs a page that accesses a database, then suspect permissions problems immediately. Every time you move a database to a new server that uses SQL Server, you have to set up the relevant permissions for the NETWORK SERVICE for the `App_Data` folder. The reason you have to do this is ASP.NET 2.0 runs under this particular service, and so if ASP.NET 2.0 wants to access the database, a request to access it will come from this particular service.

> **In ASP.NET 1.1, you would add permissions for the ASPNET account to do this. In ASP.NET 2.0, the NETWORK SERVICE account does the same. However, there have been occasions in the beta where enabling NETWORK SERVICE didn't work and ASPNET permissions had to be enabled as well. If, after enabling permissions for NETWORK SERVICE, things still don't work in the way intended, you might want to enable permissions for the ASPNET account, in the same way as outlined next for the NETWORK SERVICE account. You can find more details about this in Appendix B.**

You can enable these permissions in two ways, either via Windows Explorer or via SQL Server Enterprise Manager.

Enabling Permissions via Windows Explorer

Go to the folder of your web application in Windows Explorer, right-click your application, select the Properties, and click the Security tab, which is shown in Figure 16-9.

Figure 16-9

Here's an important note for Windows XP Home Edition users: There is no Security tab visible because something called Simple File Sharing is enabled by default. To turn off Simple File Sharing, you need to restart your PC in Safe Mode (by pressing F8 before XP starts) and then log in as Administrator. You'll get a warning about running in Safe Mode. Click Yes to accept it and then turn off Simple File Sharing. To do this, double-click My Computer, click Tools⇨Folder Options, click the View tab, and then select the Use Simple File Sharing (Recommended) check box. Then you can locate the folder whose permissions you want to change, right-click that folder, select Properties, and change the permissions.

Click the Add button to bring up the Select Users or Groups dialog box (see Figure 16-10). Type **Network Service** and click Check Names. (If you don't type in the correct case, it will capitalize the name for you.)

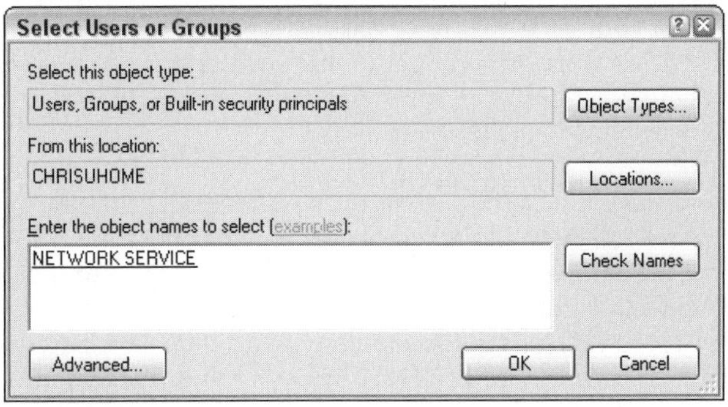

Select Users or Groups

Select this object type:

Users, Groups, or Built-in security principals | Object Types...

From this location:

CHRISUHOME | Locations...

Enter the object names to select (examples):

NETWORK SERVICE | Check Names

Advanced... | OK | Cancel

Figure 16-10

Click OK. In the Properties dialog box (refer to Figure 16-9), make sure the Write check box is checked (it is unchecked by default) and click Apply. It's as simple as that.

If the machine is joined to a domain, the user must select the Locations button and pick the current machine, rather than the domain. That's because NETWORK SERVICE is an account on your machine. By default, the dialog will attempt to add the domain name, rather than the machine name.

Enabling Permissions via SQL Server Enterprise Manager

This method will only work if you have SQL Server installed. If you bring up SQL Query Analyzer, you can run the following script (just type in the following code to SQL Analyzer), substituting in the name of the database you want to grant access to (note that you will need to log in to the database as an administrator first):

```
sp_grantlogin 'NT AUTHORITY\Network Service'

USE aspnetdb
GO
sp_grantdbaccess 'NT AUTHORITY\Network Service', 'Network Service'
```

```
USE aspnetdb
GO
sp_addrolemember 'database_you_wish_to_grant_access_to, 'Network Service'
```

Click Run to run the query, and this will have the same effect as the previous instructions.

Is Your Application Offline? (Using App_Offline.htm)

This is one of those things that I saw in the beta that really tripped me up; on one occasion I ran my Wrox United application to test it and was staggered to find that every single page returned an HTTP 404 error. Even stranger, I was browsing them from within Visual Web Developer at the time. It took me a few hours and help from the other people on the book to figure out what had happened. It actually turned out to be a really useful feature.

If you need to take your site offline very quickly, you can place a file called `app_offline.htm` in your main application folder. This makes your web site unavailable to everybody. You can place in the HTML file the text that you want your users to be able to view for the duration of the site's downtime. The advantage is that ASP.NET is working throughout this downtime, and you are able to test the site without having to worry about what users can see in the outside world. However, there are times when this file is created for you, which led to the problems I had.

Apparently during some operations, the `app_offline.htm` file is temporarily copied to your application folder and then, in theory, it should be removed when the operation is completed. A crash during an operation can leave the file behind. Unfortunately, this was a zero-length file in beta 2, and this provided no clue to the user as to what occurred. The user was just left with every page in their site returning 404 errors. Normally, the `app_offline.htm` file should not be left behind, but unfortunately in some cases, it gets left over. In the final release of ASP.NET 2.0, there is a message that informs users of what happened so they know to remove the offending item (see Figure 16-11).

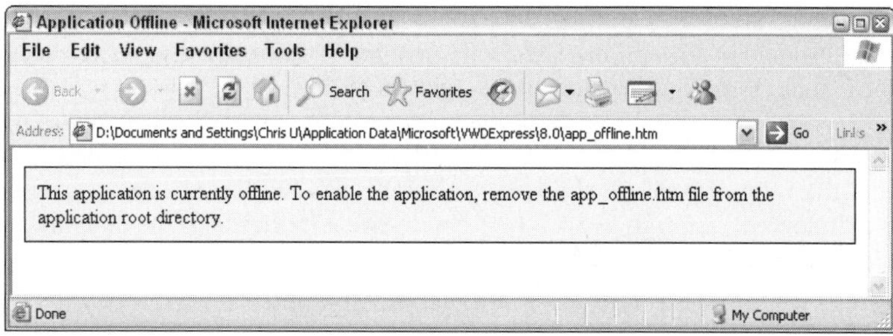

Figure 16-11

This can turn up quite a few times if your application is being unruly, so be warned. It will turn up in the root folder of your application folder. In Figure 16-11, you see the version of it that comes with Visual Web Developer by default.

Problems with IIS

Of course, if you test your site with ASP.NET Development Server, you might encounter some problems when you deploy your site on IIS. First, make sure your application is configured as a virtual directory (this process is described in Appendix B). Occasionally IIS doesn't work in the way it should, and often non-specific errors can be fixed if you run the `aspnet_regiis` executable with the `-i` switch.

To do this, go to the command prompt and go to the `C:\Windows\Microsoft.Net\Framework\v2.0.50727` folder. From this folder, type the following and press Enter:

```
aspnet_regiis -i
```

This quite often sorts out non-specific problems such as HTTP 500 errors.

Trial and Error

If you still have no success, go back, delete all the files, and try it again. If you are getting a particular error consistently, look up that error on `http://support.microsoft.com` and see if that has any solutions. If this doesn't fix things, then another way is to copy the text of the error and paste it straight into Google or your favorite search engine. This usually comes up with some other people experiencing the same problems and solutions more often than not. If not, try posting on one of the online forums recommended later in this chapter.

Testing and Maintenance

After you've successfully negotiated deployment, you might be excused for doing a quick double take. Testing, haven't you already done that? Given that this is the 21st century, you might have expected attitudes toward testing to have improved considerably — however, if anything, trends have reversed. For example, several very popular games arrived on the market in a practically unusable state because they hadn't been tested correctly. Hastily compiled patches of 20–50MB were required to rectify the situation. However, as a developer, you will probably not have this luxury. You will probably see your client week in and week out, and if the application doesn't work they will tell you about it and maybe withhold payment until the problem is rectified. They might still not grant you any extra time to test, but that is the name of the game.

Testing Before and After

Of course, while you're building an application, you should test every component, but once the build is deployed and completed, you should also make time to test the application as a whole. In particular, you should sit alongside your prospective users and watch them test it. Some clients believe that testing is the whole responsibility of the developer, but the relationship the developer shares with his code is similar to that between the author and his text. You wouldn't expect an author to be able to adequately edit his own text, and if an author uses incorrect grammar, then it's quite likely that they won't be able to spot their own incorrect grammar usage. If a developer creates a piece of logically unsound code, there's a fair chance they might not be able to spot it either. Only in hard testing, when a user who puts in often totally unpredictable values, are some errors revealed. Some textbooks will tell you to put aside as much time as you took to develop the application for testing it. This isn't over-cautious — the bigger the application, the greater the likelihood of bugs creeping in, and the longer it can take to find them. If possible with a web site for a client, get them to test it in-house, on a test server before they put it on a live server. And don't be worried to admit to bugs. Finding bugs isn't the sign of a bad developer — a bad developer is one who refuses to admit to the possibility of any bugs in the first place. The best advice is get your clients to test the application thoroughly and make sure they have time to do it. A couple of testing methods are worth mentioning here.

Unit Tests

Unit tests are a particular form of testing where you write a test for every non-trivial function or method in the code. You can separate the different sections of the program and demonstrate which parts are working in this way. Unit tests make it easier for programmers to change individual pieces of code because they can go back to the code and test the unit independently. So if you suddenly think of a new feature, you can add it without worrying about having to break the entire application.

Writing a Test Plan

Because unit tests, or indeed the whole practice of testing, can be time consuming, it's best to have a test plan up front to aid the organization of testing. A *test plan* is simply a systematic written approach to testing, detailing the experiments and tests you want to perform on the code. Test plans don't just apply to computer programs — they can apply to any kind of engineering. A single test case in a test plan for a dishwasher might be, "Test what happens when you open the dishwasher door halfway through a working cycle." Some dishwashers would shower you with scalding water, some would refuse to open, and some would stop mid-cycle and let you retrieve the last cup in the house. There isn't necessarily a right answer to what should happen, but you should write a list of scenarios that you would like to test, and record the outcomes and check that the scenarios and outcomes are what you both want, and what your end-user thinks is satisfactory.

Maintenance

Maintenance is the practice of keeping your site up and running after it has been successfully deployed. In some ways, it's like a glorified debugging process — some bugs might not show up until long after the site's deployment, but you'll still be expected to fix them. In other ways, maintenance will be about performance monitoring: how fast is your site running? How many users is it handling? Can it cope with that? This is a science in itself. This is one area where ASP.NET 2.0 has come on in leaps and bounds, with the addition of instrumentation, and the capability to instrument your application.

Instrumentation and Health Monitoring

Instrumentation or *instrumenting* is a term you will come across if you have to do any monitoring or maintenance of your system. The instrumenting of your application is the monitoring of your system or your application's function, checking to see that all is working the way it should be.

ASP.NET 2.0 has a lot of instrumentation features for the developer. You've already looked at the ability to run traces and logging and learned that there are performance counters that you can use, but are beyond the scope of this book. However, there is another new feature that is of great interest and of particular use after your application has been deployed, and that is the introduction of the `<healthMonitoring>` element.

The `<healthMonitoring>` element can be used at the system or application level and enables you to monitor when specific events have occurred and write notifications of these events to an event log, a

SQL Server database, or even to e-mail the administrator. Events that might be of interest could be a failed login, or an error occurring in the application. Besides logging events, the `<healthMonitoring>` element enables you to test the "health" of the system via a `heartbeat` attribute, which sets up an event that is generated at a predefined interval—if you can "hear" the heartbeat, you know your application is working fine. If you don't receive this heartbeat, you know there might well be problems.

To enable health monitoring, all you need to do is place the `<healthMonitoring>` element in your `Web.config` file and set the `enabled` attribute to `true`. Health monitoring is handled by three elements within `<healthMonitoring>`, which have a close relationship with each other:

- The `<providers>` element specifies where you want to send the information you have collected, which can be an event log or a database.
- The `<rules>` element specifies the name of the provider you want to write your information to and the event name you want to instrument.
- The `<eventMappings>` element specifies a name of event you want to monitor, and maps it to an actual event or set of events. The settings of this element must correspond to a valid event type. A list of valid types is contained within the `<eventMappings>` element in the `Web.config.comments` file.

It just takes a couple of attribute changes to alter an application that writes to the event log for failed logins, to one that e-mails the administrator with details.

Monitoring for Events

You can test for a range of events using the `<healthMonitoring>` element. These are as described in the following table.

Event Name	Description of Event
`WebHeartbeatEvent`	A regular event that provides statistics about the application or system.
`WebManagementEvent`	A base class event for all events that carry application and worker process information.
`WebApplicationLifetimeEvent`	An event generated by every *significant* event that occurs in an application's lifetime, such as startup, restart, and shutdown.
`WebRequestEvent`	An event that is raised with every web request and contains information about the request and the thread on which it's executing.
`WebBaseErrorEvent`	A base class event for all health monitoring error events.
`WebErrorEvent`	An event generated when there are problems with configuration or application code.

Table continued on following page

Event Name	Description of Event
`WebRequestErrorEvent`	An event that is raised when an error occurs during a web request. This ignores common types of error such HTTP 404, and focuses on things like unhandled exceptions.
`WebFailureAuditEvent`	An event generated upon the failure of a security-related event, such as a file authorization, a URL authorization, or a login authentication.
`WebSuccessAuditEvent`	An event generated upon the success of a security-related event, such as a file authorization, a URL authorization, or a login authentication.
`WebAuthenticationFailureAuditEvent`	An event generated upon an unsuccessful login authentication.
`WebAuthenticationSuccessAuditEvent`	An event generated upon a successful login authentication.
`WebAuditEvent`	A base class for all audit events, both authentication and authorization.
`WebViewStateFailureAuditEvent`	An event that is generated on view state failure. The failure may indicate an attempt to tamper with the view state, or its reuse from another machine with a different key.

There is also a broad range of providers (sources) to which you can write your event information. These can all be found in the System.Web.Management namespace, and are detailed in the following table.

Provider Name	What the Provider Holds
`MailWebEventProvider`	Writes to an e-mail.
`SimpleMailWebEventProvider`	Writes to a simplified e-mail.
`TemplatedMailWebEventProvider`	Writes to a templated e-mail.
`TraceWebEventProvider`	Writes to a trace.
`EventLogWebEventProvider` (the default provider)	Writes to the Event Log.
`SqlWebEventProvider`	Writes to a SQL Server database.

Which Events Are You Interested In?

You have a list of events, and a list of possible places where you can write the events about how they were monitored. However, at the moment this is information overkill. You need to get back to basics and answer a simple question: Which events are you interested in monitoring?

Unfortunately, the answer is open-ended. It depends on what you want to monitor your application for. A lot of the events in your list generate huge numbers of events, both when the application is working correctly and when it isn't.

A good place to start would be security. If you aren't regularly changing code in your application, then most likely the greatest threat to your application's longevity and well-being is someone trying to hack. A key to finding good security events to instrument for is to locate which events under normal circumstances shouldn't be generating a large number, but in the event of an attack or suspicious data being provided, will generate a lot of events. When your system is being attacked, you are likely to see a number of such events, which in turn can help act as an early warning system.

The key events that monitor the security-related aspects of the application might be as follows:

- `WebErrorEvent`
- `WebAuthenticationFailureAuditEvent`
- `WebRequestErrorEvent`
- `WebViewStateFailureAuditEvent`

The `WebError` event should be monitored because any code failure is suspicious. The `WebAuthenticationFailureAuditEvent` should be monitored because any suspicious login activity should be carefully monitored. `WebRequestErrorEvent` and `WebViewStateFailure AuditEvent` might have failures if a hacker is trying to intercept responses from the server and forwarding his or her own fraudulent page in response. By default, the `WebErrorEvent` and `WebAuthenticationFailureAuditEvent` are turned on. This means that in the case of any failure, they are automatically logged to the Event Log. So if such an error (for example, a division by zero error) occurs in your application, you would see what's shown in Figure 16-12 in your Event Log under Application, under the source ASP.NET 2.050727.0 (or whichever version of ASP.NET is being run).

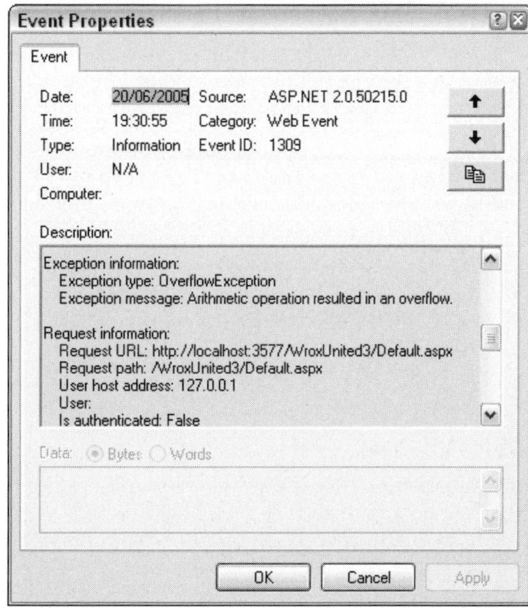

Figure 16-12

Because failed logins are written to the event log by default, take a look at how you could also log successful logins to your application in the Event Log. In this Try It Out, you track when a user logs in to Wrox United successfully, and you write details about it to the Event Log.

Try It Out Adding Health Monitoring to Wrox United

1. Open `Web.config` in the Wrox United application for this chapter. In `<system.web>`, add a `<healthMonitoring>` element as follows:

```
<healthMonitoring enabled="true">
</healthMonitoring>
```

2. Create another child element inside `<healthMonitoring>` called **<rules>**:

```
<rules>
<add provider="EventLogProvider" name="Success Audits" eventName=" LoginSuccess" />
</rules>
```

3. Create another child element inside `<healthMonitoring>` underneath `<rules>` called **<eventMappings>**:

```
<eventMappings>
<add name="LoginSuccess"
type="System.Web.Management.WebAuthenticationSuccessAuditEvent,System.Web,Version=2
.0.0.0,Culture=neutral,PublicKeyToken=b03f5f7f11d50a3a"
 startEventCode="0" endEventCode="2147483647"/> </eventMappings>
```

4. Run the application and login as **Dave**, password **dave@123**.

5. Go to the Control Panel and select Administrative Tools⇨Event Log, and you'll see the screen shown in Figure 16-13.

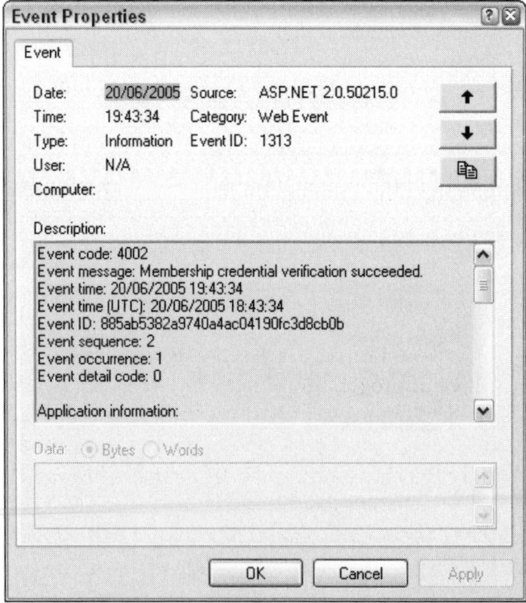

Figure 16-13

How It Works

The <healthMonitoring> element in the Web.config file does all of the work for you. You start by enabling <healthMonitoring> and then placing three elements inside it to make it work.

The <rules> element is used to map an event onto a provider. The <rules> element has three compulsory attributes: provider, name, and eventName. The provider attribute matches the name attribute specified in the <providers> element. You specify the Event Log in this element and a name for your rule, "Success Audits":

```
<rules>
<add provider="EventLogProvider" name="Success Audits" eventName="LoginSuccess" />
</rules>
```

The <eventMappings> element specifies a user-friendly name for the event and the specific type of the event you want to monitor. The type has to contain the system assembly details as well as information about that assembly such as the Version number, Culture, and PublicKeyToken:

```
<eventMappings>
<add name="LoginSuccess"
type="System.Web.Management.WebAuthenticationSuccessAuditEvent,System.Web,Version=2
.0.0.0,Culture=neutral,PublicKeyToken=b03f5f7f11d50a3a"
startEventCode="0" endEventCode="2147483647"/> </eventMappings>
```

Inside the global Web.config, you will find a tallying <providers> element, which is referenced by your <rules> element. The <providers> element specifies details about the source you write the error information to, such as Event Log or SQL Server database. Providers always have two compulsory attributes: name and type. The <provider> must use a name attribute corresponding with a name specified in <eventMappings>. Providers may have other compulsory attributes, but these will vary depending on the type of provider. The EventLogProvider only requires the name and type attributes. The EventLogProvider looks like this:

```
<providers>
<add name="EventLogProvider"
type="System.Web.Management.EventLogWebEventProvider,System.Web,Version=2.0.0.0,
Culture=neutral,PublicKeyToken=b03f5f7f11d50a3a" /></providers>
```

If you scroll down the Event Log entry, you will see a whole stack of useful information about the login. This information includes the event message, the time the error occurred, the location of the error, the error message, the user's IP address, whether or not they were authenticated, and much more.

Mailing an Administrator

Wrox United now writes to an Event Log, but this is only of use if the administrator is on hand to check the Event Log. A more proactive approach might involve e-mailing the administrator each time the monitored event takes place. Doing this requires only minimal alteration of the <healthMonitoring> element. You only need to change the rules of which provider you are indicating and the provider itself, and also add a SMTP section to the Web.config file (if there isn't an existing one). You can simply change the details of the <rules> element and the <providers> element and add an SMTP section.

Note that this Try It Out requires a working SMTP server. You will only be able to do this exercise if you have IIS installed with the SMTP service (done via the Add or Remove Programs section of Control Panel), and it must be set up to relay e-mail. Relaying e-mail can be set up by right-clicking the SMTP server in IIS, selecting Properties, choosing the Access tab, clicking the Relay button, and making sure the number 127.0.0.1 (the number for localhost) is granted permission for relaying mail.

Try It Out — Mailing the Administrator

1. Open `Web.config` and alter the `<rules>` element so that it reads as follows:

```
<add provider="EmailProvider" name="My Failure Audit" eventName="Failure Audits" />
```

2. Go to the `<providers>` element and change it so that it reads as follows:

```
<add name="EmailProvider"
        type="System.Web.Management.SimpleMailWebEventProvider"
           from="myemail@myserver.co.uk"
        to="myemail@myserver.co.uk"
        subjectPrefix="Failed Login Attempt:"
        buffer="true"
        bufferMode="Notification" />
```

Replace `myemail@myserver.co.uk` with your own SMTP server's domain name. If your machine is `TESTONE`, replace it with `myemail@testone.com`.

3. You'll also need to add a section to `Web.config` to configure the SMTP section. An example setting would look like the following, and of course you'd need to substitute in your own mail server's settings:

```
  <system.net>
    <mailSettings>
      <!-- these settings define the mail server settings
        from: the user name from which the email is sent - this is the application
that is sending the message
        host: the name of your mail server
        userName: the name the application will use to log into the mail server
        password: the password for the above user name
      -->
      <smtp from="admin@your-domain.com">
        <network host="your-mail-server-name"
                 userName="your-user-name"
                 password="your-password" />
      </smtp>
    </mailSettings>
  </system.net>
```

4. Run the application and wait. You should receive an e-mail within a minute.

How It Works

Instead of placing something in the Event Log, you are now e-mailed the details that you previously viewed in the Application section of the Event Log. To do this, you changed the rules and provider elements to specify a different provider.

The health monitoring features of ASP.NET 2.0 are a real plus for those of you trying to maintain an application and for either tracking down security breaches or hard-to-find bugs.

Scalability

The last scenario you might have to consider is what happens if the web site takes off. What happens if instead of the anticipated hundreds or thousands, you get millions of visitors? On one level, this might hit the performance of your application, it might exceed limits within your application, and it also might exceed the limits of your hardware.

For software considerations, it's best not to impose small limits on arrays and databases when you create them. You should always take care to close any open database connections. If you open up too many connections, you can end up with a Connection Pooling error. Unlike classic ASP where it was common practice to set the connection to Nothing, all that's needed is to close any open connections once you've finished them. The number of open connections that can be maintained is finite and connections are reused from a pool. If you have only one unclosed connection on a small site, you might never notice it, but on a large site, your users certainly will when they encounter this error.

For hardware considerations you might have to upgrade your server or servers, or even end up having to move your site onto a *web farm* (a collection of servers, any one of which can receive a request and deal with it). Web farms can have repercussions for the way you handle sessions, and you might be forced to change settings in `Web.config` to accommodate this. Normally ASP.NET handles sessions in memory, known as inproc, but you can change this so that either SQL Server or a separate state server process handles sessions. These options, though, can slow your site down. However, when creating your first site you're unlikely to have to worry about these considerations, but it never hurts to make sure.

Where to Now?

Perhaps the most difficult question to answer in this entire book is "What should you do next?" You've built an application, and if you've managed to do the exercises as well, you will have a fairly good grounding in ASP.NET 2.0 already, but probably not one that will let you walk into a well-paid job. So how can you improve on it? If you follow some philosophies, you can find yourself signed up for thousand-dollar courses, or with a booklist the size of a wardrobe. Although these might be helpful, they aren't essential or advised courses of action.

I'm often asked by readers what is the most important part of becoming a developer or programmer, and the answer I give is hands-on experience. You read about coding and coding techniques until you're blue in the face, but until you're faced with a problem that you have to solve, you can't really get a feel for coding. The first tentative steps on most coders' route are taking an existing application and modifying it. Improving it. Adding to it. That's what you should start now. Go back to the Wrox United application and start amending it. Think how you could improve it. Would you change the design, the way it works? Add some news articles, some new players, and some new graphics, and get comfortable with the way it works. Then go away and think of an application that would be useful to you, but not too ambitious, and start creating that. If you can't think of anything, then e-mail your friends to see if they've got anything that needs doing.

Developing is a very proactive job. The idea of a coder sitting in a room and just writing an application from start to finish and delivering it with no contact to the outside world is an outdated one. If your code is being used by thousands of people, you should at least be talking to a fraction of them. If you talk to people, they will undoubtedly have a million ideas you'd never have considered.

References

A lot of a developer's time will be spent on the web looking up new concepts or error messages. Here's a list of some good places to start:

- `http://p2p.wrox.com`: The Wrox forums and first place to ask with trouble on the book.
- `www.developerfusion.co.uk`: The UK developer community for ASP.NET.
- `www.asp.net`: The official Microsoft ASP.NET web site.
- `http://msdn.microsoft.com/asp.net/`: The MSDN reference for all things ASP.NET-related, and an essential reference for any developer.
- `www.15seconds.com`: A great magazine-like site with loads of free articles on ASP.NET 2.0.
- `http://beta.asp.net`: Microsoft's coverage of the latest version of ASP.NET.
- `www.dotnet247.com`: A compendium, online cross-reference of all the Usenet newsgroups, including all of the ASP.NET 2.0 groups.
- `http://msdn.microsoft.com/coding4fun/default.aspx`: MSDN's site on fun coding topics.
- `www.codeproject.com`: A good resource for free source code and tutorials.

Summary

This hasn't really been a chapter about a particular subject, but rather an extended wrapping up and welcome to the real world. To those ends, this chapter discussed the following:

- How you can go about deploying the Wrox United site with both Visual Web Developer and the command-line prompt tool.
- The importance of testing your application after it has been deployed and getting your potential users or your customer to test it as well.
- Maintenance, and very briefly, ASP.NET 2.0's new instrumenting feature, the `<healthMonitoring>` element, and how you might go about using it.
- A quick recheck of the Wrox United application and what you learned from it.
- Some suggestions about what you should do next after finishing this book.

You're now ready to start developing without our help.

Exercise

1. You are now developer and maintainer of the Wrox United web site. What else would you add to the Wrox United site? Make a list of possible add-ons, and prioritize them with the simplest to do first. Implement some of these add-ons. Just to get you thinking, you could add a facility to post pictures or video clips from Wrox United matches, or you could add player biographies. The possibilities are limitless here, so be creative.

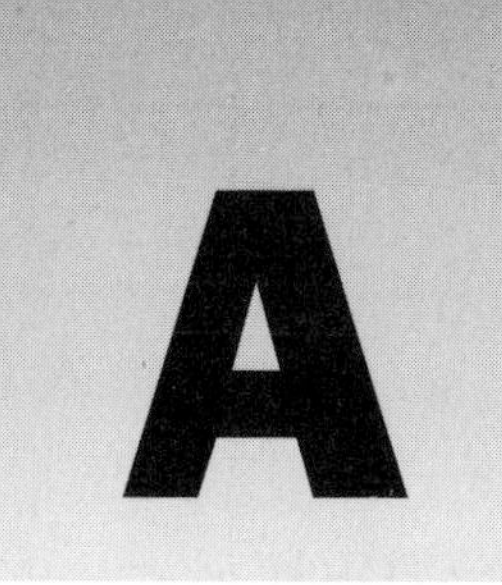

Exercise Answers

Chapter 1

Exercise 1

Explain the differences among the .NET 2.0 Framework, ASP.NET 2.0, VWD, and IIS.

Solution

The .NET 2.0 Framework is a very broad set of code (contained in classes) that is used by many Microsoft products, including servers, database managers, and web servers.

ASP.NET 2.0 is a subset of the .NET 2.0 Framework that holds the classes used to create dynamic web pages.

VWD is a tool used to create ASP.NET 2.0 web pages.

IIS is a web server that can execute the ASP.NET 2.0 code to create dynamic web pages.

Exercise 2

List some differences between ASP.NET Development Server and IIS.

Solution

IIS is a powerful web server designed to support publicly deployed sites. IIS scales to heavy loads, multiple servers, and multi-processor machines. It has a robust security model. The user of IIS is a special account named ASPNET. IIS does not expect pages to be in development while it is serving them, so it does not lock pages.

ASP.NET Development Server is a lightweight web server designed to give developers a quick and easy way to serve a page on their development machine. ASP.NET Development Server cannot handle more than a small number of visitors simultaneously. The user of ASP.NET Development Server is whoever is logged in to Windows at the time, and thus the security model is weak. ASP.NET Development Server locks a page in VWD while it is being served.

Exercise 3

When you drag the title bar of the toolbar it will only go to certain locations and certain sizes. How can you put the title bar where you want it?

Solution

Select the toolbar and choose Menu⇨Windows⇨Floating. You can now place the toolbar in the size and location you desire.

Exercise 4

How can you copy a .jpg file in `C:\MyPhotos` into your site for display on a page?

Solution

From VWD Solution Explorer, you can right-click the receiving folder and then select Add Existing Item. Navigate to `C:\Photos` and select the photo of interest. Click OK.

From Windows Explorer, you can copy the .jpg file from its original folder to `C:\Website\MyWebName`.

Exercise 5

You want to add a subfolder to your site, but folder is not one of the items listed in Add Items. Why?

Solution

Adding a folder has its own entry in the menu that appears when you right-click a folder in the Solution Explorer.

Exercise 6

Microsoft has written extensive code to make it easier for programmers to create web pages. How does a programmer actually use that code?

Solution

The code is available in server-side controls. These are tags that look like HTML but start with `<asp: ... >`. Within the control you can set properties to determine the appearance and behavior of the control.

Exercise 7

Why are there no tools in the General panel of the Toolbox?

Solution

The General panel is a place for you to place snippets of code that you copy from a page and expect to use again later. It starts out empty.

Chapter 2

Exercise 1

Describe the functional difference between the `Web.config` file and `Global.asax`.

Solution

`Web.config` contains values (settings), whereas `Global.asax` contains code.

Exercise 2

What files discussed in this chapter are in XML format?

Solution

`Web.config` and `Site.map`.

Exercise 3

Take a look at the code for a Content page. Why does it lack directives and tags?

```
<!DOCTYPE HTML PUBLIC "-//W3C//DTD XHTML 1.0 Transitional//EN"
"http://www.w3.org/TR/xhtml1/DTD/xhtml1-transitional.dtd">
<html xmlns="http://www.w3.org/1999/xhtml">
<head ></head>
```

Solution

This code lacks directives and tags because those are supplied by the Master page.

Exercise 4

What values must match between a set of Master and Content pages?

Solution

The Content page's first line directive of `MasterPageFile` must match the name of the master file.

The value of `xxx` in the Content page's `<asp:content ... ContentPlaceHolder ID="xxx">` must match the ID of the Master page's `<asp:ContentPlaceHolder ID="xxx">`.

Chapter 3

Exercise 1

Practice using the drag-and-drop functionality of VWD to put together a simple web page that displays the following information:

- The WroxUnited Logo (available for free download from `www.wrox.com`—or just use any small image of your choice).
- The names of the players and some information about each of them, arranged in a table. Refer to Figure 3-44 for a visual reference.

Solution

The finished page should look like Figure A-1 when it is run.

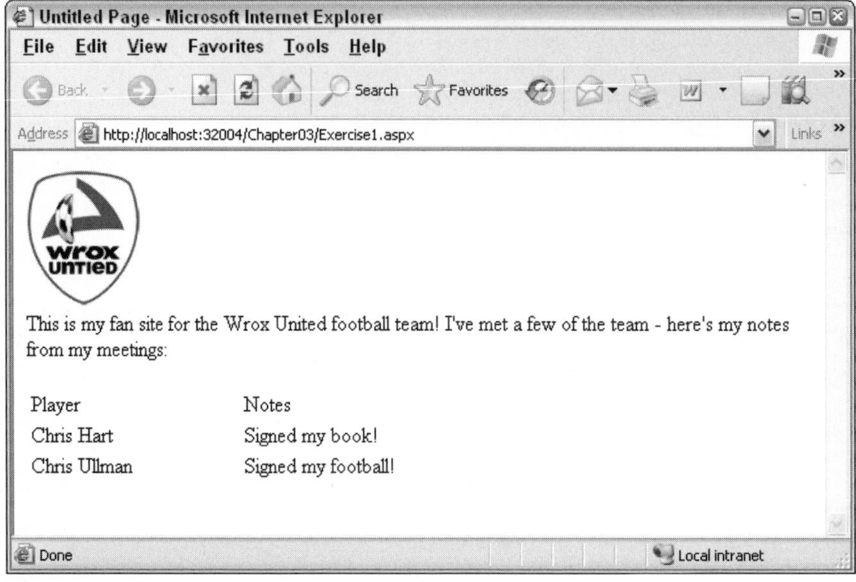

Figure A-1

The HTML that generates this page will vary according to how you set up your table, but it should be similar to the following code:

```
<html xmlns="http://www.w3.org/1999/xhtml" >
<head runat="server">
    <title>Untitled Page</title>
</head>
<body>
    <form id="form1" runat="server">
  <img src="badge.gif" />
  <br />
  This is my fan site for the Wrox United football team! I've met a few of the team
  - here's my notes from my meetings:<br />
  <br />
  <table width="600" cols="2">
    <tr>
      <td style="width: 150px">
        Player</td>
      <td style="width: 400px">
        Notes</td>
    </tr>
    <tr>
      <td style="width: 150px">
        Chris Hart</td>
      <td style="width: 400px">
```

```
            Signed my book!</td>
        </tr>
        <tr>
          <td style="width: 150px">
            Chris Ullman</td>
          <td style="width: 400px">
            Signed my football!</td>
        </tr>
      </table>
    </form>
    </body>
    </html>
```

Exercise 2

Return to Wrox United and go to the Master page. Try deleting the `Menu` control and replacing it with a `TreeView` control. Bind that control to the `siteData` data source, and you should see a fully populated tree of items, both in Design View (refer to Figure 3-45) and when you run the page (refer to Figure 3-43).

Solution

Changing the `Menu` control to a `TreeView` control is a swift process, and you can see the results in Figure A-2.

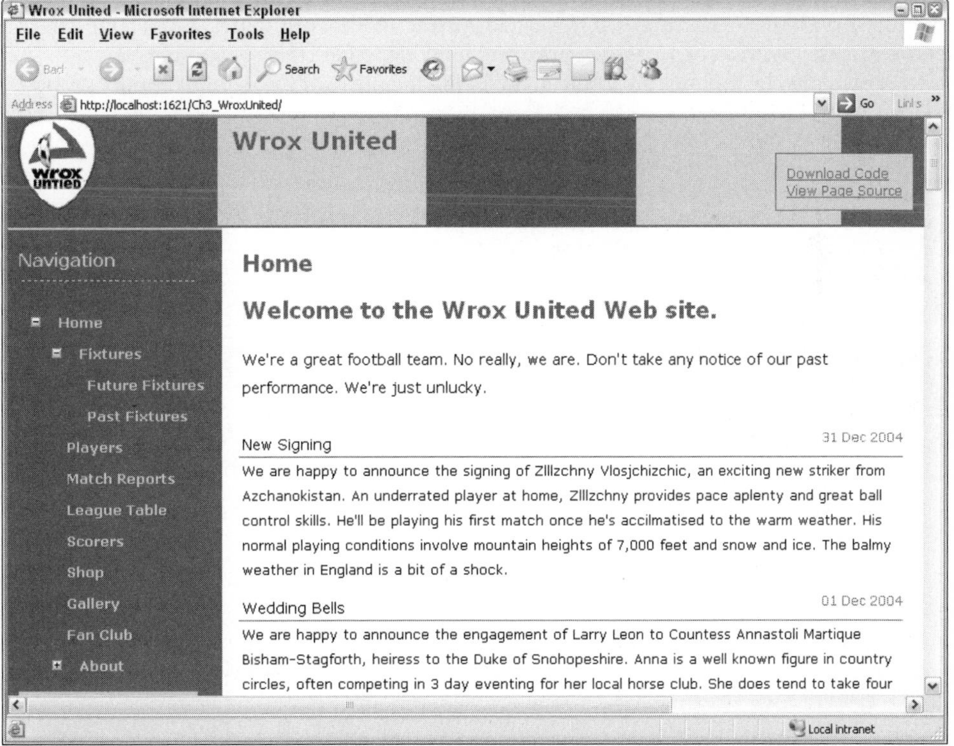

Figure A-2

After you have a siteMap data source, it's simple to plug in compatible controls and change the functionality of the site with minimal effort.

Chapter 4

Exercise 1

Change the configuration of your Chapter 4 web site to allow anonymous access, but to deny access to one specific user account.

Solution

Run through the Security wizard for the site and change the permissions as described, or modify the Web.config file. If you are successful, you will have code similar to the following in your Web.config file:

```
<roleManager enabled="true" />
<authorization>
  <allow users="?" />
  <deny users="chrishart" />
</authorization>
```

Exercise 2

Add a subfolder to the Chapter 4 web site called **Admin**. Within this folder, add a page called **MainAdmin.aspx** with a LoginName control on it and any other controls you might want. Change the access permissions for that specific folder so that only members of the Administrators group can view the page.

Solution

The MainAdmin.aspx page should have code similar to the following:

```
<form id="form1" runat="server">
  <div>
  This is the administration page for the Chapter 4 site.
  <br />
  <asp:LoginView ID="LoginView1" Runat="server">
    <LoggedInTemplate>
      You are logged in as <asp:LoginName ID="LoginName1" Runat="server" />
       <br />
    </LoggedInTemplate>
    <AnonymousTemplate>
      You are currently anonymous.
    </AnonymousTemplate>
  </asp:LoginView>
  <asp:LoginStatus ID="LoginStatus1" Runat="server" />
  </div>
</form>
```

The Web.config file for the Admin folder should have the following code:

```
<?xml version="1.0" encoding="utf-8"?>
<configuration>
    <system.web>
        <authorization>
            <allow roles="administrators" />
            <deny users="*" />
        </authorization>
    </system.web>
</configuration>
```

Chapter 5

Exercise 1

You have an ASP.NET `Label` control on a page. The label has a `font-italic="true"` attribute, and a `CssClass="maintext"` attribute:

```
<asp:label id="myLabel" CssClass="maintext" font-italic="true"
```

```
  text="This is a label"></asp:label>
```

The page has an associated CSS style sheet (not associated with a theme) that defines a `.maintext` style class has the following attributes:

```
.maintext
{
  color: Navy;
  font-family: Verdana;
  font-weight: Bold;
  font-style: normal;
}
```

How will the label appear when it is rendered?

Solution

You should see some text rendered in bold, blue Verdana, and italic, as shown in Figure A-3.

Figure A-3

The `font-style` attribute in the CSS style sheet is overridden by the element-specific style in the page.

Exercise 2

You add a `Theme="ExerciseTheme"` to the preceding page. You place the CSS style sheet from the previous exercise within the ExerciseTheme theme folder. How will the label control appear now?

Solution

The `Theme` attribute specifies that the page should now inherit all styles within the ExerciseTheme theme folder, but the style attribute added to the element remains, and the font appears in italic.

Exercise 3

You define a skin for all labels within the ExerciseTheme theme folder and specify the following attributes:

```
<asp:Label CssClass="maintext" runat="server" font-italic="false"></asp:Label>
```

How will the label appear now?

Solution

This time around, the `Label` control's italic style will override the page's style, so you will see what is shown in Figure A-4.

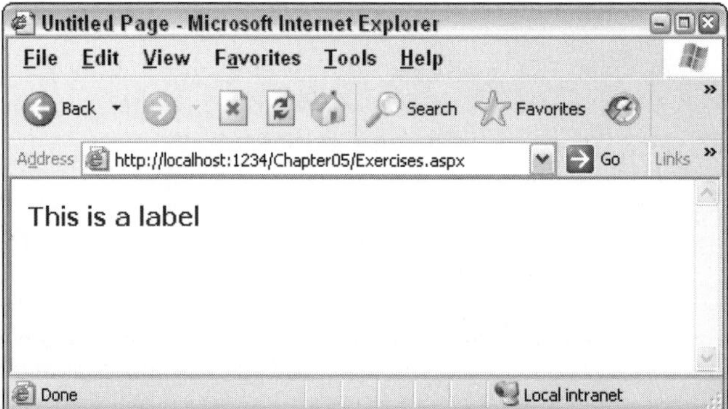

Figure A-4

Chapter 6

Exercise 1

In the Chapter06 project, create a new Web Form called **Lists.aspx**, add a `ListBox` control to the page, and add three list items with values of **One**, **Two**, and **Three**. Add a `Label` control and a `Button` control to the page. In the `Click` event of the `Button`, display the selected value of the `ListBox` in the `Label`.

Solution

The controls you add to the page should be as follows:

```
<asp:ListBox ID="ListBox1" runat="server">
  <asp:ListItem Text="One" />
  <asp:ListItem Text="Two" />
  <asp:ListItem Text="Two" />
</asp:ListBox>
<br />
<asp:Button ID="Button1" runat="server" Text="Button" />
<asp:Label ID="Label1" runat="server" Text="Label" />
```

For the `Click` event of the button, you should have the following:

```
protected void Button1_Click(object sender, System.EventArgs e)
{
  Label1.Text = ListBox1.SelectedValue;
}
```

This event procedure relies on the fact that there is a property on the `ListBox` that identifies what the value is for the selected item — the `SelectedValue` property. In fact, there is also a `SelectedText` value, because a `ListBox` has both a `Text` and a `Value` property. The `Text` is what's displayed, whereas the `Value` is stored in the page and not shown to the user. This is useful for values that come from a database, where the `Value` would be the ID of the item and the `Text` would be the description. The same is true for a `DropDownList` control.

Exercise 2

Modify Exercise 1 so that just selecting an item in the list posts back to the server (meaning you don't need to click the button). You'll need to add an event procedure to the `ListBox`, and in that event procedure you can use the same code from the `Click` event of the `Button` to display the selected value in the `Label`. Hint: The terms *postback* and *automatic* might be useful in your hunt for correct properties.

Solution

To allow the `ListBox` to post back automatically, you set the `AutoPostBack` property to `True`. Now when a list item is selected, the postback will happen right away, rather than waiting for a button to be clicked. On its own, this just posts back, so you also need an event procedure for the `ListBox`, and for this you use the `SelectedIndexChanged` event, which is raised when the selected item changes. The event is only raised when the selected item changes, so repeated clicking of the same item will not cause unnecessary postbacks. The event procedure should be as follows:

```
protected void ListBox1_SelectedIndexChanged(object sender,
         System.EventArgs e)
{
  Label1.Text = ListBox1.SelectedValue;
}
```

The advantage of this event over a postback from a button event is that you can have your page change depending upon the user selection. For example, you could have a grid filter the data shown depending on the value in a list box.

Exercise 3

Modify the EditSquad.aspx example so that the GridView is refreshed when a new player is added to the squad. The technique is similar to the code you already have, but you'll need to use a different event. Remember that you can use the drop-down lists in the code view to find the events.

Solution

To refresh the GridView when a new player is added to the squad, you need to use the Inserted event. Just as when the data for a SqlDataSource control is updated, the Updated event is raised, and when a new row is inserted, the Inserted event is raised. You can create this in the same way as you did for the Updated event, and use the same code in the event procedure.

The code for the Inserted event procedure is as follows:

```
protected void DetailsDataSource_Updated(object sender,
        System.Web.UI.WebControls.SqlDataSourceStatusEventArgs e)
{
  GridView1.DataBind();
}
```

Chapter 7

Exercise 1

Describe the general capabilities of data source and data-bound controls.

Solution

Data source controls connect to the source of data and enable communicating to the database the information for behaviors such as reading, editing, and deleting.

Data-bound controls render spaces on the page that interact with the user, either to display values or to accept input for changes to the data.

Exercise 2

Which data-bound controls render data in tables?

Solution

GridView (one datum in each cell), DataList, and Repeater (all fields of one record in each cell).

Exercise 3

Compare and contrast the DetailsView and FormView controls.

Solution

Both present data in a tabular form with only one record displayed at a time. Both controls support reading and changing values, as well as creating and deleting entire records. The DetailsView control has a built-in default template, whereas FormView has no default template.

Exercise 4

Describe how a `GridView` control can limit its records to only those that match a player's name selected in a `DropDownList` of last names.

Solution

The `DropDownList` control displays names in its `Text` property, and holds the player's ID number in the `Value` property. The `GridView` control has a `SelectCommand` that contains a `WHERE` clause that sets the ID equal to a parameter (prefaced by the @ sign). The `GridView` control also has a parameter tab containing a parameter that is filled with the value of the selected item of the `DropDownList`. Set `AutoPostBack` to `TRUE` in the `DropDownList` box so the following behavior is automatic:

- When a user changes a selection in the `DropDownList`, ASP.NET 2.0 automatically places the value of that selection into the `GridView` control's parameter tag, which means it will be employed in the `SelectCommand` `WHERE` clause.
- ASP.NET 2.0 will then cause the `GridView` control to create a new request for data using the new `SelectCommand`.
- The data returned will only have records that match the ID of the player selected in the `DropDownList`.

Exercise 5

Which data source control is best suited for the `Menu` or `SiteMapPath` data-bound controls?

Solution

The `SiteMapDataSource` is best suited for the `Menu` and `SiteMapPath` data-bound controls because it is optimized to read the XML file holding the site description information.

Chapter 8

Exercise 1

Enabling the capability to write to a database requires changes to the properties of a data source control, a data-bound control, or both?

Solution

Both.

Exercise 2

Describe the difference between an `asp:Parameter` and an `asp:ControlParameter`.

Solution

An `asp:Parameter` holds the value that came from the record of the database. An `asp:ControlParameter` holds a value that was entered by the user into a control.

Exercise 3

What problem does the `DataKeyNames` property solve?

Solution

Some fields hold values that uniquely identify them among all records. When a user changes values in those fields, there is a conundrum in that ASP.NET 2.0 needs the old values in order to find the record, and the new values for the writing. `DataKeyNames` are those fields for which ASP.NET 2.0 will hold both original and new values. When an update is made and a change is made to an ID field, ASP.NET 2.0 uses the new value for the `SET` part of the command (which writes) and the old value for the `WHERE` part of the command (which finds the one record to change).

Exercise 4

A page needs to delete the date of birth value from one record. Which command should be used?

Solution

Update. Delete would only be used to eliminate the entire record, not just one value in the record.

Exercise 5

What tags must be added to a page to allow a `GridView` to create new records?

Solution

This is a trick question because a `GridView` cannot perform inserts. But the `GridView` can have a button that opens a `DetailsView` in `Insert` mode, which can create a new record.

Chapter 9

Exercise 1

Create a class and shared method (called `DeliveryDate`) to calculate a delivery date given the date of an order. All deliveries should be made within three days of the order. Create a class and shared method to calculate delivery date given the date of an order. All deliveries should be made within three days of the order.

Solution

```
public class Orders
{
  public static DateTime DeliveryDate(DateTime OrderDate)
  {
    return OrderDate.AddDays(3);
  }
}
```

This simply uses the `AddDays` method of the `DateTime` type to add the required number of days.

Exercise 2

Modify the `DeliveryDate` method to take into account that deliveries do not happen on the weekend.

Solution

```
public class Orders
{
  public static DateTime DeliveryDate(DateTime OrderDate)
  {
    DateTime deliveryDay = OrderDate.AdddDays(3);

    if (deliveryDate.DayOfWeek == DayOwWeek.Saturday)
      deliveryDate = deliveryDate.AddDays(2);
    else if (deliveryDate.DayOfWeek == DayOwWeek.Sunday)
      deliveryDate = deliveryDate.AddDays(2);

    return deliveryDay;
  }
}
```

Here the delivery date is calculated and checked to see if it falls on a Saturday or Sunday, in which case the delivery date is moved to the following Monday.

Exercise 3

Modify the `DeliveryDate` method to take into account that an order takes three working days to process. So orders falling on a Wednesday will be delivered on the following Monday, and orders from Thursday will be delivered on the following Tuesday.

Solution

```
public class Orders
{
  public static DateTime DeliveryDate(DateTime OrderDate)
  {
    switch (OrderDate.DayOfWeek)
    {
      case DayOfWeek.Monday:
      case DayOfWeek.Tuesday:
      case DayOfWeek.Wednesday:
        return OrderDate.AddDays(3);
      case DayOfWeek.Thursday:
      case DayOfWeek.Friday:
      case DayOfWeek.Saturday:
        return OrderDate.AddDays(5);
      default:
        return OrderDate.AddDays(4):
    }
  }
}
```

This version of the method uses the `switch` statement to calculate different dates depending upon the day of week on which the order was placed.

Exercise 4

For each of the following Boolean expressions, say for what integer values of `A` each of them will evaluate to `True` and when they will evaluate to `False`:

a. NOT A=0

b. A > 0 OR A < 5

c. NOT A > 0 OR A < 5

d. A > 1 AND A < 5 OR A > 7 AND A < 10

e. A < 10 OR A > 12 AND NOT A > 20

Solution

a. `True` for all integers except 0. Without the `NOT`, the answer would only be 0. When weyou add the `NOT`, it reverses to be all numbers except 0.

b. `True` for all integers. The left side alone would be `True` for all integers greater than 0 (only 0 and negative integers would be false). The right side includes all integers that are less than 5, including 0 and negative integers. With the `OR` clause, an integer has to be within one of the two expressions in order for the entire expression to be `True`. When you combine these two sets of answers, you get all integers. (The integers 1 through 4 are included by both expressions.)

c. `True` for integers 5 and below. Integers 6 and above will evaluate to `False`. The issue here is precedence between the `NOT` and `OR` operators. The `NOT` is only applied to the expression on the left of the `OR`. Think of this problem as `(NOT A > 0) OR (A < 5)`. On the left, you have `True` for any numbers that are not greater than 0, so `True` is for 0 and negative numbers. On the right, you have `True` for any number that is less than 5. With the two sides of the `OR` combined, you have `True` for all negative numbers and 0, and positive numbers up to 5. Numbers greater than and including 6 are `True` for either side and thus resolve to `False`.

d. `True` for 2, 3, 4, 8, and 9 only. Like the previous problem, the issue is to establish the precedence of the operators. Think of this as `(A > 1 AND A < 5) OR (A > 7 AND A < 10)`. On the left of the `OR`, you can see that only integers 2, 3, and 4 would fit both criteria. The right side of the `OR` the situation is similar: only 8 and 9 meet both criteria. When you consider the `OR`, you have to combine those two answer sets.

e. `True` for all integers 9 and below (including 0 and negatives) and for 13 through 20 inclusive. `False` for 10, 11, 12, and all integers above (and inclusive of) 21. Think of this problem with some parentheses. The `OR` is the last to be evaluated, so your parentheses are `(A < 10) OR (A > 12 AND NOT A > 20)`. First look at the right side of the `OR`. Integers must meet both tests when there is an `AND` clause, so that would be 13 through 20 are `True`. Now look at the left side of the `OR`. Any number less than 10 will be `True`. The final answer is the combination of those two answer sets.

Chapter 10

Exercise 1

Create a new web site and a new page called **CodeBehind.aspx** with a single label, but making sure that you don't check the box marked Placed Code in a Separate File. Now create a code-behind file manually for that page that displays the content of the label.

Solution

Create a class called `CodeBehind.cs`. Add the following line of code to `CodeBehind.aspx`:

```
<@Page CodeFile="CodeBehind.cs" Class="CodeBehind" %>
```

In the `CodeBehind.aspx` file, add the following within the `Page_Load` event:

```
Label1.Text = "Hello World";
```

Exercise 2

How would you go about adding an image to accompany each news item? Note that it shouldn't display if there is no news image present for that article.

Solution

Add the following to `newsusercontrol.ascx`:

```
<span class="newsContent">
    <asp:Image style="float:right" ID="NewsImage" Runat="server"
        ImageUrl='<%# Eval("PictureURL", "~/NewsImages/{0}") %>' />
    <%#Eval("Description") %>
</span>
```

Add the following event handler that is called when an item of news is bound:

```
void NewsItem_DataBound(object sender ,
System.Web.UI.WebControls.RepeaterItemEventArgs e)
    DataRowView row;
    Image img;
    if ((e.Item.ItemType == ListItemType.Item) || (e.Item.ItemType ==
   ListItemType.AlternatingItem)
       {
        row = (DataRowView )e.Item.DataItem;

        if (row("PictureUrl").ToString().Trim() == "")             {
            img = (Image )e.Item.FindControl("NewsImage");
            img.Visible = False;
        }
    }
}
```

Chapter 11

Exercise 1

Create a new user account called **Admin**, and make this user a member of all of the groups. Log in to the Wrox United site as **Admin** and test to see whether you can access all of the different pages in both the fan club and the administration section.

Solution

Launch the ASP.NET Web Site Administration Tool and configure the Admin user as shown in Figure A-5.

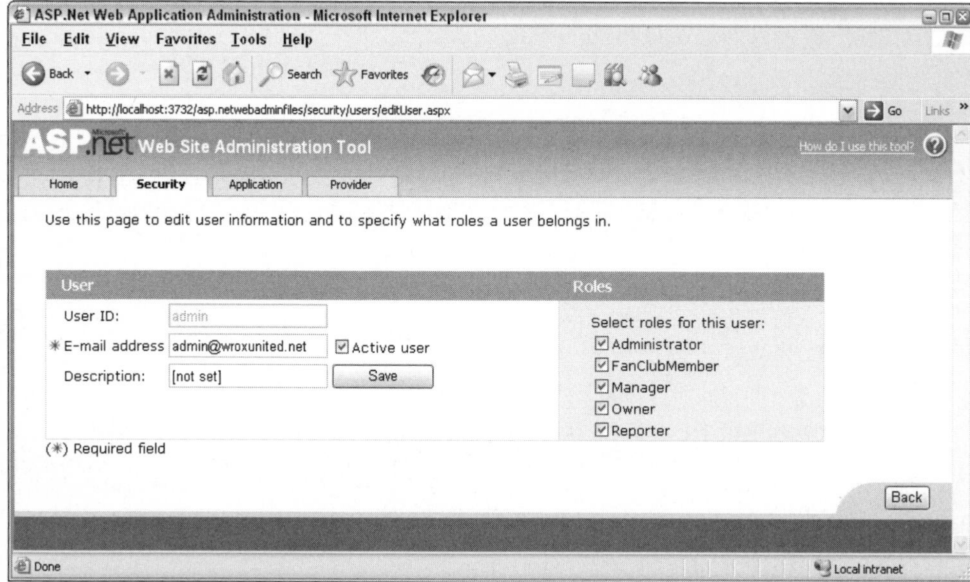

Figure A-5

Exercise 2

Remove the Admin user from any role other than the Administrator role and test the site again. Ensure that you can access the following pages:

- `Admin.aspx`
- `EditNews.aspx`
- `UpdateProducts.aspx`

Solution

The Admin user account should now have the configuration shown in Figure A-6.

If you try to access the Wrox United site, you'll see the links in Figure A-7 within the Administration section.

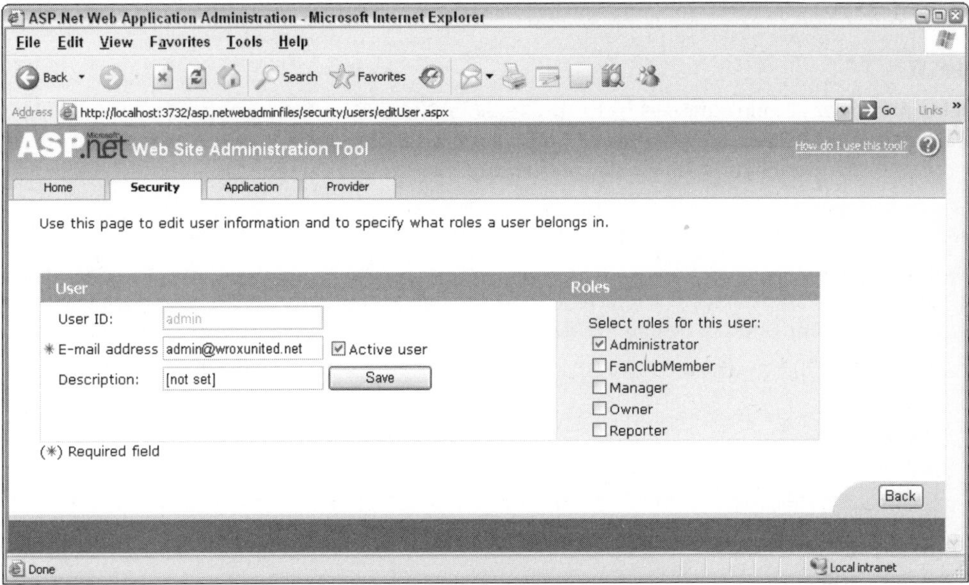

Figure A-6

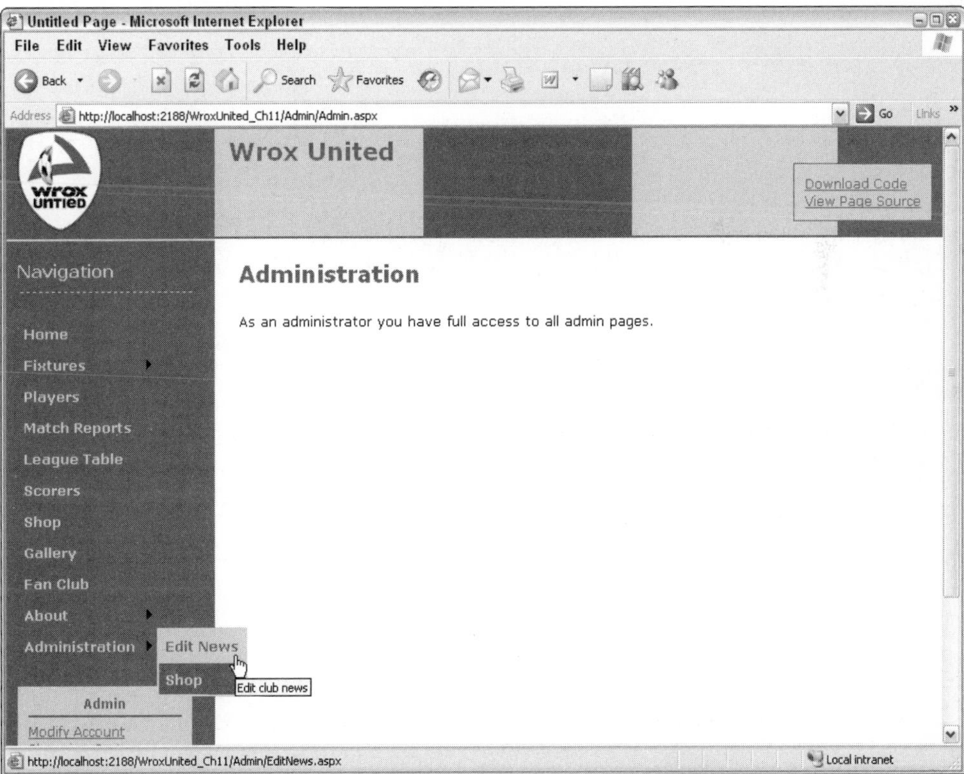

Figure A-7

Not only can you see these links, but clicking these links will take you to the appropriate pages.

Exercise 3

The Admin user has had a request by a reporter out in the field — he's uploaded a score for a match, but the score has just changed. Unfortunately, the reporter's laptop has run out of battery, so he's asked the Admin user to update the score for him. Make sure that the Admin user can update the score of a match.

Solution

You have two options. First, you could add the Admin user to the Reporters role, thereby enabling the access to the page as desired. The alternative is to enable access to the `UpdateScore.aspx` page on the site to all site administrators by making the following change to the `Web.config` file within the root of the Admin folder:

```
<location path="UpdateScore.aspx">
    <system.web>
      <authorization>
        <allow roles="Administrator, Reporter" />
      </authorization>
    </system.web>
  </location>
```

Whichever method you decide on, the Admin user needs to be able to access the `UpdateScore.aspx` page. If you are successful, you will see Figure A-8.

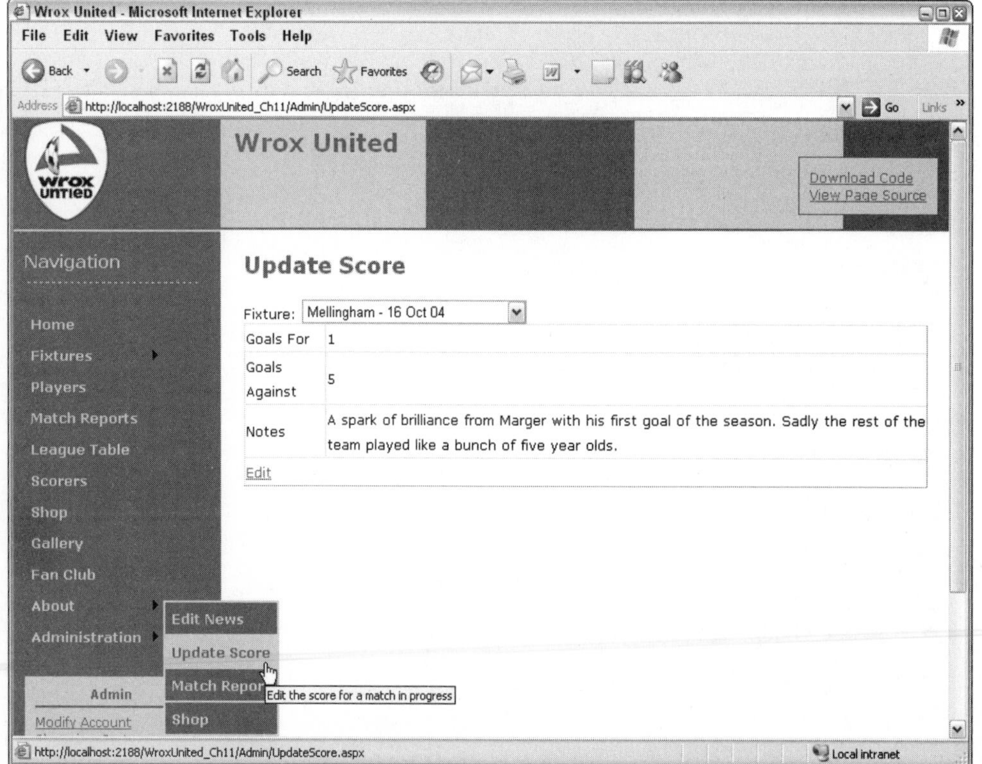

Figure A-8

Exercise 4

Add a field to the user profile for the Wrox United application called **DateOfBirth**. Give this property a data type of `System.DateTime`. Add an input field to the `FanClub.aspx` page so that users can update their date of birth. Note that you will need to convert the value entered in a text box to a `DateTime` value when you save the data — you might want to try the `DateTime.Parse()` function for this purpose. To retrieve the data, use the `Profile.DateOfBirth.ToShortDateString()` function.

Solution

1. Add the following highlighted line to `Web.config`:

```
<profile enabled="true">
  <properties>
    <add name="MemberName"/>
    <add name="Name"/>
    <add name="Address"/>
    <add name="City"/>
    <add name="County"/>
    <add name="PostCode"/>
    <add name="Country"/>
    <add name="Mailings" type="System.Boolean"/>
    <add name="Email"/>
    <add name="DateOfBirth" type="System.DateTime"/>
    <add name="Theme"/>
    <add name="Cart" serializeAs="Binary" type="Wrox.Commerce.ShoppingCart"
allowAnonymous="true"/>
  </properties>
</profile>
```

2. Modify `FanClub.aspx` to include a text box for entering and displaying the date of birth:

```
<span class="boxFloat">Name:<br />
  Address:<br />
  <br />
  <br />
  <br />
  City:<br />
  County:<br />
  Postcode:<br />
  Country:<br />
  Subscribe to email updates:<br />
  Email:<br />
  Date of Birth: <br />
  Membership Alias:<br />
  Theme:</span><span>
    <asp:TextBox ID="txtName" runat="server" Columns="30" />
    <br />
    ...
    <asp:TextBox ID="txtEmail" runat="server" />
    <br />
    <asp:TextBox ID="txtDoB" runat="server" />
    <br />
    <asp:TextBox ID="txtAlias" runat="server" />
    <br />
    ...
  </span>
```

3. The code file for the `FanClub.aspx` page also needs some changes. First, modify the `btnSaveChanges_Click` event handler code:

```
protected void btnSaveChanges_Click( object sender,  System.EventArgs e)
{
  Profile.Theme =
    ((DropDownList)FCLoginView.FindControl("ThemeList")).SelectedValue;
  Profile.Name = ((TextBox)FCLoginView.FindControl("txtName")).Text;
  Profile.Address = ((TextBox)FCLoginView.FindControl("txtAddress")).Text;
  Profile.City = ((TextBox)FCLoginView.FindControl("txtCity")).Text;
  Profile.County = ((TextBox)FCLoginView.FindControl("txtCounty")).Text;
  Profile.PostCode = ((TextBox)FCLoginView.FindControl("txtPostCode")).Text;
  Profile.Country = ((TextBox)FCLoginView.FindControl("txtCountry")).Text;
  Profile.Mailings = ((CheckBox)FCLoginView.FindControl("chkMailing")).Checked;
  Profile.Email = ((TextBox)FCLoginView.FindControl("txtEmail")).Text;
  Profile.MemberName = ((TextBox)FCLoginView.FindControl("txtAlias")).Text;

  TextBox DoB = (TextBox)FCLoginView.FindControl("txtDoB");
  if (DoB.Text <> "")
  {
    Profile.DateOfBirth = DateTime.Parse(DoB.Text);
  }

  Server.Transfer(SiteMap.CurrentNode.Url);
 }
```

Note that you need to check that the text box is not empty (if you try to save with an empty text box, you'll see an error page due to an exception).

4. Add the following code to the `DisplayProfileProperties()` method:

```
private void DisplayProfileProperties()
{
  TextBox NameBox = (TextBox)FCLoginView.FindControl("txtName");

  if (NameBox != null)
  {
    ((DropDownList)FCLoginView.FindControl("ThemeList")).SelectedValue =
      Profile.Theme;
    ((TextBox)FCLoginView.FindControl("txtName")).Text = Profile.Name;
    ((TextBox)FCLoginView.FindControl("txtAddress")).Text = Profile.Address;
    ((TextBox)FCLoginView.FindControl("txtCity")).Text = Profile.City;
    ((TextBox)FCLoginView.FindControl("txtCounty")).Text = Profile.County;
    ((TextBox)FCLoginView.FindControl("txtPostCode")).Text = Profile.PostCode;
    ((TextBox)FCLoginView.FindControl("txtCountry")).Text = Profile.Country;
    ((CheckBox)FCLoginView.FindControl("chkMailing")).Checked = Profile.Mailings;
    ((TextBox)FCLoginView.FindControl("txtEmail")).Text = Profile.Email;
    ((TextBox)FCLoginView.FindControl("txtAlias")).Text = Profile.MemberName;
    ((TextBox)FCLoginView.FindControl("txtDoB")).Text =
      Profile.DateOfBirth.ToShortDateString();
  }
}
```

This code will convert the `DateTime` value stored in the user's profile into its string representation so that it can be displayed on the screen. Because users are unlikely to know the exact time they were born, you can ignore the time part of the date—which is why you used the `ToShortDateString()` instead of `ToString()` method. After you are finished, you can test it out on the user of your choice. Figure A-9 uses Alan the Admin.

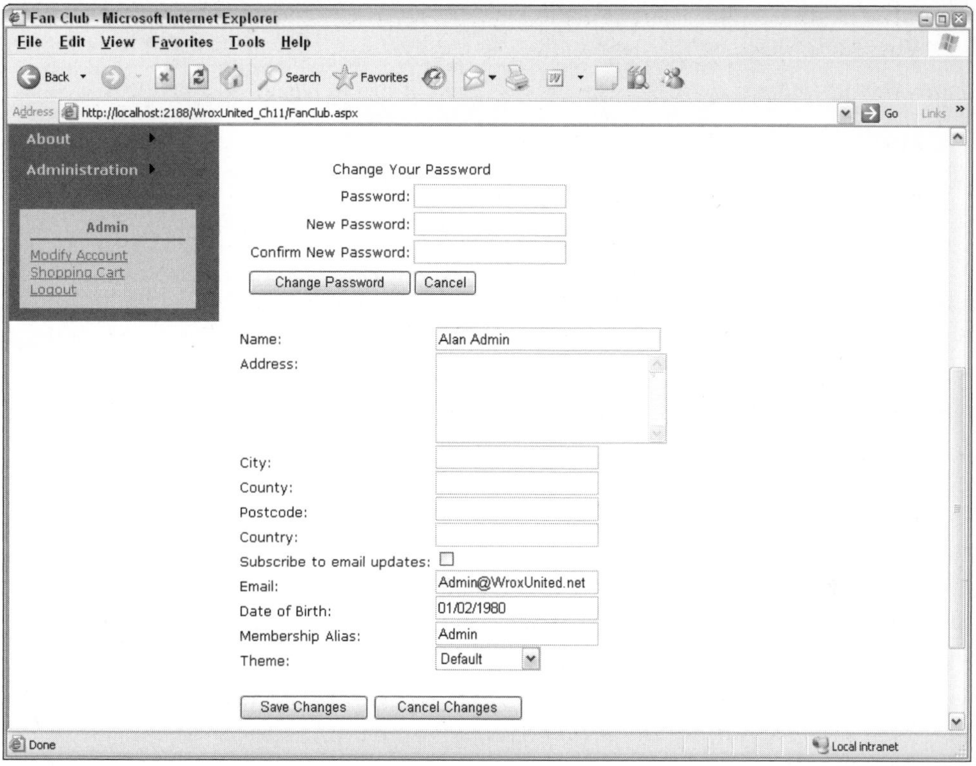

Figure A-9

Chapter 12

Exercise 1

What is the role of `SOAP` in web services?

Solution

`SOAP` is a framework for exchanging messages. Its role in web services is to parcel function calls and parameters to enable you to call the web services remotely in a standardized way.

Exercise 2

Create a web service that retrieves a Wrox United score whenever they've scored more than one goal.

Solution

```
[WebMethod]
public DataSet Fixtures() As
{
```

```
        SqlConnection conn = new
SqlConnection(ConfigurationManager.ConnectionStrings["WroxUnited"].ConnectionString
);
        SqlDataAdapter adapter = new SqlDataAdapter("SELECT FixtureDate, Opponents,
FixtureType, GoalsFor, GoalsAgainst FROM Fixtures WHERE GoalsFor>1 ORDER BY
FixtureDate", conn);
        DataSet ;

        adapter.Fill(ds, "Fixtures");

        return ds;

    }
```

Exercise 3

Create a page that consumes the third-party weather forecast for Birmingham, United Kingdom. (Hint: You will also need to discover this service first.)

Solution

Add a Web Reference first via the Add Web Reference function and discover the service by typing the URL `www.webservicex.net/globalweather.asmx`

Create a blank page and add a label called Weather Label to it. Then add the following code to the code-behind:

```
partial class WeatherPage :System.Web.UI.Page
{
 protected void Page_Load(object sender , EventArgs e )
  {

        net.webservicex.www.GlobalWeather wsConvert = new
net.webservicex.www.GlobalWeather();
        wsConvert.Credentials = System.Net.CredentialCache.DefaultCredentials;
        WeatherLabel.Text = wsConvert.GetWeather("Birmingham", "United
       Kingdom").ToString();
}
}
```

Chapter 13

Exercise 1

The member discount is something that is applied to the shopping cart as you add items to the cart. What do you need to add to the `ShoppingCart` object to make sure it can store a discount of 10% for fan club members? You can assume that you can detect a fan club member with the property: `HttpContext.Current.User.IsInRole("FanClubMember")`.

Hint: You will need to create a subtotal as well.

Solution

You need to create a `MemberDiscount` property first:

```
public class ShoppingCart
{
        private single const MemberDiscountPercentage = 0.1;
        ...
       public readonly double MemberDiscount()
            get
                if (HttpContext.Current.User.IsInRole("FanClubMember"))
                 {
                     return SubTotal * MemberDiscountPercentage;
                 }
                else
                {
                     return 0;
                }
            }
        }
}
```

Then you need to create a `SubTotal` property because between the total and the individual prices of the items, you need to show how you arrive at your figures — otherwise, it will just look like your shopping cart doesn't add up correctly:

```
public readonly double SubTotal()
            get
            {
                double t
                if (_items == null}
                {
                     return 0;
                }
                foreach (CartItem Item In _items)
                     t += Item.LineTotal;
                }
                return t;
            }
        }
```

Then you'll need in Source View to add a Panel called **DiscountPanel** and add two labels, one called **SubTotalLabel** and another called **MemberDiscount**, and make sure both contain nothing to begin with and that both are visible.

You'll also need to add some extra parameters to the `checkout.aspx` page called **@subtotal** and **@memberdiscount**, and make sure they are added as part of the `INSERT` clause in this page.

Exercise 2

How can you display the member discount details on the Shopping Cart page so that only a fan club member will see them?

Solution

You need to check to see whether a user is in the role FanClubMember, and only if they are do you then apply the extra formatting to show the subtotal and the member discount items. Last, you display the discount panel:

```
if (Context.User.IsInRole("FanClubMember"))
    SubTotalLabel.Text = string.Format("Sub-Total:{0,35:C}",
    Profile.Cart.SubTotal);
    MemberDiscount.Text = string.Format("Member Discount:{0:C}",
    Profile.Cart.MemberDiscount);
    DiscountPanel.Visible = True;
}
```

Chapter 14

Exercise 1

Convert the two shop pages, `Shop.aspx` and `ShopItem.aspx`, from using SQL statements to stored procedures.

Solution

For `Shop.aspx`, you need to create the following stored procedure:

```
CREATE PROCEDCURE dbo.usp_Shop
AS
  SELECT ProductID, Name, Description, Price, PictureURL
  FROM Products
  ORDER BY Name
```

Next, change the `SelectCommand` from the SQL to `usp_Shop`.

For `ShopItem.aspx`, the stored procedure should be as follows:

```
CREATE PROCEDURE dbo.usp_ShopItem
  @ProductID int
AS
  SELECT *
  FROM Products
  WHERE ProductID = @ProductID
```

Next, change the `SelectCommand` from the SQL to `usp_ShopItem`.

Exercise 2

Add caching to the `ShopItem.aspx` page, so that the page is cached. Note that you need to take into account that this page shows different products, so the cache needs to be varied by the product being shown.

Solution

For this you simply add the `OutputCache` directive to the page, but because the product being shown is defined in the querystring, you need to vary it with the following querystring:

```
<%@ OutputCache Duration="3600" VaryByParam="ProductID" %>
```

Chapter 15

Exercise 1

Add defensive coding to the `GenerateThumbnail` method of the `ImageHandling` class stored in the `App_Code` directory.

Solution

Having learned what you have about defensive coding and exceptions, you might be tempted to change the code for `GenerateThumbnail` to what was shown in the chapter, where both defensive coding and exception handling were used. However, during the chapter, you used the `Application_Error` event to centrally log exceptions, so the explicit logging within `GenerateThumbnail` isn't required. But you still need to code against a missing source file, so the code could be changed to the following:

```
public static void GenerateThumbnail(string SourceImagePath,
                                     string TargetImagePath)
{
  if (!File.Exists(sourceImagePath))
    return;

  using (Image image1 = Image.FromFile(SourceImagePath))
  {
    short num1 = (short) Math.Round((double) (image1.Height * 0.25));
    short num2 = (short) Math.Round((double) (image1.Width * 0.25));
    Image.GetThumbnailImageAbort abort1 =
      new Image.GetThumbnailImageAbort(ImageHandling.ThumbnailCallback);
    using (Image image2 = image1.GetThumbnailImage(num2, num1,
                                                   abort1, IntPtr.Zero))
    {
      image2.Save(TargetImagePath, ImageFormat.Gif);
    }
  }
}
```

This assumes that a failure generating the thumbnail isn't critical, which may not be a correct assumption. Thumbnails are generated when pictures are uploaded to the site—pictures such as products for the shop, match photos, and so on. The site can run quite well when these images are missing, so it isn't critical, and any exception would be logged by the central code so the site administrators would know about it.

Exercise 2

Add validation controls to the Checkout page, the part that accepts the delivery address. There is a check box to copy the address from the membership details of the user, but there is nothing to ensure that all of the fields are filled in.

Solution

To ensure data is entered into the address boxes, you can use `RequiredFieldValidator` controls. You can add a validator for each `TextBox`, adding it next to the field it validates:

```
<tr><td><asp:TextBox id="txtName" runat="server" />
        <asp:RequiredFieldValidator id="rfv1" runat="server"
          ControlToValidate="txtName" Text="*"
          ErrorMessage="You must enter a value for the delivery name" />
</td></tr>
```

You will also need a `ValidationSummary`, which can be put after the table containing the address fields:

```
  </table>
  <asp:ValidationSummary id="vs" runat="server" DisplayMode="BulletList" />
</asp:WizardStep>
```

Exercise 3

Use the debugger.

Solution

This exercise is more important than you realize, because learning how to debug is critical, especially when you are a beginner. When learning, you tend to make more mistakes, or perhaps code less efficiently than you do with years of experience. That's only natural, and learning how to quickly track down bugs will make you a better developer, not only because you'll be good at finding bugs, but also because, in finding those bugs, you learn what the problem was and how to avoid it next time. So in finding bugs you become a better coder.

Chapter 16

Exercise 1

You are now developer and maintainer of the Wrox United web site. What else would you add to the Wrox United site? Make a list of possible add-ons, and prioritize them with the simplest to do first. Implement some of these add-ons.

Solution

There is no hard and fast solution to this exercise, but to get some ideas for add-ons to your site, or to compare notes with other developers and the authors of this book, go to `http://p2p.wrox.com` and look for this book's discussion board.

Setup

The ASP.NET 2.0 runtime comes as part of the Visual Web Developer Express download. ASP has undergone an evolution in terms of setup, each version being simpler (although often larger and lengthier) to install than the previous one. In classic ASP 2.0, ASP was separate even from the IIS web server itself, both of which had to be downloaded and attached manually to IIS. By version 3.0 of classic ASP, ASP had been integrated with the web server. With ASP.NET 1.x, you had to download the .NET Framework separately to get ASP, and enable IIS, which by then was part of the operating system. However, throughout each of these iterations, you still had to download and install a database solution separately.

With ASP.NET 2.0, all four parts come together in one easy-to-install package — Visual Web Developer Express 2005. ASP.NET 2.0, the web server, development tools, and the database are all installed at the same time. The web server is a test-development server nicknamed ASP.NET Development Server (after the discoverer of the gaps and particular matter in the rings of Saturn) and can run without IIS, alongside IIS, or you can choose to use IIS in place of the ASP.NET Development Server.

System Requirements

Before you install VWD Express, you should check that your system meets the minimum requirements. We have taken the requirements from the Microsoft web site. They are listed in the following sections.

Processor

- **Minimum:** 600 megahertz (MHz) Pentium processor.
- **Recommended:** 1 gigahertz (GHz) Pentium processor.

Operating System

VWD Express can be installed on any of the following systems:

- Microsoft Windows 2003 Server, Service Pack 1
- Windows XP (Home Edition and Professional), Service Pack 2
- Windows 2000 (Professional and Server), Service Pack 4
- Windows x64 editions
- Windows Vista

RAM

- **Minimum:** 192 megabytes (MB)
- **Recommended:** 256MB (512 MB or more with SQL Express)

Hard Disk

- **Minimum:** 500MB
- **Full Installation:** Up to 1.3GB of available space may be required

CD or DVD Drive

This is not required.

Display

- **Minimum:** 800x600 256 colors
- **Recommended:** 1024x768 High Color — 16-bit

Mouse

You need a Microsoft mouse or compatible pointing device.

As with plenty of Microsoft technologies, you'll find that it may well work on other older setups; however, we cannot recommend this and we won't answer questions about it either.

Visual Web Developer Express Installation

Follow these steps to install Visual Web Developer Express:

1. Go to the following URL: `http://msdn.microsoft.com/vstudio/express/vwd/`.
2. Click the Download Now link, and from the next page, click the link to download from here. You will see the page shown in Figure B-1 asking you whether you want to run or save the file.

> **If you're using a dialup connection, remain connected after you have downloaded this file, because you will still need an active connection later during the installation process.**

Figure B-1

3. Click Run and you will see the dialog box shown in Figure B-2 after the `vwdsetup.exe` file has fully downloaded. If you are using Firefox, you only need to download and double-click it.

Figure B-2

4. You will be asked whether you want to submit anonymous information about your setup experiences (see Figure B-3). If you want to send information about your setup experience, check the box. If not, click Next.

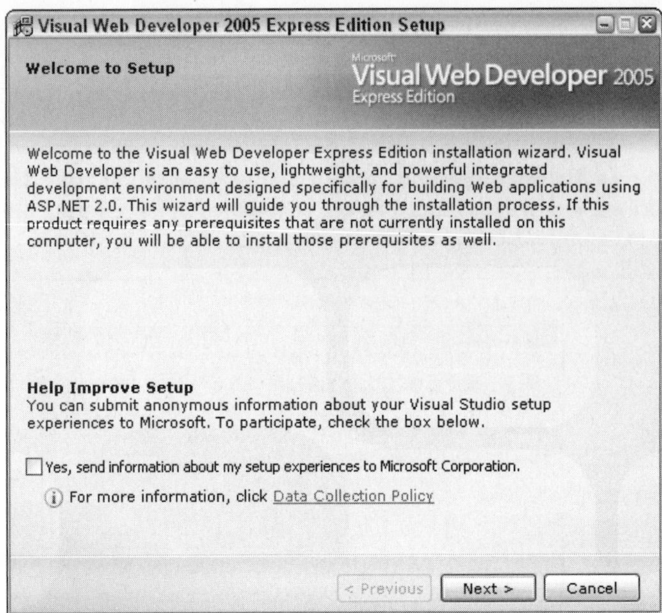

Figure B-3

5. In the next screen, shown in Figure B-4, you will see the end-user license agreement (EULA). You have to agree to this to continue, so check the box and click Next.

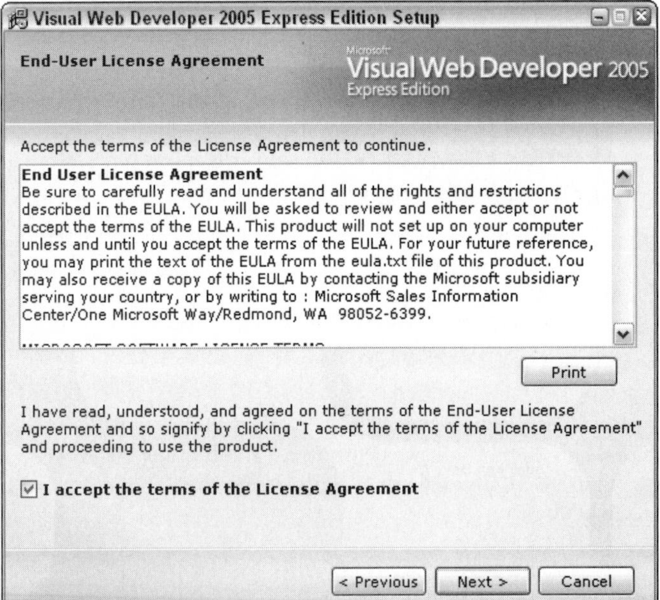

Figure B-4

6. After accepting the terms of the EULA, you then specify which installation options you want to install in addition to .NET 2.0 and Visual Web Developer Express. The only compulsory option for this book is SQL Server 2005 Express. As shown in Figure B-5, select that option and click Next.

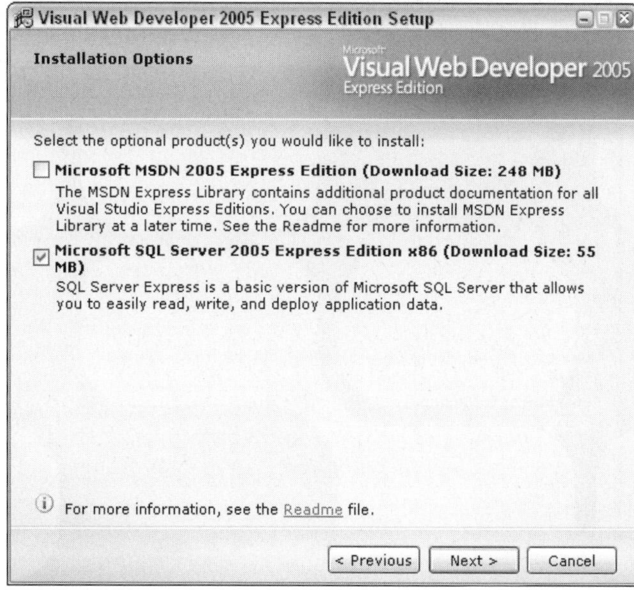

Figure B-5

7. Specify where to install VWD (see Figure B-6). We suggest selecting the default, which is `C:\Program Files\Microsoft Visual Studio 8\`, and clicking Install to begin the setup. (Don't worry if the default is something other than C on your machine — this makes no difference).

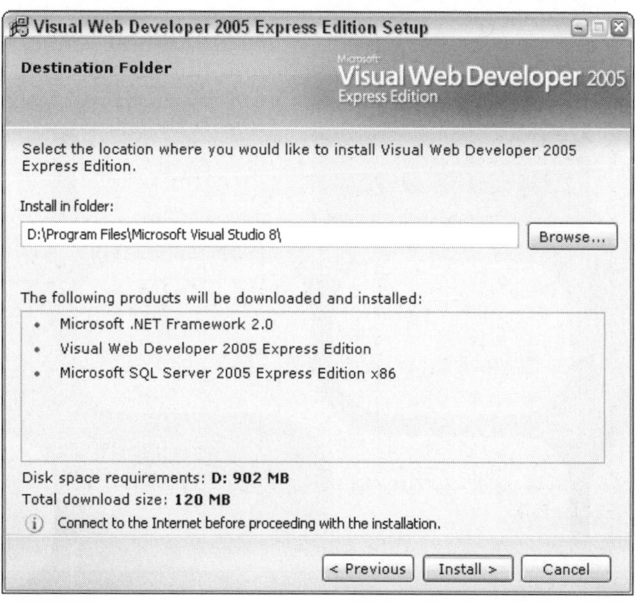

Figure B-6

Unfortunately, downloading of all the components must now commence (see Figure B-7), and with 120MB, this can take quite a while.

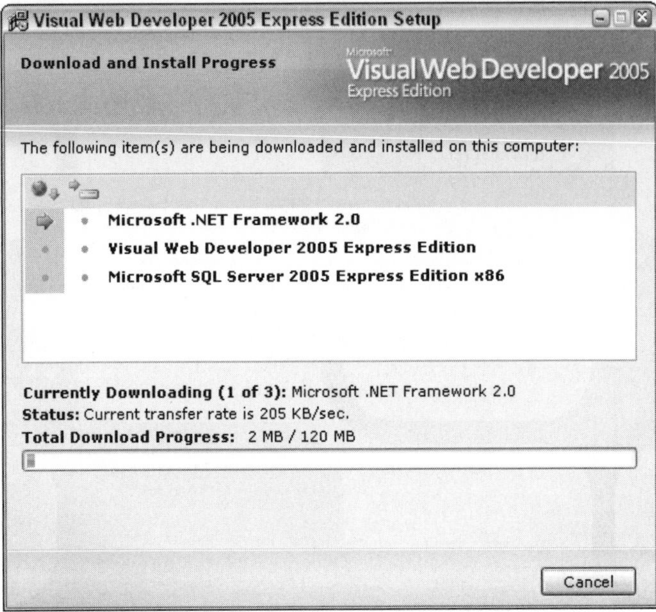

Figure B-7

Don't be surprised to see Microsoft .NET Framework 2.0 continue to download for quite a while after reaching the 120MB—this isn't unusual. After it has completed this stage, it will begin installation of the downloaded components, shown in Figure B-8.

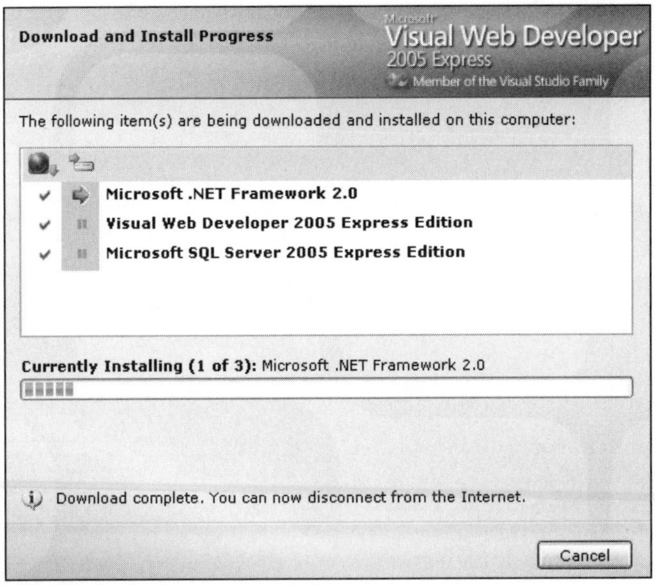

Figure B-8

SQL Server needs Internet access during installation, so make sure it can access the Internet. Otherwise, the installation will fail.

8. At the end of this installation, you should see the screen shown in Figure B-9, asking you to restart your machine. You should oblige by clicking Restart Now.

By chance, you may not see this screen. As a general rule, you shouldn't restart more often than necessary, so if you're not prompted to restart, don't do it.

Figure B-9

9. After your machine has restarted, the dialog box depicted in Figure B-10 is displayed, notifying you of a successful install (or any problems that were encountered) and reminding you to register the software within 30 days.

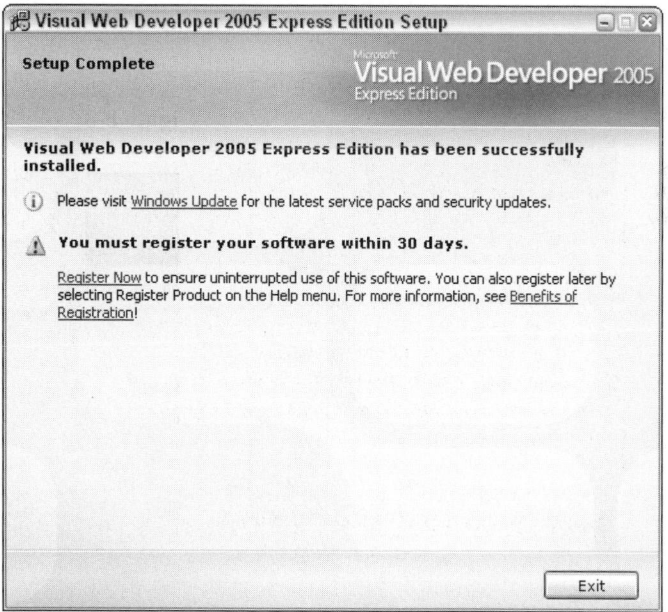

Figure B-10

10. Click Exit and you will now be able to start up both Visual Web Developer and SQL Express.

Web Site Folder Setup

Next, set up the Websites folder with Windows Explorer, and create the folder `C:\Websites\WroxUnited` (or use whichever drive is appropriate to your setup).

> **To create a folder in Windows Explorer, select File⇨New Folder and type in the name Websites.**

IIS Setup (Optional)

As we've already mentioned, Visual Web Developer Express comes with its own web server: the ASP.NET Development Server, nicknamed Cassini. However, some of you might want to use IIS anyway. Note that it isn't possible to run two versions of the web site concurrently, one on IIS and one on the development server, because the database attaches itself to the ASP.NET Development Server and you will find you can't run it with IIS without detaching the database first.

To use IIS, you must have Windows XP Professional, Windows 2000, or Windows 2003 Server installed. Windows XP Home Edition comes without IIS, and it isn't possible to install it on Home Edition if you do manage to get a copy of IIS. To begin the install, follow these steps:

1. To install IIS go to the Start menu, navigate to Settings⇨Control Panel, and click Add or Remove Programs. From the left-hand menu of the dialog box (shown in Figure B-11), select the Add/Remove Windows Components icon. This will bring up the Windows Components Wizard.

Figure B-11

2. Make sure the Internet Information Services option is selected, as shown in Figure B-12.

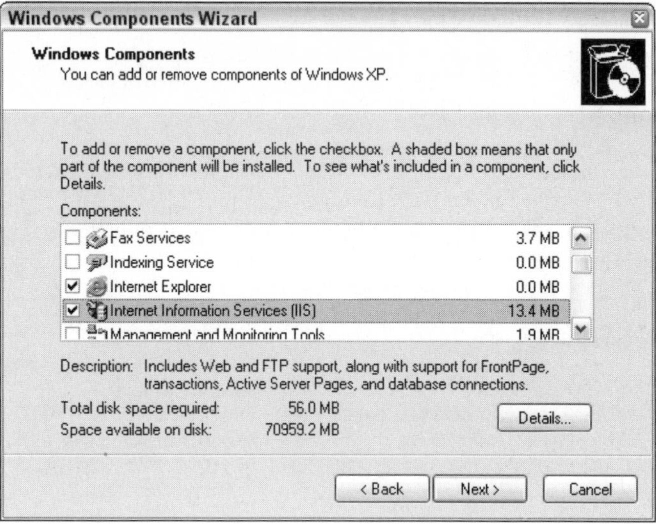

Figure B-12

3. Click Details and you can select which of the options to install (see Figure B-13). You won't need all of the options, although you can install them separately at a later point. However, you *must* make sure that you select the Common Files, the IIS snap-in, the Front Page Extensions, and the World Wide Web Services options, because these are necessary to work with ASP.NET 2.0 and Visual Web Developer Express.

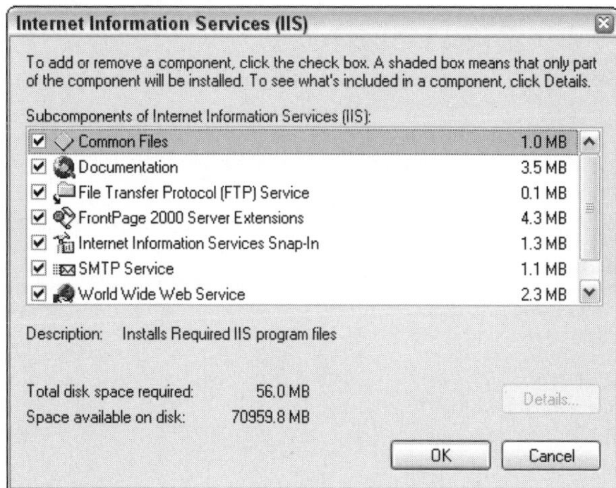

Figure B-13

4. Click OK and make sure you have the Windows CD handy for the installation.

Create Alias

If you choose to install IIS and want to use the Wrox United sample web site on IIS, you will need to create an alias so that IIS can recognize which application you mean and serve it accordingly. The following steps walk you through creating an alias:

1. From the Start menu, select Run. Type **MMC** in the text box, and click OK. In the MMC dialog box that appears, select File⇨Add/Remove Snap In. Click the Add button and select IIS Internet Information Services from the dialog box that appears, as depicted in Figure B-14.

Figure B-14

2. Expand the Internet Information Services, as shown in Figure B-15. Under that will be your computer's name. Expand that as well as the Web Sites option.

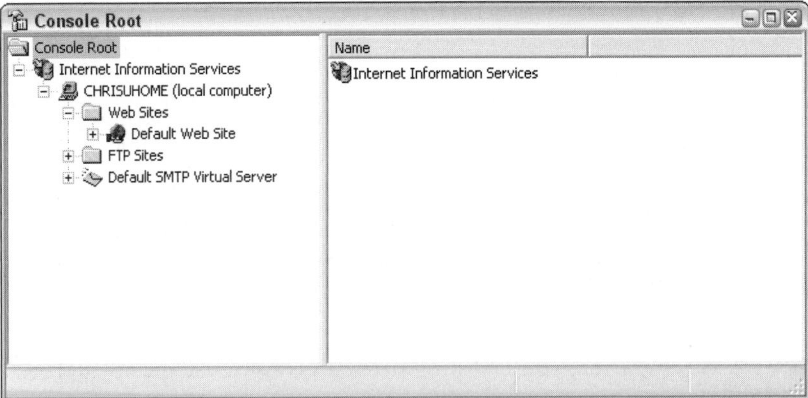

Figure B-15

3. Right-click Default Web Site, and select New➪Virtual Directory from the menu to start the wizard. Type **WroxUnited** as the Virtual Directory Name as in Figure B-16.

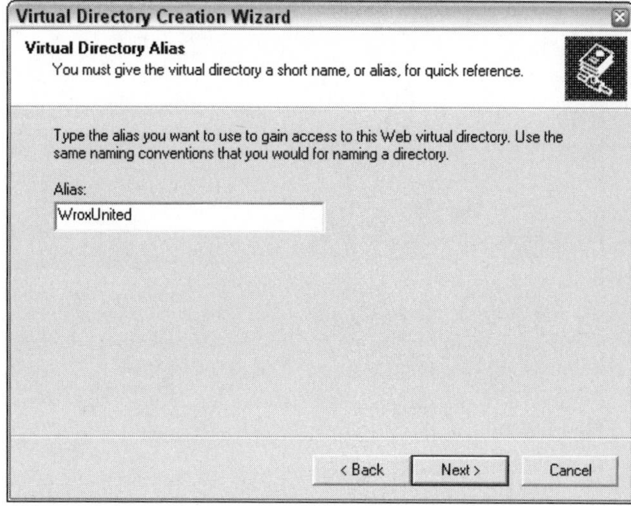

Figure B-16

4. Click Next and browse to `C:\Websites\WroxUnited` as the local path, as shown in Figure B-17.

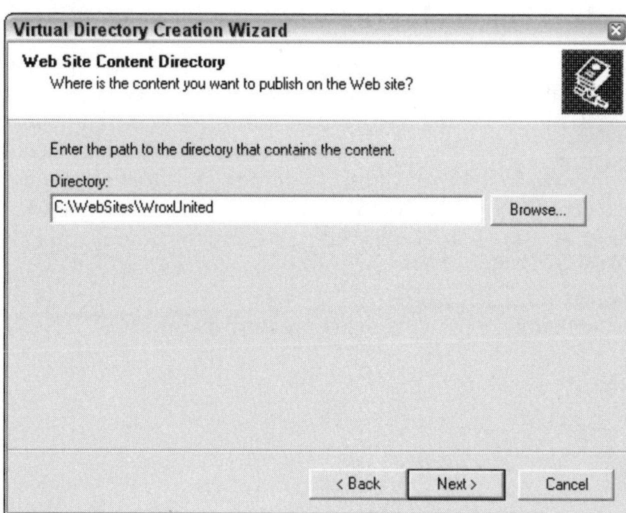

Figure B-17

5. Click Next and make sure the boxes are selected as shown in Figure B-18. Then click Next.

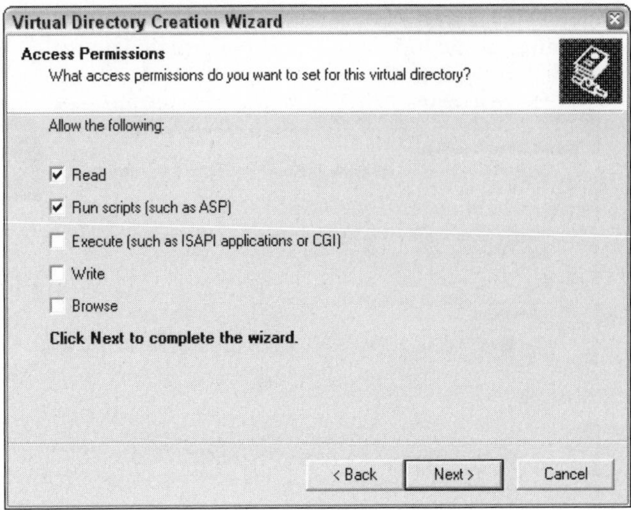

Figure B-18

6. Click Finish. Close the MMC Console. A save is optional, and you can supply a name if you so desire.

Wrox United Installation

Go to `www.wrox.com` and search for the dedicated page for Beginning ASP.NET 2.0 with C++ (ISBN: 0470042583). When you are there, you can download the Wrox United application, which comes as a single downloadable zip file containing the database and application. Download the zip file and save it to the `C:\Websites\WroxUnited` folder you created earlier. Next, unzip this file to `C:\Websites\`. It will automatically put files in the WroxUnited folder for you, so be careful not to extract it to `C:\Websites\WroxUnited`, because you could end up with `C:\Websites\WroxUnited\WroxUnited`. In Windows Explorer, make sure that inside your `C:\WebSites\WroxUnited` is an `App_Data` folder and that it has four files.

In particular, make sure that the following file names are present:

- `WroxUnited.mdf`
- `ASPNETDB.mdf`
- `WroxUnited_log.ldf`
- `ASPNETDB_log.ldf`

If not, go back and try downloading the zip file again.

Network Service Enabling

The last step before you can test the application is that you might need to add Write permissions to the Network Service account. This will allow ASP.NET to use the database and to read data from it and write data to it, as is routinely required throughout the course of this book. You can skip this step if you are using Windows Server 2003, because the Network Service account has these permissions already enabled by default. If not, then you will almost certainly have to enable Write permissions first. Here's how:

1. Go to Windows Explorer and select the `C:\WebSites\WroxUnited\App_Data` folder. Right-click it and select Sharing and Security. Select the Security tab, shown in Figure B-19.

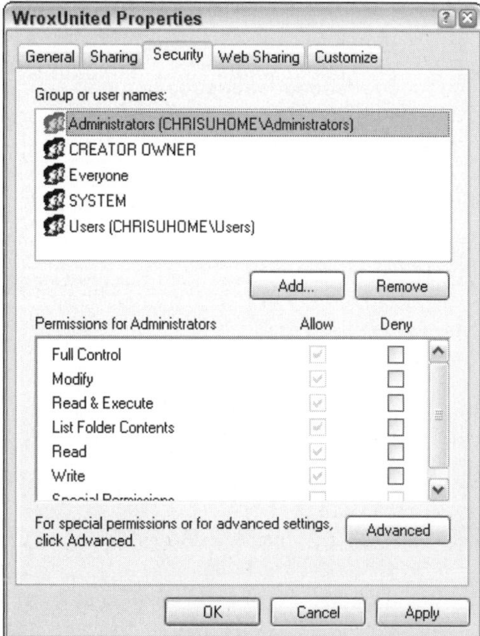

Figure B-19

If you can't see the Security tab, this is because you have Simple File Sharing switched on. To disable it, select Tools⇨Folder Options from Windows Explorer, and select the View tab. Scroll to the bottom and uncheck the Use Simple File Sharing option (see Figure B-20). If you can't see the Simple File Sharing option, this is because you have Windows XP Home Edition installed and it has Simple File Sharing switched on permanently, and you cannot change it. Instead, you will have to take another course as outlined in the next section.

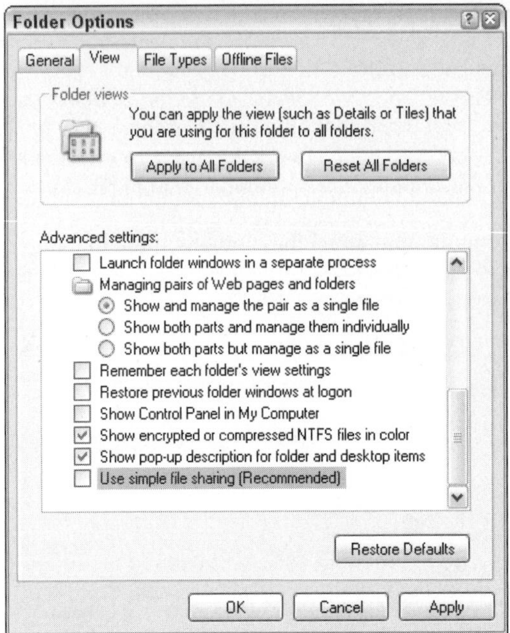

Figure B-20

2. Click the Add button in the Wrox United Properties dialog box and in the Select Users or Groups dialog box that appears. Type **NETWORK SERVICE** into the text box and click Check Names. NETWORK SERVICE will become underlined, as shown in Figure B-21.

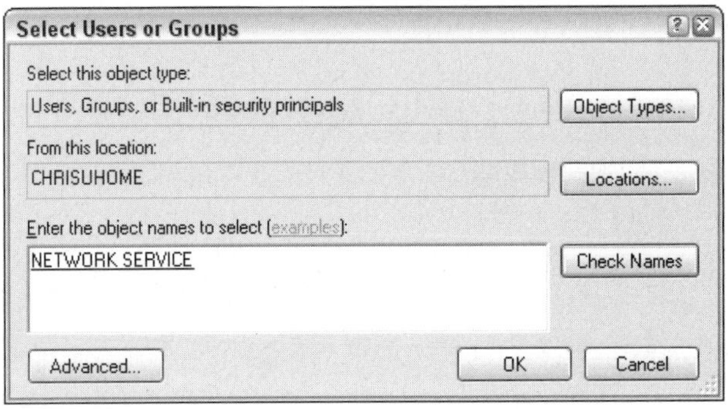

Select Users or Groups
Select this object type:
Users, Groups, or Built-in security principals
Object Types...
From this location:
CHRISUHOME
Locations...
Enter the object names to select (examples):
NETWORK SERVICE
Check Names
Advanced...
OK
Cancel

Figure B-21

If the machine is joined to a domain, you must select the Locations button first and pick the current machine, rather than the domain. That's because NETWORK SERVICE is an account on your machine. By default, the dialog will attempt to add the domain name, rather than the machine name.

3. Click OK. You are returned to the Wrox United Properties dialog box. This time, select the new NETWORK SERVICE option. Scroll down and check the box next to Write (see Figure B-22). Click Apply, and then click OK.

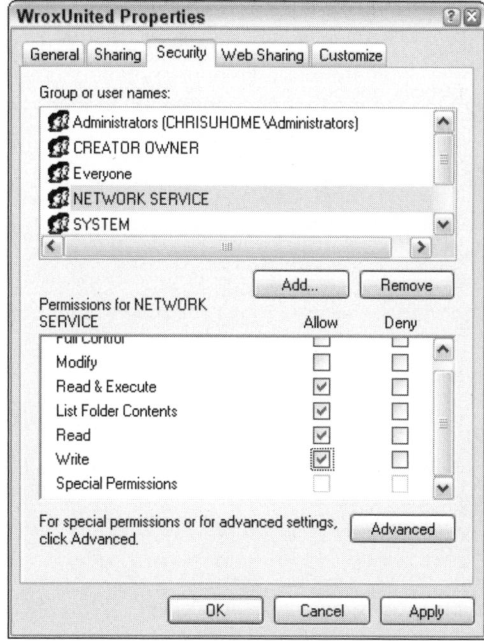

Figure B-22

This will enable your account to access the database.

Windows XP Home Edition Users Only

If, when you come to browse for a Security tab in Windows Explorer, you can't find one, this is because you have Windows XP Home Edition installed and you have a slightly more complex route to enable the correct permissions. Apparently, Windows XP Home Edition users just aren't allowed to have the same kind of power as their XP Professional counterparts. To get around this, restart your computer in Safe Mode.

To do this, restart your machine, and before the Windows XP logo appears, hold down the F8 key and select Safe Mode. Let XP continue and then log in as **Administrator**. You'll receive a warning about running in Safe Mode, but click Yes anyway. Locate the C:\WebSites\WroxUnited folder in Windows Explorer and right-click the `App_Data` folder. Select Properties and select the Security tab that has now appeared. Now go back to step 1 in the previous section and follow the instructions from there on. At the end, though, shut down and restart your machine in normal mode before you continue to the next step.

Checking the Installation with VWD and the ASP.NET Development Server

After you have successfully downloaded the Wrox United zip file, unzipped it, and enabled the Network Service, you are ready to check your installation. Follow these steps:

1. Select the Start menu and navigate to All Programs. Select the Visual Web Developer 2005 Express Edition Icon at the bottom of the menu. VWD will open.

2. Select File➪Open Web Site, and browse to C:\Websites\WroxUnited and click Open. When the web site has loaded into Solution Explorer, double-click `default.aspx` to open the file. Press the F5 key to run the page and observe it in a browser. You should see what appears in Figure B-23 in your browser.

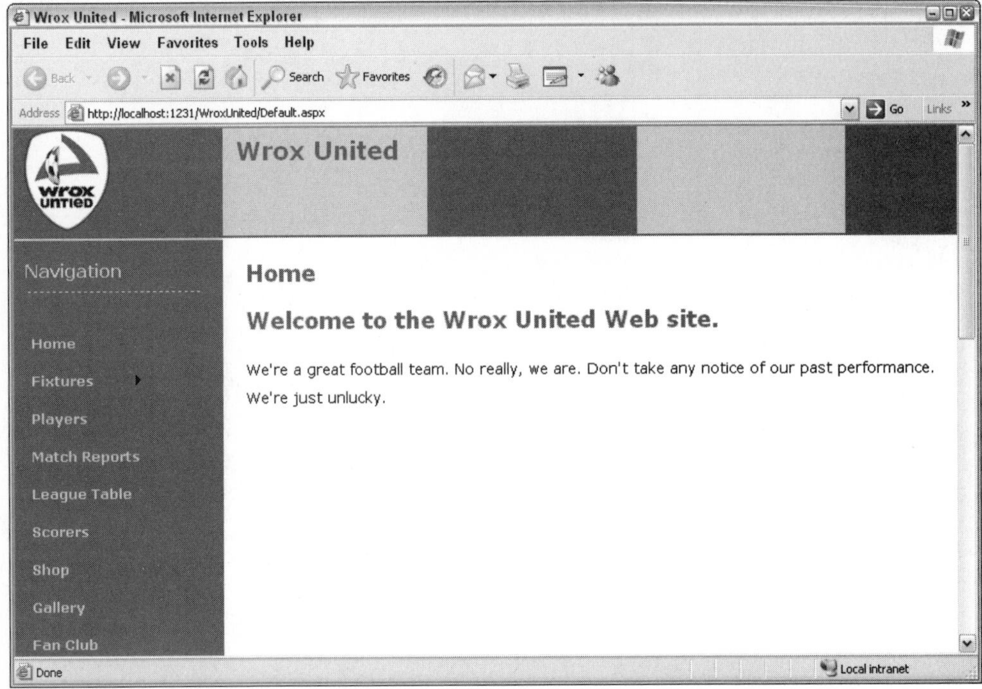

Figure B-23

Checking the Installation with IIS

Follow this step only if you have installed IIS and intend to use it as your main web server. To open WroxUnited with IIS, start Internet Explorer and type **http://localhost/WroxUnited** into the Address line. The web site should start and display what's shown in Figure B-24.

Please note that while Figure B-22 is seemingly identical to Figure B-21, the Address line reveals a small difference. If you are running your site on ASP.NET Development Server (the free web server with VWD), you will get the following line (potentially with a different number):

```
http://localhost:1231/WroxUnited
```

This indicates that the web server is running on port 1231. The ASP.NET Development Server will arbitrarily assign a port number in the URL. If you are running the web site on IIS, then you see the following line:

```
http://localhost/WroxUnited
```

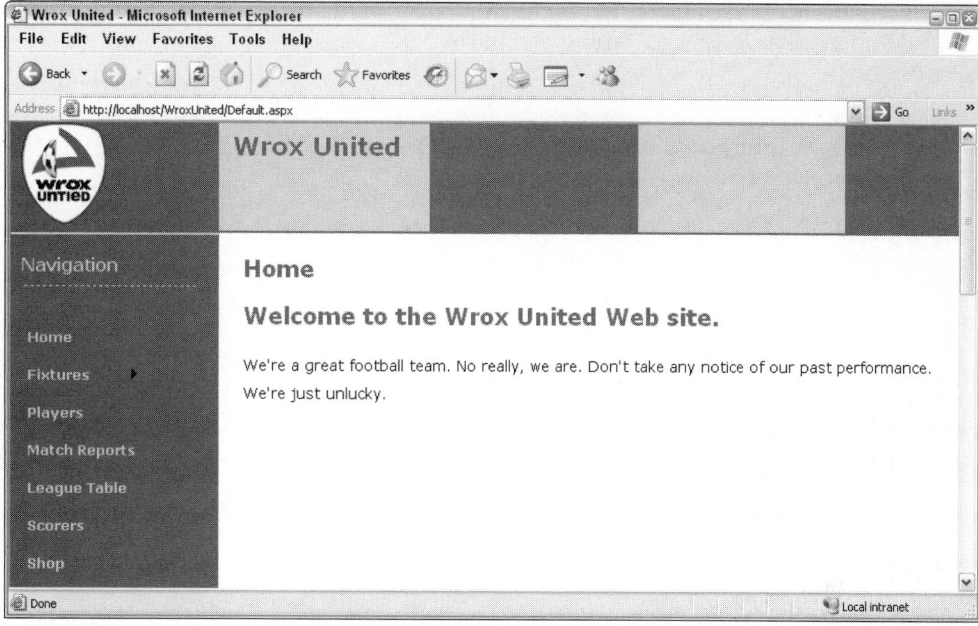

Figure B-24

IIS by default runs on port 80, and this doesn't need to be specified in the URL.

Occasionally, if port 80 is taken by another process, IIS will default to `http://localhost:8080`, or you might have to specify it yourself if you get an error message saying `Unexpected error 0x8ffe2740 occurred`.

This means that another application is using port 80. To alter this, you need to start the IIS manager from Administrative Tools in the Control Panel, right-click the Default Web site in the left panel, and select Properties. From the Web Site tab, change the number there from 80 to **8080**, or if 8080 is taken then **8081**, or the first one free above that number.

Troubleshooting

By and large, installation with SQL Express and the ASP.NET development is straightforward. However, if you are trying to use SQL Server 2005 rather than SQL Express, you should run through the following extra steps:

1. Add `[machine\ASPNET]` and `[NT AUTHORITY\NETWORK SERVICE]` as logins, substituting machine with your machine name.
2. Attach the database (`wroxunited.mdf`), making ASPNET the `db_owner`.
3. Add `[machine\ASPNET]` and `[NT AUTHORITY\NETWORK SERVICE]` as database users.
4. Change the connection strings in `web.config`. That should be all for the WroxUnited database. Then there's the providers, which can be added to either the WroxUnited database or to a separate one.

5. Run `aspnet_regsql` (in the framework directory), to add `user/roles/etc tables/procs` to the appropriate database.
6. Add provider sections in `web.config`, for `<membership>`, `<roles>`, and `<profile>`, setting the default provider for each to the new provider added. These providers should point at the ConnectionString for the database (which will be either WroxUnited or a new connection string if you're using another database).

Note that if you are using a different version of SQL Server than 2005, it isn't possible to just attach the database to the different version. If you are using the full version of 2005 and you encounter the following problem:

```
Server Error in '/WroxUnited' Application.
Failed to generate a user instance of SQL Server due to a failure in copying
database files. The connection will be closed.
Description: An unhandled exception occurred during the execution of the current
web request. Please review the stack trace for more information about the error and
where it originated in the code.
Exception Details: System.Data.SqlClient.SqlException: Failed to generate a user
instance of SQL Server due to a failure in copying database files. The connection
will be closed.
```

you will need to do the following:

1. Reboot windows.
2. Log in as **Administrator** (if you aren't running with Admin privileges).
3. Delete the `C:\Documents and Settings\username\Local Settings\Application Data\Microsoft\Microsoft SQL Server Data\SQLEXPRESS` directory.

You might need to logout and log back in as a "normal" user if you normally run with non-admin privileges.

If this doesn't work, try the following solution—there is a known problem with remote logging on and SQL Express, which the following steps should circumvent:

1. Go to the SQL Configuration Manager.
2. Right-click SQL Express and select Properties.
3. From the Logon tab, change the account from Network Service to Local System.
4. Try to run it again.

Apart from that, if you encounter a problem go to `http://forums.asp.net` or `http://p2p.wrox.com` and check to see if your problem is addressed there.

Wrox United Database Design

Throughout this book, you've seen examples based on the fictional Wrox United soccer team web site. The application relies on a SQL Server database, supplied with the code downloads for this book (available at `www.wrox.com`). This database stores details of the players in the team, fixtures and results, news items, orders from the shop, and so on.

This appendix is not intended to provide a thorough overview of database design principles, and as such, we recommend that you read Wrox's *Beginning Database Design*.

The database schema looks like Figure C-1.

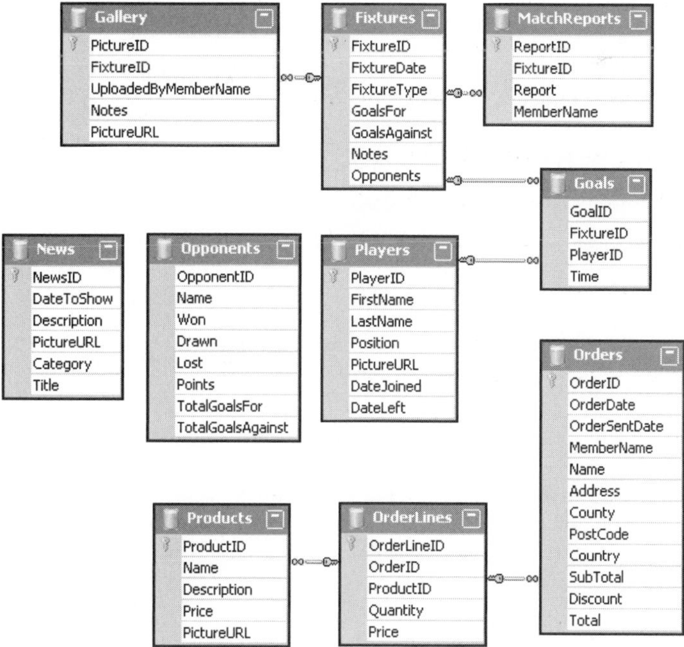

Figure C-1

This diagram illustrates the tables that exist within the database, and the relationships between those tables. For example, players score goals, goals are scored at fixtures, match reports are written about specific fixtures, and so on. Many tables relate to other tables in the database, but there are some tables that stand on their own; for example, the News table, which stores news articles. This table doesn't link to data stored in any other table. Notice also that the Orders, Products, and OrderLines tables are separate from the rest of the database — these tables are used to store data relating to orders from the Wrox United shop.

This appendix walks through the structure of each of the tables in the database and describes the relationships between them.

Players and Matches

The players on the Wrox United team are involved in many fixtures, and several related tables in the database store related data for matches. Take a look at these tables first.

The Players Table

The following shows the structure of the Players table.

Field	Data Type	Allow Nulls
PlayerID (Primary Key)	`int`	No
FirstName	`varchar(25)`	No
LastName	`varchar(25)`	No
Position	`varchar(50)`	Yes
PictureURL	`varchar(255)`	Yes
DateJoined	`datetime`	Yes
DateLeft	`datetime`	Yes

This table is typical of all database tables in that it has the following:

- A *primary key* field that uniquely identifies each row in the database
- Fields designed to store textual data about each player (in `varchar` fields)
- Fields that store date and time information
- Flags indicating whether or not different fields require values

In this table, the primary key is the PlayerID field, which stores numeric values (integers) that are unique to each player in the database. This field, along with the FirstName and LastName fields, is marked as not allowing null values. In other words, if you enter a row of data in the table, you must enter values for each of these fields. However, the PlayerID field will be filled with an auto-generated number for you (due to the way it is configured), so the only data you must enter when you create a new row is the full name of the new player. The remaining information describing the player is optional. You don't have to specify which position the player occupies, and you don't have to specify when he or she joined.

> *Note that a* `varchar` *field is a field that stores character data of varying length. The number in brackets is the maximum number of characters that can be stored in that field. If the field contains less than the maximum length, it occupies less space in the database. A* `char` *field, by comparison, always takes up the same size in the database, no matter how much of the available space is filled with data.*

Figure C-2 shows an example of some data from the Players table.

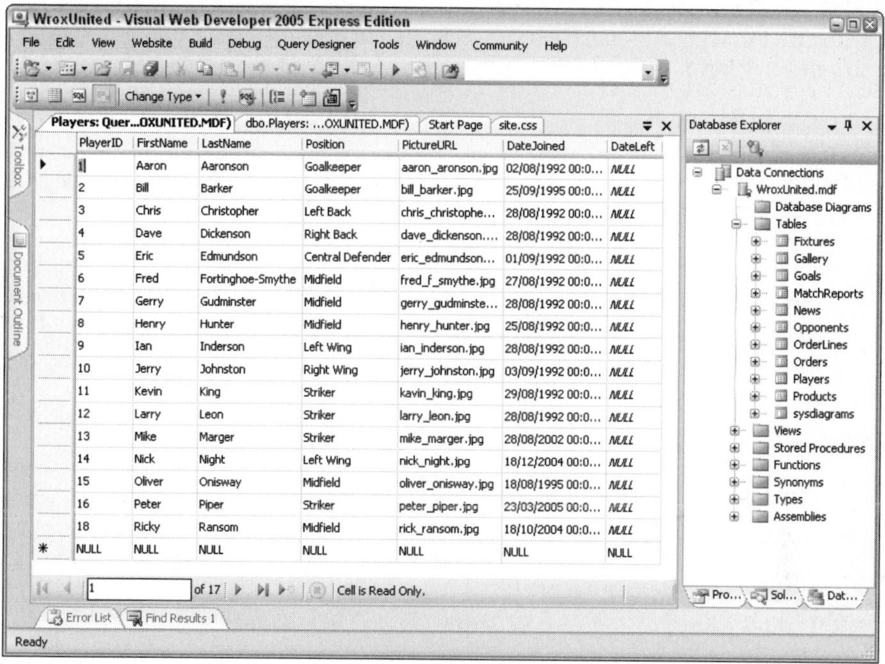

Figure C-2

This screenshot comes straight from Visual Web Developer. You can right-click any database table in the Database Explorer and select Show Table Data to try this out for yourself.

The Goals Table

The Goals table relates directly to the Players table, because players score goals during a match. The following shows the structure of the Goals table.

Field	Data Type	Allow Nulls
GoalID (Primary Key)	int	No
FixtureID (Foreign Key)	int	Yes
PlayerID (Foreign Key)	int	Yes
Time	int	Yes

Notice that one of the fields in this table is the PlayerID field, which will store an integer value corresponding to the ID of one of the players in the Players table, so if Dave Dickenson scored the first goal for Wrox United, the goal in the table with GoalID of 1 will have a PlayerID of 4. Dave could later score another goal for Wrox United, so another record in the Goal table would be created with another unique value for GoalID, but with the same PlayerID. This type of field is called a *foreign key* because it relates directly to a primary key in another table.

There is another field in the Goals table for storing ID values, which is the FixtureID field. This links each goal to a particular fixture. Because players could score many goals at a single fixture, the relationship between the Fixtures table and the Goals table is similar to that of the Players table and the Goals table.

This sort of relationship — where one fixture can contain many goals, or where one player could score many goals — is known as a one-to-many relationship.

The Fixtures Table

The Fixtures table is structured as shown here.

Field	Data Type	Allow Nulls
FixtureID (Primary Key)	int	No
FixtureDate	datetime	No
FixtureType	varchar(10)	Yes
GoalsFor	smallint	Yes
GoalsAgainst	smallint	Yes
Notes	text	Yes
Opponents	varchar(50)	No

For each match played by the Wrox United team, there is an entry in the Fixtures table. Because fixtures can be arranged several months in advance, the fixture date has to be entered as soon as the fixture is arranged, and the opponents have to be entered. The number of goals scored can be entered later, after the match has been played.

The MatchReports Table

After each match has taken place, it's up to the reporters to write up the details of the match so that fans can read all about it later. These reports are stored in the MatchReports table, which is structured like as shown here.

Field	Data Type	Allow Nulls
ReportID (Primary Key)	`int`	No
FixtureID (Foreign Key)	`int`	No
Report	`text`	Yes
MemberName	`varchar(50)`	No

This table also links to the Fixtures table by including a FixtureID field in this table, linking a match report to a specific fixture. The MemberName field stores the name of the reporter.

The Gallery Table

The Gallery table is used to store details of pictures uploaded by fan club members. The fields defined in this table are shown here.

Field	Data Type	Allow Nulls
PictureID (Primary Key)	`int`	No
FixtureID (Foreign Key)	`int`	Yes
UploadedByMemberName	`varchar(50)`	Yes
Notes	`text`	Yes
PictureURL	`varchar(50)`	No

Each picture can relate to a specific fixture (notice the FixtureID field); however, because this field allows the use of null values, this implies that pictures do not necessarily have to relate to fixtures.

Standalone Tables

The two standalone tables in the database are the Opponents table and the News table.

The Opponents Table

The Opponents table stands on its own in the database, and is defined as shown here.

The reason the Opponents table is on its own is a bit unfortunate, but the opposing team may decide to change its name at some point in the future, which would change the name of all fixtures that Wrox United played against them in the past if they were related. By keeping the tables separate, and only using a name for each team, the name of the opponent in any particular match is preserved.

Field	Data Type	Allow Nulls
OpponentID (Primary Key)	`int`	No
Name	`varchar(50)`	Yes
Won	`int`	Yes
Drawn	`int`	Yes
Lost	`int`	Yes
Points	`int`	Yes
TotalGoalsFor	`int`	Yes
TotalGoalsAgainst	`int`	Yes

This table can be updated with results of matches to maintain a tally of how well the Wrox United team is performing in the league.

The News Table

The News table, described here, contains all of the news stories from the front page of the Wrox United site.

Field	Data Type	Allow Nulls
NewsID (Primary Key)	`Int`	No
DateToShow	`datetime`	No
Description	`text`	Yes
PictureURL	`varchar(50)`	Yes
Category	`varchar(50)`	Yes
Title	`varchar(50)`	Yes

Notice that each news item requires that a date be entered for each story, so that a story can remain hidden until a certain date has passed.

Wrox United Store Tables

The online shopping experience on the Wrox United site relies on data stored in three tables: the Orders table, the Products table, and the OrderLines table. These tables are heavily reliant on each other.

The Orders Table

The Orders table, described here, contains a unique ID containing the main order details for an order.

Field	Data Type	Allow Nulls
OrderID (Primary Key)	Int	No
OrderDate	datetime	No
OrderSentDate	datetime	Yes
MemberName	varchar(50)	No
Name	varchar(50)	No
Address	varchar(255)	No
County	varchar(50)	No
PostCode	varchar(15)	No
Country	nchar(10)	No
SubTotal	money	Yes
Discount	money	Yes
Total	money	Yes

In this table, you'll notice that most of the fields are marked as mandatory (not allowing null values). This highlights the fact that orders must have full address details before an order can be fulfilled. A couple of less familiar field types are in here too. The `nchar` data type will always take up 10 characters space in the database, and the `n` in the name indicates that the data stored could contain Unicode characters. The other unfamiliar data type is `money`, which (as the name implies) can be used to store monetary values.

Notice that there are no details in this table about which products have been bought in a particular order. This information is stored in the OrderLines table.

The OrderLines Table

The OrderLines table, described here, links the Products table to the Orders table, indicating which items have been bought in a particular order.

Field	Data Type	Allow Nulls
OrderLineID (Primary Key)	int	No
OrderID (Foreign Key)	int	No
ProductID (Foreign Key)	int	No
Quantity	smallint	No
Price	money	No

Because an order can contain one or many products, there is a foreign key link here to the Products table. However, because many different orders can be for the same product, there is also a foreign key link here to the Orders table. This means that an individual line in this table stores details of one item, and one order number. If you order more than one of a specific product, the Quantity is increased for the order line, but you won't end up with a new OrderLineID.

The relationship between the Orders table and the Products table is a many-to-many relationship. In this situation, there has to be a central table that has one-to-many relationships to both tables, and this is called the Join table.

The Products Table

The Products table, described here, contains details of all of the products that can be bought from the shop.

Field	Data Type	Allow Nulls
ProductID (Primary Key)	`int`	No
Name	`varchar(50)`	No
Description	`varchar(255)`	Yes
Price	`money`	No
PictureURL	`varchar(255)`	Yes

This simple table provides data about products, and is used both when users are browsing the shop and when they're buying items from the shop.

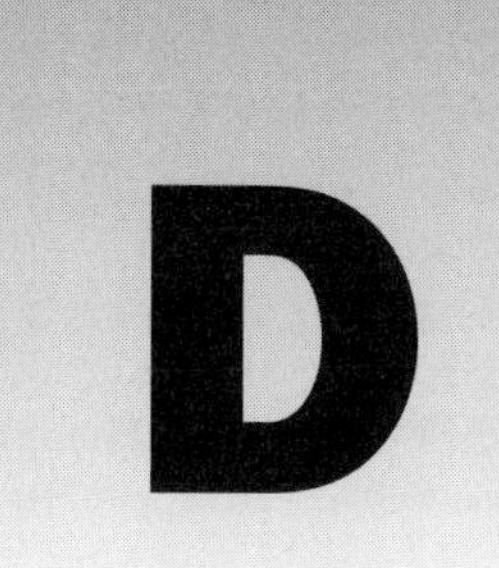

VWD Database Explorer

When you're designing pages that work with data, you frequently need to check the metadata, for example, to confirm the data type of a field. You also want to test your pages by quickly modifying the data in tables. Furthermore, in some cases, you want to add a small and simple table to a database, such as a list of shippers. In the past, these database tasks required that you leave your web editor to open a second window with a database management tool. Visual Web Developer offers a built-in tool named the Database Explorer that can perform these tasks without the need for a separate management tool. Some functions are performed directly and others invoke a wizard to step you through the task.

This appendix covers the various techniques for working with the Database Explorer.

Opening the Database Explorer

You can view the Database Explorer either by choosing Menu⇨View or by pressing Ctrl+Alt+S. After it is open, the Database Explorer by default stacks on top of the Solution Explorer on the right side of the screen. You can move it to a new dock location by dragging its title bar.

> **If you mess up the layout, you can return to the default by choosing Menu⇨Windows⇨Reset Windows Layout.**

Adding an Existing Database to the Database Explorer

The technique to connect the Database Explorer to a database depends on the type of database. The following three sections cover the Microsoft databases. Most other databases (such as Oracle or MySQL) will be the same as connecting to a SQL Server.

Accessing Files

Follow these steps:

1. On the Database Explorer toolbar, click Connect to Database, and from the first page of the wizard, select Microsoft Access Database File, as shown in Figure D-1.

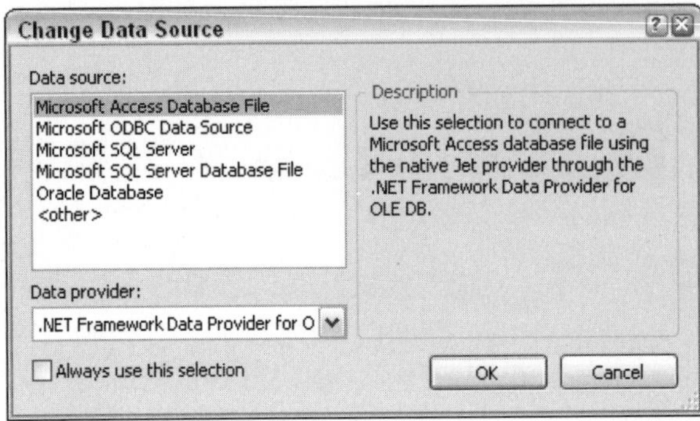

Figure D-1

2. Browse to the file, and then add logon information if needed (see Figure D-2).

Figure D-2

3. You have the option to test the connection and then it is added to your list in the Database Explorer.

SQL Databases on a SQL Server (Including SQL Server Express)

Follow these steps:

1. On the Database Explorer toolbar, click Connect to Database, and in the first page of the wizard (shown in Figure D-3), select Microsoft SQL Server.

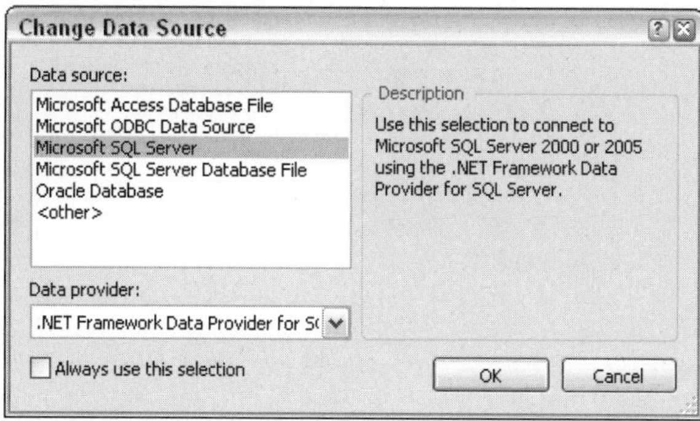

Figure D-3

In the next dialog box, the Data Source section is locked — it actually means the kind of data source, not the name of the database.

2. Continuing on the Add Connection screen, for the Server Name text box, there are two options. If you are using a full install of SQL Server, select the server name. If you are using SQL Server Express (as we do in this book), type the following syntax exactly: **(local)\SQLExpress**, as shown in Figure D-4.

Figure D-4

Note the potential confusion when using SQL Server Express. Your PC name will be listed in the drop-down box of servers, but that is not the server you want to specify. You must type into the server name box the specific syntax to point to your local machine's instance of SQL Server Express.

3. Keep the choice for logon information set to Windows (see Figure D-5) unless you have developed an authentication table in SQL Server.

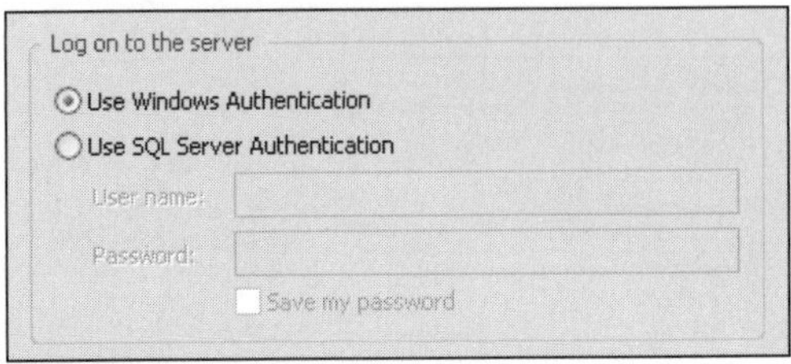

Figure D-5

4. After you have selected the server name, you can drop down the list of databases. Test the connection and then click Finish to see your new data connection.

Saving SQL Databases as an MDF File

For highest performance, data is kept in SQL Server without an external file structure. But for portability, a database can be configured to save its data in a Windows file that can be copied to a new server. The file will have an extension of .mdf. We use an .mdf file to distribute data in this book. (The alternative would be to have you download a long SQL script that would build the entire database internally in your server and populate its data.) Connecting to an .mdf file is very similar to connecting to Access Files. Just follow these steps:

1. On the Database Explorer toolbar, click Connect to Database, and select Microsoft SQL Server Database File, as shown in Figure D-6.

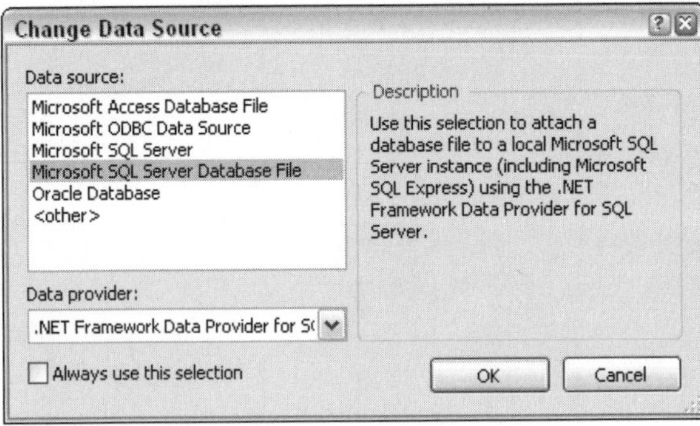

Figure D-6

2. Browse to the file and add logon information if needed (see Figure D-7).

3. You have the option to test the connection and then it is added to your list in the Database Explorer.

Figure D-7

Viewing Database Diagrams

The VWD Database Explorer provides a visual presentation of your database's objects along with the capability to drill down into each object's properties. Follow these steps to walk through a diagram of your database:

1. Within the Database Explorer, expand your Data Connections and then expand your database. When you expand the Database Diagrams (see Figure D-8) the first time, you may be asked to establish yourself as the dbo (database owner). Click Yes. Right-click the Database Diagram object and add a new diagram. If asked, accept the creation of elements needed to build the diagram.

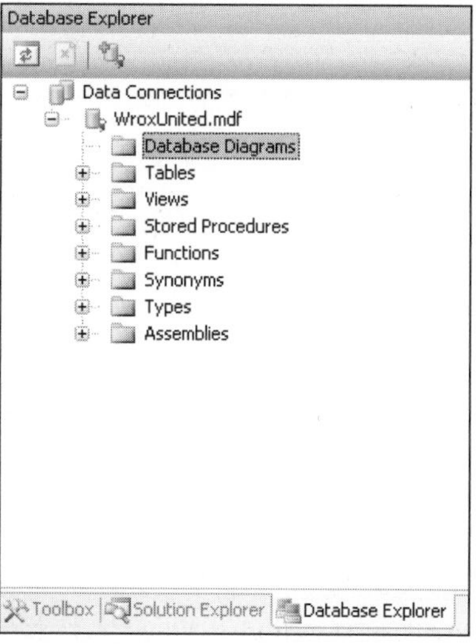

Figure D-8

2. Add tables as desired and close the Add Table dialog box (see Figure D-9).

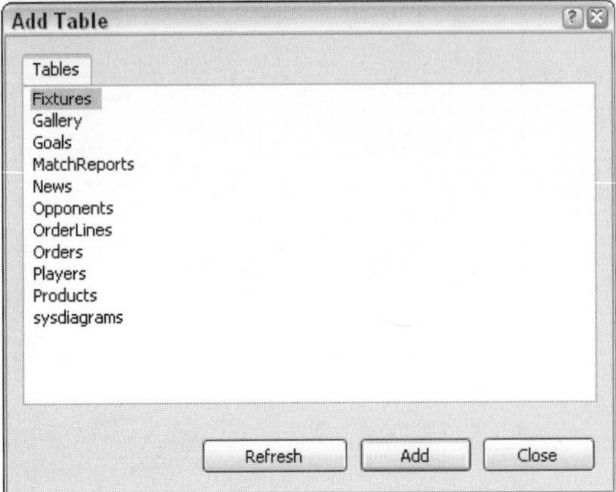

Figure D-9

The diagram can be so large that it is easy to miss tables. Note the Windows-standard horizontal and vertical scroll bars to navigate the diagram (see Figure D-10).

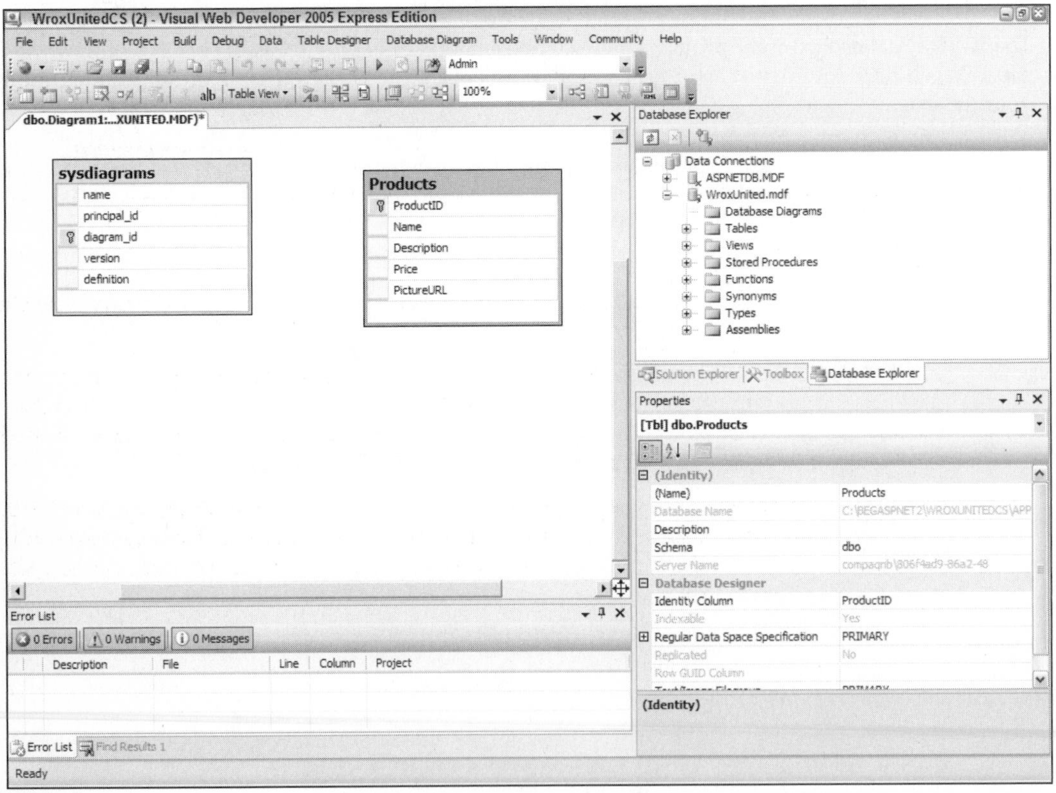

Figure D-10

3. You can rearrange the tables (the relationship lines will automatically adjust). Start by changing the zoom size to 30% or so to be sure you see all of the tables and then do some rearranging. The zoom window is on the diagram toolbar, shown in Figure D-11 set to 30%.

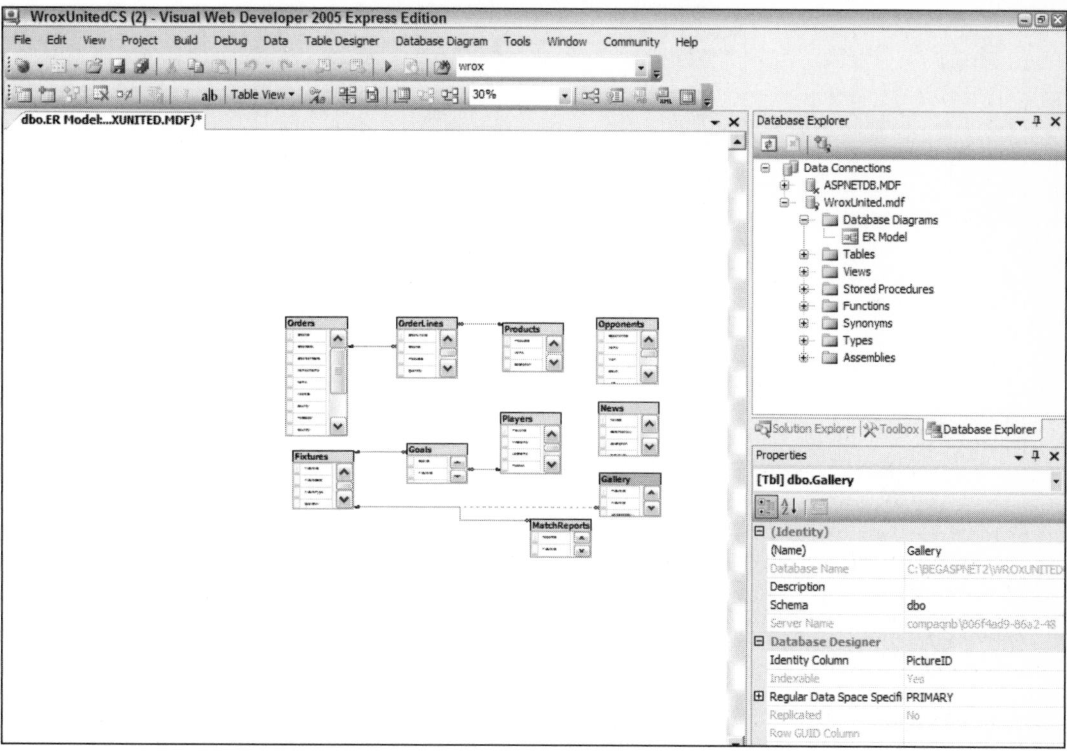

Figure D-11

4. Increase the zoom size to be able to read the data. For example, after rearrangement, 70% shows all the tables for Wrox United, as shown in Figure D-12.

5. Right-click the title bar of a *table* (for example, Players) and select Properties from the menu. In the Properties box (in the lower right of the monitor), you can view parameters such as the Identity column. Right-click *one field* (see Figure D-13) of a table and select Properties to see how that column has been configured, including the data type and length.

6. Carefully place the tip of the mouse arrow on a relationship line (for example, between Fixtures and MatchReports) so that the mouse arrow changes to a horizontal double-ended arrow. Right-click this *relationship* and select Properties to view data on the relationship, including enforcement rules, as shown in Figure D-14.

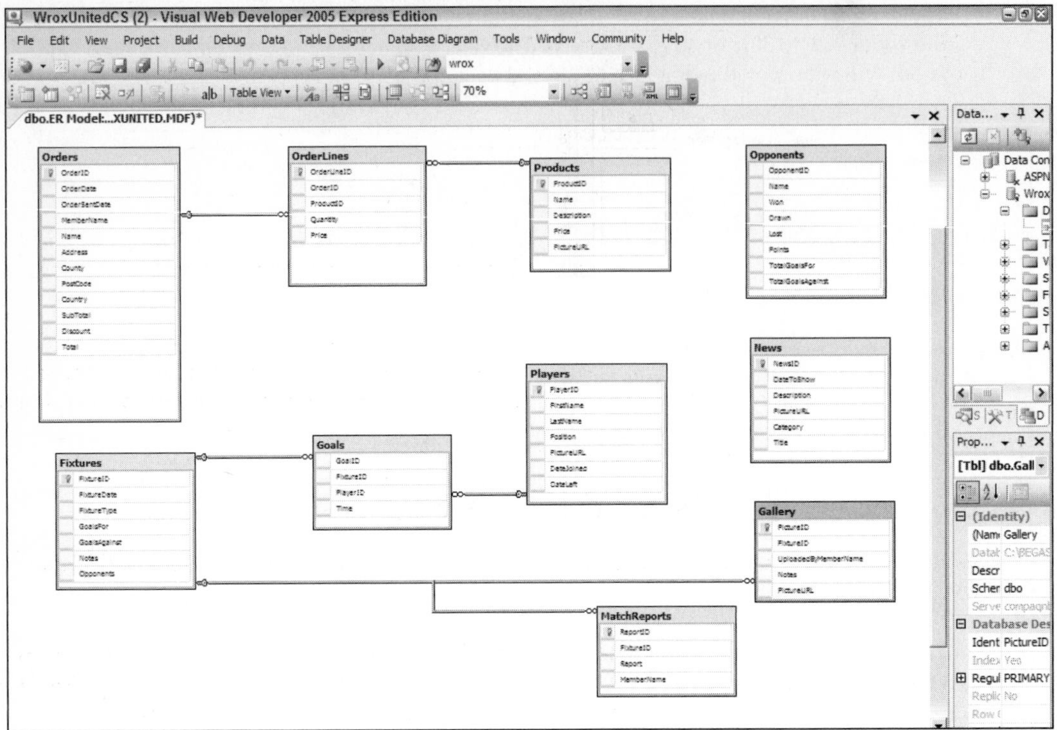

Figure D-12

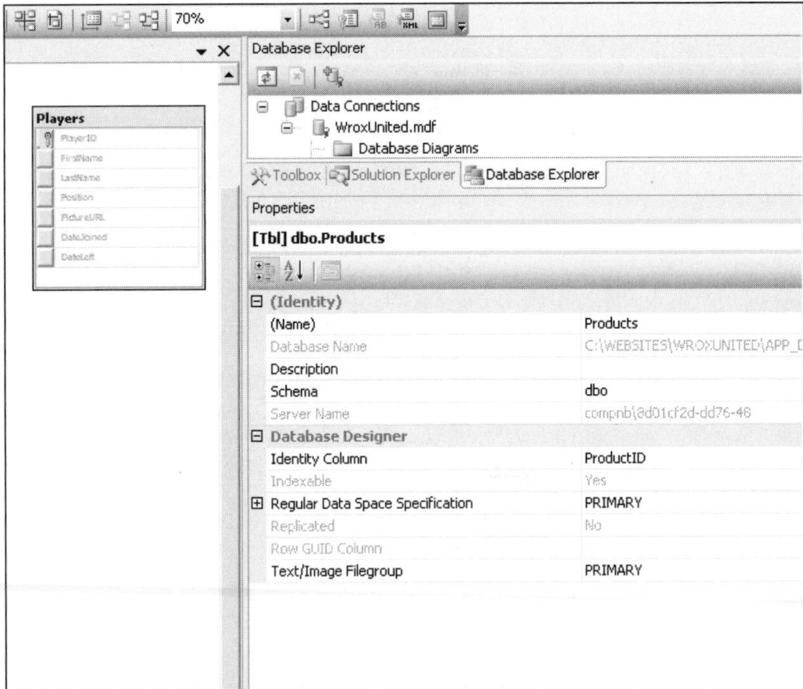

Figure D-13

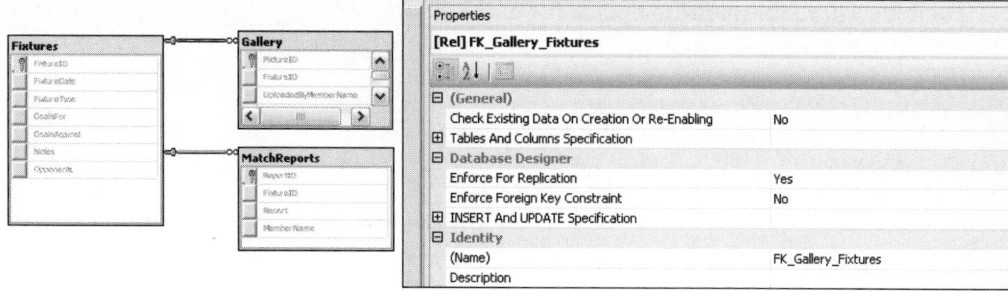

Figure D-14

7. You can also print the Database Diagram or save it to include in documentation for the site. Note that there are tools to position page breaks at specific axes of the diagram, as well as a tool that allows you to add a text box of notes.

Exploring a Table's Structure

In addition to the Database Diagram, you can look at tables through the Table node of the Database Explorer, as follows:

1. Starting in Database Explorer, expand the list of databases and then the database of interest. Expand the Tables node and select a table name (for example, MatchReports). In the Properties window, shown in Figure D-15, you will see the approximate number of records.

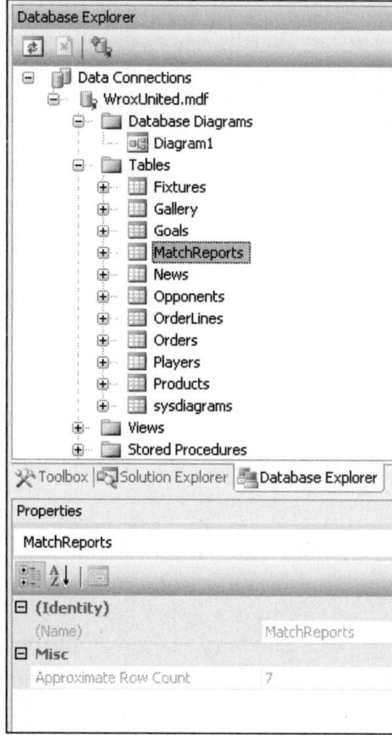

Figure D-15

2. Double-click a table name to open a list of the columns (fields) and populate the Properties windows with data on the table as a whole, as shown in Figure D-16.

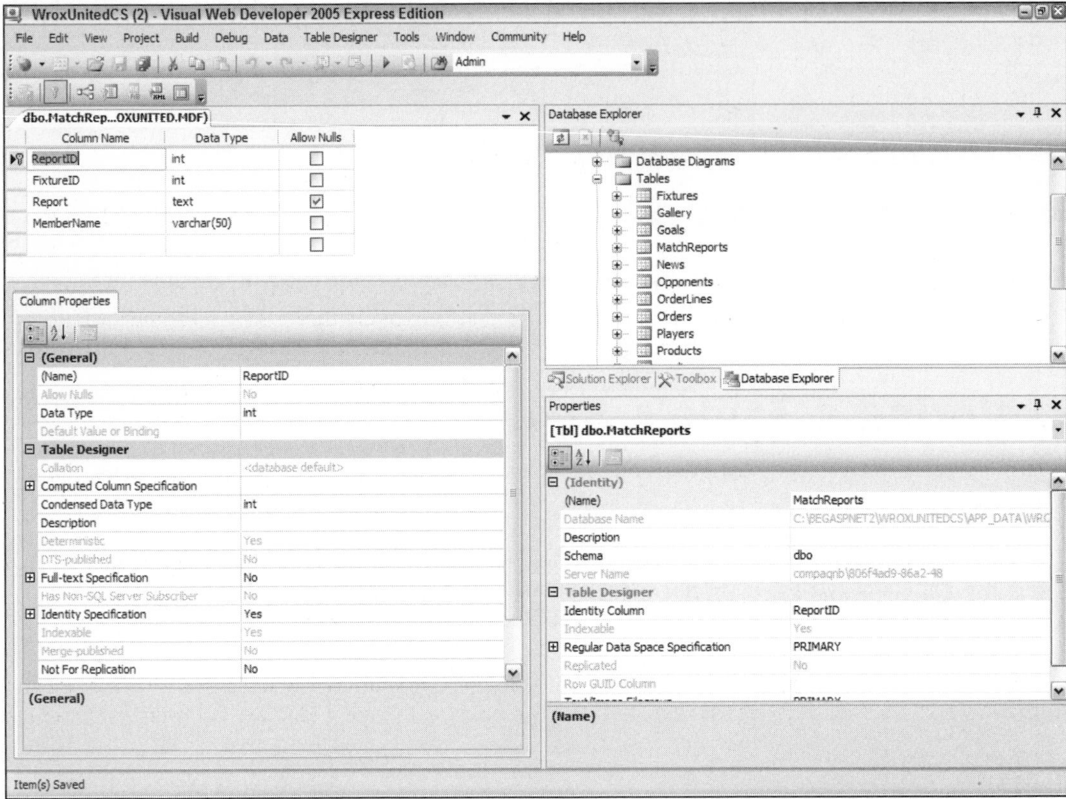

Figure D-16

These metadata can be changed in this view, assuming that you have the rights to make changes to the database structure.

Observing and Editing Data of Existing Tables

If you right-click a table name in the Tables node of Database Explorer, you'll see an option to Show Table Data. This is a quick way to find out if your data-enabled web pages are actually carrying out their tasks. You can also add, modify, or delete records to test results in data-reading pages.

Be extremely careful about changing data with the Show Table Data tool. For example, deletions or changes of customers may divorce them from their orders. In some databases, the addition of a record may require the addition of a partner record in another table. A simple correction to a spelling mistake may cause a failure to properly look up data that is based on the old spelling. If you thoroughly understand the schema and are changing independent data, you may avoid trouble. But in most cases, it is better to make revisions based on the interface that ensconces proper validation, limits, and controls.

Creating a New Database

It is rare that you will use VWD to create a database from scratch. Good databases require the kind of planning and implementation tools that come with your database management system. However, in the case of a small and simple database, VWD does offer the necessary planning and implementation tools. You can add a new database in two ways: directly in the Database Explorer or by adding a SQL Database through the Add New Item menu in Solution Explorer.

Follow these steps to create a database in Database Explorer:

1. In the Database Explorer, right-click Data Connections and select Create New SQL Server Database.
2. Select a server. If you're using SQL Server Express, use this exact syntax for the server name: **(local)\SQLExpress**. Use Windows authentication unless you have created an authentication scheme internal to SQL Server Express. Type the name of the new database into the bottom text box.

   Database Explorer will automatically add the database to its list and you are ready to create tables and add data.

You can also create a new database directly in the Solution Explorer. This technique is very similar to the preceding procedure except for the first few steps:

1. Start in the Solution Explorer and right-click the root of the web site. Select Add New Item and select the template of type SQL Database.
2. When prompted, agree to add to the `App_Data` folder.

   VWD will now roll you over to the Database Explorer where you will see the new database and folders for its objects (albeit empty). You can now create tables, add data, and perform other tasks.

Creating a New Table and Adding Data

Tables can be added and populated in the Database Explorer, as follows:

1. Expand the database, right-click the Tables node, and select Add New Table from the menu shown in Figure D-17.

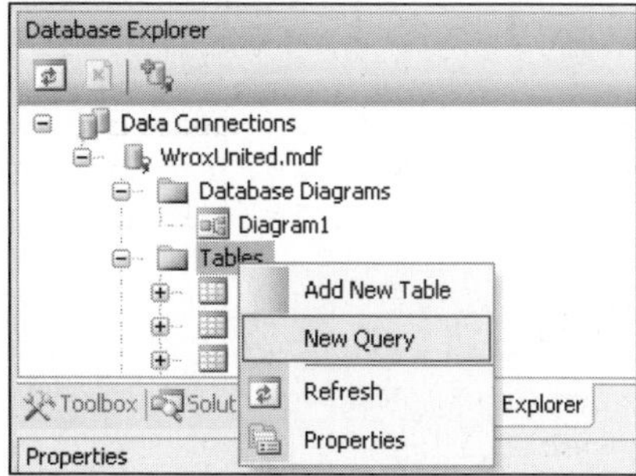

Figure D-17

2. In the resulting list of columns, enter the names and data types. For example, as shown in Figure D-18, a new table that holds a schedule of reporter's interviews with the players would start with a column (field) for InterviewID.

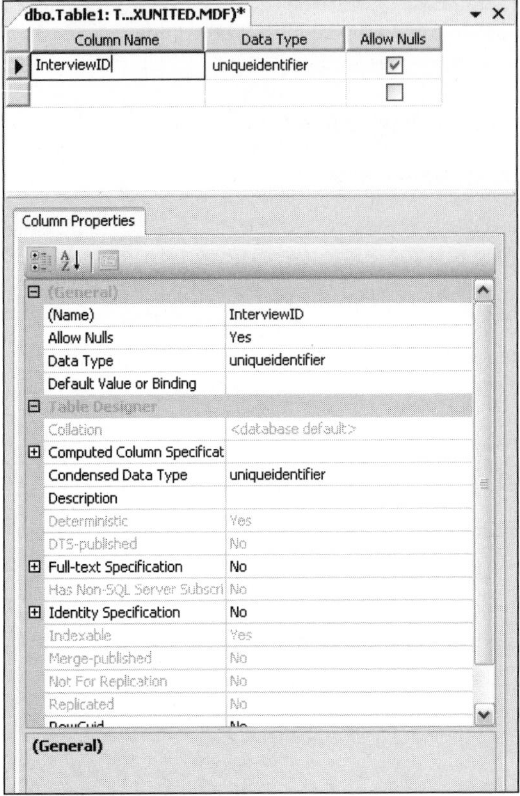

Figure D-18

Note that under Data Type, you can scroll down to find the UniqueIdentifier type, which is similar to AutoNumber in Access.

3. In the panel below the columns list, you will find additional properties for the current column such as default value and length.
4. Set the primary key by selecting a field and clicking the key tool in the table's toolbar.
5. Finish by choosing Menu⇨File⇨Save Table.

Examining and Creating Views

Views provide a set of data. Instead of returning information directly from a table, a view returns only certain fields, modified fields, or records. In many databases, the security rules will allow a web site to request a view but not directly request data from a table — this provides a level of control for the database administrator. For example, a table of employees may hold a field for salary level. A view that is authorized for the accounting department would include that field, but other users only have access to views that do not include the salary data. Views are also useful for creating hybrid data, such as combining a NameFirst field and a NameLast field to show both names in a single field of a list box.

You can do a basic exercise where you create a view that would support a selection ListBox of Players. You want the view to create two fields — the first is the player's ID and the second is a combination of the player's last and first names, separated by a comma. Follow these steps:

1. In Database Explorer, expand your database, right-click the Views node, and select Add a New View. This opens the designer for a new view in the background, and in the foreground, the Add Table dialog (see Figure D-19) will open.

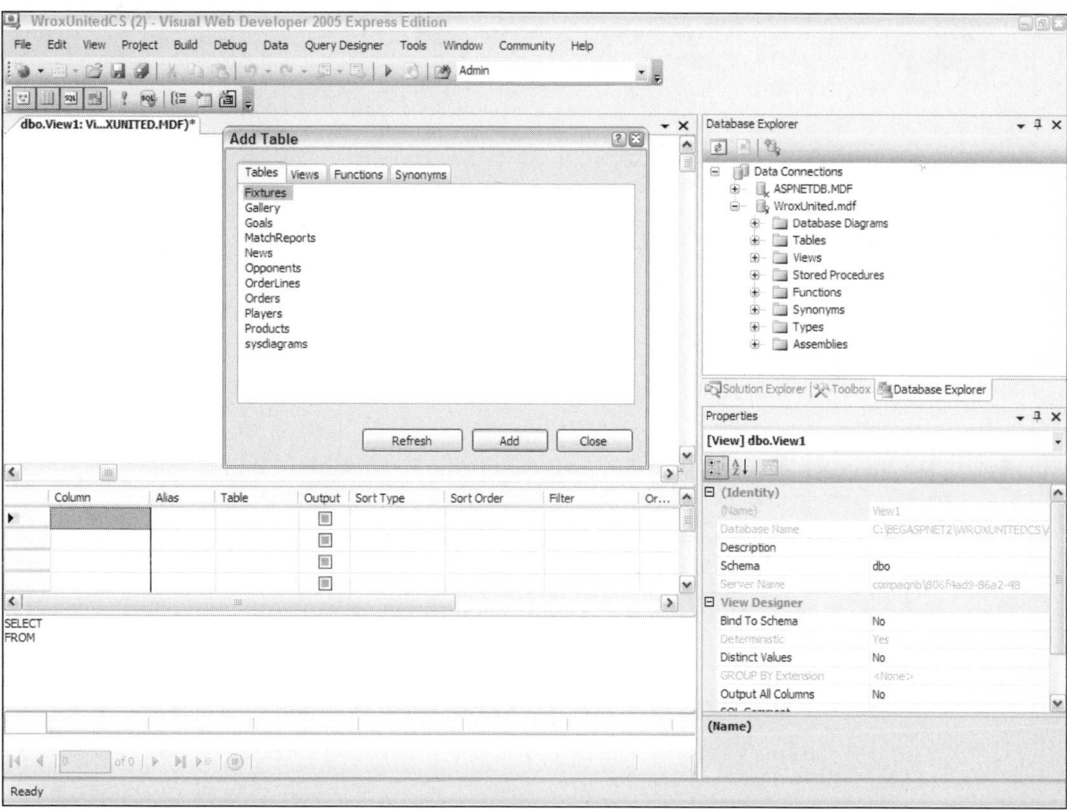

Figure D-19

2. In the Add Table dialog box, select Players and click Add. Close the dialog box.

3. Before you go on, experiment with turning on and off the panels to display a view. From left to right, they are the Diagram, Query, SQL Statement, and Results. Because you are making a small view, you can display all four. Figure D-20 shows the four panels. On the top is the pane of tables, showing just the Players table with the single field of PlayerID selected. The next panel down is the query designer, which shows the single field selected. The next panel shows the very simple SQL statement: `SELECT PlayerID FROM dbo.Players`. The bottom panel shows the results of choosing Query Designer⇨Run to produce the results table.

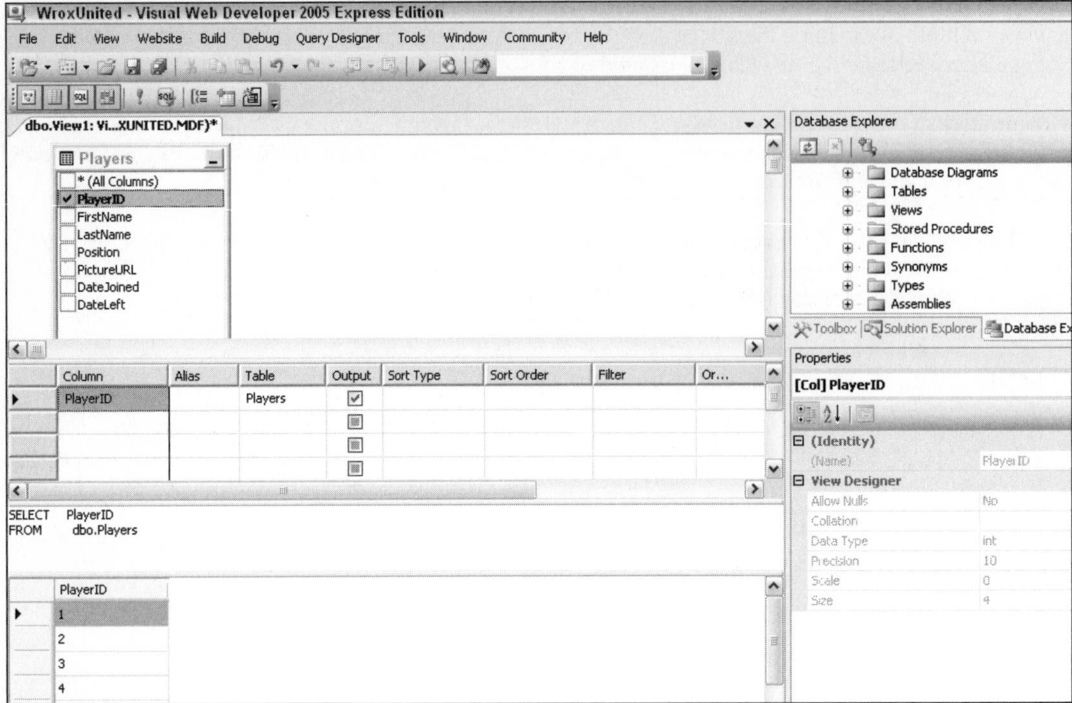

Figure D-20

4. Click the check box next to the PlayerID field in the Player table of the Diagram View (the top panel) and note that the field is added to the Query and SQL Statement panels.

5. In the Query panel, go to the second row and type **FullName** into the alias cell. In the left column, type **LastName + ', ' + FirstName**.

6. Click the execute SQL tool (the red exclamation point) to see the results, displayed in Figure D-21.

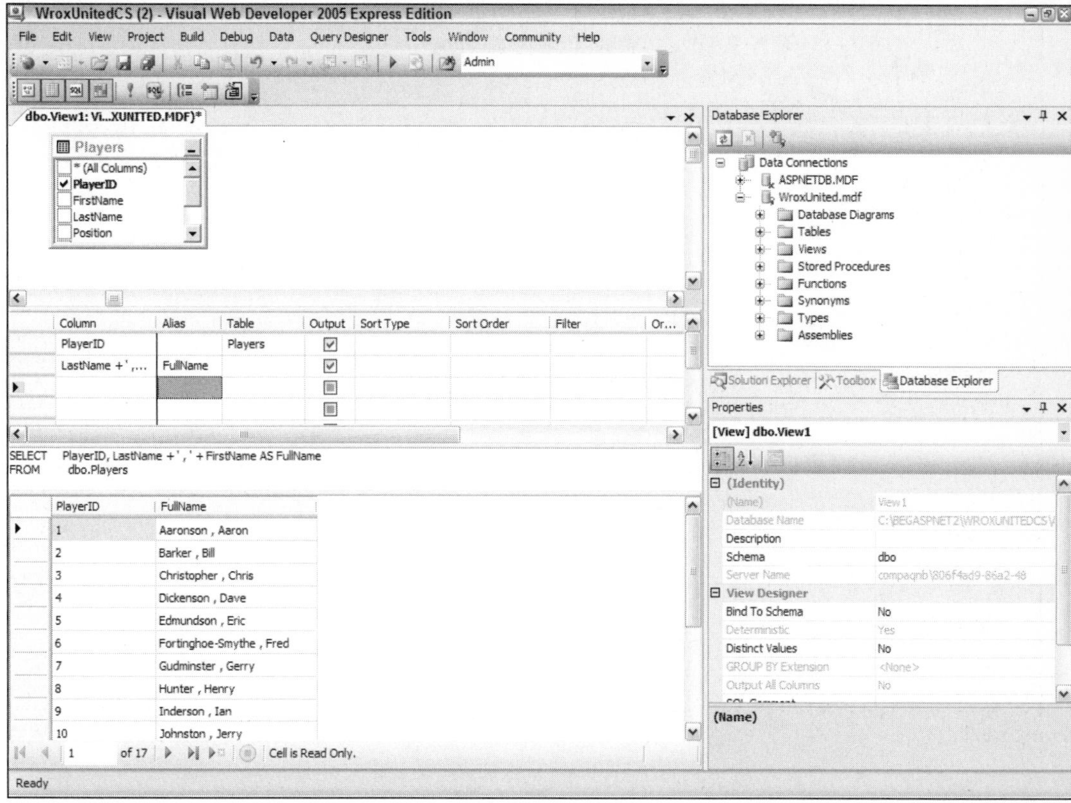

Figure D-21

7. Order the players' names by last name. SQL does not like to order on a created (or alias) field, so go to the third row of the Query panel and add the LastName field. Turn off its Output option. Set the Sort Order column to 1, meaning this is the first criterion for sorting. In the Sort Type, VWD will automatically set the order to Ascending. These four changes are shown in Figure D-22. This step tells SQL to sort according to the last name, but not to output the LastName as its own field. Execute the SQL.

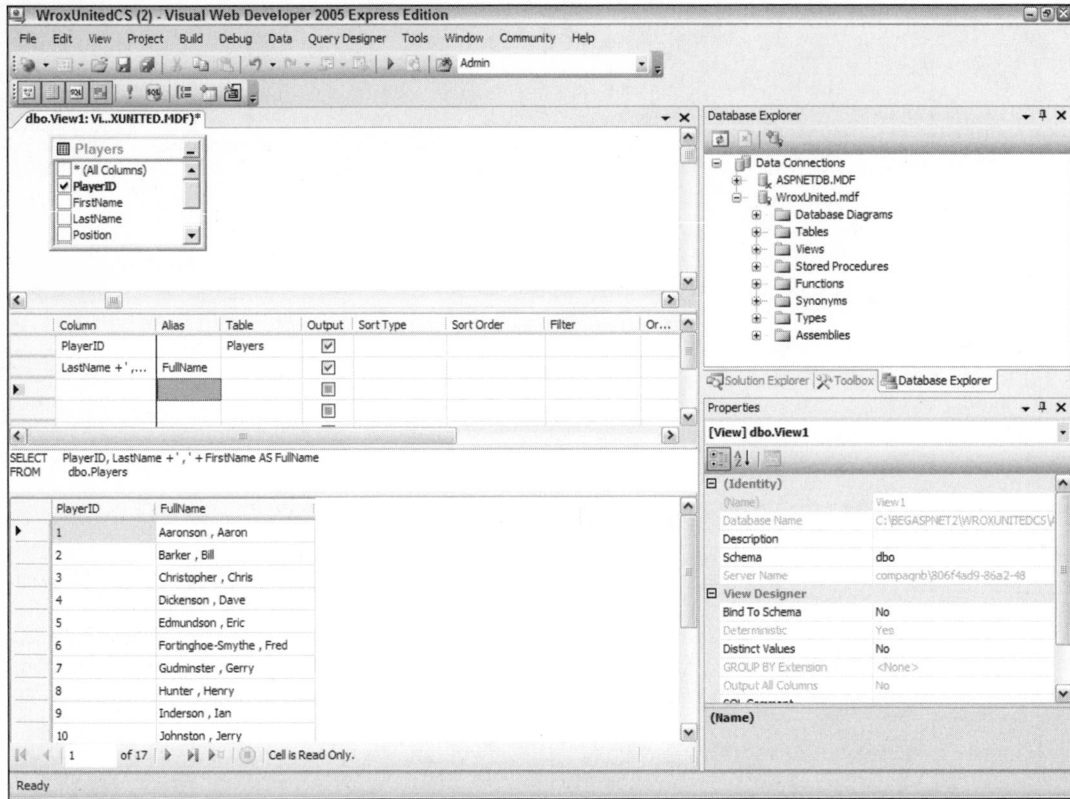

Figure D-22

8. Press Ctrl+S and save the view as **PlayersForSelectionList**. You now have a new view that can be used in a selection list of a web page — for example, `PlayerDetails.aspx`, for which the data controls follow. Note that in the `DataSource1` (supporting the list box), you are not reading from the Players table. Rather, you read from the PlayerSelection view. That view includes your new field FullName, which you can set as the `DataTextField` in `ListBox1`:

```
<asp:ListBox ID="ListBox1" runat="server"
 DataSourceID="SqlDataSource1"
 DataTextField="FullName"
 DataValueField="PlayerID"
 AutoPostBack=true>
</asp:ListBox>

<asp:SqlDataSource ID="SqlDataSource1" runat="server"
ConnectionString="<%$ ConnectionStrings:WroxUnitedConnectionString %>"
SelectCommand="SELECT [PlayerID], [FullName] FROM [PlayerSelection]">
</asp:SqlDataSource>
<br />
<asp:DetailsView ID="DetailsView1" runat="server"
```

```
DataSourceID="SqlDataSource2"
 ...
</asp:DetailsView>

<asp:SqlDataSource ID="SqlDataSource2" runat="server"
 ConnectionString="<%$ ConnectionStrings:WroxUnitedConnectionString %>"
 SelectCommand="SELECT * FROM [Players] WHERE ([PlayerID] = @PlayerID)">
        <SelectParameters>
                <asp:ControlParameter ControlID="ListBox1"
                DefaultValue="1"
                Name="PlayerID"
                PropertyName="SelectedValue"
                Type="Int32" />
        </SelectParameters>
</asp:SqlDataSource>
</asp:Content>
```

Examining a Stored Procedure (SPROC)

Like the other objects explored in this appendix, you can examine, edit, and create stored procedures, or SPROCs. SPROCs are a set of one or more SQL commands that, as a group, carry out a task. The Database Explorer offers a node for SPROCs, which can be expanded. A single click selects a SPROC and shows, in the Properties window, if it is encrypted. A double-click opens the SPROC, which can then be edited (assuming you have the rights to change the object).

The design of SPROCs is beyond the scope of this text, but you can take a quick look at one. For example, in the Database Explorer, you can expand the WroxUnited database and then expand Stored Procedures. Then you can double-click usp_OrderAdd to open it and view the following code. In this simple SPROC, only one actual SQL statement gets executed:

```
ALTER PROCEDURE dbo.usp_OrderAdd
(
 @MemberName varchar(5),
 @Name varchar(50),
 @Address varchar(255),
 @PostCode varchar(15),
 @County varchar(50),
 @country varchar(50),
 @SubTotal money,
 @Discount money,
 @Total money
)
AS
 INSERT INTO Orders(MemberName, OrderDate, Name, Address, County, PostCode,
Country, SubTotal, Discount, Total)
 VALUES (@MemberName, GETDATE(), @Name, @Address, @County, @PostCode, @Country,
@SubTotal, @Discount, @Total)

RETURN SCOPE_IDENTITY()
```

This SPROC has three parts. The first and last lines establish the frame of the procedure and declare its name. The second section, within parentheses, names the parameters that will be used to carry out the procedure. The third part, the `INSERT INTO` statement following the `AS` command, describes the one SQL statement to actually execute.

Summary

VWD provides the Database Explorer for the creation, modification, and examination of databases. Generally, a web site will use an existing database, so the examination features are most useful. However, when you're testing a new site, you can go to the VWD Database Explorer to see if your pages are updating data correctly, or you can modify data to see how the pages handle the rendering. In addition to introducing the Database Explorer, this appendix discussed the following topics:

- You can examine both data and metadata. The latter includes the list of fields in a table and details about how those fields are structured, including their exact spelling, data type, size, and other parameters that will be important when designing a page to use the fields.
- When creating a database, table or view, or SPROC, the Database Explorer will kick off a wizard to guide you through the process. Keep in mind that when referring to your SQL Server Express install, you must use the syntax of `(local)\SQLExpress`.
- For two reasons, use particular caution when modifying data or metadata for existing databases. First, others may be expecting the database to be in its original state for their Web Forms or Windows forms. Second, you may not be aware of the constraints and relationships that can be ruined by incorrect changes in the data or structure.

CSS and HTML Quick Reference

This appendix provides a quick reference to CSS and HTML. It's not meant to be an exhaustive and complete list of all HTML controls, their properties and the CSS properties, but rather to give the most common uses.

Styling Pages and Controls

You can style controls, or change their look and feel, in two ways: with properties of the control or with Cascading Style Sheets (CSS). Ultimately, both achieve the same thing, making the control look the way you want it to, but in practice, they are very different. Both Visual Web Developer and Visual Studio 2005 use properties when setting the style for controls. For example, if you drop a `GridView` onto your page and AutoFormat it with the Autumn format, you get the following:

```
<asp:GridView ID="GridView1" runat="server" BackColor="White"
  BorderColor="#CC9966" BorderStyle="None" BorderWidth="1px" CellPadding="4">
  <FooterStyle BackColor="#FFFFCC" ForeColor="#330099" />
  <RowStyle BackColor="White" ForeColor="#330099" />
  <PagerStyle BackColor="#FFFFCC" ForeColor="#330099"
    HorizontalAlign="Center" />
  <SelectedRowStyle BackColor="#FFCC66" Font-Bold="True" ForeColor="#663399"
/>
  <HeaderStyle BackColor="#990000" Font-Bold="True" ForeColor="#FFFFCC" />
</asp:GridView>
```

Here the `BackColor` sets the background color, and `BorderColor` sets the color of the border. The same sort of thing applies to the style for parts of the control, such as the `FooterStyle` and `RowStyle`.

Although the approach of including the individual style attributes works fine, there are some issues:

- It makes the code hard to read. Not only is it more text to read through, but the properties aren't always in a logical order. For example, on FooterStyle and RowStyle, the BackColor and ForeColor are next to each other, but on the HeaderStyle, there is a Font-Bold attribute between them.
- There is extra text, bulking out the page. With lots of styling applied to lots of controls, the page size can increase, which can lead to performance degradation.
- It's hard to amend if you decide to change colors. AutoFormat works fine, but if you want custom colors, you have to change each property individually.

CSS solves this problem by abstracting the actual styling away from the control, leaving the control with just a simple reference to the styles being used. This is the CssClass property for web controls or the class property for HTML controls. The GridView could now be as follows:

```
<asp:GridView ID="GridView1" runat="server" CssClass="MyGrid">
  <FooterStyle CssClass="MyGridFooter" />
  <RowStyle CssClass="MyGridRow" />
  <PagerStyle CssClass="MyGridPager" />
  <SelectedRowStyle CssClass="MyGridSelectedRow" />
  <HeaderStyle CssClass="MyGridHeader" />
</asp:GridView>
```

Immediately you can see that this is easier to read. The class names can be anything you want, and it is best not to be control-specific, because CSS classes can be used across controls. For example, if the FooterStyle and RowStyle needed the same styling, you could do the following:

```
  <FooterStyle CssClass="MyGridStandard" />
  <RowStyle CssClass="MyGridStandard" />
```

Here the same style name has been used, allowing the centralization of the styling. Style names should also not contain things like color names. For example, don't call a style TextRed just because it outputs text in red. What happens if you want to change that text from red to blue? You can simply change the style, but the class name would be misleading. Calling it TextHighlight is acceptable.

Creating Inline Styles

To create inline styles, you use the <style> element, which is usually placed within the <head> element. For example:

```
<head>
  <title>My Styled Page</title>
  <style>
    styling goes here
  </style>
</head>
```

When using Master pages, you have to put the styling in the Master page, because Content pages don't allow a <head> element. Adding the style to the Master page is sensible though, because if all pages use the Master page, they automatically get the styles.

Linking Style Sheets to a Page

Another, and better, way to add styles is to use linked style sheets. In these cases, the style sheet is created as a separate file (with a .css suffix) and linked to the page like so:

```
<head>
  <title>My Styled Page</title>
  <link rel="stylesheet" type="text/css" href="site.css" />
</head>
```

The CSS is stored in `site.css` and the `<link>` element links this style sheet into the page at runtime. Another great advantage of linked style sheets is that they can be cached by the browser, so the first time a page is requested, the style sheet is loaded and cached. Subsequent pages that use the same style sheet won't need to reload it from the server because it's already loaded.

CSS Inheritance

One of the core concepts of CSS is that inheritance is implicit in the styles. In many ways, the concept is the same as inheritance in classes, in which a child class can inherit features from its parent. CSS works the same way. This allows styling to be applied at the top level and inherited by contained controls. For example, say you defined the paragraph tag (`<p>`) to have blue text like so:

```
p {
  color: blue;
}
```

Any child tags would inherit that style:

```
<p>Hello everyone. I'm a paragraph with a <b>bold</b> word.</p>
```

The paragraph would appear in blue, including the bold word, because it inherits styles from the parent. A bold tag not inside a paragraph would not be blue:

```
<b>this is bold</b>
<p>this is blue <b>and bold</b></p>
```

The first line would be bold only, whereas the second line would be blue, including the bold word. The `<b>` tag changes its style depending upon the context.

The technique of inherited styles reduces the amount of styling that needs to be done, and is especially useful for setting default fonts and font sizes.

CSS Styles

Whichever method you use to add CSS styles, the styles themselves are the same, and are best seen by an example. Take the example of blue text on a paragraph. The style could be as follows:

```
p {
  color: blue;
  font-weight: bold;
}
```

Every paragraph would now appear in bold blue because this style sets the style for the <p> element. Only the element name is used, and the angled brackets aren't included. So p defines the element for which the style applies, and the styling is surrounded by curly braces. Styles appear as a list separated by semicolons. Styles are context independent, so they can be all on one line or on separate lines. Likewise, the curly braces can be on separate lines.

In this example, two style properties are set, and the style is separated from the value by a colon. The first, `color`, defines the color of the text, and its value is set to `blue`. The second, `font-weight`, defines the weight of the font — how heavy it looks — and this is set to `bold`.

This technique enables styles to be set for HTML elements, and is typically used for the base elements. For example, the Wrox United style sheet defines the following:

```
html, body {
  background-color: #fff;
  color: #000;
  font: normal 90%/1.8em 'Lucida Grande', Verdana, Geneva, Lucida, Helvetica,
Arial, sans-serif;
  margin: 0;
}
h1 {
  font-size: 1.8em;
  font-weight: bold;
  margin-top: 0em;
  margin-bottom: 0em;
  color: #a83930;
}
h2 {
  font-size: 1.6em;
  margin: 1.0em 0em 1.0em 0em;
  font-weight: bold;
  color: #a83930;
}
h3 {
  font-size: 1.2em;
  margin: 1.0em 0em 1.0em 0em;
  font-weight: bold;
  color: #a83930;
}
p {
  font-size: 1.1em;
  line-height: 1.8em;
  margin: 1.1em 0em 1.1em 0em;
  text-align: left;
}
```

This defines the styles for the `html` and `body` elements, which due to inheritance become the default for the rest of the page. Next are the headings and then the paragraph. The colors are described in the "Colors" section later in this appendix.

CSS Sizes

One thing you may have noticed in the previous style sheet is the use of `em` as a size, for both fonts and margins. There are many ways of sizing things, including points, pixels, inches, and percentages or for fonts, predefined sizes. One of the problems with defining sizes is that they mean *different* things to *different* people, especially if they use *different* browsers or *different* platforms. The sizing you can use are as follows:

- Points (`pt`), which are a unit of print rather than a unit of the screen. Different browsers render the same point size differently, giving different font sizes.
- Pixels (`px`), which represent an individual pixel on the screen. This again depends on the platform and screen, because they define how many pixels per inch there are. The biggest drawback with pixels is that they are not user scalable. For example, in Internet Explorer, you can select Text Size from the View menu and change the size of the text being browsed, but if the page designer used pixels, you have no way to resize the text.
- Physical units (`in`, `cm`, `mm`), which is a physical size. This again gives different results on different sized screens.
- Named sizes, such as `small`, `medium`, `large`, `x-large`. These provide relative sizes, with `small` being smaller than `medium`, and so on.
- Percentages (`%`), which define the size as a percentage of the default size (`medium`). So a font size of `200%` is twice the size of the default size.
- Ems (`em`), which represent the default font setting. `Ems` are user-resizable. `1 em` represents one unit of the default font size.

In the Wrox United application, `ems` have been used because they provide the best flexibility, and are suitable for user resizing, which allows users with visual impairments to change the size of the text. You may read much on the pros and cons of setting sizes for fonts, but as Frog Box Design (who did the CSS and images for the Wrox United site) says:

> *We use relative sizes and* `em` *units because they scale better for people using larger fonts, but we do set a relative percentage size, too.*

Percentages are particularly useful when defining the width of block elements. For example, a width of 100% means the element will be the full width of its parent element. This is useful for things like grids where you want them to be the full width of the screen.

Fonts

Deciding on which fonts to use can make a big difference to the readability of your site, because certain fonts are easier to read on the screen than others. You can define many different aspects of the font including the style (normal, bold, and so forth), the size, and the family. In the Wrox United style sheet, the main font is defined as follows:

```
font: normal 90%/1.8em 'Lucida Grande', Verdana, Geneva, Lucida, Helvetica, Arial,
sans-serif;
```

This has three parts:

- The style, which is `normal`.
- The size, which is `90%/1.8em`. This means a font size of 90% and a line height of 1.8em (1.8 times the normal font size), providing nice spacing between the lines. The size of the font isn't directly related to the line height, and this declaration is a shortcut that allows both to be specified at the same time.
- The family, which defines the fonts to be used, if they are available. If a font is not available on the browser, the next in line is tried. Here `Lucida Grande` will be tried first, `Verdana` next, and so on. Fonts that have spaces in their names must have quotes around them.

These three parts could also have been defined like this:

```
font-style: normal;
font-size: 90%;
font-family: 'Lucida Grande', Verdana, Geneva, Lucida, Helvetica, Arial, sans-
serif;
line-height: 1.8em;
```

The single-line form is just a shortcut.

Colors

Colors can be predefined or you can specify the red, green, and blue values. For example, for blue text, any of the following could be used:

```
color: blue;
color: #0000ff;
color: rgb(0, 0, 255)
color: rgb(0%, 0%, 100%);
```

These all produce the same result. The first uses a defined name, and the second uses a hexadecimal notation where `00` represents no color and `ff` represents full colors. There are two digits for the red component, two for green, and two for blue. So `0000ff` means the following:

- `00` for red, so no red
- `00` for green, so no green
- `ff` for blue, so full blue

Using `rgb` enables you to specify this either in decimal (`0` is no color and `255` is full color), or as percentages.

You might also see a shortcut form of the hexadecimal notation consisting of only three digits. This can be used if the two digits for a color part are the same. So blue could be `00f`.

CSS Selectors

Earlier, you saw how a paragraph could be styled:

```
p {
  color: blue;
  font-weight: bold;
}
```

The `p` part is defined as the *selector*, and this can be an element, an element ID, or a class name, and the way they are defined is different. To define an element ID, you place a hash sign (#) before the selector:

```
#header {
  height: 100px;
  padding: 0 10px 0 10px;
  . . .
}
```

This would then correspond to an element with that ID:

```
<div id="header">
```

ID-based selectors can only be used by a single element because IDs have to be unique, so this should be reserved for things that will only appear once. In the Wrox United style sheet, this is used for items such as the header, sidebar, and so on.

To use a class name, you precede the selector with a period:

```
.title {
  color: #a83930;
  text-align: center;
  . . .
}
```

This matches a `CssClass` property for a web server control, or the `class` property for an HTML control:

```
<asp:Label id="Label1" runat="server" CssClass="title">My Page</asp:Label>
<div class="title>My Page</div>
```

Because the class name can be used by multiple controls, you should use it for common styling across elements. The named selector can be designed to apply to all elements (as in the previous code), or just selected elements:

```
div.title {
  color: #a83930;
}
```

Here the selector only applies if a `div` element is given a class of `title`—any other element would not get the style. The following line will be styled:

```
<div class="title">This will be styled</div>
```

However, the following line will not be styled:

```
<span class="title">While this will not be styled</span>
```

Selector names are case-sensitive.

Multiple Selectors

You can also define multiple selectors to have the same style by having them as a comma-separated list at their definition:

```
span, div {
  color: #a83930;
}
```

This defines both the span and div elements to have the same style. Multiple selectors work with elements, ID-based, and class-named forms.

Contextual Selectors

Selectors can also be contextual, meaning that they can be defined to only apply depending on the context in which the element appears. For example, what if you wanted to style list elements (li and ul), but only if they appear within the navigation bar at the left of the screen (#nav)? Your style could be as follows:

```
#nav li {
  color: #a83930;
}
#nav ul {
  color: #a83930;
}
```

With these rules, the li and ul elements will only be styled if they are within a control with an ID of #nav. Outside of the #nav control, no style will be applied.

Floating Elements

Sometimes you want to position elements to the left or right of others. You can't achieve this with placing them one after another, because HTML is a flow-based layout, and elements are placed in their declaration order. One way around this is fixed position, which positions elements directly, but this has problems with users resizing their browser window, because the positioned elements may be outside the new window size.

An easy way to do this is to use floating elements, and although they are restricted in what they do, they can often provide the solution. For example, on the Wrox United home page there are news items, and the date of the item is shown at the right of the page. Resizing the browser keeps this at the right, because it has been floated to the right. The style for this is as follows:

```
.newsDate {
  font: normal 0.9em/0.9em 'Lucida Grande', Verdana,  Geneva, Lucida, Helvetica,
Arial, sans-serif;
  float: right;
  color: #666666;
}
```

Ignore the font and color — the important point is the float element:

```
float: right;
```

This states that the element should be placed at the right of its containing control. So however wide the parent control is, the news date will always appear at its right. Elements can also be floated to the left of others. If you want to learn more about floating elements, it's best to consult a specialized CSS book, but details of some are included at the end of this appendix.

Pseudo Classes

In addition to standard classes, some special classes (called *pseudo classes*) apply to actions rather than the anchor element. These allow specific classes to be applied to links. For example, consider the following:

```
a:hover {
  text-decoration: none;
}
#nav a:hover {
  text-decoration: none;
  color: #a83930;
  background-color: #fdea12;
}
```

Here the `hover` pseudo class is used, which indicates the style to be applied when the cursor is hovering over a link. The first class sets the `text-decoration` to `none`, which removes the underline from links, but only when they are hovered over. For links in the navigation area though, additional styling is done.

In addition to `hover`, three pseudo classes exist for links:

- `link` defines how an unclicked and unvisited link should be styled.
- `visited` defines how a link that has been visited should be styled.
- `active` defines how a currently active line should be styled.

There are other pseudo classes, but support for these in Internet Explorer is limited, so coding to use them always requires a lot of effort. For that reason, they aren't described here.

CSS Reference

The following table describes the CSS properties, but it does not include the aural properties for screen readers. These should be supported on most modern browsers.

Property	Description
`background`	Changes the background color and image.
`background-attachment`	Determines how background images should scroll. `background-attachment` supports three values: `scroll`, `fixed`, and `inherit`. The default value is `scroll`, which indicates that images scroll. Specifying `fixed` means that images are fixed. Specifying `inherit` indicates that images inherit behavior from their parent.

Table continued on following page

Property	Description
background-color	Defines the background color.
background-image	Defines the image to show in the background of the element.
background-position	Defines the position of a background image. It is defined as two values to specify the horizontal and vertical positioning. These can be top, center, or bottom for vertical alignment; left, center, or right for horizontal alignment; percentages; or fixed values.
background-repeat	Indicates whether a background image is repeated and can be repeat, repeat-x, repeat-y, no-repeat, or inherit.
border	Defines the properties of the border of an element.
border-color	Defines the color of a border.
border-collapse	Indicates whether borders in tables collapse onto each other. It can be one of collapse, separate, or inherit.
border-spacing	Defines the amount of space between borders in a table.
border-style	Defines the style of a border, and can be one of none, dotted, dashed, solid, double, groove, ridge, inset, outset, or inherit.
border-top border-bottom border-left border-right	Define the properties of a single border of an element.
border-top-color border-bottom-color border-left-color border-right-color	Define the color for an individual border of an element.
border-top-style border-bottom-style border-left-style border-right-style	Define the style for an individual border of an element.

Property	Description
border-top-width border-bottom-width border-left-width border-right-width	Define the width for an individual border of an element.
border-width	Defines the width of the border for an element.
bottom	Defines the distance to offset an element from the bottom edge of its parent element.
caption-side	Defines where a caption is placed in relation to a table, and can be one of `top`, `bottom`, `left`, `right`, or `inherit`.
clear	Clears any floating in action, and can be one of `none`, `left`, `right`, `both`, or `inherit`.
clip	Defines how much of an element is visible and can be a rectangle `rect[n,n,n,n]`, `auto`, or `inherit`.
color	Defines the foreground color of an element.
content	Defines the type of content and how it is to be displayed.
counter-increment	Defines the property and amount for auto-incrementing lists.
counter-reset	Resets the numerical value of auto-incrementing lists.
cursor	Sets the shape of the cursor when over the element. It can be one of `auto`, `crosshair`, `default`, `pointer`, `move`, `e-resize`, `ne-resize`, `nw-resize`, `n-resize`, `se-resize`, `sw-resize`, `s-resize`, `w-resize`, `text`, `wait`, `help`, `inherit`, or a URL to an image.
direction	Indicates the direction for letters, and can be one of `ltr` (left to right, the default), `rtl` (right to left), or `inherit`.
display	Determines how to display an element, and can be one of: `block`, `inline`, `list-item`, `none`, or `inherit`.
empty-cells	Defines how empty table cells are shown, and can be one of `hide`, `show`, or `inherit`.
float	Indicates how this element floats within the parent element, and can be one of `left`, `right`, `none`, or `inherit`.
font	Defines the attributes of the font for the element.
font-family	Defines the font family for text.
font-size	Defines the size of the font for text.
font-size-adjust	Defines the aspect value for a font element.

Table continued on following page

Property	Description
font-stretch	Defines how expanded or condensed a font is.
font-style	Defines the style of the font, and can be one of italic, normal, oblique, or inherit.
font-variant	Defines whether the font is displayed in capital letters, and can be normal, small-caps, or inherit.
font-weight	Defines the thickness of the font, and can be absolute weight values (100 to 900 in steps of 100), bold or normal, bolder or lighter, or inherit.
height	Defines the height of an element.
left	When using absolute positioning, this defines how far from the left edge of the parent the element is placed.
letter-spacing	Defines the amount of space between letters.
line-height	Defines the height between lines.
list-style	Defines the properties for list elements.
list-style-image	Defines the image to be used as the marker for a list element.
list-style-position	Defines the positioning of the list relative to the list itself, and can be one of inside, outside, or inherit.
list-style-type	Defines the type of marker for the list, and can be one of circle, decimal, disc, square, lower-roman, upper-roman, lower-alpha, upper-alpha, none, or inherit.
margin	Defines the amount of space between the border and the parent element.
margin-top margin-bottom margin-left	Define the amount of space between the border and the parent element for an individual side of an element.
margin-right	
marker-offset	Defines the distance between the border of a list marker and the list itself.
marks	Defines whether crop marks are shown, and can be one of crop, cross, both, none, or inherit.
max-height max-width	Define the maximum height and width of an element.
min-height min-width	Define the minimum height and width of an element.

Property	Description
`orphans`	Defines the minimum number of lines or paragraph that must be left at the bottom of a page.
`outline`	Defines the properties of a button or form field that has focus.
`outline-color`	Defines the color of a button or form field that has focus.
`outline-style`	Defines the border style of a button or form field that has focus.
`outline-width`	Defines the border width of a button or form field that has focus.
`overflow`	Defines the visibility of content if it doesn't fit within the element, and can be one of `auto`, `hidden`, `scroll`, `visible`, or `inherit`.
`padding`	Defines the distance between one or more sides of the content area and its border.

`padding-top`
`padding-bottom`
`padding-left`
`padding-right`
	Define the distance between a side of the content area and its border.

`page`	Defines the page type (such as regular or landscape) for printed content.
`page-break-after` `page-break-before`	Define how the browser should insert page breaks, and can be one of `always`, `auto`, `avoid`, `left`, `right`, or `inherit`.
`page-break-inside`	Defines whether page breaks split an element across pages, and can be `auto`, `avoid`, or `inherit`.
`position`	Defines how an element is positioned relative to the flow of the document, and can be `absolute`, `fixed`, `relative`, `static`, or `inherit`.
`quotes`	Defines the type of quotation mark to be used within embedded quotes.
`right`	Defines the distance an element should be from its parent's right edge.
`size`	Defines the size of the printing area in a page.
`table-layout`	Defines how the width of table cells is calculated, and can be `auto`, `fixed`, or `inherit`.
`text-align`	Defines the alignment of text, and can be one of `center`, `justify`, `left`, `right`, or `inherit`.

Table continued on following page

Property	Description
text-decoration	Defines the decoration on text, and can be one of blink, line-through, none, overline, underline, or inherit.
text-indent	Defines the amount of space to indent the first line of a paragraph.
text-shadow	Defines the amount of shadow to apply to text.
text-transform	Defines the casing to use on text, and can be one of capitalize, lowercase, none, uppercase, or inherit.
top	Defines the distance between an element and its parent's top edge.
Unicode-bidi	Defines Unicode text as having bidirectional characteristics.
vertical-align	Defines the vertical alignment of the element.
visibility	Defines how, or if, the element is shown, and can be one of collapse, hidden, visible, or inherit.
white-space	Defines how white space should be treated, and can be one of normal, nowrap, pre, or inherit.
widows	Defines the minimum number of lines that must be left at the top of a page.
width	Defines the width of the element.
word-spacing	Defines the distance between words.
z-index	Defines the depth of an element to allow overlapping elements.

Common HTML Tags by Category

Following is a list of some of the most commonly used HTML tags by category. When you know what you want to do, but you're not sure which tag will achieve the desired effect, use the following reference tables to put you on the right track.

Document Structure

Tag	Meaning
<! >	Allows authors to add comments to code.
<!DOCTYPE>	Defines the document type. This is required by all HTML documents.
<base>	Specifies the document's base URL—its original location. It's not normally necessary to include this tag. It can only be used in the <HEAD> section.

Tag	Meaning
<body>	Contains the main part of the HTML document.
<comment>	Allows authors to add comments to code.
<div>	Defines a block division of the <BODY> section of the document.
<head>	Contains information about the document.
<html>	Signals the beginning and end of an HTML document.
<link>	Defines the current document's relationship with other resources. Used in the <HEAD> section only.
<meta>	Describes the content of a document.
<nextid>	Defines a parameter in the <HEAD> section of the document.
<span>	Defines an area for reference by a style sheet.
<style>	Specifies the style sheet for the page.

Titles and Headings

Tag	Meaning
<h1>	Heading level 1.
<h2>	Heading level 2.
<h3>	Heading level 3.
<h4>	Heading level 4.
<h5>	Heading level 5.
<h6>	Heading level 6.
<title>	Defines the title of the document.

Paragraphs and Lines

Tag	Meaning
 	Line break.
<center>	Centers subsequent text and images.
<hr>	Draws a horizontal rule.
<nobr>	Prevents a line of text breaking.
<p>	Defines a paragraph.
<wbr>	Inserts a soft line break in a block of <NOBR> text.

Text Styles

Tag	Meaning
<address>	Indicates an address. The address is typically displayed in italics.
<b>	Emboldens text.
<basefont>	Sets font size to be used as default.
<big>	Changes the physical rendering of the font to one size larger.
<blockquote>	Formats a quote — typically by indentation.
<cite>	Renders text in italics.
<code>	Renders text in a font resembling computer code.
<dfn>	Indicates the first instance of a term or important word.
<em>	Emphasized text — usually italic.
<font>	Changes font properties.
<i>	Defines italic text.
<kbd>	Indicates typed text. Useful for instruction manuals and the like.
<listing>	Renders text in a fixed-width font.
<plaintext>	Renders text in a fixed-width font without processing any other tags it may contain.
<pre>	Preformatted text. Renders text exactly how it is typed — carriage returns, styles, and so forth, will be recognized.
<s> or <strike>	Strikethrough. Renders the text as deleted (crossed out).
<small>	Changes the physical rendering of a font to one size smaller.
<strong>	Strong emphasis — usually bold.
<style>	Specifies the style sheet for the page.
<sub>	Subscript.
<sup>	Superscript.
<tt>	Renders text in fixed width, typewriter-style font.
<u>	Underlines text. This is not widely supported at present, and is not recommended, because it can cause confusion with hyper-links, which also normally appear underlined.
<var>	Indicates a variable.

Lists

Tag	Meaning
<dd>	Definition description. Used in definition lists with <DT> to define the term.
<dir>	Denotes a directory list by indenting the text.
<dl>	Defines a definition list.
<dt>	Defines a definition term. Used with definition lists.
<li>	Defines a list item in any type of list other than a definition list.
<menu>	Defines a menu list.
<ol>	Defines an ordered (numbered) list.
<ul>	Defines an unordered (bulleted) list.

Tables

Tag	Meaning
<caption>	Puts a title above a table.
<col>	Defines column width and properties for a table.
<colgroup>	Defines properties for a group of columns in a table.
<table>	Defines a series of columns and rows to form a table.
<tbody>	Defines the table body.
<td>	Specifies a cell in a table.
<tfoot>	Defines table footer.
<th>	Specifies a header column. Text will be centered and bold.
<thead>	Used to designate rows as the table's header.
<tr>	Defines the start of a table row.

Links

Tag	Meaning
<a>	Used to insert an anchor, which can be either a local reference point or a hyperlink to another URL.
<a href="url">	Hyperlink to another document, the location of which is specified by the `url`.

Table continued on following page

Tag	Meaning
<a name="name">	Link to a local reference point, the location of which is specified by the name.

Graphics, Objects, Multimedia, and Scripts

Tag	Meaning
<applet>	Inserts an applet.
<area>	Specifies the shape of a hot spot in a client-side image map.
<bgsound>	Plays a background sound.
<embed>	Defines an embedded object in an HTML document.
<img>	Embeds an image or a video clip in a document.
<map>	Specifies a collection of hot spots for a client-side image map.
<noscript>	Specifies HTML to be displayed in browsers that don't support scripting.
<object>	Inserts an object.
<param>	Defines parameters for a Java applet.
<script>	Inserts a script.

Forms

Tag	Meaning
<button>	Creates an HTML-style button.
<fieldset>	Draws a box around a group of controls.
<form>	Defines part of the document as a user fill-out form.
<input>	Defines a user input box.
<label>	Defines a label for a control.
<legend>	Defines the text label to use in box created by a <FIELDSET> tag.
<option>	Used within the <SELECT> tag to present the user with a number of options.
<select>	Denotes a list box or drop-down list.
<textarea>	Defines a text area inside a <FORM> element.

Frames

Tag	Meaning
`<frame>`	Defines a single frame in a frameset.
`<frameset>`	Defines the main container for a frame.
`<iframe>`	Defines a floating frame within a document.
`<noframes>`	Allows for backward compatibility with non-frame-compliant browsers.

HTML Common Attributes to the CSS Property

The following table cross-references common HTML attributes with their corresponding CSS values.

Attribute	CSS Values	Description
`align`	`text-align`	Specifies how the element is aligned with respect to its containing element, or to the rest of the page.
`alink`	`:link pseudo class`	The color for active links in the page. A link is active while the mouse button is held down over the link.
`background`	`background:`	Specifies a background picture that is tiled behind text and graphics.
`bgcolor`	`background-color`	Specifies the background color to be used for an element.
`border`	`border`	Specifies if a border is to be drawn around the element, and sets its thickness.
`bordercolor`	`border-color`	The color of all or some of the borders for an element.
`clear`	`clear`	Causes the next element or text to be displayed below left-aligned or right-aligned images.
`color`	`color`	The text or foreground color of an element.
`face`	`font-family`	Sets the font family or typeface of the current font or base font.
`height`	`height`	Specifies the height of the element that is to be drawn on the page.

Table continued on following page

Attribute	CSS Values	Description
hidden	visibility	Forces the embedded object to be invisible in an <EMBED> tag.
hspace	margin	Specifies the horizontal spacing or margin between an element and its neighbors.
link	:link pseudo class	The color for links.
left	left	Position in pixels of the left-hand side of the object in relation to its container.
leftmargin	margin-left	Specifies the left margin for the entire body of the page, overriding the default margin.
marginheight	margin-top	Specifies the top and bottom margins for displaying text in a frame.
marginwidth	margin-left margin-right	Specifies the left and right margins for displaying text in a frame.
nowrap	white-space	Indicates that the browser should not perform automatic word wrapping of the text.
rightmargin	margin-right	Specifies the right margin for the entire body of the page, overriding the default margin.
size	size	Specifies the size of the element.
top	top	Position of the top of the element. It also returns topmost window object.
topmargin	margin-top	Specifies the margin for the top of the page, overriding the default top margin.
valign	vertical-align	Specifies how the contents should be aligned vertically within the element.
visibility	{visibility: visible | hidden}	Defines whether the element should be displayed on the page.
vlink	:visited pseudo class	The color for visited links in the page.
vspace	margin	Specifies the vertical spacing or margin between an element and its neighbors.
weight	font-weight	Defines the weight of the font used to render the text.
width	width	Specifies the width of the element that will be drawn in the page.
z-index	z-index	Position in the z-order or stacking order of the page — the z coordinate.

Recommended Reading

If you'd like to learn more about CSS, and we recommend you do, the books listed in the following tables will be useful.

Title	***Beginning CSS: Cascading Style Sheets for Web Design***
Author	Richard York
Publisher	Wrox Press
ISBN	0-7645-7642-9
Description	As part of the Beginning series, this is a natural companion to this book, covering all aspects of how to use CSS for web site design.

Title	***Accessible XHTML and CSS Web Sites: Problem–Design–Solution***
Author	Jon Duckett
Publisher	Wrox Press
ISBN	0-7645-8306-9
Description	This book is aimed more at how to make your web site accessible to people with visual impairments or who use screen readers rather than standard browsers. It's something we should all aim to do when creating web sites.

Title	***Core CSS Second Edition***
Author	Keith Schengili-Roberts
Publisher	Prentice Hall
ISBN	0-13-009278-9
Description	This is a pure reference book to the whole of CSS, including some of the future enhancements. It's definitely not a learning book, but it provides good examples as well as being an excellent reference.

Title	***Designing with Web Standards***
Author	Jeffrey Zeldman
Publisher	New Riders
ISBN	0-7357-1201-8
Description	A book for the more advanced user. It contains a wealth of information, especially about the practicalities of CSS and their use in the real world. It includes lots of material on cross-browser issues, such as sizes.

Another good resource is the web, and there are plenty of CSS tutorials. A good place to start is `www.w3schools.com/css/`.

Index

SYMBOLS

A

B

C

E

F

G

H

I

M

N

Q

R

T